ARUNDEL

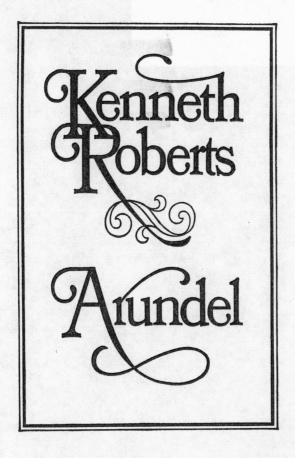

Kenneth Roberts

Arundel

Doubleday & Company, Inc.
Garden City, New York

This is Volume I of a 4-volume slipcased edition, KENNETH
ROBERTS READER OF THE AMERICAN REVOLUTION,
published by Doubleday, 1976.

ISBN: 0-385-12149-0

TO

G. T. R.

CONTENTS

PROLOGUE

Having no wish to pose as a man of letters, but earnestly desiring to see justice done, I, Steven Nason, of the town of Arundel, in the county of York and the province of Maine, herein set down the truth, as I saw it, of certain occurrences connected in various ways with this neighborhood.

Erroneous tales have been told of exploits that I, together with the notorious Cap Huff, have performed, and concerning powers I am supposed to possess.

My relations with the Indian girl Jacataqua have been misrepresented. There have been doubts cast on the loyalty of Natanis. There has been loose talk, among armchair warriors, of how Colonel Enos left us in the wilderness, and overmuch gabble among old wives about my search for Mary Mallinson and the manner in which I settled my affairs with Henri Guerlac de Sabrevois.

Above all, because of the lamentable occurrences at West Point, the countryside is filled with men of mighty hindsight who speak with scorn of Colonel Arnold, whose boots they were not fit to clean, and belittle or ignore the expedition to Quebec. That achievement, to my way of thinking, is unequaled in all the many histories of campaigns that my grandson has obtained for me from the library of Harvard College, and that I have read carefully during long winter storms, when the breakers roar on the ledges and beaches, and the pines behind the summer camping place of the Abenakis are frosted with snow, calling to my mind the gables of lower Quebec, and the bitter days through which we lay and watched them against the snow-plastered cliff beyond.

I have small skill in writing, being more fitted for wood trails than for a knee-hole desk, and my hand better shaped for handling an axe than for anything as delicate as a pen. Nevertheless I am constrained, as Colonel Arnold was given to saying, to have a shot at it, so to set these matters right.

In so doing I accept the judgment of my father, who was wise in woodcraft, and somehow versed in the ways of mankind at large, though he had traveled little except to Louisbourg on Cape Breton, where two thousand of our colonists drank untold quantities of rum and captured the city from the French. It was from Louisbourg that he brought home as booty our silver sugar bowl and the large white pitcher with the raised figures of dancing countrymen around it: the same pitcher we now use for cider on a winter's night, when the ice cakes click and scrape on the sand beyond our garden at the mouth of the Arundel River.

If you have something to say, my father held, say it without thought of anything except the truth. If it is worth saying, those who read it will not complain. If it is not worth saying, then there will be few to read it, and fewer still to vex you with complaints.

Therefore I am hopeful that those who come upon this book will disregard its faults and read it for the things that seem to me worth saying.

II

The way in which our family came to Arundel is a matter I set down, not to boast of my own people, since we have been simple farmers and smiths and innkeepers and soldiers and sailors, always; but so my great-grandsons may know what manner of folk they sprang from, and feel shame to disgrace them by taking advantage of the weak or ignorant, or by turning tail when frightened, which they will often be, as God knows I have too frequently been.

My grandfather, Benjamin, was a blacksmith and gunsmith in the Berwick section of the town of Kittery, his grandfather Richard having come there in 1639 from Berwick in England.

In those days the frontiers were steadily pushing eastward and northward; and to the eastward of Kittery lay the town of Wells, gradually growing in size, though populated by shiftless and poverty-stricken folk, dwelling in log huts without furniture, and constantly at odds with the Indians.

In order to obtain a blacksmith, the town of Wells, in 1670, sent to my grandfather a paper, which I still have in my small green seaman's chest, guaranteeing him two hundred acres of upland and ten acres of marsh if he would settle in Wells within three months, remain there for five years, and do the blacksmith work for the inhabitants for such current pay as the town could produce. This my grandfather did, albeit he spent less time at blacksmithing than in hunting with the Abenakis, by whom he was liked and trusted, as was my father to an even greater degree. It is my opinion that he was justified in spending little time in his smithy, since the only current pay the town could produce was promises that were never kept.

My father, then, was born in Wells; and when he had reached the age of seventeen, he was skilled in the arts of the blacksmith, the gunsmith, and the hunter. He had, furthermore, been blessed with nine brothers and sisters; and wishing to enjoy the pleasures of married life without falling over a child not his own whenever he turned around, he looked about and took thought for the future.

Three leagues to the eastward of Wells, along the hard white crescent-shaped beaches so plentiful in the southern portion of our province, is the Arundel River. This is a narrow river, but deeper than most of those that cut across our beaches. Therefore it has a bar farther out at sea, less easy to pass than many river bars, so that travelers view it with trepidation.

My father frequently hunted and fished near its mouth, going with friends from the Webhannet tribe of Abenakis, chiefly with young Bomazeen, the son of the wise sachem Wawa. I have heard him say he took more pleasure in the place than in any other section that had met his eye. Most men say the same thing concerning their homes; but few, to my way of thinking, have the reason for saying it that my father had.

In the spring there are quantities of salmon running upstream, easy to take with a spear because of the narrowness of the river bed. When the salmon are finished there are fat eels lying in the current riffles at low tide, so thick that in an hour one boy with a trident may fill a barrel, which is a feat I have frequently accomplished, being addicted to smoked eel with a gallon of cider before meals, or during them, or late at night when the nip of autumn is in the air, or indeed at any time whatever, now I stop to think on it.

After the eels are gone the green pollocks come up the river by the millions, fine fish to salt and dry, especially in a manner discovered by my father, which ripens their flesh to a creamy consistency, uncommonly delicious.

After the pollocks come small spike mackerel; and between seasons, when the tide rises on the bar, beautiful flat flounders lie in the sand with eyes popped out, amazed like, to betray their presence.

In the autumn come deer to paddle in the salt water, and hulking moose deer, and turkeys occasionally; also teal, black ducks, and Canada geese in long lines and wedges; while always our orchards and alder runs are filled with woodcock and that toothsome but brainless bird, the partridge, who flies hastily into a tree at the approach of a barking dog, and stays there, befuddled, until the dog's owner walks up unnoticed and knocks him down.

In the late summer, and in the spring as well, there are noisy flocks of curlews and yellow legs and plovers, wheeling above the sands in such numbers that a single palmful of small shot will kill enough for one of the juicy game pies my youngest sister Cynthia takes such pride in making and I such delight in eating.

At the mouth of the river my father found an oblong piece of farmland, set off by river and creek and beach into an easily defended section, and presenting opportunities for trade and a modest income. Since there was no white man dwelling thereabouts, probably because of the numbers of Indians who came in the summer to fish and to lie in the cool sea breezes, he took it for his own; and the Indians were content, since he traded honestly with them.

On the seaward side of our farm is a smooth white beach, half a mile in length, shaped like a hunting bow. This beach appears to face straight out to sea; but because the seacoast swings outward near this point the beach in reality faces south, toward Boston. Thus the hot winds of summer, which are southwesterly, blow in to us across the ocean, and so are cool and pleasant.

At the western end of the beach is a tumbled mass of rocks, fine for the shooting of coot or eating-ducks in spring or fall, or for capturing coarse-haired seals for moccasins, or for taking the small salt water perch which we call cunners. These we take at any season, whenever we crave the sweetest of all chowders. I have eaten the yellow stew that Frenchmen in Quebec call boullabaze, or some such name, and brag about until their tongues go dry; and I say with due thought and seriousness that, compared with one of my sister Cynthia's cunner stews, made with ship's bread and pork scraps, a boullabaze is fit only to place in a hill of green corn to fertilize it, if indeed it would not cause the kernels to grow dwarfed and distorted.

At the eastern end of the beach and of our farm is the river mouth; and directly across the river the rocky headland of Cape Arundel pushes out to sea. Two hundred yards upstream a generous creek bears back to the westward, parallel to the beach, into a long salt marsh.

Thus our farm is protected on the south by the ocean, on the east by the river, on the north by the creek, and is open only on the west, in which direction lie the settlements; so with slight precautions one need fear no attack from any ordinary force of enemies. Even on the side toward the ocean my father found protection from French raiders; for offshore is a semicircle of reefs, hidden at full tide in a calm sea, but raising a smother of foam and roaring regiments of breakers when the wind blows from the east or northeast.

These ledges, covered with tangled growths of seaweed, cause the delicious odor peculiar to these parts in summer; for the prevailing winds, blowing across them, bring to shore a perfume that seems to come from the heart of the sea—an odor I know of in no other place, though there have been Frenchmen pass through here who declare the same heartening smell may be found on the coast of Brittany. This may be true, though I would liefer hear it from an Indian than from a Frenchman if I had to depend upon it.

The truth is I love the place; and if I seem to talk overmuch of it, it is because I would like those who read about it to see it as I saw it, and to know the sweet smell of it and to love it as I do.

On the highest point of this farmland my father, at the age of seventeen, with the assistance of my grandfather and Bomazeen, the son of Wawa, and a carpenter from York and Abenakis from the camp across the creek, built a sturdy garrison house out of logs.

From the back door he looked down on the creek and the glistening dunes that border the river mouth and the beach, and on the brown rocks of Cape Arundel, over which the sun came up to warm him at his early morning labors. From the front door he saw the sweeping crescent of sand, and the reefs with creamy breakers gamboling around and over them, and the flat salt marsh to the westward; and far away, beyond the beach and the reefs, he saw what I see today and what you, too, may see if you will come to Arundel: the blue expanse of Wells Bay with the gentle slopes of Mt. Agamenticus behind it; and to the left of Agamenticus the mainland of Wells and the cliffs of York, small and blue above the water, and soothing to the eye.

It was a luxurious house by comparison with those roundabout at that time; for it had floors of boards, and bedsteads in the sleeping rooms, with mattresses resting on cords and stuffed with corn husks. In each room was a chest and a chair, and in the kitchen a table and a carved court cupboard and stout chairs. The place was a boon to weary travelers; and it was surprising how often those who passed that way were overcome with weariness at our front door.

Beside the garrison house was a smithy where my father could ply his trade when occasion rose, and sheds for horses, the whole stock-

aded against hostile Indians. On the river bank was a skiff for ferrying men and horses across; and the town had given my father, in
consideration for his living there, the sole right to conduct a ferry at
the river's mouth.

III

Of my father's first wife I know little. She came from Wells and
was a melancholy female, given to upbraiding my father for going
alone into the wilderness during the winter months. He did this in
order to trade with the Indians for beaver skins and to seek out paths
and locations for Sir William Pepperrell and Governor Shirley and for
the Colonial Government, which knew less about the country to the
north and east than a rabbit knows about fish.

Although my father never said so, I suspect he went into the wilderness to escape his first wife, and so formed the habit of roaming in
the woods and living in wigwams for weeks on end—a habit from
which he never recovered.

She was a sickly woman, troubled with indigestion, and bore my
father no children, which was a cross to him. She was intemperate
with the Abenakis, frequently attacking them with her brush broom
when they came into the kitchen uninvited, as Indians always do unless at war, when they hide in bushes near the house and wait, usually in vain, for someone to stumble over them and be killed. This,
too, was a source of trouble to my father. Indian wars have started
with no greater provocation; and for weeks after his first wife had
beaten an Indian with her brush broom he never left home without
fearing that on his return he would find the house burned down.

She was finicky and would allow no servants to assist her, although
my father, having accumulated a respectable amount of money
through ferrying and the sale of beaver skins, would gladly have obtained one for her. This was the more annoying because the house
was like to be full of travelers seeking a night's hospitality, to say
nothing of the soldiers stationed there at any rumors of Indian troubles, so that his first wife was perpetually complaining and groaning
about the work to be done, and there was no peace in the house.

Worst of all, she was a bad cook. Perhaps I should not set it down
here, but it was a good thing for her and a good thing for my father
and a good thing for the Indians and certainly a good thing for me,
since without it I would never have been born, when she died of a
consumption.

My father had little leisure for grieving after she had gone, even though he had been so inclined.

Settlers constantly increased, and hostile Indians from the north came more frequently to harass them; so the garrison house was too small to harbor those who sought refuge and provender. Therefore my father built a sawmill on the creek behind the house; and in this he sawed the King's pines that stood on his land; for in common with many in our province, he believed the King had no right to trees standing on a settler's land, even though they were the King's by law. Holding this law to be a foolish one, he broke it whenever he could break it unobserved, as is the custom with all of us. From these King's pines came boards forty inches wide, as free of knots as mahogany from the Sugar Islands.

With them he enlarged the garrison house, so that forty persons might live in it in comparative comfort. He covered the logs with narrow overlapping boards and erected a symmetrical ell on each side, and made a new room out of our old kitchen, a gathering-room cool in summer and warm in winter. It had a fireplace so large that six people might sit within it on each side of the fire, as fine a place as ever I saw for drinking buttered rum on a cold night provided the drinker is careful, as one must always be, not so much with the rum as with buttered rum, for it is the butter, as all drinkers of this concoction know and say, that wreaks the harm. And so, when the fireside drinker must be hearty with buttered rum until the butter makes him topple, it were well he took thought to topple sidewise or backward rather than slither forward into the fire.

The walls within were sheathed with broad boards of pumpkin pine with the edges shaved thin and overlapping, so that no crack could appear, howsoever the boards might shrink; and my father obtained the services of two shipwrights, and had them make small oval-topped tables, which might be drawn before the fire and gripped between the knees by one who wished to come to close quarters with a juicy black duck or a steaming clam chowder.

From the town he had a license as an innkeeper and a permit to dispense spirituous liquors; and all who came by the beaches stopped at the inn. In the town of Wells he secured a black woman named Malary, who had been freed from slavery along with six other slaves; and Malary was held in esteem for her cooking, in especial her manner of baking beans, a trick that has been nobly acquired by my sister Cynthia.

All this I know from what my father told me in my boyhood evenings; and yet how little it seems, now, that I know of him and of those times. Almost anything in the world is readily forgotten after ten years. After the passage of fifty years a happening so fades into the mists of antiquity that little is known about it except by those who took part in it; and that little is mostly wrong. Of how my grandfather Benjamin lived and what he ate and what he wore I know next to nothing, nor do I know anything about my great-great-grandfather Richard, except that he was an ensign of Kittery in 1653, and one of three men to lay out the boundary between the towns of Kittery and Wells in 1655, because I have seen his name cut on the rock at Baker's Spring. Of how he cooked his black ducks and prevented the curse of chilblains, and whether he escaped the cruel burden of rheumatics, and what he thought about certain passages in the Bible I must remain in darkness. Yet my great-great-grandfather, of whom I know so little, was at the height of his powers a mere one hundred years ago.

IV

When Sir William Pepperrell in 1745 sent out his call for troops to attack the French city of Louisbourg on Cape Breton, my father, being without financial cares, and having nothing of import to do at the moment, rode to the town of Berwick and enlisted in the company of Captain Moses Butler. There he met the captain's daughter Sarah.

She was tall, with brown hair and dark brown eyes and a manner of drawing in her chin when she laughed and touching her upper lip with the tip of a slender tongue, as if in delight at what had been done or said. Unlike the women of Wells and Arundel, she had schooling and had read the works of Plato and Horace and Plutarch, as well as the writings of Shakespeare and Congreve, albeit the latter, she told me, had been done secretly, and after stealing the book from beneath the mattress of her mother's chamber, where it was kept hid. She could speak in French; and from her I learned a few words in that tongue, which stood me in good stead in later days.

For her education I thank God. Without it, and without her desire to see me possessed of some thoughts other than those of fish and weather and sleep, I would be crying out, along with various of my fellow-citizens of Arundel, against the useless expenditure of fifty pounds a year for the education of children in our district.

When Captain Moses Butler's company marched off to Boston,

Sally Butler and her mother followed in a one-horse chaise; and before my father set foot on the ship that carried him to Louisbourg, he and my mother were betrothed.

On his return from that drunken and successful holiday they were married; and ten years later, in the garrison house between the golden sands and white breakers of the Arundel beaches and the swirling glass-clear waters of the mill creek, there dwelt, beside myself, my father and my mother, who was the sweetest woman and the kindest, bar one, that I have known, and my sister Hepsibah and my sister Jane and my brother Ivory and my youngest sister Cynthia and my seal Eunice and my dog Ranger, who was my first dog of that name but not the last, all of them half setting dog and half spaniel, entirely black save for a white waistcoat.

Those days were happy and far less luxurious than at present, what with the stagecoach that now speeds down to Boston from Portland in two days' time, and the chinaware on our tables and our plastered walls. Yet I cannot truthfully say those times were better, though many think they were. The war is over, and the roads are easier to travel; our tools are better so that our crops are larger; and though the youths are said to be growing softer and looser from too much luxury and money, I know they will fight as bravely as ever we did, once the need of it arises; and I hope fewer of them will run away.

BOOK I

RED AND WHITE

I

Iᴛ ᴡᴀs on the 6th of September in 1759 that I reached my twelfth birthday. I think I would have remembered the day because of the new eel spear my father had made for me, and the hunting shirt of buckskin my mother had cleverly stitched, with fringes at shoulders and skirt, and decorations of porcupine quills, even if for nothing else. But memorable as those things were, there was something else to keep me from forgetting.

There was a ring around the sun, and it had been there all the day before, a ring like a watery, ghostly rainbow; and with us, except in dry spells, when all signs fail, such a ring is an unfailing sign of rain.

This presage I was not pleased to see; for always, after the first hard rain of September, the Abenakis across the creek packed up their wigwams and their summer's picking of sweet grass, their dried fish and dried corn and newborn puppies, and traveled again to their winter hunting ground. This lies near Ossipee Mountain, and is a fresh-water country, abounding in beaver and otter and moose deer, but gloomy, to my way of thinking, empty of the shimmer and freshness of our blue ocean and long sands and salt marshes threaded by shining inlets.

Mindful of the sun's ring, I had been going about my duties, bringing dry white sand from the beach to place on the floor of the gathering-room, and replenishing the water jugs from the well, and occasionally pausing to speak to my young seal, Eunice. I had taken her from the rocks in the spring when she was little more than a foot long, and she now considered herself one of the family, privileged to hunch and squatter along behind me, coughing and hawking and imploring me for fish, to Ranger's disgust.

Knowing the time was short before the Abenakis departed for their winter grounds, I had it in mind to cross the creek after my chores were done and accompany young Mogg Chabonoke, the sachem's son, on a hunt for male night herons so that we might bring home their slender white plumes, I to my mother, and Mogg to Fala Ramanascho, granddaughter of the chieftainess Ramanascho, who is reputed to have owned all the land hereabouts at one time.

Therefore I was not overjoyed to hear a fretful bellowing for the ferry from the far side of the creek; for no boy wishes his labors to be increased when there is play afoot. The man who shouted was a smallish man named Mallinson. He had appeared in our parts from God knows where and availed himself of a grant of land a short distance up the river, and had since been held in esteem by the townsfolk.

He was a man of serious visage, who spoke with a portentous frown, so that it seemed a tedious and important thing when he so much as passed the time of day or affirmed that it looked like rain. Yet when, with this ponderous look, he said the east wind was chilling him, the breeze, like as not, came from the west; for he was usually wrong. In truth, he had no wisdom at all, poor man; but since folk are given to judging the wisdom of any person by his demeanor while in utterance and not by the utterance itself, he was generally held as among the wisest.

Twice he had acted as one of a commission of three men to represent the residents of Arundel; and on each occasion he had talked mighty wordily concerning Arundel's needs. The first time he got for Arundel an increase in taxes, and the second time a demand to provide more men for the militia. When the townsfolk referred to these matters, they spoke only of the fervor of his oratory, whereas my father dwelt more upon its unfavorable effect. All in all, I took no pleasure in Mallinson's hoarse and lengthy calls to be ferried across. Yet, since he wished to come to our inn, I could not in duty continue to affect an utter deafness; so I pushed the light skiff into the creek and sculled across, with Eunice playfully diving under and over the oar and making me wish to crack her on the head with it, which I never could do because of her agility in the water.

With Mallinson was his daughter Mary, a shy child with yellow hair bound around her head in braids, as the Indian women bind their own tresses when moving through the forest. After the manner of children little acquainted, she and I had nothing to say to each other, nor was there reason why we should: a few times only had I seen her, and then we had but eyed each other from a distance. Mallinson, however, bespoke me with condescension, observing weightily that we should now have fine September weather, which I knew we would not because of the ring around the sun.

Mary folded her hands in her lap and crossed her sunburned legs beneath her dress of faded blue calico and gazed sidewise from under lowered lids at Eunice, who swam and blew noisily alongside the skiff and stared with round-eyed curiosity at the two strangers, as is the custom of seals; for they will follow travelers for miles along the beach, peering out of the surf at their every movement.

When I had beached the skiff in the wiry grass that grew on the top of the creek bank, and dragged it beyond the reach of the tide, Mallinson stumped off toward the inn, between the corn patches we have always planted on its landward side. Mary, after making as though to follow him, turned back to watch Eunice who, with an apprehensive look in her large brown eyes, was dragging herself onto the bank with difficulty, because of her fatness.

At this her father called back to her that she could play a little while with me if we would be careful not to fall in the river and drown. I was well able, even at that age, to swim to the mile rock and back. Therefore I declared to myself that Mallinson was wrong in this, as in all things. Mary could not play with me because I would not be there to play with, but would be off for something more manly.

But Mary slipped down in the cool grass at the edge of the creek and said in a thoughtful tone, as if to herself, and yet freely allowed, "He will be drunk again to-night." Eunice, as though comprehending, which she could not, of course, flopped herself up on the bank and over to Mary and looked at her sadly out of round brown eyes that seemed brimming with tears. It appeared almost that some communion were established between the gentle animal and the bright-haired child. I thought I saw a tear steal down Mary's cheek, whereat I was filled with revulsion, and determined to flee me instanter from two such sentimental females.

Before I could turn, Mary looked hard into my eyes. She smiled, and her eyes seemed to cling to mine, so that I couldn't, to save my life, have looked away. I knew only that her eyes were blue, that her smile caused a roaring in my ears, and that simultaneously there was befalling within the middle of my chest a flopping, such as that which comes from Eunice's tail when in a spasm of fright she hurls herself from a rock into the water.

I stood like a frozen lummox, unable to tear my eyes from her. Eunice rolled over on her side and held up her flipper for Mary to scratch under it, which Mary comprehended and did; and at that, when I had stolen a glance at the inn and at the Indian camp, and had seen no one was watching us, I decided that if young Mogg

Chabonoke hunted for herons' plumes that afternoon he would hunt alone.

It was a pity, Mary said, that one as big and clumsy as I should keep captive a poor seal, instead of freeing her to rejoin her friends and kin. At this I told her how I had once taken Eunice to the long ledge to the southwestward, where the seals lie on sunny days to heat their fat sides, and how, on that occasion, she had followed me home again: how I had then taken her four miles to sea and pushed her overboard; then quickly and painfully rowed ashore to find her caracoling on the beach, squawking and bristling out her whiskers and getting under foot at every step.

When Mary held out her hand to be helped to her feet, her wrist and arm were smoother and softer than anything I had ever felt. Because, possibly, of long sitting, she wavered and stumbled against me. Then she looked at me hard and straight, as if she sought something, and smiled again, and again my middle chest was full of Eunice-like floppings.

We walked along the beach to the river, she and Eunice and Ranger and I. It was low water; and at the river's edge the rocks stood high and dry. Seaweed fringes hid their bases, reminding us that it had been long since breakfast, and that food was to be had for the taking.

We groped beneath the weed curtains until the feel of a hard shell or the pang of a nipped finger apprised us of the presence of one of the small lobsters that lurk under the rocks, whereupon we dragged him forth, flapping his tail and clattering his claws.

Having taken six small ones, we went to the dunes, which are always to be found on the westward side of the mouth of any river, provided it runs into the ocean through a sandy beach. At the mouth of our river they rise up like small mountains, abrupt and close together, eight and nine and ten feet tall. Among them are valleys; and in the warm lap of one of these valleys we built a fire on flat stones.

We split each lobster lengthwise with my hunting knife; and when we had banished Eunice to the top of the mountain pass leading into the next valley and set Ranger to watch over her so she could not splatter us with sand, and when the fire had burned down, we put the lobster-halves on the embers and let them stay until the flesh was white, with a milky look.

We ate them with a feeling of coziness and domesticity, a feeling somehow heightened when we saved the last two for Eunice and Ranger, and Eunice, in descending from her mountain fastness to obtain her portion, slipped and rolled against the hot rocks, set up a horrible hoarse outcry, and flounced off across the dunes to cool herself in the river.

Now I cannot say how we came to speak of marriage. It may have been because Mary told how her mother had died of a cough, and how her father had obtained an Indian woman to cook and keep things tidy, and how she hated the Indian woman, so that she hoped soon to be married.

At any rate, she asked me when I would take a wife. After having been well at ease with her, I became voiceless. I could not even look at her, for the very knowing of how she looked at me; I stood swallowing, and for better ease coughed, scratched myself, and coughed again. Then, and I think it was hoarsely, I told her I did not know, but supposed I would wed at eighteen or thereabouts, as seemed to be the custom.

She asked me whether, in case I found a woman who pleased me, I would be married at fifteen; but what could I say save that I did not know? Thereupon she declared that the man of her choice must be tall and strong, and skilled in the ways of Indians, and without hair on his face and broad in the shoulders and slim below them: that she would have only two children, and travel to Portsmouth and Boston and wear pink brocade and fine lace: and if these things could be so she would marry at any age soever.

I remained silent, which is a fair thing to do under such or any circumstances, and was glad that since I knew so little what to reply to her I had told her so much about my wide knowledge of birds and beasts.

Shortly thereafter I became aware that Mary was kneeling beside me, looking into my face; and what she said took not long in the saying, but remained long in my memory.

"Oh, Steven," she said, and an odor of sweet grass came from her, an odor I have always loved, and I discovered later that she braided wisps of sweet grass into her hair, "Oh, Steven, I want to kiss you."

Now it may have been my age, or it may have been a heritage from my great-great-grandfather Richard, or it may have been ordinary stupidity; but whatever it was, it led me to say something I have remembered with little pride late at night when lying awake. God knows I wanted her to kiss me; and yet I had to say, probably somewhat dourly, though I am not certain on this point, "Nobody's looking, and I don't care."

I closed my eyes, and felt her draw closer, felt her hands on my shoulders, and so waited for what might come; but naught came save a small voice saying, "Steven, open your eyes."

I opened them and saw her blue eyes and the long brown lashes around them; her heavy braids of yellow hair; her soft skin with small faint freckles across the top of her cheeks; her red lips. There was a faint, sweet smile on those lips; and she said softly: "Steven, put your arms around me."

So I put my arms around her. I remember now how little but how mightily pleasant she felt to me. She slipped her hands around my neck, and my eyes blurred as her face came close. I had kissed my sisters and my mother a few times; and once, in the woods, Fala Ramanascho had asked me to kiss her, and we had kissed each other; but none of them ever kissed me as Mary did.

Suddenly she sprang from me and laughed and said, "Why don't you kiss me better, Steven?"

Whereat I, foolishly, in simple earnest, said to her: "Where did you learn so much about kissing?"

She leaped up and stamped her foot, crying, "I hate you! You're a baby!" She fled across the dunes and toward the stockade, and I after her. It was time, for the wind had turned into the east and the prophecy of the sun's ring was borne out by the spitting rain drops that were falling in the gathering dusk.

Nor would she speak to me as we ran, so that I was well aware what a clown I was, and could only lead her to the small hole under the rear of the stockade, which, since I had cut it for my own and Ranger's benefit, it was my duty to close each night with a little gate of logs.

She fell to her knees and crept through, still saying nothing; but when I crawled after her, and my head and shoulders were through the hole, so that I could not move, she was waiting for me, still on her knees. As I looked at her she took my face between her hands and kissed me again and said, "Are you going to marry me?"

"Yes," I panted, and I meant it. "Yes! Yes! Yes!"

She kissed me quickly again: kissed me yet once more. Then she scrambled to her feet and ran into the kitchen.

I think I meant it as I had never meant anything in my life.

THE gathering-room was full of clamor and bustle; for travelers who might otherwise have continued their journeys had taken warning from the east wind and made themselves snug indoors for the night.

In this they were wise; for the paths through the woods, though proudly called roads, were little better than successions of bog holes, uncomfortable to travel on horseback, with the horse perpetually slipping into the muck up to his withers, and a matter for powerful cursing when the rider pitched from his horse, as he often must.

The country was sparsely settled; and the settlers, lured to the wilderness by false statements on the part of land speculators in Boston, were in large part poor, ignorant, and embittered folk, living in dark and cheerless cabins; so that a traveler who sought hospitality among them might suffer from gloom for a day and from a quinsy for a week, and be robbed in the bargain.

We were still at war with the French and Indians; and some few of our people, weary of their monotonous life and hopeful of booty, had gone away with Lord Jeffrey Amherst to attack Quebec from one direction while young James Wolfe attacked it from the other. So the French were striking where they could; and dark and rainy nights provided excellent opportunities for the French-inspired red men from the north to reach out silently from the underbrush and seize a likely colonist who could be hurried captive to Canada and put to work for the further glory of the King of France.

Often had my father warned me not to go alone on the roads on a dark or rainy night, unless I went with friendly Indians. He himself wouldn't do so except for the best of reasons; for being a blacksmith and a gunsmith, and as strong as he was wise, he was desired by the Northern Indians, who were eager to take him, since they would be well rewarded by their French masters for providing them with such a workman, as well as for depriving the colonies of his services.

So all the chairs in the gathering-room were occupied; and Malary and my mother and sisters ran here and there in the kitchen, preparing supper, and my oldest sister Hepsibah stood guard over the bean pots to make sure the pork was on the top for its final browning, which is one reason for the toothsomeness of the bean as cooked in our family. Coarse fare though beans may be, I would liefer have them as Malary cooked them, and Cynthia still cooks them, than all the ragouts and French flummeries you can show me.

On each side of the fire, which was small because the night was mild, sat the two commissioners from Wells and the two commissioners from Arundel, Mary's father being one of these, sipping often at their rum, and gravely dusting tobacco ash from buckskin shirts with hands that seemed to me to fumble somewhat.

In the corner was my father in his barrel chair, saying little but missing nothing. The trestle table had been put together, and around it sat a goodly company, shouting and laughing and pounding on the board as always occurs when a gathering is dry and snug, and of its own choice awaiting the passage of evil weather.

There was Lieutenant Wattleby, detailed with two militiamen to the garrison house for duty; Thomas Scammen, a master shipwright from across the river; Humphrey Bickford, whose knowledge of herbs and simples was such that all the townsfolk sought him for medical advice, there being no doctor at all in our poor neighborhood; Ezekiel Kezer, the Indian trader on his way from Falmouth to Boston to lay in supplies; and Ivory Fish, one of the militiamen assigned to the garrison with Lieutenant Wattleby.

Among them was a man I had never before seen. He was younger than any in the room, and yet had a look of being older, as though weary of seeing many things, but amused by all of them, though faintly, because of his weariness. He was slender, with a pale, pleasing face and an odd manner of throwing back his head and staring with cold eyes at the person he addressed. Even Noah Gooch, who carried beer and spirits to the wayfarers, walked carefully around him, and neither stumbled against him nor spilled rum on him, which was a miracle if ever there was one. Noah was the clumsiest of men, and could manage to slop small beer on a customer, even if the two were alone in the room with a brig's mainsail hung between them. Yet the stranger gave him no warnings or reprimands, but only looked at him with a frosty smile.

It was not the stranger's dress that made him conspicuous; for, like any trapper, he wore a buckskin shirt stained the warm yellow color of ferns when the life first goes out of them in the autumn, and a worn and wrinkled pair of buckskin breeches, and moccasins, and a light, tight-fitting summer cap made of brown rabbit skin. It was his speech and manner that set him apart from those about him. His speech lacked the flatness peculiar to our part of the colonies, and had a delicate swishing note to it, that called to mind a snake moving through dried grass. His manner had something I thought of then as high and biting, or disdainful. There was distinction in it; and all in all he was so different that those at the table must often be broadly staring at him. But when they met the iciness of his look they would turn their heads and cough, as if to say they had no interest in him.

The noisiest person at the board was Cap Huff, whose name was thought to be a military title. This belief, indeed, he encouraged, never correcting those who miscalled him Captain. Yet he was not a captain, but only a hugesome, bawling, swaggering young man from Kittery, not skilled in anything except the singing of ribald songs and the coining of bawdy phrases with which to insult the Indians, for whom he had no liking whatever, and a gift of tale-telling that would keep a dozen men hanging on his words and slapping themselves with delight at his injudicious statements, in which, in spite of himself, as it were, there was often a little truth.

To give him his due, he was not bad as a woodsman, being accurate with a musket; but he was given to walking carelessly into perilous straits without taking the trouble to reckon the possible cost. He trusted, it seemed to me, too much on his large, face-encompassing smile; and when this failed, he was quick to fall back on the use of his fists, at which he was proficient.

For all that, I took frequent pleasure in the company of Cap Huff when fate threw us together in after years. I know he was not thought well of in Kittery or in Portsmouth, where he had early occupied quarters in the gaol; but I disagree with those who claimed he would steal anything not securely fastened to wall or floor. He earned his living by carrying goods and messages between Portsmouth and Falmouth and the intervening towns; and what is more, he carried them safely, always. I have heard it said he sometimes returned from journeys with more packages than his commissions entitled him to have; and I noticed his visits to a locality coincided with thefts of minor articles like a sucking pig, or a pair of pistols, and sometimes a keg of brandy. Yet never did he steal from me, except small things I could easily spare.

I could not in all conscientiousness hold him up before my grandsons as a model of the manly virtues, especially in the matter of bathtaking, at which he was more lax than most of our townsfolk, some of whom boasted there were parts of their bodies that water had never touched; yet I can freely say that although Cap Huff had something of a smell, I would liefer fight beside him than beside many a man who bathes as much as twice a week and would not steal even a kiss from a willing maid.

Cap Huff knew little and cared less about the origin of his parents; but in 1725 the people of this neighborhood helped to relieve the survivors of that gallant fray known as Lovewell's Fight; and I know from my father that when the colonists returned from that long hard journey they brought with them, out of the Indian country, Cap's father and mother and two children, one being named Much Experience and the other Little To Depend Upon. The family was deposited in Kittery, where they subsisted on clams and fish entirely; and shortly thereafter this son being born, he was named Saved From Captivity and called Cap for convenience. His taking advantage to be called Captain I have ever regarded as a harmless whim, and have humored him in it, especially when among strangers.

I had brought into the gathering-room an armful of logs from the tall pile beside the kitchen door; and Cap, perspiring gently and nursing a pewter measure of rum so that it looked fragile between his great brown hands, was telling of his adventures on his most recent trip.

I slowly stacked the wood beside the fire so that I might listen to Cap's discourse; for I have always taken pleasure in it, even though accused of having low tastes for so doing because of the vast deal of meaningless profanity with which his tales are interlarded. He used it, obviously, as others use punctuation.

He spoke of an Indian neighbor of ours to the southward, a harmless Abenaki named Ockawando. Cap declared Ockawando was illbegotten and verminiferous, and an eater of bugs to boot, though in all my goings and comings among the Abenakis I never saw one of them eat an insect of any sort.

Cap, it appeared, had observed a bear cub engaged in reaching meditatively for honey in the crotch of an elm tree. The elm tree was close to Ockawando's wigwam—so close, Cap swore, that Providence must have had a hand in it. Not being one to disregard a hint from above, he said, he had hunted out Ockawando and offered him four shillings, hard money, if he would climb the tree and capture the bear. Inflamed by the generosity of this offer, Cap said, the bugeating Ockawando had readily agreed.

They had gone to the tree, which Ockawando had ascended. When he laid hold of the bear's tail the bear not only objected, but the bees failed to distinguish between the bear and Ockawando, and the two fell to the ground with a hideous outcry.

When Ockawando again laid hold of the bear's tail, eager for his four shillings, the bear clawed at him protestingly. Thus Ockawando was obliged to retain his hold of the tail and still remain out of reach of the claws, which is easier to say than to do.

"There he was," Cap said, "going round and round and round, and shouting to me to help him let go of the bear!"

"Did you help him?" asked Lieutenant Wattleby.

"Not me!" Cap said contentedly. "I come away and left him there, going round and round and round."

"Did you pay him the four shillings?" my father asked.

"Now Steven!" said Cap with an injured air, "how *could* I when there wasn't any way of telling whether he was going to catch the bear or the bear catch him?"

In an undertone he added, as though to himself, "I hope it was him as got caught, the dirty bug-eater! He *is* a bug-eater. I've seen him eat snails, and snails is bugs!"

Heartened by the guffaws that followed, Cap absent-mindedly helped himself to the stranger's flask, cupping his thumb and forefinger around the top of his pewter measure so that a full half inch was added to its height, and pouring until the liquor overran his hand.

The stranger looked at him coolly. "I wonder if it was not a gentleman named Ananias who first told that tale? Will you do me the honor to accept a drink?"

Cap hurriedly filled his mouth with liquor, and holding it so, without swallowing, he once more poured a generous cupful from the ironically proffered flask. When he swallowed he looked up appreciatively, exclaiming: "Brandy! Hot stuff!"

"Hot?" the stranger asked incredulously, feeling of the flask and placing it well beyond Cap's reach.

"Hot stuff," Cap repeated, staring at the stranger with knitted brows.

He cleared his throat, wiped his mouth with the back of his hand, threw back his head and bellowed:

"Come, each death-daring dog who dares venture his neck,
Come, follow the hero that goes to Quebec;

And ye that love fighting shall soon have enough:
Wolfe commands us, my boys; we shall give them Hot Stuff.

"Ain't you heard that?" Cap persisted. "That's what they're going to give 'em at Quebec. Ain't you heard the song they're singing?"

"No," the stranger said, "I haven't heard it. One who buys lumber in Falmouth hears few war songs."

"That's strange you ain't! Everybody 'twixt here and Boston knows it. Quebec's about the only place where they ain't heard it."

At this my father moved out from his corner and tapped Cap on the shoulder. "Cap, this here's our country, and we got to live in it. Ockawando's all right. He's square with us and we're square with him. If you go shoving your big fat face into his affairs he's liable to come over here and scare the gizzard out of these women. You know what Indians are."

"Gosh Almighty, yes!" Cap cried. "They do anything; they're dirty bug-eating——"

"They ain't as dirty as you are," my father interrupted calmly. "Ockawando takes a sweat bath twice a week for the rheumatiz, and I bet you ain't had any kind of bath since Pharaoh's army took one in the Red Sea."

"Hell, Steven, I never got wet there," Cap protested. "Anyways, you needn't be afeared I'll hurt your damned Indians; but if they ain't what I say, I'm a Frenchman!"

"To the pure all things are pure," the stranger murmured enigmatically.

Cap looked at him again. It seemed to me the two men were erecting a screen of cold air around themselves: a chilling, burdensome screen that made their movements slow and unpleasant to watch.

"If you're in lumber," Cap said, "we might sing 'em that song about Benning Wentworth they're singing up in Portsmouth."

"We might," the stranger said graciously, "but I don't sing."

"You don't say! Well, mebbe you could put me right on how much Benning paid the surveyor gineral to get out of his job, so's he could grab it himself and get the money. You're in lumber and you ought to know."

"Indeed," the stranger said, and the dry, swishing note in his voice sounded more than ever like a snake in dead leaves, "some say one thing and some say another."

Cap smiled into his empty cup and flapped his huge paw at Noah Gooch, whereat Noah came stumbling up with the rum jug, carefully avoided the stranger, and lurched against Cap's shoulder, pouring until the rum overran Cap's thumb and forefinger, whose width had again been added to the cup's height.

"What's the song, Cap?" asked Humphrey Bickford. "Lieutenant Wattleby's got a tenor."

"Hot stuff," said Cap, "and if he don't use it right, you can all hit him with a rum jug." He shot a glance at the stranger's cold smile and then went on: "What you think of a man that'll be governor of a province and then turn around and buy the surveyor gineral's job? Pays two hundred pound, that job does; and there's so much money in it, waiting to stick to a man's fingers, that Benning, the old rat, paid him two thousand pound to get out!"

Kezer clicked his tongue admiringly against the roof of his mouth. "Better'n trading," he opined.

"Trading!" Cap Huff exclaimed. "It's better'n smuggling or privateering! Less trouble and more money!" He tilted back in his chair, grinned widely and sang the song, which I remember well, for he was given to singing it in after years, when things were going a little wrong with us:

> "Now old Benning Wentworth is full to the chin
> Of pride and position and brandy and tin:
> He'll pick out a job for his mother and wife
> And then he can dream for the rest of his life—
> Asleep down in hell on a bed of hot pitch:
> Oh, Gosh! Ain't old Benning a-making 'em rich!"

He sang a dozen more stanzas, enjoying himself the more, the louder and longer he sang; and as he sang his companions banged on the table with fists and pewter measures, so the song was a stirring one, albeit I was uncomfortable at hearing such ribald things about the governor of New Hampshire, who must, I thought, since he was rich and powerful, be also good.

"It's harmonious," said Lieutenant Wattleby, when the pleased shouts had subsided, "but if you go on singing it, Cap, they'll be citing you for slander."

"Slander hell!" Cap said. "Let somebody try it if he wants his nose pushed around into his ear! There ain't no law court powerful enough to stop me saying what I think!"

Here my mother came in and ordered the men to the stockade, so that she might clean the room and place the supper. The stranger leaped to his feet and bowed politely, and all of us were offended

and displeased, without knowing why. I think it was because he
made us feel rough and uncouth. At all events, we had the desire
to be even more uncouth and rough before him than we hitherto
had been.

The others followed him out; and Cap stumbled clumsily over his
own feet and shrank sheepishly from my mother, so that she threatened him in fun with an iron spoon and restored him to composure
again.

The fire was made bright, the floor swept smooth and resanded;
and Malary set on the table two pots of beans with a relish of
chopped cucumbers steeped in brine and flavored with onions, and
two haunches of venison, and brown bread hot from the oven, and
butter fresh from the churn. Close beside the table, on wooden scissors, was a barrel of my mother's small beer, though I know not why
they call it small, for scarce a man can drink a gallon of it without
a thickening in his speech.

Also there were six mince pies laced with rum, and a bowl of
creamy cheese made from sour milk. If I had been a rich man in
those days I would have traveled far to enjoy such a meal as that;
for good provender was hard to come by; and our inns were rightly
called ordinaries, especially in the matter of their food, which was
so coarse and grease-laden as to bring on heartburn or even apoplexy.
Nor was the charge of one shilling that my father made for supper
an unreasonable sum, considering that poor travelers were never
pressed for payment, and that those who supped at the inn might
buy an oval flask of rum for one shilling. Such a price was possible
because my father's shipmaster friends bought rum in the French
Sugar Islands for two pounds a keg and smuggled it from their brigs
at our back door.

I do not know that Cap spoke ill of the stranger to the others
during the time they spent in the stockade; but when they returned
for their supper, it seemed to me, they stared at him even more furtively and suspiciously. It seemed to me, also, that his smile grew
colder and colder, and yet that he took pleasure in saying things
that befuddled or inflamed the wits. It gave me such a feeling as I
have had at seeing a swordsman playing with a country bumpkin,
threatening him with a cruel wound from the shimmering tongue of
steel in his hand, and unconscious that the bumpkin, in rage or despair, might beat down his guard by main strength and hack him in
pieces.

Mallinson, far gone in liquor when supper was over, told my father with an air of drunken pride that he had signed an agreement with the commissioners from Wells establishing the boundary between Wells and Arundel at the Arundel River, and that this question would no longer vex us. Upon that my father roared violently and brandished his fist under Mallinson's nose. He must be a fool and worse, my father shouted; for by this agreement the town of Wells would be seven miles in length, and Arundel less than two.

"Nay," Mallinson said, "we'd been here so long we had no money to pay our reckoning! The Wells commissioners paid for us. What could we do but let 'em put the boundary where they pleased?"

My father grew purple with rage. The others stared at Mallinson with dropped jaws for being such a drunken zany; all but the stranger, who smiled his hard, bright smile and said that since the people of Maine had been willing to fight a barbarous war over so small a thing as fish, he feared for their future if they must hereafter be confronted with such serious matters as this.

The company forgot Mallinson. A muttering arose among them, an angry muttering, at the stranger's words, even though they could not quite understand them.

To me he had become hateful. He put me in mind of a hostile Indian, the way he lurked silent and motionless for a time; then shot a knife-tipped dart among us.

"Well, now," said my father, moving behind a chair, which he did when violence was brewing, "those here know little concerning wars over fish, and less concerning barbarities except those inflicted by Indians from the northern settlements."

"The dirtiest crew of bug-eaters outside o' hell!" interposed Cap Huff, mopping his plate with a piece of bread.

"Surely," said the stranger, with an air of wide-eyed surprise, "surely you haven't forgot the siege of Louisbourg, as well as the wars before it, came about over who should have the taking of fish on the Grand Banks."

"Fish me no fish," my father said. "I was there! I helped to take the Grand Battery and haul the cannon across the great swamp on sledges, which men said couldn't be done. I went to Louisbourg because of no fish. I went to Louisbourg because the French pestered me and my father and my grandfather with their damned pirate sloops and brigs out of Louisbourg, and because they paid their sneaking red men to hatchet and murder and steal our women and children, and keep our whole damned country in a stew!"

"None the less," said the stranger, smiling frostily, "there's been naught but fish at the bottom of these wars, as you'd know if you spoke with men whose knowledge goes beneath the surface. What, then, will be our future if our neighbors throw away our children's land?"

"Now God knows I'm a frail reed at argument," said my father, "but I like not your use of the word 'our.' From your speech you're not one of us at all. Over half the men that took Louisbourg were from this little part of Maine. It was our war, by God, and if you'd had a part in it, you'd have seen no fish anywhere about it."

"Give him hell, Steven," said Cap Huff, planting his elbows on the table.

"Furthermore," my father said, "the disposition of our land is something we'll settle peaceably among ourselves. There's enough of it hereabouts to supply our children for hundreds of years to come, even with psalm-singing deacons from Boston gobbling it up for speculation by the million acres. You spoke, though, of a barbarous war. Since I had a hand in it, I don't choose to hear it so miscalled in this house."

"Why," said the stranger in a tone like the swishing of a whip lash, "I'd been thinking how Parson Moody chopped the altar and the images in the French church at Louisbourg, and how the Boston troops killed Father Rale at Norridgewock."

"Well, God alive!" my father cried, "and what's the reason for all this delving into ancient history! I only know Parson Moody was a bigot from York, crabbed and irritable; but I saw the French troops march safely out of the fortress, after we'd taken it, with all their arms and colors. There was nothing barbarous about it, except the stupidity of the French commander. If you must talk about barbarities, talk about the way Frenchmen stood silent at Fort William Henry and watched their stinking Northern Indians murder our women and children. As for Father Rale, the Boston troops that killed him were told he had promised the Norridgewocks eternal salvation in return for colonial scalps, and headed them himself, musket in hand, like that rat LeLoutre of Acadia. It was Rale's life or the lives of defenseless women and children from our own people, or so they thought. So they did what anyone else would do: they lodged a ball in his brain and counted the deed well done."

The stranger lifted his shoulder; and his smile belied his words.

"Such things must happen, belike, when good Calvinists are chosen by God to do his work. We aren't to blame if things go wrong when we joyously attempt, as we so often do, to teach papists and other sinners their duty with our pens, our voices, or our bombshells."

Those at the table looked furtively at each other, and their glances foretold upturned tables and broken bottles.

"I'm no Calvinist," my father growled. "I hate all praying hypocrites; so have done with this talk of what it is we do. Speak for yourself: not for us!"

"Are you not," the stranger asked lightly, "held beneath the thumbs of the praying hypocrites in Massachusetts? Do they not intend to use you to take Canada from the French? And that being considered done, and you lively witted country fellows made into disciplined, silent soldiers, what else will there be for you to do but fight England? The English and the New Englanders will hold all the land, and cannot think alike on any subject; and you must agree it has become our way to fight all who think not as we think."

He smiled coldly and continued. "If you make war against England with the Massachusetts bigots, you must have help; and the only help to be had will be that of the papist French, who will fight even on the side of Boston bigots to be revenged on England. So there you'll be—you who hate all praying hypocrites and all papist French, fighting side by side with hypocrites and papists!"

His hearers glowered at him, baffled and silent; and the stranger's pale smile, I now know, was one of contempt for the slow-wittedness of those on whom he exercised his sharp tongue and agile brain.

Cap Huff's chair creaked noisily as he moved uneasily beneath the stranger's scornful glance, and he spoke heavily to his next neighbor. "What was it he said we were? He said something about what kind of country fellows we were, didn't he?"

"Yes; he said we were lively witted."

"Did he?" Cap said. "I didn't like the look on his face when he said it. Listen!" He reached across the table and dropped his ham-like hand on the stranger's arm. "Did you say lively witted or light-fingered?"

The stranger, with no alteration in his frigid smile, looked Cap in the eye and said: "I would be better pleased without your hand on me."

Cap took his hand away slowly and examined it with an air of mild surprise. "He must have said light-fingered," he muttered. He leaned forward again. "Listen, stranger——" He stopped there and seemed to rack his brain for something proper to say, but racked it in vain, for he said nothing more.

It was then that Mary came running in from the kitchen to seek her father. He, poor weak-willed man, had fallen forward at the table with his face in some splashings of his rum, and was snoring lustily. Seeing what had happened, Mary sat beside me on the fireplace step, and her hair shone in the firelight, brighter than the buttons on Lieutenant Wattleby's coat. Shamed at her nearness, I turned from her and so saw the eyes of the stranger looking at her. Their lids half covered them, and they glowed like those of a dog staring into a tree to find a raccoon. He spoke to Kezer, the trader, who sat beside him: "Very pretty, on my soul! A sweet morsel for a cold bed!"

I began to tremble suddenly, though I was not sure of his meaning; I hated him, and if I had known how I would have done him a hurt. I had no need to think of hurting him, however. He was in trouble with others, and more capable than I.

Cap Huff stood up, rubbed his lips with his vast hands, and gave a hitch to his eelskin belt.

"He *did* say light-fingered! I'll eat two dead sea gulls and a live crow if he didn't!" He leaned forward and dropped his hand hard on the stranger's shoulder, so that he turned his eyes from Mary and looked at Cap, very high and mighty; then rose slowly to his feet.

The room was as breathless as a summer afternoon just before a black storm rolls up from the west; but I saw that if the stranger read the sign he did not heed it.

"May I again call your attention to your hand! I'm unused to so much affection from gentlemen!"

"Affection!" Cap repeated slowly, and his face grew fiery red. "Affection!"

He seemed to mull the word over in his mind, seeking the other's meaning, and it seemed clear he found it; for suddenly he uttered a surprising bellow: a great shocking roar.

"Affection! By God, I'll show you some!" Before the stranger could move, this mountain of a man had dragged him across the table; then, seizing him by the collar of his buckskin shirt and by his nether part, he lifted him from the floor.

"By God," Cap bellowed, "I'll show him some light-fingered affection!"

As I ran ahead and opened the doors, Cap charged through them with the stranger helpless in his grasp, while behind him all the company streamed from the inn, uproarious and cursing with excitement.

The tide was out and the mud of the creek showed faintly luminous in the dull night light. Bellowing still, Cap placed his foot against the stranger's back and propelled him heartily into the slimy creek bottom. He landed with a mighty slap, slid a foot or more, and lay motionless until our laughter began to fade.

He got slowly to his feet and faced us, and the burst of mirth that had followed his descent ceased entirely.

His features were hidden because of the black mud that covered them, and he was horrible to see. He was like some proud animal disfigured by an ignominious wound, enraged and deadly.

And so, though all of us within that very moment had been screaming with laughter, we no longer saw any fun in the matter.

He uttered no word: he just eyed us; and we stared at him for the length of time it takes a breaker to curl and fall. Then he turned and dragged himself through the clinging muck toward the Abenaki wigwams on the other shore; and somehow his going was more sinister and more menacing than any threatening gestures could have been.

We stood looking after him until he vanished, and I heard my father beside me breathing deeply. At length he spoke harshly to Cap, though it seemed to me his voice was softer than his words.

"Why don't you go for a pirate, where you belong? God knows what ill luck you'll bring on us yet. Come in and keep quiet, and I'll give you enough buttered rum to make you peaceable from helplessness."

III

I think I would have slept until long past sun-up on the following morning, and so had my face dowsed with water by my father, had not Cap Huff fallen over me as I lay warmly on my bag of straw by the kitchen door, and knocked sleep and wind from me at the same time.

He gave me a sheath knife, sharp as a razor, when I had let him out as quietly as possible; but quiet was beyond him because he was full of hoarse complaints of his head, which he said held seventeen rusted nails driven through from ear to ear. His tongue he damned for being henceforth useless—it had grown to the size of a fair codfish, he said, and then, not content with its prodigiousness, had perversely got itself besmeared with glue and besprinkled with sand until he could scarce so much as waggle it, and feared it were best out at once and he dumb and done for.

As for the knife, I seemed to remember seeing it on the stranger's thigh before Cap hurled him into the mud. It may be Cap, in the heat of battle, had thoughtlessly plucked it from his opponent's belt; and that reminded me to scrutinize him lest he might be carrying away with him a poke of my mother's sugar, which would have inconvenienced us somewhat.

The wind was still in the east as Cap bawled his farewells and rode westward toward the beaches and the curved blue line of the Wells shore. The rain had ceased and the crows were hard at work squabbling among themselves and breakfasting, dropping mussels from a height onto the hard sand, so the shells might be broken and the meat exposed, and this they seldom do unless the weather be about to clear.

I turned from them to find the house astir. My sisters and Mary had carried their straw bags, along with mine, to the penthouse behind the kitchen and were wiping their faces with a damp huckaback towel at the bench beside the kitchen door. I was filled with dissatisfaction at the sight of Mary, for I knew she would soon be leaving;

and the world, instead of seeming homelike and gay, became forlorn.

All my life, since then, that same feeling has come back to me as if it kept a mournful anniversary on such an autumn morning, when the dawn is silent because the songbirds have gone away to the South, and approaching winter has set its cold fingers on the house, and the crows carouse at sun-up in the open meadows and on the beaches.

It is a feeling of impending loss, of wasted days, of vanished friendship; and the only cure I know is to fare into the marshes and woods and shoot enough partridges and teal ducks so a pot-pie may be made from their breasts, and to eat the pie before a roaring fire on a sharp night and wash it down with a gallon of mulled cider.

Angry at Mary because I wished to be alone with her and was not, I hung my head, passed her by in silence, and went into the house, where I was sulky to my mother when she gave me corn bread and milk for my breakfast. When I came out I carried the sand buckets with me and said, in a voice I tried to make gruffly indifferent, that I was going to the beach for sand for the floor; but Mary neither looked at me nor spoke; so I plodded alone through the sand dunes with Ranger galloping along to inspect rat and rabbit holes that he considered it his duty to observe daily.

Eunice lay off shore, raising her bullet head and her shoulders high above the rollers and anxiously scanning the beach; and when she saw me slip down from the dune grass into the soft sand she dove through the surf and flopped herself to me, coughing as though afflicted with a consumption, and pressed her wet nose against the calves of my legs. Not being kindly disposed because of my gloom, I kicked her fat side, whereat Mary appeared as if from nowhere and pushed me sharply in the back.

"You stop!" she said. She sank to her knees and put her arms around Eunice's wet neck, and Eunice blew affectionately in her face.

"Phew! Fish!" Mary cried, sitting back on her heels and pulling Eunice's stiff whiskers. Offended, the foolish creature hunched herself out of reach to lie on her side and wave one flipper in the air and stare at the sun and make distressful choking sounds, after the manner of seals.

There were many things I would have liked to say to Mary, God knows; but like most children I could never say what I wished, and so said nothing, but silently filled my buckets with sand. She came and stood quietly beside me for a while. Then she murmured: "My father's well now. When he's finished his beans and pie, he'll take me home."

I knew this was so, and Mary must have known I knew, and surely I showed I was not happy over it. Thinking there was nothing to be said, I continued to fill the buckets and to say nothing.

She waited for me to speak, but getting no word out of me she put her foot on the edge of a bucket and overset it. When I looked at her in surprise she ran from me, laughing, so I ran after her.

Swift as she was, I was soon close enough to catch at her. Thus I was taken unawares when she stopped and turned. My arms were around her before I knew what had happened, and she was pressed close against me. Shamed, I dropped my arms and moved away to dig holes in the sand with my moccasin. I could feel her looking at me, but could not look at her, though I wished to do so.

She turned and scrambled up into the dune grass at the top of the beach. I was angry at her for going, even though I had given her no cause to stay. She stood there without moving for a time: yet I would not look at her, but continued to make holes in the sand and to wish she would come down again.

At length, in a small voice, she said, "Did you mean it last night?" and I, wishful of saying "Yes!", stubbornly shook my head. Hearing no further sound, I looked up and found her gone.

My surliness left me. Forgetful of the buckets and all else, I leaped up the bank and saw her speeding toward the stockade. Nor, in spite of my cries of "Mary, I meant it! Mary, I meant it!" did she slacken her pace until she came in sight of Ivory Fish on guard at the stockade gate.

Then, walking sedately until I came up with her, she said: "Are you glad you promised last night?" Although fearful that Ivory might know what it was I had promised, I said at once I was glad. Still she was not content, and asked: "Will you hunt for spruce gum with me?"

I knew the woods were not safe, so said, "No: there might be strange Indians from the north." With that she halted in the very face of Ivory Fish and declared I had not meant what I said if Indians could stop me. I said hastily I would come and had meant everything, which I had.

There was no pleasing her. She must needs imagine impossibilities and ask if I would come to see her even though her father moved far away, to Portsmouth or Boston, or even to Mt. Desert. I said

"Yes" to all her questions, caring not how much Ivory Fish might suspect of our affairs. I think she might have made me promise to follow her to the Sugar Islands or to London; but before she could think of these places, her father emerged from the kitchen and beckoned to her. At the same time my mother came out and called to me that I should ferry them across the creek because my father was busy on the river; and I could tell by the way she flapped her apron toward Mallinson that she was eager for his departure.

As I went down to launch the skiff I saw the Abenakis on the far side of the creek had taken down their wigwams, so I knew most of the women and many of the fighting men had already set off for their winter town. Before the day was done, they would all be gone. This added to my sadness, for the Abenakis had always been kind to me, and I could ask no merrier companions than young Mogg Chabonoke and Fala Ramanascho, nor kinder ones.

They often brought me gifts: an arrow, or a medicine stone against drowning, or a bracelet of horsehair to keep aches from the shoulders in wet weather. They had taught me how to make a fire from a bow and rawhide; how to speak in the Abenaki tongue; how to turn my feet back under me in paddling a canoe so that the posture could be endured for hour on hour.

In return I could give them next to nothing: a pinch of salt or sugar; a bead; a piece of calico; a little powder and ball; yet they would have been my friends if I could have given them nothing at all, and I was loath to see them go.

Mallinson came pompously to the bank, followed by Mary, and stared at me out of eyes like those of a dead shark, but redder, and suspended in pouches of flesh that seemed to hang from the ends of his eyebrows.

"Don't rock the boat, little boy," he said, with his weighty frown. "What I ate last night sits discomfortably within me." Lowering himself stiffly into the bow, he clambered around me where I stood holding to the bank with the oar.

If he had not been Mary's father I might have been tempted to jab him with the butt of the oar for calling me a little boy, or for blaming the effects of his rum-guzzling on my mother's cooking; but I lost my spite at him when Mary jumped into the skiff and as she slipped past me, pressed my arm.

So powerfully did she affect me that I felt no pain when Mallinson observed that we would probably have more bad weather, and that because of the departure of the Abenakis from the creek we would have no further troubles with Indians until spring. The poor man should have known that the east wind was passing around to the south, which means fair weather always, and that with the departure of the friendly Abenakis there would be more opportunity for the hostile Indians from St. Francis and the French settlements to fall upon us without warning.

Yet I gave no thought to these matters, what with staring at Mary and waiting for her to lift her eyes, which she did from time to time. Once, indeed, when her father was peering over his shoulder at the Abenaki camp, she wrinkled her nose at me so pleasantly that my strength failed and my oar turned sidewise in the water, so I was near to pitching in the river.

It was well I stared at Mary while I could; for no sooner had the skiff touched the shore than Mallinson clambered out without a word of thanks, took Mary by the hand, and hurried her up the bank and into the narrow path that led through the high pines. Twice she looked back and smiled: then the brush hid her. Never, I thought, had the pines seemed so tall and dark; never before had our garrison house and its stockade looked so cold and cheerless against the broad expanse of sea.

Long I stood staring after her, while those two backward looks of hers warmed me with the sweetness of them, yet stung me with longing. Then slowly I turned; and Ranger barked for me on the far bank.

But I sat in the skiff with my head down.

Mary was gone.

*　　*　　*

That day was unlike any other I had known. My friends turned stupid and unreal in my eyes. Ivory Fish, on guard at the gate, seemed a grinning lout; and the talk of Lieutenant Wattleby, whom I had respected as a brave soldier, appeared senseless. Even my mother I deemed slow-witted because she smiled blithely and took no notice of my leaden heart, that was gradually ceasing of its own weight to beat.

As for my father, going about his business in the smithy, it seemed to me he was a sort of dull monster, the very sight of which hurt me so I was breathless.

I did, it is true, contrive to make my way weakly to the house with the sand buckets; but when I saw Malary place on the kitchen table a platter of hash, brown on top and moist in the center, and a plate of corn bread flanked by jugs of maple syrup, I knew that life was over for me. There had been few things to stir me as deeply as hash, followed by syrup on corn bread; and yet, of a sudden, these foods seemed coarse and repulsive: I could not touch them.

That day was long. At mid-afternoon the sun came out and the wind blew fresh from the southward. I was working listlessly in the cornfield, turning back the husks from the ears and braiding them together so they might be hung from the ceiling of the kitchen to dry, when young Mogg Chabonoke ran out of the woods and down the path on the opposite side of the creek. He stood on the bank, whistling shrilly through his fingers.

I ran to launch the skiff and sculled over to him. He jumped in, looking at me curiously, and said, "My father sends to your father, Steven." He showed me a strip of birch bark with Abenaki writing on it—though I have heard many wise men say the Indians have no written language, even after I have told of receiving hundreds of written messages from them.

As soon as we landed, he ran straight for the smithy, and I followed when I had made the skiff fast. My father came out of the door, taking off his leather apron as he came; for whenever an Indian runs as young Mogg was running it is a sign that everyone had best prepare to do the same.

He took the birch bark from young Mogg and studied it. Then he looked up and said: "Stevie, Indians killed Mallinson and scalped him after he left here this morning. There was another man with them—a white man. They took Mary and started north."

He turned to Mogg. "Tell, son of my dear friend."

I went and sat down against the smithy and heard young Mogg's voice hazily through a fog, just as I heard the beat of surf on the beach.

There were eight, he said, and a white man had joined them with half-dried mud on his clothes. They had lain all night under the ledge of rocks to the west of the high point on the path.

"Waiting for someone," my father said, "or they'd have been off at daybreak."

I was thinking back at Mary: of the pressure of her shoulder against mine; of the faint freckles across the top of her cheeks; of the way she held my face between her hands and kissed me; of the firelight behind her bright hair when the stranger had looked at her with glowing eyes. The fog lifted in my head, and I interrupted Mogg. "Waiting for the stranger Cap threw in the mud!"

My father frowned. "It was last night he was thrown in the mud. There was no need to wait this morning."

"He made them wait. For Mary. He wanted Mary."

My father looked at me abstractedly. Then he nodded and walked toward the house.

I got up heavily and followed.

My father went into the kitchen, where my mother was knitting a long woolen stocking. She looked up as he entered, and, seeing his face, would have risen; but my father pressed her back in her chair.

"Mallinson was killed and scalped this morning, Sally, and them that did it took Mary away to the north."

My mother drew me to her. "Oh, I feared some evil would come of throwing that man in the mud!" she cried.

My father reached up over the fireplace and took down his long-barreled musket and the wampum belt of the Norridgewock Indians that hung from its lock. My mother pressed me closer. "You think you must go, Steven?"

"I got to do it. I know the Indians and they know me. I can talk their lingo. You know there isn't much danger for me, Sally; but if these other folk tried it their scalps would be dripping by nightfall. Somebody's got to let 'em know that we go out after murderers."

"Ma," I said, "I got to go too."

My mother laughed and touched her upper lip with the tip of her tongue, as though she heard something absurd.

"Well, I *got* to," I said. "I *got* to help hunt for Mary."

My mother glanced at my father as if to see what he thought of my craziness, and for the first time discovered that he was regarding me seriously. Her look grew frightened, and she shook my shoulder. "What makes you say such a thing, Stevie?"

"Because I *got* to, Ma. I promised her I'd marry her when we're growed up. I *got* to. I'll die if I don't, Ma!"

My father nodded. "It'll do him no hurt and he'll come to no more harm than I will myself."

"He's too young, Steven."

"No," my father said, "he's able to handle himself in the woods. He's as big as I, and he knows the Indian signs and the lingo and the tricks of the weather. He needs experience, Sally. When he's got it he'll be better able to look after you and the girls."

"Then if you must take Stevie take others too. Take Lieutenant Wattleby and Ivory Fish to guard against an ambush."

"No," said my father again. "Wattleby and Fish are on duty. For that matter, we can do better alone. More than the two of us would go blundering through the woods, and we'd lose time. Stevie and I can go where others can't. With my belt, we'll be welcome in the Norridgewock towns. The main thing's to overtake 'em."

He raised and lowered the hammer of his musket. It clicked sharply in the still kitchen. "When we find 'em, we can send back for help, if need be."

Sighing, my mother got up and kissed him. "I'll have Ivory Fish's brother to work around the place, and Ivory can help when he isn't on duty. But see you hurry back to make the house snug for the winter."

She bustled about for salt and extra flints and fresh woolen stockings and the tight-knitted woolen shirts my father wore under his buckskin in the woods, even in warm September weather, and for other small oddments we were like to need on our travels.

I ran to unwrap the oily rag from my light musket. My father made a package of needles and metal beads and brass rings as gifts for his Indian friends, filled our patch boxes and our shot pouches, and encircled our belongings neatly in the brown blankets we carried on our backs.

The sun was still bright and warm when we set off for the creek, accompanied by my mother and my sisters and Ivory Fish and Lieutenant Wattleby and Malary; yet it seemed to me, such was my impatience to be off, that we had wasted hours of valuable time.

I fretted while my father reminded my mother of things to be done in his absence, such as banking brush around the bottom of the house to keep out the shrewd winds of autumn; and I thought ill of him because he cast about in his mind to make sure he had forgotten nothing.

I endured my mother's kisses with ill grace, my thoughts being with those who were hurrying Mary from me. It was not until Ivory Fish had set us across, and the pines loomed black before us, that I looked back with a pang of regret at the small group waving to us from the other shore, brilliant in the golden afternoon sun against the green of the meadow and the cornfields: fat Lieutenant Wattleby with his blue militia coat unbuttoned; black Malary with a red cloth about her head; my mother all in gray, a white kerchief at her throat and her hand pressed against her lips; Hepsibah and Jane and Cynthia in their brown homespun clinging to her skirts; and Ranger, with his white shirt front, sitting apart, his muzzle in the air, howling dolefully at being left behind.

The thought came to me that never before had I been separated from my mother and my sisters. It is likely something showed in my face, for my father dropped his hand on my shoulder and pressed me onward. "One thing at a time, Stevie. What we do, we do for them. The sooner we do it, the sooner we'll come back."

Both of us turned and waved once more, then moved on into the pines to seek for Mary.

IV

FROM our creek the path wound crookedly along the high land until it reached the narrow ferrying place where now stands the bridge that is ever tumbling into the water on spring tides. Midway between the creek and the bridge lived Hiram Marvin, recently returned from the massacre at Fort William Henry with an arrow through his shoulder and a tomahawk gash in the muscles of his back, such was the deviltry of the Northern Indians.

He was a good man, my father said, but petulant with his wife and six daughters because of the inflammation that afflicted his wounds whenever the weather changed and obliged him to seek relief in rum to which had been added an infusion of tobacco to let him know, as he said, that he had been drinking something.

Marvin's house was a small one of two rooms, a pistol shot from Mitchell's garrison house, which stood nearest in the direction of the ferry; and some of the garrison folk were sitting along the front of Marvin's house in the warmth of the westering sun, along with Marvin and his youngest daughter Phoebe and Mogg Chabonoke the sachem, and young Mogg, who had waded the creek ahead of us and gone to tell his father we were coming.

It was Phoebe who had seen Mallinson drawn into the grass by the roadside, where he had been killed by a knife thrust and his scalp taken. She had likewise seen a white man in mud-stained garments run after Mary, stop her mouth with his hand, and carry her back into the brush. I sickened at her tale and at her eagerness to tell it.

I had long misliked the girl Phoebe, who was noisy and previous, dark and thin and so quick in her jumping about that one never knew where she was. Within the year she had been milking her father's cow in the field when she saw an Indian lurking behind near-by bushes, preparing, no doubt, to steal the milk, of which all Indians are enamored. Flying into a passion because the Indian watched her, she dashed at him and banged him so outlandishly with the milk pail that he went away in a panic, leaving a fine French blanket behind him. This she made into a winter dress, which she wore with an air of knowing that all who saw her were speaking of her exploit, which indeed they were far too often for her vanity; for her vanity was unbearable.

She was froward, and given to asking impertinent questions and to laughing inaptly at statements of her elders. She also had a vile habit of applauding her own quips with prolonged and hoydenish tittering; so that often I wondered her father had not preferred to leave his scalp and his life in the swamps of Lake George, rather than come home to such a daughter.

She jumped up and down and hugged herself in telling how she had run screaming to the spot where Mary had disappeared, and how she had seen one Indian vanishing through the trees while two others, stationed to guard the escape of the party, rose from bushes on either side of the path, closed in behind him, and vanished also.

The two guards, she said, had painted faces, a green splotch in the center of each cheek, surrounded by an irregular yellow star whose points crossed the eyelids above and ran down onto the neck below, offensively unattractive.

Of the man who had taken Mary she saw nothing, she said, nor of Mary either; so she ran to give the alarm.

I could find no fault with her tale, for she had taken note of what she had seen, which is something that few of our people are able to do. Thus they are ever speaking of armies of Indians when only small bands are on the warpath, and of packs of wolves when any woodsman knows that wolves run in families rather than in packs.

Furthermore, she told only what she had seen, whereas most of our white people wag their tongues in all directions in order to impress their hearers with their knowledge of affairs, all afeared to admit they don't know, even when they know nothing. Because of this I long ago learned it is wiser to seek information from an Indian or from a black slave, if the exact truth is desired, than to accept it from a white man.

It was Phoebe's manner of telling her tale that I misliked. It seemed to me she took pleasure in the stealing of Mary, and somehow assumed an air of superior righteousness and importance in being the discoverer of the theft instead of its victim.

My father looked at old Mogg Chabonoke when Phoebe had finished, and when Mogg approved her tale with a nod my father

tweaked her hair and told her she was a good girl; whereupon, laughing her shrill laugh and pulling at his thumb so hard that he slapped
at her, she danced out of sight around the house.

The sachem told my father there had been eight Indians and the
white man in the party. Two guards had been stationed as Phoebe
had said, and the stationing of guards was the manner of retreat
used by French officers who had fought in Acadia two years previous.

The manner of cheek-painting that Phoebe described, old Mogg
said, was peculiar to autumn war parties of St. Francis Indians, who
are the Abenakis who live under the protection of the French on the
St. Francis River near Quebec; and the arrangement of green and
yellow paint on their faces made it possible for them to lie behind
a leafy shrub and look full into the eyes of their quarry without
being observed, so closely did their painted countenances resemble
the colors of the autumn leaves.

"A French officer, he might be," my father said, "gathering information on the colonies for Vaudreuil in Quebec. A damned spy,
belike, striving to stir up dissension, as we saw last night, and too
much of an aristocrat to conceal his brain. How will he go back, my
friend?"

Old Mogg scratched his chin thoughtfully. "I would go up the Connecticut and down the St. Lawrence to Quebec."

"You're growing old, Brother," my father said. "You'd go up the
Connecticut and down the St. Lawrence because the way is easy."

"I would be carrying a white girl."

My father shook his head. "Jeffrey Amherst is before Quebec on
the west, and that madman Wolfe is still attempting it on the lower
side. God knows what they're doing; but with Wolfe's fevered brain
at work on the siege, they're up to some wild feat or other.

"This Frenchman is young and strong and full of the devil. Knowing Quebec may be in danger, he'll go neither around by the back
door, through Amherst's men, nor around to the front door, by sea
and up the St. Lawrence through Wolfe's fleet. He'll go straight to his
goal, I think, by the side door, and damn the obstacles and damn
the white girl and damn the Indians. They'll do the work and he'll
drive 'em, Cousin, by way of the Kennebec. If hell was quicker, he'd
go by way of hell."

"Easier that way than up the Kennebec," Mogg said. He smiled
affectionately at my father.

"Maybe," my father said, "but am I right?"

"You are a wise man, Steven," old Mogg said. He turned from my father and touched the shoulder of young Mogg, who was asleep beside me.

Being in distress from thinking of Mary, I took old Mogg by his leggin and asked, in a voice I strove to make casual: "Where will they carry Mary?"

Old Mogg stared at me for the space of time that it took young Mogg to dig the sleep out of his eyes; then shrugged his shoulders.

"Quebec," he said. His glance flickered over my shoulder. I turned and saw that Phoebe Marvin had come around the house. She was sitting close beside me, looking as though butter wouldn't melt in her mouth.

When he turned away, old Mogg touched my forehead with his forefinger to wish me luck, as did young Mogg; but I was doubtful whether old Mogg was speaking to me or to Phoebe when he added, over his shoulder, "Quebec is good place for girls."

If he was speaking to Phoebe, I would have had him mention a more distant and unsavory locality than Quebec; for when I rose to join my father I found the brat had made fast my hunting shirt to a nail in the side of the house, leaving me to bob at my moorings like a lobster buoy.

At this she set up one of her shrill cackles of laughter, for which I could have killed her with few qualms, and pretended to busy herself in freeing me, though she worked an unconscionable time at it. She had done at last with her fumbling and cackling, whereat I ran off after my father without a word to her, but loathing her profoundly.

When we reached Mitchell's garrison house, where four women were milking under the eye of militiamen who had come across the river at the news of Mallinson's death, Phoebe was waiting for us, having run through the woods to head us off. For a time I ignored her cries of "Stevie! Oh, Stevie!" but at length, thinking she had repented of her spitefulness, I looked up to bid her a neighborly farewell, whereat she leaped up and down with delight and screamed after me: "Stevie likes Mary! Stevie likes Mary!"

At that there was no evil out of hell I wouldn't have wished on this female monster; but she was not through. "See you in Quebec, Stevie!" she squealed hideously, and once more gave herself applause of heinous laughter. As I padded after my father along the pine-scented path which leads toward the Saco Road and the Indian country to the eastward, I thought how true it was that whenever the Indians captured white children they took only the paragons and passed over the pestiferous creatures who could most easily have been spared.

❋   ❋   ❋

It was one o'clock in the morning when we came along the Neck and into the town of Falmouth, now called Portland for some mysterious reason. Despite the lateness we were well content, having done thirty miles, in the dark, heavily burdened with muskets and packs, in something over seven hours.

I have done it more quickly since, but I had less on my shoulders and was older. Now that I look back on it, I was as small and wet, then, as a newly born bear cub. I wonder I did it at all until I remember my determination to come up with Mary and take her back to Arundel with me.

My father led me down Queen Street, past Love Lane and Meeting House Lane to Fiddle Lane and thence into Turkey Lane which leads off Fiddle Lane and runs into King Street; and while I gawked at the houses, he pounded on the door at the sign of the Red Cow until Jane Woodbury, its owner, poked her angular face out of the window above our heads, calling, "Who's there at such an hour?"

"Steven Nason of Arundel," my father said.

"Law! Why couldn't you say so?" protested Mistress Woodbury, leaving us to feel we had been at fault in permitting her to ask.

Five minutes later we were tucked into a warm bed and I was listening in drowsy wonderment to the noises of a great town—the cry of the watch, the kicking of a horse against the side of his stall, the footsteps of two people passing on unknown business, the mournful wails of argumentative cats: a tumult that would have kept me long awake in Arundel.

We were up at dawn, and so, too, was Mistress Woodbury, not only to see us fed but to learn our business; for she was a gossip with a reputation to sustain. When my father told her of the killing of Mallinson and the theft of Mary, she made with her tongue a sound like a dog walking rapidly through sticky mud.

"How'll you find this Frenchman," she asked, "when you know nothing about him?"

"I think we'll find him," my father said grimly.

Mistress Woodbury placed her hands on her fat knees and rolled her eyes upward, as if to find assistance on her eyebrows.

"There came here last night," she said, "a trader, Britt, just down from the Plymouth Company lands. His speech was full of petrified giant moose, and salmons as big as poplar logs, and sea serpents, and God knows what other Abenaki tales, so I paid mighty little attention to him, knowing he'd spoken to nobody for months except squaws. You know what that does to 'em when they come out to a big town like this!" With her tongue she briefly walked a dog through the mud. "Seems to me, though," she added, "he had something to say about a Frenchman who struck the Kennebec yesterday with some Northern Abenakis. Maybe I'd better get him down here."

She sailed upstairs, and her knocks and cries filled the house. She brought back a gangling, sheepish-looking man with a bristly mustache which, when he was in thought, he constantly forced down with his forefinger, caught lightly and almost voluptuously with his outthrust lower teeth, and immediately released, so that it snapped back into place. He pulled up a chair, cut the flaky crust of the apple pie that Mistress Woodbury placed before him, and plunged into his tale.

"You could have knocked me over with a feather," he said, sucking at his mustache. "I come down from Merrymeeting Bay over the trail last night with two Assagunticooks. There was a moon, and me thinking of nothing, only some good Christian food when I got into Falmouth instead of bear fat and hominy, when a young feller stepped out of the brush into the middle of the trail, not three feet away."

He looked quickly over his shoulder at the fly-specked wall. Mistress Woodbury walked her dog through the mud. Britt laughed sheepishly, catching his mustache with his lower teeth and releasing it slowly.

"Give me a start!" he said. "Thinks I, it's Pamola, the evil one that comes in the night, or Pulowech, or one of those men that pop out of rocks, like the Abenakis always talk about." He bit ferociously at his apple pie.

"Did he have eyes like coals of fire?" my father yawned.

"Hell," Britt said, flicking pie crumbs from his mustache, "he had something better'n that. He had a watch with diamond initials on it."

"What were they?" my father demanded.

"Couldn't see 'em, only the last one. There was two letters; then 'de S.' This Pamola the Abenakis talk about: he never carried a watch."

"No, it probably wasn't Pamola."

"Probly not," Britt agreed. "He was a thin young feller with a pale face and his chin in the air, and kind of a mean way of talking.

Had some Abenakis with him. They spoke to my Assagunticooks. French Indians. St. Francis. They had a white girl with 'em. You could have knocked me over with a pine needle!"

"That's the man," said my father. "What did he want?"

"News. Nothing but news. He wanted news of a man who'd went up the Kennebec ahead of him."

"What man?"

Britt didn't know, and my father couldn't guess what could lead a Frenchman to appear from nowhere, pursuing a man up the river, toward Wolfe, instead of down the river, away from Wolfe.

"Well," my father said at length, "it doesn't matter. What matters is that he's on the Kennebec. We'll have news of him at Swan Island or Norridgewock. If we don't get a crack at him after all this, I'm a Frenchman!"

He began to strap on his pack, as did I. Britt said: "If you ain't following a trail, you'd best take a whaleboat express from Preble's Wharf at seven o'clock this morning. One goes across Casco Bay into Maquoit Bay in two hours if the wind's right. You walk up to Brunswick over the Twelve Rod Road in an hour."

Grateful for this information, which would save us a day's tramp over the evil trails northward from Falmouth, we bade farewell to Mistress Woodbury, who waved aside my father's demand for a reckoning, declaring she would seek payment in kind at our inn when she traveled to Boston for fripperies.

I was bemazed by the size and activity of Falmouth, and by the wealth of the place. Men went freely about the streets, wearing embroidered waistcoats, lace cuffs, silver shoe buckles. From the stores on King Street came odors of all sorts of foods and drinks and merchandise; and the street itself was five rods wide. So great was the traffic that the whole road was churned into mud or dust and scarce a blade of grass grew anywhere.

There were houses of three stories, meeting houses, public buildings, all built of boards, with no logs showing, some painted red, though mostly unpainted. I wondered how the people of Falmouth could spend their days amid such noise and excitement without losing their minds; and I resolved then, nor have I ever changed, that I would hold to the peace of the country and leave the tumult of cities to folk of stronger nerves.

Never had I seen such hustling and bustling as surrounded the wharves of Fore Street—wharves so large that the largest whaleboats seemed small beside them; and even brigs of a hundred tons burthen, that would have crowded the eels and pollocks out of our Arundel River, were nothing to waste time over.

The whaleboats lay at the pier-end, one loading supplies and parcels for the Brunswick fort, and the other taking on goods for forts and settlers along the Kennebec. There were four men to row, two on each side, and a helmsman with a musket beside him, and a boat captain in the bow with a musket and a fish spear, prepared for any sort of encounter.

At seven, after a deal of shouting and swearing, the tarpaulins were stretched over the packages, and our boat pushed out, her passengers besides ourselves being a trader and a young militiaman from the Brunswick fort who had been home to visit his parents. For the first time since the afternoon of the preceding day my gloom fell from me at the thought we were about to enter the wild Indian country, and that somewhere within it—anywhere within it—we might find Mary and snatch her from her captors and carry her back to Arundel to be my love forever.

My father, too, I thought, seemed better pleased than I had seen him in some time; and he looked approvingly at the green islands in the bay and the high Yarmouth shore on our left as the whaleboat edged out into deeper water and pointed her bow a little to the north of east.

"To-night," he said, "we'll sleep with friends on Swan Island, if we can find two Assagunticooks to carry us into the Norridgewock country." With that he asked the young militiaman where in Brunswick the Assagunticooks could be found.

"God's truth," the boy said helplessly, "I know none of these red devils by name. They all look alike! If left to me, I'd have 'em wiped out, so to stop 'em yowling how we stole their lands, and put an end to their thieving and rum-guzzling!"

And this, indeed, is the manner in which the great Abenaki people are regarded by those who have had no means of knowing them, as well as by many who have had opportunities to know them but cannot, through bigotry or prejudice, see beyond the ends of their noses. Since I must frequently speak of my dealings with Abenakis during the course of this tale, it is fitting I should write down the facts that I and my father before me gathered from them and concerning them.

Little enough is known of them now, God knows, and most of that erroneous; and I fear that in another hundred years the only memory of them will be the names they gave to ten thousand hills and headlands and bays throughout our eastern country.

The Abenaki nation is a confederation of tribes living in the river valleys of our beautiful province of Maine, moving up the rivers in the autumn to hunt and gather furs, and down the rivers in the spring to fish and be cool. Between times they plant and harvest their crops on fertile spots along the rivers. The Micmacs of Acadia belong to the Abenaki Confederation as well. They are a coarser breed than our true Abenakis because of mixing their blood with slant-eyed, round-faced Indians from the cold countries. The same is true, to a less degree, of Abenakis living in the eastward of our province—the Penobscots and Passamaquoddies. They, too, are inclined to be ruder and rougher than the rest of the Abenakis, as a man from the deep woods is ruder than one from the settlements. I think it's because they're adventuresome, and have traveled among the wild tribes in the north, intermarrying with them.

However that may be, there is a relationship between all Abenakis. The land of our province belongs to all of them in common, so that a Passamaquoddy may hunt in the valley of the Kennebec if it pleases him, and a Kennebec may hunt on the Penobscot if so inclined. There's a similarity in their speech, so that an Abenaki from the valley of the Saco can understand an Abenaki from the valley of the Penobscot, though he may have difficulty. Thus, a Kennebec Abenaki calls a salmon *cobbossee*, whereas the Penobscot word for salmon is *karparseh*. The words are the same: yet they are a little different.

Our chief rivers, going from Boston toward the easternmost end of our province, are the Merrimac in Massachusetts; then the Saco; then the Androscoggin and the Kennebec together, the Androscoggin flowing into the Kennebec at the pleasant inland tidal lake known as Merrymeeting Bay; and finally the beautiful Penobscot.

In the Merrimac Valley were the Pennacooks, who went early to Canada to live on the St. Francis River because of the manner in which white men crowded them. In the valley of the Saco live the Sokokis, the Abenakis who come to Arundel for the summer fishing. In the Androscoggin Valley are the Assagunticooks, and in the Kennebec Valley dwell the Kennebecs, sometimes called the Norridgewocks, because the largest of their towns is at Norridgewock on the Kennebec. To my mind the Sokokis, the Assagunticooks, and the Kennebecs are the finest of all Abenakis, just as the Abenakis are the finest of all Indians.

Farther to the eastward, in the Penobscot Valley and on the shores of Mt. Desert, which places have no equal for beauty in any of our provinces, live the Penobscots. Beyond them, along our wildest and foggiest shores, are the wigwams of the Passamaquoddies. All of them together, with the Micmacs of Acadia, which is also called Nova Scotia, form the Abenaki Confederation.

*　　*　　*

It has been one of the peculiarities of our colonists that they have never kept faith with Indians. They have either stolen their lands outright, or made the Indians drunk and persuaded them to sell vast stretches of territory for a few beads and a little rum and a musket or two; and they have made treaty after treaty with them—treaties which have always favored the white men; and never has there been a treaty that the white men haven't broken.

Everywhere throughout New England the colonists lied to them, cheated them, robbed them—an easy matter, since the Abenakis are brought up from childhood to think that all their possessions are safe; that no locks or bars are necessary to guard them. In trade they are fair and honest. Nothing causes them greater astonishment and perplexity than crimes white men commit in order to accumulate property.

For an Abenaki to tell an untruth to a friend, except in jest or in the making of medicine, is accounted a crime. When an injury is done to one of them, all his friends make common cause against the guilty person. In friendship they are faithful and ardent, and grateful for favors, which never vanish from their memories; and if these be not returned in kind, then the Abenakis become contemptuous, revengeful, dangerous.

Because of these traits the English might easily have gained and held their friendship and had their assistance against the French. Instead of that, by insults, cruelties and constant frauds they early aroused the enmity of many of them and drove them over to the French; and the French, by flattery and fair dealing, made them into faithful friends.

This, then, accounts for still another body of Abenakis known as a tribe, but actually composed of fragments of tribes. Even before my father was born there were Abenakis south of us—the Pennacooks, of whom I have spoken as living in the valley of the Merrimac. When many of these were massacred without reason by the white settlers, the remnants departed to Canada, where the governor, knowing they would be valuable in warfare, welcomed them and made a treaty with them—a treaty that has ever since been kept. They were given lands on the St. Francis River and at Beçancour, near Three Rivers. After the attack on Father Rale and the Norridgewocks in 1724, the most bitter Norridgewocks departed for St. Francis and Beçancour; and many of the Sokokis joined them after Lovewell's raid on Pequawket in the following year. Still later many Assagunticooks removed to St. Francis.

These Indians became known to us as the St. Francis Indians or the Northern Indians; and while they were Abenakis, like our own Abenakis, they were led by French officers and longed for revenge on those who had abused them. Yet they spoke the same musical language; read the same wampum rolls in the same way; told the same pleasing tales of the good hero-giant Glooskap and his pet loon, the evil wolf-giant Malsum, the mischief-making Indian devil Lox, the great sorcerer Pulowech, the partridge, and Pamola, the evil one.

From all this it may be seen how a white man might be led astray in his estimate of the Indians; how, if he knew only the Sokokis, he might fall a victim to roving bands from St. Francis; how, if he knew only those from St. Francis, he might be at constant odds with friendly Assagunticooks and Penobscots.

My father knew them all except the braves from St. Francis. Even to them he was known by reputation; and since he had dealt honestly with them, giving fair measure and true weight, never watering his rum or sanding his powder, trusting them, helping them when they were in need, scrupulously keeping his promises to them, holding them to be honorable men in all his relations with them, they in turn dealt amiably and honestly with him.

Not only had the Norridgewocks and other tribes given wampum belts to my father, but they had erected private monuments of stone outside our stockade wall at Arundel; and so long as these monuments were not pulled down, my father's family was at peace with the tribes who raised them.

❋   ❋   ❋

As the morning wore on, a breeze sprang up from the west. We stepped a mast with a small sail that hurried us past all the islands and into the end of narrow Maquoit Bay, where we disembarked and set off for Brunswick over a path so clear that in an hour we had reached the banks of the Androscoggin and presented ourselves before the captain at the fort.

He had seen, he said, no trace of St. Francis Indians, or of a French-

man such as my father described, or of Mary; nor, he added, would
he be likely to do so, since they would be sure to move around the
fort in the concealment of the forest. Yet he offered us supplies, and
summoned Warriksos and Wheyossawando, tall Assagunticooks in
buckskin leggins without shirts, who readily agreed to carry us toward Fort Richmond on service of benefit to the colonies.

We embarked under the warm mid-morning sun, and slipped
down stream through trees touched here and there with frost. In less
than an hour we met the salty odor of the rising tide: then entered
the broad reaches of Merrymeeting Bay, with its red blaze of maples
close down along its edges. Instead of pressing against us, the tide
swung to the northward and carried us into the Kennebec.

Flocks of teal and black ducks skittered from the water to scale
off into guzzles and marshes on either side. The banks and headlands drew closer. The river split into two channels, leaving between
the channels a marsh shaped like an arrowhead. The base of the
marsh lay snug against the high curved headland of an island—an
oak- and birch-clad island—as an arrowhead rests against a flexed
bow.

"Swan Island," my father said, and I thought the sight of it made
him happy.

There were guzzles through the marsh; and my father told Warriksos to leave the river and follow one of them to the headland.
When we were close to the point we saw Abenakis behind the trees,
watching. As we neared the beach a tall girl hurried down the bank
and into the water toward us. Men, unarmed, splashed in behind
her, laughing and shouting, "Steven! Brother Steven!"

They took the canoe by the thwarts and ran it up on the shore;
and from the pleasure in their faces and the look in the eyes of the
tall girl it was apparent even to me that my father had done more
than give them a few glass beads and pieces of red flannel.

V

THE lower headland of Swan Island, high above its arrow-headed marsh, was used as a lookout by the Swan Island Indians, who are Abenakis and a part of the Kennebec tribe, though they live by themselves and have little traffic with the Abenakis who dwell in the town of Norridgewock. So lofty is the headland that one who stands on it sees spread out beneath him all the winding guzzles in the marsh and the pools through which they pass, as though he gazed down upon a vast map. He sees at once whatever pools contain swans or geese or brant or ducks, no matter how low the tide has fallen below the marsh grass, and can steal out to them in the small flat boats that Swan Island huntsmen use for killing wild fowl.

Behind the front edge of the headland is a deep swale in which there is a good spring. Beyond the swale the land rises again to a pleasantly wooded plateau on which the wigwams were placed, some twenty of them. They were strewn irregularly among the oaks and birches, and were made of poles and bark, except for three houses. These were of logs, one a Long House for meetings, the others for the sachem and the *m'téoulin,* or Indian who possesses magic power, which is also known as *m'téoulin.*

Of *m'téoulin* I know nothing whatever. I know I have difficulty in keeping a straight face when a great *m'téoulin* is mystifying an audience with some such amazing piece of *m'téoulin* as causing a strip of calico to vanish in his hands, for I can do the same thing by drawing it up my sleeve with a piece of string. Yet, when badly cut by the razorlike hoofs of a deer and burning with fever, I have had a *m'téoulin* sing a *m'téoulin* song over me and singe a wolverine's whiskers and a loon feather in a clam-shell, and have gone to sleep and awakened without fever, which is a piece of *m'téoulin* I couldn't do, even though offered a partnership in the Plymouth Company for doing it.

The sachem of the Swan Island Indians was a woman, Rabomis,

an unusual state of affairs among the Abenakis; for a sachem must be wise, brave and a successful hunter. It was Rabomis who ran into the water to greet my father, calling him "Steven" and gazing at him proudly, as a woman eyes a pleasing jewel on her finger. I couldn't understand how she could be a sachem. She was too young and beautiful, I thought, to be wise or a good hunter.

It seemed to me our arrival on the island was in the nature of a homecoming, for Rabomis clung to my father's arm, going with him around the point of the headland and up the slope to the wigwams; and behind them came the rest of us, squaws carrying our packs and braves carrying our muskets lest a squaw, by handling them, should rob them of strength and cause them to shoot inaccurately, and all laughing and talking together about my father.

I know little concerning these things, because I was young in those days and content with my father, who was both brave and good. Whatever he did, I knew, was done for excellent reasons. He went often into the Northern forests while his sour-faced first wife was alive, returning always with a store of beaver and otter skins; but whether he went always to Swan Island, I cannot say. He said little to me about it, save in praise of Rabomis, to whom he had taught tricks of hunting and governing, so that she had more skill than any of the braves; but I learned from the talk of the Indians that he had planned the building of the three log houses and supervised the work, and had given instructions in the erection and maintenance of latrines, and in the value of skins and methods to be followed in trading.

At any rate, it seemed to me my mother would be as happy if she heard nothing concerning Rabomis, so I afterward remained silent on the subject. In truth, I think all of us would be better off if we spoke and speculated less concerning the private lives of other folk, since we cannot know the whys and wherefores of their actions, and too often impose upon them standards of conduct that we don't impose on ourselves. Nor would I mention these things now, only they are bound up with my tale.

I think my father must have been a great joker with the Indians. As we came to the cabin of the *m'téoulin*, the *m'téoulin* stood in the door wearing his swan headdress, its drooping white wings puffed out around his head and shoulders. He held an empty kettle toward my father.

"We greet you, Brother," he said, taking a rawhide drum from the door post and clapping it over the kettle. "If you find our kettles empty you will send word to Glooskap, and Glooskap will hear your message and bring us riches. Here, Brother, is a messenger."

He lifted the drum, and in the kettle was a rabbit which fell to the ground, scrambled to its feet drunkenly, thumped with its hind leg, and scuttled off through the trees. The Indians behind my father howked appreciatively, and my father gravely extended his hands toward the *m'téoulin*.

"I have sent," he said, "and thus the answer returns." He showed the back of his left hand and the palm of his right: then he showed the palm of his left hand and the back of his right. Both hands were empty. He moved them quickly in the air, drawing the left hand slowly over the right, and in the palm of the right hand lay a new clasp knife. This, as the Indians whooped and slapped their thighs, he dropped into the *m'téoulin's* kettle.

Rabomis drew my father on toward her own cabin, but waved the others to the Long House. "We will return for a council," she said, and then she opened the door for my father and me to enter.

It was a good cabin, warm, with a stone fireplace, and hung with skins. On the floor was a bearskin. A small girl sat by the fireplace, playing with a doll made from the thigh-bone of a deer. There was something about the girl, even though her skin was a soft brown, that made me think of my sister Cynthia.

"Jacataqua," Rabomis said.

My father nodded and looked around the cabin. "No change," he said. His glance lingered here and there, and stopped at Rabomis. "No change," he repeated, and smiled at her.

"No change," said Rabomis. She leaned over suddenly and kissed me, the act being without reason, so far as I could see.

My father went to the fireplace and squatted by the child Jacataqua, who regarded him solemnly. When she showed no alarm, my father picked her up and sat on the bed with her in his arms.

"Stevie," he said, "I'm as good a magic-maker as any *m'téoulin*. I can see this girl is like you. She will never get up in the morning unless she must, and it will be years before she will admit she likes to be kissed. Therefore I declare her your sister and you her brother. Say the words, Stevie."

I knew my father must be joking; yet I felt he was not. I said the words of the ritual: "She is my sister: I am her brother."

"At all times and in all places," my father insisted, "until the squirrel again grows greater than the bear."

I repeated the words. My father pricked my little finger with his knife and placed a drop of my blood on Jacataqua's tongue, and she became my sister.

Rabomis smiled what seemed to me a tremulous smile, and said: "If all the English were like you, Steven, and all the French were like the Frenchman who stopped here yesterday, we'd be fighting with you against the French, instead of doing as we are."

My father eyed me stolidly, and I tried to look stolid too, like an Indian.

"So," my father said, "the French captain is on his way home!"

Rabomis nodded. "Traveling by night, to escape the forts."

"He was not liked by our brothers to the south," my father said, "because of his high-and-mighty airs. I think it would have been better for this captain—ah—bah, his name slips my tongue——"

"Henri Guerlac," said Rabomis.

"Of course! Guerlac! It would have been better, I think, if this Captain Guerlac had taken lessons in common decency before he came into these parts, so he wouldn't have looked with such contempt on all of us, or made war on unarmed men and children."

"The little girl seemed happy with him," Rabomis said.

This was more than I could bear. "She was not!" I shouted; "she was not!"

My father told me to keep quiet. "Here's the truth," he said to Rabomis, "and you never knew me to speak aught else. This Guerlac came among us two nights past. He killed my neighbor and carried away his daughter, who was the dear friend of my son. This is apart from the war: an evil done to me and to my house. We must come up with him and take the child back and finish him if we can, and avenge ourselves. There can be no end to it until this is done."

"You'll rest here to-night, Steven, and go at dawn?"

"No," my father said, "later we'll return; but this wrong has been done and we must go. Cook ducks for us and help us on our way."

"What do you want from us, Steven?"

"A canoe and two short bows and two braves to paddle."

Rabomis hesitated, but seeing the tears rolling down my cheeks, she kept silent and led us to the Long House, where all the braves were assembled. There was a stir and a murmur of welcome when my father entered, but Rabomis faced them silently until they too became silent. "Our brother," she said, "asks for help. Hear him and judge."

My father stood straight before them, as young as any man there, it seemed to me.

"In times past," he said, "I gave you help and you called me brother. Now I claim the rights of a brother. Murder has been done by the Frenchman Guerlac, who has gone north, and my son and I are afoot to right that wrong. This is a private matter between the Frenchman and myself. If there is fighting between us, my son and I will do it without help. Give us only the means to overtake the Frenchman."

"The Frenchmen are also our brothers," a young brave objected.

"That's idle talk," said the *m'téoulin*, "and unless we are dogs we must do as he asks."

"Give him a canoe and two men," said an ancient Abenaki. "He has been wronged and he is our brother. That is talk we can understand, and if we speak all day we'll come no nearer the heart of the matter."

"You'll catch them above Cushnoc," said Rabomis, "and Natawammet knows the river above Cushnoc. Say if you'll go, Natawammet, and who you'll take."

"Woromquid," Natawammet replied and stalked from the Long House.

We went out, all of us, and down to the beach. The canoes leaned against the high bank, overturned, and the *m'téoulin* pointed to a small, slender one. It was fast, the *m'téoulin* said, patting its side—fast. My father stooped beneath it, picked it up by the thwarts, swung it over his head; then lowered it into the water.

A brave brought us a moosehide bow case, two quivers, and a bundle of broad-head arrows with grooved shafts. In the case were three short hunting bows, four extra bowstrings, and a ball of sinews. Tied to the case was a bag of arrowheads.

The bows were short, barely four feet long, made of cedar backed with hickory, and the hickory in turn backed with rawhide. My father tried one of them, borrowing three blunt-head arrows from a child, and the Abenakis watched him closely, for he draws a bow to his jawbone, shooting accurately at targets, whereas the Abenakis of the Kennebec draw to the breastbone with the bow held diagonally before them, shooting miserably at targets but well enough at game.

He shot at a block of wood on the edge of the marsh, twenty paces off, and knocked it spinning into the water. Then he shot at a red squirrel on a pine branch, striking the branch and causing the squirrel to fly raging into the air with tail and fur a-bristle, at which my father declared the bow had lost its cast: the arrow was badly

made: a gust of wind had taken the arrow at the last moment. The
Abenakis, accustomed to excusing bad marksmanship with all these
complaints, cackled loudly.

He loosed his third arrow at a black duck swimming in a guzzle
some sixty paces off; but the duck, hearing or seeing the approaching
shaft, sprang into the air as it arrived and struck it somehow with his
wing so that he became tangled with it and fell flopping into the
guzzle; then flew off squawking.

When Natawammet and Woromquid had placed our packs, our
muskets, and two extra paddles in the canoe, the men gathered in a
circle around the *m'téoulin*, who drew a map in the sand.

"The Frenchman left here with two canoes at dusk last night," he
said, "so to pass the forts unseen. The tide was against them. In the
dark they could make four miles an hour: maybe less. Cushnoc is
twenty-two miles, though some say eighteen who have never paddled it. There they must carry, going silently so the garrison at Fort
Western won't be alarmed.

"Above Fort Western the water is swift and shallow. They won't
travel by night, not knowing the river and fearing to break their
canoes. To-day they have gone on cautiously, pausing at each bend
to guard against soldiers moving between Fort Halifax and Fort
Western. To-night they lie south of Fort Halifax. To-morrow morning they carry, a long carry, around Fort Halifax and past the Five
Mile Ripples, going carefully and slowly to avoid disaster. This is
the last of the settlements. Once beyond this they are safe and the
way is clear to Norridgewock and beyond.

"Now at Ticonic Falls, by Fort Halifax, there is a trail through the
forest. This trail is known to Natawammet and Woromquid. It cuts
across a bend in the river and comes out above the Five Mile Ripples. Two leagues from the ripples there is an island. On one side
of the island the water is shoal and quick. On the other it's clear,
with trees overhead and good shelter on either side. There's where
you can catch the Frenchman. If you don't catch him there, you
won't catch him at all. To do this you must reach Ticonic Falls by
dawn. That is a journey! I know of nobody who has made it in any
such time."

Natawammet and Woromquid gazed impassively at my father.
He motioned me into the canoe and went around the circle of red
men, holding each one for a moment by the upper arms. "You are
my brothers," he said. "When I return we will feast together." He
climbed over me and sat down, and Woromquid stepped into the

bow. Natawammet pushed the canoe into the guzzle and guided it through the marsh. Behind us Rabomis called: "We shall be happy when you return."

The sun was halfway down the sky as we put it at our backs and swung into the broad Kennebec. The tide ran strongly upward, carrying with it the clean smell of salt water. My father looked around at Natawammet kneeling in the stern. "The Frenchman," my father said, "is bad. If we pass over the trail above Ticonic Falls before the sun is an hour high, I will make new muskets for you and Woromquid." Natawammet rose to a half-standing position, and at each stroke of his paddle the canoe lifted in the water, and ripples hissed along its side.

As twilight approached, flocks of wild fowl passed over, moving south, and heavy-headed moose deer watched from the shallows. We came across black bears fishing at the water's edge. When we slapped water at them with paddles, they galloped into the forest, snorting and whistling in terror.

To hold the beat of our paddles in time, Woromquid sang the ancient Abenaki song of Wuchowsen the Wind Blower, who sits on a lofty rock at the edge of the sky and causes the winds by flapping his wings.

When the great lord Glooskap came among men, sang Woromquid, he often went in his canoe to shoot sea fowl. At one time the winds blew violently each day, so that he shot with difficulty. Then it grew worse. Then it blew a tempest, and he could not go out at all. So Glooskap said: "Wuchowsen, the Great Bird, has done this!"

He went, therefore, to find him; and after many days he found him, a large white bird, sitting on a pinnacle of rock.

Then Glooskap spoke to him, saying, "Grandfather, you are too hard upon your children; be easier with your wings, for the wind is too strong."

But the giant bird replied: "I have been here since ancient times, and I moved my wings ere aught else moved or spoke. I shall beat my wings as I please."

Then Glooskap, angered, rose until he touched the clouds, seized the bird-giant Wuchowsen as though he were a pigeon, tied both his wings, and hurled him to the bottom of a rocky cleft.

Now the Indians could go out in the canoes all day, for there was no wind. But the waters became stagnant; they became thick with scum, so that Glooskap could not paddle his canoe.

So, bethinking himself of Wuchowsen, he went again to the cleft in the rock and drew out the great bird, who had suffered no hurt, being immortal.

Untying one of his wings, he put him on his rock again; and since that time the winds have never been as terrible as in the old days.

❄   ❄   ❄

Darkness had fallen when our ears caught the roar of the falls at Cushnoc, at the foot of which lies Fort Western, the best of all the Kennebec forts, not only in the way it is placed, but in the way it is manned. A sentry hailed us at the landing place. Across the river burned a fire, so that the sentry could see, against the path of light in the river, any person who sought to pass the fort. My father gave our names and went up the path with the sentry to see Captain Howard. When the captain heard we wished to reach Fort Halifax before dawn, he shook his head doubtfully but had food brought so we could eat as we scrambled around the falls.

The traveling above Cushnoc was bad. The water was swift and shallow, and hour after hour was a nightmare of low falls and high falls and broken, tumbling water: of high banks, roaring rapids, jagged rocks; of pushing and fending and poling and straining with paddles; of leaping into icy water and scrambling back again; of fighting yard by yard, rod by rod, mile by mile up the river, with smooth stretches so few and far between that after we had passed them we forgot they existed.

The darkness weighed upon us; there were troublesome noises of wild animals among the thickets at the water's edge; our shoulders, stomachs, backs and legs ached from chill and exertion.

How we got through the night I cannot say. For my part I think I could never have done so but for the hope of finding Mary on the morrow. I said to myself God knows how many times that nothing on earth could tempt me to such labors again: that the effort was useless. Then I thought how my father was doing this because a wrong had been done, not to him but to his community, and how Natawammet and Woromquid were doing it for friendship and a new gun; and I knew there was no way of telling what a man will endure, or why.

When the gray light of the false dawn appeared through the trees at our right, Natawammet and Woromquid poled the canoe behind a ledge on the west bank of the river, and above the clatter and babble of near-by rapids I heard the distant vibration of falls.

"Ticonic," Natawammet said. We had come two miles an hour for eight hours, and I hoped I'd never see quick water again.

The Indians drew the canoe onto the high bank and dropped on the ground beside it. In half an hour the real dawn came, and the red men picked up the canoe and moved into the trees, hunting for the mark of the trail—saplings scored with a small triple slash inclined slightly to the left.

We clambered through the woods for three hours, burdened by our packs and muskets, whipped by branches and briers; holding saplings from the canoe and clearing rocks and vines from under the Abenakis' feet. At the end of the three hours we came to the Kennebec again, and found it running clear, without rapids, and no sign of other travelers on it.

We drove upstream, peering cautiously around each bend, never knowing when we might stumble on the Frenchman. The *m'téoulin,* we found, had told the truth, for shortly we came to a pleasant island where the channel to the right was passable by a canoe, but the one to the left was all ledges, wholly impassable.

The Abenakis put us ashore on the island with our muskets and bows; the canoe, with our packs, they took to the far bank, beyond the shallow channel.

Having seen the lay of the land, we made our plans hoping our labors hadn't been in vain: hoping we'd outdistanced Guerlac.

Being the better shot with arrow and musket, my father guarded the high bank; while I, being quick in the water and a fair swimmer, lay by the river with a branch thickly grown with leaves. If the canoes came he was to whistle the mournful cry of the yellowleg, and I was to roll into the current with the leafy branch over my face, so that I could see without being seen. When the first canoe reached me, then, I was to upset it with a hand on the gunwale and seize Mary while my father attended to the rest.

＊   ＊   ＊

We waited interminably; and I knew that all the hunting I had done, for geese or turkey or moose deer, was as nothing compared to the excitement of hunting man.

The sky was overcast and the morning still. The muted calls of chickadees and the scolding of jays were loud, and my heart was low, for I was sure Guerlac had gone on toward Quebec ahead of us.

When my hopes were lowest I heard my father whistle mournfully, the four dropping notes of a yellowleg. I rolled into the river with the branch over my face and my heart pounding as though to tear my ribs apart.

I worked out toward midstream and could see nothing. I was trembling and shivering under water, fit to shake myself to pieces.

Then I saw the canoe, with four paddlers rising and dipping, rising and dipping. They were brown and naked, feathers bound upright to their scalp-locks, green and yellow paint on their faces. My throat was dry and rough, and I sank in the water until I could scarce breathe.

The canoe came straight for me, the brown men rising and dipping, rising and dipping.

It loomed high above me. I looked into the white eye of the bow paddler: saw the deep groove at the corner of his lips. I came up under my branch, reached for the gunwale and missed—reached and caught it and pulled hard.

I heard Guerlac's cold brittle laugh. There was a shout from my father and the twang of a bowstring. A blaze of white light exploded in my brain.

VI

Tʜᴇʀᴇ was a shifting before my eyes when I awoke—a billowing green sea out of which a dusky red wall advanced until it threatened to crush me; then withdrew, writhing and fluttering. My tongue lay in my mouth like the ball my mother makes from a pair of woolen stockings when she has mended them; I could have drunk the hogshead of rainwater that stands by our kitchen door in Arundel.

I was, I thought, slipping down an endless waterfall, turning slowly in my descent; but as I strove to reach out and grasp the swollen objects past which I swirled, I ceased to slide. I lay on a bed of fir tips in a canoe. The surging green sea resolved itself into the trees along the river bank; the dusky red wall was the naked back of Woromquid, rising and dipping with each paddle stroke.

My head felt overtight, as though a squirrel had crawled in to share it with me; and though I vaguely knew there was a matter of importance to consider, I could only squeak for water. The canoe swerved inshore. My father climbed out and held up my head to let me drink from a birch bark cone. My skull was bound like a bale of beaver skins. My father cut more fir tips and slipped them beneath me, ordering me to sleep. When I woke again, the setting sun blazed red in our eyes and the canoe was pushing through a guzzle at the tip of Swan Island.

There was talk from folk on shore—dim, distant talk which angered me for no reason. The canoe was lifted with me in it, carried up a hill and into a cabin. Before I fell asleep again, I saw Rabomis and the *m'téoulin* and my father gathered around me. There was a soothing softness on my overcrowded head. I was pleased to be among friends, but unbearably oppressed by something that continued to escape me.

It was not until morning that my senses returned sufficiently to let me remember that our pursuit of Mary and Guerlac had failed because Guerlac's canoe had not been spilled at the first attempt.

Guerlac, my father said, had risen from the bottom of the canoe when I had dragged at the thwart, and had driven his hatchet toward my head. My father had shouted and loosed an arrow at his face; but the arrow, flying to the left as arrows will when too light or the bow imperfect, had slashed Guerlac along the right cheekbone and split his right ear—enough of a hurt to turn his hatchet a little so that by the grace of God I was struck with the flat of the blade instead of with the edge. The canoe turned over and my father set up a shouting in different voices to make the Indians think there were more of us. Mary, he saw, was not in this canoe at all; so he knew too late our ambush was badly planned.

He loosed two more arrows and fired a musket, striking one of the Indians in a spot that would oblige him to kneel or stand while eating.

Then, roaring and shouting, he had dashed into the river and pulled me out, emptying the water from me while the Indians were helping Guerlac to the opposite shore. In that moment he had seen the second canoe at the bend below us. The Indians, ignorant of our numbers, drove it against the bank and took to the woods, and with them they carried Mary. He fired the second musket and two more arrows toward them, to make them cautious. Then he gathered up the muskets and bows, swung me over his shoulder with my face streaming blood, and set off in search of Natawammet and Woromquid and our own canoe.

My father was frightened by my appearance, he said, for my face, where it was not covered with blood, was as white as a loon's belly, and my breathing no stronger than a kitten's, so he thought best to go down at full speed through the Five Mile Ripples.

If our canoe should be broken on them, he figured, we would be no worse off than we then were; whereas if we passed them safely we could catch the outgoing tide below Cushnoc, and by hard effort win through by sundown to Swan Island, where Rabomis and the *m'téoulin,* having some knowledge of remedies, might heal my head.

My father declared he couldn't say how Natawammet and Woromquid guided us through the quick water without disaster, for mostly he was afraid to look, and he was busy supporting my head when we bumped over the ripples, which are not ripples at all, but curling waves with sharp rocks lying among them like sharks' teeth. When Natawammet and Woromquid went to the council house to act out their adventures for the other Abenakis, according to custom, Woromquid insisted that he had been unable to turn the bow of the canoe from a pointed rock, until my father shouted at him with such violence that he found the strength to lift the canoe entirely out of water. If my father was frightened he was frightened to good advantage, which is a form of fright that harms nobody.

At this time I cared for none of these things, nor for the repeated declarations of Rabomis that Guerlac's hatchet had made a crack in my skull and that I had been only the thickness of a gnat's wing from death. I was alive, so there was no occasion, it seemed to me, to speak of death.

I wished only to hear how we might overtake and recapture Mary; I wanted to do nothing except start again in pursuit of her. Yet my head pained villainously and my father said I was too sick to travel. I would have climbed out of bed, but couldn't move an inch. When I was fully recovered, my father said, we would travel to Norridgewock for further news of Mary and Guerlac.

The *m'téoulin* brought a sheet of thin green moss that grows on dead logs, spread on it a jelly made by boiling the roots of the linden tree, and fitted it to my head, holding it in place with a cap of buckskin whose thongs tied beneath my jaws like an old wife's nightcap.

For six days the *m'téoulin* placed moss and linden jelly on my head, forbidding me to leave the cabin; and the days passed somehow. My father sat often with me, molding bullets or discussing magic with the *m'téoulin;* and Rabomis brought the wampum rolls of the tribe from their hiding place and read the ancient tales of the Abenakis: how they had fought wars with the Iroquois before the white men came; how the great lord Glooskap made man from an ash tree; how Glooskap created the squirrel too large, and so made him smaller; how the geese are divided into tribes and how they hold their council with Wuchowsen the Wind Bird concerning the weather, and despatch expresses to inform the tribes of their decisions; how the Weewillmekq' or horrible horned worm grows under water to the size of a moose; and how Lox, the crafty Indian devil, rose from the dead.

Years before, Rabomis said, there had been many more of these tales, but some of the most ancient of the wampum rolls had been lost or destroyed, and some had been carried to Canada by turbulent warriors who wished to live in St. Francis or Beçancour, where they might obtain gifts from the French in return for making war on the Engish settlements. Once the wampum rolls were lost the tales were soon forgotten, except for fragments that had no value other than to entertain children on a winter's night.

My father puffed at his pipe and said that in a few score years there would be many things forgotten about the Abenakis in addition to their tales; that this was only fair, since the Abenakis preferred their own manner of living to that of the white men. The white man, said my father, wrote down his thoughts and his customs, so that his children might profit by them. Since the Abenakis would not do this, and lived only as it pleased them to live, their thoughts and customs must vanish as trees vanish.

"It may be," said my father, "that your way of living is pleasanter than our way. If you find it so, you must be satisfied with the pleasure and not fret over the future, as does the white man."

Rabomis, slender and straight in her long deerskin jerkin, belted tight around the waist with a band of wampum, put her hand on my father's shoulder. "There are some," she said, "who live as they do because they are not allowed to live otherwise."

My father, seeing Jacataqua and myself staring, stooped to knock out his pipe on the hearth, so that Rabomis's hand fell from his shoulder; and for some reason, whenever people since that time have spoken to me of the Abenakis as savages, which they have done more than a million times, the memory of Rabomis comes into my mind.

Her face was oval, and a clear brown in color, like that of Phoebe Marvin after a summer of her deviltries in the water at the mouth of the Arundel River. Below her eyes there was a flush of red, as though a warm light shone up at her. Her black hair was bound by a narrow ribbon of wampum. Her deerskin jerkin was open at the throat; and around her neck were strands of bright blue wampum.

Her English speech was soft and pleasing, and broken a little by queernesses of pronunciation learned from her father, a Huguenot from France, who had become the master of a vessel that was wrecked at the mouth of the Georges River, near Monhegan. Her manner of expression was pleasing, too; for the Abenaki speech is involved and flowery, and it was her custom to speak in English as she would have spoken in Abenaki.

I cannot understand why white men believe that the Abenakis and all other Indians speak in gutturals, with perpetual *ugging* and *gugging*. I know little of the speech of the Western Indians, who are despised, probably incorrectly, by Abenakis for living in filth and indulging in obscene practices; but I know the Abenaki speech as well as my own, and there is no speech softer to the ear. I have spoken with Frenchmen of some position concerning this matter, and they have said there is no language in Europe as well adapted to express the niceties of diplomacy and the gentlenesses of society as is that of the Abenakis of the Kennebec, the Androscoggin, and the Saco rivers.

Indeed, it is impossible for me to hear the Abenakis called savages without recalling their honesty, generosity and steadfastness: without remembering the abuse and treachery they suffered at the hands of the lustful, foul-mouthed traders and trappers who fattened on them.

It may be I shall be damned for saying so; but unless I have misread my Bible, I have found more Christianity and human kindness in Rabomis and Hobomok, the *m'téoulin,* and Natawammet and Mogg Chabonoke and Natanis and other of my Indian friends than in the venerated and violent Cotton Mather of Boston, who has declared in his writings that all red men are Scythians, and that the practising of cruelties on them and the breaking of treaties with them are justified in God's sight.

There have been many Abenaki children stolen by white settlers during my lifetime and reared in white settlements as servants and slaves. Similarly, there have been many white children stolen by Abenakis and reared along the Androscoggin and the Kennebec and the Penobscot as sons and brothers of their captors. Now this is odd, but true: in nearly every case the Abenaki children who were stolen by the whites have sooner or later escaped and gone back to their own people, too frequently taking with them the evil traits of their captors; whereas the white children who were stolen by Abenakis have either refused to leave their captors, or have been desperately unhappy on returning to the settlements and so have rejoined their red brothers whenever the opportunity offered.

The fearless sachem of the Androscoggins, Paul Higgins, was stolen from the white settlements in his early youth. He said to me once that if he should have to return to the settlements and toil forever at the same tasks, year after year, he would feel like a broody hen, endlessly doing the same useless thing with iron perseverance, and would soon go crazy.

Even the food and the cooking of the Abenakis proved to be better than endurable. During my illness we lived on venison, which at first I refused to eat without salt, though my father devoured it in the Indian manner as eagerly as did Rabomis and Jacataqua, by dipping it in sugared raccoon fat.

Seeing the pleasure my father took in this food, I tried it and found it had merit, though I shall never prefer it to three or four platters of my sister Cynthia's baked beans, well dowsed with my

mother's sauce made from cucumbers and onions. Yet I believe that
if the Abenakis had their way they would live forever on venison
thus prepared.

From them, at this time, I discovered if a person has only one
variety of food to eat over a long period he will never weary of it.
Likewise that venison or moose meat, eaten with salt, as we eat it,
has no nourishment; and if naught else be eaten for a week or more
the body will be weakened because of certain things the meat lacks.
But eaten with sugared fat, in the Abenaki manner, it is nourishing.

There is good reason for their method of cooking wild ducks,
which, some people believe, they savagely eat raw. What they do is
roast a duck for ten or fifteen minutes, which is long enough to roast
venison, even. At the end of this time the meat on the duck's breast
is red and tender. If cooked for another fifteen minutes, as is usual
among those who consider themselves more civilized, the meat is
mealy and rich, and repulsive if eaten twice in succession. But cooked
the shorter time it is like rare beef, and can be eaten day after day
without distress.

❖   ❖   ❖

Each day the pains in my head grew less. After six days, Rabomis
and the *m'téoulin* examined my wound, bathing it with warm water
and ashes. Then the *m'téoulin* brought his conjuring tools, which
were tobacco, a pipe made from the tooth of a moose, the wishbone
of a black swan, the shoulder blade of a wildcat, and several dyed
feathers. The shoulder blade he rubbed with the wishbone, after
which he blew smoke on it from his pipe. He heated it before the
fire, brushed it with the feathers, and studied its surface. What he
saw appeared to satisfy him, for he declared that to remain longer
in the cabin might bring sickness to other parts of my body. He meant
I might go out on the morrow and sit in the sun, but he would take
no blame if the experiment proved unsatisfactory.

The Abenakis set great store by their wise men who are gifted, or
pretend to be gifted, with *m'téoulin;* but I have observed that those
who predict by means of the wildcat's shoulder blade are careful to
obtain as much knowledge as possible before predicting. If they predict the outcome of the next day's hunting they take care beforehand
to examine the countryside for signs of game. If they foretell the results of a battle they first ascertain the strength of the enemy. Furthermore, they use language understandable in more ways than one;

then if their predictions go wrong they say the fault lies in the understanding of those who sought their help.

On the following morning I went out to find a light wind from the southwest, and a fog off the sea, and a honking and quacking and squattering of wild fowl. From high up came the trumpeting of swans, far out of sight and too powerful to need rest. From lower down sounded the melancholy clamor of geese, weary from their flight against the head wind, and conversing dolefully concerning the possibility of alighting for breakfast. Lowest of all, on every side of the headland, sounded the garrulous gossip of the ducks, thousands upon thousands of them.

Seeing Jacataqua and other Abenakis drifting toward the lookout ridge, I followed along behind them, and found the women sitting along the ridge sewing moccasins and beading buckskin shirts, and looking down at my father, who was preparing to kill ducks for the whole encampment. On an earlier visit to Swan Island, the women said, he had made a narrow flat-bottomed craft out of elm bark, by means of which he was able to outwit the geese and ducks, even when they were at their wariest, and most determined not to be approached by hunters.

This flat craft lay in the guzzle which led to a pool far out in the marsh. Stretched on his back, in the bow, was my father, his own musket and mine beside him. In the stern, crouched behind a shield of marsh grass, was Rabomis with two more muskets; for, being a sachem, she could be cleansed by the *m'téoulin*, and so, unlike other Indian women, was not suspected of casting a curse on every weapon she touched.

From the lookout we could see that every pool in the marsh was alive with ducks—mallards and pintails and scaup and redheads and teals, all yelling at the top of their lungs about God knows what; and here and there a few hundred geese, standing up above the ducks, silent and watchful, like giant sentinels surrounded by frivolous dwarfs; but none of them in my father's pool.

Eventually, off to the west, I heard the sad cries of a flock of geese, beating down through the fog. They came dimly into our vision, moving slowly across the marsh; then turned toward us with doleful plaints, some two hundred of them, set their wings, and coasted with sprawling feet and high-raised heads into the pool at the end of the guzzle. Rabomis put the flat craft in motion; then, with the paddle stuck through a hole in the stern, she sculled closer to the pool with no movement of her own to be seen.

From our elevation we could see them draw nearer and nearer to their quarry; we could see the geese, alert but unsuspicious, and the addle-pated ducks splashing themselves with water and pursuing each other, all as thick as mosquito wigglers in our hogshead of rain-water in Arundel.

They stopped eight yards from the pool, concealed by a turn in the guzzle. My father rose to a sitting position and Rabomis stood behind him. The geese and the ducks leaped upward, and both my father and Rabomis shot into the mass of rising birds, out of which the dead fell by scores. While still they were thickly bunched my father and Rabomis picked up the other muskets and fired again; and again the wild fowl fell back into the pool and marsh like a storm of melons. Ducks and geese by the thousand and hundred thousand sprang into the air, Merrymeeting Bay being one of their favorite resting stations on their road to the South; and so, complaining and protesting, they resumed their journeys. Six canoes pushed out to pick up the dead and wounded, and returned with more than forty geese and seventy ducks.

The women went away to prepare the fires for smoking and dry-ing the meat; for flies, like mosquitoes, are thick along the Kennebec; and unless meat is immediately eaten or smoked, it is blown by the flies and spoils at once. Of all the meat the Abenakis smoke for win-ter provisions, the breasts of ducks seem to me the best; for they are small to carry, like chips of wood, and when boiled they swell and become tender.

Had it not been for my eagerness to set off again in search for Mary it would have pleased me to remain weeks on Swan Island; for each morning hunters went out after deer and bear and beaver and otter, which were plenty on the island and on both sides of the river; and boys under sixteen, not allowed to hunt with muskets, hunted with bows for bear and wild turkey and raccoons, and for foxes for fur, and for woodchucks for soup and dog meat and fire bags.

I was permitted to go with Hobomok, the son of the *m'téoulin,* a fat and amiable youth, three years older than I. He was fat because of the maple sugar and sweetened bear's fat brought to the *m'téoulin* by grateful and hopeful patients, and because he would not hunt far afield for game, like other boys, but preferred to sit and wait for game to come to him, even though he had to wait forever. Yet he was more successful in his hunting than many of the more active youths; more successful, even, than some of those whose age permitted them to carry muskets.

Hobomok would be a great *m'téoulin,* my father said, because a *m'téoulin* is the only Abenaki who does not hunt unless so disposed. Even a sachem is obliged to hunt when food is scarce; but a *m'téoulin* can sit in his cabin or in the medicine house and make *m'téoulin* to attract game and bring good luck to the hunters. As soon as Hobomok learned about this, my father said, he would make twice as much *m'téoulin* as anyone ever made before.

My father was right when he said Hobomok would be too thoughtful of his own comfort to let me exert myself overmuch. We took heavy short bows of cedar backed with hickory, blunt arrows for small game, and a few broad-heads for safety; and most of our hunting was done while sitting or lying down. Hobomok picked a likely stand of birches near the river, and we sat quietly among them until a covey of partridges walked up and flopped themselves into trees to feed on birch buds. When Hobomok whistled at them, they struck attitudes and waited patiently to be shot.

We moved, then, to a grassy swale, from the middle of which flowed a spring of cold water. This, Hobomok said, was turkey country; and if we waited a little, there would certainly be turkeys come here to drink. So we waited, lying behind a log with broad-head arrows nocked on our strings. Flies crawled on my hands: chipmunks scuttled across my legs: twigs bit into my stomach and elbows: the shadows lengthened until I feared Hobomok's waiting might extend through the night, or even through an entire week.

And then, at sundown, three cock turkeys came out of the birches at the head of the swale, all with long beards, haughty and deliberate, and stared about them suspiciously between greedy snatches at grasshoppers. As they neared us they looked huge: gargantuan hens from a bad dream. At the spring they were twelve yards away; we could see their red wattles, the fuzz on their heads and the bronze glint on their shoulders. When Hobomok touched my leg we rose up and drove arrows through two of them. The third stretched himself out as long and thin as an otterskin tippet, and fled back up the swale as fast as Ranger can run. Each of us loosed two shafts at him, and our second ones struck him in the back. Hobomok was pleased at this, for no feathers—not even goose feathers—equal the first six feathers from a turkey's wing for fletching an arrow.

Because of my sickness, and because a three-day rain set in from the northeast at this time, as it does each year, most unpleasant, I was obliged to linger in the camp for yet a little while, strengthening myself on ducks and partridges and venison and hominy, and such delicacies as moose nose and beaver tail. The time was not wasted. I learned from Rabomis how to make five-gallon jars from the skin on a deer's neck, taking off a cylinder of skin over the head, removing the hair, drawing one end tight together and gathering the other around a small hollow stick, then blowing through the stick until the skin is inflated like a bladder. This, when dried, is good for transporting raccoon or bear oil.

Hobomok instructed me in the making of fire pouches, which is done by cutting a slit at the back of a woodchuck's neck and drawing the body through the slit, so the skin is left whole. Then the skin is turned back from the skull, the skull is cleaned and scraped and pushed again into the skin. Thus the head becomes a knob; and when the knob is tucked under the belt the pouch is supported by it and never falls. The fire itself is contained in two large clam-shells, lined with clay, a small hole being left for escaping smoke. Between the shells is packed rotted yellow birch, which holds fire for a day. The shells are bound together and placed in the pouch; and by this means fire is carried safely through the heaviest rains.

But the thought of Mary was in my mind; so when the northeaster had blown itself out I again begged my father to set out on the trail of Guerlac and his Indians. The only reminder of my wound was a jagged scar that ached before a storm, which it has done ever since.

That night my father made up our packs and instructed Rabomis concerning the gathering of beaver and otter skins against his return, saying he would give better prices than Clark and Lake, the traders on Arrowsic Island, who had cheated the Swan Islanders for years.

Also the *m'téoulin* came with his dyed feathers, wildcat's shoulder blade and moose-tooth pipe, to prophesy about our travels; but when he had rubbed the shoulder blade and blown smoke on it and warmed it before the fire and brushed it with the feathers, he grumbled because the bone was covered with the images of soldiers instead of with our own figures. My father asked idly how the soldiers were dressed; and the *m'téoulin*, whisking busily with the feathers, said some were dressed in red and some in white.

And what, asked my father, was happening? The *m'téoulin* said one army was fleeing before the other, though he could not say whether the red uniforms fled, or the white ones.

At this my father said everyone knew James Wolfe and Jeffrey

Amherst were trying to capture Quebec, and if he thought to impress us with a prophecy that was not a prophecy at all he was grievously mistaken. He would do better, my father told him, to go into the woods and kill another wildcat with a bigger and more prophetic shoulder blade.

The *m'téoulin* laughed, for he liked my father and knew my father liked him. He said he could see on the bone that we would have a long trip and that all those who began it would return safely.

Since that was the case, my father remarked, he would take the *m'téoulin's* son Hobomok on this long trip, to provide companion-ship for me. The *m'téoulin* stared doubtfully at his wildcat bone; but when my father laughed derisively he said quickly: "Hobomok will go and learn from you."

"Good!" said my father. He stretched himself and yawned and let down the bearskins across the inner part of the cabin, in which Jacataqua and I slept.

In the moist, biting cold of the next dawn we set off in a long canoe, Woromquid and Natawammet in the bow and stern as before, and Hobomok in the bow close to Woromquid, wearing nothing but a blanket over his belt cloth, so he could leap out when the occasion demanded. Behind me was my father, his back against a bundle of dried venison and smoked duck breasts. There was a villainous wail-ing from the whole tribe; louder even than the outcries of the mil-lions of wild fowl that sprang from the marsh as we pushed down the guzzle. I would have wept myself at the grief of Rabomis and Jacataqua if it had not been for the stony face of my father, which reminded me of his saying that if one makes no display of grief he recovers sooner from it.

VII

IF I had a beaver skin for every reason that has been given to me for the name of the river Kennebec I would have enough to make a robe that would go many times around the one I most love, she being slender and smooth and straight like a musket barrel, but not so hard and cold.

Some say it was named for a chief, Cannibis, who lived along its shores; but I misdoubt the whole river would be named for one man.

Others say it is from the Abenaki words *quen-ne-bec,* meaning, "long blade"; yet there is no resemblance between the Kennebec and a long blade, unless it be a long blade of dried seaweed—the last thing to which a river would be likened by anyone save a fish.

The truth is more simple. Westward of Montreal there are Indian nations that make medicine to the rattlesnake, regarding him as sacred. When they find one, they sit in a circle, blowing pipe-smoke at him. They hail him politely as Manitou Kinnibec, praying he will send them good hunting and good crops. This often proves pleasing to the rattlesnake; and if he shows signs of amiability, the Indians think their prayers will be granted.

So I say that our river was named by the Indians after Manitou Kinnibec; for the Kennebec twists like a serpent sprawled in the sun on a tilted ledge. At its head its tongue is forked; and far away, at its smaller end in the Northern forests, it has its rise in small lakes strung together like rattles on the tail of Manitou Kinnibec. Likewise, the men of Maine, though they write its name "Kennebec," speak always of it as the Kinnibec, and always will, because that is the fashion of their speech. Also there are some of us who, though we love it, must think of it, at times, as of Manitou Kinnibec—cold and sinister and dangerous, threatening torture and death to the unwary.

In the fold of one of its greatest serpent curves, beyond the outer edge of the meager white settlements, and a third of the way to the St. Lawrence, a flat point of land, shaped like the quarter part of one of my sister Cynthia's pies, juts out into the river from the pine-clad hills behind. Above it, so close that the noise of their brawling fills the air, are the falls of Norridgewock.

Here on this point was the Abenaki town of Norridgewock, open to the sun as soon as the chill Kennebec mists had lifted from the river, and surrounded by a country rich in trout, salmon, bear, deer, turkey, raccoons, and hardwood ridges. Norridgewock was more substantial than other Indian towns. Around it was a stockade; and its lodges, made of logs, were arranged on streets like the towns of white men. At the northern end of the town, toward the falls, was a wooden chapel, with a belfry surmounted by a cross; for during the days of Father Rale the Norridgewock Abenakis were known as the most Christian of all the Kennebec Indians, though to my way of thinking it changed them from the Abenakis of Swan Island and the Androscoggin only in making them, for a time, more eager to take the scalps of settlers.

*   *   *

My father always said he could not blame the Abenakis overmuch for their anger against the white settlers and that cold-blooded body of Boston speculators known as the Plymouth Company.

The trouble, he said, arose from the inability of each side to understand the other, and over the natural kindliness of the Abenakis as opposed to the natural greed of white men. God knows I am sick of hearing the tale from the Abenakis; for I cannot go in their lodges without one of them fatiguing me with a long harangue about the theft of their lands. Yet their tale agrees with my father's, so I will put it down and have done with it:

The Abenakis possessed all their lands together, and any Abenaki had a right to use any land belonging to the Abenaki nation. Their territory was never divided, and each one of them owned an equal part, which was an imaginary part and never defined. Thus no Abenaki could sell land, because every piece belonged to every other member of the nation as much as to him. He could not understand, even, how one person could own the entire rights to a piece of land and, if he desired, banish all others from it. The Abenaki mind cannot grasp it, any more than the mind of my dog Ranger could grasp it if I told him he could only chase rabbits within certain boundaries.

Consequently, when a white man asked an Abenaki sachem to sell property to him the sachem could comprehend the sale of nothing save the right which he himself possessed—the right to hunt and fish on that piece of land, and dwell on it, in company with its other possessors. For that reason the Abenakis, in good faith, showed their kindness to white men by repeatedly selling the same piece of land to different people. There was no dishonesty about it; for there are no people more honest or greater respecters of the rights of others. Until dishonest white men came among them, they hung their beaver and otter skins on racks in the forest, secure in the knowledge that no other Abenaki would ever take them.

That is why the Abenakis have sold, as the saying goes, their choicest tracts for next to nothing—for a keg of powder, or a bottle of rum, or a pair of blue cloth trousers.

Old Mattahannada, an Abenaki sachem of the Kennebec almost a hundred years before I was born, sold a million acres on the lower Kennebec to William Bradford of the Plymouth Company for two kegs of rum and a barrel of bread. Only an idiot could believe that a sachem—a wise man—would be so witless as to sell all the rights on a million acres of land for such a sum. Not even the worst robbers among the traders have been able to trick the Abenakis into selling beaver skins for a lower rate than one blanket for twenty pounds of beaver, one pair of scarlet cloth pantaloons for fifteen pounds of beaver, and one shirt for ten pounds of beaver.

I say again it was not the land that Indians sold, but the right to hunt or fish on the land. Every white man that bought land rights from Indians knew this was so, but persuaded the Indians to sign papers that would make an outright sale of the transaction when brought before a judge.

If the Plymouth Company were still in its full strength and vigor, as in the days when it persuaded Governor Shirley of Massachusetts to build the forts on the Kennebec, I would be less free with my words. It was the heads of the Plymouth Company that persecuted Roger Williams and drove him into the wilderness because he attacked the company and denounced it for robbing the Indians of their land. They were dangerous men, preying on weakness and hiding behind pulpits, and one needed to be wary with them unless he wished to lose his possessions and his good name.

At no time during my life, however, would it have been necessary for me to be wary with the Norridgewocks, even though they are known far and wide as savages, whereas the members of the Plymouth Company are admired as Christian gentlemen.

❖   ❖   ❖

As we swept around the bend in the river and up to the pleasant point of Norridgewock, there was a movement of reds and blues among the cabins; for the Norridgewock braves, many of them, wear tunics of red or blue cloth except when hunting, having been encouraged in this manner of dress by Father Rale. The women wear mantles of red or blue cloth falling below the knee, and above their moccasins a sort of stocking of white deerskin. Around their heads they bind a light cloth knotted at the back and hanging to the waist or lower, peculiar but becoming, and not common to any other tribe of Indians anywhere.

The sachem of the Norridgewocks, Manatqua, was an old man with no hair, a rare thing among the Abenakis. He had taken from the cheek of a wildcat the piece of skin from which the whiskers sprout, and stuck it to the top of his head with pitch. The gray tuft was divided in three parts, like a scalp-lock, each part decorated with a wampum band and an eagle's feather. In appearance it was unnatural, and seemingly there was an insecurity about it in Manatqua's mind, for he dropped his forehead against the heel of his hand from time to time, as if in thought, and fingered the edges of his artificial scalp-lock to assure himself it was still there.

Some twenty of the Norridgewocks came to the river to see us disembark, Manatqua among them, and it seemed to me they proposed to prevent us from landing. They gathered in a half-circle on the pebbly shore and stared at us grimly, with no signs of welcome in their faces. My father drew out his Norridgewock belt and stepped from the canoe, holding the belt toward Manatqua, and said the Abenaki words of greeting—"You are my friend."

Now the answer to this should be: "Truly, I am your friend!" but Manatqua did not say the words, only felt meditatively of his scalp-lock and said, "We have looked for you during the passage of ten suns," this being their flowery and pompous way of speaking.

"Cousin," said my father, continuing to dangle his belt before Manatqua, "I bring you the belt given to me by your people for sending corn when you had neither corn nor skins with which to buy it. Now when I come again with your belt, I am met with sour faces, as though I had poured sand in your sweetened bear's fat.

"Cousin, I do not need to be a wise man to know that you have talked with the Frenchman Guerlac, and that he has lied to you about me. You have taken the word of a stranger concerning a friend to whom you have given a belt. You have done this without waiting to hear the explanation of the friend. It is not to the honor of Manatqua or the Norridgewock tribe that they should flutter to every wind that blows, like smoke above a wigwam."

My father stopped and looked around the half-circle of faces, then dropped the wampum belt back into his shirt.

"You," he said to Manatqua again, "are my friend."

"Truly," Manatqua replied grudgingly, "I am your friend, but the French are the brothers of Manatqua and his people. My friend has insulted our brother the French captain and lifted the knife against another brother who went from these lodges to St. Francis, wounding him so sorely that he must lie on his face in pain."

My father made an impatient gesture. "Cousin," he said, "the brother from St. Francis was unwilling to sit in your own lodges, and so went to St. Francis. Why, then, do you cry out because I make him unable to sit in a canoe?"

Now the frequency with which the braves from Norridgewock were leaving the tribe and departing for St. Francis was in no way pleasing to the Abenakis who remained behind, even though those who went were usually headstrong and quarrelsome; so there was silence at my father's words until a squaw at the back of the circle tittered loudly and vainly attempted to cover the titter with a cough.

Manatqua glowered at the titterer, but spoke to us. "Cousins, come to the Long House where we can talk in peace, without the squalling of jays to distract us."

He set off for the cabins, my father and I with him, while Natawammet and Woromquid and Hobomok carried our canoe to an empty cabin and overturned it above our packs.

My father lost no time. I heard him say to Manatqua: "Cousin, there came a man from Boston to my wigwam some moons ago, wearing fine hair on his head. The hair did not belong to him, yet it seemed to be real. Each morning he put on the hair, holding it to his head with a wafer of wax, and each night he put it off; yet no wind could blow it from him."

"*M'téoulin!*" the sachem cried, fingering his scalp-lock.

"No," my father said, "it is the habit of the Bostoners to make these things, as they make shirts. If beaver skins should be sent to me by your braves, and you should return to Arundel with me to receive money and paint and shirts in payment, I could send a letter to Boston demanding that hair of this sort be returned for your wearing."

"Brother," the sachem asked, "what color is the hair?"

"The color you wish," my father said. "Black or white; or red, for that matter, unless you desire blue or green."

The sachem made no answer, but it seemed to me an eager light gleamed in his eye. He despatched a boy to ring the bell on the church, so that the braves might be summoned to a council; and all of us went to the council cabin, which was no larger than the other cabins, but contained more skins to sit on, and smelled more powerfully, though not badly enough to cause more than a heavy feeling in the head. My father had with him a rope of tobacco, and this he gave to Manatqua, who crumbled a part of it into a bowl containing powdered sumach leaves and red willow bark, which makes tobacco more to the taste of the Abenakis, though for my part the odor of the mixture is like a hot shoe pressed against a horse's hoof.

When the pipe had been smoked Manatqua spoke to my father more amiably.

"You are our friend," Manatqua said. "This we knew many years ago because of the winter when you gave us corn to replace the seed that was eaten. Also, we know it from our brothers on Swan Island, where you lived among our people and gave good advice. But twelve suns ago this Frenchman came here with eight of our brothers from St. Francis and a small child. He showed us the marks on his braves, and the torn ear and cheek you had inflicted on him without warning. Since we are his brothers in war, he laid upon us the duty of turning you back if you came in pursuit, or of raising the hatchet against you if you persisted in going on. This, he told us, would bring us great rewards from the white chief in Quebec.

"Cousin, you have been our brother in past years, and we cannot raise the hatchet against you. Yet if we do not turn you back we will suffer in two ways. We suffer now from the Bostonnais, who push farther and farther into our lands, building forts and destroying the game, so that we feed ourselves with greater and greater difficulty. If we do not turn you back, then the white chief in Quebec will send war parties against us, or close his lands to us when we have been crowded from these.

"Cousin, you can see empty cabins around you. When last you came among us, they were filled with braves. They have gone to St. Francis to live under the white chief in Quebec, for here they have been robbed of their hunting by your brothers from the south.

"Cousin, these are the thoughts in our minds. Now we will hear your thoughts."

If I had been skilled in reading faces, I would have known, even before my father began to speak, that there was no anger against him among the Abenakis; for their heads were dropped a little forward and their lips not tightly closed as they looked up at him, showing they listened gladly to his words. But at that time I was too young to know, and so shivered for fear we would not be let to go in pursuit of Mary.

My father wore his Norridgewock belt tied around his arm, so that when he shook his fist at them, which he did to strengthen his statements, their own hieroglyphics of gratitude flashed blue and white and black before them.

"Brothers," he said, "I have many times heard bitter words on the tongues of the Abenaki people because white men are liars. That is good. I have dealt with you and I have dealt with your brothers on Swan Island, not only in the buying of skins but in the giving of advice, and you know whether or not I am a liar.

"Now the French captain who came among you was a liar. I do not say he was a liar in all things. I do not say he lied to you about his name and about his business, though he may have done even that. Tell me, my brother, how he called himself, so I may know whether he lied in this also."

"He did not lie," said Manatqua craftily, "because we asked separately of our brothers from St. Francis who accompanied him. It was as he said. He is Henri Guerlac de Sabrevois, a captain in the regiment of Béarn, a wealthy captain with estates across the water, though he has bought a seigneurie on the Island of Orleans."

My father shook his head reluctantly. "In this he was no liar, but it is probable he lied about his business."

"No, no!" Manatqua said. "He pursued an officer of Rogers' Rangers—may the Weewillmekq' devour them! We saw the very man. He passed this point at the end of Wikkaikizoos, the moon in which there are heaps of eels on the sand. He stopped to pitch the seams of his canoe; then vanished like the shadow of a cloud. A Mohegan from Stockbridge paddled him in a small canoe, light as a feather."

My father laughed. "An officer of Rogers' Rangers! A likely tale! What was he doing here? Hunting the magic pouch of Glooskap?" At his words, his hearers laughed as well; for according to the Abenaki tale, the magic pouch of Glooskap is filled with hundreds of beautiful girls, all eager to overwhelm with love the rash person who releases them.

Manatqua shook his head. "He traveled to Quebec, bearing a letter to the white chief Wolfe from the white chief Amherst at Crown

Point. He would have gone by the Richelieu and the St. Lawrence, but that road was blocked by Bourlamaque and his French regiments, who occupied Isle Aux Noix. Therefore he took the other road—from Crown Point to Massachusetts; thence up the Kennebec, over the Height of Land and down the Chaudière."

My father stared hard at Manatqua. "And Guerlac knew about this officer of Rangers?" he asked incredulously.

Manatqua looked uncomfortable. "He knew. He knew, even, of the letter that the officer carried. All things, he said, were known to him and to the white chief in Quebec."

My father smiled pityingly at Manatqua; then sadly turned his eyes to the red men who sat before him. "Brothers," he said, "listen to me. The words of the French captain were foolish words. He is a foolish man, without sense. He spoke foolishly to you, and he behaved foolishly to me. Judge, yourselves, of his foolishness. Not long since he came unheralded to my inn; and such was his folly that he held us in contempt, as being ignorant folk. His tongue wagged like that of Kwe-moo the loon, until all of us were in a rage at the foolishness of his speech.

"Among us was a rash man, such as you have among you. When the Frenchman taunted him, the rash one rose up and threw him in the mud of the creek."

The Abenakis laughed and slapped themselves; for it pleases them to see others thrown in the mud.

"Brothers, continue to listen," said my father. "Having eight braves with him, the Frenchman attacked an unarmed man and stole his daughter, my son's friend. We pursued him, my son and I, to bring back the daughter. We fought him, and came within a whisker of wiping him out. Now he complains to you that the attack was unjust.

"Is it unfair for my son and me to attack nine warriors? If this is unfair, then I am a giant, as great as the great lord Glooskap!

"The Frenchman lied to you about this, Brothers! He lied to you about what the white chief in Quebec would do for you. To-day, in Quebec, there is a French chief, Vaudreuil. He, too, is a foolish man, for he is dishonest, and steals the food from the mouths of his children. His white children do not grow in numbers, as do those of the white father in England. We do not need to look on the shoulder blade of a wildcat to know what must happen in Quebec. In a few moons, though I do not know how many, the children of the white father in England will push the French chief into the sea, and there will be no French chief in Quebec. Because I am your friend I advise you that nothing be done to arouse the anger of the children of the white father in England. In numbers they will be like the salmon that come up out of the sea in Amusswikizoos, the moon of fish-catching.

"And now listen to one more word, my brothers. I go north; for it is something that must be done. Soon I shall return. If your beaver skins are saved for me, and otter skins, especially sea otter, I will buy them from you, taking Manatqua to Arundel to receive money and goods in exchange. I will pay you double the price paid by the traders of the Massachusetts Company.

"For beaver I will pay you eight shillings a pound, or two knives; or one tomahawk for two pounds, a shirt for four pounds, a pair of pantaloons for five pounds, a blanket for ten pounds, a musket for twenty pounds, and other things in proportion. These are good prices. They are the prices I pay my Abenaki brothers from Ossipee; and since the winter is before you, there is time for you to take many skins in addition to those you sell to me. These others you can sell to the company or to Clark and Lake, and so will not arouse their anger. Brothers, I have finished."

My father sat down, and there was silence in the council house while the braves counted on their fingers. After Manatqua had felt his scalp-lock, he rose pompously and burst into an oration, in which he made the usual hullabaloo about land that had been stolen from the Abenakis, and about the bravery of their brothers the French, and about the bravery of the Abenakis, along with several pointed references to his own bravery and his skill as a hunter, after which he spoke bitterly about white men who lie to their Abenaki brothers and thus forfeit fraternal rights.

He closed by declaring the words of the white brother from the south to be honorable and wise. He had no doubt his braves would consent to send their beaver skins to Arundel. He himself, even, would return with the white brother and bring back paint and muskets and shirts to comfort his people during the coming snows.

These words were received with such yells of pleasure that my eardrums rang; and immediately there was preparation for a feast and a dance.

The mist that rises from the Kennebec in the autumn is one that bites into the bones; therefore the squaws built fires on the unpaved street between the houses, so that we could sit along them on either side. Mats of rushes were brought from the cabins to give us seats.

Over the fires were hung pots, hominy in one and trouts in another
and venison in a third. On iron plates they made pone, which the
squaws make thin and crisp out of corn, first crushing the corn on
a large rock with a small rock.

After the feast had been cleared away, the braves danced the
Beaver Dance, which is danced only in the autumn before they go
to hunt the beaver.

Hanging from their belts, when they danced, the braves wore
beaver skins; and bound around their heads were dried flags, while
in their hands they carried sticks of white birch, which they clattered
in unison. The squaws, seated in a long row between the fires and
the dancers, beat on drums with gourds filled with dried peas, thus
making the noise of water trickling over the beaver dam; and to
imitate the sound of the beaver slapping the water with his tail, they
slapped themselves violently on the thighs.

Around the dancers circled two *m'téoulins*, wearing wolverine
skins hanging from their heads. These, said Hobomok, represented
Lox, the Indian devil, a mischievous animal. They played tricks on
the dancers and the squaws, clown-like, so that I laughed until my
head hurt. Hobomok said they were not as skillful in their mer-
rymaking as they might have been. The *m'téoulins* of the Norridgewocks, he declared, had lost their skill at *m'téoulin* because of
the many years that the tribe had asked help from Father Rale's
God instead of depending on reliable *m'téoulins*. His own father, he
said, was a great merrymaker; if I should see him taking the part of
Lox in the Beaver Dance, I would ache all over from laughing.

I have since noticed, however, that Hobomok was critical of all
m'téoulin except his father's and his own, and I have had occasion
to think that if it had not been for his loyalty he would even have
carped at his father's magic.

Manatqua went with us to our cabins after the dance, fingering
his scalp-lock, and asked my father whether it would be possible for
him to have two heads of hair from Boston, one black and one vermilion. My father told him he would arrange for the two scalps, and
would even, if he wished it, get him one that would be spotted like
the skin of a young fawn, or ringed in circles of different colors,
which was only permitted to chiefs of the most important station.
Later my father told me that he would not offer so much as a chipmunk skin for the life of any brave who attempted to prevent
Manatqua from accompanying him back to Arundel.

The squaws gave us hominy and pone at daybreak the next morning; for hunting parties were already starting upstream with the intention of swinging northwestward from the Kennebec onto the Carrabasset and into a country full of beaver. By sun-up we had carried around the falls; nor did we mind when cold gray clouds shut down on us, for the river became rougher and the carries longer and more frequent, and we had little opportunity to become chilled.

Ten leagues we made the first day; and Hobomok, running ahead of the canoe at the carries, killed twelve partridges and a raccoon for supper. We camped that night by the brook at the foot of the sugar-loaf mountain, where the Kennebec turns off to the eastward; and to the westward lies the twelve-mile carry that leads to Dead River. We lay on spruce boughs with a fire at our feet, all of us close together. There was a spit of snow in the air, and a dank chill that bit into us. When we untangled ourselves the next morning there was a glare in our eyes; for the first snow of the year clung to the pines, and flakes were still falling.

We lost no time getting our lines in the water. Hobomok pounced on the trouts as we threw them on the bank behind us, stripped them with his thumb, spitted them on a maple wand, and hung them by the fire.

We traveled fast over the carry, with dry moccasins; for the snow had not penetrated beneath the towering pines.

While the day was yet young we dropped our canoe into Bog Brook and pushed down it to the black and sluggish current of Dead River. That river, the west branch of the Kennebec, winds like a serpent in the direction of the distant place that every traveler to Quebec most deeply dreads—the Height of Land.

Toward noon we reached a high point that thrust itself into Dead River from the north, so that the river makes a half-circle around it. Here, the snow having stopped, we landed to build a fire and eat warm food. As was his habit, my father raised his head slowly above the level of the high ground, hoping to surprise a deer or moose. Then, to my consternation, he yelled horribly, leaped up the bank, and dashed across the flat land beyond.

Following him up, I saw, against a growth of pines at the back edge of the open point, an Indian youth, long and scrawny, naked except for a belt cloth and moccasins, clinging to the neck of a young buck and striving to drive a knife into its throat. The buck leaped and pitched. While I watched and primed my musket the arm of the Indian youth slipped from the buck's neck, and he fell. A hoof slashed down across his side, and as if by magic the trampled snow around him was crimson with blood. The buck reared again. My father shouted and waved his arms, having covered less than half the distance.

Knowing the hoofs of a deer are sharp as a scalping knife, I shot at its shoulder before it could slash a second time. By good fortune the ball struck its shoulder blade, and it fell down across the boy. My father cut its throat and pulled it off the Indian, who was Hobomok's age or thereabouts. We took him under the arms and dragged him to dry ground under a clump of spruces.

VIII

NATAWAMMET skinned the deer, Hobomok built a fire, and Woromquid and I cut spruce branches for a bed. My father brought blankets,
and needles from his pack to sew up the gash in the Indian's side.
We bandaged the wound with sheets of the green moss that grows on
dead logs. He was thin and weak, and his moccasins were in tatters,
showing he had come far. Also, in spite of his thinness, his paunch
was swollen, so we knew he had eaten little in a long time.

My father took the liver from the deer, wrapping it in a strip of
fat and roasting it on a stick over the fire, after which he fed a little
to the Indian. We prepared our own dinner, and then my father fed
him a little more, but only a little, so he might not sicken. He fell
asleep; and when he awoke, my father fed him again before asking
who he was and from where he had come.

Natanis, he said, was his name. We understood little he said at
first; but soon his speech became clearer to us. He was from the town
of St. Francis, on the St. Francis River, above Quebec. Although his
grandfather had been an Abenaki from the Pennacook tribe on the
Merrimac River, his words had a French twist because of his tribe's
association with French priests and traders.

During the last moon, he said, the English general on Lake Cham-
plain had sent two English officers to the town of St. Francis with
gifts, thinking they might be allowed to pass through to Quebec. The
braves of St. Francis, however, had seized the officers and taken them
to Montreal and delivered them to the French. As a result the English general had been angry, and so had sent Rogers' Rangers, two
hundred of them, to destroy the town.

The Rangers, he said, had fallen on the town just before dawn,
after marching a vast distance at high speed, killed his people by the
hundreds and destroyed the town. His father had been killed, and his
mother and a brother. Another brother and a sister had been captured and carried away by the Rangers. Those who escaped had fled
into the woods and down the St. Francis to the St. Lawrence. He him-

self, he said, had reached the St. Lawrence wearing only his moccasins and his belt cloth, and unarmed. He had continued down the river, thinking to cross to Quebec where he might find friends among the Abenakis who were helping to defend it; but he had found the Canadians in a panic, fleeing and hiding and rushing up the river in small boats, so he dared not cross.

"In a panic?" my father asked. "What were they in a panic about?"

"Because Montcalm was dead," said Natanis, "and the French army had fled across the St. Charles, away from the city, and Wolfe had taken Quebec."

My father got up with a glum face and walked rapidly back to the canoe. I followed, not knowing what had got into him. He hoisted his pack to the shore and rummaged in it until he found his flask of rum.

"Stevie," he said, "rum's a curse, and you know I hate the stuff. Keep away from rum, Stevie, because there's more hell in a gallon of it than the devil could pack into a hogshead. Still and all, Stevie, there's times you've got to do something violent or bust, and this is one of 'em."

He held up the flask, and I could see it was full. "Here's to Wolfe," he said. "He's a great man. He did something there was only one chance in a million of doing. Here's to Wolfe, the man that took Quebec!"

He tilted up the flask and there was a gurgling like rainwater pouring into our hogshead at Arundel during a thunderstorm.

When he took the flask from his lips, he screamed violently, after which he passed it to me.

"You know how I feel about it, Stevie. Don't ever drink more than you have to; and be moderate about it, or you'll make a fool of yourself. And don't ever say I countenanced it, Stevie. But I suppose some day you'll take a drink, like everybody else; so go ahead and take a suck of this. Then all your life you can say you took your first drink to red-headed James Wolfe for taking Quebec. That's as good a reason as you'll ever have for taking one."

So I took a little drink. It made me gag and I have never liked rum since that day, though I have had my share of it to stave off the cold.

My father put the flask back in his pack and looked thoughtfully at me. "I ought to have another! I ought to drink the whole flaskful and then swallow the flask! Think what it means, Stevie! No more Frenchmen to bother us! No more war! No more rotten English gen-

erals, like Braddock and Abercrombie and Loudon and the rest of
'em, to lead our men into ambushes and get 'em slaughtered for nothing! No more damned Indian raids! When your ma wants to walk
over and see the neighbors she can do so without being afraid one of
those red devils from St. Francis will stick a hatchet in her.

"I'm against it, Stevie, but I'm going to take a little drink to your
ma, God bless her!"

He got out the flask again and took a small drink without screaming, after which we walked back to where Natanis lay beside the fire,
and found all four of the Indians pretending not to have heard my
father's scream.

My father gave Natanis a slice of liver and patted him on the shoulder. "Your talk is good. Tell more, and say whether you saw the
French captain Guerlac, who traveled with a small girl and a band
of your brothers from St. Francis."

Natanis corrected my father. "De Sabrevois; not Guerlac. A celebrated seigneur and captain, traveling with the small girl, his sister,
and wounded in the cheek and ear from fighting a strong detachment
of Bostonnais troops and defeating them with his few braves."

To hear Mary spoken of, even, stirred me as though a hand had
squeezed the blood from my heart.

My father nudged me to make no sign. "That is the man," he said.
"Where did you meet him?"

But like all Indians, Natanis could not leap about in his tale, but
must tell it in order, like my mother telling what she was doing and
thinking when she saw a mouse run across the floor.

He said he had no fire until, in a brook, he found a striped water
snake. With the snake skin he made a string for the twirling of a fire
bow and got fire, after which he hunted along brooks for trouts to
tickle with his fingers, and in this way got a little to eat, but not
much, for the trouts were small, the large ones having gone down
into the St. Lawrence. The nights, he said, were cold, so when he
came suddenly on a black bear he tried to kill it with a club made
from the root of a birch tree, so that he might take its skin; but the
club broke and the bear got away. He could have skinned the bear,
he said, with a chipped flint, which makes a better skinning tool than
a knife, since it cuts more readily.

He tried to beg a knife from a Canadian whose cabin was on the
bank of the river; but the Canadian, in a state of excitement over the
fall of Quebec, fired at him with a musket and set a dog on him, at

which Natanis fled, fearing the dog might rob him even of his belt cloth.

After that he would not approach any cabin for help, but kept on to the cove where the Chaudière flows into the St. Lawrence, intending to ascend the Chaudière until he came to the settlements of the Southern Abenakis, or to autumn hunting parties from the Kennebec.

At the mouth of the Chaudière he saw a camp of Indians, and, on joining them, found they were Guerlac's six braves.

"Six?" my father asked. "I thought there were eight."

"There had been eight," said Natanis, "but one, Eneas, had been struck by an arrow so that he had difficulty in sitting, and another, Sabatis, had been hit in the shoulder; and these two had been left behind with a canoe at the Chain of Ponds, so the others might travel faster without them."

The six Indians, Natanis said, had agreed to take Guerlac and Mary down the river that night, hiding by day and pressing on when darkness fell, until they should encounter a French vessel, or until Guerlac should find means of getting back to France.

"For," Natanis explained, "the French captain wished to settle his affairs in France and place his sister in a convent, and so could not run the risk of falling into the hands of the English, who sometimes kill prisoners and eat babies."

"Who told you that?" my father asked sharply.

"De Sabrevois," Natanis said, "but it is also something that has been said by all Frenchmen since the English prisoners were killed at Fort William Henry."

"A tale for frightening children," my father said. "We will charge Guerlac for it when the day of reckoning comes. Get on with your story, my son; and remember that we, who saved you from the buck and give you this food, would also be called English by your French friend."

Natanis, who was quick-witted, smiled and nodded, and received a small piece of liver at my father's hands.

He had asked the braves for a knife and a blanket, he said, and they had given him a knife, but would not give him a blanket because they had cut pieces from their own to make a dress for the little girl. He had lain by their fire that night and watched them, when it became dark, set off down the St. Lawrence. In the morning he had pressed on, fearful that Rangers or Wolfe's troops might pursue him, pushed up the Chaudière to Lake Megantic, and in three days crossed the Height of Land, traveling rapidly to keep warm, and living on next to nothing—a few small trouts, a porcupine, thorn apples, partridge berries.

He said he could not find Sabatis and Eneas at the Chain of Ponds, and since he felt less strong he dared not stop. Along Dead River he jumped the same deer three times; therefore, since there was the smell of snow in the air, he set out to run it down, knowing that with snow on the ground, he could tire it out provided his own strength held.

He ran it all day. That night a light snow fell; so at dawn the next day he jumped it once more and kept close on its heels. At last it rested too long, and he caught it as we came up. Lacking the strength to hold it fast, he would have been cut to pieces save for us.

Having told his tale, he smiled confidingly at my father and asked for more liver, which my father gave him, saying that it was the best of all meats to give him back his blood, provided he took it in moderation.

Natawammet, Woromquid, and Hobomok, hunkered down around the deerskin, which they were scraping and rubbing with ashes, spoke admiringly to Natanis for what he had done; for to run down a deer without the help of snowshoes and deep snow is a great feat, only to be accomplished by a skillful hunter. He deserved admiration; for I have never known an Abenaki or any other Indian whose knowledge of the forest was as great as his.

To learn that Mary had been taken away where we could not follow, and where I could not know what was happening to her, filled me with a feeling of heavy emptiness, as though my stomach had been replaced by a bag of bullets.

My father knew how I felt. "Stevie," he said, "you want to remember to-day isn't everything. That's what Abenakis can't remember, and that's why they're Indians; why they haven't a chance with white men. There's to-morrow coming, to-morrows aplenty, and we'll find Mary on one of 'em, and Guerlac too, if we want to find him. That's sure, Stevie, because whatever you want, you generally get, if you want it hard enough."

I didn't say anything; only snuffled.

"Now Stevie," my father said, "your ma's waiting for us, and Cynthia and the rest of the girls; and there's Ranger and Eunice hanging around the back door, same as always; and we'll get back just as quick as we can, only we might as well pick up a few beaver skins, so to help get your ma a piece of silk from Boston, or some kind of flummery.

"There's another thing, Stevie, and that's this Natanis. It seems to me he isn't what you'd call wallering in blessings. I guess things don't look any better to him than they do to you, and maybe they don't look so good. You got a ma and a dog and your sisters and a good house to go home to, but he hasn't got anybody or any place. It's only a few days ago they killed his pa and his ma and his brother, and burned down his house. He's pretty near starved to death, and a good deal banged up. If you ask me, he probably feels worse about it than you do about Mary. I don't rightly know how these Indian boys do their thinking; but I know a little something about the squaws, Stevie, and they can't be much different; so it's my guess he lies awake at night and feels awful bad over the way things turned out."

My father walked me down toward the canoe. "This boy Natanis has done a lot for us: more than you realize. He's saved us a terrible trip—one I wouldn't have considered taking if it hadn't been that I'd promised you, Stevie, and of course you've always got to keep your promises.

"I figure we owe him something, you and me, and it's kind of up to us to pay it. Besides, he's a good boy. I should judge he's the best Indian boy we've seen in a long time; and we've seen some good ones. You notice he didn't brag about traveling three days without much food and then running down a deer. If Manatqua had done that he'd have quit hunting for the rest of his life and just sat around talking about himself. The others would have fed him, of course, to keep him from talking, at least while he ate.

"It won't do you any harm to have this Natanis for a friend, Stevie; so if you'd feel like it we could stay here a few days and kind of keep him company and build him a cabin and get him started, and maybe pick up a few beaver skins for your ma, and have a good time doing it."

He stopped at the edge of the bank and looked out over the sunny bend in Dead River, and the meadows beyond, to the hulking sides of Dead River Mountain—the one they now call Mount Bigelow—that seemed to block our homeward path. Its pines were frosted green in the afternoon sun, and the maples at its base were as red as the vermilion face paint of a brave, with the yellow flames of the birches licking through the red. From the point we could see both up river and down, for the river made a sharp turn around it; and in both directions the black water was broken by the circles made by feeding fish. Far off we saw the broad arrowheads made by swim-

ming minks or otters; and a cow moose with a calf came out of the
brush, well upstream, and pawed through the thin snow for fodder.

"It's as pretty a spot as you'd want," my father said. "The King
himself couldn't get a nicer place for a hunting cabin if he ordered
it special. You could probably learn a lot from this Natanis, too; but
if you wouldn't choose to stay here that long we can figure out something else."

We went back to Natanis. My father gave him more liver and told
him to go to sleep, and said at night he could have a large piece, and
the next day we might even kill a moose and let him eat all of it.

Natanis grinned and went to sleep, whereupon my father set me
to staking out the cabin at the back part of the meadow, on a knoll
and near a spring, so located that anyone coming to it must walk for
some distance across the meadow, exposing himself to those inside.

Natawammet and Woromquid overturned the canoe and rested it
on stakes, raising a lean-to of spruce boughs against it, with sides of
boughs at each end, so that we had an excellent shelter, open to a
fire in front. By sundown the logs were cut; so venison was hung before the fire to broil, and Hobomok made birch-bark plates and a
birch-bark bowl for melting sweetened bear's fat.

Natanis looked enviously at our venison when we ate; but my father held him to his liver, explaining to him meanwhile the thoughts
that were in his mind.

"My son," he said, "you have given us useful information. Therefore I will repay our debt in what manner I can, as well as with advice. You have come here to a good hunting ground, rich in beavers,
otters, fish, deer, and everything needful, open to the sun, and safe
for many years from people who might wish to steal your land. If you
desire to go farther south, I will take you to Norridgewock or to Swan
Island, where there are many Abenakis; but I advise you to remain
here. In the south your people are more closely pressed each year by
the white people, whose ways are different. The beavers and the
deer daily become more timid, and go farther into the forests, where
they are harder to find. Here the beavers and the deer are unfright-
ened. I advise you to remain here in the cabin we build; and I also
advise Natawammet and Woromquid to remain through the winter,
trapping beavers and otters with you. Nowhere near the Androscoggin can they find as many pelts. Thus you will not be lonely. When
the snows melt, the three of you will be rich in skins, and I will buy
them at such prices that you will be able to have fine muskets and
traps and shirts and pantaloons, and knives and kettles and toma-

hawks such as you never saw before. Also the cabin will remain here, so that nobody will occupy the land in your absence; and Natanis can return to it after he has sold his skins. We will build a canoe, and leave powder and shot, knives and hatchets, arrowheads and bow-strings. Everything that can be spared, we will leave; and in the spring you can repay with skins. Think about this and then speak your mind."

"Father," Natanis said, "I will stay. I am grateful."

My father waved his hand as if to signify there was no cause for gratitude, and looked at Natawammet and Woromquid. Before they could answer Hobomok spoke, folding his hands comfortably over his stomach. "I, too, will stay. The fish in the river are salmon."

"That is good information," my father said, "but you will go home to your father and learn to be a great *m'téoulin*, with a scream that will paralyze all who hear it, as should be the case with good *m'téoulins*. I would like you to stay, to confound your father, who predicted all of us would come back together, and also so you might become less fat. Remember my words, Hobomok, and become thin. It is hard to believe in the magic of a fat man."

Hobomok smiled benevolently. "My father did not predict that all of us would come back together."

"Indeed!" my father said. "That is how I remember it."

"No," said Hobomok, "he predicted that all who began the trip would return safely, but he did not say when."

"Hobomok," my father said, "you will be a great *m'téoulin*, and it would be a pity if you sullied your hands with ordinary toil. You will return in the canoe with me; and none of your *m'téoulin* tricks, either."

Natawammet said ruefully he could not stay unless my father would stop at Swan Island and persuade his wife to join him at Dead River; but Woromquid said he would remain, since his wife had re-cently left his wigwam and returned to her parents, and he wanted never to see another woman, or at any rate not until spring. My father said he would attend to Natawammet's wife, sending her back by a hunting party, and arranging to have her carry an additional musket for Natanis, together with such blankets, moccasins, and leggins as would be needed during the winter.

Hobomok caught salmon for us in the morning, fine fish that will saw off one's finger if it becomes looped by the line; and these Natanis was allowed to eat, provided he ate often, and not much at any one time. I feared there would be no more salmon left in the river after we had been gone a week; for he ate as a mill eats corn.

In the afternoon Natanis hobbled painfully into the forest with me, looking first, like all good hunters, at the spot where he had jumped on the deer, so to see how he might have done it better. He carried my father's hunting bow with him, and soon he sat on a stump and made a peculiar noise with his lips against the back of his hand, a sort of muffled squeak. A raccoon came out from behind a stump and looked at him. He tried to draw the arrow, but could not because of his side.

With each passing day Natanis grew stronger, eating until I feared he might explode, and even hanging a piece of venison above his head at night so he might wake and eat it. To this, however, my father put a stop after a porcupine came clattering in to look for the meat while we were all asleep, and stumbled over my father, leaving a dozen quills in his leg.

While my father, Woromquid, and Natawammet labored at a birch canoe, Natanis went into the woods with Hobomok and me, hunting for beavers and otters, and for linden trees for snares and medicines.

Never, in the woods, have I seen a person as skilled in the ways of Nature. To him the forest was as full of signs as the roads of Falmouth. The tops of pines, he said, incline toward the east; the largest number of limbs grow on the south sides of the trees; moss grows toward the roots on their northwest sides; a red moon is a sign of wind, and a pale moon a sign of snow or rain. Whatever he saw, he remembered: the spots where certain red squirrels habitually sit to eat pine cones; branches on which night herons roost; trees favored by partridges; marks on rocks; oddly shaped limbs on trees. When he had seen one of these things he recognized it instantly again, even though he approached it from another side; so he was never lost in the woods, but could always return the way he came.

He declared that animals and birds conversed with each other, and that he could talk with them; and I think this was so. He was silent as a shadow when he hunted, taking care where he placed each foot, and looking around him before he stirred. Yet sometimes he found it necessary to move quickly, so that noise was unavoidable; and when he wished to do this, or to signal to one of us, he would talk to the crows. This he would do by cawing a few times like a crow, and suddenly changing the note of his caw, so that it dropped into a hoarse lower key. Instantly a crow would come from somewhere, cawing at the top of its lungs, whereupon Natanis would repeat his hoarse call. Then more crows would come from a distance to circle the trees under which he stood, all of them hawing and cawing. While this went on, Natanis said, it was possible to walk carelessly, even in leaves or dried twigs; for animals near by would think the noise was caused by two crows on the ground engaged in combat over a she-crow. Those overhead, he declared, were urging the lady crow to leave her two ruffianly friends and come away with them.

He said the bluejay was the tattle-tale of the forest and told everything he could see. The bluejay had one call, he said, that meant "Here comes a hunter," and another that meant "Here comes a wolverine," and another that meant "Here comes a hawk"; and Natanis could give these calls.

He said that when a rabbit was in pain it called to other animals for help. This call, he said, was the squeak he made by pressing his lips to the inside of his clenched fist and sucking sharply. Whenever he did it, an animal came to look: either an apprehensive rabbit; or a squirrel cursing and flirting its tail; or a wildcat or a mink or a wolverine, licking its lips hopefully at the thought of the troubled rabbit.

The greatest talkers, he declared, were squirrels and partridges. By listening carefully to a squirrel one could tell whether he was jeering at a wildcat, a fox, a hawk or a man. Also, with practice, one could speak with partridges, telling them when to stop feeding and watch for danger, when to run for shelter, when to fly, and when they could safely come out of hiding and resume feeding.

Even the beavers, he said, though the dumbest of all animals, making no sound except by slapping the water with their tails, converse together by means of odors; and to that end the female beaver has two sets of glands from which come different smells. One set Natanis called bark glands, and the other oil glands. By mixing the juices of these glands he was able to call beavers to his traps, which he made out of logs delicately held up by fibres from the linden tree, so that they fell at a touch.

When we hunted, he took exception to Hobomok's carelessness in the woods. It was no use grumbling at me, he said. White men are more impatient than red men, unwilling to crouch motionless for hours in order to obtain food; averse to hunting without garments, so to avoid noisy contact with branches; scornful of eating no fish previous to a hunt, so there might be less odor for animals to detect—of eating, in fact, almost nothing on the day before, so the senses might be keener and the desire for game greater. Everywhere in the

woods, he said, there is game fleeing before a hunter; so that for every
animal the hunter sees, there are ten that see him.

He talked with me often about Mary; for seemingly his eyes understood not only the forest signs, but also my heart and that which
was near it. Each day he would tell how the pieces of blanket had
been fastened together to make her dress; how her hair, because of
catching on twigs at the carries, had been hacked close to her head
with a hunting knife; how her worn-out shoes had been replaced by
rawhide moccasins and leggins; how her face and hands had been
scratched by branches; how she would not sit at her food with De
Sabrevois, but wandered about with venison in her hand, examining
Natanis and thrusting out her tongue at De Sabrevois when he ordered her to be still. These tales made me both sad and happy; I
couldn't hear them often enough.

"The French captain has known the forest and cannot stay across
the sea," Natanis said. "He must come back. When the time arrives
we can go together to see him, if my brother wishes." This he often
repeated, seeing that I did wish it.

At the end of a week we had done what we could for Natanis, his
side being healed enough to leave off the bandage. The cabin was
finished, a roomy cabin with a fireplace and a chimney of sticks
coated with mud, and the chinks between the logs stuffed with moss.
The wind was west, sharp but pleasant, with a feel peculiar to our
Northern woods in autumn: one that makes children squeal like colts
and run aimlessly about, leaping from elation. The air was bright
and clear, so that every leaf and pine needle on the mountain, almost, stood out sharp to our eyes. Since our work was done, my
father said, we must go. Within ten minutes our few belongings were
wrapped in our blankets and we sat in the canoe, my father in the
stern, Hobomok in the bow, waiting for Natanis to make a bundle
of six beaver skins and two otter skins.

I had left him my musket; and my father had given him his kettle
and bullet mold and our spare knitted shirts and stockings, and all
our powder and ball except enough to get us home; also fish hooks
and lines, as well as arrowheads and bowstrings, smoked venison,
ducks' breasts and sweetened bear fat.

Natanis laid his bundle in the canoe, then reached out and touched
my father and me on the arm. "I give these poor skins," he said.
"You have given me life and many riches. For me this is a good
exchange, and I shall remember." He pushed the canoe into the

stream. "In the spring," he added, "we shall talk together again in your house."

"Come in Muskoskikizoos, the moon in which we catch young seals," my father said. "Thus you'll escape mosquitoes and black flies. You can bring Natawammet and Woromquid to get the new muskets I promised them."

They shouted and waved as we slipped down the river in the bright sun. They looked small and lonely on the high bank with the vast expanse of dark forest and rolling mountains beyond them; and when the first bend in the river hid them from us I knew from the feeling of loss in my own heart that their memories of us would be fond and lasting.

*   *   *

Through the bright morning we bent back and forth with Dead River Mountain clinging at our shoulders, lost it as we turned off at Bog Brook, and took trout at noon from the east pond on the twelve-mile carry.

We camped that night at the mouth of the Carrabasset; and early the next morning, before the mist was off the river, we came to Nor-ridgewock, where Manatqua gave us hot hominy.

My father, eager to be gone, made short work of loading beaver and otter skins; and so precipitately was Manatqua hustled into the canoe that he lacked fresh pitch for his scalp-lock, and traveled with it all askew.

So we came again to the settlements through the red and yellow flames of the maples, passing the houses built by Dr. Gardiner for those who settled on his lands, and the wharves at the mouth of the Cobosseecontee where Dr. Gardiner's people take sturgeons in the spring of the year for shipment to England in hogsheads; and my father said we should come in the spring to eat sturgeon eggs, they being the most delicious of foods, as the Abenakis well know.

Opposite Pownalborough, where Dr. Gardiner had given land to German settlers, good farmers but stubborn beyond belief, we met the smell of the sea from Merrymeeting Bay, and with it a black topsail schooner, running upstream.

Seeing us, she rounded into the wind and dropped jib and anchor; so my father ran alongside. The name on her stern was *Black Duck*, New Haven.

Four men stood at the rail. One was swarthy, chunky, blue-eyed and young, with tremendous broad shoulders, and wearing a bright tasseled cap like a stocking and a gay blanket coat belted at the waist with a sash, such as Canadians wear in winter.

"Good day to you, Captain," he said to my father. His eyes flicked to Manatqua, who was attempting to straighten his scalp-lock. "I see," he added, "that scalps are barely holding their own this morning."

"Yes, sir," my father said, "and from the indications there'll be a falling off before night."

The swarthy young man nodded, widening his eyes like a dog that has caught sight of a cat. "Captain," he asked, "could you spare me a little information?"

My father considered, studying the young man and the schooner. "Why, yes, sir. I can spare some; and I'll trade it for a little trip in your schooner, if it so happens you're going back to sea again."

"Aha!" said the young man. "A trader! Well, I'll trade if I can get good value. What way might you be going, Captain?"

"I might be going to Arundel, seven leagues or so south of Falmouth."

"Hm! And would you be bargaining for the transport of your crew and cargo as well?"

"I would."

"I think," the young man said, "I should look at your wares. They'll have to be good to pay for such a trip."

"I'll give you a sample," my father said. "Wolfe took Quebec!"

If he expected to astonish his hearers he was disappointed, for the swarthy young man and his companions merely nodded.

"You knew it!" my father cried. "I've stocked the wrong goods!"

The young man seemed sympathetic. "Where'd you get your news, sir?"

"On Dead River, sir, from a St. Francis Indian whose town was destroyed by Rogers' Rangers."

"There's information! Where the devil is Dead River?"

"Will this information apply on my passage?" my father asked.

The young man laughed, a brilliant laugh that lengthened his face oddly, giving him the appearance of slenderness, height, fairness, instead of breadth and shortness and swarthiness. "Tell me where Dr. Sylvester Gardiner lives, and I'll carry you to Arundel for four otter skins."

"Hell," my father said courteously, "I'd rather swim than pay four otter skins for such a trip. It's worth no more than the information you seek. I'll give you that for nothing. Gardiner's holding lies on the west side of the river where the wharves run out at the mouth of Cobosseecontee stream. He'll be in Boston at this time of year. From your masthead you can see Gardinerstown."

The young man seized the ratlines on the inside and went up them hand over hand, not moving his feet: as quick and agile as the monkeys that Spanish sailors carry. At the top he swung his leg over, and in a second was clinging to the mast, smiling down at us. "From here?" he asked, and looked upriver. He seemed to slip, caught himself, swung under the ratlines, and dropped to the deck as light as a squirrel, looking at us as though to say: "You couldn't do that!" and I wouldn't have sworn we could.

"I'll have a shot at it," he said. "I'll tell you what I'll do. I'll take you to Arundel, and you can pay me what you think it's worth."

An older man with a chin whisker made some sort of protest, in which I caught the word "dirty."

"We've been a month in the woods," my father said quickly. "To-morrow we'll be cleaner than you are."

The young man paid no attention to my father, but rounded on the chin-whiskered man with a face suddenly dark as a blackamoor's, and puffy, as though rage surged knobbily to his cheeks. His voice was startlingly shrill. "This schooner's under charter to my employers! I take whom I please and go where I please. Hoist your jib and anchor and get under way!"

He turned to my father again, his face lightening and lengthening extraordinarily. "What's your name, sir, and where'll I pick you up to-morrow when I drop down on the early tide?"

"Steven Nason, sir; innkeeper and trader, of Arundel. We'll lie off the southern tip of Swan Island."

The jib slid up and the schooner's head payed off.

"To whom am I indebted, sir?" my father called.

The young man, gay in his white coat striped with blue on the sleeves and skirt, waved to us "Benedict Arnold of Norwich, Connecticut, sir, newly come from Quebec." The schooner slipped off upriver as smoothly as her namesake.

My father bent to his paddle, chuckling. "That boy's a trader, Stevie. That was good trading you listened to, and your pa sort of out-traded him."

IX

I HAVE often wished we could have left Natanis a day earlier or a day later, so that I might have escaped a store of grief at a far distant period; but it may be that by doing so we would have encountered other and greater evils than the Reverend Ezekiel Hook.

There was an odd silence among the waiting Swan Islanders when we came down to the tip of the island and pushed through the guzzle; then Hobomok shouted that we had left Natawammet and Woromquid in a place of countless beavers, and that the sachem of the Norridgewocks was escorting us home. Thereupon there was a bedlam of whooping and firing of muskets, and the entire encampment rushed down the slope of the headland to welcome us. When Rabomis sought to take my father by the shoulders, he held her off, saying he would talk to nobody until the two of us had gone into the sweat house and freed ourselves of pitch and grime.

The *m'téoulin* ordered squaws to heat stones for us; and he himself led us to his cabin. On the way we saw a white man in rusty black garb standing alone on the ridge, looking sourly at us as though our talk and laughter had something unrighteous about it. This man, Rabomis said, was an exhorter sent from Boston to talk to settlers who had no meeting houses, and to lead the Abenakis to follow the white man's Great Spirit, if they did not already do so. That afternoon, she said, he had paddled over from Pownalborough and spoken to them. They held a council, she said, and now the *m'téoulin*, being an orator, would reply. Since she interpreted badly, she begged my father to interpret.

My father said he wanted nothing to do with it; and we went on with the *m'téoulin*, who brought with him a kettle full of water in which herbs were steeping. This we took into the sweat house, a small wigwam at the edge of the river. Two squaws put in hot stones; then left us clean moccasins and blankets, and carried away our clothes to be washed and our leather shirts to be scoured with sand.

My father trickled the water on the stones, and a sweet-smelling steam arose, so that perspiration poured from us. In this stifling place we stayed fifteen minutes, after which we jumped in the icy-cold river, and came out feeling strong and elated: ready, my father said, to ride a bob-cat.

We cut each other's hair, and my father was scraping bristles from his chin when the *m'téoulin* came in to say the white man wished my father, in the name of his Great Spirit, to interpret the words of the council.

I could see my father was reluctant; and if I had known what would come of it I would have gone back into the sweat house and stayed until the stones grew cold. But I could not know, nor could the *m'téoulin* with all his knowledge of magic; so we wrapped our blankets around us and went to the council house. The minister Hook eyed us disapprovingly, making me feel undressed, like a person driven from his home by a fire in the dead of night.

Hook was thin and hunched, so that he looked like a heron waiting for a fish. The skin over his forehead was tight and glossy, as though it might easily burst. He said to my father, in a harsh voice, that he had told the red men, earlier in the day, how he had been sent by the great missionary society of Boston, not to get away their lands or goods, but to instruct them in worshipping the Great Spirit. There was only one religion, and unless they embraced it, they could not be happy. They had lived in errors and darkness all their lives, and he had come to save them. Other Abenakis were awaiting the decision of their older brothers on Swan Island, so if they had objections to the true religion he wished to hear them.

My father, wrapped in his red blanket, nodded soberly and signaled to the *m'téoulin* to speak.

"Brother," the *m'téoulin* said, "the white men came here to enjoy their own religion in their own way. We gave them corn and meat; they gave us poison. They called us brothers. They wanted more land; they wanted our country. We became uneasy; Indians were hired to fight against Indians. Your white chiefs have offered large sums for the scalps of the women and children of our brothers to the east. Your people brought strong liquor that stole away our senses and even killed our friends.

"Brother, our country was once large and yours was small. You have now become a great people, and we have scarcely a place left to spread our blankets. You have got our country but are not satisfied; you want to force your religion upon us.

"Brother, continue to listen: you say you are sent to instruct us how to worship the Great Spirit agreeably to his mind, and if we do not embrace the religion which the white people teach we shall be unhappy hereafter. You say you are right and we are lost. How do we know this to be true? We understand your religion is written in a book. If it was intended for us as well as for you, why has not the Great Spirit given it to us? And not only to us, but why did he not give to our forefathers the knowledge of that book, with the means of understanding it rightly? Why has the Great Spirit permitted our forefathers to live wrongly since the olden time? We only know what you tell us about it. How shall we know whom to believe, being so often deceived by the white people?

"Brother, you say there is but one way to worship and serve the Great Spirit. If there is but one religion, why do you white people differ so much about it? Why not all agree, since all read the book?

"Brother, we do not understand these things. We are told your religion was given to your forefathers, and has been handed down from father to son. We also have a religion which was given to our forefathers, and has been handed down to us, their children. It teaches us to be thankful for favors we receive: to love each other, and to be united. We never quarrel about religion.

"Brother, the Great Spirit has made us all; but he has made a great difference between his white and red children. He has given us a different skin and different customs. Since he has made so great a difference between us in other things, why may we not conclude he has reason for giving us a different religion? The Great Spirit does right: he knows what is best for his children. We are satisfied.

"Brother, if you white men murdered the son of the Great Spirit, we Indians had nothing to do with it. It is none of our affair. If he had come among us we would not have killed him. We would have treated him well. You must make amends for that crime yourselves.

"Brother, we do not wish to destroy your religion or take it from you. We only want to enjoy our own.

"Brother, you say you have not come to get our lands or our goods, but to enlighten our minds. We are told you have been preaching to white people along this river. These people are our neighbors: we are acquainted with them. We will wait a little while and see what effect your preaching has upon them. If we find it does them good, makes them honest and less disposed to cheat Indians, we will then consider again what you have said."

* * *

Seldom have I seen a man so infuriated as Hook when my father had interpreted the last sentence. His rage, for some reason, was directed more against my father and me than against the *m'téoulin* or the other Abenakis. I think he suspected my father of putting words in the *m'téoulin's* mouth. His eyes reddened and his knees trembled; he shot his head forward and croaked, "Blasphemy!", looking more than ever like a heron about to pounce on a fish.

My father would have gone from the council house had not Hook gone up close to him, shaking with wrath, and said: "These sons of Belial have blasphemed against our religion and our God. Say to them they cannot speak thus!"

My father shook his head. "Reverend Hook," he said, "I'm no minister of the gospel to rebuke these people for their beliefs. I'm a trader and innkeeper, and sometimes, against my will, an interpreter." Again he made as though to leave the cabin, but Hook stopped him, his lips compressed, and his forehead shiny like the dried bladders my sisters throw about at Christmas.

"Or," asked Hook, his voice shrill with rage, "are you yourself a heathen, damned forever with these imps of hell?"

"Now, now!" my father said soothingly. "I take comfort in the Good Book; and according to my lights I'm what they call a godly man. I think, even, I'm as godly as your Boston saints and deacons who speculate in land and trade in human flesh and specialize in bribery under the protection of a special God."

"A special God!" Hook croaked, raising his hands, as though undecided whether to call on heaven for help or to take my father by the throat.

"Why, yes," my father said, "a special God; the God of Boston. We're sick of your Boston God, and we're sick of your Boston merchants with their special privileges we common people can't have; with their money bags filled out of wars we little people make; with their yowling and yelping that we who want a voice in the affairs of the colony are thieves and rascals!"

"A special God!" Hook whispered, with an air of expecting to see my father struck dead.

"Just so," my father said: "a God like the God Jonathan Edwards wrote and preached about, without mercy or decency, rejoicing in human misery and suffering, cruel beyond belief to little children, and condemning the greater part of mankind to eternal torment.

There's no place for any such God in my life; for Jonathan Edwards' God says my son here"—he dropped his hand on my shoulder —"is evil, was born evil, and is doomed to hell fire. Therefore if I believed in Jonathan Edwards' God my son would be wasting his time in striving to lead a decent, godly life, being damned to begin with. And if I told these red men about the existence of such a God, they'd say he was worse than Malsum, their evil wolf-god. They'd fear to speak his name, lest he come back to earth to do mischief to innocent people."

Hook stared from my father to me. I have never seen hatred more bitter, not even on the faces of men with whom I have fought for my life. He moved to the door, peering back at us with hard heron-eyes. "The sins of the fathers!" he rasped. "You and your son and your son's sons shall burn in hell!"

"I reckon we will," my father said calmly, "if your say-so can do it!" He snorted a little, seeming to imply that Hook's influence was not sufficient to cause him distress.

While Hook stood glaring, the *m'téoulin* went to him and offered his hand in farewell. Hook said bitterly, "There can be no fellowship between the religion of God and the works of the devil!" He flung out of the cabin and paddled back to Pownalborough in the dark, causing my father to remark that he had his faults, but cowardice, seemingly, was not one of them.

That night we feasted on venison and beaver tail, comfortable in our newly washed garments and our scoured buckskins; and after the feast the squaws brought all the drums in the camp to play upon for what my father called a Bragging Dance, which is what the Abenakis always have when a sachem from another nation comes to visit.

When Manatqua rose up to sing his bragging song there was no way of telling his enormous powers of endurance, for his knees were wrinkled and seemingly insecure, and his voice quavery. Yet he grew stronger and stronger, going back many years and fishing up mighty exploits that my father said may have happened to Manatqua, but more likely happened to Noah on the Ark.

All of us near died with laughter we could not show; for in the heat of his dance his scalp-lock came unstuck and fell off, and he was forever striving to stick it on again, only to have it slip to the ground at once. So to conceal our mirth we whooped and shrieked as though in applause, thus spurring him on to renewed endeavor.

* * *

We went down to the guzzle at slack tide in the morning and climbed into a long canoe, with Manatqua and the *m'téoulin* and all their skins, and two braves to paddle us.

When the black topsail schooner came slipping into sight around the bend Rabomis kissed me. "Come back soon, Stevie," she said, "and bring your father." We both looked at him, but he stared stonily ahead and signaled for the canoe to be run out. Hobomok splashed into the marsh beside us and gave me a pouch made from mink skin. The marsh grass hissed as we moved through it. Clouds of ducks and water hens went up around us with a vast whispering of wings, and little short-tailed birds blundered helplessly among the reeds.

I knew, when I looked back at the silent throng on the beach, that I could live happily at Swan Island if I had no other home, and no mother or sisters, and no Ranger or Eunice to draw me back to Arundel; and if, above all else, I had no Mary Mallinson to drag my thoughts to her from any place at all.

* * *

Arnold gave my father his hand when we came alongside the *Black Duck*, while Manatqua and the *m'téoulin* scrambled up and stowed the skins under a tarpaulin. Before we knew we were aboard, almost, the schooner had slipped past the end of the marsh, and our friends were dark specks against the broad expanse of red-rimmed river.

My father and Arnold soon became thick. My father wanted news of Quebec, and Arnold asked what he knew of military matters, whereat my father said he had been at Louisbourg in '45. At once they united in cursing the stupidity of the English for giving back to the French that which had been won by the colonies with so much labor.

Arnold told my father he had gone as a soldier to Lake George four years before, when he was sixteen, but had sickened of inaction under the overambitious Shirley, and so had deserted and returned home.

Together they damned the English officers who had been sent to fight the war against the French, and it was plain to see that either of them would prefer to take a rattlesnake to bed with him than to trust himself in our forests with an English general, barring always James Wolfe and young Lord Howe.

By the time the schooner had dropped down Merrymeeting Bay and passed through the narrow water-churn we call the Chops into the broad lower reaches of the river, they seemed like old friends; and Arnold had told my father how he had sailed up to Quebec, arriving just before it fell, with a load of medicines from his employers, the Lathrops, of Norwich, who imported drugs from Europe, and sold much of them to the English army.

"Drugs, eh? So that's why you went up to see Sylvester Gardiner!"

"Aye," Arnold said. "Private business! If I can make a trade with Gardiner in Boston I can get him a market for his drugs at a round price and be the gainer myself, with nobody the worse for it." He winked at my father, placed his hands on the hips of his white blanket coat, stuck his right leg straight out in front of him and squatted suddenly, so that he was sitting on his left heel. Then, as easily as I get off a bench, he raised himself again on one leg and looked inquiringly at me.

"Can you do that?"

I tried it, but fell over on my side; and I was months learning to do it as easily as he did. He was forever performing such tricks: reaching up, when talking, to the rung of a ladder or the edge of a doorway and chinning himself with one hand; or holding his left foot with his right hand and hopping through the circle thus formed, all so easily and gracefully, that I was lost in admiration of him.

"How's trade in Quebec?" my father asked.

Arnold's eyes rounded until they looked like snowballs stuck with bits of blue glass.

"Why," he said, "the city was stove to pieces by Wolfe's artillery, and the people of the town robbed and cheated for years by two of the greatest thieves unjailed, Vaudreuil and Bigot. They need everything; and any price in reason looks cheap after those they've had to pay." He drew himself up a rope, as we had seen him do the day before, and dropped lightly back again. "Everybody in Quebec is either a gentleman, a thief, or a dolt. It's the easiest place to make money I ever saw! If I had the capital I'd trade nowhere else; and almost before you could spit I'd have a fortune."

My father nodded. "Did you ever hear the name Guerlac or De Sabrevois in Quebec? Henri Guerlac de Sabrevois, captain in the regiment of Béarn?"

My heart pounded as I waited for his answer.

"I know that name," Arnold said. "He has a seigneurie on the Island of Orleans. He bought one of the bomb-proof houses in the upper town. He's a stinker, pale and haughty; a devil with the women."

"Not so pale," my father said quickly, "since I scarred his cheek and ear with a hunting arrow!"

Try as I would, I couldn't keep the tears from my eyes. Seeing this, Arnold sat beside me on the deck house, clapping his hand on my shoulder and looking inquiringly at my father.

"He came through Arundel a month ago," my father said. "Out of cussedness he stole a little girl who lived near us; and his damned French-led Indians killed her father. We've been after him, but we lost him. Now we hear he's sailed back to France."

Arnold patted me on the shoulder and rounded his eyes at my father again. I find it hard to describe this quick, fixed stare of his, gone almost as soon as it appeared; but it was a little like the hunting glare of an animal, or the fixed look in the eyes of our cat when she peers up into the corners of our kitchen at night for things we cannot see.

"What was the name of this little girl?"

"Mary Mallinson."

Arnold repeated the name, then picked me up by the upper arms and jounced me down on my heels so that my teeth jarred together. "Now, now!" he said. "Everything'll be all right! I'll keep my eye on your Frenchman myself, and save him for you. When you get bigger you can shoot off his other ear. Some day we'll walk right into his house and throw him through his bomb-proof roof. Listen!" He tapped my chest. "Your girl won't like Frenchmen any more than you would!" He paused impressively. "They eat frogs' legs!"

Cheered by this knowledge, I sat with Manatqua and the *m'téoulin* and only half heard Arnold tell my father how Wolfe had found a path up an impassable precipice at Anse du Foulon, and taken his entire army up it in the dead of night; how Montcalm, fearful of being cut off from all supplies, had come out from behind the impregnable walls of the upper town and fought Wolfe in the open fields; how Vaudreuil, the lying, timorous, braggart governor, had failed to go to Montcalm's support, so that the French were routed; how they had fled through the town and thirty miles beyond in an insane panic; and how both Montcalm and Wolfe had been killed.

They spoke of warfare, too, and my father told how the Abenakis begin to train their children in the art of war when they are twelve years old—the art of war being the art of ambushing and surprising an enemy.

"You seem to think," said Arnold, "that if they were properly disciplined they'd fight better than the English."

"They're already disciplined," my father said. "They're under good command, and punctual. They cheerfully execute orders, and march abreast, without disorder or confusion, in a line a mile long, with a space of twenty feet or more separating each man from the other. It's their discipline to annoy the enemy to the greatest degree, while saving their own men and their equipment. That's against all the rules of the white man, who regards war as an excuse to follow unwise counsel, and to waste as much money as possible to no effect, just as the English think it's discipline to have their men slaughtered in the woods, and to no result.

"Look," my father said, "at the defeat of General Braddock when he tried to take Fort Duquesne four years ago from the French and Indians. He had nine hundred men killed, while the six hundred Indians who defeated him lost seven! That battle was planned and executed by Abenakis from St. Francis. I've heard from Virginians who fought in it that when they took trees to protect themselves in the Indian manner, Braddock beat them back into line with his sword, to be shot down like cattle. Discipline! That's no discipline! That's organized murder!"

"Then you'd discipline our people in the Indian manner?" Arnold asked. "Encourage them to run like dogs when they lose a few men?"

"Oh, no!" my father said, "I'd train them in both the Indian and the English manner, so they'd always protect themselves as much as possible, behind trees in the woods and in holes in the open plain, but arrive somehow at their objective, if worth having, despite all losses. There's no other sensible form of warfare, if any sort of war is sensible. If we could teach our militia to fight that way, I think they could whip the finest armies of all Europe, though we'd be called a cowardly rabble by the foreign officers who were being whipped."

At a later day, when we picked Burgoyne's army to pieces at Saratoga, under Arnold in reality, I thought often of those words, and of the wide hunting stare of that swarthy-faced young man; but on this autumn morning I cared little for world affairs or the fate of armies. We passed the low shores of Arrowsic, Georgetown Island and Phippsburg, and rounded out past Popham Beach into the long swells of the open sea. The broken hills of Casco Bay lay on our right, and the high sun glittered on the little waves. Straight ahead was home—a thought that set me to shivering under my blanket with excitement, and made time flap by on leaden wings, as it never fails to do when I am returning from far places.

We raised the sandy spit of Winter Harbor and the rock ledges beyond; then the pine-clad islands of Cape Porpus. When we rounded the cape, Wells Bay opened out before us, the breakers creamy on the reefs, and the soft blue bulge of Agamenticus rising from the distant shore.

Standing in around the rocks of Cape Arundel, we saw the garrison house behind the dunes where I had sat with Mary. A little figure of a man stood by the skiff at the ferry landing, staring; and though we bawled and waved at him, he stood doltishly watching us, unmoving.

Around the corner of the stockade came Ranger, looking at us, his head high. We shouted again, and Ranger moved closer to the water. The anchor went down, and a third time we shouted. Ranger ran back and forth at the river's edge. I knew he was whining to get to me.

The doltish figure, Ivory Fish's brother Jethro, came to life, flapping his arms, and hurried to the house, while Ranger plunged in and swam toward us.

Then there was a hullabaloo. My mother and sisters and Malary and others came running to the beach; and Jethro Fish set out after us in the skiff. Ranger was dragged aboard, and leaped on me, knocking me down to lie wetly on my chest, striving to lap the skin from my face. Manatqua and the *m'téoulin* piled the skins into the skiff; then all of us, bidding Arnold good-bye, got in as well.

Our new friend stood at the rail, his white coat unbuttoned in the warm sun. My father looked thoughtfully at him. Then, pulling two otter and two beaver skins from the bales, he handed them up.

"I find," my father said, "I'm not as good a trader as I thought."

Arnold took them, nodding gravely. "We New Englanders," he said, "are sometimes overburdened with conscience."

The schooner's crew stowed her anchor and she moved off toward York, Arnold's white coat gleaming above the *Black Duck's* sides.

"We'll be looking for you some day," my father shouted.

Arnold nodded and waved.

❋   ❋   ❋

When I leaped at her from the bow of the skiff my mother screamed, then passed her hand lightly over the scar on my forehead before she kissed me. My father picked her up in his arms, and my sisters pummeled me, looking doubtfully at Manatqua and the *m'téoulin;* and with Ranger careering about us in a frenzy of joy, we started for the house, followed by Malary and Ivory Fish and Jethro Fish and Lieutenant Wattleby and a few others whom I scarce saw in my excitement. Among them, suddenly, I was amazed and horrified to become conscious of brown-faced Phoebe Marvin, in her dress made from a French blanket. She was quiet enough when I looked hard at her, so I thought no more about her until I went off the path to inspect a hole that Ranger was imploring me to see. Thereupon this skinny creature moved quickly after me and said in a high, mocking voice, though not loudly: "What did they do to Mary?"

I leaped for her in a fury. She fled around the stockade into the dunes and I after her. After some dodging and leaping, I caught her attempting to duck past me.

I held her by the arms, shaking her rigid body and saying over and over, "If you weren't a girl I'd pound your face in." Then I felt her go limp, and saw her staring at the scar on my forehead.

"What's that?" she asked.

I took my left hand from her to feel the scar. "Why," I began, "it's nothing much . . ."

With that she jerked free, fetched me a clout on the side of the jaw that hurt me more than Guerlac's hatchet, and fled with an eldritch scream of laughter.

I put her quickly from my mind; for Eunice came coughing to the kitchen door and got under my feet so that I fell on her. For dinner we had baked beans with my mother's cucumber relish, and I was given small beer to drink in recognition of the hardships I had endured. But despite all these things, which should have made my happiness complete, I knew, when I laid myself on my mattress that night, lapped in the kitchen's warmth and the sweet, faint odors of dry pine and spices and coffee and wood smoke, that Mary was fixed so firmly in my heart that I could neither forget her nor give her up: that only through finding her could I find ease for the hurt within me.

BOOK II

THUNDERHEADS

X

WINTERS in Arundel and all our Eastern country lie hard and burdensome on idle folk. There are heavy skies and spittings of snow in November, a weighty fall or two in December, and through January and February and March enough snow and ice and bitter wind to make the devil himself press close up to the flames of hell, and still feel a chill on the side removed from the fire. The birches are bent out of shape by the weight of snow. Ancient pines, weakened by rocky soil or overcrowded by their neighbors, sink to their knees under the snow bundles on their exposed polls, thus forming the deadfalls that madden us when we travel forest trails.

Our winters are not, as some would have you think, seasons of silence and stagnation. There are splitting sounds behind the walls of our garrison house, as though a furtive giant tested boards across his knee. The eaves drip, seeming to weep for the sins of those the roof has sheltered. At night the mournful plaint of horned owls—*whoo; who-who*—emerges endlessly from the pines across the creek, punctuated occasionally by the howls of hunting wolves or the distressing scream of a wildcat. When there is ice in the river, it complains and ejaculates as the tides rise and fall beneath it. There are always chickadees clinging upside down to trees and bushes, sometimes alighting on one's musket barrel in their trusting blindness, forever uttering their dreary, weary song. There is always the quawking of ducks and geese and night-herons; the wailing of gulls; the abrupt tapping of woodpeckers; the squeaking and clattering of mice between the floors; the moan of the wind fingering at the sashes.

I have long held that if a person plans chores to keep him busy, he will find our Eastern winters a time of relief from the blinding sweat and the countless small tasks of summer, instead of a stagnant period during which each man comes to hate his neighbors, his family, and at last himself.

For all that, I am glad, in late March or early April, when the first thunderheads of the year roll up over the long blue coast line of

Wells, and the rumble of distant thunder comes to us from the towering masses of silver-edged clouds. We know then that within the
week the last of the drifts and the slabs of ancient ice must vanish
from the easterly side of ledges; that the salmon are in the rivers;
that mayflowers will soon lie hid among their rough leaves at the
edges of clearings; that before we know it the baby frogs will set up
their pipings in the roadside pools. They are a sign, these first thunderheads, that a new world of rich harvests, lush meadows and billowing groves is on its way to replace the barren fields, bleak
outlines and devouring chills that have so long oppressed us.

❀   ❀   ❀

That first winter after my father and I returned from our pursuit
of Guerlac and Mary, whenever I could steal a few moments from
my chores, I practised the tricks I had seen Arnold perform aboard
his schooner; but toward the end of the winter a terrible occurrence
put an end to such practising, and left no part of any winter hanging
heavy on my hands.

It was a bitter afternoon in February, with the wind in the north
and a dirty scum of gray clouds across the sky, when my father heard
a blast on the horn that hung from a post on the far side of the ferry.
Being in his smithy, he called for Jethro Fish, but got no answer;
so he went himself to the skiff and pulled across. The tide was low,
the water running out swiftly in the narrow bed: so as he swung
the skiff alongside the tall, gangling passenger who stood on the far
bank, he leaned over and set his oar in the sand to hold it in place.
Feeling by the motion of the skiff that the man was aboard, he withdrew his oar and dropped it into the oarlock, looking up at his passenger as the skiff swung off into the stream. The passenger was the
Reverend Ezekiel Hook.

Hook recognized my father at the same moment and stepped
backward, croaking, "I'll cross with no blasphemer!"

It may be that in staring so intently at my father he forgot the
skiff had left the bank and thought to step off, or he may have lost
his balance; but for whatever reason, he fell backward over the
stern. From the way he bobbed beneath the surface and up again,
beating the water with his arms, rigidly, his mouth open to scream
but emitting only gasps and gurgles, my father saw he couldn't
swim; so he pulled alongside him, reaching down to grasp his coat.
Hook gave a convulsive flop, clutched him, and pulled him in as
well.

Unable to cope with his thrashing arms, my father hit him on the chin and knocked him unconscious, breaking his jaw at the same time, I am happy to say, though it would have been better for all of us if he had broken his neck. He pushed him into shallow water; then struck out after the skiff, which was whirling downstream. Overtaking it, he climbed in, pulled back, picked up the senseless Hook, and rowed him to our shore. When he had drawn up the skiff and made the rope fast, he carried Hook to the house, where my mother bound up his jaw and put him to bed.

It must be my father had sucked overmuch bitter cold air into his lungs on top of a throat trouble he had caught from travelers—such a trouble as spreads out of the cities, now and again, like a flame running through the woods—for he fell to shivering and shaking and burning up with fever. Hook departed the next day, saying nothing because of his bound jaw, but glaring maledictions at my mother and myself. My father had taken to his bed, breathing with difficulty, so we sent Jethro Fish posting to Portsmouth to pray a doctor there to come at once to my father's relief; and to make sure he came, we sent him an otter skin.

That night my mother called me to her room, where my father lay between the feather mattresses. As well as he could, because of the pain in his chest, he told me how I must be governed by my mother in the management of the inn and the ferry; how I should invest our earnings in beaver and otter skins, and especially in sables when I could get them, always sending word to the governor's house in Boston when there was an accumulation of sables, so that the Boston bloods could ride down for them, and get drunk doing it; how my mother and I should continue to deal with Captain Callendar of Boston, sending skins to England by his brig, so that with them he could buy tea in Holland, wine in Portugal and molasses in the French Sugar Islands, and smuggle all of them into Boston, like so many of the Massachusetts and Connecticut merchants; and how we should add to the gold in the barrel buried under the kitchen until we had enough to build a brig of our own.

With that he patted me feebly on the arm and motioned to my mother to send me away.

I went into the kitchen and sat unhappily with Malary. Late that night the doctor came from Portsmouth, half frozen. He put blisters on my father's chest, but shook his head, for my father recognized neither him nor my mother. The next morning, just after the sun had risen and the wind had swung into the south, my father died.

*   *   *

We made out after a fashion. Seemingly Guerlac's hatchet had released some spring in me; for I shot up to a great height for one of
my years. From necessity I worked in the smithy when there were
musket locks to be mended or horses to be shod; and betweentimes
I raced from the smithy to the sawmill, and from the sawmill to the
ferry, getting this done and that done by asking those who worked
for us to show me how they should be done; for my father had often
said to me that people in our part of the country were independent-
minded, and wanted less to be told how things should be done than
to tell others how to do them.

Indeed, it often seemed to me, as the seasons rolled on, that the
independent-mindedness of many of our people would have better
borne another name—opposite-mindedness, belike, or cussed-mind-
edness.

We had hard times when the French wars were over. There were
two years of drought and no more selling of supplies to the English,
so the farmers could not get shut of their corn. They were in debt
to the merchants for stock and supplies, and too often in debt for
their land as well, though they could usually find enough for a glass
of rum. Rich men in Portsmouth and Boston and Connecticut were
investing in land speculations in the distant West, along the Susquehannah and farther. It was possible for settlers to get Western farm
lands for fifty cents an acre, since the speculators obtained it for a
cent an acre, or less, by stealing it from the Indians. Therefore there
was no demand for land near old settlements, such as our own; and
the value of our farms sank so low they could scarce be given away.

When some of our farmers came to the inn of a winter's evening
and filled themselves with French rum, you would have thought
from the way they pounded the tables and cursed that they were
going to march to Portsmouth or Boston the next day and carve their
initials on the livers of the land speculators who were causing them
such grief, and making it difficult for them to get their hands on
ready money, and thus robbing them of their liberty.

Those who worked in the shipyards, and some of the fishermen,
too, got wind of a way to make money, just by printing it and giving
it to people who would pledge land as security against the money
they received, or some such foolish scheme. They went yelling and
squalling around in a teeter of excitement, always in a rage because
the sensible merchants who had the right of voting, which these

crazy-headed people didn't have, refused to let them print money. They were angry against the merchants, and angry because they had no votes with which to beat the merchants and get paper currency. One who heard them ranting about liberty in the tavern of nights would have thought that liberty was somebody like a female relative, and that she had been assaulted around the corner somewhere a few minutes before and had her scalp taken.

For the matter of that, they seemed to have some reason on their side. I could see no good cause why the town meetings of our New England towns should be controlled by a lot of overwealthy robbers who had made themselves rich while less careful and less godly men had fought in the wars, and the mass of people in the towns, including those who did the fighting, have no voice in elections.

When the paper-money roarers and anti-capitalist bellowers had finished pounding on tables, the English-haters would begin pounding; and it was hard to tell which of them could pound hardest. On some nights, when I had been busy serving out rum and copying accounts from the board on the wall until my brain was all thick and curdled, it seemed to me I must get down my hatchet from the slot over the front door, where I kept it in case Guerlac should come back again, and sink it into the head of the next man who bawled "Sugar Act" and banged the table with his fist.

For years everybody in Arundel and the other New England seacoast settlements had traded wherever he pleased and with whomever he pleased, and thought no more about it. Our New England rum was made out of molasses smuggled into Portsmouth and Boston from the French Sugar Islands, there being insufficient molasses in the English Sugar Islands to supply our rummeries; and the French molasses being cheaper to boot. Also our sugar for hot rum punches and other purposes came from the French Sugar Islands, as did our French rum, all of it being smuggled, since only a madman would pay duty on what everyone was smuggling; and since any customs officer, for the gift of a pair of shoe buckles or a new hat, would close his eyes to anything. Everybody south of Halifax who owned a vessel larger than a hash-chopper had busied himself at smuggling at one time or another, even though not pretending to such operations as Peter Faneuil or John Hancock of Boston, and the other merchants with plenty of money made from the wars.

Then, of a sudden, after the Sugar Act against smuggling had been ignored by everyone for more than a generation, the lunkheaded English decided that the ancient, bewhiskered, forgotten law must be enforced. The merchants in Boston, not wishing to be disturbed in their smuggling, hired a man to travel around and explain the evils of the law. He stopped at our inn one night and outbawled and outpounded all those in the gathering-room, buying rum for them and telling how a duty on molasses and sugar would ruin both the distilleries and the fisheries, which were our greatest industries.

He did more than curse England and her mouse-headed lawmakers. He told the open-mouthed crew of drinkers in our gathering-room how, if the Sugar Act should be enforced, five thousand New England seamen would be turned out of employment and would starve; and how other workmen who depended on the seamen would also suffer—coopers and farmers and tanners and shoemakers and sailmakers and innkeepers and God knows who-all. From that night onward, then, the wild folk who bawled for paper money, forgetful of their rage against the merchants, began to join with them in bawling that England was crushing their liberty; and our inn was in an uproar every night.

*   *   *

Always, since my father's death, I had sought eagerly for news of Mary and Guerlac, thinking to go to Quebec as soon as I felt myself sufficiently strong to clout Guerlac on the head when I found him, and carry Mary away with me to wear figured brocades and rule over my kingdom at the mouth of the Arundel River—though I knew I would have to banish the bawlers and table-pounders before I could provide the proper kingdom for her.

For a time, though I spoke with every passing trapper who had set foot in Quebec, I could get no word whatever of Mary, nor of Guerlac either. Natanis came to see me, bringing sable skins which I sold to the governor of Massachusetts, Bernard, who sent his scented secretary to get them. Natanis brought me news of Manatqua; how his pride at the two wigs he had received from my father had been so great that he dared not leave either of them in his cabin lest it be stolen or lost. He would wear one and hold the other in his hands, and do no hunting at all, hardly, so that the Abenakis had deposed him as sachem, a pitiful case. Natanis gave me reports, too, of Hobomok and Jacataqua; how Hobomok had learned to outscream every *m'téoulin* in the valley of the Kennebec, and how Jacataqua was becoming beautiful, slender and straight like her mother. Learning that I had heard nothing of Mary, he offered to travel to Quebec; and that summer he did so, but could discover nothing save that Guerlac was in France.

Even had I learned anything, I doubt that I could have availed myself of it. My mother and sisters were half distracted because of the noisy and discontented gatherings that cluttered our inn; and it was my task to keep order, since a woman could not make herself heard, while hired men like Jethro Fish, instead of keeping order, would join in the arguments and become as tumultuous and contentious as any of the others.

I doubt, even, that these discontented folk, when full of rum, would have consented to be kept in order by any but myself; but me they regarded as a boy; and since I had some strength from working at the forge and practising Arnold's tricks, I could haul them from the house when their feet became unmanageable, slap their faces to bring back their senses, and dowse them in the creek, all with an apologetic air, and all without arousing their displeasure.

Also my mother, still having her looks because my father had not made a pack horse and a brood mare out of her, as is the custom in our section of New England, and being the owner of a tidy property, was constantly snuggled up to by widowers and bachelors who hoped to be supported handsomely for the remainder of their days. Being a woman of gentleness, and having an eye, furthermore, to our earnings, she forbore to send these snugglers about their affairs, and so had little time to watch over the inn's business.

To me, however, she spoke her mind about those who pursued her, saying that my father had been the only man in all New England, she believed, who would not hurry out to get a new wife within five minutes after his previous wife died; and that there was no distinction in men's minds between a shirt and a wife; almost anything would do; and they were to be worn out, both of them, and replaced at once if lost; and few cared whether or not they were ever washed so long as they were serviceable.

When, therefore, Phoebe Marvin came to the inn one morning and asked to be allowed to work for us for a dollar a week, with some instruction in letters thrown in, I could not make the protest I would otherwise have made.

She was less unendurable than she had once been, but I still found her capable, at times, of trying the patience of Job. She was thin, but with a compactness about her thinness that came, I think, from the hours she spent in the water during the warm weather, when there was scandalous talk about her because her swimming garment was

an ancient gingham dress, cut off above the knee and sewn at the
bottom so that it ended in pantalettes instead of a skirt. Scandal-
mongers had trouble seeing her because of her persistence in remaining under water when onlookers were about, swimming on her
back so that nothing showed but her nose and chin, and emitting
derisive jets of water from time to time between pursed lips; but
those who had seen her complained that she went about in the sun
with the top of her dress unbuttoned.

All the day she was in the water or on it, fishing from a crazy skiff
she had dug from the mud and patched with pitch and rotten canvas,
and calked with rags and old rope. In this fearful craft she sailed in
and out of the river and around the reefs until every seaman in the
place threw up his hands and swore that by rights she should have
been drowned ten times each month. Because of this, doubtless, she
was a golden color on those portions of her that could be seen, as
well, I suspected, as on several portions that could not be seen: a
most unmaidenly color, wholly unlike the beautiful whiteness of
Mary.

She had recovered from her hellish manner of bursting into
eldritch screams or hoydenish titterings at her own rude remarks;
and she had even learned to be silent in the presence of her elders and betters. Yet there came often into her eyes, which were
gray and could seem as hard as the ledges that crop out in our pine
forests, a look in which was concentrated all the rudeness and jeers
she had been wont to express aloud.

One evening I came on her looking out of a window into the red
clouds in the west and weeping silently. Being, as I have shown, of
a forgiving nature, I put my hand on her shoulder and asked her why
she cried. Since she did not move, and since the twilight bent me
to gentleness, I reached around her and turned her against my
breast, repeating my question. She was as taut in my hands, when
I turned her, as a bowstring, and as unyielding as a quiverful of arrows; and her eyes examined me as though from a distance, with a
scoffing look in them that made me take my hands from her and
cry, "Don't you say that!" Not with a torrent of words and eldritch
screams of laughter could she have sneered at Mary more effectively.

She wished to work for us, she said, because she must have schooling which she could not get elsewhere; but I think it was because
she knew my father had liked her father, and was sure I would give
her rum for him—rum he needed for dulling the pain in his arrow-

pierced shoulder, but could no longer buy. Otherwise I doubt she
would have worked for anyone; for our girls are so independent that
some of them will starve rather than take orders from strangers. In
a way I counted myself fortunate to have her help, though she irked
me so sorely, with her jeering glance, that I often longed to hit her
with my mother's wooden pestle.

We put her to helping in the gathering-room of nights; and her
squirrel-like quickness stood her in good stead when the men tried
to maul her. She knew more tricks to escape from a man than any
wench I ever saw. If it had not been so my mother would have refused to let her stay there, just as she refused to let my sisters go
into the gathering-room when the men had commenced on their
rum.

*   *   *

When it seemed as though the unrest and cantankerousness of our
farmers and fishermen could grow no more, there began to be even
louder rantings over a damnable business called the Stamp Tax, and
bitter complaints concerning press gangs from English ships of war,
which were coming into any port and snatching up our seamen to
round out their crews. In talking of these things the talkers raked up
all the other matters concerning which they had been ranting since
the fall of Quebec—the need of paper currency; the Sugar Act; the
damned Virginia and Rhode Island land speculators with their Ohio
Company and their Susquehannah Company, sending colonists out
to countries so wild that armies had to be maintained to protect
them; the special privileges of the great merchants; the King's trees,
set apart for masts for the King's navy and so not to be cut by the
settlers on whose lands they stood, though most of the settlers persisted in cutting them because they were the best trees; the senseless
English law against making hats or iron goods in our colonies. It
seemed as though every man had a bitter grievance for which he
longed to bash someone over the head; and through all the talk there
ran the moan that our liberty was being taken from us, and that no
nation or people had the right to steal liberty from other people.

I could not help but see that those who talked the loudest about
their loss of liberty were those who had lost the least, or had the
least to lose, being the poorest and wretchedest of our people, with
little land, less money and no vote. Yet I learned from travelers that
this was the way of it throughout New England.

＊   ＊   ＊

In the spring of my eighteenth year, when all this hullabaloo about
liberty was swelling like the incoming tide in a creek, there came a
warm, glittering day with the wind in the southwest, and a flight of
sickle-bill curlews, large, slow-flying birds, near as big in the body
as a partridge. Moved to hatred of the inn and all its works by the
soft odors of marshland and sweet grass and mallow, I took my musket and old Ranger and his young wife Ginger and went to the beach
to kill a few curlews for supper and speak to Eunice, who had grown
so fat from a surfeit of salmon, pollock and bluefish that she could
no longer come to the house, but lay in the wash of the breakers and
barked hoarsely for me with tearful eyes.

While I stood on the beach, kicking Eunice gently in the side and
making her groan with pleasure, a traveler rode up over the high
land at the far end of the beach, and along the white crescent of
sand toward me. There was something about the hugesome manner
in which he towered over his horse and bulged out on each side that
made me think of Cap Huff, though years had passed since I had
seen him. As he drew near I saw it was indeed Cap Huff, as enormous and jovial and sweaty as ever, his buckskin shirt so wrinkled
and stained that it might have been the same one on which he wiped
his hands after throwing Guerlac in the creek. But in place of his
ancient coonskin cap he was wearing a three-cornered hat with gold
lace on it, and beautiful jack boots where once he had worn leggins
tied with eelskins.

He told a strange tale when he had done bawling curses at me
and roaring his pleasure at seeing me again. There was, he said, a
secret organization called the Sons of Liberty spreading through
Massachusetts and Rhode Island and Connecticut. Recently the
Sons of Liberty had been formed in Portsmouth, and he was one of
the leading Sons—so much so that the Portsmouth Sons had now sent
him to Arundel to select and instruct other Sons in their secret duties.

"By God, Stevie," he roared, banging me on the shoulder, "there's
none of these damned merchants can put me in gaol any more, because if they do, my Sons of Liberty'll tear their old hell's gaol to
pieces, and tar and feather 'em into the bargain!"

When I asked whether the secret duties of the Sons of Liberty
were to keep him out of gaol, he became mysterious.

"Stevie," he said—and I knew from the way his eyes turned inward that he was fishing out words he had learned from other folk

—"it's this matter of the Stamp Tax. If the English can take a shilling in the pound from me without my will, why not twenty shillings? Why not my liberty or my life? If anything of ours can be taxed, why not our lands? Why not the produce of our lands?"

"Since when have you had lands?" I asked, but he waved my question impatiently aside.

"If these things can be taxed," he continued, becoming fiercely virtuous, "why not everything we possess? Why not the kettles in your kitchen or the coat on your back or—or—" he cast around vainly for other taxable articles, and finally ended, weakly—"or your little dog, playing on the sand?"

"Well, why not?" I asked, watching Ranger scratching at the back of his neck and looking with lackluster eyes at Eunice. "I wouldn't have to pay it, would I, any more than I pay taxes on our smuggled rum?"

"Ah ha!" Cap shouted in a great booming voice, "then the English could run their ships into the mouth of your river and make slaves out of you, if they saw fit. There it is, Stevie! Sam Adams says that's what we'll come to: slaves! We'll all be slaves, unless we look out! That's the reason for the Sons of Liberty!"

Still I could not see what he was driving at, and said so.

"Look here, Stevie," he said, wiping his mouth with the back of his hand and clearing his throat, so that I knew he was dry from talking, "everybody talks and nobody does anything. The merchants whoop and howl, but they don't *do* anything, only write letters to each other and to the Boston *Gazette*. Well, to hell with that, Stevie! What we got to have is men that'll *do* something when it's time to do something, and not write a letter to somebody about it. By God, Stevie, if I had my way there wouldn't be a man in the Sons that could write a letter!"

He thrust out his right leg and gave his new jack boot a resounding slap. "See this boot, Stevie?"

I could no more have overlooked it than I could have overlooked a brigantine in the river.

"Last week," he bellowed, "there was a merchant in Portsmouth who said the Stamp Tax was reasonable and all right, and he was in favor of paying it." Cap slapped his boot again, thrust his hands in his belt, and eyed me knowingly.

"What happened?"

"Well, the Sons went down to his store and turned it inside out and pulled it down. Then they left a sign on the door saying 'Enemies of Liberty Beware.'" He took off his new hat and eyed it moodily. "It was a boot store, and it had a few hats, but there wasn't a shirt in the place."

"What did the merchant do?"

Cap replaced his hat. "I ain't heard. He's still getting the tar and feathers off him."

"Won't he have you put in gaol?"

"My gosh!" Cap shouted, "ain't I told you? This is a secret organization, and anybody that lets out the secrets, like who's in it, gets treated the same as a merchant or anybody else who's willing to see Sons of Liberty made into slaves. Sam Adams says all we got to do is hang together, and we can get rid of England and be our own masters. Then nobody can make slaves of us."

"Get rid of England!" I protested. "What in thunderation would we want to get rid of England for?"

Cap Huff jabbed me in the chest with a forefinger like a marlin spike. "You blamed idiot! Can't you see there ain't nobody around here any more that's got a chance to make money or do anything, except the merchants? Sam Adams says if we take the government in our own hands, and everyone gets a chance to vote, we can stop the merchants from hogging everything and pick up a little something for ourselves. Sam Adams says we got to fight England to do it. He says it's coming, sure as shooting!"

"Sam Adams says!" I objected, befuddled by his talk. "Sam Adams! Sam Adams! Sam Adams! Who in hell is this Sam Adams? And what do we want to fight England for? I don't know what you're talking about! If you talked about fighting the French, now, it would mean something. They've been fighting us for a hundred years, and my father said there never was a bunch of dirtier, underhandeder, rottener fighters than the French! I'd rather fight the damned Virginians, with their high and mighty airs, and every cheap drunkard telling about being a Cavalier! I'd rather fight the Rhode Islanders! There ain't meaner white folks anywhere than the Rhode Islanders, and everybody knows it!"

"Listen, boy," Cap said. "You're living back in ancient times! Sam Adams is the biggest man in the colonies. He's the people's friend. He knows everything. He says there's Frenchmen over here now smelling around to see if we're willing to fight England, and he says France'll help us whenever we're ready."

"Well, if they come smelling around here," I said, "I'll treat 'em the way you treated the one that stole Mary."

Cap looked at me blankly. "I don't know what you're talking about, but I'll tell you one thing: after I get the Sons of Liberty organized, you want to be careful what you say! Don't get rambunctious with any Frenchmen! If you and your father weren't friends of mine I could bring my Sons of Liberty over here and wreck your place, just on account of what you've said. Say, how *is* your father?"

"He's dead," I said. "He died because he tried to save the life of a man who hated him."

"That's the way it goes," Cap said. "That's the sort of thing the Sons of Liberty aim to change. We aim to kill off the ones that need killing, so the good ones can stay alive."

"You're aiming pretty high," I said.

"There you go again," Cap said, "talking too much! After the Sons of Liberty are organized you don't want to say anything. Not *anything!* You want to keep your mouth shut so tight you can't get a knife into it without hammering it in." He eyed me appraisingly. "Of course, I could make you head of the Sons in Arundel; only, being as how you run the inn, I guess maybe you'd have to keep all the other Sons in liquor, and that wouldn't help you any."

We went up to the inn, and at once Cap lighted on a worker from the shipyard above the upper ferry—James Dunn, who had come to town three years since, and lived mostly on ship's bread and greens that he picked himself in the spring, putting them in a barrel with salt and pressing a board on them with a rock, so they could be eaten at any time, providing one had the stomach for them, though as for me I had as lief eat poison ivy.

James Dunn was such a man as we have in most of our New England towns—grave and determined in appearance; tall and gaunt; kindly-looking, yet obviously a man of inflexible will and passionate intensity; a quiet man, smiling at times a little bleakly, as if disillusioned by clear judgment and profound wisdom; but underneath it all the greatest nincompoop that ever tried to puzzle out his left hand from his right.

I don't know where James Dunn got his nobility of face; but he looked wise enough to give advice to the King of France without half trying, whereas my dog Ranger could solve any ordinary question in less time than it took James Dunn to decide whether he should first take a bite of greens and then a bite of bread at his dinner, or first a bite of bread and then a bite of greens.

I know well that if James Dunn could confront those given to talking about the character to be seen in people's faces they would guess him to be a general or a governor, or the sagest of theologians, instead of a humble adze-wielder in a shipyard, and such an adze-wielder that Thomas Scammen, the master shipwright across the river, declared he often longed to hit him over the head with an adze, but dared not for fear the blade would be shattered and ruined.

Cap selected James Dunn to be secretary of the Arundel Sons of Liberty, nor would he hear any word from me against his choice; so it may be he knew what he was about, and planned to use James for his own ends. For the rest of the members, he took all the noisy brawlers and table-bangers, so long as they had no property to speak of. He was especially pleased to get the wild and foolish fellows who had no vote and had screamed the loudest for paper money; and he went so far as to send to the Upper Village to summon three other paper-money brawlers, so they too could be made Sons of Liberty.

When he had made his selections, he herded them into our big upstairs room along with a barrel of French rum. As I passed back and forth between the gathering-room and the kitchen, I caught the rumble of such words as "Stamp Act" and "slaves" and "slavery" and "taxation" and "Liberty" and "Rights of Man," all in Cap's thunderous bellow, and such salvos of cheering as our inn had never heard before, not even on the night when my father told how Wolfe took Quebec.

When the Sons of Liberty emerged from their secret meeting, flushed and noisy with rum, Cap Huff clapped me on the shoulder before them all and said I was doing secret duty for him, and must be guarded carefully, which was his way, I suppose, of keeping me from harm in case I spoke overfreely of subjects displeasing to the Sons of Liberty.

It was that night that Cap, happy at his success with the Sons and feeling amiably disposed toward all, slapped at Phoebe as she passed him with a hot rum punch, thinking to strike her toward the base of her spine or thereabouts, according to his playful custom. In some way she whirled so that Cap pitched forward, and the hot rum punch fell down the back of his neck, almost as though she had studied how to do it. If I had not held him by the slack of his breeches and given her time to run into the kitchen, I make no doubt he would have caught her and squeezed her to death in good-natured play.

That was my introduction to the Sons of Liberty. In the beginning they were the poorest and scurviest knaves that our village could boast, so that instead of being called Sons of Liberty, they were more often called Sons of something entirely different, when mentioned by respectable folk. Yet they were no different, travelers told me, from the Sons of Liberty in Massachusetts and Connecticut and the rest of our colonies, and I have no doubt it could not have been otherwise, if they were to do the work they did.

Late that night Cap Huff came to my mattress in the kitchen, smelling powerfully of sweat and rum and his new boots, and asked me what I meant, that afternoon, when I spoke of the Frenchman that stole Mary. What Frenchman, he wanted to know, and who was Mary? I told him the whole tale, while he sat rubbing his bulbous knuckles in silence. When I had finished he got up and fell against the stove, upsetting some pots. He righted himself and scratched his neck thoughtfully.

"He was the one," Cap said, "that talked of affection. What I said about Frenchmen to-day is said as a statesman. I can talk differently in my private capacity. When I've tended to this Liberty business, we'll make a social call on Guerlac and stuff him up his own chimney."

There were times when I thought I could, if I wished, raise a regiment to punish Guerlac for his sins.

XI

I<small>T WAS</small> the next day that I unexpectedly had my first news of Mary and Guerlac. Cap Huff and I were in a corner of the gathering-room, and Phoebe was resanding the floor and wiping off the tables and benches, while Cap Huff soothed his tongue—swollen, he said, from unaccustomed speechifying—with a quart of my mother's small beer to which a tot of Hollands had been added to give it body. Cap was telling me in his usual violent language of the times he had been thrown for no reason at all into the Portsmouth gaol, a disgustingly verminiferous gaol, too, he declared, when two fine gentlemen rode up from the beach on horses that gleamed sleekly in the morning sun.

They came into the gathering-room, handsome, tall young men in plum-colored coats, doeskin breeches and riding boots of Spanish leather, and bowed so politely to Cap and me that we became sour and doltish, as is the custom of our New England people when they encounter manners that seem somewhat overperfumed. One of them smiled sweetly and prayed we would inform him where he might encounter Monsieur the *propriétaire* of the inn. Thus we knew he was French.

Cap, hunched down over his beer, waved a huge paw in my direction. The Frenchman took a letter from his pocket and handed it to me. It was signed "Sam'l Adams," and urged the recipient to reply freely to all questions asked by the bearer, Raoul de Berniers, since such replies would promote the interests of the colonies in America.

"Sir," I said, when I had shown the letter to Cap Huff, who stared at it amazed-like, "I'll tell you whatever you want to know, because of this letter of Sam Adams, who is the greatest man in all New England, and also because I had a friend, a Frenchman, who left me a gift I still have."

"Truly!" said De Berniers, and smiled and bowed, having no way of knowing I spoke of the scar on my forehead.

"It may be," I said, "you knew the gentleman—Henri Guerlac de Sabrevois, of the regiment of Béarn?"

"But certainly!" cried De Berniers. "It was our regiment, Béarn! De Sabrevois we knew well! Perhaps he will come again to this great country, so you may renew your friendship." When De Berniers said this, I caught him looking drolly at his companion, whom he called Sharl, as if to say a friendship between De Sabrevois and this country bumpkin would be worth seeing.

"Your friend has been in France, then, these past six years?" I asked, not caring what he thought or how he looked, so I had news of Mary.

"No, poor fellow," De Berniers said. "He was captured by the damned English, he and his sister. They were sent to Elizabeth Castle on the Island of Jersey as prisoners, they and some others, among them the good Abbé le Loutre, who was villainously treated, in spite of his holy orders."

Now this Le Loutre was a hound of hell if ever there was one, a brutal man and a murderer, responsible for the death of hundreds of English in Acadia because of his fiendish persistence in sending Indians against them. When Cap Huff heard him called "the good Abbé" he sprang up in a rage, bawling "Good!" in violent tones of protest. Fortunately I could kick him hard on the shin, so he changed his cry to "Good God!" and sat down again, shaking his head as if in despair at the cruelty of mankind.

"I didn't know," I said, "that he had a sister!"

"Ah, yes!" said De Berniers, "and how Marie is beautiful, with golden hair and all the graces of an angel, but none of Henri's coldness! Wholly charming, all white and gold: a beautiful flower, nodding and swaying in the sun; eh, Sharl?"

Sharl nodded vigorously. "A true lily of France!"

Cap, doubtless unnerved by this unexpected contact with fine gentlemen, choked on his small beer and was taken with a horrible, whooping fit of coughing, so that he lumbered hurriedly from the room. I would have liked to hug the thought of Mary, white and gold like a lily, to my breast; but something impelled me to look around. I looked straight into the face of Phoebe Marvin. She was jeering at me with her eyes so that I could have rubbed her face on the sanded floor and thought no shame of myself for doing it.

"Bring rum!" I shouted, banging the table with the flat of my hand. "French rum!"

When she brought it, Sharl smiled warmly at her, which was a surprise to me, for I would have thought her swarthy face and her thin, straight body possessed no attraction for any except the easily pleased folk who gather at our inn, and little enough for them.

De Berniers told me, over our glasses, that De Sabrevois had now been in France for three years, and that his opinion concerning the state of mind in the colonies regarding England was much sought at court. Therefore, said he, if feeling grew stronger against England, De Sabrevois might return to watch and to assist. "For," said De Berniers, "he hates the English. The thought of them is poison to him."

He asked me the feeling in our neighborhood toward England; and I told him as well as I could: that our people were discontented at all things, including England's acts, and that they would not pay taxes to England, or pay the duties that England might think to collect. I told him there had been no talk of war against England; that no man in our neighborhood with good sense would think the colonies capable of fighting England's mighty army and navy, but that there were more people without sense in our town than there were people with sense. Also that those without sense were the most reckless and daring; so that if the merchants declared against war the reckless, senseless folk might declare in favor of it to show their hatred of the merchants.

All this time Sharl was nodding and smiling at Phoebe, who stood out of my sight; and when they got up to go, Sharl, looking meaningly at Phoebe, said to me: "Sir, we have been much taken with the custom you call bundling. I regret we cannot remain here to enjoy its benefits."

Now there may be parts of our colonies where bundling is widely practised; but it is frowned on in Arundel; so to pay Phoebe for her jeering glance, and maybe to save her the trouble of answering Sharl, I said quickly: "Sir, there's no bundling here save with me."

At this we all laughed understandingly, and I escorted the two Frenchmen to their horses. Cap Huff came around the corner of the house and bade them farewell in a voice so mealy that it aroused my suspicions. He expressed the hope he might some day see them at his home in Newburyport, which seemed to me strange, since he lived in Kittery.

When the Frenchmen had gone on toward Falmouth, Cap followed me into the gathering-room, saying he must be off to rejoin his Sons of Liberty. He drew a cambric handkerchief from his breeches, unknotted it, and took from it a number of gold pieces, which he pushed over to me.

"Here," Cap said, "this is to pay for my lodging and for a little rum, now and then, for the Sons."

I studied the coins. They were French louis, newly minted and beautiful. After a while I tossed them back.

"Now listen, Stevie," Cap said, "these Frenchmen came over here to help us. That's so, because Sam Adams said so in his letter. Well, ain't it helping us if we use their money for the Sons of Liberty?"

"Where was it?"

"Clear 'way down in the bottom of their saddle bags. I only took a little out of each one. They got plenty left. They won't miss it any more than they'll miss this." He reached inside his belt in back and dragged out a ruffled shirt. "I got this off of Sharl," he added proudly.

"Well," I said, "I don't want their dirty money. I'll take anything of Guerlac's I can get, but nothing of theirs."

Cap stared at me in disgust, then bawled hoarsely for Phoebe. She came in at once. "Look here, Phoebe," Cap said, picking up the gold and handing it to her, "Stevie and I had an argument over this. You keep it till he's ready to build a sloop or something; then buy into it. Then he'll have it, only he won't have it."

Cap laughed his hoarse, bellowing laugh, stood up and hitched at his belt, rubbed his face briskly with his huge hands, and went swaggering out of the house, bawling his lewd song about old Benning Wentworth. We could hear him roaring it as he set off on his horse, and even until he got down into the dunes, where the southwest wind caught it and whirled it into fragments.

*   *   *

I felt little like looking at Phoebe when Cap was gone. After I had cleared my throat with some effort I told her I had meant nothing by what I said about bundling, but was irritated with her and Sharl, and so said the first thing that entered my noddle.

"I guess you know," I told her, "how I feel about Mary. Some day I've got to find her; and my feelings being what they are, there's times I could knock your jaw out of joint for looking at me the way you do."

Phoebe nodded, chinking Cap's gold pieces together. "Steven, I guess I don't want to work here any more."

"My land, Phoebe! I told you I didn't mean anything!"

"I know, Steven, but it's spring, and I don't believe I can stand it unless I can have the sun and the water and all. Your ma's taught me how to read and figure. I studied through the whole of the *British Mariner's Guide,* Steven."

Not knowing what she was driving at, I said my mother would miss her, as indeed I knew she would.

Phoebe chinked the gold pieces more rapidly. "Steven, I heard your ma speak about building a brig some day." She hesitated; then shot her words at me so fast I was near graveled.

"I can sail a boat better than these thick-heads around here, Steven! I can cut a ledge closer than any fisherman on the cape. I know every bar and every reef 'twixt Porpus and the Nubble! I can learn 'em from Frenchman's Bay to Sandy Hook in a week! I can sail circles around these people, Steven! Don't wait for a brig! Get a sloop—and let me sail it! I'll make it pay. I'll make it pay so much you can get your brig twice as quick. I'll sail it for nothing, Steven, if you'll give me a little interest in it. If you do I'll make money for you and myself, too. I can read and figure and navigate, Steven, and that's a sight more than anyone around here can do, except old Coit that took a privateer out of York. If I can't sail rings around old Coit I'll kiss a pig! You can put in this gold of Cap's, and I'll watch Scammen build it, and there won't be a sloop in Maine waters to touch it."

Now this girl was one of the most importunate creatures I had ever encountered, but I couldn't escape the fact that there was something in what she said. It was nigh impossible to get an able man to captain as small a vessel as a sloop, and be a trader into the bargain, and do it to show a profit, whereas Phoebe could sail a boat better than anybody I ever saw, and she was afraid of nothing and nobody. Furthermore, she could swim as well as Ranger, only faster; and as I well knew, she had a tongue in her head, which is no drawback to any person who follows the sea.

"How much of an interest," I asked, "would you consider fitten and proper for yourself, in case I talked to my ma and we decided maybe this could be done?"

"Oh, Steven," she said, and she stood there in front of me with her fists clenched so tight that I feared she might tear herself to pieces in case I crossed her wishes, "I don't care! Give me what's right. I'll do it for anything!"

"Would you do it for a tenth?" I asked, wanting to be sure she meant what she said.

"Oh, Stevie!" she said with a sort of gasp, "you'll do it!" She had a look as if she might hang around my neck and cry, so I went in to see my mother. The upshot was that we gave Phoebe a fifth interest in the sloop, which was a square trade for both of us, in case she fancied herself with good cause. That night my mother and I talked with Thomas Scammen in the kitchen about the building of it. Phoebe, my mother said, should have a word in the matter; but it was more of a sermon she had than a word.

She had ideas aplenty, claiming it ought to be sharp like a knife instead of round like a tub, and deep, so to let her crack on canvas. She had ideas about the cabin, vowing she had never had comfort anywhere, and was now going to have it, since there was every reason why a sloop's cabin should be richer in comfort than any room on land. Scammen snorted at these ideas, and Phoebe grew outrageous, wagging her finger in his face and telling him how he had built vessels all his life the way every other damned fool built them, and never thought of the whys and wherefores of what he did, only *whooshed* like a frightened buck when somebody wanted to build a craft more sensible than any he'd ever laid adze to.

What Phoebe asked for and what we agreed on was a sloop of one hundred and twenty tons or thereabout, of fifty-eight foot keel, twenty-two foot beam, and eleven foot hull, built with all white oak above water and all good oak below water, the outboard plank not under two and one-half inches thick, and the mast and bowsprit good white pine of such dimensions as Phoebe Marvin might direct. For this we agreed to pay Thomas Scammen two pounds, thirteen shillings and fourpence for each and every ton that she should ton when built, one fifth in cash, one quarter in West India goods, and the remainder in English goods or provisions as desired, New England rum to be two shillings a gallon, molasses one shilling eightpence a gallon, cotton wool one shilling eightpence a pound, coffee one shilling fourpence a pound, chocolate one shilling sixpence a pound, pork four pounds ten shillings eightpence a barrel, and codfish seventeen shillings a quintal.

Little good it did poor Scammen to waggle his head and moan that no man had ever seen the like of the rising generation for wildness and cussedness; for Phoebe was at his shipyard the next morning, and there she stayed until the sloop was finished, peering at every knee and plank and pin that went into the hull, and whizzing around the blocks like a squirrel to watch each adze stroke, screaming at Scammen like a demoniac when displeased.

She was better off out of the house; for from the day when the

Sons of Liberty were born the scenes in our gathering-room of nights
took on the air of feeding time in a den of foxes, and any woman
who went into it was like to be pounded to pieces; not from deviltry,
but from the waving fists with which the Sons, in their excitement,
emphasized their determination to be freed from slavery.

Our people fell into a veritable frenzy over the Stamp Tax and
the English. Whatever happened to a man during this time—a bad
harvest, say, or a torn coat or a foot cut on a clamshell, or anything
at all—was blamed by our Sons of Liberty on the English and the
Stamp Tax. Yet this frenzy, travelers said, was no different from that
into which the people to the south of us had fallen, all the way to
Boston and through Rhode Island and Connecticut and beyond.

Such was their frenzy that they were no longer content to fulmi-
nate over their rum, but must set forth in mobs to visit their wrath
on officers of the crown or any man who held views opposed to their
own. First there would come word from Portsmouth that the Sons
of Liberty had seized on a wealthy shipowner who counseled moderation, and stuffed him into a hogshead full of ancient fish. Then
there would be advices from Boston that a mob of wild men had pil-
laged and wrecked the grand mansion of Chief Justice Hutchinson.
Then, in another month or so, there would be news from Connecticut
that the stamp distributor had been whipped in effigy by the Sons of
Liberty and hanged to a gallows fifty feet high. Still a little later we
learned from New Haven that our friend Benedict Arnold, having
discovered a man to be an informer concerning smuggled goods, had
stripped him naked with his own hands, tied him to the whipping
post, and given him forty lashes, while the Sons of Liberty looked on
and howled for joy.

Despite these tumults, I continued to inquire of trappers and
traders concerning Guerlac, thinking the unrest would soon be at
an end, so I could leave my mother and sisters to conduct the affairs
of the inn while I went off on my own business. Yet there was no
word of him, nor was there any lessening of the riots and disorder,
even though the Stamp Act was repealed while I was still in my
nineteenth year.

Indeed, the unrest grew worse; for those Sons of Liberty who were
without work and money—which most of them were, since they were
the poorest and least responsible of our people—began to attack the
homes of wealthy men for no other reason than to take possession
of their belongings. Thus other wealthy men, fearing for their own
persons and possessions, raised a rumpus against the Sons of Liberty,

so that they were made stronger and more violent by opposition.

On top of everything, in my twentieth year, the King's customs officers in Boston were such fools as to think they could begin to enforce duties which they had never before enforced, having theretofore been content to take bribes. With that the mobs went rampaging through the town, beating customs officers, helping shipowners to land cargoes, wrecking the houses of the King's sympathizers, threatening those they misliked with tar and feathers, and even defying the courts and the governor of Massachusetts.

Now the Sons of Liberty had set up committees of correspondence in all the different towns, and the committee in every town would write to Sam Adams in Boston, telling him what was happening; and Sam Adams would write to the committees of correspondence in the towns, informing them of all important circumstances.

It was a cool September night, that year, when James Dunn stood up in our gathering-room and said he had a matter of interest to lay before the people. On account of the coolness, a greater number than usual had come to warm themselves with a dram. Some of them were folk who had shown no friendship toward the Sons of Liberty, though they, like myself, had taken care to say nothing against them lest they have their barns burned and their cattle scattered in the woods. All of them fell silent before the solemn, sagacious face of vacant-headed James, and he then read a letter from Sam Adams. It said the English government, on the grounds of rescuing the government of Massachusetts from the hands of a trained mob, would shortly send a regiment from Halifax and two regiments from Ireland into Boston to enforce order. Believing, said the letter, that the colonists would prefer to put their lives in their hands and cry to the Judge of all the earth rather than to be the slaves of England, it urged all well-disposed colonists to provide themselves with firearms.

Having read this letter, James Dunn sat down without further comment, which indeed he was incapable of making; and I might here add that this sort of incapacity of his was of great value in giving him his reputation for wisdom; as whenever he could find nothing to say, people were impressed with the idea that he was engaged in powerful thoughts. The other Sons of Liberty remained silent as well, staring into their tumblers, but looking as though their ears were athrob to hear how the rest of us would take it.

Now God knows I had been a peaceable citizen, deploring the violence of the Sons of Liberty; but when I heard these words out of James Dunn I knew no fat King in England could throw me an order

and then send troops to jam the order down my throat, not so long
as decent men like Sam Adams and John Hancock and Benedict
Arnold said there was no need to obey the order. Therefore I stood
up and said I was provided with enough firearms to stand off our
share of English troops, and would undertake to furnish the residents
of Arundel with muskets, powder, and bullet molds at their exact
cost, and show them my books into the bargain so they could not
accuse me of growing rich out of them, which they otherwise would
be sure to do. Such a wild hurroaring and hurrooing arose at this
that it cost me a small keg of French rum; and the very next day I
despatched Phoebe in her sloop to Portsmouth for additional muskets, powder, and lead.

It had been a stroke of fortune for my mother and myself when
we made Phoebe the master of the sloop *Eunice*—a name Phoebe
had bespoke on the day her keel was laid. From the look in her
eye I suspected she wished this name so that I would not call it the
"Mary M.," which I would not have done, though I had given some
thought to calling it the "White Lily," but decided against it for fear
of what Cap Huff would say in case he saw it.

Knowing how pestilential she could be if crossed, I agreed to the
name Eunice, whereat she set Thomas Scammen to work carving a
seal's head for a bow ornament. This head she herself decorated with
whiskers, having me make nails at my forge so she could drive them
into the side of the nose, causing the head to appear to pout and
bristle, very realistic, like Eunice imploring me for fish.

She carried two hands on the sloop, selecting always the stupidest
men she could find; for she said she wanted a crew that would take
orders without knowing enough to try to think for her because she
was a female, or to be afraid. Thus she got her men cheap; though
after she had taken me out in a brisk southwesterly breeze and run
me so close to the ledges, dodging in and out among them, that they
would have rubbed off my finger nails had I thrust my hand over the
lee-gunnel, it was in my mind that her crew would need to be wholly
witless to sail under her for any amount of pay at all.

She carried our lumber and fish to Boston as fast as they could
be carried, and faster than most folk said was possible. There she
exchanged them for such goods as I needed in the inn, trading discreetly, and holding the high respect of those with whom she traded,
even though she persisted in wearing sea boots like a man. She might,
indeed, have been mistaken for a small-waisted boy save for the East
India chains and necklets she was forever wearing, in especial a

string of stones called cat's eyes that she had from an East India
sailor in trade for two stone hatchets and a magnifying glass which
she had swapped for a gray parrot from God knows where.

The sloop's business, however, was Phoebe's and my mother's. The
inn kept me busy—far busier than I wished; for if ever I wanted to
be an orphan child with no responsibilities to weigh me down, it
was on the second occasion that Benedict Arnold's path crossed mine.

*   *   *

I had been off around Cape Arundel in my flat-bottomed skiff
to cut ash poles, in the spring of my twenty-second year. On returning up the river and into the creek with the rising tide, I saw a
crowd of people—my mother and sisters and James Dunn and several
others—standing near our front door. As I watched, a man among
them made a short run and took two steps up the sheer side of the
house, so that he was above their heads; then threw himself backward
in a somersault, landing neatly on his feet. Instantly there flashed
into my mind the memory of a man in a white blanket coat going
hand over hand up a rope as easily as I could walk up a staircase;
and I knew I was looking at Arnold once more.

I shouted and ran up, happy to see him, and found those about
him entranced by the tricks of skill he had been performing. Even
while he greeted me my sisters clamored for him to do a feat he had
done for them. Nothing loath, he went to the cart on which we
dragged our whale boat from the creek to the beach at low water,
measured the height of the wheel with his outstretched hand; then
backed away, ran lightly at it, and vaulted completely over without
touching hand or foot to either wheel. Never have I seen another
man who could do this, though many tried it in after years, especially
when elevated by rum, and narrowly escaped breaking their necks.

Though I could see he took pleasure in the amazed head-wagging
of those who watched him, as who would not, he beckoned James
Dunn to give him his broadcloth coat and three-cornered hat,
donned them, and clapped me on the shoulders, saying he had come
from Cape Porpus to see me. As soon as we were by ourselves in the
inn, he flipped the back of his fingers against my chest, lengthened
his face in the smile I well remembered, and shot at me abruptly:
"I've seen your girl!"

Now any faint suggestion of Mary was enough to constrict my
heart as though a hand had closed around it. I could only gawk at
Arnold and whisper, "Mary Mallinson?"

Arnold shook his head. "Marie de Sabrevois. Slender and golden-haired, with freckles across the top of her cheeks like yellow dust on a lily."

"Mary Mallinson," I said again, and closed my eyes to see her on her knees, holding my face between her hands.

"Marie de Sabrevois," Arnold repeated, tapping his forefinger on the table, "sister to Henri Guerlac de Sabrevois! The only fair-haired daughter the house of Sabrevois has ever known: fair and beautiful and a Catholic!"

The kitchen door burst open. Phoebe Marvin, thin and dark and quick as a cat, whirled into the room and stood with her back against the door, dried salt spray showing white on her high sea boots and brass-studded pirate's belt. The string of cat's eyes glowed and dimmed on her breast from the quickness of her breathing.

"There's hell to pay in Boston," she cried. "The troops shot into the Sons of Liberty on King Street and killed a mess of 'em!"

Arnold jumped to his feet, upsetting everything on the table. "What did they do to the soldiers?" he shouted, his face darkening until it was well nigh the color of Malary's, and growing strangely bulbous.

Phoebe looked at him coolly. "Nothing! The mob fired first."

Arnold groaned. "The mob! Mob! Citizens like you and me, peacefully pursuing their lives and liberty!"

"Well," Phoebe said calmly, "there might be two ways of looking at that. I saw it, and it was a mob, with a half-breed negro at its head; but they got no business to turn the King's troops on 'em. It was terrible!"

"Terrible!" Arnold cried, striding to the wall and hitting it such a blow with his clenched fist that the pine sheathing split. "It's wanton, cruel, inhuman murder! Good God! Are Americans all asleep, and tamely yielding up their liberties; or are they all turned *philosophers,* that they don't take instant vengeance on such dogs?"

"To hell with that!" I said. "What about Mary?"

Arnold whirled on me. "Mary! Mary! You want to talk about a damned little baggage sniveling in a convent school when troops of a foreign tyrant tramp over stones bespattered with your countrymen's brains! Mary! My God!"

I reached around and took hold of a stool, ready to brain him for speaking so of Mary. Arnold's pale blue eyes widened, like a cat's, fierce and waiting. My senses came back to me and I dropped the stool.

"Sir," I said, "I'll go against any English troops with any man, or alone, anywhere; but I've waited as many years as I can remember to have word of Mary. I'm sick of waiting!"

Arnold stared at me for another moment, then moved his thick shoulders in his blue broadcloth coat, as though to loosen them, smiling so the darkness and bulbousness passed from his face, leaving it light and gay.

"Why," he said, "you're all right! When the time comes they'll find us ready for them if we can keep from each other's throats—if we can work together instead of at cross purposes!" His face darkened again. "That's the devil of it—cross purposes! D'ye know what happened in New Haven? A dirty informer set the English on me for evading their damned laws, and I lashed him! Gave the English a lesson in what they'd get if they didn't let Americans alone! You'd think my own people would thank God someone had the heart to stand up to their oppressors, wouldn't you? Wouldn't you?"

He thrust his face almost into mine and eyed me furiously; then, not waiting for an answer, went on again. "Cross purposes! Cross purposes! Even my own people can't see what's plain to be seen! They're so used to oppression that they won't consent to stop being oppressed! They fined me fifty shillings and rebuked me publicly. Rebuked me, damn their cowardly ratty souls to hell! Rebuke! I'll give 'em something to rebuke me for!" He shook the table until it clattered on the floor, drew a deep breath, held it a moment, then expelled it gustily and smiled again.

"Well," he said, "the way of it was this: I went into the drug trade in New Haven for myself, after I brought you down from the Kennebec. Then I began to export horses to the Sugar Islands, and bring back such cargoes as all of us bring back nowadays—molasses and sugar and rum. Having learned the ropes in Quebec, I took goods there, drugs, the best of drugs; and having sold them I bought horses, which I know as well as any man, and sold the horses in the Sugar Islands. Do you remember I told your father, and a fine man he was, how easy it was to make money in Quebec?"

I nodded, wondering when in God's name he'd get to Mary.

"I was right," he went on. "In New Haven I have a fine home and a sweet wife and two children, as pretty as you'll see anywhere. I own three brigs—one in Cape Porpus, that I captain myself, and two others at sea, one between New Haven and the Sugar Islands, and t'other bound home from England. On top of all this, the young bloods in New Haven elected me captain of the Governor's Guards, who'd fight the devil in hell or the troops of that fat swine King George. It's all one to us!"

He tilted back and looked at me contentedly, and with reason; for this man I had thought to clout with a stool was the equal in property and position of any in our colonies.

Satisfied, seemingly, with my round eyes, Captain Arnold got at his tale. "No man knows," he said, "when special information may prove valuable; so I've never gone to Quebec without asking for your friend De Sabrevois. Until this trip I learned little I didn't know already. He'd been taken by an English corvette and carried to Jersey; and on the signing of the treaty he went to France.

"At first the English planned to seize his estates—a seigneurie on the Island of Orleans and a house in the upper town; but having their silly damned ideas about pacifying the people of Canada, they decided to interfere with neither property nor religion. So De Sabrevois comes posting over to Quebec with his beautiful sister Marie and settles down among his iron stoves and fur rugs, pleasant as pie to all the English, and prodigal of his wines because of his delight, he says, at having the odors of his dear Canadian forests in his nose. Then around come the handsome English officers to look at this beautiful gold-flecked lily, Marie, his sister. Such is the intensity with which they look that the lonely brother, who has a slit in his cheek and nick in his ear as if a stoat had been chewing at him, has never a chance to see her from morning to night."

Arnold's eyes popped out at me; then slipped instantly back to their usual state.

"Now," he said, "I don't know whether De Sabrevois was displeased at this, or whether he was bitten by another reason. I know I wouldn't be displeased if a troop of young officers crowded around my sister, whom I love dearly. At any rate, he sent the beautiful Marie to a nunnery in Montreal, saying she wished to perfect herself in astronomy."

"Astronomy!" I said, trying to remember whether the word had to do with the study of flowers or cookery.

"So, too, said I," Arnold declared, smiling a knowing smile. "From what I saw of the lady, the stars have little to fear from her investigations."

"You saw her before she went to Montreal?" I asked eagerly.

"Why, no," Arnold said, with a reckless look I was to know better before our acquaintance ended. "I heard all this from friends. Since the gentleman was so insistent that the beautiful Marie was his sister,

I thought it might be to my advantage to have a shot at it to see whether it was so or otherwise. When I sailed up to Montreal I took with me four English uniforms for four of my seamen; and one night I called at the nunnery, accompanied by four red-coats, and commanded the mother superior to open in the name of the King and produce for my inspection the person of Marie de Sabrevois." He laughed, silently and slyly, and his broad shoulders shook.

"She was produced," he went on, "and the reports I'd received in Quebec were borne out. She was as sweet as a cluster of arbutus with the leaves peeled off: fresh and pink and delicious; and her bright hair bound around her head like a rope. She was so soft in her gray gown that if I'd taken her by the waist I'd have looked for her to hang limp across my arm, like my sister's cashmere shawl."

I could hear Phoebe go stumping to the door in her sea boots, but I threw her not even a glance, having no interest in knowing whether she was jeering at me, or how she felt.

"I spoke to her in English," Arnold said, hitching forward and prodding the air before him with his forefinger. "I said I was come from her friends in Arundel. She answered in French, vowing she didn't understand. I said, still in English, that since she wished to adopt this attitude I'd call my men and take her away, so she could be questioned at our leisure. She looked at me piteously out of round blue eyes and said in English that she had no friends in Arundel; that if any considered themselves so, she prayed I'd tell 'em to interest themselves in their own affairs and leave her in peace."

Arnold leaned back, nursing a knee and staring at me foxily. "That gave me a hold on De Sabrevois, if ever I should need one, so I came away."

"For God's sake! When you had her, you fool, why didn't you take her!"

"A little less emphatic, if you please," Arnold said. "I have business in Montreal and Quebec. Why should I steal a young lady who might be unwilling, to thrust her on you, who might be ungrateful? There may be other and weightier business in Montreal and Quebec, before long, for all of us, and De Sabrevois might be of great assistance. Why should I sacrifice that assistance for your private affairs? You exaggerate their importance!

"I explain these things after being called a fool," he added, his head lowered between his massive shoulders, "because you're unbalanced by love, which is worse than the throat distemper, since it unhinges the brain."

"Sir," I said, "I ask your pardon again. Now I must do what I always planned—go to Quebec after Mary."

Phoebe went to tapping on the floor with her boot. I was surprised to find her still in the room. "Your mother can't manage this inn alone," she said.

"Let James Dunn help her," I replied. I had employed James to watch over the gathering-room of nights, since his dignified appearance and his position with the Sons of Liberty had a value in those troubled days.

Phoebe shook her head. "You know James Dunn as well as I do."

Arnold pulled me down onto a seat again. "I came here for one purpose: to tell you these things before you should hear them in another way, and go galloping off to roil the waters and frighten the fish for others."

"I've got to get Mary," I protested. "I've waited all my life for the chance."

"A body'd think you were tottering on the verge of the grave!" Arnold cried. "Listen to me a minute. We're going to fight England! You people here in the backwoods may not know it, and some of the cowardly money-hoarders in the cities won't believe it; but fight England we must!"

"How do you know?"

"It's in the air," Arnold whispered. "You can feel it in the crowds. You can hear it in their talk. They want to be let alone. They don't want to be interfered with, except by their own people, and damned little by them. They're angry: waiting to strike, like rattlesnakes."

His voice rose and sent a stirring along my spine. "And look at England blundering along! What does she know about us? Nothing! What has she ever known about us? Nothing! What will she ever know about us? Nothing! Who does she send to govern us? Fools or knaves! Everything she's done has been wrong! She can't change. Everything she does will be wrong. Wrongs piled on wrong! More wrongs added to the pile! More and more and more! And then war! For God's sake, can't you see it, here in this inn? Can't you hear it in the talk of nights?"

I nodded.

Arnold gathered the front of my shirt in his hand and shook me. "Wake up! You can't go traipsing into Canada at a time like this, trying to break into nunneries, and bellowing through the streets of Quebec! You know Indians; you know the country. How many do? We'll need everybody who knows such things. I wish to God your father was alive! You wouldn't catch *him* running off to Canada at a time like this!"

I nodded again, caught in a spell by his words.

"Mind what I say," he said. "You're needed here. When it's proper for you to go, I'll tell you. You stay here until you have word from me. Don't you move until then! I'll take care of you! I'll get you to Quebec some day, but you've got to wait!"

"All right," I said reluctantly, "I'll wait."

"That's a bargain!" Arnold said. He seized my hand and shook it: then at once made preparations to be on his way.

Phoebe offered to carry him to Cape Porpus in the sloop; but he protested he had ridden over, leaving his horse on the other side of the river. With that, being both pestilent and froward, she said she would set him across in the skiff. She swaggered ahead of him like a boy in her clumping sea boots and high brass-studded belt, her shirt open at the throat; and as they went, they laughed and jested together. When I would have followed them, it came to me suddenly that Phoebe might be making game of Mary, and so I stayed behind lest she provoke me into pushing her into the river.

XII

THERE were times when a blind rage came over me at this girl's wilfulness. If I had been her father I would have stripped off my belt and laid her over my knee, though I would have had a care lest she put my nose out of joint before I did what was necessary.

If I spoke to her with disapproval about the wearing of breeches as being unmaidenly, which I sometimes did, she would say she had been meaning to get a brocaded dress with a bustle to wear down to Boston in the next sou'wester, which is no answer at all; or she would ask some pert question, such as how would I like to shorten sail in a westerly squall with a skirt tangled between my legs, which had nothing to do with the matter.

Or she would urge me to draw a picture of the sort of dress she should wear on the sloop in place of breeches, so she could have it made in Boston and call it her slooping gown, all as frivolous and meaningless as the mewing of a seagull.

Indeed, I was like to find myself infuriated whenever I held speech with her; but I was prepared for no such piece of outrageousness as she announced to me shortly after Arnold had gone off to the Sugar Islands.

I was hard at work calking our whaleboat when she came up and lolled importantly against it, one hand in a pocket of her bold and hateful breeches like a man, and the other playing with her string of cat's eyes, so that I begged her to behave either like a man or a woman. At this she said soberly she was thinking of taking a husband, and knew no better way of behaving like a woman.

"Now why," I asked, tempted to throw my calking knife at her, "do you want to go and do that! You're living on a sloop as you want to live, more comfortably than you can live with any man in this town, and laying by enough money so in time you can own a sloop in your own name, or perhaps even a brig. Yet you must go and wreck this arrangement of ours, which is making money for all of us, when it was only for you that we let Thomas Scammen build the damned sloop. Where, for that matter, can we get another master for her? I believe before God there never was such a contrary, harassing hussy as you!"

"But you don't know who I intend to marry."

"No, nor care! Whoever he is, he'll only put you to raising brats, a thousand of them, like all good husbands here! He'll set you to hauling water out of the well and cooking and spinning; and you, being only half-sized and quarter-witted anyway, and thin as a crow to boot, will be an old woman, all wrinkled and gray and dirty, like the potato James Dunn carries in his pocket against rheumatism, before you're a dozen years older! He'll never let you go about in breeches and boots and a shirt open at the throat, as I do; so all in all I think you've been affected by the sun! What oaf is it you're taking?"

"James Dunn," Phoebe said, whirling the string of cat's eyes around the forefinger of the hand that was not in her disgusting pocket.

"James Dunn!" I cried; and then, in stupefaction, I once more gasped, "James Dunn!"

"Yes, if you prefer to pronounce it so. James Dunn!" With that she imitated me, which to my mind is a loathsome trick for anyone to perform, and especially so with Phoebe; for there was never any mistaking her imitations.

"But you can't marry James Dunn! He eats dandelion greens and ship's bread!"

"That means less cooking," she said calmly.

"He can't count above five," I protested; "not above four, I do believe! When he stood beside Thomas Scammen a few nights since, a tray in one hand and a pitcher in the other, and Scammen handed him a shilling, he couldn't think how to take it without dropping either the pitcher or the tray! So he dropped the pitcher because it was in his right hand, and therefore easier to drop!"

"That's easily remedied."

"Indeed! And how would you go about it at Dunn's age?"

"That's simple," Phoebe said, peering down her unbuttoned shirt and removing a fleck of dust from her chest with her little finger. "I'd never hand him a shilling."

"Bah!" I said.

"What's more, I'll sail the sloop as in the past and if I have need of a seaman I'll carry James along, thus saving wages. If I don't need a seaman, he'll remain here, doing as he's doing now. I've spoken with James about these things, and he agrees with me it would be well if I continued to be master of the sloop, as well as"—she looked at me maliciously—"to wear breeches and boots; a garb in which he sees no harm."

"He sees nothing in anything!"

"He seems to see something in me."

"Pah!" I said. "What sort of marriage is that?"

"I've heard it named in Boston. There they call it a legal marriage."

She went off, whistling, her hands in her pockets, the most hateful thing I could see in all Arundel.

＊　　＊　　＊

These two, Phoebe and James, were a strange pair. Phoebe would be gone for three and four days, or even for a week, leaving James to blunder along as a helper at the inn. When she came home they would never moon together among the dunes, like other lovers; but she would come and sit in the gathering-room of the inn, giving James little problems to do for the improvement of his brain, she said, speaking of that which was not there. James, a needle-witted scientist in appearance, would brood over them and shake his head in perplexity, while Phoebe would try to make them clear to him. Or she would ignore James and come into the kitchen, where I would be working at my accounts, and spend hours telling my sisters how she had seen a woman in Newburyport or Salem or Boston wearing thus and so, after the manner of all women.

Why they were so slow in marrying I could not see. The times seemed to be growing more peaceable, and there was less talk of mobs in Boston and elsewhere. Also the wild men among the Sons of Liberty fell into greater disrepute than ever, and merchants, here and there, began to say a war with England would be ruinous. In view of all this I might have broken my promise to Arnold and gone off to Quebec; but whenever I spoke of it to Phoebe she said she was of a mind to be married in a few weeks, and would want to take James from his work in the inn, so they could go on a wedding trip. At that my mother would shake her head sadly, and I would have to sit furiously and bide my time.

Such thoughts were driven from my head in earnest when Phoebe, in the third year of her engagement, returned from Boston with the news that the East India Company, having a surfeit of tea in England, was to be allowed to bring tea direct from India to America in its own ships and sell it to our colonists. Thus, Phoebe said, the company would be able to sell tea cheaper than our merchants,

who had to buy theirs in England: cheaper, even, than those who
had been smuggling it from Holland.

This news, she said, had thrown all Boston into an uproar. The
merchants, scenting ruin in having their trade taken from them, had
forgotten their fear of a war with England and were bellowing as
loudly as any of the Sons of Liberty.

Furthermore, she said, the Sons of Liberty, greatly encouraged,
had taken on new life; and the mobs had started up again, tarring
and feathering customs officers, and hurling buckets of filth through
the windows of those whose sympathies lay with England.

Once more our gathering-room was full of bawlers and table-
pounders of nights: bawlers who grew warlike at the news that a
mob of Indians had seized the first of the East India tea ships and
spilled tea to the value of ten thousand pounds into Boston Harbor.

I have heard folk say our war with England started over the tax
on tea. I think these folk are addle-pated, for our merchants had
been paying a tax on tea for two years before the cargo of the *Dart-
mouth* was tossed into Boston Harbor. I know for my part that the
rumpus over tea excited me not at all. But it was another matter, a
little later, when the English declared the port of Boston would be
closed to all shipping until the citizens had repaid the East India
Company for the ruined tea. Not only did they close the port, so that
Phoebe was forced to land her Boston cargoes at Salem, but they
further declared they would seize Sam Adams and take him to England for trial.

I could not think about these things without my shirt growing
moist along my spine; and none of our Sons of Liberty whooped
more loudly than I when word came to our committee of correspondence that a Continental Congress had been formed and that towns
near Boston had sent it a message demanding that troops be raised
to disarm the English parricide, meaning King George, for pursuing
our guiltless countrymen with unrelenting severity and pointing the
dagger at their bosoms.

There were rumors, most of them wild and false, of the coming
of countless troop ships and how the English would transport us all
to Canada or the Sugar Islands, or take our children as hostages;
how no arms or ammunition would be sent to us ever again; how
they planned to seize us and sell us for slaves; how all our towns
would be put to the torch, and all the Indians of the West turned
loose on us. A frenzy of rage and hatred filled us—not all of us, but
those of us who had our anger fed each day by more news and more

news, and by the growls of our neighbors sitting together over their glasses of rum.

Cursed with inactivity, we grew constantly more bloodthirsty, crying out for the infliction of terrible deaths on those against whom we raged. When we had word from Portsmouth on a clear December day, telling how Cap Huff had stormed and rampaged into the King's fort with the Sons of Liberty and seized a hundred barrels of gunpowder, we were disgusted because he had let the garrison off with their lives, and not torn them limb from limb. Since then I have learned that those who cry loudest for blood are those who stay at home, making war with their mouths; but in those days we opined Cap had grown weak and womanly from being overlong out of gaol.

* * *

The ice still lay in the lee of the rocks that spring when we learned that English troops, marching out of Boston to prevent the powder in Lexington and Concord from going the same way as that in Portsmouth, had been met by our Minute Men in Concord and driven back into the city with scores of red-coats left dead and dying by the roadside. Those who drove them back, said the letter, had camped at the barricades at Boston Neck, so that the English could not come out again. This was another matter; and it was a silent crowd that night in the gathering-room. There was scant table-pounding, and no bawling at all; and some of the voices seemed querulous and at times given to unexpected cracking; while men laughed, when they did laugh, a little tremulously.

A few days later an express rider galloped up from the beach, flung me a handbill with a shout of "Nail this up!" and clattered on toward Falmouth.

I stood and stared at it; and one by one the folk in the house came out to see what it was—my mother and Phoebe and my sisters and Jethro Fish and James Dunn and Malary.

In Congress, at Watertown, April 30, 1775 [it read]
GENTLEMEN:

The barbarous murders on our innocent Brethren Wednesday the 19th Instant has made it absolutely necessary that we immediately raise an Army to defend our Wives and our Children from the butchering Hands of an inhuman Soldiery, who, incensed at the Obstacles they met with in their bloody Progress, and enraged at being repulsed from the Field of Slaughter, will without the least doubt take the first Opportunity in their Power to ravage this devoted Country with Fire and Sword: We conjure you, therefore, by all that is dear, by all that is sacred, that you give all

Assistance possible in forming an Army: Our all is at stake, Death and
Devastation are the certain Consequences of Delay, every Moment is infinitely precious, an Hour lost may deluge your Country in Blood, and
entail perpetual Slavery upon the few of your Posterity who may survive
the Carnage. We beg and entreat, as you will answer it to your Country,
to your own Consciences and above all as you will answer to God himself, that you will hasten and encourage by all possible Means the Enlistment of Men to form the Army, and send them forward to Head-Quar-
ters, at Cambridge, with that Expedition which the vast Importance and
instant Urgency of the Affair demands.

JOSEPH WARREN, President, P. T.

I left them reading and went into the kitchen, where I took my
musket from the wall and sat down to clean it. My mother came in
and looked at me; then went to her spinning wheel and fell to spinning. The whir and click of the wheel got into my head, in some
unaccountable way, so that I could never go on a march after that,
or move toward an enemy, without a whirring and clicking starting
in my brain and keeping time to my movements.

Malary came in snuffling, so that my mother began to sing to
drown her out; and at this I went into the gathering-room to have
quiet. I found none; for James Dunn was sitting at his counting desk
in the corner, a bland and kindly smile on his face, as though he had
done some noble work of charity, which he had not. Before him
stood Phoebe, her back as straight and flat as a board.

"Jethro Fish is going," she told him. "He went home to get his
musket and leave word at Lord's and Towne's and Cluff's and
Merrill's. When he comes back I'm going to run him down to Newburyport."

James Dunn sat silent, as benevolent as a minister who has saved
a soul from hell fire.

"Why don't you say something?" Phoebe wanted to know; but
James Dunn just sat there looking indulgent; and since both of them
ignored me, I went at my musket again.

"Can you shoot a musket?" she asked James.

After some deliberation he nodded gravely and said he could.

"You're a Son of Liberty," she shot at him, clutching his counting
desk. "You're one of the ones that wanted a war, and now you've
got it! You've got to go! That's what you joined the Sons of Liberty
for! You promised to go, just by joining!"

James Dunn seemed to turn this over in his mind like a bass
goggling its eyes and rolling a minnow in its mouth.

"He can go down with me," I said.

Phoebe whirled. I thought she was going to wrench the musket out of my hands and clout me with it. "What are you talking about? You can't go! You promised to wait! You told Arnold you'd wait till you heard from him! He may need you!" She raised her fists and shook them. "Lord! Men are terrible!"

"I know that, Phoebe, but I thought I'd find him quicker in Cambridge. I wouldn't feel good staying around here with others going."

"Oh, so you wouldn't feel good!" she jeered, but with no sting in the jeer. "It'll be good practice for you! There's going to be plenty of times you won't feel good before you chase the English army out of New England!"

James Dunn leaned forward with the look of a judge about to render a decision affecting the welfare of nations. "I could go if you married me, I guess."

Phoebe hesitated. I thought she had an air of listening; but whatever she listened for, she failed to hear it. "All right!" she snapped finally. "I'll marry you right now, and run you and Jethro down to Newburyport together. Go get the minister!" She stamped into the kitchen and banged the door behind her, making as much noise as though she were twice as big as Cap Huff, instead of little enough to walk under my arm, sea boots and all.

*   *   *

So Phoebe was married; nor had she ever exasperated me more than when she stood up to James Dunn in our gathering-room, like a swaggering little kingbird standing up to a big wall-eyed owl, answering "I do" impatiently, and saying to James Dunn, immediately it was over, "Hurry up with your pack; the tide's running out!"

If I had married a slip of a thing like that, and she had bespoken me so, I would have shaken her until her teeth cracked. I think my feelings must have shown in my face; for she kept turning to look at me; and when she flung into the kitchen to gather up her belongings for the journey, she thrust out her tongue at me, as provoking as ever, more fitted to be a cabin boy than a wife—especially the wife of James Dunn.

Jethro Fish came back with his brother Ivory and four of his friends, all laden with packs and muskets and powder horns, and all hullooing and pushing and tripping each other, uncontrolled and prankish, as if off to a curlew hunt instead of a war.

I set them out to the sloop in the skiff; and they kept on with

their whooping and skylarking, cuffing each other and jigging to
keep warm in the brisk east wind, with James Dunn standing, noble-
looking and faintly amused, among them, a major general in appearance. I envied them and thought ill of my promise to Arnold,
who might be dead for all I knew, and said privily I would wait a
day or two; then go myself.

Among them was one Asa Hutchins, a wild and lazy Son of Liberty, who sometimes condescended to go a-fishing when he could
get no more credit from tavern keepers. While I leaned on my oars,
watching them, Asa shouted: "Better get married, Steven, so there'll
be somebody to send you down to Cambridge too!"

Phoebe came scrambling aft and twitched him around to face her.
She said something I couldn't hear; then doubled her fist and drove
it so hard into his stomach that he folded up like a flail and sat
himself over the side of the sloop with a prodigious splash.

I salvaged him and threw him on the deck.

"I want no time wasted," I said, shaking my finger at Phoebe, "in
rowdiness and fighting! If you can't keep this sloop peaceable I'll
sail her myself and leave you on shore in a skirt, where you belong!
See you have her back here to-morrow for another load. There'll be
a kit and caboodle of our people waiting to set out."

Phoebe turned indifferently in the middle of my words and busied
herself with the raising of the anchor. When the sloop was under
way, she looked at me from under the jib and said, in a mincing
tone, "Was there anything else?"

*   *   *

I was in no good humor when I rowed ashore to humdrum tasks
while the others pranced off to Boston on a holiday. In a cabin near
us lived Joseph Denico, a poor worthless Frenchman who had been
sent out of Acadia many years before with all the other Acadians;
and with him lived his sons, John and Joseph, both clever at hunting, traveling frequently into the Indian country. I bargained with
John to set off for Ossipee Mountain and bring Mogg Chabonoke
to me on urgent business; and with Joseph to carry a copy of Warren's
handbill to Turbat's Creek and Cape Porpus, telling the townsfolk
on the way that those desiring to travel to Cambridge to join the
army might go as far as Newburyport without charge on our sloop.

All through that night our townsmen straggled into the inn, laden
with muskets and packs, most of them happy and many of them
boisterous, since it became at once the fashion at all inns and ordinar-

ies not only to give double drams to those who were going for soldiers, but even, in some taverns, to refuse pay from such persons when they felt the need of rum.

They sat in our gathering-room until dawn and long after, pounding on the tables with rum mugs and singing such songs as "Lillibullero" and "Benning Wentworth" and "Hot Stuff" and "Yankee Doodle," all out of key, many fancying their voices were tenor when they were not; while some who considered themselves poetizers insisted on writing new verses for the songs, all of them horrid.

Shortly after dawn other stragglers appeared and some military genius conceived the idea of greeting each one by marching him to the beach and having him yell curses at King George, who was supposed to be listening and seeking protection beneath the royal bedstead across the water. I think we marched back and forth to the oceanside twenty times betwixt dawn and sun-up; and I know we laughed immoderately at the profanities addressed to the fat King of England. Whether his ears burned I do not know; but if all of us could have blown our breaths on him at close range that night, he must have died the death.

I had forgot how our little town had grown until I saw the numbers who poured out like hornets, to help hold the English in Boston—three Wildes, one a ship captain, and the Hutchins twins; Cleaves, the blacksmith's son; Jesse Dorman and his brother, and the two sons of the Murphy who was an ensign at Louisbourg; my cousins Joshua and Edward Nason from the Saco Road, and Carr whose brother was a sailor and went later on the *Chesapeake;* Miles from Turbat's Creek, and the Abbott who had come recently from Scarborough, and the unmarried Adams, and the son of Deshon who came from France as a linguist; Nathaniel Davis and his son Nathaniel, the latter being only thirteen years old, but as good a marksman as any of us, as the English discovered when he lay behind the rail fence on Bunker Hill in six weeks' time. Also James Burnham who had twelve children, and Noah Cluff and poor Nathaniel Lord; an Emmons, a Tarbox, two Townes, a Lewis, two Dearings, a Perkins, a Burbank, an Averill, and some others that have gone from me. These were only the ones who went at once. Many more went later, volunteering or being drafted, or being hired by those who from necessity or timidity wished to avoid the draft.

Phoebe returned with news for me. Arnold, she learned, had gone to Cambridge with his New Haven company immediately on hearing of the battle at Concord, and had proposed to the Massachusetts

Committee of Public Safety an expedition to capture the English forts at Ticonderoga and Crown Point. To this the committee agreed, and made him a colonel. In Newburyport she spoke with an officer, newly sent from Cambridge to urge all sloops and schooners to scour the New England coast for volunteers; and he, she said, told her Arnold had just now departed on the mission.

"You'll be mighty big," said Phoebe, putting her hands on her hips and staring up at me as though in admiration, which I knew she did not feel; "grand and important, being the adviser of a colonel."

"Do you suppose a man like that," I asked her, "would remember what he said to a country innkeeper long ago? I'm a fool to stay here when I ought to be in Cambridge, carrying a musket against the English!"

"You'd be a fool to be in Cambridge," she said. "They'd put you to peeling potatoes, since you know how to manage an inn; or set you to making the colonel's bed or washing his shirt. Stay here where you were told to stay, so when you go to war you can fight, and not be nursemaid for a horse! If Arnold forgets you, which he won't, I'll go to him and snap my fingers under his nose and ask him why he hasn't put you to leading men through the forest toward——" She stopped and clapped her fist against my breast, bringing my mind back from Mary, toward whom it had instantly flown when Phoebe spoke of going through the forests.

"What if he sends for you? What can you tell him about the Indians, or about other things he ought to know? If he's gone to Ticonderoga he'll need news of every road to Canada!"

"It seems to me," I said, "that a hussy who thinks on some matters as you think might have thought more carefully before marrying James Dunn."

"Will you answer me!" she cried, stamping her hulking sea boot within an inch of my foot.

"I've sent for Mogg Chabonoke to carry messages to Natanis and Paul Higgins. And will you answer me?"

She played with her string of cat's eyes, and shot a jeering glance at me. "He's a handsome, good man. With a little learning he'd be equal to any Boston statesman."

"Bah!" I said.

"And unless I've misheard the words you yourself have spoken, his brain is no worse than those of many British generals sent here in past years: General Abercrombie and General Braddock in particular."

This being the truth, I was unable to make a quick reply, where-upon she added: "And you've told me that always, when such a general was sent over, a woman contrived it."

"What are you getting at?" I asked, feeling it was time either to shake her or slap her.

She placed one hand coquettishly on her brass-studded belt and daintily drooped the other at arm's length before her; then stepped affectedly in front of me with a simper that aped a modish lady. "What has been done before can be done again. I'll make him a general and have him sent to conquer Spain."

I reached for her, but she squeaked and backed away. "Steven," she said, retreating before me, "I either had to send a man or go myself."

"Then why didn't you send a man!" I bellowed, furious at her.

"He'll be all right, Steven," she protested. "You can see he goes where you go; and between us we'll look after him!"

"Us! We! *We* look after him! There's no reason why I should look after him, and I won't do it! If it's in your mind to go tagging after an army, making a nuisance and a spectacle of yourself, get it out of your head before I put you over my knee and drive it out of you with a butter paddle!"

With no further words she left me and went to gathering her human cargo from the dunes and the beach, where they were dozing in the sun and recovering from their military evolutions of the night before.

*   *   *

For the next two weeks there was constant traffic, from the east-ward, of men bound for Cambridge, some going by land so they might have free rum and food along the road and kind looks or better from the girls; others hunting for schooners and sloops to speed them more quickly to Cambridge. There were some in ancient blue militia uniforms, and some in homespun, and many from the back settlements barefooted and unkempt, but all with muskets and blankets, and all panting for a shot at gilt buttons on a red coat.

The traffic dwindled when the news of fighting slackened. To-ward the end of May we learned how Arnold, lacking men of his own, had gone with Ethan Allen to the taking of Ticonderoga; and then, having received a few Massachusetts troops, had gone and captured St. John's alone. In June we had the news of Bunker Hill: how our men stood face to face with British regulars, which the

British had said we were too cowardly to do, and twice drove them down the hill in disorder before our powder gave out, killing them in heaps and suffering some loss ourselves. Of those from Arundel, Israel Dorman was stuck with a bayonet where he sat down, and Nathaniel Davis was shot through a rib; while young Nathaniel, his son, having picked off eleven Britishers in the three charges, sent word home it was easier than killing squirrels, but more fun.

At this there was another outpouring, and our sleep of nights was again broken by whoops and occasional musket shots from those who pressed toward Cambridge; while I daily grew more fractious from puttering over the affairs of the inn when all the rest of the world went adventuring.

Mogg Chabonoke had come in from Ossipee Mountain, bringing me a leather hunting shirt from his wife, Fala Ramanascho, and had gone off with messages from me to Paul Higgins, the white man who had become the sachem of the Assagunticooks on the Androscoggin; also to Natanis in his camp on Dead River. To each of them I sent a gift of hand mirrors, scissors, awls, and needles, asking whether they were still my friends, and saying I needed their help against my enemies. Mogg returned with a belt from Paul Higgins and a message saying he would come with thirty warriors whenever the time was ripe. At Swan Island, Mogg said, he had found a town of Abenakis, Jacataqua being the sachem and Hobomok the *m'téoulin*, a powerful *m'téoulin* able to scream so that those who heard him could not move. But he had found the town at Norridgewock abandoned; and when he reached Dead River he could not find Natanis though his cabin had been occupied within the month, and there was dried venison hanging from the ridgepole. Therefore he left my message drawn on a piece of bark.

August found us fretful from heat and mosquitoes, and ill at ease because General Washington had come to Cambridge to command the troops. A scattering drift of men was wandering back from Cambridge, swearing it was better to desert than to be drilled and drilled through scorching days by a Virginia disciplinarian.

Sick of everything, I rolled a blanket, with hunting shirt, razor, and extra stockings in it, and thought to myself I would go off to Quebec without saying anything to anyone, though I caught Phoebe watching me and misdoubted I would be able to do it. While I pondered the matter a horseman in a blue coat and doeskin breeches came up off the beach with his horse in a lather of sweat and began to bawl for Steven Nason. I asked him what he wanted.

"I want beer!" he said. "Here's an express from Colonel Arnold to Steven Nason."

He went off bowlegged after his beer. I clawed at the message, which lies to-day in my green seaman's chest.

To Steven Nason in Arundel [it read]
DEAR SIR:

As I make no doubt of your being hearty in the cause of liberty and your country, and mindful of certain messages that I left with you at an earlier period, I should take it as a particular favor if you would come down at once to Cambridge. I shall be at the hdqtrs. of Gen. Washington, and shall hope to learn of your arrival there no later than three o'clock to-morrow afternoon. Pray hurry on as fast as possible, and under no circumstances hazard any opinions concerning your movements or concerning the object of this message to any except your own family. I am, dear Sir, your friend and humble serv't,

B. ARNOLD.

"Mary!" I said, and went to get my musket.

XIII

Pʜᴏᴇʙᴇ put me into Newburyport that night, pestering me all the way to take her to Cambridge, so she might see James Dunn.

"This is beyond me," I said. "First you dawdled for years, threatening to marry him but not doing it. Then you up and married him and sent him off in a half-hour's time, all brisk and businesslike. Now you want to tag along to see him when you have this sloop here to tend. You'd be a horrible nuisance to me and everyone else. You said once that men were terrible; and I say to you now that women are worse, for they change their minds every two minutes, and still they're bound to have their own way in spite of hell and high water!"

"Then you won't take me?"

"That's what I'm trying to say. If you can't understand my thoughts after the way I've spoken, I'll unship the tiller and pound them into your head."

When the sloop nosed into Tracy's wharf at Newburyport I wasted no time in farewells, knowing she'd pester me. As I went up the wharf she called: "I'll wait here until I have word from you."

I turned and ordered her back to Arundel, while she played with her string of cat's eyes and stared abstractedly at the peak of the mainsail. When I started onward, she let me reach the end of the wharf; then again said: "I'll wait here until I have word from you!" I'd have spoken my mind freely, but when I turned to do it she was vanishing into the cabin. I said to myself she could lie there, for all of me, until the *Eunice* had barnacles on her bottom as thick as the mud on Ranger's belly in the spring.

All Newburyport was astir: candles in the windows; carts rumbling through the streets loaded with provisions for the army; up and down the walks a passing of people, many of them hallooing to me when they saw my musket, wishing me good luck.

By Davenport's Inn a man came out of a side street, carrying three muskets. He drank from a flask, and stood watching me as I swung toward the turnpike. Then he hailed me, calling me Brother and asking whether I was bound for Cambridge. He joined me, and between us we emptied the flask. Soon, he said, we must beg a ride in a provision wagon or a rum cart, so he could be relieved of the weight of his three muskets.

He had a hare lip, poor fellow, and was hard to understand; for when he wished to say "Brother" he actually said "Mruther." I gave him a lift with one of his muskets, a cheap thing, expressing surprise that he should travel so heavily armed, whereupon he said: "Mruther, ain't you min oun oo Amridge yet?"

I said I had not yet been to Cambridge; so he explained there was a shortage of muskets in the army, some of the farmers having arrived armed with rusty swords, bayonets on rake handles, and muskets that had needed cleaning and repairing since the days of the Plymouth Colony. Muskets brought such prices in Cambridge that he had come home and bought two for twenty-two shillings, lawful money. These, he said proudly, he would sell for fifty or sixty shillings apiece, lawful money.

While I was turning this over in my mind a cart came clopping up behind us. I surmise the driver, a villainous-looking man with matted hair and a drooping mustache, would never have stopped for us if we had carried fewer weapons. He looked even less amiable when my companion, after climbing into the cart and poking into the hay, uncovered four kegs. They held rum, the driver said; and he gave us a drink of it. It tasted something like rum, and was made, my companion said, from a little rum and a lot of water, to which had been added burnt sugar, tobacco, and certain chemicals to make it more powerful, so that those who drank much of it awoke on the following morning feeling as though the sweepings of a barber shop had been burnt in their mouths.

He downed a pint of it and then said gloomily he didn't know what the world was coming to: that soon nobody at all would be honest.

I broke into his meditations on the growth of dishonesty by asking a question that had been preying on me: how, in short, it had been possible for him to leave the army in order to go home. This, he said, was simple: you told your captain you had to go home to tend to your haying, though you might have to promise to harvest the captain's hay as well. When I asked him whether or not his crop had been good he said, "Hell, Mruther, I ain't *ut* no hay: I'm a whew maker!"

"A what maker?"

"A *whew* maker!" he replied impatiently. "Whew! Whew! What you wear on your feet!"

At Ipswich we left the clean, fresh smell of the salt marshes and struck the broad fields and rich farms of Wenham, the odor of new-mown hay lying heavy and sweet under the maples and elms. We dozed through the long hills of Danvers and awoke at Salem to a great hurly-burly, for though dawn was not far off, the provision sloops and schooners were unloading, privateers were stocking up, and brigs that had stolen in from the Sugar Islands were discharging cargoes. Here my hare-lipped friend proposed we buy two gallons of rum and make it into five gallons with water and molasses and a substance he would buy at an apothecary's: then sell it in Cambridge at a round profit.

Having no time for such diversions, I left him and went into a tavern, the Anchor and Can, to have a slab of bacon with eggs. There my attention was caught by a small, graceful young gentleman in a tight uniform. It was not his being somewhat in liquor that took my eye, nor the way in which he tongue-lashed the landlord with such an amiable smile that his words sounded like compliments. I think he was the prettiest man I had ever seen, his ears small as a girl's, and his mouth large with smooth red lips. He looked a little like a well-shaped woman in his close-fitting doeskin breeches and blue broadcloth coat. The chief thing that drew me to him was his declaration, made in elegant language to the innkeeper, that if the chickens were not packed in five minutes he would go elsewhere, since he wished to be in Cambridge by breakfast time. At this I asked him politely to advise me how I could most speedily arrive in Cambridge.

"With pleasure!" he replied quickly and happily, being, as I have said, somewhat in liquor. "By running!"

"That would be bad training for the future," I said.

The young man nodded. "True, but you Massachusetts men should be trained for all emergencies."

"Sir, I'm from Maine, not Massachusetts."

The young man struck an attitude. "Incredible! Don't tell me you're not a colonel—not a Massachusetts colonel!"

I had no idea what he was getting at; but liking his looks and knowing I was at liberty to show Arnold's letter so long as I kept silent concerning the reasons behind it, I fished it from my pocket. The young man accepted it, declaring, even while he opened it: "I've met hundreds of Massachusetts men, and they're all colonels. The blow of meeting, in the very heart of Massachusetts, a man who's neither a colonel nor a Massachuser is like to unnerve me."

He glanced through my note. "Oh, ho!" he cried. "To Mr. Steven Nason from a colonel, but not a Massachuser colonel! Oh, ho! Oh, ho! And secrecy in the air! Ah, hah! Well, sir, I'll get you up to Cambridge behind the cleverest black gelding that ever outran a Massachuser colonel, and my name's Burr, from New Jersey. We'll have a drink on it, a drink of Spanish wine that doesn't lie in your stomach for days, like this damned New England rum, a drink for ditch-diggers and pirates."

"Captain Burr," I said, "I think you've never drunk your rum buttered."

"Not captain! Plain Aaron Burr of Princeton in New Jersey, sir. Since I've seen these Massachuser colonels strutting and blowing about, and giving all the rest of us to understand that God made Massachusetts first, working hard at the task, and then tossed off the rest of the world as a sort of adjunct to Massachusetts, sir, I don't want to be any sort of officer unless I can be greater than a colonel. What's more, sir, I know as much about buttered rum as the next man, and I say the drinking of rum, whether hot, cold, buttered, or unbuttered, is no better than swallowing a mouthful of powdered flints. To hell with rum and to hell with colonels, sir."

"To hell with 'em, so far as I know," I said, "barring Colonel Arnold."

"Quite right! Quite right!" Burr said. "He keeps slipping my mind, what with the flux of Massachuser colonels! I except Colonel Arnold with pleasure; but since you wish to be specific, I'll put another in his place—and a general."

"A general? One of our generals?"

"Yes, sir," Burr said, steadying himself against the table, "a general! Imposing manner—noble face—but one of the greatest windbags, sir, ever blown up! A stuffed weskit, sir: nothing but a stuffed weskit!"

While I puzzled over this injudicious speech he shouted for the landlord, who came running in with two baskets, one filled with chickens and ham and new-killed lamb and a goose, and the other with Spanish wine. "For a little dinner to-night," Burr said, winking slyly at me, "with my friend Matt Ogden and some Cambridge young ladies whose mothers don't know they drink. We'll have one of the bottles and be off."

He told me about his health, which was not good, he said, inasmuch as his digestion was bad, so that he could eat only the finest

and most delicate foods. I never knew a man so proud of a weak
stomach, or so desirous of discussing it. He looked as slender and
pale as though he seldom ate anything more substantial than chicken
wings; but the two of us were only half an hour in wrecking a leg of
lamb and two bottles of Spanish wine. That done, we got ourselves
into a light wagon with the hampers. Burr cracked his whip smartly
and we went off across the Lynn marshes in the rosy light of dawn,
skirting slow-moving provision wagons and shouting greetings to
travelers already on their way to join the army or visit friends in it,
or match their wits against its seasoned traders.

With his tongue well loosened by his final bottle of wine, Burr
dropped the subject of his delicate stomach and spoke largely of the
Pennsylvania troops, whom he called a mongrel breed, and the
Rhode Island troops, who were, he said, the meanest human beings
ever spawned, and the Connecticut troops, whom he regarded as
eaten up with hatred and spleen. He waxed eloquent concerning
officers and men from Massachusetts, holding them to be braggarts
and bigots, unbearably democratic and thoroughly unreliable; while
the Virginians, in his opinion, were imitation cavaliers, and poor imitations to boot.

He had even more to say about the young men of Harvard College,
a lot of loose-living, rum-guzzling rakes with an offensive and un-
founded air of superiority; whereas the young gentlemen of the college which he had attended, at Princeton in New Jersey, were vastly
superior persons, both aristocratic and democratic at the same time,
as well as brave and learned, with only the natural instincts of gentlemen for wine and the companionship of the fair sex.

It further developed he had a strong dislike for General Washington, though he admitted there were few to share this opinion with
him. Nevertheless he held to it that General Washington was a stuffed
weskit.

I thought to myself it would not take him long to discover that
the Maine troops, including myself, were somehow distressing, so
there would be nobody in the world but himself and his friends from
Princeton with whom he could be pleased. Yet he seemed sensitive,
and I feared to speak my thoughts lest he burst into tears on my
hands.

The gelding whirled us through the single long street of Malden
and the rummy odors of Medford. When we had crossed the Mystic
marshes and come into Cambridge the breakfast fires of the army
were sending out a haze of smoke; and sharp odors of burning pine

and coffee and roasting ham brought the water to our mouths. Burr dropped me at the beginning of the tents, so I could look for our Arundel men. He leaned down to shake hands. "We're sick of this stale and dreary life, Sam and Matthias and the rest of us. If you know about this business of Colonel Arnold's, give us a hint."

"I know nothing," I said, "but if you go along with him you'll find little that's stale and dreary about it."

Burr saluted me with his whip, cracked it over the gelding so that it sounded like a pistol shot, and went racketing down between the tents as though off in a hurry for Colonel Arnold's headquarters, which he may indeed have been.

* * *

This camp of ours was a strange sight, like a county fair, or a mass of Indian towns stretched out on either side of the road. Here and there were proper tents and marquees; but for the most part the men were housed in huts manufactured from sailcloth or from boards, or from boards and sailcloth put together, or from anything available. There were huts of sods, and huts of stone, huts of brick and of brush fastened together with laths. Three tents were made from the wicker casings of rum bottles; and near by were others built of willow withes in the manner of a basket, the doors and windows neatly wrought in the same material. Straw was used for the lower sections of some; likewise hay; and one was made from the joined halves of molasses barrels, still fragrant.

The soldiery, too, had a peculiar look of being masqueraders at a rout. A few boasted ancient blue militia uniforms, but more wore canvas smocks, or leather hunting frocks, or hickory shirts with the sleeves lopped off.

Seeing a gaunt man crouched over a fire, stirring strips of bacon in a pan with one hand and waving a swarm of flies from his head with the other, I asked him whether he knew the whereabouts of men from near York in Maine.

"Brother," he said coldly, "they're around these tents too much o' nights, looking for anything stealable. If you're going to join up with 'em, keep away from these tents unless you want to be buried alive in our latrine."

"You're not from Maine, then?"

"Brother," he said, removing his bacon from the fire, "if I was one of those mean Mainers I'd be ashamed to show myself in public. I come from Connecticut, Brother, where we eat civilized and act civilized and talk civilized." He held a strip of bacon above his head and dropped it into his mouth.

"Well, sir," I said, "I've just arrived, and I'm unaware of these things. Till now I'd always heard you Connecticutters hated everyone else, and sold clay coffee beans for a living. I'm glad to hear you're growing civilized."

When I started off, he called after me, his mouth full of bacon: "How'll you trade for that musket, Maine?"

I shouted back I couldn't for fear of being paid with wooden nutmegs, and at this he bellowed that I'd find my friends in Colonel Scammen's regiment, three streets down and two streets over, and to sew up my pockets before I went there.

I found them comfortable in tents made of boards and sailcloth; and when Jethro Fish, looking up from mending a pair of shoes, bawled that here was Steven Nason come from Arundel, the Arundel men came out of their tents and away from their morning chores as though an Arundel man were as rare a sight as the great Cham of Tartary.

First they satisfied their curiosity as to how their corn was looking and whether the pollocks had been running and was there plenty of seaweed for fertilizer and how their children and wives were doing and whether anybody else was going to join the army and when money would be raised for the purchase of uniforms. Then they began to acquaint me with their own troubles; for our Arundel people are disgruntled, whatever their condition. I truly believe that if ever our Arundel men become angels in heaven, they will complain that the clouds are over-lumpy for sitting purposes, and that the golden harps are too small for good harping and out of tune to boot.

One thing that irked them was the need of serving under officers they had not elected themselves, so that they were unable to consult with them and advise them as they might otherwise have done. We New Englanders like to choose our own leaders; and I know that in past wars many Maine men wouldn't fight unless they could name their commanders.

"Why, hell, Steven," said young Pierce Murphy from Cleaves's Cove, "this Colonel Scammen, he's a good enough soldier, I guess, but I don't know him and I can't go up to him and call him Charley and tell him he's *got* to let me go home for a couple of weeks, same's I could if *you* was colonel, or Jesse Dorman, or somebody I *know!*"

"Yes," growled Noah Cluff, "and not knowing 'em, you got to salute 'em. Hell, I've saluted so many of these dod-rotted colonels since

George the First took holt that my trigger finger's all stiffened up!"

"George the First?"

"Washington," Nathaniel Lord explained.

"What's the matter with him?"

"Oh, hell; nothing!" Sile Abbott said. "For a Virginian, he's pretty good."

"He'd be good, even if he was a Connecticutter," said Murphy. "General Ward, he commanded before Washington. You never saw old Artemas Ward out on the lines all day, the way Washington is. Ward kept himself planted in a chair so tight that if Washington hadn't come along he'd have sprouted. Washington don't pay attention to cannon balls, any more'n he would to mosquitoes. Only thing wrong with him, he's a crazy fool about saluting. What I say is, if you know an officer, it don't do no good to salute him. If you don't know him, what's the use?"

"Anyway, he's got the British bottled up so's they can't move," said Dorman proudly. "He runs a couple thousand of us up on a hill around dusk, and by daylight we got a new fort dug."

"Those lousy British take a month to dig what we dig in a night," Noah Cluff said.

"They can't get no food nor nothing," Nathaniel Lord told me.

"Yes," said Abbott, "and there ain't anything for us to do except watch to see those damned Connecticutters don't steal the locks off our guns! I'm sick of hanging around here digging forts and saluting! I want to go home!"

"Who don't?" growled one of the Burbank boys.

James Dunn's face rose impressively behind his fellow troopers. "If we're not going to march, I'd ruther work in a shipyard. People in shipyards ain't as mean as soldiers."

"By gravy!" Murphy said, "that ain't far wrong! I don't know how they got so many downright mean men in this army! The Rhode Islanders ain't a damn bit better than the Connecticutters; and there ain't *nuthin'* meaner'n a New Yorker."

"Except a Pennsylvanian," Cluff observed dryly. "If the British don't come out, I'd just as lief fight the Pennsylvanians."

"I was directed here," I said, "by a soldier who complained Maine men would steal anything."

My neighbors looked baffled.

"We borrowed a barrel of cider from the Rhode Islanders a couple nights ago," Abbott admitted.

"It wasn't a Rhode Islander. It was a Connecticutter."

A contemptuous growl greeted this information. "We caught three Connecticutters trying to steal our extra stockings last week," Jesse Dorman complained. "They'd cut the buttons right off your pants if you didn't watch 'em!"

Our conversation was interrupted by a rasping shout of: "Don't you ever salute officers?" It came from a red-faced man in a blue militia coat, with a yellow band on his sleeve. He hated us: no doubt of that.

"This is a deliberate insult," he said loudly. "After all the orders issued concerning saluting, you turn your backs on me! It's intolerable!"

He was rewarded by vacant stares and a thick silence.

"I demand an answer!" he roared, looking blue around the gills.

"Sir," Jesse Dorman said plaintively, "we didn't see you!"

"That's no excuse! A soldier's expected to see what's going on around him. You'd be in a fine pickle if you didn't see the British sneaking up on you some night!"

"Colonel," said Noah Cluff, "our backs was to you."

"Well," the officer said, "they ain't now! You see me now, don't you!" He stared at me, prodding a fat forefinger toward my chest. "Why don't you salute?"

"Sir," I said, "I'm not in the army. I don't know how to salute."

A shrill whisper came from somewhere behind me. I recognized Asa Hutchins's voice. "Kiss him, then!" it said.

The colonel, purple as a huckleberry, peered furiously at the line of expressionless faces, but seemed to find them little to his liking. Muttering something about "whooping, holloing gentlemen soldiers," he took himself down the street, and I, misliking the appearance of his back, set off in the opposite direction.

Desiring no trouble, I touched my hat to everyone I passed and so arrived without incident at the common, where I was shown the square house in which General Washington had his headquarters.

My all-night journey had made my eyes sticky, so after washing down a pork pie with two quarts of beer at the Laughing Dog Tavern, touching my hat to every man who bore a military air and several who did not, I went into a hay field, put my arms around my musket and pack, so no Connecticutter or Rhode Islander could steal them from me, and slept four hours.

I was awakened by what I thought was a slamming door; but on hearing a louder slamming near at hand, I knew it for an explosion. Here was the war at last, I thought; so I hastened to General Washington's headquarters, preferring to be under a roof with others if there was to be any extensive dropping of cannon balls.

There were sentries in the general's headquarters, neatly uniformed, like Mr. Burr, and extremely military, rattling and slapping muskets whenever an officer passed. I showed one of them my letter and was directed to the office of General Gates, Adjutant General of the army. He was a fussy-looking man with a sly eye and stringy gray hair: better fitted, it seemed to me, for sewing buttons on General Washington's shirts than for fighting his battles. None the less, he received me politely, bidding me wait in a corner room.

I waited an hour, dozing in the warmth of the late August afternoon, when there was a prodigious clatter and crash in the hall. Thinking a British shell had burst through the wall of the house, I snatched up my musket and pack and fled into the entryway. There, rising from the floor, was the hugesome bulk of Cap Huff, gorgeously attired in a gold-laced blue coat, doeskin breeches and shiny black boots, a sword at his belt and spurs on his heels the size of cookypunches. He greeted me with a clanking of spurs and accoutrements, and by tripping over his sword.

"By God! Stevie!" he shouted, clapping his vast paws on my shoulders and giving me a squeeze that almost broke my neck, "I bet they're going to give us another clout at that fox-faced Frenchy!"

"Look here," I said, pushing him away with the butt of my musket, "have they made you a general? What are you doing, falling down this way?"

Before he could answer, the door of the front room was jerked open and the face of Colonel Arnold popped out and glared at us from round eyes; then popped back again.

At the same time General Gates came up beside Cap and said coldly: "Colonel, may I know your name and organization?"

"Why, yes," Cap said carelessly, "Huff."

"*Colonel* Huff?" Gates persisted.

"Yes; Huff!" Cap declared.

Seeing something was not as it should be, and fearing I might be somehow hindered in my interview with Colonel Arnold if Cap grew restive under this questioning, I swung my musket butt against the small of his back. Cap groaned and sank to one knee. Dropping my musket and pack, I caught him and steadied him.

"Sir, I think the heat made this gentleman ill," I said.

"I think he's mad!" Gates said.

"It may be," I admitted. "With your permission I'll take him outdoors." It was in my mind to guide him to the field where I had taken my nap, and tie him so he'd be there on my return. My planning went for nothing when the door of the front room was again jerked open by Colonel Arnold.

"General," he said to Gates, "General Washington asks that these two gentlemen, whom I've had the pleasure of meeting, be admitted to his room."

"Certainly, Colonel!" Gates said, "but I fear, Colonel, the gentleman in the colonel's uniform is ill."

I kicked Cap as hard as I could and helped him to his feet. He blinked and felt of his back. "Sir," I said to Colonel Arnold, who was examining Cap's uniform with as much interest as Gates had shown, "he's recovering: he'll soon be himself."

Colonel Arnold nodded and led the way to the front room, into which he ushered us, Cap still leaning against me, groaning and pressing his hand to his back. General Washington sat behind a long table and watched us come in. He was an imposing man with broad, square shoulders, powdered hair and a ruddy face a little marked with smallpox—taller than Cap Huff, though smaller seeming from the fineness of his features and the lack of coarseness about his hands or waist. I thought, when I saw the straight line of his lips and the intentness with which he watched Cap, that I wouldn't like to give him reason for speaking harshly to me.

"General," Colonel Arnold said, when he had closed the door, "this is Steven Nason of Arundel, who had been far up Dead River when I first met him, as I told you, and has reasons to wish to go safely to Quebec. And this gentleman," he added, pointing at Cap, who passed his hand clumsily over his face, "is Squire Huff of Portsmouth, who helped seize the powder in Fort William and Mary, as you already know."

General Washington nodded. "I hadn't heard," he said to Cap in a pleasant, deep voice that vibrated as though from overmuch giving of orders in harsh weather, "I hadn't heard you'd been made a colonel."

Cap shook his head like a dog with a fly on his ear. "Who hit me?" he asked.

Colonel Arnold tweaked his sleeve. "The general asked you a question."

Cap fumbled for his sword and leaned on it. "I hadn't heard it, either," he said, "and damned good reason! A scurvy rat in Portsmouth bribed the gaoler to lock me up and let no word reach my friends. I've heard nothing since Jonah got out of the whale!"

"Then you're not a colonel?" General Washington said impassively.

"Why, hell, General," Cap growled, "I've been in gaol! If it hadn't been for Colonel Arnold sending me a letter I wouldn't have this sword or this uniform, or be out of gaol, even, the dirty weasels!"

"In time of war," General Washington said, "a person found within the lines in a uniform to which he's not entitled is liable to be shot for a spy."

"A spy!" Cap bawled. "I'll go back and kill that damned son of a goat!" He threw his sword on the floor with a clatter, and wrenched an arm from his coat.

General Washington got up from behind his table and placed a hand restrainingly on his arm. "Let's have the full tale," he said. He glanced grimly at Colonel Arnold; but it suddenly came to me there was no grimness about his look; merely a sober intimation that what he was about to hear would be enjoyable.

"Well, sir," Cap said, "there ain't much to tell. There was a tailor that dealt with the British officers, and I suspicioned he'd been the ringleader of them as put me in gaol. So when I was let out I went to his house and took him by the collar and held him over his stove, and he promised to make me a uniform. Well, General, he done it, and gave me a sword and a hat to boot. Yes, sir, and to show his affection he let me have a silver tea set and a bag of hard money that your honor might find handy for the army." Growling ferociously, he finished stripping off his coat and threw it on a chair, placing his sword across it. Under the coat he wore a shirt of India goods. I wondered where he got it. "Anybody that wants that coat can have it," Cap said.

"We're all needy," the general said. "I make no doubt we can find a taker."

"Is there anything the matter with it?" Cap asked.

"Why, no," the general said. "It's fitting enough, in the proper place. It happens to be the field uniform of a colonel in the Royal Marines—the rarest of all military ranks. There are only four marine colonels in the entire British army. I think, sir, you'll find a leather hunting shirt more suited to your needs."

He turned to me then; and I repeat now what I have always said: that a man had to be careless and thoughtless not to straighten up under his cold blue eye and do the best he could.

"Sir," he said, "Colonel Arnold tells me you set off for Quebec as a boy by way of the Kennebec."

"Yes, sir."

"You had no fear of making this trip successfully?" he asked.

"Why, no, sir. My father was with me."

"Would you be as sanguine to-day, without your father?"

"Certainly, sir, if I could pick my companions."

"So you wouldn't travel that route to Quebec with anyone?"

I studied for a time. "Sir, I'd prefer to go with somebody who knew the woods or had some special desire for going. Then I'd be sure of getting there."

"Would you be willing to go with Colonel Arnold?"

"Not only willing, sir, but happy."

"And with your friend here?" The general meant Cap Huff.

"I'd count myself fortunate."

General Washington turned to his desk and consulted a small map. "Now," he said, "when you traveled toward Quebec as a boy did you experience any difficulties?"

"No, sir. Not while our canoe was driven by good paddlers."

"How did it happen you never got there?"

"We learned the man we pursued had got clean away."

"But you could have made it?"

"Easily, sir, so far as we knew."

"In how long a time?"

"From Swan Island, near the mouth of the Kennebec, in eight or nine days, sir, if all went well."

"What do you mean by 'If all went well'?"

"If we found no drought, sir, and no floods. If we got food when we wanted it. If we hit no rocks—kept from spilling in rapids. If all our muskets weren't lost, and none of us broke a leg."

"And if such things happened?" the general asked. "How long would you be then?"

"God knows, sir."

"Do you know others who made the trip?"

"Yes, sir: the Abenaki Natanis, my friend, made it several times."

"Several times?" the general asked quickly. "Then this Natanis has been in Quebec more than once since the British have held it?"

"Yes, sir," I said. I saw him shoot a quick look at Colonel Arnold.

"Do you know of others?" he asked.

"Many others. Lieutenant Hutchins of Rogers' Rangers took a message from Amherst to Wolfe by way of the Kennebec three weeks

before my father and I went up. I've read the wampum rolls of the
Abenakis, and seen the records of how Father Drouillettes went
twice from Cushnoc to Quebec and back, and how Father Rale went
up from Norridgewock. There was an Englishman named Montresor
who traveled that road a year after my father and I. Natanis says
Montresor drew a map, though I never saw it. Many Norridgewock
Indians traveled to Quebec each year to trade or see relatives. Now
all of them have gone to St. Francis, which means they went by way
of the Kennebec, squaws and all. Assagunticooks from the Androscoggin make the trip often. It's no great trick for a woodsman; but
no one ever made it without knowing he'd been on a journey that
near graveled him."

"Let me ask you, sir," General Washington said, "whether there
are men in your section capable of making such a trip?"

"Plenty, sir; good woodsmen and hunters, hardy in the woods."

"Then if we could get an army of such men, they'd all be capable
of making it?"

"An army!" I cried.

"An army, sir, capable of taking Quebec."

"What would it do for food?" I asked, thinking of the tumult an
army would make in passing through the forest; thinking of the tumbled mass of rocks at the carrying places: of the bogs, the rapids,
the trackless wilderness.

"It would carry its own food," the general said, "but that's not the
question. The question is whether, if we could get an army of men
like Colonel Arnold and you and Huff, it would be capable of traveling to Quebec by way of the Kennebec?"

"Gosh all hemlock, Stevie!" Cap exploded. "Yes! Capable of traveling there and carrying Quebec away in our pants pockets!"

"Sir," I said, "with favorable conditions, I think an army could do
it."

Colonel Arnold had sat gnawing his nails while the general questioned me. Now he spoke. "General, we'll make our own favorable
conditions!"

"Colonel," the general said, "I know you'll try, and I hope you'll
have better fortune at making favorable conditions than has fallen
to my lot when I've attempted it."

XIV

GENERAL WASHINGTON spoke through tight lips, which made him seem angry, though I learned later he compressed his lips to prevent his teeth from slipping or clacking, they being badly fitted to his mouth and therefore insecure. "You're familiar with this Northern country, gentlemen," he said, "and I'd like to ask you a few questions."

"General," Cap roared, obviously attracted to him, "you go right ahead and ask anything!"

The general studied a paper on his desk while I might have counted five. Then he eyed Cap grimly. "I have been told by Colonel Montgomery, in whom I repose great confidence, that every New Englander is a general, and not one of them a soldier. Therefore I'm pleased to find a New Englander who invites questioning, but doesn't insist on forcing his opinion on us."

While Cap Huff stared blankly, the general turned to me.

"What, in your opinion, should be used for the transportation of the supplies of such an army: bateaux or canoes?"

"Both," I said, thinking of the labor of transporting heavy Kennebec bateaux across the Great Carrying Place.

"I'm told," the general said, "that the roughness of the water and the sharpness of the rocks would endanger supplies carried in canoes."

"They might," I admitted. "And they might be dangerous for bateaux, too. Those who make the trip always go by canoe. You don't know what the carries are like, sir! Miles of 'em! Miles! To carry bateaux would be—would be——"

"You'll have to admit," the general said, "that wherever a canoe can be carried, a bateau can be carried too."

I was silent, unwilling to say either Yes or No.

"A bateau, General, requires less skill than a canoe," declared Colonel Arnold. "Canoes are more easily broken."

"Sir," I said, "I can find you enough Indians to take canoes safely wherever we'd have to go."

General Washington got up to stand at the window, staring out at the dusty elm on the common and the knots of militiamen and officers who straggled back and forth beneath it. Then he turned to us, speaking over our heads, so I couldn't tell whether he spoke to Colonel Arnold or me. "Sir, I know Indians. They're cowardly, plundering, murdering dogs, contemptuous of treaties, devoid of humanity. On the darkest day of my life, twenty years ago, when we were retiring from Fort Necessity, where the damned French had spotted my honor with tricks of words, I was deserted by Indians, threatened by Indians, attacked by Indians, my medicine chest destroyed by Indians, and two of my wounded murdered and scalped by Indians."

"Dirty, ill-begotten, diseased, bug-eating sons of goats!" Cap Huff muttered.

"For years," the general said, "I saw those red hellions let loose on us by the French, in defiance of all the rules of civilized warfare. I won't have it said I'm responsible for their use in this war."

"Sir," I protested, "you're speaking of another breed of Indians. The Abenakis of the Kennebec and Androscoggin are honest and brave. I've lived among 'em and traveled with 'em. They'd be our friends. There's no man could give us more help in reaching Quebec than the Abenaki Natanis and the Abenaki Hobomok and the white man Paul Higgins, a sachem of the Assagunticooks."

"You see!" the general said to Colonel Arnold. Then he turned to me. "Unknowingly you've damned yourself out of your own mouth. We've had reports from the Kennebec. This Natanis is one of the spies of Carleton, who commands at Quebec. The help he'd give you would be to carry information straight to Carleton, and our army would never cross the St. Lawrence."

"Sir," I said, "I don't believe it! Where'd you get your information?"

"When did you speak with him last?" the general snapped.

"Not for two years—for three years; but I saved his life, and I sent a message to him only this summer, saying I wanted his help against my enemies."

"Ah," the general said, "and what was his answer?"

"Why, he hasn't answered yet; but no answer's needed. I saved his life."

Seeing from the amused glint in his eye that he took little account

of what I said, I would have pressed the matter further, but he
stopped me with a peremptory gesture.

"One more thing. I gather Colonel Arnold wishes to use you as a
guide and counselor. It seems to me your friend here, being less
familiar with the upper Kennebec, ought to be subject to your orders.
What rank, should you say, would be likely to make you most valuable to such an army as we have discussed?"

I recalled the purple-faced colonel who wished to be saluted, and
Burr's remarks about officers, and said I would wish to remain as a
guide with no rank at all, so that there might be no jealousy of my
movements, and freedom from the supervision of small and ignorant
men.

"Then, gentlemen," General Washington said, "I make both of you
guides, with the seniority going to Nason. You shall have a captain's
pay, with the chance of a commission at the end of the campaign,
if this seems satisfactory."

"All I want," I said, "is opportunity to go to Quebec."

"If you're asking me," Cap rumbled, "I'd ruther be a colonel on
this journey and nothing afterward; or nothing at all on this campaign
and a colonel afterward."

"I greatly hope," said General Washington politely, "you won't
be disappointed." He turned abruptly to Arnold. "Take them along,
Colonel, and give them their orders. It's a hazardous enterprise; but
if successful it will realize results of the utmost importance. It may
be of the greatest consequence to the liberties of America; and on
your conduct and courage, and that of your officers and soldiers, may
depend not only your own success and honor, but the safety and
welfare of the whole country."

To us he added: "There's another thing to remember: we're engaged in a war with a people so depraved and barbarous as to be
the wickedest nation on earth. They're ruled by a king who's a tyrant,
and ministers who are scoundrels. The British people, inspired by
bloody and insatiable malice, are lost to every sense of virtue; and
it's essential that no news of this proposed army reach the ears of
the enemy."

At this he gave us his hand and we came away, Cap absent-mindedly picking up his sword and coat as he came. He might even have
donned them again had not the general called after him to leave
them, together with his spurs, in General Gates's office.

As Colonel Arnold hurried us to his headquarters near the college
buildings, he was saluted respectfully by everyone we passed, which

led me to say we had heard in Arundel of his brave attack on Ticonderoga and St. John's, and that Maine was proud of his success.

He made no reply until he had led us into his reception room and thrown himself down at his desk. Then he scowled at us, his face as black as newly plowed earth, and puffy from anger.

"Success!" he cried sharply. "Didn't you hear how they investigated me?"

We shook our heads.

He thumped the table with his fist. "By God!" he said, "it was I who suggested taking Ticonderoga; but because I waited to be commissioned by the Massachusetts Congress, so to do it legally and in order, I found the Bennington mob ahead of me, acting on money supplied by Connecticut. A mob: that's what it was: without commissions or standing, and headed by three of the greatest boors that ever lived—Ethan Allen, James Easton, and John Brown! The Green Mountain Party, they called themselves, and they fired on me twice, by God, for refusing to obey their thieving orders! Rum and loot was what they wanted; and before I could make a start on fortifying the places we'd captured, I had to bring matters out of the confusion caused by Allen's men, save citizens from being plundered of their private property, and make it possible for persons to go about without being constantly in peril of abuse and death at the hands of these Green Mountain Boys!"

He seized the edge of the table, lifted it six inches and thumped it down again. "And what did *they* care about fortifying Ticonderoga and Crown Point?" he demanded. "What did *they* care about strengthening them so they couldn't be recaptured by the British? Not a thing! Not one damned thing! What Easton and Brown wanted was position, and titles that would let them wear handsome uniforms! Those two Berkshire yokels wanted to be colonels—Colonel Easton and Colonel John Brown—when they were no more fit to be colonels than Job's turkey was! They wanted to be colonels—wanted to get me out of the way so they'd have a free hand; and to do it they resorted to politics!"

"Politics?" Cap Huff asked. "Ain't this a war? It was politics got me put into Portsmouth gaol! I dunno as I want to be in a war if there's anything as dishonest as politics connected with it!"

Arnold snorted. "A politician can't keep politics out of anything! You ought to know that! Easton and Brown got a Connecticut colonel on their side—poor, weak, helpless Hinman; and then they let it be known that the Connecticut troops who had come up to help garrison Crown Point and Ticonderoga objected to serving under me. I held a Massachusetts commission, they said; and Connecticut troops would suffer keenly if obliged to serve under an officer who had been commissioned by Massachusetts! So I got 'em together and talked to 'em. All they had to do, I said, was show me a better leader, and I'd get out and let him command in my place. And by God, sir, Easton—Easton, the coward, who wet his gun when we crossed the lake to attack Ticonderoga, and so had to go into hiding and dry it out while the rest of us attacked—Easton, by God, had the effrontery to say the Connecticut men would feel safer under him! Safer!"

Arnold laughed sourly. "I took the liberty of breaking his head; and on his refusing to draw like a gentleman, he having a hangar by his side and a case of loaded pistols in his pocket, I kicked him heartily and ordered him from the Point!"

"But," I protested, "a man like that couldn't——"

"Listen," Arnold said, "a dirty politician can do anything! Anything! God protect me from a country politician! Even with two thirds of his body paralyzed, he can be twice as dirty as any city politician! Easton and Brown are country politicians, and they're dirty! They ran to Massachusetts and Connecticut, playing dirty politics in holes and corners; and just as I was making a start on fortifying Crown Point, sir, up came three gentlemen from the Massachusetts Congress to investigate my spirit, capacity, and conduct! *My* spirit, capacity, and conduct, for God's sake, when spirit, capacity, and conduct are as rare in these colonies as blue horses! What was more, they had full authority, and they ordered me to turn over the command to Hinman—to Hinman and Easton and Brown!"

"I'd 'a' seen 'em in hell first!" Cap Huff bawled.

Arnold nodded. "That's what my men said. They mutinied at the order, and I had to disband 'em! God help the man that's hounded by a dirty politician! There's no lie too black for him to tell: no insinuation too foul for him to make! At all events, Easton and Brown got what they were after; and Ticonderoga and Crown Point are just as I left 'em! Not one stroke of work did Hinman or Easton or Brown do on either place!"

"I hate a man like that man Easton," Cap declared, "always getting people investigated and interfering with peaceable folk! All you got to do is show him to me, Colonel! I'll pull his hat down over his nose so he'll never get it off!"

The colonel smiled faintly, so that the lumps and knobs of anger were ironed from his face. "Oh, well," he said, "it's ancient history now! We have other business on hand, and it's time you were off on it. I'm obliged to you, and so is the general, for confirming our opinions of the expedition we're undertaking."

"His opinions about bateaux are wrong," I said. "Also about Natanis."

"His opinions are my opinions, sir," Arnold reminded me. "The loggers on the Kennebec use bateaux; and we'll use bateaux. That's been decided, and the bateaux ordered."

"Sir," I said, "I've waited years to go to Quebec. It's the same to me whether I go by canoe or bateau or dough-trough. However we go, I'll get there. I'd have advanced no opinion unless I thought my advice was needed as well as asked."

"That's better," said the colonel genially. "Now here's the plan." He unrolled a bad map of New England and the St. Lawrence.

"It's the same old scheme of a double attack on Canada, with one element added: that of surprise. General Schuyler, an able soldier, will come openly down the St. Lawrence and attack Montreal, thus drawing all available British forces in Canada to the defense of that city. Meanwhile, we'll ascend the Kennebec, a route regarded as impossible by the British. We'll come down the Chaudière River onto the St. Lawrence directly opposite Quebec. The fortifications of Quebec are crumbling; the armament bad; the French inhabitants disgruntled; there's no garrison of any moment. With speed and good fortune we can walk into Quebec as you'd walk into an inn on a winter's night. We'll unite all of North America against the English—leave them no spot on which they can land men and supplies unless they can first wrench it from us and then hold it."

My brain was a tumbled scroll of brilliant pictures—of Mary, lovely and slender and golden-haired, lying in my arms; of my father on the deck of the *Black Duck,* telling Arnold how the Abenaki art of war was the art of ambushing and surprising an enemy; of Guerlac, with his pale face and his slit ear, standing helpless, my bayonet at his breast; of our close-packed ranks, blue-clad and soldierly, passing between the palaces of Quebec while laughing men and beautiful women cheered us; and finally there slipped into my mind, unbidden, the cruel cleft in the rocks up which canoes must be dragged in carrying over Skowhegan Falls—that, and Phoebe Dunn in her jack boots and broad brass-studded belt, jeering and jeering with her eyes.

I was brought back to earth by a gusty sigh from Cap Huff. "Quebec," he said, scratching his nose contemplatively, "will be richer than Portsmouth." I knew he was thinking of the capacity of his breeches' pockets.

"What we'll do," Colonel Arnold went on, disregarding Cap, "is take three companies of riflemen to lead the way, Morgan's Virginians for one. They'll make you New Englanders look like old women in the woods, if you aren't careful. For the rest we want woodsmen who can handle bateaux and axes; who can stand hardships. We want a lot of Maine men—tough Maine men. I know all Maine men are tough, but we want 'em extra tough. That's the first thing I want you to do. Go to your friends here in this camp and select a few. Tell 'em what's wanted. Tell 'em to be cautious about it, but to spread the news. And tell 'em when the time comes, to volunteer. I want the best men in the army, and I'll see they have the best officers. I guarantee it: the pick of the colonies—Christopher Greene of Rhode Island, Timothy Bigelow of Massachusetts, Henry Dearborn of New Hampshire: fit to be generals, all of them! Daniel Morgan, a leader for Virginia to be proud of—Thayer from Rogers' Rangers—Roger Enos, who made his mark in the British army: there's no better men anywhere in the world! Understand?"

We nodded.

"Very good!" Arnold got up and prowled restlessly around the room, swarthy and broad-shouldered and powerful, as light on his feet as a girl who walks down the street with the eyes of twenty men on her. He looked up at the top of the doorway, and I felt it was in his mind to leap up and chin himself on it, but that the dignity of his position restrained him.

"Do this to-day," he went on, throwing himself down at his desk again. "Then, to-night, start for the Kennebec. The bateaux will be built by Colburn at Agry's Point, below Fort Western. Go there. Watch them. Get what intelligence you can. Talk with the Indians. Find suitable clothing for me. Get me some means of rapid transportation. Within a week or ten days we'll follow. We'll go by land to Newburyport, then by sloop and schooner to Fort Western, and thence by the river to Quebec."

He flirted his hand, as if it would be done as easily as travelers cross our river at low tide. "To be sure all's understood, you might repeat your orders."

While I repeated his instruction to me he wrote two letters for us. Mine I have yet in my green seaman's chest. I prize it as being from the bravest man I ever knew.

To those engaged on the Expedition to Quebec:

GENTLEMEN—This is borne by Steven Nason of Arundel, who is gathering intelligence and furthering our interests. On his secrecy you may depend, and I should take it as a particular favor if you would give him what assistance, information, and trust he may require. Your compliance will much oblige, Gent., Your friend and humble serv't.

B. ARNOLD.

He took a tin box from a drawer of the desk, unlocked it, flipped out a roll, and caught it deftly in mid-air. "Here's fifty Spanish trade dollars. Buy what you must, and ask for the rest in the name of the United Colonies. Now be off, and expect me at Fort Western in ten days."

"Sir," I said, preparing to go, "we spoke once of a Quebec gentleman named Guerlac. Is anything known of him?"

Arnold's eyes widened. "Why, yes. Guerlac, I understand, occupies himself innocently in Quebec. I'm hopeful you and I may pay a pleasant call on him and his charming sister, and at no distant date. Until then, sir, I'll take it as a favor if you'll forget his name and his very existence."

Cap Huff brooded over this remark as we set off up the street. "Colonels," he growled, "are a plague. They may be necessary to some, but not to me! We'll have to rid ourselves of this one of yours if ever we hope to show Guerlac any more light-fingered affection. Pleasant calls, hell! When I call on Guerlac it'll be as pleasant as a dog-fight!"

A sutler's cart caught his eye, and he left me to speak to the sutler. I could see he was displaying his new jack boots and doeskin breeches, so I suspected a trade was brewing, and was not surprised when he told me to go on: that he would join me later. I gave him the address: Ivory Fish's tent in Colonel Scammen's regiment, next to the Connecticut troops, and went on without him.

I had finished enthusing Noah Cluff and Nathaniel Lord and Jethro Fish over the Quebec expedition, and was eating lamb stew and dumplings with the Arundel men in front of Jethro's tent, when Cap Huff popped around the corner hurriedly, ignored our greetings, and said hoarsely: "You don't know me and never saw me and never heard of me." With that he dodged into Jethro's tent.

While we puzzled over this announcement, four soldiers ran down the street, one of them saying, "He came this way!" I recognized him as the Connecticut trooper who had warned me against the thievery of Maine men.

"Hey, Maine!" he said, his sallow face bitter. "Where's the big man that came past here just now?"

"Nobody came past here. What man was it?"

"Look, Maine," the Connecticutter said angrily, "if I knew what man it was I wouldn't be asking you! He talked like one of you lousy Mainers, but if we catch him he'll look like cold pork!"

"What did he do?"

The Connecticutter cursed foully. "He came staggering down the street, all smeared with dust. When he got in front of our tents he caved in. We went out to look at him, and he said some Virginia riflemen had jumped him and tooken his coat and musket. He said he was dying, mebbe. We drug him into a tent and went to get a doctor, and when we came back he'd slid out under the back with a musket and a powder horn and two shirts and a knife and a blanket."

The Connecticutter's three companions had gone along; so he favored us with a suspicious stare, and joined them.

After we had eaten our lamb and dumplings a sutler's cart drove up. "This Jethro Fish's tent?" the sutler asked, peering at us nervously. He threw a bundle at our feet, whereat two jack boots and a pair of doeskin breeches sailed out of Jethro's tent. We passed the bundle into the tent, and handed the breeches and the boots to the sutler. I thought he intended to turn and go back the way he had come; but he was stopped by a hoarse whisper from the tent. "You'd better be moving out of Cambridge."

The sutler nodded, looking apprehensively behind him.

"Just a minute," said the whisper. "We'll go with you."

I bade my Arundel friends good-bye, and mounted beside the sutler. In a moment Cap Huff, clad in leather breeches, woolen stockings, and stout buckled shoes, emerged from the tent with a rifle and a pack. He burrowed into the back of the cart, which sagged and wobbled under his weight. Jethro, with a smothered exclamation, raced into his tent and struck a light; but since he emerged calmly a few moments later, I knew his belongings were intact.

We squeaked off into the warm, sweet August night. When we reached the salty odors and the cold air blanket of the Mystic marshes, Cap emerged from the back, rubbing the sweat and dust from his face, and squeezed himself onto the seat with us.

"You see, Stevie," he said, sensing my disapproval, "it ain't as if we all stood on an equal footing. Here we were, going off on a hard trip. Well, I *had* to have something to wear, Stevie; and after what the colonel told us about Connecticutters, seemed as if they was the ones that ought to have things tooken from 'em. My gosh, Stevie, they'll be getting free uniforms and everything they need before you know it!"

"Say," the sutler exclaimed, "did that coat belong to you?"

"That was my coat," Cap assured him. "When I left it with General Gates I didn't know I'd have any more use for it. Did the general say anything when you asked for it?"

"Well," the sutler said, "he made me sign a paper saying it was for the colonel."

"What colonel?" I asked quickly.

"Easton," the sutler said in some surprise. "Didn't you say Easton? I wouldn't want to get into any trouble—not over just one coat!"

Cap eyed him doubtfully. "Was it Easton or Hinman?" Then he brightened. "That paper won't mean anything if you let your beard grow."

"I can't grow a beard until November," the sutler said unhappily. "It makes my face itch in warm weather."

"Well, my gorry!" Cap bawled. "Ain't it worth a itch? Those clothes of mine are worth fifty dollars, hard money, if they're worth a farthing; and these things you handed me for 'em ain't worth a cent over twelve dollars!"

The sutler gloomily refused to proceed farther than Malden, so we hailed an empty provision wagon whose driver agreed to let us ride provided we would drive and let him sleep. It was a good thing that I was along; for Cap, having a long trip in prospect and unknown expenses to meet, would otherwise have placed the sleeping driver gently on the Lynn marshes and sold the horse and cart in Salem for what he could get.

By plundering a score of orchards and kicking two score dogs that came out to protect them, Cap contrived to keep from starving until we reached Newburyport, where we found the *Eunice* anchored off Tracy's wharf, trim and cozy-looking in the early morning sun.

Cap let out a bellow as we came onto the dock, and Phoebe, in her old gingham swimming dress, whipped up over the stern like a golden otter, and down into the cabin.

She sculled over to us a little later, sea boots, brass-studded belt, cat's eyes and all, a blue cotton handkerchief knotted around her wet hair. She had beans and mustard pickles for breakfast, she said, and one of us must go to the bakery for two loaves of hot bread. This I did, bringing back an apple pie to top off with, thinking to

please Phoebe with it, but found her so busy with Cap, slapping him
for his uncouth remarks about the color of her skin and eluding his
great grasping hands, that she seemed to care as little for me as for
the pie. I spoke to her harshly, saying that if she was not interested
in my return she might at least show some interest in the welfare of
her husband.

She gave the oar to Cap and scrambled over to sit beside me,
slipping her arm in mine.

"I *am* interested, Steven, but I hated to start talking to you because
then I'd have to tell you I couldn't take you back to Arundel."

"You've got to," I said. "Why can't you?"

"Because, Steven, Nathaniel Tracy had orders from General Washington, and there's eleven sloops and schooners obliged to stay here
to take an army to Fort Western. The *Eunice* is one, Steven, and I
can't leave without orders."

"If that's all," I said, "I'll see Tracy so you can carry us up. What
Cap and I don't know about that army isn't worth knowing, is it,
Cap?"

"Hell, no!" Cap roared. "George couldn't have done anything about
it unless we agreed to help him; hey, Stevie?"

"George who?" Phoebe asked.

"George Washington, of course," Cap said. "Why, when we left,
George said: 'Now remember, boys, this is practically your army, so
take good care of it and don't mislay it.'"

"Behave, Cap!" Phoebe said.

"Hope to die!" Cap bellowed. "When we was leaving, George was
that overcome he said to me, 'Captain Huff,' he said, 'go on in and
see Gates on your way out and leave some little thing I can remember you by: a coat or something, so's I'll have something to remind
me there's a few brave, honest men in the world when I look around
at these lousy, thieving rascals from Connecticut and Rhode Island
and Maine.' Didn't he, Stevie?"

"Those were his very words."

"Steven," Phoebe said after a little pause, and she seemed fearful
of my answer, "is this army for Quebec?"

"It's a secret, Phoebe, but that's where we're for: Quebec."

She said nothing. We clambered into the sloop, getting out of our
clothes as soon as Phoebe had lowered the mainsail a little to make
a screen for us, and going over the side to rid ourselves of the sweat
and dust of our journey. Cap, holding to a rope made fast to the stern
davits, sloshed himself up and down in the river like a wild-eyed

sea cow, blowing spray halfway up the mainsail and thumping on the vessel's side with his ham-like fist until Phoebe thrust her head out of the hatch in a fury, threatening to burst the bean pot on his noodle unless he gave over.

If there is a better or tastier breakfast than beans, mustard pickle, coffee, hot bread and an apple pie with cinnamon, I have never found it in many years of traveling—unless, of course, the beans be badly baked, so that they rattle on the plate or swim in grease, as always happens with cooks who don't understand the trick of baking them.

When we had taken off the sharp edge of our hunger on the beans and divided the pie into three equal pieces, Phoebe wanted more information, nor did I consider she had been overexpeditious about it.

"Did you see James?" she asked. I told her I had and found him no different than might be expected. Since I had expressed myself on the subject of James before they were wed, I forbore to add to this explanation, except to say he was weary of camp life, and desirous of marching in a soldierly manner.

"Where does he want to march to?" Phoebe asked. I told her I didn't know, any more than he did; that he would doubtless be content to march in a circle.

"Does he plan to march to Quebec?"

"I don't know. I said nothing to him about it, because I wouldn't wish to have my life depend on his quickness in a fight. Those who volunteer will be taken, and God knows there'll be many among us no better than James Dunn, and maybe not as good."

"Poor dear!" Phoebe said. "Would it be better for him to stay in camp, Steven, or go with this army?"

"How do I know? I've heard my father say there never yet was a New Englander but went half crazy in a camp, what with homesickness and smallpox, and who didn't thrive on a campaign provided his generals weren't British donkeys like Braddock or Abercrombie. Yet I can't tell what this campaign might be. It's a more serious business to march to Quebec than to walk to Falmouth for a gingham dress."

She showed no further disposition to question me, so I took the punt and sculled ashore to see Nathaniel Tracy. I found him in a brocaded dressing gown, pottering among the tall phloxes in the front yard of his mansion, built out of the earnings of a score of brigs and schooners.

"Sir," I said, when he wrinkled his eyes at me good-naturedly over the top of eight-sided spectacles, "I was with General Washington and Colonel Arnold yesterday afternoon, and Colonel Arnold gave me this letter."

"Yes, indeed!" Mr. Tracy said, taking the letter and pushing his spectacles up on his nose where he could see through them. "Yes, indeed! I know, I know, I know!" He peered carefully at my face and ears and shirt, started to read, then looked back sharply at my breeches and shoes, as though they might conceal some clue not contained on my upper sections. He completed his reading of the letter, murmuring "Yes, indeed!" a score of times.

"Sir," I said, seeing it was his intention to commit himself to nothing until I had said my say, "I have a sloop lying in this river: the one with a girl as master."

"Yes, yes, yes, yes!" Mr. Tracy said. "Yes, yes, yes! Yes, indeed! The *Eunice!* Yes, yes!" He groaned slightly, as if the machinery that produced his yesses had run down. "A baggage, sir! Quick brain! Active! Works ahead of herself! Make a good chess player! You play chess?"

I said I didn't, and waited for him to go on, but he grunted obstinately and examined a pink phlox.

"Sir," I said, "Colonel Arnold has ordered me to Fort Western. I'd like to sail there in my own sloop. If you'll do me the kindness to release the *Eunice,* Phoebe'll take us there and return here before Colonel Arnold arrives."

"Bless my soul!" he said. "Yes, yes, yes, yes! Thought you wanted money! Go right ahead and send her right back! Yes, indeed!" He growled amiably at a cerise phlox. "A baggage, sir, but clever! Brain well oiled! Smart! Sees everything! Great help to a man! Go after her myself if it wasn't for having asthma! She your sister?"

"No, sir," I said, bemazed to hear him run on at such length about Phoebe, and thinking how frequently men, to their undoing, will imagine qualities in a woman, especially in a young woman, that don't exist.

"Hm! Hm! Well! Well! Not your wife, of course! Never married, that baggage! Tell that easy enough! Hrrump! Hmp!"

"Yes, sir. She married a man in the army, just this summer."

Mr. Tracy shook his head and hrumped violently. "Don't understand it! Sailing your sloop and married to another man! Something wrong with one of you! Hrump! Well, none of my business! Nothing to do with me! Well out of any such mess! Come, come, come! Get

along, now! Got to have that sloop back before Arnold gets here!
And tell that baggage I want to see her when she gets back! Teach
her chess! Probably beat me after one lesson! Get along, get along!"

I got along, leaving Mr. Tracy hrumping among his phloxes; and
all the way to the wharf I puzzled over what could ail him.

If Phoebe had been gentle and fair-haired, like Mary, I might have
understood his enthusiasm; but it seemed to me she had few of the
things one seeks in a woman, her skin being as brown as an old
law-book, and her black hair cut off at the nape of her neck for
greater freedom, and scorched by the sun to a rusty color. Her body
was hard and flat like a boy's, so I had as lief put my arm around
a spruce mast studded with brass nails, for all the pleasure I would
get out of it.

At the wharf I banished the matter from my mind and shouted to
Phoebe that it was all right. By the time I had sculled out to the
sloop Cap had raised and stowed the anchor and was getting up the
jib, interlarding his labors with further accounts of our council of war
with General Washington.

"You could see," he said, "that George was depending on Stevie
for everything.

"'How do you think we ought to get up the Kennebec?' he said
to Stevie, sort of anxious, as if afraid Stevie would say we oughtn't
to go at all.

"'How do you mean?' Stevie asked, not wanting to make any mistake on such an important matter.

"'What I mean,' George said, 'is do you think we ought to swim
up, or go up in bateaux?'

"'Well,' said Stevie, being a diplomat, 'how was you thinking of
getting up?'

"'Why,' George said, sort of undecided, 'I kind of thought bateaux
would be best.'

"'Did you order any bateaux?' asked Stevie, feeling his way along,
as you might say.

"'Yes,' George said, 'I ordered two hundred of 'em.'

"'Well,' Stevie said, 'in that case I tell you frankly I know the
Kennebec from keelson to whiffletree, and my advice to you, though
you can take it or leave it, and God knows I don't care which, being
as how I'm a free and independent resident of Maine, is to use
bateaux.'

"With that George pulled out his handkerchief and mopped his
forehead. 'Sir,' he said, 'this is a great relief and I'm certainly obliged

to you, though for a time you had me fair stonied for fear you was going to recommend using blowed-up bladders!'"

"Well, what could I do?" I asked sourly.

The *Eunice* slipped down the river, passed Plum Island, and danced across the vicious chop on the bar. "Did you think they ought to use canoes?" Phoebe asked, letting the sloop run before the warm west wind.

"Of course they ought to use canoes! An army can't stop to calk leaky bateaux, the way lumbermen can: not if it's going somewhere in a hurry. After they've been dragged over a few rocks there won't be any way of telling whether the river's outside trying to get in or inside trying to get out!"

"You can get a canoe for yourself," Phoebe said.

"You can get anything you want for yourself in the army," Cap grumbled, gazing darkly at the Isles of Shoals off our starboard bow, "but you don't keep it if it's any good. The one that keeps it is a colonel."

XV

Cᴀᴘ ʜᴜғғ refused to let us put into Portsmouth, saying he had nothing there worth getting. I suspicioned there were other reasons for his indifference, having to do with the gaol and those who had put him there. So we ran on to the eastward, rounding the Nubble into Wells Bay and dozing in the warm, smoke-laden land breeze, which brought us swiftly to Arundel on the flood tide that night.

There was a pother on our arrival. Having felt the bitter white Kennebec mists of autumn, I put my mother and sisters to work knitting woolen stockings for the two of us out of double yarn, long enough to reach a foot above our knees, and short ones to wear over them. There were woolen shirts to be collected, and tools to be assembled for carrying in my pack, as well as fish-hooks, needles, awls and mirrors for Hobomok and Paul Higgins and the others.

Wherever I moved Ranger moved with me, knowing I was going away, and pressing against my legs so that I fell over him a thousand times. My mother and the girls, with their hands and eyes busy at their knitting, moved like folk in a dream, so that we fell over each other as well. By midnight our dispositions were so near to souring that I declared I would make no more preparations, even though we froze and starved for it; so Cap and I sat before the fire in the gathering-room, with knitting needles clicking around us like maple branches after an ice storm, and told my mother and sisters, between draughts of flip, how our camp at Cambridge had seemed, and how General Washington had looked and what he had said, and how our men had plenty to eat, and how the British in Boston had next to nothing to eat, and how we could beat them if we had powder, which we had not, and what General Washington had worn, and how he was beloved by all, and all the other things that womenfolk must have recounted to them so they in turn can recount them, with their own additions, to the neighbors.

When I turned to my mother's affairs, and spoke of the difficulties she would have in managing the inn, she scoffed.

"*Tchah!*" she said. "What is there about this inn, with Malary and the girls to help me, that's more difficult than the managing of any house! Put your mind at rest! All our drinkers will be gone to war, and there's money at hand—what your father left, and what we've earned from trading in furs and from the sloop."

"If that's so," I said, "why was it, when Phoebe was engaged to James Dunn, that I could never leave this place for fear of her getting married and leaving you helpless?"

My mother started up, exclaiming she had forgotten to put the beans to soak, and Phoebe yawned, declaring we should all be abed if we proposed to go out with the early tide. My sisters, who had reached the heels of our stockings, went off upstairs with her, gabbling over nothing; so Cap and I sat alone by the fire, drinking our flip and hoping the days to come would find us in no worse circumstances.

The next morning, when we dropped down the river and across the bar, we looked back at what we were leaving and wondered, as I think those who go away to war have always wondered and always will wonder, when we should see it again—my mother and sisters and Malary on the hard gray beach at the turn of the shore, waving and smiling, though I well knew they felt little like smiling; young Ranger, the image of his father, his ears erect and his tail moving slowly back and forth, hopeful until the last of being called to follow me; the garrison house, gray and comfortable behind the dunes, smoke rising in a blue plume from its squat chimney; the little early-morning waves dropping weakly on the beach, as if in patient sorrow at our going; the ledges brown and glistening on the pearly surface of the sea, and the water near the shore so glassy and so sheltered from the soft west wind that the far blue line of Wells and York seemed floating in the air.

That night we dropped anchor at Parker's Flats, off Georgetown Island in the Kennebec, Phoebe declaring it was better to take our time about it than to hang ourselves up on a ledge. We took ten fat flounders from the flats, and Phoebe made a chowder from them, adding pork scraps and sliced potatoes and ship's bread and butter and an onion, so that we put in our time profitably.

We helped her to weave an instrument to wear on her wrist—four musket balls wrapped in leather and enclosed in braided strips, the strips narrowing to a tube, and ending in a bracelet. When the bracelet was on her wrist the tube lay in her hand, projecting six inches beyond it. At the end of the tube were the musket balls, tightly laced in place.

Men, Phoebe said, were a pest, continually clawing and mauling at a woman; and with this in her hand it would be easy to discourage them.

"Ho!" Cap roared, slipping his arm around her waist and pulling her so tight against him that she looked like a coonskin against a barn door, "what could you do with *that* when a man does *this* to you?"

He bent his big red face down toward hers. Misliking his rudeness, I set out to pull him away and throw him overboard, when Phoebe flicked up her hand so that her new machine tapped against the back of his head. He released her, his eyes as loose and rolling in their sockets as those of a bass staring up at a grasshopper; and after he had wobbled around, as though he had drunk too much rum, he leaned against the mainsail and slid sidewise onto the deck, where he lay looking thoughtfully at the stars.

*   *   *

We came to anchor the next morning off the lower tip of Swan Island; and before the anchor rope had done thumping on the deck a canoe put out from the headland and twisted toward us down a guzzle. The Indians in the canoe were young men, strange to me, so I ordered them back with word that Steven Nason had come to visit with Jacataqua and Hobomok. They shook their paddles at me, shouting "Brother!" to let me know my father's name had not been forgotten, and when they had taken word back to the headland, five canoes returned.

I recognized Jacataqua among the paddlers, for she was like her mother, only smaller and rounder; but Hobomok I would never have known. He had grown thick through the chest and shoulders, and his face was loose-skinned and deep-lined, like that of a clergyman addicted to discourse and praying.

They brandished their paddles and whooped at me, keeping up a doleful howling until they had swarmed over the sloop's thwarts, when Hobomok seized me by the wrist as though it had been a pump handle, and Jacataqua took me by the waist and wedged her shoulder under my arm. She was pleasing and soft, with the same red glow on her cheekbones that her mother had, as though a light were shining up at her; and neat, too, with blue wampum at her brow and throat, and a deerskin jerkin over her leggins, such as her mother wore.

For one who so powerfully disliked Indians, Cap Huff's behavior was strange. Engulfing Jacataqua's arm in his bear's paw of a hand, he pointed first to me, roaring, "Brother!" He then pointed to himself and said, "Brother!" after which he poked Jacataqua in the chest, unnecessarily hard, it seemed to me, and bellowed, "Sister!" Jacataqua laughed, threw her arm around his neck, and kissed him, at which this hulk of a man whooped more loudly than any Indian and scrambled up the sloop's mainmast in an excess of emotion.

Phoebe scrutinized Jacataqua with care, and from time to time coughed a hard, dry cough, which I had long ago learned was a sign matters sat ill on her. Therefore I put an arm around each of them, saying to Jacataqua, "This is my sister."

Phoebe pulled away, saying, "No! No! No sister!"

Jacataqua smiled up at me. "I speak English better than my mother." She went and sat by Phoebe, picking up her hand and holding it. "Steven knew my mother," she said. "His father made us brother and sister long ago, when they were following the white girl." Phoebe freed her hand, then put it back in Jacataqua's again.

"How did you learn to speak English so well?" I asked.

She laughed. "Boys come to see me from Gardinerstown and Pownalborough; sometimes from Fort Western and Arrowsic Island and Brunswick—oh, many places."

Cap Huff descended the mast and regarded her with admiration. "Wait till you see what's coming up from Boston in a week or so," he said. "You'll speak two or three languages after that."

"What languages?" Jacataqua asked, wide-eyed.

"Oh, Irish," Cap said, "and Connecticut, and Harvard, maybe."

"I speak a little German," Jacataqua said.

"German!" Cap bawled.

"*Gottverdamte!*" said Jacataqua. "There's nothing but Germans across the river in Pownalborough."

"Well, I'm a—I'm a sculpin!" Cap muttered.

Jacataqua couldn't keep her hands off Phoebe's cat's eyes and brass-studded belt and the rest of her odd belongings, so I left them for Hobomok, and found Natawammet squatting with him on the sunny side of the hatch, looking little different than I remembered him. His throat was scrawnier and his knees showed signs of wear. I was glad to see them; and from the tone of their voices when they called me "Brother," they were equally glad to see me.

Rabomis, they told me, was dead, having pitched from a canoe in the Five Mile Ripples and broken her neck against a rock. Jacataqua had been made sachem in her stead because she was known and liked in all the adjoining settlements, and received many favors from white men. Woromquid had set off for Quebec two years before with three Assagunticooks, and none of them had ever been heard of again. All of the Norridgewocks had gone to St. Francis and Beçancour to live, and most of the Swan Islanders too, for the settlements had pressed so close around them that there was game for only a small number.

With the turning of the tide Phoebe left us, declaring she couldn't lose the favoring wind. We sent two men with her, to ride through the Chops on the sloop and make sure she came to no harm. Beyond the Chops I knew the wind would take her safe to Arundel.

I watched her at the tiller, fingering her cat's eyes and squinting into the west, little more than a shadow larger than on the day when she fastened my hunting shirt to her father's cabin; and I wondered what it was that Nathaniel Tracy had seen in her. I was reminded, too, to ask Cap, some day, what possessed him to want to put his sweaty paws on her.

✳   ✳   ✳

Fearful of what cussedness Cap might inflict on my friends because of his dislike for Indians, I consulted Hobomok, saying it might be well to tranquillize Cap by showing him something he couldn't understand. Also I said I had heard Hobomok had become a skilled *m'téoulin*, able to walk ankle deep in rock and scream terribly.

I have never learned why these two things—screaming and seeming to walk ankle deep in hard earth or rock—are the signs of a great *m'téoulin* among the Abenakis; but it is so and always has been so. There is no trick about the screaming, which a *m'téoulin* practises in remote places, starting when a young man, so that in time he is able to scream fearfully, in a manner beyond the comprehension of those who have never heard the scream of a *m'téoulin*. About the walking there is a trick, though I have never learned it; nor have I understood why it should so fill the Abenakis with amazement and terror. When a *m'téoulin* walks thus his feet appear to sink deep into the ground, as though he walked in the soft sand at the bend of a tide river; and I have heard it said that the footprints of a powerful *m'téoulin* are often found sunk deep in stone.

When I invited Cap to smoke a pipe in Hobomok's cabin, he protested that he would not smoke with a dirty bug-eater, especially since the tobacco would be mixed with rat's fur and stink-bush leaves; but I told him that even though what he said were true, which it was not, we had been sent to make ourselves useful, and this was a part of it.

We entered behind Hobomok, who took a pipe from a shelf at the far end of the cabin, filled it, and gave it to me while Cap looked on, grumbling. Then he turned from us without a word and left the cabin.

"Now what ails this ill-begotten bug-eater?" Cap asked; but in that moment Hobomok rejoined us. He seemed to swell and tower upward toward the roof, and his face was hideous. He took three short steps toward us, dragging his legs like a man wallowing through a snowdrift. I could feel Cap, breathing hard, fumbling at his waist for his knife. Before he could reach it, a convulsion swept Hobomok's face and body. His eyes bulged, and from his contorted mouth came a shriek so piercing and so awful that, although I had prepared myself, it came against me like a clammy hand, drawing frozen fingers along my spine, and piercing my ears like knitting needles.

Then he turned from us and went out. I looked at Cap, and found him staring glassy-eyed at the door, his hands and his mouth half open. I had heard my father say that when a good *m'téoulin* screamed unexpectedly in a room, no person in that room could move. Perhaps the strange walk of the *m'téoulin*, followed suddenly by his scream, first holds and then numbs the attention of those who hear him. It may be that which happens to a hen when a boy holds her beak against a board, draws with a piece of charcoal a long straight line from the tip of the beak outward along the plank, and presses her head against it. The hen remains there, helpless and unmoving; and so, too, did Cap stand until I shook him. During the remainder of the time we were together he called no Indian either lousy or ill-begotten until he had first looked over his shoulder to see whether he was overheard.

*   *   *

What with the vagueness of Colonel Arnold's orders, and General Washington's mislike for Indians, and the low opinion both those officers held concerning my thoughts on bateaux, I scarce knew what to do. I considered myself handy with a paddle; but I could no more navigate the upper Kennebec without Indians who knew the waters and the country than I could visit Boston without breeches. The

Kennebec country is wild: more tumbled and torn than can be im-
agined by any man who has not struggled through it. Therefore I
decided I would do for Colonel Arnold what I would do for myself.

Leaving Cap at Swan Island to get information from the women
and make sure they made proper buckskin garments for Arnold, I
set off up the Androscoggin with Natawammet to ask help from Paul
Higgins and his Assagunticooks—the assistance he had promised
months before.

From the start we seemed doomed to disappointment; for we paddled into a northeaster that drove buckets of water down the front
of our shirts; and when we came to the falls of the Androscoggin,
where Paul Higgins's people had always pitched their wigwams, we
found nothing but a piece of bark wedged in a cleft stick, and on
it a drawing showing that the town had been removed to the southern end of Cobosseecontee Pond, which lies between the Androscoggin and the Kennebec.

When we had labored on to Cobosseecontee and around its winding shores until we had come to the Abenaki camp, we found only
women and boys and old men. We smoked a pipe with the old men
and learned that Reuben Colburn had paddled in from Gardinerstown and persuaded Paul Higgins to travel to Cambridge with his
warriors and offer his services to Washington. Higgins, they said, had
at first refused, saying he had promised his help to me; whereupon
Colburn had told him, and rightly, too, I thought, that he would
obtain more credit by going to Cambridge himself, since any orders
I might give would also come from the great chief in Cambridge.

As a result of this, Natawammet and I sat down with them on the
shores of Cobosseecontee to shoot deer and ducks and await Paul
Higgins's return; for knowing General Washington's opinion of Indians, I suspicioned that Higgins might be received in Cambridge
without overmuch courtesy, and that unless I did something about
it, his help might be withheld when we needed it most.

On the afternoon of our third day of waiting we had returned
from across the pond with two bucks and were skinning them on the
shore, surrounded by gabbling squaws and noisy boys, when a silence
fell, and the women scuttled off into the bushes like so many chickens
at sight of a hawk overhead. I looked up to see Paul Higgins, in
leggins and belt cloth, standing silently on the bank with his hands
on his hips, glowering at me instead of leaping down to thump me
on the back in his accustomed manner. Behind him were a score of
Abenakis, all gloomy. Thus I knew I had been correct in my sus-

picions. I made a to-do over him, dwelling on the feast we would have with the venison and raccoon fat I had got while awaiting him, and going at once for the mirrors, awls, and scissors I had brought as gifts—gifts Paul needed. It had been long since he had trimmed his hair or beard. He looked more like a walking juniper bush than a man.

I liked Paul Higgins, despite the sneers of his white neighbors who pretended to find fault with him because he was overly free with his wives, marrying a squaw one year and putting her aside after the lapse of three or four years. I noticed, though, there was little complaint from the squaws; and I had reason to believe the white men who were bitterest against him would have done the same, if marriage customs among us were as lenient as those of the Abenakis.

Having been taken by the Indians when small, he had few of the white man's evil habits, being neither foulmouthed over nothing, nor a drunkard, nor given to spreading malicious reports concerning his neighbors. For that matter, there was little of the white man about him. He was browned by exposure to the sun, and spoke with the softness of the Abenakis instead of with the nasal rasp of our own people.

At all events, I took pleasure in his company; and knowing this, he bore no grudge against me for his misfortunes, so we feasted harmoniously together.

He spoke bitterly of his journey to Cambridge. With him, he said, had gone nineteen of his braves, as well as Swashan, a sachem from St. Francis who had come to offer his help against the English. When they were admitted to the presence of Washington, he said, he had spoken quickly and to the point, saying they had lived at peace with their neighbors for many years; and now having been told the freedom of the land was at stake, they offered themselves to assist in preserving it.

"When the great chief had heard us," Paul said, "he thanked us in fine words, and told us if there was need for our services he would send a message. Then he let my braves come away without food or drink or presents. Yet I know he is sending an army against Quebec. If there is no need for us now, there is no need for us ever. We resent this, my brothers and I. It sits ill on us to be held in such low esteem."

For my ears he added angrily, in English, "Let 'em go to hell in their own way!"

I couldn't blame Paul for his anger, knowing how I would have felt if I had offered my services and had them put aside in this manner; neither, knowing a few of the difficulties of the road to Quebec, could I let him be lost to us if I could hold him. I had liefer try to sing under water than speak in public, but I knew I must make the attempt, so I got perspiringly to my feet.

"Brothers," I said, "many years ago I heard my father speak of war to the white chief who will lead this army against Quebec. In this talk he said the Abenaki method of making war was better than the white man's method, and that white men, in making war, perpetually sought excuses to follow stupid counsels.

"Brothers, Washington is a great chief, just and fearless, but he has taken bad advice. He has taken the counsel of men who pretend to know the river Kennebec and its ways, but do not know it. They have told him to use bateaux instead of canoes. I have said to him, Brothers, that canoes are better than bateaux, but the advice he has had seems better than mine, so he must follow it. Now this cannot be changed; but it's not my business to weep because bateaux are being used. My business is to go in a bateau.

"Another thing, Brothers: many years ago the great chief was traitorously used by Western Indians. This is something I mention without pleasure, but I do it so you may know I speak the truth, as my father spoke it to your fathers. The great chief doesn't know the Abenakis of the Kennebec and the Androscoggin as I know them and as my father knew them. I ask my brothers if it wouldn't be better to find some way of letting this knowledge be known to all the world, rather than to sulk like children because the great chief thinks all red men are like the red dogs of the West."

With this I sat down, quaking internally and hoping the St. Francis chief, Swashan, would be silent, but fearing he wouldn't because his conscience was too vulnerable.

No sooner was I down than he was on his feet, important and indignant. "Can my brother give this counsel," he demanded, "when he knows my people have stood firm against the English for tens of years? A slight has been put upon the honor of my tribe——"

With this I broke the rules of Abenaki speech and got to my feet. "I answer my brother before he goes farther than is wise," I said. "My brother knows the St. Francis Abenakis were a thistle under the belt of all New England for many years, when my friends of the Androscoggin and the Kennebec were living at peace with us and suffering unjustly for crimes their St. Francis brothers committed!"

"Micmacs: Etechemins from the Penobscot: Passamaquoddies!" broke in Swashan, glowering at me.

"St. Francis Indians!" I insisted. "Ask Hobomok! Ask Paul Higgins! In their time I had this," and I struck the red scar on my forehead, "because Indians from St. Francis murdered my neighbor and stole his daughter."

"Led by a Frenchman," he growled.

"Yes, Brother," I said, "led by a Frenchman. But what did we care who led them? Murderers led by a hangman are no worse than murderers led by a priest. Within our memories your St. Francis people have done things we hate. All the more reason, then, that you should cease to babble of your honor and look for a way to put yourself right before the world."

They were silent, staring at me with beady black eyes. I could feel they were pleased rather than angry at my attack on Swashan, and were turning over in their minds how they could save their pride and still, as I had suggested, set themselves right with the world. At the same time, I knew that whatever they did, no matter how brave or self-sacrificing, they were doomed forever to be naught but Indians to most—one with Mohawks and Micmacs; Sacs and Foxes; Nipissings and Pottawattomies and Winnebagoes.

"Brother," Paul said at length, "the great chief didn't want us. This we cannot forget or change."

"Brother," I said, "that's not the question. The question is this: If an army marches to Quebec by the Kennebec, does it need you? If it needs you and you don't give it help, then I may think what I please. It pleases me to think you offered help to further your private ends, and not to assist this country and your white brothers."

Again there was silence while the braves, huddled in their blankets, watched me with glittering eyes.

"I have traveled toward Quebec," I said, "with Hobomok and Natawammet and Woromquid. There was never a moment that I was not in need of them and helped by them. The army that goes to Quebec will need the help of every Abenaki on this river."

Paul Higgins shook his head. "I won't go with this army," he said. "We have met coldness already, and I won't risk meeting open disgrace."

"Brother," I said, "answer me a question."

Higgins nodded.

"Soon it will be time to begin your autumn hunting."

Again he nodded.

"Where shall you hunt?"

He waved his hand to the northward. "Throughout the Abenaki country," he said, "wherever our parties know there are deer and bear and beaver."

"Carrabassett?" I asked. "Moosehead? Carritunk?"

He nodded.

"Dead River?"

"Some," he agreed.

"Paul," I said, "go beyond Dead River and hunt on the Height of Land. Go soon, saying nothing to any man, and stick to the Height of Land. When this army crosses the Height of Land it will either need you badly or need nobody's help. If it needs nobody's help, you have hunted on good hunting grounds. If it needs help, you will be there to give it. I ask this in the name of friendship."

"It will need help," Higgins said.

There was a murmur of assent from the other braves.

"I think," Higgins said, "I'm willing to hunt on the Height of Land."

A brave on the opposite side of the fire howled furiously, rounding off the howl with shrill yips. "I will hunt on the Height of Land," he announced. With that there was a general howling, significant of pleasure and approval, following which the fire was replenished and a Bragging Dance was held, with Swashan bragging louder than any three of the Assagunticooks put together.

XVI

Natawammet and I left Paul at dawn, followed the winding sixteen-mile course of Cobosseecontee Stream and came out into the Kennebec at Gardinerstown, six miles below Fort Western.

On the Kennebec we found rafts of lumber moving down river toward Reuben Colburn's shipyard, which was in a turmoil of shouting and pounding. The shore was covered with bateaux, acres of them, knee deep in shavings and smelling of fresh-worked pine. The place was alive with carpenters, swinging adzes and nailing pine boards to white oak ribs and bawling at each other to keep out of the way and pass the nails.

Of all rowing boats I know, I hold the Kennebec bateau in the lowest esteem, because of its weight and clumsiness. In Arundel we use a boat called a dory: a high flat-sided affair with a narrow bottom, clumsy-looking, but easy to row because of the small resistance to the water, and almost impossible to overturn, even by standing on the gunwale. The Kennebec bateau, which had its origin with the lumbermen of the lower Kennebec, is double the size of our dories, and somewhat the same shape, the bow pointed and overhanging, the stern flattened and less overhanging than the bow, but the sides built of overlapping boards, whereas the sides of a dory are smooth, the boards fitted tight together. To my mind, this overlapping of boards is a defect if there is to be rough going among shoals and reefs, since the boards catch easily against rocks, and there is more likelihood of leaks. It may be a good boat for lumbermen to use on the lower Kennebec, where tides are swift and rocks few; but on the upper Kennebec, where smooth water is unknown and quick movement essential to safety, I would as soon travel in a pine coffin.

Colburn was a chunky, quick man; intelligent, but overdesirous, I thought, of doing everything himself to make sure it was done properly. I had known others of a like temper, and it had seemed to me they courted trouble by thinking the things they could not do themselves would of necessity be done badly. Expecting bad results, they would select their agents carelessly; consequently their fears were frequently justified.

I was prepared to mislike Colburn as being responsible for Washington's and Arnold's fondness for bateaux; but I had wronged him.

When I said mildly that these craft were overly heavy, he kicked contemptuously at one of them.

"Green!" he said. "All green boards! Heavy as wet paper! No seasoned lumber this side of Falmouth!"

He added that time was too short to bring seasoned planks from Falmouth by schooner. "If there's delay," he said, as we walked toward his house, "let it be at the other end! Two hundred bateaux they ordered, and two hundred there'll be when Arnold gets here."

I said it seemed to me there might be worse delay if the green boards opened up in quick water.

"Mister," he said, tapping my chest, "they want bateaux, and the only way we can give 'em bateaux is to build 'em out of green boards. What you got to say to that?"

I said he might give them canoes as well.

"Hah!" he said. "They want bateaux and I give 'em canoes! Then what happens if things go wrong? God ain't to blame! The weather ain't to blame! Reuben Colburn's to blame! Just building boats is bad enough, mister. Will I get my money for 'em? God knows! I won't if we don't whip England! Sylvester Gardiner's got more brains than I've got, and he's sticking with England. Well, I believe in Washington and Arnold, mister, but I ain't going to try to make 'em take things they don't ask for!"

"What got them so excited over bateaux?"

He led me into the hall of his house, a spacious dwelling on a rise at the bend in the river. "Mister," he said, "I wish I knew; but Washington and Arnold, they keep their own counsels." He rummaged in a desk and produced a letter from Colonel Arnold.

SIR [it started off]: His excellency General Washington desires you will inform yourself how soon there can be procured or built at Kennebec two hundred light bateaux capable of carrying six or seven men each, with their provisions and baggage.

"You see," Colburn said, "they had the idea already."

I nodded, and noted, farther down in the letter, the order:

You will also get particular information from those people who have been at Quebec, of the difficulty attending an expedition that way, in particular the number and length of the carrying places, whether dry land, hills or swamp. Also the depth of water in the river at this season, whether an easy stream or rapid.

"Did you get the particular information?" I asked.

"I sent four men from above Fort Western. Conkey and Slike and two of their friends, with an Indian."

"To go to Quebec?"

"No. To go to the Chaudière and back, and see the state of things. They ought to be back now."

There was a receipt in his desk, signed Patrick Conkey, acknowledging

115 pound salt Pork, 106 pound Shipp Brad, ½ a Bushshall of Corn, 6 Gallons Rum for Journey toward Quebec.

"Good men?" I asked.

"Good as any hereabouts," he said indifferently.

"As good as Abenakis?" I asked in surprise.

"Well," Colburn said, "they talk English better than Abenakis. Me, I like Abenakis, but you know how General Washington feels about Indians. We got to remember that if people ain't accustomed to red men, they feel safer if their scouting's done by white folks, even if it ain't done so well."

"I saw Paul Higgins," I said. "He and his men say they won't go with the army."

Colburn nodded gravely. "What's done's done. I got eight rounded up to go along and paddle and carry messages."

"This Conkey?" I asked. "How far can he travel on a gallon of rum?"

Colburn laughed. "These people up here have to have rum. They'll go without corn and they'll go without bread, if their money's low; but you can't make the price of rum too high for 'em."

"Well," I said, "they're not much different down my way. What I'm wondering is how much Patrick Conkey and his friends could see or hear when they were loaded with rum."

"There'll be no trouble," Colburn said reassuringly. "It's a plain trail, sticking to streams and ponds all the way. An army wouldn't scarcely need a guide."

"Have you been over it recently?"

"No," Colburn admitted. "I haven't ever been over it, but I know about it from hearing people talk."

"Did you ever talk to anyone that had crossed the Height of Land?"

"Come to think of it, I don't know as I ever did."

"No, nor I," I told him, "only to one man when I was a boy. There's no streams or ponds to follow on the Height of Land. Nobody goes near it unless he must. I'll bet you a sable skin to a jack knife that Conkey sits down with his rum on this side of the Height of Land and never crosses it at all."

Colburn shook his head. "You can't get anything done nowadays unless you do it yourself. I've got to provide bateaux, and setting-poles for 'em, and buy sixty barrels of salt beef, and all the pork and flour on the river, and ride down to Falmouth to get the commissary that's coming from headquarters to look after supplies, and God knows what all. There's times when it seems as if they expected me to fight the whole damned war alone."

"When are they expected?" I asked, thinking of Natanis, and in a turmoil inside for fear something might go wrong to keep me, at this late day, from reaching Mary. "If there's time I might try the trip myself, with Natawammet, to see how it looks."

"You can't do it! They'll be here any time—in three days, four days —a week anyway."

Determined to have word of Natanis, Natawammet and I filled ourselves with cider and dumplings at Smith's Tavern, above the shipyard, and set off upstream for Patrick Conkey's cabin, ten miles beyond Fort Western.

By good fortune I found Conkey, dirty, unkempt, and newly returned from his scouting trip, seated on the ground outside his cabin, comfortably wriggling his bare toes in the afternoon sun and engaged in a spitting contest with his brother Michael and one of his scouting companions. In front of them, removed from the line of spitting, stood a gray stone jug. I gave them good-day and offered them my letter from Colonel Arnold. Conkey took it, looked at both sides with half-closed eyes and returned it without comment.

I asked if there had been changes in recent years on Dead River. Conkey asked who I might be. I said I was Steven Nason, as he had read in the letter. Conkey said, "I thought it was a map."

After some meditation he said he had heard of me. He spat carefully, protecting his chin by a quick outward and upward motion of his lower lip, and his companions followed his example. Conkey outspat them. I asked if he had crossed the Height of Land on this trip. He shook his head, tersely remarking, "Dangerous!"

From Conkey's thick and fragmentary conversation I gathered he and his companions had carried from the Kennebec to Dead River and there encountered Natanis, who traveled with them for one day but would go no farther, though they offered him a dollar a day. Their suspicions were aroused by his refusal of such riches. The only explanation that could reach their rum-fuddled brains was that somebody had paid him more money to remain where he was. Since there could be no one but the English who would pay money for any such service, Conkey had accused him of being in the pay of the English. Conkey declared Natanis had confessed this to be true, and had threatened to carry word to the English if they attempted to force him to go farther. Because of this, he mumbled, they had proceeded a little along Dead River, then returned to the Kennebec and come home.

I sat and whittled at a twig, looking down on the tumbling quick water of the river. Inwardly I damned this drunken, lying fool until my stomach tightened with rage. I was sure I knew how it had come about: how Natanis, having received my message, would not go far from his camp lest I come for his help and find him gone; and how, when accused of spying for the English, he had joked derisively with them, threatening to perform an impossibility—to race on ahead and tattle to the English, which would have been of no use to anyone.

"If he said he was a spy and would tell on you," I said to Conkey, "why didn't you shoot him? We're at war with England."

Conkey made no answer, but spat repeatedly. Then I knew he was a coward as well as a drunkard, and had run home with his tail between his legs without bringing a farthing's worth of information concerning the carries on the Height of Land and beyond it, as he had been told to do—bearing only lies concerning one who would be of more value to the army than a thousand Conkeys.

I knew it was no duty of mine to reach over and cram his blackened teeth down his throat. Arnold and the army would require his services, worthless as they were. My only duty, as I saw it, was to give Natanis whatever protection I could from this strange patriot. Not only was Natanis my friend; but he could, I knew, guide the army more skillfully than any other man, and so must be protected at all hazards.

We left Conkey to his drinking and spitting, and went rapidly downstream, as if hell-bent for Fort Western. No sooner, however, were we safely out of sight of Conkey's hovel than we ran ashore, made camp, and took trouts for our supper. While the trouts were broiling, skewered between slices of salt pork, I said to Natawammet: "If Natanis isn't warned that he's supposed to be a spy, he may have trouble and we might lose his help. This we can't afford. Someone must warn him; but I can't do it, for Colonel Arnold expects me to meet him on his arrival. What do you think? Can you travel alone to Dead River?"

Natawammet nodded. "Easily, if you'll give me all the salt pork and all the powder."

"You're a good friend, Natawammet," I said. "You can have whatever of mine you want. You'll have to be off at daybreak and travel fast, for there's little time remaining. When you find Natanis, tell him what we've learned. Tell him never to show himself to white scouts or war parties, for fear they might shoot first and ask questions afterward. Tell him I'm his friend and brother, always, and in need of his help. Tell him to be on the lookout for me."

Natawammet lifted the trouts from the fire and laid them on a strip of bark. "I'll stay with him," he said, "watching for you."

"One more thing," I said. "This is important. Natanis must draw a true map, showing the path across the Height of Land: showing also the length of the carries between his cabin and the Chaudière. Tell him to put it where the advance scouts will find it. They need such a map; and it may be helpful to Natanis if it's known that he provided it."

Natawammet nodded, stuffing himself with trouts and salt pork. I racked my brains, but could think of no other way to help Natanis; and I hoped nothing more would be needed.

At the crack of dawn Natawammet daubed his face with red paint, rolled his blanket, and set off afoot toward the north. At the same time I slid the canoe into the river and went back to the southward, past Fort Western and down to Colburn's shipyard.

. . . The place was busy as a beehive with preparations for Arnold's arrival; but busiest of all was Cap Huff, who had come up from Swan Island and was engaged, he told me loudly, in helping the Commissary from Cambridge buy provisions. He had risen in the world, for he had a canoe of his own, paddled by Hobomok. It was a sort of public canoe, he said, loaned to the army by Jacataqua, and when he got through with it, anybody could have it who wanted it—and have Hobomok too. Hobomok, he declared, made him nervous—not because of anything he did, but because of what he might do. The truth seemed to be that Cap lived in dread of hearing Hobomok scream again.

In his canoe Cap darted up river and down at all hours, looking

for things, as he put it, to pick up. He had picked up aplenty; not
only cornmeal packed in deer bladders to help feed us on our journey
to Quebec, but so much hard money that he had been at a loss how
to carry it, and so had stitched it in rows to the tail of his shirt, where
it covered the lower portion of his body like a sort of armor. He
was vague as to where he got it; but I gathered he had accepted
it from settlers who sought his influence to keep from being drafted
into the army.

Jacataqua was there, too, with buckskin shirts and leggins for
Arnold and his officers; but from the manner in which she avoided
the affectionate slaps aimed at her by Cap, I somehow sensed that
the two of them had not, as our Arundel people say, hit it off together.

. . . Those of us who knew the river and the Maine woods were
in a stew over Arnold's slowness in arriving. The season had been
dry, and the water was low. As is always the case after a dry summer,
the leaves turned early; so we waited amid a profusion of colors such
as can be seen nowhere else in all our eastern country—gold and
russet and crimson, flame red and orange and pink, pale green and
dark green.

They were the colors of advancing autumn—a sure sign that winter
was not far away; and autumn being what it is along the Kennebec,
we knew the need of setting off before the northern frosts took too
high a toll of us.

With each passing day we said to ourselves that Arnold was never
coming; and we fumed and swore and snapped at each other until
we forgot our hatred of England in our desire to fight among ourselves.

Cap and I, with some of the workers on the bateaux, were at
Smith's Tavern eating a dinner of soggy dumplings and corned beef,
sour because of having been killed in the hot weather, and we were
fretful because of the delay and the bad food and the flies that
buzzed about us, walking on our faces and hands, very persistent.
We bickered somewhat over the date—Friday, the 22nd of September—which is why I remember it, for Cap was bawling that all we
needed to make everything perfect was to have Arnold get here on
a Friday—when a boy rushed in screaming that a schooner and two
sloops were coming upstream.

We ran to the shipyard, leaping over the long lines of bateaux that
covered acres of the shore, and saw the reach full of sail, white and
gleaming against the glowing leaves that fringed the river.

We could see crowds of men on the decks, and among the sloops and schooners a number of birch canoes; and from all the craft there rose such a clamor of shouting and laughter that we would have started with them that minute to storm the gates of London itself, and counted ourselves certain of success, Friday or no Friday.

XVII

To SPEAK with Colonel Arnold, that September afternoon, a man needed to be quicker than a flycatcher after a gnat. When he was not among the bateaux, peering into and hefting them, he was racing along the shore, shouting orders to his lieutenant colonels, or saying whom he would see at Colburn's and whom at Fort Western, thinking of a thousand things and doing them with the speed of five men.

Downstream I saw the *Eunice;* but since she was lying off, waiting for the others to get clear, I watched the landing of the three rifle companies from the leading sloops, under the direction of Daniel Morgan, an enormous man, bigger even than Cap Huff, and harsh in his orders.

Those riflemen were worth watching. They came ashore as quick and sure-footed as squirrels: tall men, dressed in queer jackets of gray canvas.

I had heard about these men at Cambridge, for they had marched six hundred miles from Winchester in three weeks without losing a man. The other two rifle companies were from Pennsylvania, both as tough and able as Morgan's, and their shooting such as to fill our Maine marksmen with amazement.

Young Nathaniel Davis told me they were trained to load and fire their rifles while running over a broken field. While doing this they pierced targets the size of a saucer at two hundred and fifty paces— a great distance to shoot with a rifle, even when both marksman and mark are motionless.

When the *Eunice* moved inshore I walked down through the piles of packs and the waiting groups of musketmen, hoping to spend an hour with Phoebe and send messages by her to Arundel.

She was so small, pushing her way among the hulking militiamen, making fast a rope here and a rope there, that I pitied her and her swaggering foolishness of sea boots and brass-studded belt and cat's eyes and blue bandanna, and sentimentally considered giving her a kiss to take each one of my sisters as well as my mother, an act of kindness that would do me no harm.

While I watched her slipping forward and aft like a child, a waiting musketman caught her around the waist and swung her off her feet. Quick as a cat she caught at a stay with her left hand and whacked the musketman on the head with something in her right. He fell down like a log, and she stepped over him and went on with what she was doing, though I thought with less of an appearance of childishness.

I waved to her, and could have sworn her eye caught sight of me, but she gave no sign, and in a moment popped into her cabin; so I studied those who were disembarking. Among them, I saw poor Nathaniel Lord and Noah Cluff and that limb of the devil, Asa Hutchins. When I caught sight of the grave and benevolent face and dignified figure of James Dunn coming over the side, I said to myself I would drag Phoebe from her cabin and read her a lecture that would send her home in tears. Before I could do it there was some bellowing from the captain of their company, Goodrich, whereat they all hurried upstream and fell in line.

I thought of going to Phoebe's cabin, but she came out of her own accord and said something to two men who still remained on deck. They started to heave up the anchor, and Phoebe swung herself ashore and walked by me, her nose in the air, as impudent as any Falmouth baggage. Yet it was not her impudence that held me speechless, gawking at her as a dog gawks at a cat up a tree, but her garb; for she had replaced her sea dress with a deerskin jerkin and leggins and moccasins. She might have been an Abenaki except for the blue handkerchief around her head, and the cat's eyes at her neck instead of wampum.

She put down her bundle and went to fixing her waist, sliding a glance at me as she did so. I saw that under her jerkin she wore her breeches and brass-studded belt, though leggins and moccasins had supplanted her sea boots. I went to her and shook her arm.

"You idiot," I said, "what do you think you're doing? What do you think this looks like!"

She puckered her brows, seeming hurt and puzzled by my anger, though I knew she was neither puzzled nor hurt. "Now what's the matter?" she asked, peering around at herself, first over one shoulder and then over the other, as women have a way of doing. "Jacataqua made them for me like her own, and we're both of a size."

"Jacataqua!" I shouted. "Matter! Why aren't you on our sloop?

Where do you think you're going? Why did you let James Dunn
come on this expedition?"

"Don't shout," she said. "I'm not deaf!"

Now if ever I saw a human, man or woman, always able to say
the one thing that was the wrong thing, it was Phoebe.

"I'll shout all I please," I said, "and if you're not deaf, then I think
you're blind and dumb and witless to boot!"

"You won't think so," she said, "when I tell you the price I got for
the sloop."

"What do you mean, price?" I asked in a fog of rage and bemud-
dlement. "Price for what?"

"For the sloop. I sold the sloop to Nathaniel Tracy."

"You couldn't! It isn't yours to sell! I wouldn't consent to the sale
of it, and therefore it couldn't be sold."

"I spoke about it to your mother," she said. "Your mother considered it a fine trade. She owns two fifths, and I one fifth, so we voted
to sell it. If you'd refused to sell for the price we got, I think you'd
have been as great a goose as ever was."

"How much did you get?"

"Four hundred and fifty dollars. Twice what we paid; so when we
get back from Quebec we can have a fine brig, or two brigs if we
want them, or even a ship."

"We!" I exclaimed, dropping the matter of the sloop, since the
price had indeed been large. "We! What sort of talk is this? How
can you go to Quebec when there's no one to look after you? We'll
be busy enough saving our own lives without having you on our
hands!"

"It'll be a cold day, Steven Nason," she said, with an air of disdain
that made me want to lay her over my knee, "when you find *me* on
your hands."

"Now here!" I said. "This is enough! Either you set off for Arundel,
where you belong, or I'll go to Colonel Arnold and have you put out
of camp at the point of a bayonet!"

"That's a good scheme," she said, "but I've already spoken to Colonel Arnold. He said if my husband had no objections to my following
the army he saw no reason why he should raise any. You aren't my
husband, unless I'm greatly mistaken; and if you've been given the
right to speak for him, I haven't heard of it. I'm weary of all this
twaddle about having women on your hands; so I'll tell you now that
Sergeant Grier in the rifle corps has his wife along, a woman three
times my size, yet no one's raising a hullabaloo about having her on

his hands; and Warner of the rifle corps is taking his wife as well, and glad to have her. As for James Dunn, I've heard him raising no objections to my going—nor have I heard any from you over the going of Jacataqua."

"She isn't going, is she?"

"Yes, she is, is she!" said Phoebe, dropping her lower lip vacantly in a manner she doubtless felt to be an imitation of me, "and a strange thing, if you ask me, that one who goes around miawling she's your sister, and hanging to your waist like a sick ninny, should have said nothing to you about it!"

"What do you mean?"

"Sister, indeed! What I mean is clear enough! It wouldn't be so pleasant for you, would it, if a woman from your home followed this army and saw you at your innocent play with a brown hussy calling herself your sister? Sister! Pah!"

"Phoebe," I said, "there's no sense in what you say. She was a little girl, playing with her doll, when I was hurt going after Mary Mallinson. How could she be anything but what I tell you, Phoebe? There's no room in my mind for anyone but Mary!"

Phoebe shouldered her pack with a sniff. "Then you don't fear what I'll see, and don't mind my being with the army?"

"I do *not!* It would make no difference to me if you marched three feet from me all the journey!"

"Then we'll say no more about it," she said. "If you're going up to Fort Western by canoe I'll go with you."

She was bound to have the last word, I saw, and nothing was gained by arguing with her, any more than with any other woman; so we set off for the tavern together.

＊　　＊　　＊

Already order was appearing. The bateaux, drawn to the edge of the river, had been filled with packs and supplies. Strings of them were being launched and detachments of men rowing them upstream. The water was dotted with loaded bateaux, all moving toward Fort Western; and detachment after detachment was setting off afoot along the rutted wood road leading north from Agry's Point.

On a knoll at the lower end of the shipyard, surrounded by captains and lieutenants, stood a high officer of the expedition supervising the formation of three companies of musketmen. What caught my eye was the face of a man standing a little behind him—a long, sour face of a flat gray color, as though modeled in the clay from one

of our Maine coves. It called to my mind the inside of the council
house at Swan Island and the cold spring day when my father, dripping wet, dragged himself for the last time up the stairs of our inn at
Arundel. I leaped away from Phoebe, raced around the group of officers, and took the gray-faced man by the front of his buckskin hunting shirt. What was in my mind I'm not quite sure; but I know I had
often thought, in the half-dreams that lie between sleeping and wak-
ing, that I would like to take this man in my hands and pull him
slowly to pieces in revenge for what he had done to my father.

"Is your name Ezekiel Hook?" I asked, taking a tighter grip on
his hunting shirt. He looked me in the eyes, with no change of expression, and shook his head. Before I could question further I heard
a rasping shout of "Don't you ever salute officers?" It was the high
officer who shouted. He was red-faced and angry, and in him I recognized the person who had given us a dressing-down in Cambridge
for the same fault.

"Sir," I said, saluting carefully, "I ask your pardon! I thought this
man once did me a wrong."

The officer, mollified by my respect, laughed uproariously. "No, no,
no! John Treeworgy wouldn't do anyone a wrong. Always doing good,
John is. Guide, sir. Knows the Kennebec like a book. Best guide I've
got."

A messenger stood at attention before him. "Colonel Arnold's compliments to Colonel Enos," the messenger said, "and Colonel Arnold
asks him to wait here with his division for the construction of twenty
more bateaux."

I rejoined Phoebe, dissatisfied with Colonel Enos's recommenda-
tion of John Treeworgy. John Treeworgy was too like Ezekiel Hook
for my own peace of mind; and Colonel Enos looked as if he would
believe anything, provided it was told to him loud enough and often
enough.

*   *   *

I could hear Cap's bellowing voice bursting out of Smith's Tavern;
and while I wondered whether to interrupt him and carry him up
with us there was a scuttling beside me, and Jacataqua pushed herself under my arm. Her dog, a smooth-haired black animal with yellow legs and pale masklike markings around his eyes, grinned up at
me and flapped his tail against my knees, making me think back to
Ranger with a pang of homesickness.

"Here," I said, "whatever became of Ezekiel Hook?"

She shook her head. "I don't know him."

"A minister," I reminded her, "who wanted all of you to be Christians."

The name meant nothing to her.

"Do you know a man named John Treeworgy?" I persisted.

"Yes," she said, wrinkling her nose, as if at a bad odor. "An inspector for the Plymouth Company. He carried information about settlers and traders, so they often had trouble with the company. I haven't seen him for three years."

Phoebe touched me on the elbow, nodding toward the tavern. In the door stood little Aaron Burr of New Jersey, as neat and well brushed as though fresh from his tailor. Yet he looked less pretty than I remembered him, for his shoulders were stooped forward and his eyes glittered unpleasantly. Being glad to see him, I saluted; but he paid no attention. I saw he was staring at Jacataqua.

She smiled at him, swinging herself forward and backward at my waist, and said: "We can go now."

"I don't relish your distribution of favors," Burr said.

Jacataqua stared at him slack-lipped.

"Sir," I said, "you may remember me."

"Why," Burr said, "I may, but I probably sha'n't, under the circumstances."

"Under what circumstances?" I asked. His look was too offensive for my fancy.

"You know very well," he said, stepping up to me like a bantam. "I find you too free with your hands."

"Well, now," I said, "that's too bad, because if you had your way, I'd have to remove myself forever from my blood sister."

"Your blood sister!"

"Why, yes," I said. "Since she was four years old."

His hard black eyes never left mine.

"Well," I said to Phoebe, casting a look at the brassy-blue sky, "it looks a little like rain, so we'll start." I patted Jacataqua on the shoulder and took Phoebe by the arm, saying to myself that this liver-colored young whippersnapper needed a ducking in the river, and that the only thing saving him was the trembling of Jacataqua's lip.

We started away, whereat Burr came running to me, contritely holding Jacataqua by the hand. "Sir," he said, "I behaved badly; but dark eyes and cheeks like wine on amber can make the best of men, like the poorest of us, into boors. What can I do to redeem myself?"

When I had pondered his words, I said: "You might tell me about Colonel Enos."

Burr shot me what I thought was a grateful glance. "Enos is another of those lousy Connecticut colonels—a lieutenant colonel. He may not think he's God Almighty, but he considers himself a close relative."

"It seemed to me," I said, "he has a passion for being saluted. If he doesn't get over it, there might be trouble on the upper Kennebec. From what I've seen of our bateaux, they won't stand much dropping on the rocks, not even to let Colonel Enos be saluted."

"He'll get over it," Burr said, "when he has something to occupy his mind; but he'll never recover from remembering he was an officer of the King in the last war against the French, and in the expedition against Havana in 1762, when all the rest of us were infants, puling about the kitchen floor. He's stuffed to the bursting point with military lore he learned from the British, most of it not worth learning; and his age makes him cautious. When Colonel Arnold says 'Damn everything! Come ahead!' Colonel Enos says 'Wait! Let me think how we did it when I fought with the British!' To the devil with him and his caution! I can't see how caution will ever help us take Quebec!"

We went upstream close together, Jacataqua paddling Burr in a light canoe, while her dog sat in the bow, thumping his tail modestly against the bottom; and Hobomok at the stern of ours. When we slipped past the long strings of bateaux, those that rowed them bawled pleasantries at us, asking us where the dance was to be, or begging to be invited to the christening, or urging us to stop so they might kiss the bride. The whole river was a highway, bateaux moving up singly and in strings, and canoes bearing messengers and sightseers, with here and there a sloop or a schooner. On the shore detachments of soldiery threaded their way between the oaks and pines, with messengers or officers a-horseback weaving through them.

From Burr I had information concerning the army—how it consisted of a few more than one thousand men, all accustomed to fighting Indians or handling bateaux and axes, and skilled in the use of rifle or musket. They were, he declared, the choicest of the troops besieging Boston, and officered by the best the army afforded; so their patriotism and determination made up for the smallness of their numbers.

At this Phoebe thrust in her oar. "If they're all so patriotic, what ailed those aboard the sloop *Eagle* in Newburyport, struggling to get ashore once they were aboard, and guards placed over them to keep them from running home?"

Burr shook his pretty head. "A dozen of us racked our brains over that! They embarked gaily enough, and within two hours it was as though the devil bit them. One of Arnold's guides was there—a sour-faced fellow with a name like a mouthful of porridge. He thought they might have become ill from the stink of bilge."

"It takes more than the smell of bilge to turn a New Englander's stomach," Phoebe said.

"Was the guide's name Treeworgy?" I asked.

"That was it," said Burr. "Treeworgy. A name that sounds as if its owner didn't know how to spell it."

I thought so too, and said to myself Treeworgy would bear further inspection.

When I asked Burr whether he included Colonel Enos among those who were patriotic and determined, he said he did, since Enos had fought the French, and gone with the British to Havana on that dreadfully mismanaged expedition, and so must be counted a brave and able man.

But if, he said, there were shortcomings in him, they were made up by the excellences of Colonel Arnold and Lieutenant Colonel Greene, the former regarded by General Washington and General Schuyler as the foremost fighting officer in the army; one who would bring the highest military honors to our colonies.

He spoke with admiration of Major Meigs and Major Bigelow, and of the captains, any one of whom, he said, was fit to be a general. I think, with a few exceptions, he was right; for many of them became generals.

Over the rifle companies he waxed well nigh lyrical, saying they were the greatest soldiers ever seen: so far as he was concerned, he would be willing to attack Quebec with no more than three compa-nies of riflemen and their officers, and Colonel Arnold to lead them. I thought at the time he was speaking irrationally, since there are but seventy-five riflemen to a company, but I soon had occasion to change my mind. At an even later date, when we had picked Bur-goyne's army to pieces at Saratoga, I heard Burgoyne admit that Mor-gan's regiment of riflemen was the finest in the world; so I would be the last to consider Burr's judgment far off the mark.

There were horses and oxen at the foot of the quick water below Fort Western, and the bateaux were going up on sleds over the spongy wood road; so Hobomok and I overturned the canoes on one of the bateaux and traveled up in state.

The parade ground between the long wooden barracks and the river was already filled with tents and board huts, put up by the riflemen; and at one of the doors of the barracks stood Cap Huff, idly rummaging among his teeth with a splinter of wood, but scrutinizing the newcomers with prodigious attention. He darted past me and seized on a young Rhode Islander who was carrying a pair of dead chickens.

"Got a place to sleep, Brother?"

The boy shook his head.

"We got two bunks in the barracks," Cap said, "but we got to move up river right away. You're liable to be here five or six days, Brother, and get rained on if you ain't under cover."

The young Rhode Islander stared helplessly.

"Get your friend," Cap said, "and we'll trade you our two bunks for your two chickens."

What Cap said about being rained on was true; but he was not one to give up a bed so lightly. I waited for him; and in the course of time he emerged from the barracks, carrying his pack and the two chickens, and accompanied by a shambling man with a melancholy face. This man he introduced as Lieutenant Church.

"The lieutenant," he said hoarsely, "is the best scout in the province of Maine."

The lieutenant looked mournfully at the chickens.

"You better get on one of these scouting parties, Stevie," Cap continued in his hoarse whisper, "or they'll put you to dragging bateaux. Have you dragged one of 'em yet?"

He assured me with a horrified face that the Kittery gaol would be easier to drag. "I had to move one of 'em to-day," he said, caressing his broad expanse of back, "and it kind of took away my appetite."

I asked him how he had happened to relinquish his bunks in the barrack.

"Oh," he said, "they were full of bugs. The lieutenant discovered 'em."

The lieutenant poked mournfully at a chicken. "All right, Lieutenant," Cap said. "All right, we'll get right at it."

"How did you get up here so quick?" I called after him, as they moved away.

"I found a horse down at the shipyard," he explained, "so I rode it up to see if I could find out who it belonged to."

"Who did it belong to?"

"Well," he said, "I ain't had time to ask."

*   *   *

We worked until dark, getting up supplies from the foot of the
quick water. Later I sought out Captain Goodrich's company, so to
share their supper. They had drawn cornmeal and salt pork and peas,
and Phoebe had done what she could with them, which was little
enough, God knows.

As we sat by our fires and ate our rations I heard amazing tales of
what lay ahead. There was a mountain, one man said, alive with bed
bugs, enormous and rapacious, more like the hard red crabs on our
rocky coast. These insects had, for centuries, bred on its slopes; and
when it was overpopulated great armies of them set out, shrinking in
size from their exertions in swimming streams and climbing deadfalls,
until they came to settlements where they could support themselves.
Men who fell asleep near this mountain, the man said, were eaten to
death. No animal or bird could live on it.

Noah Cluff piped up to tell a tale he had heard about the Chaudière
River, which we must descend. "Chaudière," he said, "was a French
word meaning "boiler," and the name was given to the river because
along its course were holes down which the water was sucked, boiling
and steaming, into the depths of the earth; and any canoe that approached too close to a hole was never seen again.

Another said the army must march across a place called the Height
of Land which had never been crossed but by ten men; and on it
were bobcats the size of moose, and wolverines so fierce they would
attack men for the pleasure of hearing their bones crack.

At each of these tales I laughed, expecting the others to laugh with
me, as they would have laughed if I had said a sea serpent came up
the Arundel River every Sunday morning and devoured two fishermen and a dory. But the only one who laughed was Asa Hutchins,
and he would laugh at anything, even the Bible. The rest of them
grinned discomfortably, looking sideways at each other.

"Well, for God's sake!" I said. "Where'd you get these bogey tales!"

Jethro Fish poked at the fire with his bayonet. He was crowded off
the *Eunice,* he said, and came up from Newburyport in the *Eagle.*
All those aboard her had heard the tales and many more, some worse,
like the one about the meadows above the Chaudière growing on
top of rotted leaves, so those who set foot on them would be swallowed up.

"Why was it," I asked Jethro, "that men aboard the *Eagle* tried to run away after they'd embarked contentedly enough?"

Jethro said he wasn't sure; but those who tried to go ashore were Connecticut troops, men from towns, who knew less about the forests than most. It may have been, he said, they were frightened.

"Frightened by these tales?" I asked.

At this a laugh went up, a laugh of derision for folk who would allow themselves to be frightened; but I remembered how the laughers' eyes had rolled when the tales were told.

"Was there much of a stench to the *Eagle*," I asked, "of bilge or fish?"

"No," Jethro said. "She was a lumber schooner."

I asked him if he had seen the guide Treeworgy, or spoken with him. He said he had not; nor did the name have a meaning for him. There was something about the business that stuck in my gizzard; but I spoke my mind concerning the wild romances they were telling.

"Now," I said, "the truth is this: in my younger days, as all of you from Arundel know, I traveled far up Dead River. There I met an Indian, Natanis, who had come up the Chaudière from the St. Lawrence and across the Height of Land. I saw none of these things, nor did Natanis either. Your tales are fables, such as knaves tell to children to frighten them when they come to dark places in the road. If I knew who started them, I'd take off his skin with a rope end, just as I'd lash a man who found joy in frightening children. Wipe them out of your mind, and see there's no repeating of them! First thing you know, we'll have all the Connecticutters and Rhode Islanders running away, and our Maine men joining them in a panic to the shame of our province."

A messenger rode into the gate of the stockade and kindled a tin lantern so he might see the dispatch he carried. He bawled it out:

"All men to the carrying up of bateaux and stores at dawn; all captains to headquarters at Captain Howard's house, one mile above the fort, at ten o'clock; all guides to headquarters at sun-up."

Knowing we had need of sleep, I went back to Hobomok, and found he had made beds for us out of spruce branches. I said to myself, as I pulled the blanket over my face, that now, indeed, we were committed to the enterprise, and there was nothing to stand in our way, so that I could think of Mary as much as I wished. Before I could start to think I found Hobomok shaking me, and heard the trumpeting of geese overhead, and saw it was dawn again.

XVIII

I HAVE heard times without number, from folk who had no part in our march to Quebec, of the banquet held at Fort Western while we lay there waiting to start, a banquet of roasted bears and pumpkin pies and watermelons and rum punch. These tales have always come to me in after years, when the wood of our bateaux was rotting in the crevices of the river walls. If there was a banquet I saw none of it, nor did those who went with me; yet when I say so, I am rebuked by those who tell the tale. They say I wish to rob our march of its romance; but there was no romance to it that I could see, not even to that early part of it: nothing but haste that blistered our hands and toil that blinded us with sweat.

To this day I can hear the snarling bellow of Daniel Morgan driving us through the woods with our loads, and see him go charging up past us, dragging at a bogged wheel or heaving on a bateau, cursing the curses he learned as a teamster with Braddock's army when it marched to its ruin on the Monongahela.

I can see the ledge that blocked the road. Captain Dearborn, who has since become Secretary of War and a major general and an ambassador to some country in Europe, stood at the top of it, his shaggy black dog beside him, and at the bottom Captain Thayer, a most deceptive man, gentle and mild, yet an ex-officer of Rogers' Rangers, deadliest of all bush fighters. As we came laden to the ledge Thayer would push at us and Dearborn would pull, and the shaggy black dog would prance and bark, and we would bounce up the ledge as if it were no more than the feather bolster that separates children from their parents when all of them sleep in one bed.

Above all, I can hear Colonel Arnold shouting at us in a voice that was excitement itself, so that it put new iron into our sagging legs: "Get it up, boys! Up with it! No time to lose! If we lose a day we may lose everything! Get it up! Get it up!"

Those that talk of banquets never dragged up more than two hundred bateaux and the supplies to fill them, and made their camp and cooked their meals, and shifted the bateaux to starting places and loaded them, and learned their stations.

Yet I think I know how those reports of banquets had their start. Many of the officers were fed and lodged at Captain Howard's house, which he had built after he had ceased to be the captain at Fort Western; and at the end of our day of carrying, just after Colonel Arnold had passed up through us on his way to headquarters, Captain Hanchet, a Connecticut officer with an under jaw that stuck far out beyond his upper, came inside the stockade and made a hullaba-loo about pumpkin pies, looking among all of us, and even under the bunks in the barracks.

Cap Huff had come to sit beside me, somewhat moist and breath-less. He growled at Hanchet there was no use looking in the barracks, for if pies had been brought there, they would have been instantly gobbled by the vermin—which were plentiful enough to eat pies and tin plates to boot.

Eight pumpkin pies, I gathered, had been placed in the rear win-dows of Captain Howard's house to cool, and some ill-wisher had made off with them.

I would have thought no more about it had not Cap Huff whis-pered hoarsely that Hobomok had spitted a mess of partridges and ducks on ramrods, and that Phoebe was tending them by my lean-to with James Dunn, and that he had left Lieutenant Church there, and Jacataqua cooking pone, and a friend of Jacataqua's named Burr. Ravenous at the mention of partridges, I made off to the lean-to, fol-lowed by Cap; and when we got there Cap pointed up under the canoe in a meaningful manner. I dropped to my knees and peered into it. Resting on the bottom of the bow seat were five pumpkin pies.

Knowing eight had been taken, I asked where the other three had gone.

"Three!" Cap bawled. He crawled clumsily beneath the canoe to see for himself, and scrambled out roaring like a wounded bear. "You can't trust anyone!" he grumbled, staring first at Burr and then at Church, who studied his moccasins morosely. "Six there were, by God, when I went to get Steven."

"What did you do with the other two?" I asked.

"I dropped one. It fell on my foot. The other I had to eat."

"Well," Burr said, "seeing all of us must swear we don't know what you're talking about, I trust you'll control your anger long enough to let us deal with the others while we still have the chance. You should feel flattered to think you're eight times better than any of us. We made way with only one."

It was plain this thought pleased Cap, for though he continued to rumble concerning untrustworthiness, I caught him glancing admiringly at Burr from time to time. This he did, too, despite the manner in which Jacataqua leaned against Burr while she ate, looking up into his dark, pretty face so sickish-like that Phoebe withdrew from us and went to sit with James Dunn. James, embarrassed by the presence of officers, had perched himself on a log at the edge of the firelight, where he bit into a duck with such profundity that he seemed to be planning a reform of the currency.

❉   ❉   ❉

It was well Burr had spurred Cap to silence and greater speed, for we had barely finished the last of the pies when a messenger came down the path, shouting again for all guides, scouts, and officers to report at headquarters. We found Colonel Arnold laboring at a desk in Captain Howard's sitting room, checking lists and making new ones and dictating orders to his secretary and calling for this captain and that captain, no more interested in a banquet than we were in having our hair powdered.

I was called before him when the night was half done, and found Colonel Greene, Colonel Enos, Major Meigs, and Captain Morgan with him, all in blue uniforms save Morgan, who wore a hunting shirt and leggins and moccasins.

Colonel Arnold popped out his pale eyes at me. "Nason, you've been up Dead River. Give these gentlemen your opinion."

He read Conkey's report aloud.

"Do you think," he asked, "that this report is correct or that our army would be in danger from either Indians or British troops?"

"Sir," I said, "that report's worthless! I think Conkey stopped far short of his goal, and filled his report with lies. The man who made it had to carry six gallons of rum to get even as far as he did."

"So!" Colonel Arnold said, smiling blandly at the others. "I think it's plain we're safe in taking a shot at it."

"Sir," I added, "in regard to the Indian Natanis——"

"I know all about him!" Colonel Arnold said impatiently.

"Sir," I said, "in that matter the report is also——"

Colonel Arnold's face grew dark and lumpy. He slapped his desk with the flat of his hand, while Colonel Enos frowned portentously at me. "I ask for advice when I want it!" Arnold snapped.

I thanked my stars I had sent Natawammet to warn Natanis; and I resolved to keep my mouth shut about him in the future until such time as I might be forced to speak.

That night we were assigned; and of the assignments I noted only three: Cap Huff to Lieutenant Church's scouting party that was to start as soon as possible after sun-up the next day; John Treeworgy to Lieutenant Colonel Enos; and Steven Nason to Colonel Arnold.

Cap was fat and moist and pleased when he set off in the bow of one of Church's two canoes the next morning, secure in having escaped the danger of being burdened with a bateau, and red-faced from his recent glut of pumpkin pies. At the same time the party of Lieutenant Steele of the Pennsylvania riflemen set off in two more canoes to scout across the Height of Land and bring back the information that the wretched Conkey had failed to get. Of men who have lived up to their names, I think this same Steele accomplished it best; for if ever a man seemed made of metal that would never break, it was he. The world is full of statues to less deserving men than Archibald Steele; but they were fortunate and he was not; so he is statueless still.

When Steele was gone, we moved the bateaux of the first division to the starting place, halfway between Fort Western and Captain Howard's. The three companies of riflemen formed the first division, and all of them agreed to go under the leadership of Morgan. Our New Englanders, badly disciplined and more independent than a hog on ice, looked askance at Morgan because he issued strict orders and enforced them with a heavy hand. Yet the riflemen, being disciplined, took pride in him, holding him in esteem and affection, and would have followed him through hell and high water, even while calling him opprobrious names: Old Yeller-belly and Dirty Dan and Gorgon Morgan and others too foul to set down. Indeed, they held Morgan in almost as high esteem as Arnold, who was considered by all the troops to be the bravest and ablest officer, not only of our little army, but of the entire continental forces.

Now that I look back on it, I doubt that our march could have been made under any leader but Arnold, excepting Washington himself, because of the fearful jealousies that would have arisen. Arnold was a dare-devil, violent and passionate when he had cause. So, too, was Morgan, though ruder and coarser than Arnold, who had the manners of a polished gentleman when he chose to use them.

Because of Colonel Greene's high rank, Arnold placed him in command of the first division. At once Morgan raised an outcry that many

of us heard because of his booming teamster's voice. He would ac-
knowledge, he said, the authority of no man except Arnold over his
riflemen, nor would the riflemen accept it. Therefore he himself
would command the riflemen or nobody would. I looked to hear an
explosion from Colonel Arnold, but there was none. He soothed Morgan and he soothed Greene, saying Morgan had a genius for leading
quick-moving troops in forests, and was more experienced at it than
anyone. Since, he added simply, the object of the attack was to capture Quebec, and not to gain glory for any individual, he would yield
to Morgan's judgment and give Colonel Greene the command of the
second division. Thereupon there was great good feeling, Arnold and
Greene happy because they had been generous, and Morgan happy
because his claims, which were justified, had been recognized.

         ❖   ❖   ❖

On the last Monday in September in 1775, we watched Morgan's
tall Virginians launch their sixteen bateaux, laden with forty-five
days' provisions and their ammunition and axes. They traveled light
to hew out a road across the Great Carrying Place for the rest of us.

Each bateau was poled by two men, while a relief of two men
followed it along the shore. When the first bateau of the sixteen had
shrunk to a black dot upstream, the sixteen bateaux of Smith's Pennsylvania riflemen went in, riding high in the water, and set off after
them; and behind them those of Hendricks's Pennsylvania riflemen,
all the bateaumen poling for dear life, and those who marched on
shore shouting at them profanely not to let the lousy Virginians beat
them, and be careful not to run on a rock, dearie.

Among those who shouted was the wife of Sergeant Grier, an es-
timable woman with an arm as big as my leg and a rump like a
draught horse, and Mrs. Warner, a tall red-faced wench. As they
struck out ahead of their husbands, Sergeant Grier slapped his wife
affectionately on her broad seat with the butt of his rifle, so that she
went howling into the woods.

In three minutes there was no sign of the more than two hundred
men save the bateaux bobbing upstream, yawing in the swift water,
and the faint shouts of those who had been swallowed up in the
crimson foliage of the river side.

By noon of the next day the second division went up, Captain
Thayer's company and Captain Topham's company and Captain
Hubbard's company, the bateaux streaming out into the river under
the eye of Colonel Greene and Major Bigelow, and half the men

marching along the shore, strung out and making no effort to march in ranks, as indeed they could not, since the trail was churned into muck by many feet and the rain of Sunday.

With this division went young Burr, his rank that of volunteer cadet officer. He came up behind me, dapper and smiling and hampered by no pack at all, and said, "Bring up a pumpkin pie when you come."

When I asked for Jacataqua, he winked mysteriously, saying she would be along shortly. So she was, as soon as the tumult had died away, paddling bow while one of her Swan Island braves knelt in the stern, her yellow-faced dog leaning against the small of her back, yawning as though he took no interest in the prospect.

Knowing Phoebe would be off on the morrow, I traveled to the Fort to see her that night. She was cutting James Dunn's hair, while he brooded philanthropically on a log, as though he had founded a college but couldn't decide who should be president. Phoebe gave him a few extra snips around the ears, then handed him the scissors, patting him on the shoulder as one pats a child. "Take these to Jethro, James, while Mother talks to Stevie."

"For God's sake," I said, when he padded away, "go back to Arundel and take him with you. You're like two children, not knowing what lies ahead."

She shook her head. "Yesterday I thought I might. There were some men deserted from Enos's companies, and no effort made to pursue them, so I thought I might take James away with me."

"Why didn't you?"

She twirled her string of cat's eyes. "When I told him about it, he looked at me so I felt worse than a coward. 'I couldn't do that,' he said. 'Somebody might think I was afeared.' He told me he was having a good time: the best he ever had."

She swung her cat's eyes thoughtfully. "He never had a good time, Stevie. He was always put upon; always pecked at; always browbeat when there was any browbeating afoot, more than anybody else; always laughed at in the shipyard and the tavern. Now he isn't pecked at any more than anyone else; never will be again, he says, because he can always do what they tell him. Nothing to do, he says, but carry a pack and a musket and go where you're told. He can do that as well as anyone, he says."

"Isn't he afeared?"

"He says not. He says there's nothing to be afeared of if you don't think ahead: just do what you're told."

There was something in that, I decided. I knew that in my own case I sweated and groaned in my blanket when I thought, as I often did, that I might be kept from finding Mary by these endless days of delays, or by falling over a rock and breaking a leg.

"Why did you marry him, Phoebe?" I asked. It was a question that often came into my mind.

She held up one of her cat's eyes and squinted at the fire through it. "I'll tell you some day. I'll tell you after you've found Mary."

"I hope to God it'll be soon then," I said. Phoebe continued to gaze at the fire through her cat's eye, turning it from side to side, as though to catch the glow in it.

"So," I said at length, "there's been desertions among Enos's men?"

She nodded. "They say there's a thousand Iroquois ambushed on the Chaudière, waiting for us."

"They say! They say!" I shouted. "It's a lousy lie! How would the Iroquois get down through Schuyler's army, and who'd feed 'em? Why is it that none of the other divisions gets these stories, only Enos's?"

I got up in a rage, a vague idea in my mind, and started off to put it to use.

"Well," Phoebe said, "good-bye in case we get separated."

I went back and took her by the shoulders. I had seen a deal of her in the past four years, and she seemed like a young brother, a little. "We'll see each other often. Don't go falling into logans, and keep your feet out from between rocks." I looked around to see if anyone was listening. "If anything goes wrong after you reach the Height of Land, you can always find friends of mine in the woods. Understand? Red friends."

She stared up at me with a sort of trusting look in her eyes. I stooped and kissed her. Her lips were cold.

"In the spring," I said, "we'll have our brig."

She nodded.

"Good-bye, Phoebe." She didn't answer; so I went away to look for Treeworgy.

I found him sitting by a fire, gray-faced and sour-mouthed, as if he had been eating half-ripe chokecherries. If he was not Ezekiel Hook, he was the spit of him, except for being heavier and grayer. There were a few musketmen at the fire with him, all somber and cheerless. I dropped my hand on his shoulder, saying, "Hook!"

He turned and looked up at me, then grinned sourly. "Not me," he said, seeming to take no offense.

"What's all this I hear about desertions?"

Treeworgy humped his shoulders. "There's a few went home. One or two, mebbe. Homesick, likely. Got to thinking, the way boys will, they wouldn't see their mothers or their gals for months or years, mebbe; mebbe ever."

One or two of the musketmen moved uncomfortably, staring into the fire.

"There's something queer going on in this division," I said. "There's more damned lies afloat in it than Beelzebub himself could think up in a million years of hell."

Treeworgy nodded. "I heard 'em. Them about the British mining the banks of the St. Lawrence, so's to blow us all up, and Million Rattlesnake Mountain, where the rattlesnakes strike first and rattle afterward, and Boiling Water Bog, that you fall into and cook if you try to cross."

"My God, Treeworgy!" I shouted, "haven't you got more sense than to repeat these things? They're damned filthy lies, fit to scare the gizzard out of folks that don't know Dead River's as pretty a river as there is."

"That's what I tell 'em," Treeworgy agreed. "When they come to me and ask if Dead River got its name from the thousands that died on it I tell 'em it ain't so. The same with all of the stories. I don't believe any of 'em."

"You don't *believe* 'em," I said, breaking into a flux of profanity and eyeing him while I cursed. "You know there isn't a word of truth in 'em!"

"Well, now, I guess that's right," said Treeworgy, mild as a phoebe bird's song on a hot day, and seeming to pay no attention to my swearing.

"You *know* it's right! If I can get my fingers on the misbegotten spawn of hell that started 'em, I'll tear his lying windpipe out of his throat." With that, having in mind how Ezekiel Hook had shrunk before what he had been pleased to call my father's blasphemy, I blasphemed against the teller of these tales with such violence that I was shamed by my own play-acting. Yet the gray sourness of Treeworgy's face altered not a whit, so I was forced to believe he told the truth when he said he wasn't Hook.

On the next day, Wednesday, the third division went on its way, Captain Dearborn's company, Captain Ward's company, Captain Hanchet's company, and Captain Goodrich's company, all of them led by Major Meigs, whose first name was Return, so that he was scurrilously known as Back-up by the men of his division, and it was the fashion among the other divisions to shout, "Whoa! Whoa!" at them. His own men, indeed, were given to shouting, "Whoa! Whoa!" at each other. Immediately on doing so they would pole their bateaux vigorously, being men from Maine and Northern New England, skillful with setting-poles.

The river looked to be filled with the bateaux of this division, sixty-four of them, each one loaded more heavily than Morgan's or Greene's. My heart misgave me as I watched James Dunn and Phoebe marching off abreast of the bateau poled by Jethro Fish and Asa Hutchins, Asa bawling, "Whoa! Whoa!" at the top of his lungs. Phoebe looked sadly small, marching thin and straight in her buckskin jerkin and blue handkerchief behind the hulking James, an extra pair of moccasins dangling at her waist. She turned and waved to me, then vanished under the flaming leaves of a giant maple. I wondered what in God's name I could say to my mother if I had to come home without her.

And so we knuckled to the getting up of Colonel Enos's division, the fourth and last, heaviest laden of them all, since the carrying places would be cleared for them, and huts built, and camping places selected. All that day we worked like slaves, and the next morning, bringing bateaux and tents and kegs of nails and pitch; barrels of bread and pork and peas; bags of flints and salt and meal, and a whole kit and boiling of material. Still there were bateaux unfinished and supplies unassembled; and Enos was puttering about at Colburn's like an old woman or a British general.

Thursday passed, with Arnold sending messenger after messenger to Enos, his face black and lumpy, as though walnuts had been pushed under his skin, and gnawing at his nails until they were chewed straight across the ends of his fingers. He was pleasant enough to the rest of us, holding his turmoil within himself. When he told me to go down and tell them for God's sake to hurry, he said it pleasantly and calmly, with only a little twitching at the corners of his mouth to show his eagerness to be off.

Even on the next morning, a damnable Friday again, though I have no sympathy with folk who attach an evil influence to this day, there were only two of Enos's companies up—Captain McCobb's and Captain Scott's—while Enos and the commissary and Captain Williams's company and Reuben Colburn's company of carpenters were still down at the shipyard gathering up their odds and ends. At ten o'clock Arnold's adjutant, Captain Oswald, came jumping down the path from Captain Howard's house and ordered McCobb and Scott to send off their companies. "Let Enos and the rest follow when he can," I heard him say.

He turned to me, grinning like a boy who has heard good news. "Get your canoe! We're leaving for Quebec in an hour!"

Hobomok brought me up to Howard's with our packs, our meal tied into bladders, so no water could hurt it, and over our packs a bearskin. Arnold's long canoe was there, loaded, with Indians to paddle, and places for Arnold and Oswald. I asked Hobomok who the Indians might be.

"Eneas and Sabatis," Hobomok said.

I only half heard him, for Arnold came plunging down the bank, a yellow hunting shirt over his uniform. He turned a cartwheel on one hand, so that there was no military pomp about him.

"Keep close behind," he called to me. "I'm using you to carry dispatches."

In a moment the canoe was off, bouncing across the quick water toward the converging walls of red maples as though shooting into a funnel of flame.

BOOK III

MANITOU KINNIBEC

XIX

To my mind there is a serpentine beauty to the Kennebec: dappled with ledges and islands; twining gracefully among rolling meadows, towering forests, and rock-strewn mountains; slipping smoothly across levels; plunging headlong over falls; coiling quietly in pools. There is something about it, I have often thought, that captivates those who gaze upon it: something that brings them back to stare in fascination; to dare its perils; to listen at night to the dry rustlings, the chucklings, the intermittent rattlings with which it flows along its rocky bed. Sturgeons and salmon return to it each year in greater numbers than to any of our other rivers. Even wild fowl, struggle as they may to leave its glittering folds, seem drawn to it from distant places, too often falling victims to their infatuation.

Yet one must have a care; for there is a snaky chill about it all the year; and in the fall and winter this becomes a bite that tortures flesh and sinks into the bone.

Being busy with my thoughts as we went up the stream, I neither saw the beauty of the river nor felt the sharpness of waning September. It had come to me that I had first heard the names of Arnold's Indians years before, from Natanis. They were the ones who, punctured by my father's arrows, had been left by Guerlac at the Chain of Ponds when he was running for safety ahead of us.

How this coincidence had befallen was the thing that puzzled me; for Hobomok declared that Sabatis and Eneas lived far from each other, Eneas near the Height of Land still, but Sabatis in Pittston, close to Colburn's, for whom he trapped beavers and otters and so lived in comfort. My brain was in a muddle over the affair. I misliked revealing myself, as I would if I questioned them properly. God only knows what an Indian will do when he considers himself wronged; and if they learned I had been a party to the attack on them when they had been Guerlac's men, their love of vengeance might lead them to do me a hurt, and even to include my friends in their hatreds —Natanis or Cap Huff or Phoebe or Hobomok. So I said to Hobomok we must bide our time until we found Natanis. He would either know the truth or discover it for us.

Colonel Arnold signaled us to go ashore at the settlement of Vassalborough. He climbed from the canoe with water dripping from the seat of his breeches and asked in scathing tones what would have become of the army if it had used canoes.

"This thing's a basket," he said, "good for a minnow-trap, but bad for sitting! Let me have no more bark cockleshells! Get me something to keep out the water!"

He would have none of our canoe when I offered it, though it was as dry as a puffball; so Captain Oswald and I hunted through the settlement until we found a high-sided wooden canoe, a peraqua or pirogue, carved thin out of a pine log without knots, a log that must have been five feet in diameter when it was standing. In this the colonel went on more slowly.

We passed up through the bateaux of the fourth division before dusk and camped that night near old deserted Fort Halifax, whose usefulness, together with that of all the other Kennebec forts, had vanished when James Wolfe took Quebec from the French. By mid-morning of the next day we had passed the fort and found many bateaux waiting at the first carrying place, though the most of them had already been carried the third of a mile around Ticonic Falls. Here there was a tumult. The water was quick and broken so that the men were in and out of it perpetually, holding their bateaux in place and nursing them into line, slipping on the rounded stones and filling their mouths in the middle of a curse, and coughing and swearing and shouting.

I thanked God I was handling a canoe, for each bateau must be unloaded, piece by piece, and the load placed on the bank, after which the bateau was hoisted out and balanced on two carrying poles. Its crew staggered off with it, slithering in the mud, stumbling on roots and stones, and so carried it for the entire third of a mile; then returned and shouldered the load, kegs and barrels and sacks and tents and muskets, carried them the third of a mile to the bateau, stowed them in place and set off into the stream again.

Far worse were the Five Mile Ripples, just above Ticonic Falls. They come down at such a slant, and with such a turbulence of foam and leaping spray, that one who has never passed over them thinks, on looking at them, that they cannot be mounted in any craft whatever.

Knowing they must be conquered, the bateaumen belittled the

prospect, one declaring that fish went up, and that no fish was better than he; others shouting, "Whoa! Whoa!" and all plunging at it without delay, each bateau carrying four men instead of two.

Two of the men wielded poles, shoving rapidly and violently. If the head of the bateau fell away with the swiftness of the water, the other two would leap over the side and struggle to hold her bow upstream. Often they couldn't, so that the bateau would whirl downstream to bring up with a crack against a boulder. Thereupon her half-drowned crew would straighten her out and go at it again.

There were five miles of these ripples, long miles; and though all the bateaux got up eventually, they took a prodigious thumping from rocks and a power of wrenching from the current. Every last one of them sprung leaks—not one leak, either, but many. Most of the bateaumen stood calf-deep in water when they had surmounted the ripples; and if there was a dry load among them I heard nothing of it.

The dusk came down bitter, with a white mist rising from the river, a mist that stiffened arms and legs; and when we saw a line of fires we went ashore. The fires belonged to Meigs and his men. We found them inclined to be thoughtful and silent; for the result of all their laboring and wallowing and straining had been a gain of seven miles between dawn and dark.

We unpacked a tent for Arnold and lay in the woods. It was that night that the coughing started; and there was never a night after that, for months, that the sounds of the river or the forest were not broken by coughs. We fell asleep to a chorus of coughs, and we woke to more coughs. There was no end to the coughing, so that it seemed there could be no place in the world free from it.

A barrel of salted beef had been opened that night, but when we came to eat it, it was summer-killed and sour. There was noisy argument among the men, some calling it beef; others declaring it was horse or porpoise, or maybe seal; and most of them pitching the meat into the river without more ado.

I found Phoebe tending James Dunn, who sat regally before a hot fire, occasionally shaking with a chill that collapsed him like a pricked bladder. All of them were wet, Jethro and Asa and Noah and poor Nathaniel Lord, and even Phoebe; and the night was one of those cruel nights that occurs toward the end of September, when the water freezes along the edges of brooks and puddles, and the unaccustomed coldness seems to bite deeper into the marrow than the real cold of later winter.

I told them to stuff their pulpy shoes and moccasins with leaves, tight, if they wanted another week's use out of them.

"How is it up ahead?" Noah asked, careless-like.

I hated to answer. "Well," I said at length, "it ain't so good, but it might be worse."

They pondered over this. "Well," Phoebe said, "to-day might have been worse. We might have had to come through a tidal wave."

"What I think we ought to do," Asa said, "is bore holes in the bottom of our bateau, so's the water can run out as well as in."

A man bawled at us from the adjoining fire. "We got a better scheme over here! We're going to cut holes in the bow and stern. Then we can stand in the holes and walk along the bottom and hold the bateau up around us like it was our skirts."

"How's James doing?" I asked Phoebe.

"If it ain't any worse than to-day," James said, "I can keep going forever."

"It looks as if that's about the length of time you'll have to keep going," Noah Cluff told him sourly.

Seeing they were in good spirits in spite of their wet clothes and bad food, I went back to our camp and found Captain Oswald perturbed over desertions, which had begun to be noticed toward the end of the Five Mile Ripples. One bateau crew from Meigs's division, he said, had deserted in a body, vanishing into the forests with their muskets.

"What does Arnold say about it?" I asked.

"He says we're better off without 'em. He says they wouldn't fight anyway."

"That's about right, isn't it?"

"Maybe, but it gets worse farther on, they tell me."

"You haven't seen anything yet," I assured him.

"What if they all quit, then?"

"The way you and the colonel are going to quit?"

"My God!" he said, "there's nothing that'll make *us* quit."

"Well," I said, "don't forget others feel the same way."

Oswald nodded. "That's right. I guess the salted beef got me gloomy."

That was a bad night. The wet clothes froze on the men, a distressful feeling; and no man was wishful to lie abed beyond dawn. Since it was only the first of October, we told ourselves, there must be warmer weather in store for us; and since we were still in settled regions, not yet swallowed in the trackless wilderness, the traveling must improve. So we thought, but not for long.

We pushed out into quick water; and because all the bateaux passed it safely, we tried not to notice how they were racked by the passing, and how frequently their crews went ashore to bail with bark scoops.

But in time we approached Skowhegan Falls, made by the devil for the torturing of racked bateaux. Half a mile short of the falls was a right angle in the river and below it a triple whirlpool because of the force with which the water shot around the bend from the narrow channel above. Here the bateaux were strained and slammed against the rocks. How they came through the whirlpool and the narrow chute I cannot tell to this day, though I watched them passing through, the bateaumen swinging their poles from one side to the other like flails, poking and clawing and scrambling like cats. Above the chute between the ledges was a half-mile run of hellish current, quick and white; and though the crews scrambled along the shore, dragging their bateaux with ropes, there was no way to keep the clumsy craft from bumping and thumping against the sheer rocks, and sopping up water like salt bags. At the end of the half-mile run, there were the high Skowhegan Falls on each side of a craggy island in midstream. The face of the island is six times the height of a man; and in the middle of it is a cleft, which the Abenakis say was made by the tomahawk of the great lord Glooskap. The cleft is the route for carrying canoes over the falls. One man must drag, clinging with his toes and fingernails to the rock; and another must push, pressing himself against the rock sides like a snail. If either slip, then both are cruelly scraped and bruised, fortunate indeed if not hurled to the bottom of the cleft, all skin torn from them, and their canoe smashed into the bargain.

When, therefore, the bateaumen went to carrying their bateaux up through this cleft, after the barrels and packs and stores had been unloaded, there were times when it seemed men would burst like eggs between the bateaux and the rocks, and other times when apparently a bateau couldn't move another inch unless knocked to pieces with axes. Yet every bateau went up, and men lay exhausted on the point of the island above the carry, shoulders torn from their hunting shirts, knees ripped from their breeches, and crimson bandages to show where bateaux had crushed them against the ledges.

Everywhere, on both sides of the river and on the islands, men calked their bateaux as best they could; for being of green wood, and not too well made, they opened up under the pounding and wrenching as though built from driftwood. I thought it was true, what Phoebe had said to me, that she would as lief essay this journey in the ancient skiff in which she had learned to sail as a child, made out of a sunken boat patched with pitch and rotten canvas, as in one of these terrible craft.

Arnold didn't like it. "I still think they're better than canoes," he told me, "but get forward to Morgan and have him stop everyone at Norridgewock for overhauling all boats. If we don't, half of 'em'll burst in midstream and we'll lose our supplies."

Hobomok and I went up past Greene's men, struggling through the roaring water of Bombazee Rips; and by nightfall we reached the point of land my father and I had known as Norridgewock. Now it was nothing, its cabins having been leveled to make place for the farms of two settlers. We came up to Morgan at the foot of Norridge-wock Falls, where the riflemen were unloading their bateaux and pre-paring for the carry around.

Morgan was furious. He was a strange figure, having grown a bristly beard and being clad in nothing but leggins, moccasins, and belt cloth, in the Indian fashion. Across his bare back were the criss-crossed scars of a whipping received from British officers in his younger days—a whipping that caused him to hate the English with a bitter hatred, and that cost them dear before Daniel Morgan had done with them.

"By God!" he roared, and his voice reverberated above the rumble of the falls, "it's high time! Look at this!" He seized one of his bateaux by the thwart and heaved it on its side, so that its load of barrels and tents and bags and litter of tackle slid out in a dripping heap. Then he banged the side with his fist, sinking one of the boards below the other, slipping his fingers into the opening, and with a jerk of his arms loosened the upper part of the side from the lower as easily as the backbone of a broiled mackerel is lifted from the meat.

"A puking baby could build better boats out of blocks!" he shouted, pounding the boards back into place with two mighty blows. "Show me the perfumed dressmaker that basted these for men to risk their lives in, and I'll calk a boat with his skin!" He named the carpenters violent names; foul names from dark recesses of his mind; so that I was filled with amazement to know so much profanity had been hidden from me.

Nor were his riflemen milder in their anger. Their supplies were soaked; and they themselves had been drenched by day and frozen

by night since they had left Fort Western seven days before, so that
illnesses were breaking out among them, dysenteries and throat dis-
tempers, and rheumatisms that swelled their joints.

Some of them told me in all seriousness that they thought of waiting until the carpenters should come up, and then binding them and
carrying them to the top of the falls and sending them over it in the
worst of their bateaux.

"No," I said, "the fault lies farther back. The one to blame is the
man who persuaded General Washington and Colonel Arnold that
the Kennebec could be navigated in these boats."

"And who's that?" asked a tall Virginian, his wrists so swollen with
rheumatism that he held his hands before him as if seeking appro-
bation.

"I don't know," I said, "but some day I'll find out."

"When you do," he said, "we'll skin him for you, unless you'd rather
have him covered with clay and baked in a hole in the ground."

These men wouldn't rest, saying they must cut the roads for the
others because they were better woodsmen than our little weaklings
from Connecticut and Maine, which I think they were, though Maine
woodsmen are by no means useless. At dawn the next day a part of
them carried their baggage up the steep rocky hill of Norridgewock
—a hill a mile in length, as rough and cruel as the ledges of Arundel.
The rest went to calking and pitching their bateaux. As soon as a
bateau was finished, four men would hoist it to their shoulders and
stumble off up the carry. By the time Arnold reached us that night
the entire first division had gone over.

The other divisions came up slowly, in worse condition, I thought,
than the first. They were more heavily laden, and the men less powerful, man for man, than the riflemen, so their bateaux had been less
skillfully handled and were almost wrecks.

Never did I see a greater mess than these bateaux. Some carried
dried codfish as provisions, stuffed loosely around casks and barrels.
The fish, soaked for days, had disintegrated. Water had leaked into
the barrels containing dry bread, so that the bread had swollen and
burst the barrels. There were casks of dried peas, poorly coopered.
The peas had swollen and forced the staves apart; and the bottoms
of the bateaux were filled with a soup of fish, bread and peas, trampled together and smeared over the rest of the baggage.

Now Norridgewock was less than a third of the distance to Quebec; and beyond Norridgewock, until we should reach the French

settlements far down the Chaudière, there was no house, no road, only unbroken forests to which axes had never been laid since the beginning of the world. Therefore I misliked this wrecking of our food supply. It left us with nothing except flour and pork, and not too much of that; and I had seen no disposition on the part of any of our soldiers to be sparing with their rations, nor did I look to see them so while there was any left; for their independence was such that if told to eat less food, they ate more out of cussedness.

Yet Colonel Arnold stayed cheerful, nor did I ever see him in an evil mood so long as he could go forward. At a delay he was in a frenzy of anxiety and querulousness; but while he could move toward his goal there seemed to be no blow great enough to lower his spirits.

"Now," he said, when I reported to him the bursting of all but two of the bread barrels in the third division, "now they'll travel faster; for they'll travel lighter and be more eager to come to food." Nor could I quarrel with his determination to press on, for I had long ago made up my mind that I would press on to hunt for Mary, even though every man in the army turned back and left me to go alone.

Knowing what I knew about our food, I tried to send Phoebe back. I found her perched beside James Dunn in the warmth of a roaring fire, like a half-drowned mouse sitting beside a sleepy dog. She was roasting strips of pork on the end of a stick, wrapping them in cakes made of flour and water, and pushing them into James's mouth. There was mud on her face, and a welt across her throat where a briar had slashed her. From her breast to her moccasins she was black with water and muck, and her extra moccasins had been fastened at her neck, where they hung under her ears like pendulous lobes.

"Where are your cat's eyes?" I asked.

She popped a piece of pork into her own mouth and went on feeding James, pausing only long enough to show me a lump tied into the toe of one of her extra moccasins.

"Phoebe," I said, "take James and go on home before food runs short. There's no houses beyond here."

James Dunn regarded me calmly. "When are you leaving?" he asked.

"That's my James!" Phoebe said thickly, her mouth full of pork.

"Why," I said, surprised at this unexpected burst from the silent James, "I'm not leaving, but I don't want to see you two get into trouble."

"Of course you don't, Steven," Phoebe said. "None of us would have dreamed of coming with this army if we'd known there'd be trouble."

"I'm used to trouble," James said.

"We wouldn't know what to do if we couldn't be in trouble," Phoebe said.

"You know what I mean," I told them.

"From the way you talk about us going back," James remarked, "you must think we're a couple of rats from the Fourth Division."

"No," I said, taken aback by James's newly found independence and willingness to use his tongue. "No, no! No, no, no!"

"I've got the flux," James said. "My stomach's ached me for two days, but even so I can march better than most of these soldiers. There ain't none of 'em passed me. I'm as good as any of 'em. There ain't any of 'em that'll do better, not while I stay alive."

"Good!" I said, wishing I'd never touched the subject, and earnestly desiring to speak of other things, but unable to think of anything.

"If there ain't food," said James with an air of thoughtful meditation that made his face almost beautiful, "I can eat dandelions, or pine cones, maybe; maybe leaves."

Phoebe slipped another slice of pork into James's mouth, jeering at me with her eyes; so I left them hurriedly, swearing I would interest myself no more in the affairs of so unaccountable a female as Phoebe Dunn.

The colonel stayed at Norridgewock for seven days—seven dreary days of rain and cold; of whistling winds and brown leaves that whirled out of a leaden sky, smelling of sadness and the dying year—seven days of driving each division at top speed in the repairing of its bateaux; in the sorting and repacking of its diminished provisions; in the dreadful mile-long carry up the rocky sides of Norridgewock Falls.

Not until late on the seventh of October did Colonel Enos's division get the last of its baggage across the carry. All his men were grumbling bitterly because they were more heavily burdened than the other divisions. I looked for Treeworgy and found him carrying loads as weighty as any man; albeit with a face so gray and dolorous that if I had been forced to see it often by my side I would have sickened with sympathetic misery.

*   *   *

I have often wondered what evil of Nature is the most unsup-
portable. There are times when I think heat is the worst; times when
I'm sure there is nothing so bad as bitter cold. But oftenest I have
been led to feel that long-continued rain is the foulest of all, with its
gloom and discomfort, the trees and rocks and houses weeping and
weeping until every man's spirits are lowered in fellow feeling: the
earth a morass that plucks at the feet; the bodies of men and animals
steaming and reeking with the chilly damp from which there's no
escape.

It rained hard the day we wished to leave Norridgewock, which
was the eighth of October. We could get no foothold in the mud
of the steep carry, and feared to burst our canoes and supplies by
falling with them. We waited until the ninth, hoping for a let-up;
but there was more rain, so the colonel decided we must have a shot
at it. This we did, coming through safely, and so set off after the
army.

If all our journey could have been through country as rich as that
between Norridgewock and Carritunk Falls, and over water no more
violent, we might have made a picnicking party of it, regardless of
the rain. The stream was full of trouts, which we caught by thousands. There were grassy islands in the river; and the banks were
fertile and sloping, cut with the indentations called logans on the
Kennebec. Above the logans were stands of oak and maple, elm,
beech and ash, as well as pines and hemlocks; so the army struck
up on the slope to avoid the logans and marched through this un-
spoiled forest, free of rocks and tangled undergrowth.

We camped on a high island covered, like all this section of the
Kennebec, with a blue joint grass that grows six feet tall. Out of this
we made soft beds. We caught trouts and dried ourselves by driftwood fires, saying to ourselves that marching through the wilderness
wasn't bad, once we were hardened to it.

*   *   *

We have days, on the coast of New England, that are beautiful
and cloudless, with scarce enough wind to flutter a poplar leaf. Folk
of small experience are ravished by them; but those whose daily
habits are governed by the weather know they're weather-breeders,
forerunners of storms, though we find difficulty in explaining how a

weather-breeder can be distinguished from a fine day, and usually do so by saying it's too good. If from Arundel we can see the White Hills, eighty miles away, it's a weather-breeder.

When we woke to a bitter dawn, stumbled around Carritunk Falls and embarked on a river shallower and more rock-strewn than any portion we had yet found, it came to us that the easy journeying of the preceding day had been a weather-breeder: a period of unnatural calm before a tempest.

We found ourselves among mountains capped with snow, overbearing country, with cold gray clouds pressed tight against the hilltops. The water was so shoal that bateaumen dragged their clumsy craft, which is hard on the stomach muscles. It is equally hard on bateaux; for after one of those poorly built things is banged on a rock a hundred times, and wrenched across ledges, and jerked a dozen miles over the gravel beds of the upper Kennebec, it becomes as porous as my mother's nutmeg grater. Not even canoes could be driven through the shoalest spots; so we were perpetually in and out of the icy water, the colonel and Oswald included. By dusk we kindled our fires with no further remarks concerning the pleasurable features of wilderness travel.

I know that I, for one, took a deal of joy in the sight of Sugar Loaf Mountain dead ahead the next morning, after we had fought the current less than three hours; for the Sugar Loaf is the landmark of the Great Carrying Place.

All along the westerly side of the river were the bateaux of the first three divisions, piled in tiers and sticking out of the brush, and their baggage and provisions, and fires for the cooking of the trouts that hung by forked twigs from trees and bushes, so that a hungry man needed only to help himself. It was noisy, what with the unloading of bateaux and the shouts of those whose craft had been crowded into undesirable positions by new arrivals, and the curses of those who found their provisions spoiled by the water.

Colonel Greene and Captain Morgan came down to the shore and beckoned the colonel to a landing place. Behind them stood Lieutenant Church, gloomy and morose, waiting to submit his report. I looked for Cap Huff, knowing he had accompanied Church, but I could see nothing for the arm-waving of a gaunt, bearded man who stood beside the lieutenant, both hands full of trouts. When this tall, pale man bawled at me in evident irritation, I looked at him more carefully. It was Cap Huff, wasted away almost to a shadow, though to a person who had never seen him before he would still look as large as two ordinary men.

"Come ashore!" he bawled, wiping trout from his beard. "There's some beautiful walks around here!"

XX

A<small>T ITS</small> upper end the Kennebec holds to the Northern wilderness by two tails, one a short, false tail bearing off to the northeast and losing itself in Moosehead Lake; the other a healthy, main tail branching off to the west, contorting itself among cold hills and mountains with its tip pressed tight into the great rock barrier of the Height of Land. This tip is a chain of ponds: irregular, close-packed ponds, strung on the nethermost end of the coiled, undulating river like the rattles on Manitou Kinnibec.

Some, who know the river well, speak of this true tail as the West Branch, and of the shorter one as the East Branch. Others, because its appearance differs from the rest of the Kennebec, as the tail of a serpent grows darker and loses its markings, have given it a name of its own. They call it Dead River because of the slowness of its current. This name has stuck to the West Branch, and so I shall call it, though it is truly the Kennebec.

For a river supposed to be dead, this west branch behaves perversely. It wriggles along smoothly until another sixteen miles of wriggling would bring it into its companion stream; then it rears backward, twisting as though in agony. After twenty miles of tumbling northward over ledges, no more dead than a bobcat after a rabbit, it swings to the east for another twenty miles, and is thenceforth known as the Kennebec.

Always, since there have been red men or white to follow these highways of the wilderness, travelers to and from the trail over the Height of Land have shunned the northwestward leap of Dead River, and carried their canoes straight across the Great Carrying Place from the Kennebec to the point where Dead River turns to the north. In the carrying they are helped by three ponds that lie between the two streams; so that those who travel light, with small packs and bark canoes readily borne by one man, moving softly and taking fish and game for food, find little to discommode them.

Yet there was something about the looks of Cap Huff that spoke ill for the carry, which Church's party had been surveying, nor did his appearance improve on closer examination. His hunting shirt was ripped, his breeches torn, and his moccasins roughly bound with strips of moose hide. He led me to a fire, where he skewered a trout and set it to broil. He stared at me out of round goggle eyes and passed the back of his hand across his brow, ejaculating, "Whew!"

"What's the trouble?"

"Everything!"

"Do you mean there's something wrong with Church? Or was it the traveling that was bad? Or the food?"

"Food!" Cap said hoarsely, snatching his trout from the fire and biting at it, but replacing it when he found it still raw. "Food! There wasn't any! Not enough to call food, that is. Just a little here and a little there."

"Didn't *anybody* have food?"

"Of course not," Cap said. "If anyone had, I'd 'a' got it."

"What became of it? You had plenty when you left."

"We *thought* we did," Cap said, "but it disappeared like smoke. And the damned beef was sour. The bread got wet, too." He looked at me suspiciously. "Have you been getting rain?"

"All there was."

He nodded, relieved. "We got so much I was afraid there wouldn't be any left for the rest of you. It got into our bread and bust the barrel." He sampled his trout again; then looked up at the wisps of gray cloud caught on the hilltops across the river. "It's about rained out, ain't it? It's got to stop, ain't it?"

I said I didn't know: the summer had been dry, and nobody could tell what might happen in the way of weather in this Northern country. Although the scar on my forehead throbbed each day, I couldn't tell whether the throbbing was a sign of worse weather to come, or the result of wet clothes and persistent labors.

"Did you see Natanis?" I asked.

"We didn't see nobody! We didn't hear nuthin! There hadn't never been no-one where we went, and we went everywhere. We clumb up on every rock and smelled it, and we jumped into every bog to see how deep it was, and we paddled around every lake and into every brook and tasted it; and if we'd had a couple more days we'd have clumb every tree small enough to get our arms or legs around, or hang onto with our teeth. Between times we'd walk five miles and measure everything. I tell you, Stevie, this man Church is terrible! If Arnold told him to survey the Atlantic Ocean he'd swim over every inch; and if I was with him he'd make me dive down and walk around the bottom like a damned ousel!"

"Didn't you hear anything of Natanis?" I asked.

"Listen, Stevie," he said, gnawing his trout as one eats an ear of corn, "who do you think would tell us about Natanis? The squirrels? Maybe Steele's men found out something. They had orders to kill him."

"Kill? Orders to kill Natanis?" My brain turned porridge-like. "Why, you're crazy!"

Cap eyed me coldly. "I s'pose so! I s'pose we're all crazy but you! Listen: it was Steele told me about Natanis. Steele said the colonel told him Natanis was a spy—a dangerous one—and gave orders to shoot him on sight."

Cap tossed the cleaned backbone of his trout on the fire and skewered another. "What I want to do now," he said, while I wondered helplessly where Arnold had got his information, "what I want to do now is get away from this man Church and pick up a nice easy job lugging a bateau."

Cap's desires had no interest for me. I forgot him, and tried to think what to do about Natanis.

Lieutenant Church came to stand dejectedly beside our fire. He stared gloomily at Cap. "Getting rested up?"

"Hell," Cap said, "it's going to take me the rest of my life to get rested up and et up."

Church winked at me sadly. "Good traveler, Cap is. Couldn't lose him in the woods."

"Good reason," Cap said bitterly. "If you'd lost me, I'd never et again."

"Now, now!" the lieutenant said, "you'd been all right if you hadn't found that salt codfish."

"What was that?" I asked.

"Why," Church said, "Cap came across a salt codfish lying around in one of the canoes, along about two o'clock one morning. Not wanting to annoy any of the rest of us at that late hour by trying to find out who owned it, he et it all."

"I saved the rest of you a lot of grief," Cap said.

"Yes," Church admitted. "We happened to be on Middle Carry Pond that night, the water all mud and bugs and smell. After Cap et the fish he near drank the pond dry. It kind of weakened him."

"It kind of ruined me," Cap said.

"Well," the lieutenant said, "we're starting for Dead River right now, Cap, so leave that trout for Nason and come ahead."

Cap immediately handed it to me, tightened his belt, rubbed his face with his hands, which had become almost bony, and set off after Church without a word.

When I went back to the colonel's tent, pitched on the rising ground north of the brook that runs in at the start of the Great Carrying Place, I found him busy writing dispatches, keeping an eye meanwhile on the activities of the army, and sending messengers running to his captains with orders or information.

Never have I seen such a man, at one moment occupying himself with the smallest detail having to do with the least of his men, and at another moment disregarding all details and bidding everyone else do the same for the sake of getting on. I've seen him, after a day of forcing his way through bogs and underbrush, when all of us were drenched with perspiration and weary enough to fall asleep with our mouths full of food—at such times I've seen him sit for two hours over his dispatch case, writing letter after letter as though fresh from a restful evening at an inn.

"Go over the carry," he said, smiling that queer smile of his that lengthened and lightened his round swarthy face. "You'll have to make two trips to get your own load over. Maybe more. I'll camp to-night on the far side of the first pond, but you go right ahead and wait for me at the brook that runs into Dead River." He picked up a paper.

"Here: Church says the trail to the first pond is three miles and a quarter, a bad road; then half a mile to the second pond, a rough road; then near a mile and a half to the third pond, terrible going; and finally three miles to Bog Brook, the last mile of the three a devil, muck halfway up your legs."

He waved his pen at me and went back to his writing. Hobomok and I unloaded our canoe, made the load into packs, stored a part with the baggage dump of Captain Goodrich's company, shouldered all we could handle, and fell into line with those who were crossing the carry.

Because of the difficulty of the route, each man took as much on his back as he could manage and toted it to the first pond, returning until all the stores for which he was responsible had been transported. Then the bateaux were carried to the first pond, loaded and rowed across, and unloaded again; and once more the men shouldered their clumsy freights. At first it seemed to me that the worst of all burdens was a barrel of salt pork, because of its shape, or a barrel of flour; but in the end all loads came to seem the same. Before we were through with the Great Carrying Place, the backs of all of us were bent from the weights we had borne, and some swore they'd never be straight again unless hung up by the hands for a week, with a bag of bullets tied to each foot.

For all of Cap Huff's complaints about his journey with Lieutenant Church, I doubt that either of them had properly appreciated the true nature of the road over which our bateaumen passed. Church had traveled light, before the axemen of the first division had widened the path by felling trees and leaving multitudes of three-foot stumps. If he had traveled as the army did, he would never have been content to call these roads merely bad, or very bad. Yet, if he had described them properly, he would have been court-martialed for using language.

Four hundred pounds, a bateau weighed—a grievous burden for the stoutest shoulders. The first carry was along a mountainside for three and a quarter miles. If we had been cumbered with nothing more than muskets and a few ducks, the three miles would have seemed long. Laden as we were, they seemed endless. Most of us stripped off our shirts and coats, rolling them into pads and placing them on our shoulders so the weight would fall on them. Nor was it the weight alone that bothered us. The rains had made the footing insecure, and there were spots where a man plunged his leg knee-deep in a mud hole. He'd fall; the bateau would slip, smashing against one of the countless stumps. Sooner or later every man in every bateau crew drove his shin against a stump and fell, the bateau clattered down on him, and the other three carriers went down in the crash.

By the grace of God we ate well on this carry. The first pond was alive with salmon trout, pink-fleshed and delicious, so eager for food that they came into shallow water to take a hook, four and five at a time struggling for the bait.

When we dumped our loads on the shores of the first pond we saw two Virginians poling toward us in what looked like an empty bateau. When it reached us three men got up off the bottom and climbed out, emaciated men with thick beards, their hunting shirts stained and torn; their actions slow and weak.

Among them I recognized Lieutenant Steele, who had left us two weeks before to scout across the Height of Land and to the headwaters of the Chaudière.

When he left us he was tall and slender, walking with a jaunty swing to his shoulders, smiling constantly, his cap cocked a little on the side of his head. He had been well-groomed, always; but now I hardly knew him. His cap was still over one ear; his smile was lopsided; but he stooped in his walk; and on irregular ground he tripped easily. His eyes looked rubbed with soot.

He would have started back over the long trail between the Kennebec and the first pond; but when I told him Arnold was coming in during the afternoon he threw himself down with a groan of relief. We had a greater distance to go, he told me, than any of us had anticipated—eighty miles on Dead River before we could cross the Height of Land and reach the Chaudière.

I asked him whether it was bad crossing the Height of Land. It would be a matter of food, he said. If we had enough food we could get across. Otherwise it might be bad. His own food, he said, had run out, and game was scarce: scarcer than he had ever seen it. His party had shot two moose, but the meat was without fat, like all moose meat: it filled their bellies but gave no nourishment. They had near starved, all of them, as well as breaking both their canoes.

Striving to speak carelessly, I asked him the question that seemed to me most important: Had he seen Natanis?

Steele said they had surrounded his cabin to kill him, but he was gone, though the cabin had recently been occupied.

"He left a birch-bark map for some of his Indian friends," Steele said. "We took it and used it."

A load lifted itself from my heart. That meant Natanis had received my messages and done what I asked.

"Good!" I said. "Good!"

"Do you know this Natanis?" Steele asked.

"I haven't seen him in years."

"What sort of Indian is he?"

"The best there is. An Abenaki and a good friend."

"We'd have been a week getting through the Chain of Ponds without his map," Steele said. "Just as well we didn't find him. What made Arnold so hot against him?"

"I wish I knew! He'd get us plenty of food if Arnold would use him."

"It was funny about those moose," Steele said reflectively. "They trotted right out onto us, as if they'd been driven."

"Did you see any other Indians?"

"Nary hide nor hair. That country is empty as a Tory's heart, and damned near as cold."

He fell asleep. I started back across the carry at a trot, so our canoe might be brought up with no loss of time. I wished to be free to seek Natanis—to ask his help before anything went wrong. I passed Phoebe. On her shoulder were three muskets. Looped over them was not only her blanket, but strings of salt pork that dangled to her heels. Asa Hutchins, walking behind her, bent almost double under his load, peered up at me and croaked: "What's the matter? Forget your shoe buckles?"

We met the colonel going in, making good time with no luggage on his back, and having something to say to every bateau crew and loaded man he passed. "That's the way!" he'd say. "Stick to it, boys! We'll kick up a dust they won't forget! Come on, boys! They can't beat us, boys!"

You could see the bateau crews strike out springier after they'd heard him. He was a fighter if ever there was one, and the men knew it.

We got our canoe and the rest of the baggage as far as the first pond by dusk, saying to each other we had done our share of work and must take it easy for a while; but we were new at it, or we'd never have invited misfortune by such talk. In time we came to know there was no weariness so extreme and no labor so great but what we could endure worse when it came.

When, in the morning, we crossed the first pond and carried over half a mile of ledges, we came to an evil pond; a miserable, low-lying water of a vile yellow color, surrounded by bogs and dead trees. There were no fish in it, and it smelled of decay and corruption. Most of us, dry from the heat of carrying, drank the yellow water, which affected some of us in one way and some in another, but making all of us sick.

We might have camped here to boil water and recover from our weakness; but no man, so long as he could move, seemed willing to stop—mindful, no doubt, of what had befallen poor Ervin from the first division. He was swollen with rheumatism and couldn't move, even to roll himself over in bed; so he was left in a brush hut at the second pond, with four men to tend him and turn him over when the pain became too great to bear, and he was being eaten alive by vermin to boot. After seeing him none of us was wishful of letting himself be sick.

We crossed this dirty yellow pond and pushed on toward the

third pond, the largest one, over a swamp a mile and a half long. Its surface was a tangle of roots that snared and tripped us whenever we moved faster than a crawl. While the rear bearers of a bateau fumbled with their feet for a safe footing, the front bearers would find one and lurch forward, so the two rear bearers would have to set their feet wherever chance dictated. Thus, either the front or the rear bearers were constantly tripping and falling, and the bateau sinking down and rising up. As we looked back at the line of bateaux crawling along this trail on the shoulders of their bearers it had the look of an ugly brown dragon painfully undulating between the high forest walls through which the axemen had hewn our path.

There was clean water in the third pond, and fish, too—dark, deep-bodied, square-tailed trouts. From it we could see the snow-capped top of Dead River Mountain to the westward, and knew that with one more effort we would reach Dead River. On it, we told ourselves, we could travel easily to the Height of Land; so it seemed to all of us that we were almost at an end of our march to Quebec.

❖   ❖   ❖

I have often marveled at our youthful ignorance on this journey; and I have snorted, as men will when they grow older, staring up at the ceiling in the gray of dawn, to think I could have been so callow as to think the things I thought. As we paddled over this third pond I felt it was high time to consider how I should comport myself with Mary when I popped into her house in Quebec: whether I should say nothing, but take her in my arms and kiss her; or whether I should write out a long speech, elegant beyond belief, such as my mother had read to me out of a book, and recite it to her.

It turned out there was no immediate need of preparing for this ordeal. The length of the carry from the third pond to the little brook that fell into Dead River was three miles. Three miles, we thought, with the memories of our other carries behind us, was nothing but three miles. We double-loaded our canoe, piling our stores at the ends so it might not break in the middle, and set off among the bateaumen of Greene's division. For a mile we clambered upward on the ragged withers of a mountain, so the skin on our shoulders was rubbed backward cruelly. Then for another mile we traveled easily down the opposite slope, hailing each other jocosely at the ease with which we progressed, even though our legs ached as if they might snap under us, and the skin of our faces burned from our exertions until they felt fit to fry fish. We disregarded, even, the forward chafing of our burdens, which almost flayed our backs; for ahead of us we saw a long green meadow, level and beautiful, dotted here and there with thickets and edged with spruces and cedars.

When we jubilantly set out across the meadow, it softened beneath us. The surface became a green moss, spread smoothly over a thick black soup into which our legs sank to the knee at every step.

Under the mud were jagged stumps of trees, and barbs of decayed branches—the graveyard of a forest dead from floods and fallen before mountain storms, as all ancient forests fall in these Northern woods.

The stumps and barbs tore at our water-soaked shoes and at the skin beneath. There was no way to avoid them; so we adopted the plan of letting ourselves slip down at each step, nearly to a sitting position, until our feet reached a foundation; then lifting the canoe forward eight inches or even a foot, dragging our feet from the ooze and taking another step.

Why the bateaumen were diverted by their flounderings, I cannot say; but they howled profanely at their plight, swearing loudly that somebody had hold of their feet, or that they had stepped on a dead cat, or that the mud was full of broken chairs and old bottles. They wrenched themselves along, cackling and guffawing; and from the churned muck in which they wallowed there arose a stench that might have been the parent of every noisome odor in the world.

In the course of time we came to narrow Bog Brook, its waters brown and smelling of deadness; but regardless of its odor we soused ourselves in it, clothes, head, hair and all, until the sweat and the slime and the stench were partly gone. Those whose luggage was entirely carried set off down Bog Brook; and we could hear them, across the meadow that separates the brook from Dead River, bawling at each other as they went poling up against the river's sluggish current. As for those others who had brought only a part of their belongings, they stumbled off across the dreadful meadow again, sinking through the level green moss into the foul mud, pitching forward or sideways as their feet struck the snags and barbs beneath.

When we had washed ourselves, we stored our baggage and set off down Bog Brook.

I knew, when we turned into Dead River, that there was little use in following the bateaux upstream. Natanis, I was sure, would do one of two things: either send a messenger to me at night when he had located me; or watch for me himself at the point where I must enter Dead River.

We floated silently on the slow brown current, looking about for signs.

There were three crows on a tall tree, a little downstream from us, and as we drifted the three of them sprang into the air, cawing, and flew toward a twisted bull pine on the far side of the river. They circled around it, raising an outcry that came faintly to us.

Hobomok grinned and drove the canoe downstream. "Natanis is talking to the crows," he said.

We went ashore abreast of the old bull pine; and in the thicket beneath it we found Natanis and Natawammet, glad to see us, as were we to see them. It had been years since I had laid eyes on Natanis, yet he had changed little from the boy we had rescued from the deer, save that his face was thinner and harder, and the muscles under his skin more corded. He seemed to find more of a change in me, which was nothing surprising; for my beard was ragged and my eyes hot and sunken from the sickness at Middle Carry Pond; also my hunting shirt and breeches were ripped, and the soles had parted from my shoes, so my feet stuck through in places.

"We have waited here for my brother," Natanis said, hunting in his quiver for his pipe, "since the men with rifles first came into the river. I would never have known him if my brother Hobomok, who I hear is a great *m'téoulin,* had not come with him."

"What is all this talk," I asked, going straight to the point, "that you're a spy?"

Natanis lighted the pipe and gave it to me. How welcome I found the familiar sumach leaves and powdered willow bark with which the tobacco was mixed! "We must think about this," he said, hunkering down over his fire which, like most Indian fires, was small enough to be held in the palm of the hand. "This tale comes from some man who wishes to keep your war party from having my help."

"Why do you think so?"

"Because when the stupid guide Conkey came into this country he asked immediately whether I was a spy, showing he had been told I was a spy. Since I'm not a spy, and have never been one, this tale must have been spread abroad by someone who wished your army to be suspicious of me."

"I think so," I said. "The great chief Washington and the chief of this army, Arnold, had been told in August that you were an enemy."

"I don't understand it," Natanis said. "There's no sense to it. I could not believe that Conkey spoke seriously when he asked whether I was a spy. That was why I answered him lightly, saying, 'Of course I'm a spy, because I deliver myself into your hands and sit by your fire, instead of hiding in the forest and watching your movements without danger to myself. Next I shall write on a piece of bark "I am a spy" and hang it around my neck, so there may be no mistake about it.' I thought by saying this I could show Conkey the foolishness of his question. I was mistaken; for he feared me, and went away without exploring the river or the Height of Land—without asking, even, for a drawing of them, which I'd have given him for the asking."

"It may help you to realize that Conkey was serious," I said, "when I tell you the scout Steele and his seven men had orders to kill you for a spy."

Natanis nodded. "I saw them when they came into the river. I prepared a map, as you asked; and when I was sure they'd pass my cabin, I ran ahead and left the map in a cleft stick. I watched them creep up on the cabin with cocked rifles. Natawammet and I followed them to the top of the Height of Land. When they were without food, I drove rabbits and raccoons into their path. Being hurried, they never saw those small creatures; so at length, fearing they might starve, I drove two moose into the river ahead of their canoes."

"I wish," I said, "I could learn the truth of this spy talk. Arnold is paddled by Eneas and Sabatis. Do you think either of them has reason to wish you dead?"

Natanis shook his head. "Eneas was in Beçancour visiting his brothers during the two hot moons of summer. He returned here in September, departing to hunt with Sabatis at once, so he could have said nothing to the white chief in August. Sabatis has fished and hunted on the lower Kennebec for years, and has been welcome in my lodge. He has no reason to lie about me, and would not do it."

"Well, God knows what the answer is," I said, "but there's one more thing: the winter we returned after building your cabin, my father died because of his kindness to a Boston preacher, Hook, who fished for souls among the Abenakis."

Natawammet laughed. "I remember! He was angry because we dared to have a religion of our own!"

"With this army there is a man who calls himself Treeworgy," I said. "To me he looks like Hook; but he denies it. Do my brothers know anything of this Treeworgy?"

"I will look at him," Natawammet said. Natanis shook his head.

"What about Paul Higgins and his Assagunticooks?" I asked.

"On the Height of Land," Natanis said, "keeping out of the way until the white men begin to starve."

"Do you think they'll starve?"

Natanis touched the blue welt along his side. "There's an aching in my scar. There will be storms, I think; bad storms. Food is hard to find. You might think the rabbits had been wiped out, there are so few; and the animals that feed on rabbits are fewer. Also the moose are moving to the west. I've seen nothing like it in all the years I have been here."

"Well," I said, "here's the heart of the matter. I say to Natanis that he is my brother. These men with whom I am marching are also my brothers. I'm in need of a brother's help. I expect now that my brother will help me in every way he can, and all my other brothers with me, if we come to bad times."

Natanis seemed to consider my words unnecessary. "I had my life at my brother's hands," he said. "I am ready to help him while that life is left in me."

He lit the pipe again and the four of us smoked in turn. "Now," I said, "our supplies are low, and the army cannot stop to hunt for food. When it stops, it ceases to be an army, and loses the strength given to it by the fear of others' laughter and the desire to equal others' efforts. Therefore the day may come when it's entirely without food. The bateaux are wrecks, and I doubt they can be carried across the Height of Land; so there may be no means for the army to reach Quebec if ever it gets to the Chaudière.

"This army must be watched carefully. If what I suspect is true, there must be fast men sent to the French settlements to spread the word to bring in food. There must be men set to building canoes on the lower Chaudière for the crossing of the St. Lawrence. There must be men set to watch the leaders, to see they neither stray from the trail nor die from lack of food. You must talk this over with Paul Higgins, deciding how it can best be done. Whatever happens, no word of this army should be spoken to any person who might carry the information to the English. When a decision has been reached, Natanis should return to me, looking for me by night in the camp of the white chief Arnold. No guard is kept, and it's safe for red brothers to move anywhere among the army at night. There are already more than twenty Abenakis among us, mostly Swan Islanders and braves from Arrowsic and Georgetown."

"This shall be done," Natanis agreed.

"It's in my mind," I said, "that the day will come when those who said Natanis was a spy will burn in hell. If we take Quebec, it will be further said we couldn't have done it without Natanis and his brothers."

We feasted on strips of moose meat dipped in sweetened bear's fat, a toothsome change from the salt pork and trout that had so long sustained us.

The ways of a man's stomach are beyond me. There are seasons when I turn up my nose at partridges and ducks, cooked juicily over coals, and long for salt pork and trout; and there are other times when I am like to gag at the mention of trout and pork. Yet I have seen the day when the sweetest food in all the world was a strip of pork rind, raw, that had lain for a week in the bottom of an Abenaki woodchuck-skin wallet.

XXI

For four more days the army wallowed back and forth across the stinking, moss-topped swamp at Bog Brook, all of it except Enos's Fourth Division, which fiddled along behind, dragging itself into sight when everyone else was sick of waiting. One by one Greene's rear guard washed themselves clean of mud and stench and poled off down the brook. Morgan's riflemen, their canvas jerkins torn and frayed from road-making labors, had fallen back to second place for the first time, so that Greene's men jeered at them. Yet Morgan's men, ordinarily proud of their ability and speed, had no retorts to make except perfunctory ones. I knew there must be a reason for their silence, and I wondered what it was.

Meigs's division pulled itself out of the mud and went out slowly.

For the first time every bateau carried a sick man or two, and in some cases three or four—men poisoned by the yellow water we had drunk at Middle Carry Pond, or limp from the flux, or with feet torn on the snags and barbs of the bog, or crippled with rheumatism so they could not stand.

When the men of Goodrich's company, finished with their carrying, threw themselves down on the bank, waiting for the bateaux to start, I saw Phoebe among them. As ever, she was beside James Dunn, moving around him like a sparrow moving around a log. He was stretched out at full length, his clothes in a wretched state and a gray cast to his face. Nor was Phoebe much better. Her moccasins had completely worn off, so that the upper parts had been pulled up on her legs to afford added protection from brush, and the bottoms had been replaced with bags of moose hide, lashed around her ankles and insteps with a snake skin and sacking. Her buckskin jerkin was ripped and stained, and her eye discolored. Yet there was an alert and unbeaten look about her.

"Steven," she said, "James must go in a bateau. He's not fit to march."

"I'm as good as any man," James whispered. To prove it he sat up.

His shoes were nearly gone, but there was still flesh on his ribs; so I told Phoebe it might be better for him to keep going rather than give in to weakness. He might grow stronger instead of weaker, and so leave room in the bateaux for those more in need of help.

"Are there many in the bateaux?" James asked.

"There's a sick man or two in every one," I said, "but we can always find room for you if you need it."

"I'm better than any of those sick ones," James said. He sank back against the grass Phoebe had thrown behind him.

Phoebe gave me a dumb, baffled look. Then she leaned over and patted James on the shoulder. "You're better than a lot of the well ones."

Noah Cluff, patching the knee of his breeches with a square of wet buckskin, grinned fearsomely behind his whiskers. "You ain't so bad yourself, Phoebe."

*　　　*　　　*

The scar on my forehead ached and smarted, on the fourth day of our waiting, as though newly branded with a hot iron. There was a spit of snow in the air, and a veil of it over the top and sides of Dead River Mountain. Early that afternoon we saw the colonel and Captain Oswald struggling across the meadow. Two other Indians, Swan Islanders, had replaced Eneas and Sabatis in the colonel's canoe; and from them we learned Arnold had sent Eneas and Sabatis with dispatches to friends in Quebec, sympathizers with our cause. I knew Eneas and Sabatis were best equipped of all of us to act as messengers, but I mistrusted them because they had been with Guerlac many years before.

I would be, I saw, a fool indeed to run with suspicions to the man on whose shoulders rested all the burden of our venture; nor could anyone remain in an ill temper with Colonel Arnold when he was happy at being on the move.

Seeing us on the far side of the brook, he picked up a setting-pole from a bateau and ran with it to the edge, thrusting one end against the ground and vaulting over by holding to the other end, as easy as stepping over a log.

"The worst of it's past," he said, pleased as a boy when we gave him the tails of the two beavers we had shot for him. "We'll be half-way up Dead River to-night, and at the gates of Quebec before you can say Boh to a goose!"

Yet his face lost its cheerfulness when we had been at our paddling

for a few hours; for the river twines and twists around the foot of
Dead River Mountain, dark and glistening and silent, as though
waiting to gather a victim in its coils. When a person sets out upon
it, he sees the frowning bulk of the mountain at his left shoulder. Then
he bears off to the right, and then he turns to the left and then he
turns to the right, and then to the left and right again; and at the
end of hours of twining, the gloomy mountain is still at his left shoulder, no farther away and no nearer than when he started.

Half an hour before sundown we came to the beautiful point on
which we had built the cabin for Natanis, my father and I; and my
mind turned back to the day when the two of us had taken a drink
to red-headed James Wolfe for capturing Quebec. I wished to God
my father could have been sitting in the canoe with us. I think
Hobomok read my thoughts; for he said there was a belief among the
Abenakis that when they went to war, the spirits of their fathers
went with them to give them strength and protection. Such things,
it seems to me, are vain and childish. Yet they did me no harm,
since I thought that if what he said was true no Britisher that ever
lived could stop me from going over the walls of Quebec and taking
away what I most wanted.

By nightfall we had passed well beyond Natanis's cabin and come
among the bateaux of Colonel Greene's division; so when we found
a likely meadow on the top of a high bank we camped there all
together, pleased because the snow was over and the river full of
salmon trouts, with no shallows to wet us. Only the scar on my head
stung and throbbed to a degree that led me repeatedly to lay my
fingers against it, fearful lest it might have burst open.

Before the night was over there were complaints; for companies
that supposed themselves to have three and four barrels of flour had
found no flour when they searched their bateaux. At first it was
thought the flour belonging to one company had been picked up by
bateaumen of another company; but when all the flour in all the
companies of Greene's division was scraped together there was only
enough for each man to have one-half pint—scarce enough to feed
my dog Ranger for half a day.

Hobomok and I were making cakes out of the meal we carried
in bladders for emergencies when Captain Oswald came past us in a
pother. "Did you take the flour?" he asked, eyeing our cakes suspiciously.

"Nay," I said, "not I; and I've known enough to guard what I've
got."

"Well," said Oswald, "this division's in a pretty mess, with next to nothing to eat. We've got to draw on Enos for reserve supplies."

He started off, but came back again. "What did you mean," he asked, "by saying you knew enough to guard your supplies?"

"What do you suppose I meant?" I was in bad humor because of the throbbing of my scar, which seemed to tap on the front of my brain like a hammer.

"I suppose you meant that if you hadn't watched your supplies they'd have been stolen."

"That's what I meant," I said. "I learned long ago that food, or anything else for that matter, can't safely be left near any body of men, unless they're Indians. It's becoming dangerous to trust Indians overmuch, now they've benefited by the society of their white neighbors."

"What are you trying to say?" Oswald demanded.

"I'm trying to say nothing! You're nosing about in search of a mystery, and I'm trying to help *you* say something. My opinions have no value in this army. You've seen that. All I want to do is march to Quebec with the rest of you, and help you fight in whatever way I can. Other persons can advance the opinions."

"Very well," said Oswald, "I'll advance the opinions if I can find out what maggot is crawling in your head."

"The maggot is this," I said. "Daniel Morgan's a hard driver and a proud man. You saw him refuse to serve under Greene, and God knows that's a spectacle that won't be equaled in some time: a captain refusing to serve under a lieutenant colonel. Also, Morgan's riflemen are hard men, good soldiers; no doubt the best we've got. They know it, too. If you ask 'em, they'll tell you so."

I stopped; but Oswald stood gawping at me expectantly; so I saw he was still as blind as I had been, and must have his nose rubbed in it. "It's simple enough," I said. "Morgan and his Virginians, and the rest of the riflemen for that matter, can hold first place in the line of march against us clumsy New Englanders, whether they go by bateau or by land. Before they'd give up first place to Greene's men or anybody else, without good reason, they'd work their legs to stumps and tear the flesh from their fingers."

Oswald nodded.

"Morgan's men weren't so busy at road-making," I said, "that they couldn't have held first place in the line if they wished; for Greene's men set off up Dead River less than two hours ahead of them."

"That's so," Oswald said.

"Of course it's so! Would Daniel Morgan, or his men either, have allowed Greene's division to precede them by little more than an hour without a fight, unless they had a reason for wanting Greene's division out of the way? No, they would not! Daniel Morgan would have bawled like an unmilked cow; and his men would have pushed Greene's men into the bog and trampled on them, rather than let them start first! What's more, there's good reason why Morgan's men didn't catch up with Greene in no time."

"Finish it up," Oswald said.

"So I will! Morgan's men lagged behind at the Great Carrying Place to give Greene's men a chance to pass through them. While they were passing, Morgan's men stole their flour!"

"Hm!" said Oswald.

"Yes," I said, "and then they let Greene's men start off down Bog Brook ahead of them so Greene's men couldn't see the extra flour packed in Morgan's bateaux."

"Well, the dirty rats!"

"No," I said, "there's more than one way of looking at that. I remember my father telling how the men from his company, during the siege of Louisbourg, stole thirty lobsters that had been caught by Lieutenant Benjamin Cleaves's men. Men have stolen food in all wars, even those fought by the Egyptians. These Virginians are no psalm-singing deacons, but rough and reckless citizens who'd break their rifle stocks over the heads of those who displeased them, whether Patriots or Tories. Since they hold themselves more valuable than the rest of us, which I suspect they are, there's little wonder they think nothing of preserving their health and strength by appropriating whatever food they can find. It seems to me if anyone's to blame, it's Morgan's captains for not keeping a stricter hold on their men, or Greene's captains for not stationing a guard over the victuals."

"Could you prove these things?"

"Leave me out of it. I give you the information to use as you wish."

"Then say nothing concerning your suspicions," he said, "and I'll see how to use the information."

"Indeed," I said, "I don't want to see Morgan's and Greene's divisions at each other's throats, so I'll be silent." As Oswald started away, I added: "There's one other thing. I've given you information; now give me some in return. Where did the colonel learn about his messenger Eneas and about the guide Treeworgy?"

"He had information concerning them while he was still at Crown Point," said Oswald.

"As long ago as that! Where did the information come from? Boston?"

Oswald hesitated and muttered something about secret intelligence.

"I swear to my God," I said, "I'll keep it as secret as you or Arnold could. I want it only to protect all of us from harm."

"Well," Oswald said, "he has correspondents in Quebec. This information came from one of them."

"Spit it out!" I cried, irritated by the throbbing of my scar and by the withholding of the name I hoped to hear. "Who was the man?"

"His name," Oswald whispered reluctantly, "is John Woodward."

"John Woodward! John Woodward!" I flung at him, in a rage of disappointment. "Who in hell is John Woodward! Where does he live and how does he know about Eneas and Treeworgy?"

"I don't know," Oswald said. "The colonel lets me copy letters to him in the letter book, but the address he withholds until the letters are given to the messenger. He says Woodward would be killed if it should be known in Quebec he was sending information to us."

With this, which helped me but little, I was forced to be content.

* * *

The wind was in the southwest when we threw off our blankets the next day, and I couldn't understand the unceasing throbbing of my scar, for in Arundel a southwest wind usually brings only short storms, not enough to set a small scar to burning and pounding as mine was doing.

The colonel dispatched Major Bigelow and twelve bateaux to get provisions from Colonel Enos, so that Greene's division might have food on which to proceed. Enos was still fuddling around on the Great Carrying Place, meaning that the provisions would be a matter of three or four days in coming up; so the rest of us went to catching trouts to satisfy the hunger of the entire division—an easy task because the river was alive with them, all the same size, seemingly, about half a pound apiece.

Morgan's division passed us at noon, the men poling and paddling on the far side of the river; content, for once, to hurl none of their jeers at Greene's men. They were a hardy lot, those riflemen. I called across to a bateau, asking how their flour was holding out, and the bateauman shouted back, seriously, "We're eating fish, Brother, and saving our flour." I looked for some of them to fall overboard from laughing, but not one of them so much as smiled.

Morgan alone came ashore here to pass the time of day with Arnold; and Oswald told me afterward that Arnold said only one thing to him—"Captain, I shall expect your division to be always in the lead hereafter; always in the lead!" Oswald said Morgan stared at him as if intending to be haughty or thick of understanding; then changed his mind suddenly, saying, "Sir, that's our fixed intention!" I'm sure that whatever Morgan had replied, Arnold would have said no more, lest the welfare of the army be further endangered; for if ever a man would have sacrificed pride or health or his life to see our campaign succeed, it was Arnold.

Being, as the colonel said, so near our destination, the men were put to work making cartridges and packing them in barrels. When the Third Division had come up behind Morgan's and made their cartridges and gone on, the colonel said we could serve no good purpose by longer waiting; so we too pressed on behind Meigs. The men were catching rides on the bateaux, walking across the neck of land at wide bends in the river; then begging rides until they came to another neck. I saw James Dunn lurch from a bateau, with Phoebe, strangely deformed-looking, pushing him. I shouted at them to know how their food was holding out and went closer to see what ailed Phoebe. James walked on without raising his head; but Phoebe lifted the buckskin jerkin over her hip and I saw a raccoon dangling from her brass-studded belt by his hind legs.

"Jacataqua killed it!" she called to me. "I almost had to hit Burr with this to get it away from him!" She waved her leather-bound bullets at me gaily and steered James around a young pine thicket through which he seemed about to walk.

❋   ❋   ❋

The proceedings of the next few days are grouped in my mind around a Friday—not because I think Fridays bring evil, but because so many of our calamities fell on Fridays, though God knows worse things happened to us on other days, especially on Sundays, which I have never heard called a day that brings disaster.

At any rate, it was on the day before a Friday that this bad business started: on Thursday, that is, the nineteenth day of October. It was raining when we came out of our blankets, a cold and mournful downpour, nor was its cheerlessness relieved by the appearance of the country, which seemed as flat as a salt marsh in the direction we were moving, with barren spots on the soil and the trees smaller, as if they had been starved, and all of them pines and spruce and fir, with no pleasant maples or elms or oaks such as help to make the Arundel countryside so beautiful.

The river grew narrower, with pestiferous little rapids and falls at frequent intervals; and for fear of upsetting and losing more provisions, we carried around each one, slipping on our faces in the slimy ground and dropping everything on which we laid our hands because of its wetness.

The rain came in bursts, as if the clouds were ripping in spots and spilling masses of goose shot in the water. The wind, too, blew harder and harder from the southwest, so that our skins grew numb from the driving of the drops against us. When we camped at our last portage we were more than two hours finding dry wood and starting fires.

When Friday broke the wind was higher, moaning dolefully through the spruces and dead tamaracks, and the rain was heavier. It bounced from the surface of the river and from the meadows, whirled upward by the raging wind, so we were rained on from above and below. Thinking it must let up soon, we lay snug in our lean-to's, watching Meigs's division go past, bateaux and bateaumen oozing water like ledges of rock over which a wave has just broken.

When Phoebe trudged by, sandwiched between James Dunn and Noah Cluff like a sandpiper between two curlews, I called to her to come and get dry. Her buckskins were plastered to her body and there were bluish shadows under her eyes and around her mouth, as though some of the color had run out of the handkerchief around her hair. She shook her head grimly and pulled James Dunn to his feet when he stumbled. I saw there was no sole to one of his shoes.

This, with the drenching rain and the mournful sky, led me to think gloomily on the folly of women; how they cleave most faithfully to those of us who are weakest and most worthless. Was this true, I wondered, or does it only seem true because our attentions are drawn to weak and worthless men, and our spleens aroused to see them blessed with wives or mothers as good as those of more deserving folk?

The river seemed to boil with rage, growling irascibly and sweeping away the litter of a century—hoorahs' nests of twigs and leaves; tree trunks black with age; witches' mats of roots festooned with foam. Great trouts rose from the bottom of the stream, trouts so dark that they looked purple, and rolled on the surface, snatching at grubs and worms, and slapping with their tails at those they couldn't eat.

That Friday night the rain fell as I had never known it to fall, in solid sheets, like water pouring out of a hogshead. The wind rampaged terribly among the trees, coming in bursts that increased in force, as the force of a man's breath increases when he fails to blow out a candle. With each succeeding burst we swore it could blow no harder. There was a smashing among the trees in the forest behind us from time to time; so at dawn on Saturday we made ready to depart lest the storm work some great inconvenience on us.

I have been through storms in my life fit to rank with any storms anywhere—northeasters that drove rain through the outer walls of a house and the wainscoting within; northers that whipped snow into a man's face with such force as to peel off the skin; squalls out of the southwest that rolled a dory over twice and blew the plug out of the bottom. But never have I seen equaled the violence of this storm on Dead River.

The water had risen three feet, and the falls to which we were constantly coming were white smothers of foam. When we fought our way up through the bateaux of the Third Division, blinded by the rain that smashed at us, we found them shipping more water from the downpour than they had shipped in the buffeting of the Five Mile Ripples. There was a howl to the wind that seemed made by living creatures; noises above our heads like the screaming of innumerable wildcats. There was a creaking and splitting among the taller trees that sent us scuttling past them; and all along the edges of the forests there were newly fallen pines.

In the afternoon we passed an open meadow in which stood one tall pine, perhaps two feet in diameter at the base, a stout tree. Before our eyes the whole tree rose a little in the air and fell on its side, tearing up a flat patch of earth bigger than the floor of our kitchen in Arundel. It didn't fall slowly, like a pine cut at the base; but with a violent quick fall, as a musket falls when a man stumbles over its stock.

As we passed a gentle hillslope, forested with pines and spruces, there was a rushing roar in the air, ominous and menacing. On the instant an irregular area of green trees on the slope, a tract three or four acres in extent, flattened as if sat upon by an enormous invisible giant.

At dusk we came up with Morgan's riflemen. They were camped

on a low point clear of trees, huddling in the lee of their bateaux, without fires. Misliking the nearness of the water and the lack of shelter, and eager for some place where we might kindle fires, we continued another mile onward in the gloom and the howling wind and rain until we came to a high ledge that would shelter us from the falling trees, which were going down on every hand amid a hellish tumult. Under the ledge we found dried twigs, and after three hours of labor we coaxed fires into being, got hot food into us, and warmed our wet clothes until they steamed.

It was midnight when we rolled ourselves in our blankets, too numb to think, and almost too numb to feel.

It was still as dark as the middle of a wet feather bed when I wakened to the sound of shouting. I lay there dazed, until a wave slapped me in the face. It soaked through my blanket and ran coldly down my thigh. Then I could hear others splashing around in water, and as I unrolled myself and got to my feet I felt how the river had come all the way up the bank, a prodigious rise, for we had camped more than my own height above the surface of the flood.

Our canoes were sunk, and most of our supplies and baggage. Some of it we found and dragged out, groping around under water like seals. We carried it to the rising ground behind us and sat there shivering until dawn, the rain having ceased and the wind grown colder.

Though the dawn came in two hours, it seemed like ten to me; and I fear it seemed longer to the colonel. I could hear him making little noises of distress with his tongue against the roof of his mouth, though he kept his troubles to himself. God knows he had plenty of them; for everything had happened to us that shouldn't have happened.

When Sunday came we saw a sight. Where there had been a river flowing regularly between banks on the day before, there was now a great lake with trees rising from it here and there, and falls occasionally, white and angry-looking, and a current so swift that small trees bent before it.

Morgan's division came by us at noon and Meigs's at night, struggling hard against the current and shouting out their news to us: how their bateaux had been swamped and smashed and carried off by the flood; how pork and flour out of their scanty stores had been washed away in the twinkling of an eye, nor ever found again, and muskets carried into the depths of the river. With each piece of bad

tidings our spirits grew lighter, as though the hearing of it had relieved us of another tribulation.

Our friends, as they passed, would shout at us to learn what we
had lost, and when we would shout back, "Nothing but our food!"
they would laugh hilariously and say they had lost five bateaux and
a barrel of pork and two kegs of powder. We would all double up
with mirth, slapping ourselves and declaring there was still life in
the old Dead River.

When we heard how the foot soldiers, driven inland by the flood,
had been obliged to strike back all the way to the high land in order
to go forward, you might have thought it was the gayest news since
the tea was thrown into Boston Harbor. And when we went to fishing
to eke out our scanty provisions, and found the big trouts all gone
away, probably into the newly flooded land, leaving nothing for us
to catch save minnows the size of my thumb, the dragging out of
each minnow was greeted by derisive howls. And indeed I have
found it true that parlous situations bring the greatest merriment and
peace of mind to those whose courage has not been wholly shattered
by sickness or injustice. Why this is so I cannot tell, unless it be that
all past and future worries are wiped from the mind, and the immediate present stands out absurdly clear and small against impending danger.

*   *   *

On Monday we found ourselves with Meigs's division and Morgan's
division. The bateaumen were drawing themselves along by trees
and submerged bushes, for the depth and quickness of the water
made the bateaux difficult to handle by means of poles.

We thought the worst was over, and that with the high water we
could go on quickly to the Height of Land; yet we had no sooner
started than we found the foot soldiers of Meigs's division had mistaken their way and gone traveling up a branch of the Dead River
that would lead them God knew where and leave them lost in this
terrible wilderness with no food. They must be brought back, Arnold
said; and he sent me, with Hobomok, to do it.

We had gone two leagues when we saw a squirrel, high in a tree,
cursing and flirting his tail and stamping his forepaws in a temper.
Hobomok laughed and swung the canoe; and under the tree I saw
Natanis smiling at us.

"Where does this water come from?" I asked.

Natanis raised his eyebrows. "There has been nothing like this in my memory—no such numbers of trees felled by one wind! It is bad."

"Some of our men have taken a wrong direction," I said. "Have you seen them?"

"I met them three bends above here. I led them across the stream where there were fallen logs, and sent them to the river, a three-hour march."

"Did they know who you were?"

Natanis looked pityingly at me. "I said I had been sent after them by the white chief."

"Was there a small white woman among them, wearing a blue handkerchief on her head?"

"Yes," said Natanis. "A better soldier than some of them, I think."

It might be, I thought to myself, that what Natanis said was true; yet I had her on my mind a dozen times a day, wishing she were back in Arundel where she belonged, keeping my mother company instead of making herself a nuisance around a man's army and occupying men's thoughts when they should be busy on other matters. It may be I felt more put out at Phoebe than at Mrs. Grier and Mrs. Warner for marching with their husbands among the riflemen, because it was impossible for me to give my thoughts to Mary Mallinson, as I liked to do when we steamed comfortably before our campfires at the end of the day's toil, without the thin brown face of Phoebe Dunn popping into my head and setting me to wondering about her food and her condition when I had no desire to wonder about her at all.

"There's no need to be concerned about her," Natanis added, staring at me curiously. "She has the body of a boy that can stand anything." He touched the blue scar on his side and smiled affectionately, as if to remind me what he himself had endured as a boy.

I told him quickly that I was not concerned about her, and asked him whether he had taken my messages to Paul Higgins.

Natanis nodded. "Paul sent four men down the Chaudière to make canoes and tell everyone that food must be brought to Sartigan, the first of the settlements. They'll send word to all Abenaki hunting parties along the Chaudière, and whatever they see they'll kill for the army."

"Well," I said, "I know of nothing more that can be done. Follow the foot soldiers. When we make camp to-night, come up behind our fire and we'll talk further."

We put back to Dead River and found the colonel fidgety and lump-faced from inaction. He heaved a sigh of relief when I told him the foot soldiers had cut across country. "Now," he said, "we can kick up a dust and be done with all this delay! We might have rowed these bateaux to Havana in the time it took to come up this broken-backed river!"

We pushed on against the devilish current, bawling and whooping at each other because the rain was over and the worst of our troubles behind us.

Now I'm not superstitious, and I put little faith in our Arundel habits of rapping on wood or spitting over the left shoulder in order to avert disaster. Yet I wish that instead of holloing and whooping that October afternoon we had rapped on wood until the skin was worn from our knuckles, and spat over our left shoulders until the river rose another foot.

We went two miles to a narrow place in the river with a smooth surge of water flowing rapidly over what looked like a gentle fall. The Indians call it Shadagee Falls, and it's only an hour's paddle from the Chain of Ponds.

At ordinary times there's a drop of four feet at the fall; but the high water made it seem less. There was, we thought, nothing difficult about it; nor would there have been if all the bateaux had carried paddles as well as setting-poles. We watched the first few, manned by riflemen with paddles, pass up over it. By working until their muscles must have near split, they got over without accident. Then Hobomok and I went up, and the colonel and Oswald; but before we could continue onward we heard a frenzied shout from below us, a despairing yell, so that Hobomok whirled the canoe and we shot back over the falls.

Three bateaux had gone up abreast, their crews using only setting-poles, and laboring frantically; but all together the three of them had struck a spot where their poles found no hold. Immediately the heads of the bateaux fell off and the force of the stream drove their gunwales under water.

As the overturned boats surged downstream, the bateaux behind them strove to escape, four more turning broadside in the effort. They, too, were seized and drawn down by the violent river; and in a moment their precious contents were torn loose and sucked into the raging brown flood—muskets, powder, flour barrels, pork barrels, and salt.

While we were dragging out the crews, the colonel came back to us with the set smile and hurt eyes I have seen in the faces of men who were fighting stronger men with their fists, but would never stop until they were killed, no matter how they might be battered.

"We camp here, gentlemen, for a council of war," I heard him say to his officers, "so we can decide how to live without any food at all."

XXII

I HAVE often puzzled over the difference between a brave man and a man who is not brave, and it is a thing that will always baffle me. Indeed, I dislike to say this man is brave and that man a coward, because often a man will do a cowardly thing that requires more courage in the doing than a brave thing. There are many who have done brave things because they were afraid to do the cowardly things they would have preferred to do. Also some are cowards about fighting but heroes over money; some brave before audiences but cowardly alone; some brave alone but cowardly before audiences; some deadly afeared of sickness but contemptuous of a storm at sea, and so on. When I think about these things, my brain is muddled; and I arrive at no conclusion, save that every man, somewhere, has in him the spark of bravery.

At the council of war that night there was no one, I learned from Oswald, who voted for returning. The remaining provisions, Arnold admitted, would provide scant rations for a dozen crows; but determined men, he insisted, might keep alive for days by depending on what heaven sent.

"I can get a little food from Enos," Arnold said, "and dash ahead myself to the French settlements so to send back supplies to the rest of you. All that can happen to us has happened, God knows! Anything that happens after this can't help but be a lesser evil."

At this Morgan, unshaven and red-eyed, his huge wrists covered with water blisters and his thighs all scratched and whipped above his Indian leggins, roared in his hoarse carter's voice: "Go on, for God's sake! We can feed on hope for a week!"

"I trust," Arnold said, "we can count on something more solid. Even when everything's gone, we can't help but find food in these forests and the waters we'll cross. I believe we should have a shot at it. If we're successful, it will be a feat remembered for a thousand years to come.

"More than that, General Washington depends on us. I for one don't propose to run home like a child, moaning I couldn't go where I was sent because I was hungry."

There was a growl from all the officers. Captain Dearborn, who became an ambassador afterward to some country in Europe—and a horrid sight he was, Captain Oswald declared, with tangled black whiskers that could scarce be told from the coat of the curly-haired dog between his knees, and a face as white as a clam-shell from some sickness that gnawed him—spoke up softly and said: "Sir, if I correctly gather the sense of this council, these gentlemen are for Quebec, even if they have to eat their breeches to get there."

"You gathered correctly," Colonel Meigs said, "but from the looks of my breeches, I'll have nothing to eat after the first ten minutes."

"There's one more thing," Arnold said, after he had thanked them. "It seems to me we should rid ourselves of those we can't depend on. We must send back the sick, certainly; but I'm also in favor of sending back any man who's faint-hearted about continuing."

"I have some sick," growled Morgan, "but no faint hearts! If I found any, I'd take 'em by the slack of their breeches and throw 'em all the way across the Height of Land!"

Late that night Oswald summoned me to the colonel's tent. I found him writing, as was his habit when alone at night. He stabbed his pen at me over the top of his field desk when I came in.

"Now for the reward of virtue," he said. "Back you go to a land flowing with milk and honey, and take care you don't eat yourself sick."

"My stomach's shrunk," I said. "I don't need the food I needed a month ago."

"All the more reason to beware when you find yourself among the flesh pots." He picked up two letters. "Here are messages for Colonel Enos and Colonel Greene. Greene is waiting for Enos to come up with the reserves of food; so you'll find 'em close together. This is important! Some of us are going to be in desperate need of food, and before you know it, too. Listen to this, now, in case you lose it."

With that he read me the letter to Colonel Enos, dated, "Dead River, thirty miles from Chaudière Pond," the latter being the lake my father called Megantic.

We have had a council of war [said the letter, after mentioning the extreme rains and floods], when it was thought best and ordered to send back all the sick and feeble with three days' provisions, and directions for you to furnish them until they can reach the commissary or Norridgewock; and that on receipt of this you should proceed with as many of the best of your division as you can furnish with fifteen days' provisions; and that the remainder whether sick or well should be immediately sent back to the commissary to whom I wrote to take all possible care of them. I make no doubt you will join with me in this matter as it may be the means of preserving the whole detachment, and of executing our plan without running any great hazard, as fifteen days will doubtless bring us to Canada. I make no doubt you will make all possible expedition.

"I'll start at dawn," I said, "and be as far as Colonel Greene's division by night."

Arnold rose from his camp stool to drive with his fist as though hitting at somebody. "Tell 'em to hurry! Hurry, hurry, hurry! We've been a month in the coils of this river, and a third of the distance still to go! If we could have hurried we'd have walked through the gates of Quebec by now. Get at it, and hurry; and hurry back with the news of how many are coming up!"

*   *   *

Natanis crawled into our lean-to that night and lay with us, the air being bitter cold with a feel of snow in it. Because he was a better hand with a paddle than Hobomok or myself, I determined to take him with us for speed and safety, both in going and returning. This, I felt, I could safely do because his face was known only to Eneas and Sabatis; and those two had gone to Quebec with messages from Arnold.

In the gray of the dawn, therefore, Natanis left us silently and circled behind the camp so we could pick him up unseen.

When Hobomok and I slid our canoe into the water, the sick men were coming down to the bateaux, so they could be sent back: men so weak from the flux they couldn't walk, but must be dragged to the river side; men so swollen and lamed from rheumatism that the sweat poured from them in the biting morning air when they were picked up and carried. There was one, a Pennsylvania rifleman with bones near sticking through his skin from the flux, who made such an uproar that men came from all over the encampment.

"Leave be!" he shouted, his voice shrill as a woman's from rage and weakness, "leave be! I ain't going back! There ain't nothing wrong with me that a day won't fix! I ain't going back, I tell ye!" Yet he was so weak he could not struggle with those who dragged him. "There's sicker men than I be!" he cried, "hiding and pretending to be well! I ain't going back! Leave me lay in the woods alone! I'll catch up!"

Daniel Morgan, hearing the commotion, came striding down among the ragged, bearded riflemen and looked into the face of the sick man.

"Stand him up on his feet," he said to those who had him under the arms.

They lifted him up until his feet were flat on the ground; then released their holds. He slumped down in a heap, making a panting noise, like a tired dog.

"Put him in the bateau," Morgan said. He glanced at the riflemen, glowering at their impassive stares. "Don't any of the rest of you get sick! That's an order! You men keep well long enough, and England won't know whether she's standing on her head or her fat behind!"

There may have been twenty to twenty-five sick men in all, not more. I looked for James Dunn among them, but couldn't find him, nor could I say whether I was fearful or hopeful of seeing him.

We picked up Natanis, who took the stern paddle while Hobomok moved to the bow. Thus driven we went down the swollen waters faster than I thought possible.

On both sides of the stream were sad reminders of the flood—tent canvases caught against tree trunks and draggling mournfully in the current; tangles of setting-poles and ropes jammed into the tops of bushes; boards of bateaux broken apart on the falls; chunks of salt pork turning slowly in the eddies at the base of rocks; burst barrels tilted among half-submerged trees.

By noon we came up with Greene's division, camped a few miles below the spot where the flood had hit us. Sending Natanis and Hobomok down the stream, I went in search of Greene and found him with his officers, Major Bigelow, Captain Thayer, Captain Topham, and Captain Hubbard, all talking about food; and I have found that when there is a shortage of provisions folk will talk about eatables to the exclusion of all else.

Colonel Greene tore open the message, signaling me to wait, and read it aloud. He asked in his mild voice, a voice that seemed abashed at its boldness, how we had stood the deluge, and what was the state of our food. Those who served under Colonel Greene esteemed him highly, for he was gentle, always; thoughtful of those with him; more eager to know what other folk were thinking than to air his own thoughts. There were times when all of us would have been better pleased if he had raged and roared, like Morgan; for in armies, in time of war, the noisy man is listened to first, and then the quiet man; and since wars are noisy and violent, it may take long for the ability of quiet men to be recognized, or for their voices to be heard above the bellowing of incompetents.

I told him how near we had come to drowning, and how the officers and men were set on going to Quebec, even though they must eat their breeches.

Greene smiled gently, as though someone had said the morrow would be pleasant; but Captain Thayer, a maker of perukes before he came within a whisker's width of losing his life at Fort William Henry, and the most harmless-seeming dare-devil that ever was, said mildly that the idea was all right so long as everyone ate his own breeches.

I asked where to find Colonel Enos, at which they looked at each other with the look men have when they hold someone in disregard, but feel a reluctance to speak their minds before a stranger.

"Broadly speaking," Major Bigelow said, giving me the faintest suspicion of a wink, "you'll find him in the rear."

"Broadly speaking," Thayer murmured, "he *is* the rear."

"No, no, no," Major Bigelow said genially, "he must stay where he can watch the provisions and make sure nobody ever has enough to give away."

"Gentlemen! Gentlemen!" protested Colonel Greene, as though a little frightened at his temerity. To me he added: "I think you'll find the colonel a little below us. It might be well if Colonel Arnold's message reached him at the earliest possible moment. We've heard some of his men are"—he cleared his throat apologetically—"slightly disaffected."

"I've heard," Major Bigelow said carelessly, "they're damned well scared. I've heard that if a twig snaps near one of 'em, he jumps like a doe that's backed into a thorn bush."

"Would you be so kind," Colonel Greene added, "as to tell Colonel Enos, if he asks for us, that we'll wait for him to come up with provisions."

Major Bigelow and Captain Thayer burst into an indecorous laugh, and Colonel Greene wagged his head at them in mild reproof.

Misliking these tidings concerning Colonel Enos, I was on my way back to the river when I was stopped by young Burr, ragged as to shoes and breeches, but cleanly shaved, and with his dapper appearance somehow preserved.

"Here's luck!" he exclaimed. "What's happening up ahead? Have they got any food up there?"

"Mighty little! Probably less than you, since the flood."

"Less than we! That's beautiful! That's wonderful! At last we have something smaller than nothing!"

"What are you talking about?"

"Why, bless your soul," Burr said, "the only food I've had in seven days is what Jacataqua shoots for me! Food? Why, we're on starvation rations! To-day I saw men cutting tallow candles into their gruel to give it body."

"But Enos was ordered to send up his surplus food to you!" I protested.

"Enos!" Burr cried, his eyes malevolent. "Enos! Rot him and rat him! He said he had none for himself! Gave us only two barrels of flour! Two barrels of flour to carry two hundred men to Quebec! Why, he might as well have offered us a dozen apple cores!" He called Colonel Enos names that would have turned the stomach of his reverend father who, I had been told, was the president of Princeton College.

"But what became of his surplus?" I asked. "He carried enough to cover our retreat!"

Burr laughed unpleasantly. "I think he still has it. Why do his men hang behind, never coming up with us, unless they fear we'll take supplies from them by main strength when we see how much they have? We would, too, God knows!"

I went to the river and signaled to Natanis and Hobomok. "Look here," Burr said, "is there any talk up ahead of turning back?"

"Yes," I said, "there's talk of it. The talk is that anyone who turns back is worse than a roach. A roach likes water."

Burr smiled and clapped me on the shoulder. Then he caught sight of Natanis bringing the canoe to the bank. "Ho! There's a new face! Who might your new Indian be?"

"A friend. You can call him Mr. Pitt."

"Indeed," Burr said, "I'll call him Benjamin Franklin if he'll go down and relieve Enos of a few of the barrels of flour that he's keeping from us."

I left him cursing Enos, and meaning every word of it.

*　　*　　*

We met Enos moving slowly upstream, as though he had a year to make the journey. Far behind him two bateaux straggled around a bend.

The bow paddle of Enos's canoe was in the hands of John Tree-worgy. He had been so often on my mind that I recognized his long, gray, glowering face as far as I could see it. An Indian paddled stern: one I couldn't place. Hobomok flung me the information over his shoulder: "Swashan, the sachem from St. Francis: the one you bearded at Cobosseecontee."

"Does this man know you?" I asked Natanis.

"I never saw him before," Natanis said. I took no pleasure in seeing Swashan with Treeworgy, or the two of them together with Enos. I could feel in my bones there was something wrong about Treeworgy. I had my suspicions of Swashan as well; and I would have liked to put both of them out of the way. Yet I couldn't shoot them in cold blood, no matter what my suspicions were; for even in war times it's murder to kill a man unless you can prove him an enemy.

Colonel Enos had lost none of his importance; so I was as full of politeness as a Boston hairdresser when, on coming up with him, Natanis swung our canoe alongside.

"Colonel Arnold's compliments and a letter," I said, handing it to him and keeping tight hold of his gunwale to see as much of Tree-worgy as I could. So far as I could tell, Treeworgy took no interest in any of us after his first glum nod at me.

As the colonel read, he continually scratched at his knees and made a sucking sound with his tongue to show displeasure. He read the letter twice from beginning to end; folded it and put it in his pocket; then snatched it out and read it again. "Well!" he said. "Well!" and fell to scratching himself, his forehead all wrinkled.

At length he looked up, puzzled-like. "How do the men feel up ahead? Are they for going on, Morgan's men and Meigs's men?"

"Yes, sir. Even the sick we're sending back."

"Gah!" He made a noise in his throat, such a noise as a cleanly housewife makes on seeing a kitchen in a mess, "Gah! These sick men! If I could be rid of 'em, I might do something! Sick men! Sick men! Sick men! All to be looked after and fed like a lot of yowling babies!"

He glared at me. "How do Arnold and Morgan and Meigs have provisions for fifteen days, when all I've heard from 'em is calls for food? Food! Food! Food! Don't they do anything but eat?"

"Sir," I said, "I only know what the colonel writes. They lost a deal of supplies from the flood and overturned bateaux, so they're on half rations; but they'd go on if they had no rations at all."

"Morgan and Meigs and the colonel are good officers: they wouldn't permit such a thing," he said pompously. "The first duty of an officer is to his men."

I thought of the tales I had heard of General Braddock at the Monongahela in the last war; how he beat our men with the flat of his sword to make them come from behind their trees and stand in line like good British soldiers, to be shot to shreds by the hidden French and Indians. There also came into my mind the many times I'd heard my father say the first duty of most British officers sent to America was always to themselves. But since I was facing a soldier who believed in discipline, I made no reply.

"I have no such supplies as Colonel Arnold speaks of," he said querulously. "My men have barely three days' provisions left! It's common knowledge among 'em that if they advance another day's march into this howling wilderness they'll starve whatever they do: starve if they go forward; starve if they go back."

"Up ahead," I said, "they think that since Colonel Enos's division had more provisions at the start than any of the others, it still must have more."

" 'Tain't true!" he shouted, hammering his fist on the canoe thwart. "We're near starvation ourselves! We lost food from rains and the damned leaky bateaux; then we fed the sick and gave flour to Greene's division."

"I was told," I said, meaning to be sarcastic, "that what Greene got from you was two whole barrels of flour."

"Yes," said Enos petulantly, seeing no sarcasm in it, "and now I'm told to send on as many men as I can supply with fifteen days' provisions, and send the rest back! How in God's name can I do two things at once when I haven't the means to do either!"

I gave him the message Greene had given me for him—that he was waiting for provisions. Enos made his housewifely noise in his throat, "Gah!" and prodded Treeworgy's shoulder. "I'll go ashore. Go back, Treeworgy, and tell Captain McCobb to hurry up here with the rest of the officers. I want to talk to 'em." To me he added, "I'll need you, too! There may be questions you'll have to answer."

He strode up and down the bank, rumbling to himself and making sucking sounds against the roof of his mouth, like a toothless old woman.

✿　　　　✿　　　　✿

This, Natanis told us while we waited, was good hunting country. Not far from us, on the west side of Dead River, there was a wide brook rising in two ponds, thick with beavers. On this brook, he said, he had a burying place, as well as on the next stream above, and on the fourth pond of the Chain of Ponds and the first pond on the far side of the Height of Land.

I'd almost forgotten that spare canoes are often buried in the winter by all Northern Indians for safety and preservation; that a diligent Indian in rough country, where there are many falls and bad carries, will have several canoes scattered through his territory, either buried or, in the summer, carefully covered with branches.

When the bateaux of Colonel Enos's division came up I sent Natanis and Hobomok away again, telling them to get game if possible, but to keep an eye on me in case I wished to move. There was a slow surliness about these men of Enos's. They seemed more wretched than any of those in the other three divisions, though it was impossible that they had suffered greater hardships.

Two of them, Connecticut men, came over to me to ask whether I had come from up front. When I said I had, one asked when the front divisions were starting back.

"What makes you think they're starting back?" I asked.

"Everybody says they're starving to death," he said. "Everybody says we'll starve to death ourselves if we go beyond here. They can't go on! They've *got* to come back."

"I haven't heard anybody say so," I said. "Probably you've been listening to some crazy man: somebody that never left his mother before. Some cry-baby, maybe."

"No," the bateauman said, "all the sick from Morgan's division are saying it."

"Did they say it to you? Did you hear them?"

"No," he said, "but Treeworgy was talking with them. They told him."

Well, I thought, there it was, what I had been sure of at Fort Western: Treeworgy spreading fearsome tales!

"I'll bet they didn't tell him the worst of it, though," I said, hoping they'd tell me more.

"Prob'ly not," said the bateauman. "They told how the officers have to lick the men with whips to git 'em to carry their bateaux over the bad spots, so's their backs are all bloody."

"Well, well!"

"Yes," the other bateauman said, "and how the water beyond here is poisoned by the rains so them as drinks it are all swoll up, and can't walk."

"Is everybody swoll up?" the first bateauman asked.

"You gosh-blamed idiots!" I said, "do I look swoll up?"

"No; that's what Treeworgy said," growled the first bateauman.

"What was it he said?"

"That they'd be sending back somebody as wasn't swoll up, to say everything was all right, and git our food away from us."

"There ain't going to be nobody git no more of my food away from me!" the second bateauman growled.

"Me neither," said the first.

The two guffawed. "Anybody that gits food out of us from now on," said the second, "will have to git our muskets away from us fust."

I turned to look at Enos, who stood on the bank, pinching his lower lip and staring down river.

"The damned old woman!" the first bateauman said, following my glance.

"Yes," said the second, "he's gave away enough provisions to fellers that say they're sick. To hell with him and to hell with them! If we don't look out for ourselves, nobody will!"

"Well," I said, "they don't feel that way up front. They'd rather die than give up."

The first bateauman snorted. "What's the good of that? It's like Treeworgy was saying: if it's sure death to go some place, you're more use to your country if you don't go there."

Rain had begun to fall again, a cold drizzle that might, I knew, change to snow.

"Look at this!" the second bateauman cried. "Look at this stinking country! Look at those damned mountains! I go no further!"

I heard Enos calling. Sickened by their talk, I left the bateaumen and went to him. Other bateaux had come up, and some of the officers of the Fourth Division—Williams, Scott and McCobb, captains; Lieutenant Hyde and Lieutenant Peters. A fire had been lit for them and a tent pitched, whereas I doubt there was a single tent left in all of Morgan's and Meigs's divisions. They sat disconsolate in the tent, looking out at the rain. I marveled how it was possible for men of the same size and muscle and upbringing to be so different. The minds of Morgan's, Meigs's and Greene's officers worked swiftly, seizing on favorable and happy things; but those of Enos's officers worked slowly and moved little, like a cow quivering the skin over her shoulder to drive away flies on a hot afternoon. They saw no ray of light or hope in anything.

"Here's the messenger that brought the letter," Colonel Enos said as I came up.

They glowered at me. Captain Scott, a heavy-paunched man with a thin face and a red nose on which a drop of moisture hung, asked gloomily whether I knew what lay between us and Quebec.

I said I knew from hearsay, whereupon Captain Scott asked me to tell him honestly whether I would undertake to travel the route with insufficient provisions.

"Why, sir," I said, "I'd travel it if all I had was a handful of salt and a lump of pork to cook with trouts."

"That's quibbling!" Colonel Enos said. "I detest quibbling! Answer truthfully, now: if you had provisions for only a few days, and couldn't get more, would you be willing to make the journey to Quebec from here, especially if it was your duty to conduct others who looked to you for safety?"

"Sir," I said, "you're a colonel. I'm only a guide. If I should speak out, my words might be held against me. I might be accused of disrespect. I know little about the ways of an army. Some of them seem to me to be thought out by lunatics."

"Disregard our rank, sir," Colonel Enos said. "Give us the information we're seeking."

"Well, then," I said, "there's two ways of going to Quebec: one in wartime and one in peacetime."

"Now you're quibbling again!"

"Sir," I said, "I'm not quibbling! I'd go to Quebec in wartime with no provisions at all, so long as there was another man left to go with."

"Let's get at this another way," said Captain Williams, a pleasant, polite man. "Do you know the instructions in Colonel Arnold's letter?"

"Yes. He ordered Colonel Enos to send forward all the men to whom he could give fifteen days' rations, and send home all the others, both sick and well."

"That's correct. Now let me ask you what you'd do about going to Quebec in this case: Suppose you could only send forward thirty men with fifteen days' provisions, while the rest of your men, three hundred and more, would have to be sent back with no provisions of any sort—sent back to struggle through these forests and bogs and keep up their strength for a week—two weeks, maybe—without a damned thing to eat."

"Now you're asking about an impossibility," I said.

"Not at all, sir; not at all!" Enos cried. "That's our predicament exactly! Tell us what you'd do in such a situation?"

"Well," I said slowly, "I think I'd put all my provisions in one place and count 'em."

"Just what do you mean by that?"

"Why, sir," I said, "I mean there's no doubt in my mind you've got more provisions than you think."

"Drat you!" the colonel began, purple with rage; but Captain Williams stopped him.

"We invited it, Colonel." He spoke to me politely. "We'd like you to see this as something apart from your personal desires. Our own men are sullen from fearing their food will run out. We have others to consider, too. We're obliged to support all the sick sent back by Morgan and Meigs and Greene. I suppose you think it's our duty to let these sick men starve in the wilderness?"

"No," I said, "I don't."

"Then you think it's our duty to give them enough food to get back to the settlements, because without food they'd certainly starve?"

"Yes," I said, "I do."

"Then if you think that's our duty," Captain Williams said, "you must think it's our duty to return home with the entire division."

"Oh, for God's sake!" I exclaimed in disgust.

"But we can't do two things!" Captain Williams protested. "We can't send the sick home, and go forward at the same time. You say yourself it's our duty to supply the sick with food. As soon as we do that we can't give anyone enough provisions for fifteen days. Colonel Arnold asked only for such men as could be supplied with provisions for fifteen days. It seems to me you think it's our duty to return home."

"That would be all very well," I said, choking with rage, "if you had as few provisions as you say."

"Well, do you think we're better judges of that, or you?" Captain Williams asked sweetly.

"I think I'd be, if I could count your provisions without getting a bullet through the head from one of your bravehearted boys."

"We couldn't think of exposing you to danger."

"No," I said, "and damned good reason, too! You can't think of exposing *anyone* to danger, including yourselves."

I have often waked up at night regretting what I said next; but I was in a fury at being talked in a circle by this sea lawyer of a Williams.

"Here's another thing I think," I added. "I think if I were in your place, and thought as you think, I'd pack up my bateaux even if I had provisions for a *thousand* men for fifteen days! I'd run off home with 'em, leaving the heartbreak and fighting for those who don't live by measurement: for those willing to trust to God and their own efforts to have shoes on their feet and air in their lungs and food in their bellies in a week's time."

With this I walked out of the tent, hot with anger and expecting a bullet or a club in the back of the head.

Natanis and Hobomok drove the canoe across the river when they saw me. As I climbed in, too disquieted to rejoice at the two raccoons and the bundle of fat spruce partridges that lay in the bottom, I heard Enos's peevish voice behind me. "Tell Colonel Greene to wait for me in the morning. I'll hold a council of war when I come up with him."

In his voice I sensed a number of unspoken words; and I wished I could pick up one of the partridges and jam it down his throat.

*   *   *

The rain turned to snow as we went up to Greene's camp in the semidark—a gurry of weather that made it hard to pick our way around the falls, nor could we have done so without Natanis to guide us. Even so I stumbled perpetually, my mind being on the lack of provisions of which Enos and his men complained. I didn't believe their food was as low as they claimed, nor do I believe it to-day, it being in my thoughts then and now that the men, affrighted out of all reason by Treeworgy's tales, had hid provisions so they might run home, uncovering the hoards as they ran. Yet if it was true, Enos and his officers were indeed in a parlous situation; for if they went on, leaving sick men to suffer and starve, they would be damned for cruelty; and if they turned back, leaving the rest of the army to go on without them, they would be equally damned for cowardice.

Also there rested heavy on me the knowledge that Treeworgy from the first had sown discontent among Enos's men, and that I had failed to get at the bottom of it in spite of my suspicions. Nor was it, I thought, any great comfort to know that if Enos's division turned back, Treeworgy would turn back with them.

It was dark by the time we saw Greene's campfires through the snowflakes, and I was in no pretty frame of mind, what with my anger and the burning of my feet from tramping over the carries in shoes broken in a dozen places, so that I might as well have been barefoot.

But when I left Natanis and Hobomok kindling a fire in the lee of our canoe and went with the raccoons and partridges to Greene's tent to give him Enos's message, the welcome I got was as good as warm clothes on my body and an opened window in my head to let out the darkness and gloom that had filled me at Enos's camp.

It's doubtless a fine thing to be serious-minded, preserving a dignified and ponderous demeanor toward life; but if I must fight or march I prefer to do it with frivolous, light-minded folk; for they are the ones who fight and march while others give serious thought to how it should be done.

"Dear, dear! Dear, dear!" said Colonel Greene, feeling of the raccoon absent-mindedly and passing it to Major Bigelow, who cuddled it as though it were a child, "I'm sorry to hear these tales about Enos's division, though it's no more than I expected. I'm sure the colonel will do what's best."

Bigelow, a wiry, brown-faced officer with heavy black eyebrows and a peculiar habit of breaking into imitation peals of laughter at unexpected moments, had placed the raccoon's body on his knees and was parting its hair carefully at various spots. He whistled shrilly, pointing with apparent horror at the parted hair of the raccoon. A large black flea moved languidly against the white skin. "Colonel Enos!" Bigelow said gravely.

"Moves a little fast, doesn't he?" Captain Thayer asked.

"Yes," Bigelow said. "He's going south."

"He can *go* south for all of me," said Captain Topham. "If he doesn't, and we take Quebec, we'll have to stay there twenty years waiting for him to catch up."

"Gentlemen! Gentlemen!" Colonel Greene protested.

"Gentlemen hell!" said Bigelow. He went to the rear of the lean-to and tossed the raccoon to the cook, who was working over a kettle under a pine tree. "Put this in the gruel, Luke," he shouted, "and see if you can get it strong enough to hold up a hair."

He turned back to Greene. "He's an old woman and you know it, Colonel! Don't be so easy on him! If he was a hen, he wouldn't cackle till he'd looked under himself twice to see whether the egg was really there. If I can get him behind a pine tree with nobody looking I'll kick him all the way back to Norridgewock. Don't say Gentlemen to me! I'm nothing but a carter where Enos is concerned!"

"It may be," the colonel said, "that he's out of provisions, as he says. If it's true, I don't envy him, with all our sick on his hands."

"Stuff and feathers!" Thayer said. "How *can* he be out of provisions when he started with twice what any of us carried!"

"What do you think?" the colonel asked me.

"Sir," I said, "I don't know. I was in a rage at him and Williams and McCobb, thinking they were shameful cowards; but the men are frightened and sulky, bound to save their own skins and be damned to Enos and everybody else. It may be they wasted food, cooking more than their needs. They may have hid some, unknown to Enos and the rest."

"Oh, for God's sake!" Bigelow cried, "he could chance it with *some* men, couldn't he? Do you think we'll turn back if we have less than fifteen days' provisions, such as the colonel tells us to have in his letter?" He struck an attitude. "I shall go forward even though I have provisions for only fourteen and one half days!" He burst into shrill, false laughter; and the rest of us laughed at his clowning, knowing he would go forward with the colonel and the rest of the division if he had nothing more than a cupful of flour to get him to Quebec.

* * *

I make no pretense of reading men's minds, since I have found so many of them cheerful in war when they might reasonably be sad, and sad when there seems fair cause for cheerfulness. Yet if Colonel Enos was dispirited when I gave him the message from Colonel Arnold, he had more reason for being so on the following morning.

There was a blanket of snow on the ground; and the air had an edge to it that took men piercingly in the knees and behind the ears. It may be I speak overmuch of the biting nature of the cold along the Kennebec; but I do so because it was one of the enemies we fought, as well as the British, and because it seemed a peculiar racking cold that slid down from the Height of Land, creeping and twisting along the winding coils of the river, undulating in a sort of clammy mist that clung to the valley through its whole length.

Then there were the sick men coming down on him, bateau after bateau filled with them, more than twenty-five men from Morgan's and Meigs's divisions, and some sixty from Greene's, men so weakened with the flux that they could scarce stand, and so racked with rheumatism that if they fell, which they often did when out of the bateaux, they dragged themselves along on hands and knees until someone came to lift them up.

Greene sent off his division as soon as it was light, staying behind himself with Bigelow and the other officers to wait for Enos and the council of war.

"When the council's over," he told me, "I'll give you a message for the colonel."

I watched the men set off, churning the new snow into slush. There were barely a hundred of them, all badly off in the matter of clothes, and two with no shoes at all, though I make no doubt their feet were tough as leather.

I caught Burr on the run and asked him the whereabouts of Jacataqua.

"Gone ahead to hunt," he flung at me over his shoulder. "Send your Mr. Pitt to get food if there's time. I could do with a juicy crow to-night!"

This I did, telling Natanis and Hobomok they were safe in hunting for a matter of three hours, though it was a move that did me no good. Yet I cannot rightly say I regretted it; for it has always seemed to me that if we regretted and sought to avoid all the small movements that lie behind our misfortunes and disappointments, we'd spend our lives in regrets and our days in immovability.

It was noon when Enos came up the river with his officers, Williams, McCobb, Scott, Hyde, and Peters; and after all these years I cannot set down their names without cursing them, even though I know in my heart there may have been good and sufficient reason for what they did. They were in a bateau, driven by Treeworgy and Swashan. I knew at once they were going no farther; for in the bateau was neither baggage nor provisions.

They crowded into Colonel Greene's tent, and after a time I crouched beside it, to hear, if possible, what might be going forward. Major Bigelow was speaking, as careless as though he spoke of scraping barnacles off a sloop.

"There's no use huffering and chuffering about what Colonel Arnold would have us do if we can't live up to the letter of his instructions," he said, "because Colonel Arnold has gone beyond our reach. He said he wants no sick men and no faint hearts, but must have fighters; so I'm going on, and my men with me, and all the talk in the world can't change *that!*"

"But you've got to figure," Enos complained, "that it takes three days to cross the Height of Land and two more to reach Lake Megantic and another three——"

"Begging the colonel's pardon," said Major Bigelow, "I haven't got to figure, and I'm not going to. I'm going to go, and not waste time figuring."

"That's what I'm figuring on doing," said Captain Thayer, mild and pleasant as always.

"But an officer is responsible for his men," Colonel Enos objected. "I must think of my men."

"Holy mackerel! begging the colonel's pardon," Bigelow cried. "What are you going to do if we have to ram our men against the guns of Quebec? We haven't any written guarantees from England that we won't have to. I hope we wouldn't be supposed to wrap 'em up in feather beds until the British are all dead!"

"That's another matter entirely," said Colonel Enos. "I have to think of my men."

"So do I!" said Bigelow. "I have to think of them, and of Colonel Arnold, and of the men in Morgan's and Meigs's divisions. That's why I'm going!"

"My men refuse to continue," said Captain Williams.

"So do mine," said McCobb.

"And mine," said Scott.

"Sir," said Enos, seemingly speaking to Major Bigelow, "I protest against your manner of spitting when my officers have stated a fact calculated to enable us to arrive at a decision. It's an act unworthy of an officer and a gentleman!"

What reply Major Bigelow made I never learned; for a hand touched me on the shoulder. It was Natanis.

"Where is the canoe?" he asked.

"Our canoe?"

He nodded. "It is gone, with our blankets and food."

"Treeworgy!" I said under my breath. We ran to the spot where we had camped. There was no need to look at the tracks leading to the river. Treeworgy and Swashan had robbed us. From the marks on the bank we saw they had gone upstream.

"How far," I asked Natanis, "to your laid-up canoe?"

"Ten times the flight of a partridge, on the opposite bank."

This was about a mile. "Quick," I said, "get across with Greene's bateau, you and Hobomok, and uncover it! For God's sake, hurry! This Treeworgy is up to some deviltry! He's a spy and there's no two ways about it!"

I recall no particular despair at our situation, despite our lack of food and blankets and the loss of my musket, but only a longing to have Treeworgy at the end of my sights, or my hands on his lying throat. Both Hobomok and Natanis had muskets and carried fishing lines, flints, and steel in their pouches, so that there was no danger of starvation. But Treeworgy's dash toward the front of the column was something on which I hadn't counted. There was a feeling in the pit of my stomach that it had something to do with me—something bad.

I ran to Greene when he and Enos came out of the council, followed by the other officers. Enos bawled for Treeworgy; and Bigelow and the rest of Greene's officers went off toward their bateau without so much as a farewell glance toward Enos's men.

"My compliments to Colonel Arnold," said Greene, with a look about his mouth as though he had eaten something hateful. "Tell him my division, reduced to one hundred and seven effective men, will join him with the others."

"And the council of war?" I asked.

"That's a message I hate to send," he said mildly. "Colonel Enos's officers voted against proceeding, on the ground that their provisions were insufficient and their men unruly. Colonel Enos voted with us to proceed, but yielded to the pleas of his officers and will return at the head of his division."

We stared at each other. "Is that all, sir?" I asked.

"Yes, I think that's all," Colonel Greene sighed. "It's difficult and painful. He'll have to stand a court-martial when he gets back, of course."

"That shouldn't be hard to stand," I said, "with Williams and Mc-Cobb testifying for him, and no Bigelow or Thayer to distract them."

Greene nodded and turned away, a fine gentleman, but a little overkindly and obliging, it seemed to me, for an army not officered exclusively by gentlemen, which our army wasn't, any more than was the British army.

I hid in the pines near the camping ground, watching Enos fuming and fussing in the snow and occasionally whooping for Treeworgy. At the end of an hour Natanis and Hobomok came around the bend, driving a small canoe against the current so that the water curled away from its stem, showing it was well loaded. There was an odd hump in the middle, and over it a blanket. They came up on the far side of the river: then, as I showed myself, cut across. Beside the blanketed hump lay a spare musket.

"What's all this?" I asked.

"Half a barrel of flour," said Natanis, "that Mr. Pitt was asked to get."

I heard Colonel Enos bawling behind me, so climbed in. "Here!" he shouted, as we pushed upstream, "set me down to my camp!"

"Begging the colonel's pardon," I said, mindful of Major Bigelow's military forms, "but the colonel can go to hell."

He was bawling furiously for Treeworgy when we had our last sight of him, nor did I care if I never had another.

XXIII

I HAVE, it seems to me, a fairish eye for beauty, and I have heard it said there is great beauty to the Chain of Ponds that lie against and on the Height of Land, giving rise to this river that had thrown its coils about us and battered us until we were bruised and lame. Yet they seemed hideous to me when we fought our way across them through the gales and snow of late October, so I think there is more to beauty than swelling hills or tumbled rocks or limpid waters; and I wouldn't give one acre of my ragged sand dunes in Arundel for all the mountain ponds you can show me in a week.

Nor, for good reasons, did I see beauty in any of that torn and crumpled region that lay between us and Canada, one of the reasons being that the snow stung our eyes so that for a part of the time we could see nothing but the trees about us, and another being that we made our way through such a smother of brush and fallen logs that we had to screen our eyes to keep them from being whipped out, and a third being that I long ago learned from Natanis that speed is gained and strength saved, in arduous marching or climbing, if the eye is fastened on the ground that lies before the feet, once the trail be known.

Therefore I saw less of that country than I might have seen had I gone into it to dawdle over the killing of moose or bear, with stout shoes on my feet, and a full belly thrice a day, and fires to drive the ache from muscles and joints. The main shape of it, none the less, I shall always remember; for I often find it in my dreams, when objects are swollen and distorted, unreachable and ungraspable.

What I see is a stupendous stone wall, an overwhelming enlargement of those we build in New England out of the gray rocks that fill our fields. The wall, in my dreams, lies across a bog in which the hoofprints of a million giant cows have frozen and thawed and run together; and from one division of the bog to the other, across this monstrous wall, there runs a long and twisted stalk of woodbine. Along the stalk, in my dreams, I see a throng of little red ants, groping and hesitating, fumbling here and there, straying and struggling, backing and filling, but ever moving onward.

It is like this stone wall that the cruel, stone-toothed Height of Land divides the bogs of the North. To the south are those of the Chain of Ponds, like vast hoofprints in the mud of ages, from which all the waters run to the south. To the north are those of Lake Megantic, forming the Chaudière and other streams that fall into the St. Lawrence. Our trail across it was like the tangled, twisted stalk of woodbine; and we, climbing the trail, were like the ants, creeping feebly, but somehow creeping forward.

Eager as were Natanis and Hobomok and I to overtake Treeworgy, when we left Enos shouting into the whirling snowflakes, we were held back by the snow and the gathering dusk. We passed Greene, and in time came up with Burr riding in a bateau with his friend the chaplain, Reverend Spring, a jovial young man from Princeton College, who was cursed with chilblains, an ailment he was encouraged to conceal because of his heartening effect on the men, and his failure to hear and see matters better unheard and unseen by a chaplain.

"Here," I said, as we drew alongside him, "Enos has gone back with his entire division, and here's some flour for you."

Burr broke into a flow of profanity at Enos that could have been achieved only by someone familiar with the Bible.

"Amen," said the Reverend Spring, feeling cautiously of his toes.

"Anyway," said Burr, after he had spoken freely about Enos, "I'm glad to see Mr. Pitt did his duty. We give you our hearty thanks, Mr. Pitt." He lifted his hat to Natanis, who grinned amiably. "How did they do it?" he asked me.

Natanis spoke rapidly in Abenaki.

"Well," I said, "I'd been content not to know, fearing there might have been some chicanery about it, but it seems to have been the merest chance. Mr. Pitt happened to be near some of Enos's men when a fearful screaming broke out in the forest, a horrible screaming such as had never been heard before. The men's attention was so caught by it that they must have dropped the flour, as well as a musket and three blankets that we sorely needed."

"Oh," said Burr profoundly, "that explains everything!"

"The Lord giveth and the Lord taketh away," said the Reverend Spring, huddling his feet carefully in his blanket.

❧   ❧   ❧

We were off at dawn the following morning; and though the driving snow had ceased, we were hindered and blocked at the carries by the bateaumen of Meigs's division, who clambered with difficulty through the slush. Not until noon did we come to the first of the Chain of Ponds, all of them bordered by mountains that seemed to me to blanket us with chill and darkness. I couldn't breathe easily or deeply among them, as I can among the sweet salt marshes and the silvery, curving beaches of Arundel.

Up these we went, crossing round ponds and oval ponds and ponds with points like fingers stretching out to catch at us, and ponds shaped like hourglasses strung together on a thread of a river that twisted and dwindled and hid in bogs and leaped out at us over ledges again: small ponds, medium ponds, large ponds, until we were sick of ponds—a sickness that has stayed with me to this day. I have but one good thing to say of them, and that is this: if a man have a fondness for ponds and cannot find one to suit him among them, he must be hard indeed to please.

We found Morgan's men groping around the shores of one that they insisted had no inlet at all—until Natanis showed it to them. They followed along behind us, and Natanis guided us from pond to hidden pond as surely as a Falmouth man passes from his home to the wharves. At nightfall on the last Thursday in October, and again I remember the day because the next day fell on a Friday, we came to the last of the Chain of Ponds, the last and greatest, and crossed it with the granite, tree-clad wall of the Height of Land looming dark before us.

While Natanis and Hobomok cooked trouts, I went to those of Morgan's men who had landed near us and learned that Treeworgy, with an Indian, had passed them at mid-afternoon.

"Did they tell you about Enos?" I asked.

"Nay," said a drawling Virginian, busy patching his breeches with a squirrel skin, "he went past us like a pig after a snake. What about Enos?"

I told them the tale, while all these tall men came around me and listened, chewing silently on sumach leaves or willow bark, even forbearing to spit until I had finished.

"Well," said one of them, "I hope he rots away, a little at a time, starting now, or dies plenty painful." He embellished his speech with frills and trimmings that made Burr's attempts, which I had so much admired, seem lady-like. There was a general chorus of deep, passionate cursing from the rest of the Virginians, until there was nothing about Colonel Enos or his ancestors left uncursed.

I have heard it said that cursing is not what it was in my grandfather's day, when it was considered, both by the damner and the
damned, a serious business to damn a man for a fault or a sin; whereas
it is now the fashion to damn anything and everything, whether it
deserves damning or not; so that a man will damn a twig that slaps
his cheek or a bird that twitters overloudly when he is desirous of
sleeping. This may all be so; but I could ask to hear no more polished
and intricate cursing than Colonel Enos received. If there was no
efficacy in it, then there never will be efficacy in any sort of curse
anywhere.

At dawn of Friday, the last Friday in October, we set off to cross
the Height of Land; and while I had held Morgan's riflemen in high
esteem as soldiers, the thing they did that day has set them, in my
mind, above all others. Whenever, since then, I hear them bragging
somewhat concerning their powers, which they are prone to do, I
feel that they have earned the right to brag.

The supplies of all divisions were sadly shrunk, the provisions near
gone and much of the ammunition spoiled by the leaking of rain and
river water into the powder kegs. Therefore Colonel Arnold, to ease
the crossing of the terrible five-mile wall of the Height of Land by
his half-starved army, had sent back word that each company need
carry only one bateau for medicines and a few essentials. The others
could be abandoned at the last of the Chain of Ponds.

Yet Morgan's riflemen, angered by Enos's desertion and determined to make rapid progress when they reached Canada, as well
as to save the few military stores they had so jealously guarded, said
they would carry all seven of their bateaux across the mountains on
their backs. This they did, and in doing it they wore the skin from
their shoulders, so that the bones showed through.

When we passed those men, creeping slowly up the trail, dragging
at the bateaux like ants tugging at something infinitely vaster than
themselves, I thought to myself that Roger Enos's excuse for leaving
us might prove satisfactory to all the world, but could never be anything more than the whimpering of a frightened puppy to those who
had gone on.

Knowing that the trail which Morgan's men were following had
been made by Lieutenant Steele, Lieutenant Church, Cap Huff and
the twenty axemen, I feared to follow it too far lest someone recognize Natanis and so make trouble for him, and also lest I be ambushed
by Treeworgy, who couldn't be far ahead. Therefore Natanis led us
off the trail and into a winding trace, like a deer path. Along this we

struggled as well as though we were on the snagged trail, though this, God knows, is not said in high praise.

What hell may be like, I don't know; but if it's like the Height of Land I hope I may be spared from it. I have seen evil forests in my life, but never so much evil compressed into such small compass as here.

The trees were dwarfed and starved, without a first-growth tree among them; and all of them grew from the rotting bones of other forests which had been beaten to the earth, Natanis said, by the terrible windstorms that rage across them. There were blow-downs everywhere, tangles of dead pines, with new growth binding them together, so that there was no getting through them. Nor, as one climbed higher on this terrible wall, did the moisture drain from the earth, as might be expected. Everywhere there were mire holes: wet gullies through thickets whose dead twigs snapped into our faces: devilish bogs at the bottom of ravines, and sheer precipices rising out of dark bogs with other bogs at their tops.

Along our narrow deer track, twisting around mire holes and skirting blow-downs, Natanis moved without hesitation, though it was a path I could never have followed by myself. When I said so, he showed me the Abenaki trail marks, faint ones so that they might not be used by the Montagnais or any other Northern Indians: triple slashes, little more than scratches, inclined to the left or to the right, or straight up and down, depending on the direction followed by the trail ahead. There were, he said, three main Abenaki trails across the Height of Land from the Chain of Ponds: one zigzagging across from the pond we had just left and coming out on Seven Mile Stream, which is the stream flowing from the northerly side of the Height of Land into Lake Megantic; one going to the right of this and coming out on the easterly shore of Lake Megantic; and the third going to the left and coming out on the westerly shore of the lake. These, he said, were necessary for hunting parties, and had existed for years, with cross trails connecting them. It was the first of these, he said, that we were traveling. The trail opened for the army was straighter and shorter than any of the Abenaki trails.

After we had topped the Height and commenced our descent we came to a mountain meadow, one that seemed to me a lovely sight because of its resemblance to a fragment of New England dropped into all this hellishness. It was dotted with clumps of elms, large and stately, and over it lay a thick mat of grass, so that it had a familiar look, like Ipswich common, or the green at Newburyport. Natanis

warned me not to be misled by this unexpected sight into thinking
all our troubles lay behind us. The meadow, he said, was without a
mate anywhere in that country; and from its beauty the Abenakis
believed it to be the spot where the great lord Glooskap was born. Its
lower end, he said, gave rise to the Seven Mile Stream, which, after
seven miles of winding, fell into Lake Megantic; but the country
through which it flowed was worse than the Height of Land, thick
with trackless bogs lying deep in water, so that even the Abenakis
shunned it, skirting around it on the high land to the east and west.

Through this meadow ran a new-made trail, so we knew Church
and Steele and his men, as well as Arnold himself, had passed this
way into Seven Mile Stream and so to Lake Megantic. We went beyond the meadow, watching carefully for Treeworgy, dropped our
canoe into the twisted channel of Seven Mile Stream, and slipped
silently down it through the worst swamps that ever I saw, there being no banks at all to the stream on its lower portions, only trees and
shrubs standing in water, with here and there an islet choked with
brush.

The trees and bushes ceased toward dusk, and we knew we had
come to the lake. In the distance was a plume of smoke, rising straight
in the cold air from the right-hand shore. We saw bateaux in the water, and made out five or six campfires, so we were certain we had
caught up with Colonel Arnold, which indeed we had.

We skirted around the camp so that Natanis might land beyond it
and be safe until we had need of him. Then we came back to the
camp, Hobomok running me inshore quickly; so that if Treeworgy
was there I might face him unexpectedly.

Captain Oswald stood on the point talking with Lieutenant
Church and Lieutenant Steele when the canoe shot in. They fell
silent as I jumped ashore and went up to them. "Is Treeworgy here?"
I asked, trying to look into the gloom beyond them.

Steele stared silently across the lake. Church, scratching his lugu-
brious face with his forefinger, said sadly: "What you want of him?"

Both had failed to give me any greeting at all.

"What's the matter?" I asked. At once I thought I had the answer.
"Treeworgy told you about Enos, of course! Where is he?"

Steele walked away. Church looked mournfully at the ground.

Oswald said: "You'd best hold your tongue until you've seen the
colonel." His voice was hostile.

"Why, what do you mean?" I said. "What the hell ails you, treating
me like a criminal!"

"Over there," Oswald said, pointing to an Indian cabin made of bark, sheltered from the north by a heavy clump of spruces. Light gleamed through its cracks. He and Church turned away, leaving me alone.

＊　　　＊　　　＊

I walked over to the bark house with a cold feeling in the pit of my stomach. It never occurred to me to wonder how the cabin had come there. I pushed aside the blanket that hung at the door and found Colonel Arnold inside, his field desk balanced on his knee. When he looked up and saw me, he snapped down the cover of the inkwell and threw the desk together with a bang.

"By God!" he said, "you're either a brave man or the damnedest fool alive to come into this room with me!"

"What in God's name is the matter?" I asked, near sick with apprehension.

Arnold's eyeballs gleamed white in his dark, puffy face, which had lost all its pleasing contours and become nubbly, like the green squashes we grow in Arundel. He made a hissing sound, and picked up a heap of papers from beside the stump on which he sat.

"Here," he said, slapping one of the papers and glaring at me until I thought his eyes would pop from his head. "You advised Colonel Enos that it was his duty to return to Cambridge with all his troops and provisions! What have you got to say to that, damn you!"

"It's a damned dirty lie!" I said, cold and shaking all over, and feeling as though I had no stomach inside my hunting shirt.

"Do you dare to stand there and deny——"

"Deny! Deny! I say it's a lie! I fought him, for God's sake! What are you talking about?"

"I've got it here!" Arnold shouted, banging the stump with his fist. "I tell you I've got it down in black and white! Here! Did you or did you not say this to Captain Williams before Colonel Enos, when asked for advice? Did you or did you not say that if you were in their place you'd pack up and go home, no matter how much food you had?"

"Oh, for God's sake!" I said. "Yes! But in sarcasm! In sarcasm!" A hurly-burly of thoughts raced through my head, making me near speechless from desire to speak them all and inability to know where to start. "By God!" I said, "it was Treeworgy! Treeworgy heard me!"

"Yes," Arnold said, his face furious, "Treeworgy heard you say it!"

"I tell you I didn't say it! I said other words that changed the meaning!"

"But you used those words!"

"Yes, but not as you imply. Wait: I can't remember what I said! I tell you I fought Enos and Williams! This Treeworgy—he's responsible, damn his dirty lousy soul to hell—they never would have gone back but for Treeworgy!"

"Oh," Arnold said, moving his thick shoulders under his coat and glaring at me cold and unwinking out of pale blue eyes. "Oh, so now you turn it all on Treeworgy! What was it Treeworgy did?"

"Damn him!" I said, half crying with desire to tear him to pieces. "He took my food and my musket and my canoe, and raced up here to lie about me!"

Arnold watched me with hard blue eyes. "Good reason, too! He heard you advise them to go back. He thought you intended to go back as well."

"He thought no such thing! I did *not* advise them to go back. I'd see anyone in hell before I advised him to go back! If I advised them to go back, why have I come on myself? What would Treeworgy say to that? Where is he, the damned gray rat?"

"I'll tell you what he'd say," Arnold said. I tightened my muscles, thinking he meant to jump up and take me by the throat. "I'll tell you what he *did* say. He said he took your canoe because he thought you were a coward and would go back with Enos, so that you'd have no use for a canoe. He said if you came on in spite of that, it would prove what he disliked to think: that you're a spy!"

"No!" I exclaimed, groping and groping in my mind for words, but finding little there except what seemed to me like cold flakes of metal such as fall from red hot iron when pounded at the forge. "No! It's not true! Why, you *know* me! You've been in Arundel and you've been in my home and you *know* me! You knew my father! You know my mother and my sisters! How in God's name could *I* be a spy!"

"Why, for that matter," Arnold said, glowering at me, "you're nothing but an innkeeper and a trader—a man who'll take money for almost anything he owns——"

"Damn you! You can't say that!"

"Oh, can't I? Why can't I, when I've got a thousand men on my hands to bring safely through these forests? I say it, just as Treeworgy said it to me: somebody must have got to you with money! You've taken money! You must have taken money!"

"Now wait!" I said, feeling as though some terrible thing had happened in the pit of my stomach. "Wait! Now wait for a minute!"

"You've taken money!" Arnold repeated. "I'll not run the risk of having my men endangered by such as you! I'll have no more of you!"

"Wait!" I said, fumbling for words. "Endangered! Do you think I'd endanger Phoebe or Noah Cluff or you or any friend of mine? For God's sake, wait a little! Why, here: you've known for years I've wanted to go to Quebec—to Quebec after Mary. Yes, and you've seen Mary! You went to see Mary and brought back word of her to me. Now wait a minute! You wouldn't let me go to Quebec until you gave the word! There it is: you know the both of us! You can't treat me this way! Why, Colonel, I swear to my God I've done no such thing—I've taken no man's money! What do I want of money? What object would I have in taking money to turn against my own country and my own people?"

"Object?" Arnold asked thoughtfully. "Object? Why, the best of objects from the point of view of a lovesick idiot! If you were taking British money the gates of Quebec would be open to you always. You could walk in to see this milk-faced wench of yours with no trouble, where the rest of us might have to fight our way in."

"No!" I shouted. "No! It's a lie! I'd waited years! I'd have waited years more, and you know it damned well!"

"Now listen!" Arnold said. "I can remember when you'd have hit me with a stool—me, a guest in your own house—for being slow in telling you about your doll-faced wench. Don't tell me what you'd do! There's no telling what a man in love will do! He isn't in his right mind! As soon as Treeworgy asked whether there was any woman in your case I knew he'd hit it!"

"No! For God's sake, no!" I said, striving to speak calmly. "You can't take Treeworgy's word against mine! I'm your friend, and you never saw Treeworgy before this expedition. I tell you he's a liar!"

"So!" Arnold said softly. "So! I never saw him before! And he lies about everything, does he?"

"Yes, damn him! About everything! He filled Enos's men with lies, until they were ready to turn tail and run by the time they reached Skowhegan."

Arnold went to laughing silently, his broad shoulders shaking under the deerskin shirt that covered his uniform. As he laughed he stared into my face with bulbous blue eyes in which there was no merriment at all. "I think," he said, "he sometimes tells the truth."

"No!" I protested. "Never! I tell you every word he says is a lie!"

"Ah!" said Arnold, "and is it also a lie that the Indian Natanis has visited our camps in your canoe?"

I stared back at him, speechless at the trap into which I had blundered.

"Speak up!" Arnold cried. "Treeworgy may be a liar, but you can't deny Natanis has been with you, as Treeworgy said! Do you deny it?"

"No!"

He got to his feet, his face swarthy and nubbly. "I know this much! You were warned about Natanis! Washington warned you and I warned you! We threshed that out and settled it! He's a spy; and you were told so. You knew we had no faith in him. Now you've taken him the length of our lines. You've shown him the last shred of pork and the last keg of powder we've got! You knew Steele had orders to shoot him, and yet you did these things! By God, I'll lay odds you warned him, so he escaped us!"

He moved his shoulders, as if loosening them in his clothes. "I see no good reason why I should close my ears to the things Treeworgy told me, or open them to every windy utterance of yours. And if it's of interest to you, I can tell you Treeworgy was of service to me long before this expedition started! He's no new acquaintance!"

"Sir," I repeated, my thoughts moving slowly in a circle, like a rabbit before a hound, "Treeworgy's a liar. He's a liar! Bring us together and see whether he makes these charges." Even as I said it I had the sickening feeling that Treeworgy, with his sour, pious face, would lie about me more convincingly than I could tell the truth about myself.

"I sent Treeworgy across to the St. Francis River, and down it, to carry a message to General Schuyler," Arnold snapped. "If I hadn't, I'd not trouble to question what he tells me about your treachery where Natanis is concerned. You admit it's the truth!"

"Sir," I said, "it's *not* treachery! Natanis is no spy. He'll spend his life in our cause as readily as any man!"

Arnold shook his head, and there was, it seemed to me, a pitying look on his face. "Can't you see you're either an idiot or a bought spy to persist in such statements? He admits himself he's a spy, because he said so to Conkey. Treeworgy knows it, and my advices from Quebec have said it." He shook his clenched fist at me with an air of finality. "Treeworgy must have been right about this, as he was right about the rest of it. You must have taken money, and you must be a spy!"

"Sir, for God's sake!" I said. "I tell you I'm no such thing, but willing to go anywhere and do anything under your command. It's a terrible black lie! Even if Treeworgy should run for shelter into heaven and hide himself under God's footstool, I'll hunt him out and kill him for the spy and snake he is!"

Arnold stared at me curiously. "Under God's footstool! Why, there's another true thing Treeworgy said. He said I'd get no satisfaction if I confronted you with this, only violent words and blasphemy."

"Did he say 'blasphemy'?" I asked, raging inwardly because my words and thoughts were dammed up in my head, with only small and useless things breaking loose.

"'Coward, spy, and blasphemer' was what he called you."

"Hook!" I exclaimed. "I knew he was Hook!"

"Hook or no Hook, he made no mistakes about you!"

"I tell you he lied!" I said. "I'm no more a spy than Steele is, or Morgan, or you yourself!"

Arnold's face was terrible, black and lumpy. He walked the earthen floor of the cabin like a caged wolf, sliding bitter looks at me as he walked. "Nason," he said, "I'd like to believe you; but this Natanis business is more than I can stomach. There's a chance you may be honest according to your lights. In your heart you may not be guilty. I'm not sure about you, and so I sha'n't have you shot. Yet I'm sure of this: I have an army in my care. That being so, I take no further chances with you. You're done and finished!"

I scarce heard what he said for the welter of thoughts in my head —thoughts that had to do, most of them, with Mary Mallinson. Little pictures rose in my mind, like wavelets in a cove on a rising tide, each lapping over the other until my mind was full of pictures: of Mary on her knees before me; of the last look she had given me as she vanished into the forest; of our pursuit of her; of Guerlac's braves rising and falling as they drove their canoe toward my watery hiding place; of Natanis, sick on his bed of spruce tips, telling me how Mary's dress was made of scraps of blankets; of the two Frenchmen in their plum-colored coats smiling at Phoebe Marvin and telling me of the White Lily that had returned from France as Marie de Sabrevois; of Arnold's visit to the convent, and the slender, gray-clad girl he had found there. I thought of the times I had been on the verge of setting out to bring her back to Arundel; and here was the end of it—the end of it! Accused, in a dirty hut in the wilderness, of aiding a spy and being a spy myself.

"I'll have you with us no longer," Arnold went on, his face as hard as a rock in the firelight. "And don't think, when I leave at dawn to get food for the others, that you can join them. I'll send back word so they'll know what you've done. Go on into the forests with this red spy, Natanis, and see what he can do for you—provided he's able to dodge the bullets of the riflemen!"

He glared at me. As I stared silently back at him there was a clinking in the pile of baggage behind him. He whirled to look; then went and prodded at it. Seeing nothing, he brushed by me, threw up the blanket over the doorway, and motioned me out. He looked behind the wigwam, and I heard him call for Oswald; so I moved back toward the heavy undergrowth, feeling gone inside, not from hunger, though I had eaten nothing but a flour cake since morning, but from despair.

*   *   *

I had no heart to brave the stares of Church and Steele and Oswald again, or risk words with them so long as they took me for a spy; yet Hobomok lay offshore, still, in our canoe. Nor did I know how I could reach Natanis; though I knew I must try, for the night was black and bitter cold, and ice was forming where there was water.

While I stood and pondered and took my bearings from the stars, I felt a body near me: a breath or a silent movement, something living. When I crouched and faced it I heard a voice I knew, a rough, coarse whisper, saying: "Stevie! All right, Stevie! It's me!"

"Cap!" I said. I went deeper into the brush and got him by the shoulders.

I felt his hard barrel of a chest and his stubbly beard and his huge upper arms, muscled like a horse's thigh, and sniffed at the reek of perspiration mixed with the buckskin smell of his shirt. He had his pack with him, and his musket, though I gave no thought to this strange circumstance at the time.

"Thank God it's you, Cap! I never needed a friend the way I do now." I must have been sick, because my eyes were wet, and I felt weak, the way I've sometimes felt when my dory barely rises to a breaker over the ledges.

"You big damned fool," Cap said, clapping me on the back, "you certainly went and done it!"

"Cap, I swear I'm not what he said!"

Cap growled and dragged me deeper into the thicket. The smell of pine was soft in my nostrils.

"It was all a pack of lies, Cap! They hit me like a sledge-hammer, they came so quick."

"Gosh all hemlock!" Cap whispered hoarsely, "why didn't you speak up to him, then, instead of yawping around like an old nanny goat, just bawing and not getting nowhere? Hell, he gave you a chance to talk! Anybody that gets a chance to talk ought to be able to wiggle out of anything!"

"Where were you?" I asked.

"I was around, but that ain't neither here nor there! What gets me is why you went and did something that got him sore as hell. Why didn't you let that misbegotten Natanis alone?"

He stopped suddenly and looked over his shoulder. Both of us held our breaths to listen, turning our heads and looking sideways, so to see better in the gloom.

"Anyone here?" I asked.

"Natawammet!" said a familiar voice close beside us.

My heart grew measurably lighter. "Where did you come from?"

"I built this cabin," he said. "Paul Higgins left me here to watch. I've been here five days."

"Where's Paul?"

"To the west of the high meadow at the head of Seven Mile Stream."

"Listen, Natawammet," I said. "I've been put out of the army in disgrace because a bad man spoke lies about me. You knew him—Hook, the holy man, who wished your tribe to worship his God."

"I remember," Natawammet said.

"When you see him, kill him. Because of him they say I'm a spy, and Natanis too.

"Now listen to me, Natawammet. Natanis is a mile below here, where we landed at dusk. Hobomok sits in a canoe before the cabin. Can you lead me a mile along the shore, in this darkness, and find some way of sending Hobomok down as well?"

"We'll go above the camp and call him," Natawammet said. "There's good land there."

"Cap," I said, "I'll leave you. Tell the others I'm not what Arnold thinks. I hope some day they'll know it."

"They'll find it out, Stevie," said Cap reassuringly. "Go ahead. I'll go along with you a ways."

"You'll get lost."

"No," Cap said, "I guess I'll stay along with you."

"You can't do that! It's desertion."

"No," Cap said, "it's getting lost. Anyway, it just came to me I can't go back."

"Why not, for God's sake?"

"I just remembered," Cap whispered hoarsely. "They'll find my footprints in the snow, where I listened."

"What of it?"

"Well," Cap said, "while the colonel was busy with you I got to feeling under the edges of the cabin, and I came across a couple of bottles in one of the bags."

Natawammet stopped us and went forward to the edge of the lake. We heard his signals to Hobomok: an irregular succession of the squashy squawks of a night heron.

"What was in the bottles?" I asked.

There was a thump and a sound of breaking glass, followed by a faint gurgling noise. The gurgling stopped, and Cap exhaled gaspingly.

"Brandy! I was afraid it was ink!"

He pushed the bottle into my hands. I tilted back my head and poured my mouth as full as I could without touching the broken neck. It was not only brandy, but good brandy: the first drink I had swallowed since leaving Fort Western.

"We don't want to give none of that to Indians," Cap said, taking the bottle from me. "They don't know how to handle the stuff." Again the bottle gurgled melodiously and, it seemed to me, interminably. At length it was put back in my hands. "Finish it up," Cap said with a racking hiccup.

A canoe grated on the shore and Natawammet returned to us. I could hear him sniffing, though he had no need to sniff. I have no doubt our breaths could be smelled halfway to Quebec. I explained as well as I could, because of my hiccuping, that Cap had given me medical treatment. We paddled out around the camp, putting inshore where we had left Natanis.

We found him waiting by a small fire. This we recklessly made large, in the white man's way, pooling our few remaining provisions, so to fend off the cold as best we might. Cap pooled his second bottle of brandy along with our flour and the trouts Natanis had caught. "When you divide a bottle of brandy into five parts," he declared

mournfully, "there ain't enough to hurt a pee-wit, let alone an Indian."

We sucked at the sumach leaves in Hobomok's pipe, and I told
Natanis how we had been branded as spies and how I had been
thrown out of the army.

Natanis covered his nose with his blanket and studied for a time.
"That's bad," he said at length, "but it might be worse. We are none
of us sick or wounded. We can go now to Quebec if you wish it,
arriving before the white chief Arnold."

"And what'll we do when we get there?" I asked. "Join the British
in Quebec, as Arnold thinks we mean to do?"

"We could join 'em for a time," Cap said, "until we get rested up.
Gosh almighty, Stevie, it seems as if I hadn't slept warm enough or
long enough since the year of the earthquake!"

"No," I said, "I must stay with this army, and that's where you
stay, too, so you won't get fat and die young."

"Well," Cap said, seemingly resigned to his fate, "anything's better
than working for Church and Steele. Those two men are hellions!
When we started chopping, Steele said that if anyone lost his axe he'd
have to chew down the trees with his teeth."

He grumbled and growled to himself while I spoke further with
Natanis.

"Will the army have trouble in marching, now it has crossed the
Height of Land?" I asked.

"Much trouble," he said. "In all the marches they have had and will
have, there is nothing so terrible as the swamps below the meadow
we passed to-day, the meadow that was the birthplace of the great
lord Glooskap."

"Then we must go back to the meadow and do what we can to
help them. Why are the swamps above the lake so terrible?"

Natanis gathered his meager possessions. "There is no time for
talk. Paul Higgins is watching the army, and to-morrow it may start
to come down out of the meadow. We must find Paul and hold a
council, and to do this we must paddle to Seven Mile Stream and
up it, to-night, until we come to dry land. Then to-morrow we can
get to Paul before he escapes us."

Cap and I rolled our blankets. "Here is another thing," Natanis
said. "To-morrow morning, you have said, the white chief Arnold
leaves the bark house to go down the Chaudière. This bark house
we built for men lost in the swamps. Therefore we must leave Cap
and Natawammet here. When the white chief and his men have left

in the morning the two of them must go to the wigwam and keep
a fire both day and night, so that those in the bogs may see either the
smoke or the fire. Cap can keep the fire and Natawammet can stock
the cabin with food."

"And I can sleep!" Cap sighed.

"Remember this!" Natanis warned him. "The fire must be kept
day and night until we have found all who are lost. This may be in
two days or four days, and it may not be for twenty days, and the
fire must never fail."

There was some growling from Cap as he unrolled his blanket
again, and I knew he was thinking of his vanished bottle of brandy
and the cold nights to come.

"Why are you so sure that men will be lost?" I asked.

"You'll understand later," Natanis said. "They'll be fortunate if they
don't lose their lives as well as their paths."

In the thick and frosty dark we paddled to the head of the lake,
groping from submerged tree to tree until we found the mouth of
Seven Mile Stream. We fumbled and scrabbled our way around its
countless curves, getting into backwaters and false streams, and snag-
ging ourselves on logs and bushes, but finally reaching a point where
the swamp ended and the stream flowed between banks of good
earth, firm with pine needles. There was no way to tell the time; for
the stars were hidden because snow was on the way.

To me, as I huddled in my blanket, it seemed weeks ago that we
had passed Morgan's riflemen coming up from the last of the Chain
of Ponds, their bateaux rubbing their shoulders raw; and I thought
what young men sometimes foolishly think when things look dark:
that in one day's time I had grown to be an old, tired man.

XXIV

Paul higgins, a bearskin over his left shoulder and leaves stuffed into mooseskin moccasins for warmth, was in an ill humor when we came up with him toward noon. We were hungry and ate what we dared of fat bear meat, which was not much, for we had been a week on half rations and so knew a full belly would sicken us for two days.

"This army of white men," said Paul contemptuously, for there were times when he considered himself an Abenaki, even though he was as white as I, which was not saying much because of the scabs and pine pitch and dirt on my face, "this army of white men couldn't let well enough alone last night! When I built a warm fire, a scouting party came crashing and bellowing through the forest to see what was making all the smoke!" He spoke in Abenaki, which was his custom when proud and haughty.

"Have all of them crossed the Height of Land?" I asked.

"A part came into the meadow last night," he said, "carrying seven bateaux." He wagged his head. "These are good men, stronger than moose. The others straggled in this morning, near dead."

He hitched his bearskin around him, and examined my shoes, one of which had lost its sole in crossing the Height of Land, so that my foot was bruised. "Where are your other shoes?"

"Stolen," I said, "by a rat and a liar named Treeworgy, and a spy into the bargain. I can't show my face in the army for the things he said of me."

"I know him," said Paul, going to his pack. "He's a spy by nature. He spied on both white men and Abenakis of our country, telling his God about them in the hope of having them punished."

"I knew it!" I said. "His name was Hook!"

"Hook," Paul agreed, busy at his pack. "When the white men wouldn't stop drinking rum and the red men wouldn't worship his God, and his God wouldn't punish them to suit his ideas, he was angry and went to spying for the Plymouth Company, tattling on those who wouldn't pay taxes or do work they were supposed to do.

This gave him more pleasure; for the Plymouth Company is quicker to punish than God is."

He tossed me a pair of mooseskin moccasins. "Stuff these with grass or leaves and put them on," he said, "or you'll have no feet left at the end of another day. This Hook was ashamed of leaving God for the Plymouth Company. After he changed, he claimed he was not Hook at all, but a half-brother. He was a liar. His footprints never changed. Hook walked on the inside of his heels, with his toes turning out and taking no grip on the ground, and so does Tree-worgy."

"Waste no more thought on him," Natanis said. "Steven says he must be killed. He's as good as dead. What about the army in the meadow? Did they find your fire?"

"They found no fire of mine," Paul said. "When we heard them blundering through the forest, we buried the fire a foot deep and lay behind a ledge to watch them. They were noisy and warlike, eager to shoot someone. We can't help them until they are lost and weaker."

"What's all this talk," I asked, "about everyone losing his way? Is there some law that requires a man to be lost in these mountains? And how was it, if this is so, that Colonel Arnold went quickly and safely to the lake?"

Natanis cleared a spot on the ground and sat beside it. The rest of us came around in a circle, Paul Higgins and Hobomok and two of Paul's Abenakis.

"It's seven miles," Natanis said, drawing on the ground with a stick, "from this meadow close beside us to Lake Megantic, on which we were last night. It's easy enough to go from the meadow to the lake by bateau or canoe down Seven Mile Stream; but it's a different matter to go on foot. That's the way the army must go, for no company except Morgan's brought more than one bateau across the mountains.

"If the army marches down Seven Mile Stream," he said, "it comes into the flooded land you saw last night. Through that swamp run two false mouths of Seven Mile Stream, both deep ones, making half-circles through the bog. Thus, if the men attempt to continue through the swamp they'll run into those false mouths and be pocketed among them. If they turn back and try to skirt the false mouths they'll come to Maple Leaf Pond, whose ragged shores are a nuisance. If they succeed in rounding this they'll come to more swamps and streams, and eventually to still another pond, larger than Maple Leaf Pond. It has bays and bogs protruding like fingers on a hand, so we call it Finger Lake. Those two ponds and the false mouths lie like a barrier between Lake Megantic and the Height of Land, provided one travels afoot. To reach Lake Megantic you must walk around the swamps and the ponds; but as you shall see, a man may walk forever in attempting to walk around them."

"That's true," Paul said. "Nowhere have I seen the like, nor does it mean anything to tell about it. There are no trails, because there's no land, only mounds. There are no blazes on the trees; no game except crows and chickadees. The alders are laced in the water like the thongs of a snowshoe. I wouldn't go into those bogs on foot alone for any man alive."

"They're bad," Natanis admitted. "No Abenaki hunter will go into them. The only reason I know them is because I traveled their water-courses on snowshoes, when there was heavy snow or thick ice."

"Then how is it you march around Lake Megantic?" I asked.

"Instead of going down Seven Mile Stream," Natanis said, "you turn your back on the stream, marching to the northeastward along the shoulder of the Height of Land, thus remaining above the bogs and the streams. At the end of ten miles you can come down from it, moving to the northwest, and walk straight to the shore of Lake Megantic. Even to this route there is danger, unless it's well known to the persons who follow it, for there are streams that flow down from the Height of Land. It's natural to follow these. If this is done, they also lead into the bogs of Maple Leaf Pond and Finger Lake."

"Well," I said, "I'm befuddled by your description, so let's get out of here and see what can be done. Tell me where you put your men, Paul."

Paul took a square of birch bark from his belt and showed me. "With me," he said, "there are three men. One watches now at the edge of the meadow. Two are here.

"We brought five canoes, leaving two on the Height of Land where the army would find them.

"There are four men along the shoulder of the Height of Land, on the trail to Megantic. Each night they'll light fires, so that if the army is in the swamp it may have the good fortune to see them and come out.

"We built a bark house on the first point in the lake and left Natawammet there to light fires for those who reach the edge of the lake."

"That we saw," I said. "Natawammet is still there, and my friend, Cap Huff."

"That's nine men," said Paul. "Then there are four more at the First Falls, fifteen miles down the Chaudière from Lake Megantic; four at the Great Falls, fifty miles farther down; two at Rivière du Loup, four miles from the first inhabitants at Sartigan; and six at Sartigan, spreading word on the lower river that there must be more food in Sartigan than ever before, and building canoes. That's twenty-five. Then there are four messengers on the Chaudière, two moving up and two moving down, so that those who are on their stations may be told each day what's happening. That's twenty-nine, and twenty-nine is our total number if you count Natawammet as one of our men."

"You're a good captain, Paul," I said. "I don't know how it could be done better."

"As the army passes," he added, "I'll follow in the rear. The other men will come along as soon as there are no stragglers to be pushed back on the path and no sick to be helped. When the army reaches food and shelter we'll show ourselves to Colonel Arnold, and not before."

❋   ❋   ❋

We picked up our packs and moved forward to the edge of the meadow we had crossed the day before.

It was a long, narrow field, with groves of elms at intervals through it. From its upper end rose the peaks of the Height of Land; and at its lower end the matted wild grass sloped into Seven Mile Stream. Along its center was spread the remnant of our little army, five hundred or thereabouts, in knots and clumps and straggling lines, some sitting at fires, some sleeping, some hunting in their clothes for vermin.

At the lower end of the meadow, the end nearest the stream, I recognized Morgan's company, because of their gray canvas jerkins and the seven clumsy bateaux with the men sleeping among them; but I could tell none of the other companies apart. Nowhere could I see Phoebe, though I strained my eyes to find her.

"Bring in your watcher," I told Paul, "and let's see what he can tell us."

Paul cawed a little, like a crow; and the watcher joined us at once. No one, he said, had started away to the east, along the high land. Ten companies had come into the meadow; and two had gone down the east bank of the stream on foot. He expected them to return momentarily, since they would not be able to pass through the swamps.

"When did this happen?" I asked.

"At noon. All the food was put together in a heap, and divided equally. After that the first company went down the stream on foot. Later the second started, led by a sick man with a black beard and a black dog. He traveled in one of the canoes we left on the Height of Land."

"That was Dearborn," I said. "Was there anything about the first company that would help me to know it?"

"It had one bateau for provisions, and a woman in man's dress."

"What did the woman look like?"

"I can show you," he said. "There are four women among the army. Jacataqua, near the bateau." He pointed, and I saw her with her dog, cooking at a fire. "There are two with the riflemen, the fat one and the one with sharp bones." He showed me Mrs. Grier and Mrs. Warner. "It was the other one," he said.

That meant Phoebe had gone into the swamps with James Dunn and Noah Cluff and Nathaniel Lord and the rest of the Arundel men. I knew I must do something about it. I got up and fastened my pack. Another company was forming in the meadow, a company of riflemen; and the captain looked, at that distance, like Matthew Smith.

It was he, Burr had told me, who led the men who murdered the Indians in Conestoga and then massacred those in Lancaster gaol, twelve years before; who even led a mob of a thousand ruffians toward Philadelphia to discipline the Quakers for their peaceful ways. He wasn't a bad captain; but he was hard as a turtle's back toward Indians and Indian sympathizers, holding they were of no use to anyone unless dead, and then only as fertilizer.

"I don't know," I said, "whether they've heard yet that I'm a spy, but someone must warn these people, and it had best be me."

"It *must* be you," said Paul grimly, "because I won't talk to them until I can show how I've helped them."

"Oh, I'll do it," I said, "but it appears to me you're going to find it pretty hard to help them without talking to them."

Natanis and I skirted the meadow and went rapidly to the bank of Seven Mile Stream. We could hear Smith's riflemen shouting to each other on the opposite bank, and before long Smith himself came slowly down in his bateau, two bateaumen and two sick men with him.

I stepped to the edge of the stream and called to him as he approached. His bateaumen pushed in toward me.

"This is the wrong way for the men," I said. "They'll be tangled in ponds and swamps if they follow the stream. They ought to go back on the high land."

Smith blinked. "Who says so?"

"Those that know the country. The Indians say so."

He seemed to ponder my statement. "Does Arnold know it?"

"Yes. He wants you to go by way of the high land."

"Did you come from him?"

"Yes. I was with him last night."

"Didn't he give you any written orders for us?"

"No. He was in too much of a hurry."

"Took you kind of a long time to get here, didn't it?"

"Yes," I said, "I got lost."

"Oh, you got lost! How'd you get here?"

"In a canoe."

"Where is it?"

"Down the stream a piece."

"Didn't come alone, did you?"

"No. I came with an Indian."

"Where is he?"

"Why," I said, wishing I was a better liar and had never answered any of his questions, "he went back into the woods to get food."

"It don't sound reasonable. This ain't the time to go hunting! How'd he happen to get lost if all the Indians know this country so well?"

"I don't know. Those things happen."

"If they happen to me," he said, "somebody finds a dead Indian. Did you see Dearborn?"

"Yes. That is, I know he went down, but I didn't have a chance to speak to him."

"Too busy, I suppose. You didn't happen to see Goodrich, did you?"

"No."

"He went down a little ahead of us. I suppose that was while you were lost."

"Look here," I said, "your men'll walk into bogs and have a hell of a time! Take my word for it, will you, and get them around by the high land, and get Goodrich and Dearborn back as well?"

Smith took a paper from his coat and unfolded it. "You say there's ponds between here and Lake Megantic."

"Yes, and rivers."

"I suppose you know this army is going by Montresor's map?"

"Yes, I know it."

"Well, there's no ponds or bogs or rivers on Montresor's map. I've got a copy here. This river we're on runs into Lake Megantic, clear and clean, according to my map."

"The map's wrong."

"It's been right so far. If Arnold got through this way, I can get through. If you want to know what I think——"

He hesitated, watching me, then pushed his map back into his pocket and buttoned his coat. "Get on!" he shouted to his bateaumen. "We can't hang around here all day!"

I hurried to Natanis and we went downstream at a trot. "We've got to go on," I said. "We've got to look for Goodrich's company. They're my people. They'll listen to me. I wouldn't like to see them come to any harm if we can prevent it."

"We'll find them, Steven."

"We'd better get to that canoe before Smith's bateau gets there, too," I told him. "He saw there was something queer about my story. He might take a notion to have his men pop at us. They don't miss often."

"There's no danger," Natanis said. "He must follow the curves of the stream. We can go straight."

There was neither sight nor sound of Smith or his men when we came to the cedar thicket where we had laid up the canoe. We launched it and drove rapidly toward the lake. The sky was overcast and there was a strong smell of snow, so we knew dusk would come early.

"They followed the river," Natanis said. "I know where to find them, but I'm not eager to be with them. This night will be cold."

We came to a sluggish stream that ran out of our course at right angles. "Now you see how it is," said Natanis. "Straight ahead is Megantic, maybe a mile away. This stream that runs out at right angles is a false mouth. Your friends crossed it, I think. We'll look for their tracks to make sure. Everywhere through here are swamps and bogs. If they crossed the false mouth and waded through the swamps to the lake, they'd turn to the right to go along the shore, and then come to another false mouth, very deep. Thus they'd be in a pocket, unable to go forward, or to the right or to the left: able only to wander in the swamp."

He drove the canoe into the slow water of the false mouth, skirting the shore. I saw broken branches, mud-swirls in the bog beyond the bank, a wisp of cloth caught on a jagged alder. We went ahead a mile, on a wide curve, then came to another fork, with another sluggish stream turning off to the left nearly at right angles.

"This," said Natanis, swinging the canoe into it, "is the easterly wall of the pocket. Your friends are trapped here."

We drifted slowly down this dark and dismal stream. The air was bitter cold. We felt snow-spit on our faces, flecks of chill wetness.

"Can we take them out?" I asked.

"If you think you must; but you know what happens when men climb into a canoe from a bog."

It was true. Our canoe would split, eventually, and all of us be worse off than before.

"Find them first, then," I said. "I'll build a fire on a mound, so they can come to it. You can lie at the edge of the stream in the canoe, sleeping in it so we run no risk of losing it."

Natanis stopped the canoe and we listened. The swamp seemed lifeless. There was no sound of any bird; no trickle of moving water, only the drip from my paddle, laid across the bow. At last, far away in the bog, a man shouted. Closer at hand a word was spoken: then I heard a slushing, sucking noise that I took to be men walking.

Natanis sought to force the canoe between the trees; but the thickness of the brush obliged him to stop. "There's a mound ahead," he said. "I can't reach it. You must get out."

I put my flint and steel and tinder in my cap, loosened my hatchet in my belt, and swung my pack onto my left shoulder, wriggling my toes regretfully in my dry, warm moccasins.

The water was up to my calves. There was a crispness to the moss that showed it to be needled with ice flakes. I could see the mound dimly, a small one with a few dwarf birches and pines, such as partridges love. When I stepped toward it, the bottom fell out of the marsh and I went in to my armpits. It was cold water: so cold I got my breath with difficulty.

"I'll lie behind the brush on the far bank of the stream," Natanis said. His canoe rustled against a bush and vanished.

For the most part the swamp ranged from knee-deep to thigh-deep. There were gullies between the alder roots, under water, into which a walker, if careless, would sink to his waist.

It was bad, and a part of my mind turned to Phoebe, wondering how she had passed through this water. The other part was busy timing the movements of my feet to the whir and click of my mother's spinning wheel; feel, feel, feel for the alder roots; feel, feel, feel;

step! feel, feel, feel; step! I had no time to think of the ache in knees and ankles.

When I came to the mound, a patch of land no bigger than our gathering-room in Arundel, I blazed trees, marking the direction of Natanis and the river. Then I laid about with my hatchet, glad of the opportunity to warm myself, until the treelets were cleared and lopped into burnable lengths. This done, I kindled a fire, a high, flaring fire to attract the waders.

It was dark before the first of the company reached the mound. They came out of the water like wooden men.

At their head was a butcher from York with shiny red cheeks that looked dark blue in the firelight. "Where's the bateau?" he asked huskily.

"I don't know," I said.

He stared into the fire as if drugged. The second man stood silent, contemplating a gash on his bare leg.

A third man came out, stiff-legged and grunting a little whenever he put foot to the ground, which I thought was natural since he had no shoes upon his feet. He pushed himself between the first two, who staggered as they shifted to left and right. Noah Cluff came into the firelight, one leg of his breeches flapping open where it had been torn from waist to knee. He looked at me as if we had parted ten minutes before: absent-mindedlike, and casual.

"Bring anything to eat?" he asked.

"No."

"Where's the bateau?"

"I don't know. Haven't you got anything to eat?"

He shook his head and moved around the others to stand in the warmth of the fire and stare into it.

"Where's Phoebe?" I asked, seeing that Asa Hutchins had stumbled onto the mound, and remembering James Dunn and Phoebe always marched near these two.

Noah shook his head, seemingly unable to move his eyes from the fire.

Asa Hutchins coughed a racking, tearing cough that pitched him forward on his hands and knees. He crawled to a clear place near me.

"Where the hell did you come from?" he said; and added, without waiting for an answer: "Anything to eat?"

He seemed to need no answer; for when I was silent, he observed: "Figured there wouldn't be." He reached into his hat and took out a

square of moose hide, an untanned piece. He examined his right
shoe. I saw it had broken at the heel, so that with each step the
whole lower part of the heel must have slipped from his foot. Shaking
his head, he drew out his knife, cut a strip from the moose hide,
wrapped it around a stick, and held it close to the fire.

A straggling line of men waded slowly out of the swamp and onto
the mound. One of them fell and lay still. The others laughed. The
man next to him plucked at his coat, and the fallen man rolled over
and sat up, coughing weakly.

"Where's Phoebe?" I asked Asa.

"Back there a piece," he said, drawing the moose hide from the
fire to sniff at it, and replacing it again. More men came up onto the
mound and pushed close to the fire, all of them watching Asa with
eyes that glittered in the firelight.

"Back where?" I asked.

There was a long wait before anyone spoke. Finally a musketman
who wore no stockings roused himself sufficiently to answer. "Back
near where Goodrich started from," he said, never taking his eyes
from Asa.

"Anything wrong with her?"

"Wet!" Asa said. Two or three men tittered dryly. Asa took the
mooseskin from the fire and felt it with his teeth. Then he put it on
to cook once more. Some of the men began to have paroxysms of
shivering, throwing up their heads and shaking like kestrels balanc-
ing in a high wind.

"Everybody with hatchets go to chopping," I said. "We need wood
and you need warmth." I loosened Noah Cluff's hatchet in his belt
and put it into his hands. "Try to remember where you saw Phoebe,
will you? I'll try to find her."

"Where's this place we're in, Stevie?" Noah asked.

"Right on the edge of Megantic. There's no cause to worry. We'll
all be picked up in the morning."

"They'll have to pry me up," said one of the shiverers.

"What became of the bateau?" asked the butcher from York.

"It must have gone down Seven Mile Stream and across to the
other shore of the lake," I said. "What became of Goodrich?"

Asa sunk his teeth in the crisped mooseskin and tore off a little.
"He was looking for a place to get across this river over here"—he
pointed to what might have been east: looked bewildered: then
swung his hand uncertainly toward the southwest—"and he walked
and walked, up to his waist in water, backward and forward, until he

got kind of sick." After prolonged chewing, Asa swallowed with difficulty, and held the mooseskin to the fire once more.

"I never see nothing like it," said the barefoot man.

"All our flour was in the bateau," Asa said. "We got five pints apiece to last us to Quebec."

"We have if we get it," said the butcher from York.

"How far are we from Quebec, Stevie?" Asa asked. All the men turned their eyes on me.

"I don't know," I said. "Not far."

"You're a liar," said Asa. "It's a hundred miles if it's an inch."

"Gosh!" Noah said. "We walked pretty near that far in the swamp this afternoon."

"What became of Goodrich?" I asked again.

"When he couldn't find a way across the river, so's we could get out of the swamp," Asa told me, "he took a file of men and waded out to a clump of bushes in the pond, thinking he could mebbe see somebody with a bateau and get 'em over here for us. Dearborn come along in a canoe and took him off, and I guess the men are still there—Whitten and Burbank and Stone and Nathaniel Lord and Merrill and Walt Adams and some others. He was figuring on coming back with the bateau."

"Look here," I said, "try to remember where you saw Phoebe. How's it happen she stayed out there?"

"Dunn's sick," Noah Cluff said. "We waited for him two-three times. She wouldn't leave him and we had to keep moving."

"Couldn't anyone carry him?"

"Some of us tried," Noah said apologetically. " 'Twasn't no use. I guess we ain't been getting enough to eat. It's all we can do to lug our packs and ourselves."

"Was she near the lake, or near the easterly river, or near the westerly river?"

The men looked helplessly at each other. I reminded the stockingless man that he had seen her near where Goodrich started. "Did you mean where he waded into the lake?"

"Yes," said the stockingless man, "but I disremember which way that was." He pointed, with no great certitude, away from the lake. Noah Cluff disagreed with him, pointing to the westward. Others had different ideas. I was glad I had blazed trees to tell me where the lake lay.

"Keep the fire up," I said, "and don't be afraid to use your lungs."

I waded into the swamp, knowing I would have no trouble while
I could see the light of the fire.

*   *   *

The snow was falling steadily, in small flakes, and the swamp had
scummed with ice. Ordinarily this would have been unpleasant; but
now, it seemed to me, I might find it a help in returning. As I went
I cut saplings, feeling for them in the pitchy dark and hacking them
clumsily until I could break them down; then, when they were down,
laying them in a line toward the lake, sighting back to the fire across
the stumps to make sure I was going straight.

I would not recommend walking for pleasure in any swamp on
such a night; yet it is bearable so long as there is an object to be
reached, and while the mind is occupied. Mine was busy indeed,
holding a straight course, lopping saplings, feeling for footholds so
not to sink over my waist in the icy water, and counting my steps to
be sure how far I'd come.

When the fire grew dim to my sight, I felt around for higher
ground, and found patches of icy moss through which the feet sank
little more than ankle deep. Here I stood and bellowed, "Phoebe!
Phoebe!" into the darkness until my throat felt raw.

By the grace of God I heard a sound off to the northwest, more
of a movement in the air than a sound. When I had bellowed again,
and cocked my head so my ear was toward what I heard, and raised
and lowered myself to have the benefit of air currents, I heard it
again and knew it for a voice, a weak, faint voice, but one my im-
agination said might be Phoebe's.

I went to cutting saplings again, determined not to lose my way,
and moved slowly toward the voice, shouting from time to time, and
each time getting a response that came clearer.

So I came closer and closer, laying my line of saplings, feeling
among the alder roots with my feet, the snow coming ever thicker
on my face, until I could hear Phoebe cough, and snuffle a little
after each cough, and was close enough to speak to her without
shouting.

"What's the matter with him?" I needed my breath and had no
words to waste.

"I don't know," said Phoebe, her voice thin and wavering from
cold. "Just worn out, I guess."

I could see neither hide nor hair of her or James. When I had laid
my saplings up to her, so that I could get my hands on her, I found

her crouched against a rotted stump, with James lying against her, his legs drawn up out of the water, and his blanket, wet, laid over him.

I thought at first he might be dead; but there was warmth in him, though not much, and a movement of his heart.

I felt of the handkerchief on Phoebe's head, and her flat back, and the brass-studded belt under her buckskin jerkin. A sort of tightness went out of my chest at the feel of her. She was wet from her breast down. Her ribs, under her jerkin, were like those of a lamb with the fleece off.

"You all right?" I asked her.

"I guess so. Can we get to a fire? Did the bateau come back?"

"Pick up his blanket," I said. "Let's get out of here. Listen, now: follow the cut saplings. Don't lose them. Don't move till you have your hand on one of them. Keep them on your right. It's ninety-eight of my steps to the turn, and a hundred and sixty-one from the turn to the fire. Go ahead, and don't lose the saplings."

She stumbled into the water, and I after her, with James balanced over my shoulder. I could feel this would never do. My legs bent too easily; the added weight forced me deep into the swamp.

"Wait, Phoebe. Does he know what's happening?"

"No. He's asleep. I can't wake him. Even when he wakes, he only half wakes. He makes the wrong answers, and gets angry when spoken to."

"I've got to drag him," I said. I lowered him into the water and hauled him as I might haul a canoe. After a time I stopped and buttoned his arms inside his coat to keep them from catching in alder roots. He was heavier than a canoe, and hard to hold because the hand with which I held him became too numb to grip.

"I can see the fire," Phoebe said.

"Follow the saplings," I told her. "Take no chances."

We came to the turn, and for the first time I could see Phoebe, outlined against the distant firelight, little and blundering, like a fly caught in a pan of molasses, moving forward through the swamp as though the legs would be wrenched out of her at each step.

In due season we reached the mound, where some of the men had come to life and were chopping at the fallen trees. Asa Hutchins was still chewing the last of his broiled moose hide. Some had put their feet to the fire and fallen asleep, their bodies pointing outward like the spokes of a wagon wheel, and their heads two feet or so from the swamp. I hoped the weather wouldn't moderate, letting the snow turn to rain, lest the waters rise around us and drown us into standing.

When I dragged James onto the mound, the men stopped their chopping, and gathered around us.

"Ain't done any talking, has he?" Noah Cluff asked.

"No," I said. "He just laid."

"It's been three hours since I waked him last," Phoebe said.

"He's tuckered," Asa said. "I told you he was tuckered this afternoon."

Phoebe looked down blankly at the inanimate James. "We got to do something for him. What's the best thing to do?"

"There ain't nuthin you can do," Asa said. "You just got to leave him lay."

"But he's got to be dried off! Cut poles and we'll prop him back and front and under the arms, so to stand him in front of the fire."

" 'Twon't do no good, Phoebe," Noah Cluff told her. "He's as well off wet as dry."

"You do as I say!" she cried, her voice shrill and cracked.

Some of the men silently went to cutting crotched poles. Asa knelt down and looked in James's face, then opened his coat and felt of his chest. Not content with this, he put an ear close to James's mouth; then the other ear.

He hunkered back on his heels and looked up at Phoebe. "He's dead!"

Phoebe stared hard at Asa. "It ain't so!"

She dropped to her knees and looked into his eyes; then she felt again and again of his chest; held her cheek over his mouth, and then the inner part of her forearm. She got to her feet at last, pushing close to the fire and looking half dead herself, black smudges under her eyes and the skin tight over her mouth.

"It's true," she said, and her voice was a dry whisper. "He's gone! I felt he was going, late in the day, before I got him to that stump where you found us. I felt he was going then."

Just for a minute I wanted to get away from her. I didn't know anything I could say.

I stared at the still face of James Dunn. It looked like a good man's face to me; so I just stood there looking down at him and wondering why I hadn't thought more of him than I had; for it seemed to me that I had always been pretty hard on him in my thoughts, and that there hadn't been any reason for it.

I wondered and wondered why I had ever had hard thoughts of

him; and when I thought what a good soldier he'd tried to be—tried to be so bravely right through to the end—I could only swallow and wish I could get a decently kind word through to where he was now, so that he'd know I felt sorry about the hard thoughts I'd held of him, and would like to be more appreciative of him than I had been.

But after a while I saw that just standing there like that wasn't doing any good to me or anybody else, so I turned back to Phoebe.

She'd sat down by that time, looking into the fire; and I did the same, sitting beside her and coughing now and then because I didn't know anything to say.

*   *   *

It was long, that night, what with the snow coming down on us all the while, the coughing and snoring of the men, choking and muttering in their sleep, their heads lower than their feet, and the hissing of the fire and the *chock, chock, chock* of the woodcutters.

Knowing James Dunn must be left on the mound, I smoothed a pine slab and carved his name on it, and the date, which I was hard put to it to remember, though it finally came to me that it was only Saturday, October the twenty-eighth or even Sunday, though I think it was still Saturday when he died.

Phoebe rolled herself in her blanket and lay close beside Noah Cluff. I couldn't see that she slept overmuch. She kept starting up and looking around; then lying down again and shivering in spasms, all through the night.

When it came to an end, at last, I waked Phoebe and told her I was going for someone to take them out of the swamp. "Listen carefully when I've gone," I told her. "When you hear me shout, send Asa Hutchins after me. I think I'll have trouts."

I had meant to tell her I was in disgrace: that Arnold thought me a spy, and had put me out of the army; but what with the dirt on her face, and the way she strove to square her shoulders when she looked at James Dunn, wrapped in his blanket with my pine slab on his breast, and the rents in her buckskin jerkin, and her poor attempt to smile when she saw me ready to leave, I had no heart to put any other burden on her mind, and so held her by the arm for a moment and then went into the swamp.

When I had floundered to the edge of the stream I saw Natanis fishing, as I had expected. He came over to me with all of a hundred small trouts strung on alder whips; and as he came he continued to fish, shooting his hook into the water and instantly flipping it back with a trout on it. I shouted for Asa, and went a little way to meet him, handing him the whips and sending him back to the mound goggle-eyed with amazement, but not so goggle-eyed as to prevent him from pulling off one of the trouts, squeezing out its entrails and eating it raw.

We pushed out into the lake and saw a canoe coming toward us from the direction of the bark house where we had left Cap Huff. This, I knew, would be Goodrich and Dearborn, so we signaled to them, and when they had seen us we went back up the stream again, with them following. Opposite the mound we shouted, until we heard someone splashing through the swamp.

"Here's Goodrich!" I called. "Come over to the stream!" There was a triumphant whooping from the waders, and more whooping from the direction of the mound; so we knew we could leave them and go about the rest of our sorry business.

XXV

W<small>E</small> COULD hear Morgan's riflemen coming down Seven Mile Stream in their seven bateaux, spirited and noisy from their good night's sleep in the meadow, and so for safety's sake we pushed our canoe into a clump of spruces until they had gone by.

I wondered, as I watched them passing, cuffing each other and hurling insults at the occupants of the other bateaux, whether they had made an honest division of their rations with the other companies in the meadow, or whether they had concealed some of their stolen goods in powder kegs. I say again that these Virginians of Morgan's were great fighters; though to me, at times, their high spirits were wearisome, especially when they felt the need of enlivening their fighting by playfully cutting buttons from their companions' breeches, or stealing food from the haversacks of starving friends.

In one of the bateaux I saw Burr; and the thought came to me that he had a knack for discovering which side his bread was buttered on; that he had doubtless smelled out Morgan's extra provisions and abandoned Jacataqua for them, since food can be more important than a woman to some hungry men.

There was no trace of the army when we reached the meadow, save at the lower end, where Morgan's men had lain during the snowfall. The remainder of the meadow was smooth beneath its white blanket; and from the upper end rose a thin column of smoke. While we watched it Hobomok came out from under the trees and signaled to us; so we laid up our canoe in the thickets and went to him. He had two partridges for us, and a piece of bear's fat that Paul Higgins had left, and this food we ate at once, fearful of suffering James Dunn's fate.

Many times, since those days, I have listened to windy talk from folk who have never gone hungry; and it seems to me there is more ignorance concerning hunger than any other subject. It may be that I am wrong in this, and that there is general ignorance concerning all things. At all events, I have some small knowledge of hunger, and am able to recognize ignorance concerning it.

Unlike thirst, which causes agony in the mouth and belly of him who suffers from it, hunger is little more than a dull disturbance in the interior, readily banished by the eating of fish or roots. Its greatest evil is the weakness that goes with it—a deceptive weakness that trips the legs unexpectedly and robs a man of the power to endure cold or heat, or to make the sudden violent effort that often saves him from death. I had as lief go without food for days on end, if I could sit in a chair and do nothing while going without; but if I must labor or fight or march, then I must have real food, pork and flour: fat meat aplenty. If I cannot have fat meat, then I twist into knots with hunger cramps, even though I fill myself with trouts or moose meat, in which there is no fat.

While we ate, Hobomok gave us what news he had. Two hours after we had left the meadow on the day before, he said, a messenger had come up from the lake: the guide Hull, one of those who had sat before the cabin with the rum-drinking Conkey, on that far-off day when I had gone to Conkey to learn about Natanis.

Hull, Hobomok said, had come with good news, seemingly, from Arnold; for after his message had been learned the men capered in the meadow, some discharging their muskets in the air. All of them had thereupon cooked their flour into cakes, each man having as much flour as could be picked up in a handkerchief, but nothing more. Some, Hobomok said, had eaten their cakes at once. Immediately thereafter, though there was only an hour of daylight left, all those in the meadow, saving Morgan's division, between three hundred and three hundred and fifty men, had rolled their blankets and set off to the northeastward, along the shoulder of the Height of Land. Colonel Greene and Hull were in the lead, so it was evident that Arnold had sent Hull back to guide them.

"They've started properly to go to Lake Megantic," said Natanis, "but I suspect the guide will turn down from the Height of Land too soon and lead the men into the swamps of Maple Leaf Pond or Finger Lake, which are larger and wetter than the one in which you spent last night."

Paul Higgins, with three men, Hobomok said, had followed behind the last of the marchers, leaving word there would be one Abenaki messenger always on the blazed trail to Lake Megantic along the shoulder of the Height of Land.

With no further talk we crossed the meadow and took up the trail, which led us over and around a tangled maze of precipices and gullies.

In an hour we came to the spot where the men had camped the night before. There lay before us, in place of the trackless snow, a muddy, trampled expanse, the trees slashed by the hatchets of six companies, and thirty blackened circles where the campfires had burned. From that spot onward a blind man might have followed the trail; and as we pressed ahead, Natanis pointed here and there to the boat-shaped marks of Paul Higgins's leaf-stuffed moccasins.

At the end of another hour's march we came to a brook that flowed out of a valley between two precipices. The trampled trail of the men turned at the brook and ran downstream along its bank, toward the north. Natanis pointed across the brook at a twisted bull pine; and when I looked closely at it I saw three small slashes close up under a lower branch, all of them perpendicular.

"The trail goes straight," Natanis said. "This fool guide has missed it and gone down the brook. The brook runs into the swamps of Maple Leaf Pond, where there are no trails."

"Is there a way to escape?" I asked.

"Probably not," Natanis said. "Once you are in that swamp there seem to be rivers everywhere. It's hard to tell bogs from arms of the pond, or either of them from rivers. Your friends will move to the eastward, thinking to skirt the swamp and come to Lake Megantic; but to the eastward they'll strike Finger Lake, which they'll have to round. It has so many arms, sprawled out like the legs of a spider, that to round it is like rounding the hub of a wheel by crawling out to the end of each spoke and in to the hub again, and out to the end of the next spoke and in to the hub again, time after time after time."

"You say there's no trail through these swamps?" I asked, thinking how we might bring the army out of this place before nightfall.

"It would be useless to go after them at this time of day," Natanis said, seeming to sense what was in my mind, "because there's no way of finding them except by following their tracks. We might be forever in coming up with them. Paul Higgins and his men have followed them down the brook; and tracks of one man go up the true trail. This, I am sure, is Paul's messenger."

"Go ahead on the true trail, then," I said, "until you come up with the messenger. I hope to God Paul can help them."

We went ahead, slipping and stumbling in the snow over country that grew no worse, because it was already as bad as it could be. It was beyond belief, almost, that so great an area could be so battered and crumpled, as though mauled and smashed by a giant hammer, and hurled contemptuously into this forsaken end of the world by the angry god that did it.

At a second brook, which we reached at mid-afternoon, we found a fire smoldering beneath an overhanging cliff, and in the snow a drawing of two Indians shooting at a rabbit, the rabbit being twice as large as the hunters. Thus we knew that Paul's messenger had come up with one of his advanced messengers, and that the two had gone to hunt.

Here, Natanis said, we must camp; for the brook flowed down into Finger Lake, and it was probable Paul Higgins had told his messenger to wait here, hunting for food.

"I think they need food," said Natanis gravely. "No man would draw a rabbit larger than himself unless a rabbit seemed something to be greatly desired. Therefore we'll all go hunting."

He sent Hobomok to the lower land to look for rabbits or raccoons. "When you return," Natanis said, "shoot anything, even a crow, if you have found little game. A crow is better than nothing.

"You and I, Brother," he told me, "will go back along the trail. I saw a dead tree on high ground after we passed the first brook. I think it may be a good tree for us."

*   *   *

We went back over our trail; and I swore, as we crawled and stumbled over it, that if ever I got free from this damnable land of bogs and dead shrubs with a dreadful aptitude for plucking at a man's eyes, I'd spend the rest of my life among the level sands of Arundel, and climb nothing higher than the dunes where Mary Mallinson and I had eaten our lobsters and kissed each other.

Nor, having thought of lobsters, could I get them from my mind, but brooded on them while I clambered over rotten logs and clung to ledges. I could almost smell their salty, seaweedy odor, and feel their tender shells crunching between my fingers; and I thought to myself that I could eat twelve, if they were large ones, and as many as twenty-five if they were small chicken lobsters. Indeed, when I really put my mind to it, it seemed to me I might be able to eat thirty, or even a round three dozen, provided I was not hurried, and could dip each one in a dish of my mother's fresh butter, hot from the stove, and chew a little now and then on thin corn bread, and have an occasional draught of small beer to wash it down.

What Natanis had seen was an ancient white oak that had stood alone in a cup-shaped hollow in the mountainside for many years, lording it over its domain so that no other trees grew near. A bolt of lightning had shorn off its head, and it had died, with two gnarled arms held out to the hills as if for pity. Young trees, knowing nothing of its past grandeur, and caring less, had sprung up near it, weedy and useless-looking, as all young things so often are.

Once Natanis had shown it to me, I could see scratches on the trunk. On its upper side a branch had been blasted off, and the inside had rotted, so that there was a hole in the tree, with claw marks at the edge. This, we were sure, must be a bear hole; but since the hole was forty feet from the ground, and the trunk too large to climb, and since there was no small tree tilted near to the hole, nor any we could cut for a ladder, we were obliged to take thought as to how we should get at the bear.

I have said many times I would never kill a bear cub, because of its likeness to a fat, mischievous child; and I took no pleasure in bear-hunting, their flesh tasting like coarse corned beef, and their appearance being overmuch like a harmless dog, as well as human in many ways—far more human, I often think, than some of my fellow townsmen who spend their days in slander and meanness.

It is painful to hear men brag of killing our Eastern black bears, as though they had done something fine and brave; for the bear is the gentlest creature that lives, almost, and a clown to boot, and timid as a mouse. There is scarce an Abenaki huntsman in all our province who would not willingly attack a bear with his knife alone.

Yet this bear seemed another matter. I wanted him; for we were desperately hungry, and there was sure to be thick fat beneath his fur—beautiful, sweet fat.

Twelve feet from the oak trunk was a scrawny maple, but it slanted away from the oak, so that even after it was climbed, the climber was still out of reach of the hole. We hunted, however, until we found a thicket of birches, close-grown so they were slender and tall. From these we cut a sapling three times my height, trimming off the branches. From a blown-down birch we took handfuls of dry, rotted wood, rolling it in birch bark until we had a dozen small bundles the size of my two fists.

We built a fire, after which Natanis fastened the bundles to the back of his belt and climbed the maple until he was twice my height in air. Thereupon I lighted a bundle of rotted wood, poked the end of the birch pole into it, and handed it up to Natanis.

He slipped another bundle from his belt, and lighted it from the burning bundle on the pole. Hitching the pole upward, he held it out like a fishing rod, and dropped the smoking bundle of fuel into the hollow oak. At once he placed his second bundle on the end of the pole, ignited a third from it, and dropped the second after the first. Bundle after bundle he dropped into the hollow tree, until smoke poured from it.

Soon we heard a sneezing and snuffling, and a small bear, about three times the size of Ranger, scrambled sleepily from the hole and clung to the edge of it, coughing and pouting out his upper lip with fright. I shot him under the left shoulder, and he fell down with no further movement.

This is the one pleasant thing about the killing of a bear: when shot in the head or near the heart he dies at once, unlike a deer, which may run for half a day with a bullet hole in him big enough to kill a dozen bears. Sometimes I have thought a bear may receive a wound that has no great seriousness to it, and yet die of the fright.

However that may be, we were overjoyed to have him. With the help of Natanis's carrying string we hauled him over the trail and to the overhanging ledge at the second brook, where we found Hobomok and Paul Higgins's messengers skinning two raccoons. They came shouting down the path at sight of the bear and carried him the rest of the distance for us, whooping ecstatically. When they had taken out the liver and wrapped it in the caul fat from his inside, luscious, delicate fat, they spitted it on a ramrod, catching the dripping in a bark dish. It was not much of a meal, but it stayed our stomachs and gave us strength to skin and quarter the bear.

*   *   *

At dusk two of Paul Higgins's Abenakis came up with us, one dragging a soldier at the end of a carrying string and the other urging on a second soldier, who constantly fell in the snow, as if drunk.

When we put the soldiers by the fire they became as though dead, seeming scarce to breathe for long periods.

Soon Paul himself came out of the dark, carrying two extra muskets and blankets. He reached at once for a piece of raw bear fat; then examined the two exhausted soldiers.

"This is bad business," Paul said. "Three hundred of these men, maybe three hundred and fifty, went down into the swamps soon after daylight this morning. Ever since then they have followed the bogs and the arms of Maple Leaf Pond and Finger Lake, in and out and in and out, up to their knees in water when not up to their middles. I gave over following them for fear I might be lost myself and never come out."

We waited for Paul to tell us the tale, knowing that if he had left the army it was for good reason, and not from timidity, for although I have heard Paul talk of his fear of this and that, I have never seen him feared of anything.

"Their guide," Paul said, when he had spitted a piece of bear meat and hung it before the fire alongside ours, "is a bad one, and in a panic. He has reached a point where he dares not leave the water-courses, no matter which way they run."

"Then he'll follow watercourses in that swamp the rest of his life," said Natanis pleasantly.

Paul cursed the guide in English; then took a huge bite from his bear meat, a bite big enough to feed my sister Cynthia for two whole meals.

"Here is what I did," he told us. "I don't know whether I did right, but it was as near right as I could do without going the entire length of the column to reach Colonel Greene and the guide, and being mistaken for a spy."

He laughed testily. "It may be I could never have caught up with the head of the column. It was in a frenzy to get wherever it was going." Again he swore in English. "Through those swamps and thickets, the worst traveling ever I saw, they marched not less than fifteen miles. They may have marched twenty!" He made a hissing sound. "Twenty miles! And all of them hungry and weak, and tripping at every step on the roots beneath the bogs!"

He chewed his bear meat. "They stopped for nothing after they'd been in the swamp three hours. If a man fell into a stream, or lagged from sickness, they left him and went on, hurrying, hurrying, fearing to lose their places in the line."

He got up and looked at the two soldiers again, felt their chests and nodded encouragingly. "We found four men that had fallen out. One had collapsed in a stream. He was dead. Another had sat down to rest. I took him to dry land, but he died. These two"—he pointed to the soldiers—"could go no farther. One of them lay as he lies now. The other would walk a little and fall: walk a little more, then fall again. It seemed to me they might live after they had slept and eaten."

"I think they can march to-morrow afternoon," Natanis said, "if not given too much food."

"When I saw how they would never leave the arms of Finger Lake," Paul continued, "I came out of the swamp and went to the eastward until I reached this brook, lower down. Then I went back into the swamp and hunted a piece of high land, a sizeable piece. On it I laid sticks for a fire, close under a pine so the flames would set it alight. Also I made lines in the snow, pointing to the trail, and blazed trees with proper trail marks. Toward dusk I lit the fire and went away a little, to watch.

"In a short time I heard shoutings and splashings, after which some men, led by an officer with a large forehead, dragged themselves out of the swamp and up to the fire, all of them glad to be there. The officer was thin, with lips that purse up into a laugh, as if unwillingly."

"Major Meigs," I said.

Paul nodded. "I hope these men, finding my fire and seeing my signs, will know enough to trail me. If they do, Natanis can lead them around the eastern end of Finger Lake and down to Megantic before the sun is overhead to-morrow. If not, and if they spend two more days in those swamps, it will be as bad a thing as ever happened."

He looked up at the sky and sniffed. "To-night will be cold. The swamps will freeze the thickness of my tongue——"

"Thick enough to walk on," Natanis said.

Paul glowered at him. "Not thick enough for white men to walk on: only for Abenakis with light brains. The swamps will freeze, and if they wade through them for two more days they'll die, all of them."

"We'll get them out of the swamp to-morrow," Natanis said, "no matter what happens. It may be they'll come up the brook in the morning, following Paul's tracks. Paul has done well, and is a credit to the great Abenaki people."

"Yes," said Paul, "and I'll be waiting to-morrow night to hear your jesting and your idle laughter after you've cut your shins on swamp ice for half a day."

*   *   *

We were up at dawn, hoping for sight or sound of Greene's men. We shook the two soldiers into consciousness and fed them strips of bear meat, small and thin. They fell asleep at once, wretched-looking men, heavily bearded, their clothes and shoes in shreds, and a powerful odor about them.

When we had waited another hour it was plain that the army had not followed Paul's trail.

"I'll go into the swamp," Natanis said, "and see what has become of them." He left us, traveling with no blanket or pack; and in less than two hours he returned.

"It's all right," he said, shouldering his pack and motioning for us to do likewise. "Only one company of men camped at Paul's fire. The others made fires on unflooded land nearer Finger Lake. Therefore the one company went back and joined the others. The guide is still following the arms of Finger Lake, striving to get around it. I know where they must pass in three hours' time, or maybe four."

We waked the two soldiers and fed them once more, telling them to follow when they felt strong enough, and that they'd find more food hanging from a tree at the end of two miles. We gave them their blankets and muskets and went on.

In a short time we came to a brawling stream. "This," Natanis said, "flows into the easterly end of Finger Lake, and the army must cross it eventually lower down. We'll cross it here, where it's small, continue down toward the fording place, and wait there for the army."

The stream emerged from the rocky spurs of the Height of Land into a hideous flat country, tangled with alders and a hellish growth of shrubbery. Its width may have been four rods. There was ice against both banks, but the water flowed smoothly with nothing fearsome about it.

When we stood at what Natanis said was its first shallow place, and looked toward Finger Lake, which we could not see for the growth of brush, there was a tremendous stretch of swamp at our left. Through this swamp Greene and his men were still wading. On our right were the rough, broken-faced spurs of the Height of Land.

We held a council; and this was what we decided: When the army crossed the stream, it would continue over the rocky ridges beyond, because there was nothing else for it to do. Natanis, therefore, would cross two ridges and lie on the far slope, waiting for Greene and the guide to come up. With him would go Paul Higgins and myself, to lie hidden among the rocks and do what we could in case the guide, who had seen Natanis before, should attempt to shoot him. Hobomok, with the other Abenakis, would remain at the river; and when Jacataqua passed he would go to her and tell her to make her way up to the head of the line to tell Greene she had seen an Indian: one who would guide the army quick and straight to Lake Megantic.

When this had been done Natanis would show himself. If for some reason it could not be done, Natanis said, he would speak to Greene at all hazards.

I wonder now, as I look back at it, that we should have troubled ourselves to use such care with men who were lost and starving and weak with the flux; but it may be I have forgotten the wariness that enters into a man when he has been accused of spying, and when scouts have been ordered to kill him, as in the case of Natanis. Nor did we have any faith in the guide Hull, whom we knew to be one of the worst, neither reliable nor inventive; and men of this sort are prone to sudden frights and to the reckless use of firearms.

So we climbed two ridges, bad ridges, rough and rock-strewn, and slippery with snow, and waited on the second, lying where we could look back into the deep depression between the two, a depression at whose bottom the snow had been melted by the wetness of the ground.

"In less than two hours' time," Natanis told us, "I can lead these men to the northwest a little, and then to the northeast and then to the southwest, and put them on the path that borders Lake Megantic. There they'll find the tracks of those who went ahead."

In time, far in the distance, we heard a faint, thin piping, a reedy chirping such as you may hear in the late summer in Arundel, if you lie in the tall grasses of the sand dunes and listen to insects going about their occasions. This, Paul said, was made by the army passing through the river.

❊   ❊   ❊

It may be I shall come to be an old, old man; and my memory may slip from me as it does from some when they are ancient; but there are certain things that can never fade out of my mind. One of them is my recollection of the men who crawled slowly over the ridge across from us. It was not so much the leaders, Colonel Greene and the doctor of the army, young Senter, and the guide Isaac Hull, though they, God knows, were slow and fumbling in their movements, looking helplessly about and talking together, striving to see beyond the tangled shrubs and trees that surrounded them. It was the men who came after them that I can never forget: haggard, dirty, ragged men, slipping and tripping where no man should slip or trip, lifting their feet painfully and slowly as if their legs were shackled to the ground, crawling and groping down the rocky slope like helpless insects blinded by a sudden light.

We saw Jacataqua and her yellow-faced dog come over the ridge, sliding and running in the snow, and catch up with Greene. The guide Hull sat down when she spoke, holding his head in his hands. Greene looked back up the slope, as did all the others. We could hear a murmuring from them, a babbling like the babbling of children.

Natanis came out from his hiding place and went lightly down the hill and up to Greene, who was looking for him to come from the rear. We could see Natanis smile and point; see Greene nod, he and Senter holding together for support; and beside them sat the guide Hull, his face still resting in his hands.

Led by Natanis the ragged column blundered onward. Our eyes clung, with a sort of sickness, to the miserable horde that crept among the boulders on the ridges and in the valley between: to men slowly coming to the top and falling together in a heap as they started to descend: to men standing stock still, wavering on their feet as they stared into the valley before them, as if calculating whether their strength would suffice for the descent, then moving downward, slipping, sliding, pitching head foremost into the snow, their muskets flying from their hands: to men moving to help them and falling on them in turn: to men dragging themselves upward by holding to bushes: to men losing their hold and rolling back to the bottom again, lying there motionless until a little of their strength came back: to men who had no eyes for those who had fallen from the line, but plodded on, stumbling, crawling, limping, their gaze fixed on space, brooding over God knows what: to hatless men: to men whose garments hung on them in rags: to men whose feet were bare and left blood spots on the snow.

Last of all came those who had fallen out, but had summoned another ounce of energy when the stillness of the forest had closed in on them, thin ghosts pitching and weaving along the trampled trail, dragging themselves on hands and knees when they fell, then getting to their feet once more: silent men: horrible men; but men whose faces showed no suffering and no terror; only the resigned detachment that comes, it seems to me, to all those whose marchings and whose fightings exceed the limits of their endurance.

*   *   *

When there was no more movement in the depression between the ridges Paul Higgins and I went down into it and picked up the two men who lay there. We built a fire and left them beside it, then went back along the army's trail to see how it happened that Hobomok and the other Abenakis had not come up with us.

On high ground near the river a fire was burning, and by it sat Jacataqua, roasting the last of our bear and raccoon meat. Beside her crouched her yellow-faced black dog, gnawing voluptuously at a bone; and lying by the fire were seven men, soldiers, seemingly without life.

"Don't eat too much of that," I said to her as we came up.

"Do you think I'm a pig?" she asked, without bothering to look at me.

"What happened?" I asked.

"Steven," she said, waving a greeting to Paul Higgins, who stared at her gloomily, "everything happened: every damned bad thing in the world."

At this Paul and I touched wood. I'm not superstitious, nor do I put any faith whatever in that foolish custom. If there were more bad things on the road for us, it was not reasonable to suppose that the touching of a piece of wood could save us from them; yet it seemed to me that nothing capable of averting evil fortune should be overlooked.

"Where are the others?" I asked.

"Gone after other sick men. Two fell in a bog about a mile back. One man sat down at the edge of the lake and couldn't get up. I think the two in the bog are dead."

"What about these men?" I asked, looking at the seven by the fire.

"Crossing the river," Jacataqua said. "That was bad! Some, to keep their clothes from being made wetter, took them off when they crossed. When they fell down, they found the water so cold they couldn't get up."

She added that four dead men had been left in the stream. "We can't waste strength on dead men," she said.

There was something lonely and bitter about her. It put me in mind to ask why Burr had left her and gone with Morgan's men.

She shrugged her shoulders. "He may be a great gentleman among white men, Steven, but he's strange about food."

"What do you mean?"

"You know what we do to an Abenaki who has food and won't share it with a man who has none."

Paul and I nodded.

"Yes," said Jacataqua, "that's the first thing we're taught, so I'm troubled about Aaron. He never shares his food unless he must."

Paul grunted. "Many good white men are like that. White men have strange savage customs." He spoke, as he so often did, as though his father and mother had been Abenakis instead of white colonists from Devonshire in England.

"I think," Jacataqua said, "that if Aaron had to choose between me and five pints of flour, he might take the flour."

"I know nothing about it," I said, "save that men are peculiar. I cannot understand how a woman can endure to take up with one of them for more than a week at a time. Neither do I see how such talk as this will feed these men when they wake. Let's go along the ridge and see if there's anything to kill."

"I'll go," Jacataqua said. "Tarso can help us hunt."

"Tarso?"

"Anatarso," she explained. "Humming-bird."

"Anatarso!" Paul groaned, as if to say he preferred to starve, rather than hunt with a dog named Humming-bird.

None the less, Humming-bird nosed a rabbit out of a thicket, showed us a covey of spruce partridges in a tree, and gave tongue among the rocks until we climbed up and found two porcupines. I know of things that I had liefer eat than porcupines; but their livers are delicious, and the rest of them might be worse. After we had shoved a stick through them lengthwise and burned off their quills in a fierce flame, they were juicier than beaver, and certainly better than seal.

When Hobomok and the others returned they brought three men with them, all three unconscious from exhaustion.

On the following morning, the last day of October, we left behind us at Dead Man's Camp ten live men, with two of Paul's braves to send them, when rested, on their way to Lake Megantic.

It was Paul who named it Dead Man's Camp, since those for whom it was made would have been dead except for the grace of God and Paul's Abenakis.

XXVI

Wᴇ ᴄᴀᴍᴇ out of the forest into a clear space on the high easterly shore of Lake Megantic. Natanis was there, with one of Paul's messengers from the lower Chaudière. They were warming themselves in the sun and looking back across the head of the lake at the great barrier of the Height of Land, shining and sparkling in the early sunlight.

We could see the marshes at the mouth of Seven Mile Stream protruding into the blue lake, seemingly as fair and dry as fertile meadowland; and up above the mouth of the stream, on the lower slopes of the Height, like lace on a woman's breast, shone the white patch of the Beautiful Meadow. Above this, in turn, rose the spurs of those terrible mountains. They were harmless-looking now, against the pale blue of the autumn sky; but I could not forget the bloody footprints in the snow and the rigid body of James Dunn on the mound in the swamp. To me the mountains seemed hideous and menacing, like the bared teeth of some jealous monster, snarling at those who dared invade this Northern country.

"That's over," Natanis said, as if in answer to my thoughts. "I think the Great Spirit must have watched over your brothers. They escaped from the swamps and went down the Chaudière."

"All of them?"

"All except the stragglers and the sick. Arnold went first, with a few men; then Morgan with his bateaux. Your friends were led out of the swamps by Goodrich and Dearborn yesterday. Behind them, this morning, went those we brought out last night. There will be no further losing of the way. The Chaudière will carry them straight to the St. Lawrence. There can be more trouble, though, and some is already here!"

One of Paul Higgins's messengers ran to us, drew a ball of knotted twine from his wallet and began to read it to us, unrolling it from his left hand into his right, fingering the knots and seeming to get a meaning from each one.

"The white chief," the messenger said, "was wrecked at Talons du Diable, three leagues down the river. His boats were broken in pieces. At Great Falls our people carried what was left of his boats for him.

"Later the tall loud-voiced captain whose men carry rifles came down with seven bateaux. All seven were smashed in pieces. One man was drowned. Many would have been drowned if our people had not saved them. These men have no food. We are hunting game for them, but game is scarce.

"A captain with a black dog is sick. We think he will die if he cannot have food.

"One company had all its food in one bateau. The bateau was wrecked before the company could come up with it. All the food was destroyed. The company is hungry."

The messenger rolled up his string and replaced it in his wallet.

"Is there enough food in Sartigan for all these men?" Paul Higgins asked.

"Plenty."

"How far is Sartigan?" I asked.

"From here, seventy miles. Five miles beyond where the Rivière du Loup flows into the Chaudière, and then across the Rivière la Famine. From the beginning of the Chaudière sixty-five miles."

"Is there no food nearer?"

"Sartigan is the first house," Natanis said.

If I understood the messenger rightly, it was Goodrich's company whose food had been destroyed. They must have gone foodless for two days. I thought to myself that if Phoebe must march without food for another sixty-five miles she'd be no more in my hand than the carcass of a night heron, all feathers and boniness.

I could feel, in the flesh of my palms, the ridges of her ribs as I had felt them in the dark swamp, and her thin little body fitting loosely into her brass-studded belt; and there was something terrible in the thought that she might become so wasted she could never be smooth and golden again, to slip over the stern of a sloop like a golden otter sliding up a river bank.

"Someone," I said, "must go for Cap Huff and Natawammet, and not stop to catch fish or hunt wildflowers."

"I'll go for them," Natanis said. "You can follow your friends down the Chaudière."

I hitched my pack and musket into place and hurried north along the Megantic shore with Hobomok, Jacataqua, and the dog Anatarso.

* * *

Of all the rivers I know, it seems to me the Chaudière is best named. Dead River is painfully alive for most of its length; the Sandy River hasn't enough sand, in some parts, to polish a shilling; and although Cobosseecontee means "where the sturgeon is found," there are no sturgeons in the Cobosseecontee River except at its mouth in the spring of the year. But the word "chaudière" means "caldron" in the French tongue; and the river Chaudière is a boiling, hissing caldron of water for its entire length, its bed made up of jagged rocks and ledges, with here and there a sudden roaring cataract set among rock-walled turns so sharp that the water, whirling in them, seems to smoke.

In other rapid rivers there may be white patches of quick water, followed by stretches of smooth; so that a canoe, driven by skillful paddlers, reaches for one goal of dark water after another, giving the paddlers time to think, and so come through safely. In the Chaudière the water runs white for miles, all curling waves and foam from bank to bank, with spines of rock rising above the smother like the backs of salmon in the quick water of a tide river in early spring, as they go up to lay their eggs and die.

Thus paddlers shoot for miles through this furious water, and in the end become numb to the whiteness and the danger. Their alertness relaxes, their canoe is slashed to the vitals by the sawlike teeth of a ledge or toppled headlong down an avalanche of foam, and it's a miracle if they, as well as all their belongings, aren't boiled to a pulp by the Chaudière.

Nor does the foul nature of this stream cease with its rocky bed and its swiftness. There are high bluffs on each side of the river channel. Sometimes the river runs far from the bluffs; but again it turns abruptly against them, raging and snarling, so there is scarce an inch of shore on which to find a foothold. Thus there are times when one who follows the banks of the Chaudière on foot is pushing and twisting his way through the cedar and hemlock swamps of the lowlands, wading through streams and over piles of dead trees, spewed out by floods in years gone by; and there are other times when he is clambering up a precipitous bank, catching at roots or briars to keep himself from slipping, or plunging down the face of a precipice into a tangle of underbrush at the base.

I have traveled this trail with a full belly and warm clothes, and found it a tax on my patience. When a hungry man, weak and ill clad, has passed over it, no threats of hell's tribulations can frighten him thereafter.

❋   ❋   ❋

At the end of Lake Megantic, where the Chaudière starts on its devious and rocky way, we made a fire near the trail, and went into the woods to hunt.

It may be that the passage of the troops, who were perpetually banging on kettles and shooting off their muskets for the fun of hearing the noise, had frightened the game away. Whatever the reason, we found nothing in our two hours' hunt but two great horned owls —whose only edible parts are their hearts and livers—three spruce partridges, a porcupine, and three crows. These things were not worth saving for those ahead of us, so we cleaned and cooked them. While they were broiling we saw Natawammet trotting toward us along the trail, and behind him Cap Huff, puffing and blowing to keep ahead of Natanis, who pressed close on his heels.

There was a look of almost painful neatness to Cap when he joined us. He had taken on weight since I saw him last, and had shaved off his beard. The rips in his buckskins were patched, and he was wearing new moccasins, made out of raccoon skin with the fur inside, the soles reinforced with pieces from his old moccasins, so that taking him by and large, he was a soldierly figure indeed.

When I complimented him on his appearance he said indifferently that most of it was Natawammet's doing. He spoke of Natawammet as Nat, raising his voice to a deafening bellow when he addressed him, in addition to using childish phrases and a wealth of gestures. It was seemingly his impression that if he could roar as loud as a clap of thunder, Natawammet might understand him easily.

"I've got something for you, Stevie," he said, squeezing himself between Jacataqua and myself at the fire. He turned to Natawammet, shouting, "Fat—Stevie—You—Me—Give—Get—Good."

Natawammet obediently produced a package wrapped in birch bark. On opening it I found a cake of raccoon fat.

"This Indian Nat," Cap said, "he ain't so bad."

"One of the best in the world," I assured him.

"Did you know," Cap asked, "that ants kill vermin?"

"Every Indian knows that."

"Well," Cap said, "you could have knocked me over with a horsehair!" He meditated for a time. "Those Virginians," he resumed, "were a lousy lot. Do you know what they did? They stopped off at our cabin day before yesterday. Dearborn and Goodrich got out of the swamp in a canoe and stayed overnight. Early in the morning they left all their truck in the cabin and went back to the swamp to get their men out. They left a couple pieces of pork and enough flour to fill a couple hats. After they'd gone some of Morgan's men came along."

He paused again, and absent-mindedly kneaded Jacataqua's shoulder. "You know, Stevie, I don't mind a man picking up a little food here and there, or a pair of breeches or something, but it kind of seems to me you shouldn't take a man's food if it's all he's got, any more'n you ought to take his last pair of pants, unless you got something against him."

"Look here," I said, handing him one of the roasted crows, "push that into you and come ahead! There's men starving down along the river!"

"For sure there is!" Cap said. He bit violently at the crow's breast, chewed twice, and then swallowed convulsively. "For sure there is! Those lousy Virginians, they stole Dearborn's and Goodrich's food. Just took it and walked out and said nothing, only laughed fit to die when they went off in their bateaux."

"All their bateaux were wrecked," I said.

"It serves 'em damn good and right! Those men, they'd steal *any-thing*."

"Come on," I urged him.

"Listen, Stevie," he said, struggling to his feet, "after they'd gone I begun to itch, and you know what Nat did?"

"Warmed up an ant's nest," I said, shouldering my pack.

"Damned if he didn't!" Cap said. "He built a fire around a ant hill, and they come to life, hot and mad, and I put my clothes on it. Left 'em there an hour, and ain't had an itch since!" He clapped Natawammet on the back, nodding and grinning at him violently, as if to assure him of his friendliness. "All right, Nat!" he bawled so I thought my eardrums would crack. "Good—You keep—You no give yet."

"What's all this?" I asked.

"Oh," Cap said, "he taught me how to roll Indian dice in a bowl while we waited. I licked him. He ain't got nuthin no more."

"No food, you mean?"

"No; not *nuthin!* See that musket he's got?"

"Yes," I said, mystified.

"It's mine. I won it. See his shirt and leggins?"

"Yours?"

He nodded complacently. "I let him use 'em. I like to have people grateful."

So we started down the river, hurrying insofar as it was possible to hurry over those cliffs and swamps. At mid-afternoon we spied a bateau with its side caved in; beyond that two more without bottoms. Then we saw the wreckage of half a dozen, and a fire on the river bank, with men near it.

I could hear the roaring, bellowing voice of Daniel Morgan, and see his towering figure striding up and down among the men. Here, therefore, was the rear-guard of the army; and someone, we decided, must remain always behind the rear-guard, picking up exhausted soldiers, dragging them to fires and catching fish for them. To perform this duty we left Paul Higgins, Hobomok, and five of Paul's Abenakis.

As for me, I knew I couldn't hunt for my friends among the long line of troops without going among them; so it seemed best that Cap and Jacataqua and I should try our luck with Morgan and his men, to see whether I was taken for a spy or not. If not, I could venture anywhere. Therefore Natanis went around this camp of Morgan's while we went boldly through it, only to find we might have spared ourselves all worriment, since those we passed were so weary and hungry that they cared for nothing save their own affairs.

There were bateaumen from Morgan's seven boats at this camp, and bateaumen from three other bateaux, as well as all their passengers. Burr was among the latter; and he hailed us jovially, though his swarthy face was drawn and lined, no longer pretty.

"Ho, ho!" he said, drawing Jacataqua out from between us and holding her by the upper arms, "life's not all gloom and sorrow after all!"

"Were you overset?" I asked, and braced myself for his answer, fearing I might have to run for it.

He looked at me, frowning in a puzzled way. "How did you get here? It was back in '73 that Colonel Enos ran home and you gave me the flour, wasn't it? Or was it in my first year at Princeton? I've forgot, I swear I have! You ought to be up ahead of us, oughtn't you—or have you discovered the northwest passage and gone around by it to take us in the rear?"

His eyes strayed toward Jacataqua's dog, Anatarso, snuffling at the package of raccoon fat in my breeches pocket.

"Were you overset?" I asked again.

"A thousand pardons! Things seem to slip my mind. Too much high living, I fear. Ho, ho! Yes, yes! Well, let me see: were we overset? *Were* we? Man dear, this was the greatest oversetting since Pelion was piled on Ossa! It was like the Red Sea overwhelming Pharaoh's army, except that we were rolled over more handsomely."

He dropped his gaiety. "You haven't anything to eat with you by any chance, have you?" I thought I saw a queer furtiveness in his eye as his glance returned to the dog Anatarso.

"No," I said, meaning to hold to my package of raccoon fat until there was greater need for it. "Food's none too plenty where I've been. They tell me you had extra food in your bateaux. Where'd you get it?"

"I know nothing about it. Whatever they had, they've lost it now." He released his hold on Jacataqua and reached for Anatarso, who came to him amiably, switching his rump from side to side and laying his ears back to show his appreciation of this small notice. Jacataqua caught the dog by the tail and dragged him away.

"Keep your hands off my dog, Aaron," she said, sweetly enough; but there was no mistaking her meaning. "He stays with me."

Burr gentled her arm again. "I'd do him no harm."

"You will if you can," she said, pulling free, "but you can't, because I'll damn well see that you don't. He's found game for you all along the river, and now that you're emptier you want to eat *him*."

"No, no, no! little spitfire," Burr said, striving to catch her, but not striving hard, it seemed to me; and, in truth, Jacataqua's beauty had faded in our marches. She looked draggled and hard, her tangled hair bound with a twisted squirrel skin instead of a wampum band, her back bent forward under blanket and musket, the velvety brown of her face and hands scratched and chapped from wetness and the brush through which she had scrambled, her buckskin garments wrinkled and stained.

Cap Huff, in his turn, took Jacataqua by the shoulders and shook her lightly. "Naughty, naughty girl," said he, in a hoarse but mincing voice, "why didn't you tell me! I could have saved some for your friend!"

Cap put his arm on Jacataqua's shoulder and led her down the path through the camp, while Burr listened morosely to Cap's booming voice. "There were those six raccoons," he improvised, "and the eighteen partridges and all those nice buttery catfish and that fat buck! He could have had some, just as well as not, if we'd dreamed he was hungry!"

"He's making game of you," I said, having no heart to tease a starving man, even though I mistrusted him. "Cap's as empty as the rest of us. Why didn't you get on, and where are the others?"

Burr made an angry hissing sound. "It was that damned wreck! We were half drowned, all of us: pitched out and rolled down the river for close onto a mile, banging against rocks and fighting to get our breaths and swallowing water like funnels."

He shook his head at the recollection. "I swear to God I *was* drowned! How I got out, I don't know, nor any of the others, either. All we know is that we came ashore in a little cove. Morgan found us lying on the bank as if we'd been pulled out and thrown there. We were sick, all of us: couldn't move for a day. Felt like a flame in our lungs; had aches everywhere, as if a smith had hammered us."

He moved his right shoulder tentatively and felt the back of his neck. "We saved a little food. Wet flour—a little. The footmen went on. They're fairly well off. We'll all get through, I guess. Some of the others won't."

"What others?"

"Goodrich's men. They're scattered; going it as best they can. Hurrying to get to food. Hurrying. Falling down. Bad."

"Where are they?"

"You'll come up with the best of them to-morrow. Some of the worst ones are just beyond here. Captain Dearborn's sick. He looks terrible—a skeleton with a black beard."

"Some filthy rat stole food from him," I said.

"I don't know anything about it," Burr protested. "He doesn't need to starve. He's got his dog with him: that damned big black dog. Fat, too."

"How do you know?"

"I felt him."

I shouldered my pack. "When are you starting on?"

"To-day. Soon. Some of the men are getting so they can stand. We got a few fish. The stream's so swift we can't handle 'em. Our lines break, or the current snags 'em before we can hook anything."

"Good luck," I said.

"If you want to say good-bye to McClellan," Burr added, "he's in the lean-to. We've got to leave him here."

"What," I said, "Hendricks' lieutenant?"

Burr nodded. "Didn't you hear about it? He's got the fever in his lungs. Captain Hendricks and one of the riflemen brought him over the Height of Land on a stretcher. We thought maybe he'd get well;

but he was in Hendricks' bateau, and it came down behind ours and piled up when we did. I guess he's dying."

McClellan was a good officer, young, like Major Bigelow, and cheery like Bigelow. I went in the lean-to to see him. He whispered something; but I couldn't hear for the roaring of the Chaudière. I wanted to do something for him, but could only give him a bit of raccoon fat.

"Let me have some of that," Burr said.

I gave him a piece the size of a walnut.

Jacataqua and Cap Huff fell in line behind me, and Natanis rejoined us when we had gone below the camp. Thirty miles we made that day. Toward dusk the trail was dotted with stragglers who sat by the path, asleep, or held to trees and watched us pass. Some wavered from side to side, raising their knees as though they expected to find the path higher than it was, like drunken men. Others talked quietly to themselves and at times laughed a silly laugh, a weak titter.

"We can't waste time," said Natanis, shaking his head over the numbers of the stragglers. "If we should have a change of weather, these men would die like flies!"

At nightfall we came up with some of Goodrich's soldiers. I remembered them as the poorest of the company, the most slovenly and improvident, men who could not be trusted with rations when rations were running low. They couldn't eat a little to-day and a little to-morrow, but must eat everything to-day and let the morrow look out for itself. Such men, I have found, are always the first, barring those who are sick or hurt, to lag behind.

They were merry among themselves, which is something I have ceased to explain to folk who have led sheltered lives: how one evil experience, provided it carries with it no sharp pains, is no worse than another, and how a number of them put together are things to be endured from moment to moment with the thought that eventually things must be better. It is strange to me how folk will not have it so, but wish to think that men who are, as they say, suffering must constantly bemoan their condition.

These men were clustered around a little light kettle suspended over a fire, and were talking about food: squabbling as to whether there was nourishment in boiled leather. Indeed, I could get nothing out of them concerning the rest of the company until I had given my opinion on leather-eating. Each one had cut a piece from the top of his moccasins, a strip three inches wide and eight inches long, and had washed this and his leather shot pouch in the river so they could be cooked. Some held that if roasted until crisp and scorched, they would crumble in the mouth and give nourishment when swallowed; while others held that if boiled they would become pulpy and more easily digestible.

Thinking their strength might hold out better if they amused themselves in this way, I said I thought it would be wiser to boil their leather. If it didn't dissolve, it could then be recovered and roasted; whereas if it was roasted first it would be useless for boiling.

At this they put private marks on their pieces and popped them into the kettle; and one of the men took from his pack a jar of pomatum, such as is used to grease the hair, and offered to put it in the broth on the chance that it might prove nourishing. I felt guilty about the raccoon fat in my breeches pocket. Yet it would have done these men little good, and I was determined to save it until I reached Phoebe.

While the leather stewed, one of the men deigned to answer my frequently repeated demand for information concerning Noah Cluff, but the others embarked on a discussion of cookery, in which they had evidently been involved before my arrival.

"Noah's close behind Goodrich," the soldier said. A square of birch bark was roughly stitched to the seat of his breeches.

"How far ahead?" I asked.

He had, however, injected himself into the argument. "They ain't no good unless you parboil 'em three times before you bake 'em!"

"That don't take the place of soaking overnight," another objected.

"Who said it did! Soak 'em all you damned please, only they won't soften up till you parboil 'em."

"Gosh," said another, "I could eat a kittleful, parboiled or not!"

"A kittleful!" The speaker's hair stuck out on all sides of his head like straw out of a wagon. "I could eat a barrelful!"

"With hot bread!" added a small man with no teeth in his upper jaw.

"And sour milk cheese!" said another.

A man whose coat lacked a sleeve raised an angry shout. "What you want to mess up baked beans with sour milk cheese for! You can't improve on hot bread and plain beans with lots of juice to 'em! Sour milk cheese, for God's sake!" He snorted contemptuously.

"I'll tell you this much," said the one with the birch-bark seat. "If you don't parboil 'em three times you'll get so much wind in your stummick it's apt to press your heart up against your backbone so it can't beat."

"Hell," said his wild-haired friend, "it ain't parboiling that stops wind: it's putting mustard in 'em when they're baking. You put in a couple pinches mustard and there won't be no more wind to a barrel of 'em than there would be to a humming-bird!"

"Well, by Gosh," said the owner of the birch-bark rear, "I wouldn't *tetch* a bean that hadn't been parboiled three times!"

"No, I s'pose not," the wild-haired man sneered. "I s'pose if somebody come up behind you and held a great big plate of beans, all brown and juicy and smelling of pork and all, over your shoulder, you'd say, 'If those ain't been parboiled three times, take 'em away! I don't choose to have nothing to do with 'em!' I s'pose that's what you'd say!"

The soldier with the birch-bark seat looked quickly over his shoulder, as though hopeful of seeing the plate of beans, but saw only my face.

I seized the opportunity. "How far ahead is Noah Cluff? Is Phoebe Dunn with him?"

"I dunno," he said. "I got awful tired and laid down and slept. If they ain't slept any, they're six hours ahead of us."

"Keep going," I told him. "There'll probably be food to-morrow or next day."

The wild-haired trooper called after me as I moved on. "Tell 'em to parboil it three times, or we won't eat it!"

*   *   *

Natanis had saved the body of one of our owls of the morning, and Cap had with him a piece of raccoon fat the size of Jacataqua's fist. These we divided into four equal parts, and were glad to have them. There is something, I learned, to be said for owl meat: it can be chewed longer than anything I have ever eaten, though Natanis told us it is not to be compared with a piece from the neck of a bobcat, which, if chewed discreetly, can be made to endure for a day with no noticeable shrinkage.

To this moment my memory is dim concerning the following day. We were dizzy when we started at dawn, and there were blank spots in my mind for long stretches, together with periods when I felt light and unreal, so that my feet seemed to skim the ground; then hugesome and heavy, as though I carried anvils in my shoes. Cap angered me by stumbling, then tittering like a silly girl, so that for a time I could think of nothing save when he would stumble and titter again, and in so thinking I would stumble myself. Yet we were better off than any of those we passed; for the four of us had eaten meat and fat within three days, whereas the others had eaten nothing.

It seemed as though we passed a thousand men, which was impossible since the whole army had dwindled to little more than six hundred. When I saw the snail's pace at which they traveled, and their stumblings and slippings, I knew God was good to give us fair weather on that first day of November; for if there had been a fall of snow with a bitter wind to lash it into our faces we'd have lain down and died, and nothing could have saved us.

Thirty miles we made that day, the last of it along the top of the bluffs. When we came down to the river's edge we found Goodrich's men digging in the wet gravel for the roots of water plants. Noah Cluff was stretched beside a fire, which Phoebe tended, while Nathaniel Lord and Asa Hutchins scratched feebly in the dirt. They were a miserable-looking company. Their movements were slow; their eyes sunk deep in their heads.

While we stared at them, a battered canoe shot down through the white water. In the middle was Captain Dearborn, gaunt and bearded, holding to his big black-haired dog. The canoe was guided by the chief of the axemen who had worked at clearing the portages, a Mr. Ayres, a strong and tireless man. Natanis wagged his head as he watched him, declaring he had done two great things—first to venture to take a canoe from Lake Megantic to this point, and then to succeed in doing it. Even with a good canoe, he said, it was a great feat; whereas this canoe, he could see, was worn out and on the verge of breaking in the middle. In the bow was a soldier, sitting as close to the end as he could get. When the bow dipped beneath the white surges, the water foamed against the soldier's lap and chest and fell away on either side. Otherwise the canoe would have foundered. It came inshore and grounded near the fires.

Natanis spoke quickly to Jacataqua, and she caught her dog by the scruff of the neck and held him. To me he said: "There's still enough light for us to see. We'll try to reach Sartigan to-night, so to send out all the rest of Paul Higgins's men to help these poor people. Tell them they'll reach the inhabitants to-morrow; and say to the sick captain there'll be another canoe for him at the Great Falls."

They vanished in the dusk. Cap Huff and I moved closer to the fires.

"Hey!" said Noah Cluff when he saw me. "Is that you?"

"Who'd you think it was?"

"Can't be sure of nothing nowadays," Noah said. He had trouble getting his breath. "Seemed as though the river was all mud flats this afternoon. Thought there was clam holes in it. Thought I saw water squirting up out of 'em from the clams."

Phoebe lay back to look up into my face. I was glad my mother was not there to see her and to put the blame on me—not that she'd have thought me to blame; but the sight of Phoebe would have made her angry at all the world, and she'd have known that I could best endure her anger.

She had found dried grass somewhere and stuffed it into her jerkin for warmth, and her poor thin neck and face stuck out above this swollen jerkin like a doll's head fixed on a body too large for it.

"He started to walk in and dig clams," she said, and smiled up at me. It was a terrible, strained smile. I looked at Cap, and found him opening and closing his hand, as I had seen him do before hitting someone, and I knew the same thought had come into his head that had come into mine: the thought that somebody must pay for all this.

"Can you hold out, Phoebe?" I asked. "It'll only be till to-morrow."

"To-morrow!" Nathaniel Lord whispered. "I'd like four pork chops and a chicken and two dozen ears of green corn!"

"Corn!" Phoebe cried. "I'd forgot there *was* such a thing as corn! I couldn't think of anything but pumpkin pie."

"My God!" Cap Huff said. "I never found out who stole that pumpkin pie off me!"

"Listen, Stevie," Noah said, "you don't need to worry about *her* not holding out. It was her kept me from walking into the river to dig clams!"

"You were going to give me some, weren't you?" Phoebe asked.

"Yes," Noah admitted.

"Well," Phoebe said, "I didn't want them. That's why I stopped you."

"Gosh, Phoebe," said Noah helplessly, "I don't rightly know what you're talking about!"

She edged over and slipped her arm through his. "Keep everything full and by, Mate." She smiled at me, that same terrible, strained smile. "Noah can sail on the *Ranger*, can't he, when we get home?"

"Why, yes, Phoebe. Anyone you say. That's your job."

I took the raccoon fat from my breeches pocket and held it behind my back. "Here," I said, going down on one knee beside her and speaking the lines my mother used to say to me when I was little: "Open your mouth and shut your eyes and I'll give you something to make you wise." When she did so I popped into her mouth as big a lump as I could get on my forefinger, knowing that if I gave it into her hands she'd eat none of it herself. I held her arms until she swallowed; then gave her the rest of the package. It had scarce left my grasp before she was sharing it with Noah.

"Take some, Steven," she said, before she turned to Nathaniel Lord.

I told her Cap and I had eaten recently and could hold out until the next day, expecting to hear a bitter outcry from Cap; but he was watching Asa Hutchins and a good-for-nothing rogue named Flood who hailed from Wells or York. These two were standing together, near poor Captain Dearborn, who had climbed weakly from his canoe with his big black dog clumsily striving to be kittenish before him, delighted at being on dry land again.

What ailed Captain Dearborn I don't know; but he was close to dying of it, whatever it was. All of us went about our duties for more than two weeks thinking he was dead and buried; and indeed he looked ready for burying, even now, his face dead white, and sunken around his mouth and eyes, and a ragged black beard making his face seem more waxy and deathlike than it was.

Ayres held him up and guided him, to keep him from pitching on his face. Even when guided he put down his feet as though he expected to find nothing under them.

Asa and Flood approached Dearborn, quiet and hesitant-like, as hunters steal up to a river bank. Remembering Natanis had given me a message for Dearborn, I went along behind them.

When they reached Dearborn they went around and stood in front of him. Asa did the talking, while Dearborn, being a fine and thoughtful gentleman, stopped and listened.

"Captain," Asa said, "our bateau got wrecked. We ain't had any food since the morning we got lost in the swamps. We're real hungry, Captain."

"My boy," Dearborn said, "I know it! I do, indeed! I feel for you and for all the others, and I'm sure God will soon deliver us out of these tribulations."

"Captain," Asa said, "there's a lot of us here that ain't far from dying and we'd like for you to help us."

"Why," said the captain, "I'll do what I can, but there's nothing I can do, my boy. To-morrow, I hope——"

"Captain," said Asa, "this dog of yours, he's a fine dog. We'd like for you to give him to us."

The dog, clumsy, fond creature, galloped up to us with his tongue lolling out, and blowing pleased, audible breaths. He pranced a little before Dearborn and then went over to grin amiably at Asa and Flood.

"Why," Dearborn said, "I wouldn't—do you mean to eat?"

"Damn you," said Ayres, "get out of here! You'll have food in the morning! Can't you see the captain's sick?"

"Captain," Asa said, watching Ayres warily, "I think some of us might die to-night if we can't get something into us. That dog, he'd feed thirty men. Maybe fifty. We think you ought to let us have him."

"Why, dear, dear," Captain Dearborn said, "dear, dear! He's been with us all the way! I'd no more eat him than I'd eat one of you! Why, bless me, my boy, you don't want to eat *him!*"

"Captain," said Asa, "we'd eat anything! We tried moose hide and moccasins, but they ain't no good."

"If you could only wait until to-morrow——"

"It's *now* we want food! Captain, let us have him."

I think Ayres must have made some move to go for Asa; for Dearborn stopped him. "We can't be judges," he said to Ayres. "Just because we can hold out is no sign others can. What we can do we must do." He put his hand around the dog's nose, pressing it weakly, and the dog looked up at him, grateful and loving. "Take him, my boy," he said to Asa, "but take him a long way off, and be—be merciful."

Asa hunkered down, snapping his fingers. The dog came to him immediately, taking pride in the friendship. Asa took him by the neck and led him away.

"Asa," Cap called after him, "you could wait until to-morrow and you know it. If you won't, I'll give you two weeks to fatten up in. Then I'll knock your gizzard out through your ears. You're a rat, Asa, and if I was as hungry as you claim to be I'd kill you and keep the dog."

It seemed to me there was no way of knowing how Asa and Flood were affected by their hunger, and no justification for Cap's violent language. I determined, none the less, to attend to Flood's gizzard on the day Cap dealt with Asa's.

XXVII

C‌AP and I took Dearborn down the river bank on the following morning, his canoe having softened in the middle so we dared not let him sit in it, though Ayres said he would take it as far as the Great Falls or know the reason why. Dearborn was deathly sick, his legs numb and lifeless at times, nor were ours as reliable as they might have been.

Noah Cluff and Phoebe and Asa and the rest had gone on before us. In an hour's time we heard a screaming, thin and reedy, and musketry fire, so we dropped Dearborn behind a tree and fumbled with our own muskets, fearing the British had come out from Quebec.

Then Cap began to swear; the rich, mellow swearing of relief; for four wild-eyed oxen came lumbering past us, small oxen, but oxen none the less, and two horses ridden by swarthy little Frenchmen in dirty gray blanket coats and knitted caps, from under which long queues hung down. There were sacks of meal thrown across their saddle bows.

Running with the cattle were other Frenchmen with yard-long queues and blanket coats, and Abenakis belonging to Paul Higgins's band. Thus we had escaped starvation by the breadth of a gnat's whisker.

We hurried to come up with the others, and found fifty men gathered together. An ox had been left with them, and they had shot it, stripped off the hide for moccasins, and cut the body into pieces with hatchets. The place was a shambles, the men crouched over fires with meat stuck on sticks, and the remnants of the ox still steaming beside the path. Up and down among them went officers telling them to have a care in their eating; but many wouldn't listen, only tore at their meat like dogs tearing at a gristly bone.

When we brought food to Dearborn, he couldn't eat. Being low in spirits from his illness, and from thinking, probably, how his black dog would have delighted in the fragments from this ox, he fell to weeping, saying over and over: "The poor men! The poor men!"

I might have had no trouble myself if Cap, seeing Dearborn's tears, hadn't begun to snuffle and snivel as well, and if Phoebe, seeing us, hadn't come running up with her piece of meat and divided it between us. Because of all this, and because there was a weakness in my throat from God knows what, I felt wetness in my own eyes, though I controlled it at last by shouting at Cap, calling him a lazy fool and demanding whether he intended to stand there all day when we had work to do.

We pressed on to the Great Falls, which are less than ten miles from Sartigan; and Sartigan is the end of the wilderness and the beginning of roads and houses. There was an Indian watcher at the falls, an Abenaki, who told me where to find the canoe of which Natanis had spoken, a circumstance that bemazed Dearborn, to say nothing of Ayres, who was waiting for us at the falls when we arrived.

He had no reason to doubt, Ayres said, that this was a howling wilderness, but it seemed to him a strange thing that whenever he and Captain Dearborn needed a canoe, there was always one ready for them, as though it had grown on the nearest bush.

When we had come to the end of the carry around the falls we found two more Abenakis in another canoe, bringing additional provisions to the men.

These braves asked whether Dearborn was the sick captain of whom Natanis had told them, the one who had traveled all the way from Megantic by canoe. When I said he was, one of them quoted an Abenaki saying—"It is easiest to stumble at the end of a journey"—and they unloaded their provisions, hiding them by the trail, and took us to Sartigan in the two canoes.

*   *   *

There was little of note to the place we knew as Sartigan. There were four houses, small whitewashed affairs with thatched roofs, and barns for horses and cows, and a powerful odor of manure over everything. In each house dwelt a stunted Frenchman with a queue hanging to his rump and a face the color of a black duck's belly.

These houses, unimpressive as they were, had a mighty importance in our sight. It had been thirty days since we had set eyes on a habitation: not a long time, I know; yet to some of us the thirty days had seemed longer than all the years of our lives, and we had thought too often we might never see another house again.

At the edge of a field behind the houses were wigwams; there, the Abenakis told us, we would find Natanis. Near the houses was set up a small shelter in which a young Frenchman sold food—rice and potatoes; milk and bread and chicken. He seemed pleasant, and I thought best to deal with him, since we were ravenous and had no way of knowing what Natanis had found for us.

The young Frenchman seemed glad to see us, and this, I told Cap, augured well for our travels in Canada. The young man demanded hard money for his provisions: a quart of milk being one shilling, a pint of rice one shilling, a loaf of bread one shilling, and a chicken two shillings. No wonder he was glad to see us, Cap said. At such rates he would quickly make enough to buy himself a seigneurie, provided his chickens held out. Nor, Cap added, could starving men question such prices, though for his part he considered them downright dishonest.

He pulled out his shirt-tail from what was left of his breeches, cut loose three dollars from the hard-money armor that protected his rear, and selected four chickens, two loaves of bread, a pint of rice, and a quart of milk. When the young Frenchman hid the three dollars, Cap watched him closely—so closely that I felt almost certain the three dollars might soon be attached to Cap's shirt tail again.

Natanis and Jacataqua were waiting at the wigwams; and from Natanis, while Jacataqua popped the chickens and the rice into the pot, we had the news: how Colonel Arnold had gone five miles down river and taken headquarters; how all the Abenakis had gone up river to help the army; how Natanis had sent word to Paul Higgins that he and Paul would demand a council with Colonel Arnold in two days' time. There was nothing for us to do, Natanis said, but eat and sleep ourselves back to health again.

"I'm healthy enough," I said, "and to-morrow morning I'll be as good as ever I was. I can see Cap is thin and tired, but I'm better off than he is; so I'll go back to look after the Arundel men."

Natanis laughed and took a mirror from behind a bearskin in the corner, holding it so I could see myself; and at what I saw I almost reached for my musket.

My hat was gone, and my hair matted like a last year's robin's nest. There were corrugations in my forehead, and grooves between my eyes, and the eyes themselves were red, with black smudges beneath, as though I had rubbed them after cleaning a stove. My cheekbones stuck out above a reddish beard, mottled and stained with pitch and scabs; and what there was to be seen of my lips was cracked and blackened as if from eating hot cinders. My buckskin shirt was torn in a dozen places and my breeches were wrecks, so that I might well have hesitated to appear in public without wrapping myself in a towel. There was next to nothing left of my stockings except what was hanging around the tops of the clumsy moccasins Paul Higgins had given me. All in all, I was a spectacle to make a child flee in terror, screaming it had seen the bogey man.

"You're needed at the council," Natanis said, "and there is nothing you can do for your friends that won't be done by my brothers. You'll be doing all of us a service if you clean yourself and eat and sleep."

"What does he say?" Cap asked.

Jacataqua looked up from the boiling chickens. "He says," she translated, "he wants you to run back twenty miles and carry food to those that need it."

Cap reached over and caught her by the ankle, pushing forward and upward so that she stumbled backward into his lap. "I've wore myself to a shadow," he said, holding her arms so she couldn't smack him, "and there's going to be food carried to *me* for a change." He made a show of biting her ear, baring his teeth and growling horribly.

"What do you have for Phoebe to wear?" I asked.

Jacataqua shook her head. "Nothing. These French people have blanket coats, but they're expensive."

Cap rolled over, spilling her out of his lap, and dragged his shirttail out of his breeches. "Here," he said, "take what you need."

Jacataqua eyed it thoughtfully. "No: it's not big enough to make a coat for her."

"Gosh!" Cap cried. "You ain't fit to travel in polite society! Unstitch the money before I take you over my knee!"

We had a chicken leg apiece, and a cup of broth, and slept until Jacataqua woke us to give us more. She held open the deerskin doorway as we ate, and we saw Smith's riflemen wading the Rivière la Famine and coming up to the first house, skinny, hairy, ragged men, shuffling along with no attempt at order, but whooping and laughing: glad to be alive.

It was the next afternoon when Jacataqua woke us again. A heavy snow was falling, and Phoebe sat inside the opening of the wigwam stitching at a piece of gray blanketing. Her hair was bound neatly in a blue cotton handkerchief once more, and her cat's eyes hung at her throat, so she looked more like my old-time Phoebe. There was a grimness about her mouth that hadn't been there before we started on this devil's march, but that looked as though it might remain for many a long year.

"You look *awful*," she said, seemingly able to see me out of the back of her head. "There's two weeks' sewing to be done on your breeches and shirt, and land only knows what you're like underneath!"

"Pretty bad," I said, getting myself into a better position to eat the rice and chicken that Jacataqua brought. By this time we could have more: not a meal, by any means, but enough to taste. Phoebe took my cup when I'd finished with it, and drank broth.

"You men!" she said. "Don't you ever shave unless you *have* to? Don't you ever shave just to look nice?"

"What would Mary say," Jacataqua asked, nor did I fancy her impertinence in asking it, "if she saw you with a beard like that?"

"How should I know?" I said, turning on my side preparatory to sleeping again.

It seemed to me Phoebe's voice was more cheerful when she went on babbling to Jacataqua in an undertone, a pleasant and soothing undertone. It may be her voice sounded cheerful by comparison with the subject of her chatter, for she spoke of how the men had split the ox-bones and eaten the marrow, and had even eaten the intestines; how many of them, overeating despite the warnings of the officers, had become ill, and how a few, overeating still more, had died.

To this babbling I fell asleep. That night we were allowed to have bread soaked in soup, and milk to drink, and more chicken, and the half of a partridge apiece.

While Phoebe stitched away at her gray blanket-stuff, we lay and yawned and wondered about Quebec, and whether we should take it, speaking as though it lay a matter of six or eight miles distant, so that we could trot over to it on the first clear night. When we learned from Natanis that we must still march seventy miles down the caldron of the Chaudière before we could come to the St. Lawrence, we listened helplessly to the whooping and squalling of the braves who were arriving in twos and threes from up river. Seventy miles! We slept immediately and soundly, despite the hideous outcry.

*   *   *

There was a bright light when we woke, reflected into the wigwam from snow that had fallen in the night, and in the brightest of it sat Natanis, gazing into his hand mirror and making himself beautiful with paint: vermilion, yellow, black, and white.

"Two of your friends have come," he said.

"Not Hook!"

"No," Natanis said, running a line of white down the center of his nose, "older friends: Eneas and Sabatis."

"I thought we'd never see them again. What messages did they bring back for Arnold?"

"That's a queer business," Natanis said, coloring his mouth and chin vermilion. "They say they were captured when they entered Quebec, and Arnold's letters taken from them."

"Then it's known we're coming!"

"That's not the main thing," Natanis said. "The main thing is that our people have always come and gone in Quebec as they pleased. Our help is too valuable to be thrown away by seizing us and search-ing us, and so angering us. There are a thousand ways our people can enter and leave Quebec unnoticed, provided they wish to do so. Therefore I doubt Eneas and Sabatis were captured."

I pondered while I honed my razor. If they hadn't been captured, they had freely given the letters to some man of importance. If we were friendly with them and didn't arouse their suspicions, and heaped favors on them, we might come to learn something of those with whom they had trafficked in Quebec. We might catch Hook, somehow, through them! To catch Hook, I would have gone without food for another week.

Thus minded of food, I ate half a loaf of bread sopped in broth, and longed for the day when my stomach would let me start the day properly with a cut from a fat cow and half a pie, preferably pumpkin.

Natanis had gone to work filling in the upper sections of his face with yellow, a task requiring dexterity because yellow paint soaks into black hair if allowed to come in contact with it. "There's another thing," he said, in the far-away tones of one absorbed in delicate manual labor. "Arnold shouldn't show anger toward them. If he ac-cuses them of doing what we think they've done, they may fly into a rage and leave us when we most need their help."

"He knows that," I said, preparing to scrape off my beard. "He's a wise man."

"He's a bold man, given to speaking his mind. He was not wise enough to know we weren't spies."

"He can't be blamed for that! He was scurvily treated by those he considered friends. It's natural for him to be suspicious. What could he do but suspect us of being spies if he was told we *were* spies?"

Natanis shrugged his shoulders and painted a black tortoise in the middle of his forehead. His face was so covered that there was no way of telling what his expression might be beneath the paint. "None the less, he must be told to show no anger; for it's my plan to know more about the persons who called me spy."

"It's my plan to find Hook," I said.

"Then warn him," he said. "Let him know Eneas and Sabatis are our brothers." He made a snoot at me, a horrible snoot, so that I nicked my ear with the razor. Natanis was pleased: his painting had been successful.

While I studied my hunting shirt, not knowing where first to thrust my needle, Phoebe came to the door with a bundle. Such was her elegance that I clean forgot I had on no shirt, until she said that she'd mend it, unless I was planning to boil it and eat it. With that Natanis said he had a new shirt for me, and he fished it out from the rear of the wigwam, a stout one of buckskin, without fringes or ornaments.

Phoebe wore a gray blanket coat, belted around her middle with a red worsted sash, and long gray breeches stuck into the top of moccasins. Her string of cat's eyes dangled at her throat. Cap sat up and rubbed his eyes at sight of her, swearing that if she had a queue down to her waist and a pipe in her mouth, and stunk of garlic enough to crack the wigwam apart, no one would be able to tell her from a Frenchy.

She gave me her bundle: blanket breeches and worsted stockings for Cap and myself. Cap declared he was disappointed at being given breeches, since he had planned to get the loan of a pair from the young Frenchman who had charged us so handsomely for provisions. In fact, he said, he had planned to borrow those the young man had on, if he could catch him in a dark, quiet place.

While Phoebe cut my hair we warned Cap to keep his hands off all Frenchmen, since they were our friends and we would often stand in need of their help.

"Stevie," Cap said, "you always gravel me in an argument, but these Frenchies aren't real Frenchies: they only think they are. You never saw a real Frenchy with a queue like these Frenchies. These Frenchies are more like folks from China that have tails on their heads a rod long."

"Well, what of it? They're our friends, tails or no tails, so let 'em alone."

Cap whined that he merely wanted one of the tails to take home with him: that I whistled a different tune when it came to my own pet Frenchy, Guerlac; that these Frenchies were robbers, anyway, charging double what they should for the necessities of life. Weary of his clack, I pushed Phoebe out, scrambled into my new breeches and shirt, and fled the place, reminding him that when it came to robbing, our own honest citizens on the Kennebec had been quick to sell us sour beef at four hundred per cent profit. He managed to have the last word, bawling after me that people ought to expect that when they come to Maine, whereas it should be different elsewhere.

❂   ❂   ❂

There was a fleet of twenty canoes on the river bank, brought there by forty braves, all decked out in wampum necklets and armlets, and silver wrist guards. They had fur robes, and their heads were shaved.

All of them were painted, even Paul Higgins, so there was no way of telling one from the other. Natanis said this was why Indians paint when preparing for war: so that if one of them comes close and strikes a foe, the stricken man cannot tell his assailant from any other painted Indian, and so may later be unable to take his vengeance. This may be true; but if you ask me, I think they paint their faces because they like to do it. They spend hours daubing themselves, and fly into terrible rages if their hands slip and spoil the symmetry of their designs.

Natanis, while I knew him, wore paint on his face this once, and never again; yet he enjoyed painting himself on this occasion as much as a woman enjoys putting on half a dozen petticoats and a dress that sticks out behind her big enough to make a hiding place for a pair of owls. I think they are two customs of a piece. Many Indians I know are as handsome men as you could find in a month of Sundays, whereas when they paint themselves they look like something you dream about when overly free with pie and hot buttered rum. In the same way there are women as straight and sweetly rounded as can be; though when hung with silken saddle bags and wire lobster pots underneath, they might as well have spavins and broken hocks for all anyone knows.

Hobomok greeted me at the canoes, and Natawammet, and the braves who had been with us among the swamps of Finger Lake; also Paul Higgins, whose face was yellow with a jagged black line across his forehead like the tops of pine trees against the sky.

"We left a camp full of men at the head of the Chaudière," Paul said. "Food was scarce, so we stole a horse from the French and sent it back to them. What do you think? Is it all right to steal a horse?"

"Probably they'd have given it, if you'd asked," I told him.

"Not the French," Paul said. "You don't know 'em!" I thought that if I didn't keep Paul and Cap Huff apart there might not be a French queue left on the Chaudière by the time we reached Quebec.

The trackless forests had ended at Sartigan; and the river ran between level fields, snow-covered and sprinkled with whitewashed farmhouses. Here we saw the first of many chapels, surmounted by the papist cross. These farms and chapels surprised me, since I had thought that Canada, being papist, was a heathen and barbarous country. Yet I found it neater than our own province of Maine, and the houses snugger and better than most of those in Arundel.

We went rapidly down the six miles of quick water that lay between Sartigan and Arnold's headquarters, and put in at a point where there were two whitewashed farmhouses with barns and sheds.

A number of men emerged from one of the farmhouses as we came up to it, among them Lieutenant Church and Lieutenant Steele and Captain Ogden, all of whom eyed me coldly. Lieutenant Church, staring at his moccasins with his usual gloom, asked abruptly, "Where's Cap Huff?" This was the only greeting I had from any of them.

"We picked him up," I said. "He was lost. We took care of him. He'll be down to-morrow."

Church nodded and scanned the sky, as though looking for more snow. "I cal'late!" he said. Like so many of our Maine people, he didn't explain what he calculated. I interpreted it to mean that there had been no serious doubts in his mind concerning either of us at any time.

Arnold's room was sizeable, and heated with an iron stove, so that I felt my first real warmth in a month. It sent such a wave of weakness through me that I had to hold to the wall.

Arnold was talking with his commissary when we filed in, and though I thought he might, like the rest of us, be worn and weary from the march, his face was as florid, his shoulders as broad, his hair as crinkly and jetty black as ever, albeit his hair curled a little about his ears and neck, and his uniform was stained and wrinkled from soakings.

He dropped his head to stare at me from rounded, light-colored eyes. I went to his table of loose plank and placed a piece of bark

on it. On it I'd written: "Wait before rebuking Eneas and Sabatis."
He looked at it sourly, his face dark and bulbous. Then he went
to the Indians, shaking hands with each one. Finally he shook hands
with me.

"What are you doing with these—these gentlemen?" he asked.

"Sir," I said, "my friend Natanis asked me to interpret."

Arnold nodded. "Which one is Natanis?"

Natanis stepped forward, as straight as the mast of a sloop, and I
wished his face could have been free of its mask of yellow and vermilion, to let the colonel see the wisdom and kindliness in it.

They eyed each other, the rest of the Abenakis standing silent
behind us. "Truly," Natanis said, "I am your friend."

Arnold smiled when I interpreted. As I have said before, there
was something so reckless and straightforward about his smile that
the person on whom it was turned would follow him, with little per-
suasion, wherever he led.

"Why," he said, "I've been sadly misinformed. I'm his friend as
well, and the friend of all these brave men."

"That is good," said Natanis. "There are matters we must discuss
with the white chief; matters that must remain between him and us,
and discussed alone." He glanced at the commissary, an officer from
Matthew Smith's riflemen, and a hater of Indians, as could be told
when he glowered, from time to time, at the men behind me.

The commissary went out, red as an August sunset, and hotter,
unless I greatly mistook, and I knew we must keep an eye on him
to make sure we got something besides briskets and rump when beef
was butchered.

Paul Higgins spoke first, gloomy and grand with his black light-
ning-streak across his bright yellow face; for it had been agreed that
he, being sachem of the Assagunticooks, should speak for all.

"Brother," Paul said, dropping his bearskin on the floor and sitting
on it, so that Colonel Arnold might sit as well, "you are on your way
to fight for the country in which you live. This you are proud to do.
We, too, would be proud to do this, for it is as much our country
as yours. But when we went to see the great chief in Cambridge,
offering to fight behind him, he thanked us and let us come away.
He had no need of our help."

He waited a moment, and I wondered whether Arnold would have
any answer for this. I could think of none he could make. Nor could
he, it seemed; for he only popped out his eyes like grape-shot, and
said nothing.

"Brother," Paul continued, "there's no need for a great oration. We are not talkers. We prefer to help a little and to fight a little when opportunities come. Thus we will tell the white chief certain things that have happened, so he may know he has been helped, in spite of what was said to us in Cambridge.

"Brother, the Abenaki people are a proud people, unaccustomed to be scorned when they offer help. On returning from Cambridge we would have gone into the forests to hunt deer and beaver, wounded in our feelings. But your friend Steven came to us and made an oration, telling us we must go to the Height of Land to hunt, or else be liars when we said we wished to help our white brothers, regardless of money or glory."

My face was red when I interpreted this, and Arnold shot a sour look at me, saying, "Leave nothing out."

"Likewise, Brother," Paul went on, "news was spread about that one of our brothers was a spy, our brother Natanis, whom we love dearly. Men were sent to kill him; but by good fortune he was warned by your friend Steven, and so escaped to be of service to us all.

"That's enough of that," Paul said, drawing a roll of birch bark from his belt. "We came to the Height of Land to hunt, as we promised Steven. We found the hunting bad. Our brother Natanis drove two moose into the hands of the men who had been sent to kill him. Without those moose they'd have died.

"Six of our braves"—he read the names from the bark roll—"were sent to Sartigan to say food must be brought up river against the coming of the white men. That's why my brother found more food in Sartigan than had ever been seen there before. Then they made canoes, so there might be enough to carry the white men across the St. Lawrence. They made eighteen canoes, tightly sewn and pitched. These are hidden on the west bank below the falls at St. Francis on the Chaudière, where the smooth water begins.

"Some of our men were used as messengers, Brother, between Sartigan and Megantic, and there were others at intervals from the meadow at Seven Mile Stream all the way around to the lake, all of our number being thus employed." Here he read the names of the remainder of his men.

"We did not know whether we could trust the men in your army, Brother. The life of our brother Natanis was being sought. We have heard there are some among your men who have murdered Indians without cause. Perhaps this is not true. We are glad if it is not; but we had heard enough so we did not wish to go openly to them and offer our help.

"Nevertheless, Brother, there has been help given." He consulted his bark roll again. "Our brother Natanis left a map of Dead River and the Chain of Ponds at his cabin, where soldiers found it. We built a house of bark on the shore of Lake Megantic, where it could be seen by all who came down Seven Mile Stream. You camped in that house, Brother. A good bark canoe was placed where you could find it and travel in comfort with it. When you left that house we kept a fire before it each night, so that wanderers might reach it.

"When there were men lost in the swamps your friend Steven and our brother Natanis built a fire for them in the snow and warmed them. When your guide, Hull, returned to lead the army around the swamp and to the shore of Megantic, he took them into the swamps. We followed and picked up those who fell out from exhaustion, warming and feeding them. When it was seen that many could not escape and would die in the swamps, our brother Natanis guided them to safety.

"We took twenty-two men from the swamps, Brother, unconscious or so weak they couldn't walk, and put them by fires on the trail. We took nine men from the Chaudière after the bateaux were wrecked; men who would have died if our braves had not saved them. We picked up and warmed thirty-seven men on the path down the Chaudière when they were exhausted and near death.

"We stationed guards at the long portage around the Great Falls, and my brother was helped by them, as were many others who came after him. We provided canoes for the sick captain with the black beard. Two of our brothers paddled him from the Great Falls to Sartigan, fearing he might otherwise be wrecked and drowned.

"There are other things: the carrying of provisions to the army and the stealing of food for men who must otherwise have gone without; but there is no need to go into them. It is probable my brother knows the English have destroyed all canoes and boats on this side of the St. Lawrence, so that his army cannot cross. But we have with us our own canoes in addition to the eighteen new canoes. If my brother thinks it would be a help to him, we will take all these canoes to the St. Lawrence and set the army across in them. Also, if my brother thinks it would be a help to him, we will fight with him to take Quebec from the English. Brother, I have finished."

Paul got up from his bearskin and moved back among his Abenakis.

It seemed to me, as I watched Colonel Arnold staring down at his clasped hands and moving his thick, broad shoulders inside his wrinkled blue coat, that although Paul's speech had made no pretense at eloquence, it was as eloquent as any speech could have been. Therefore I was glad when he, too, made no effort at fine speaking, but spoke simply and to the point.

"Friends and Brothers," he said to them, "I know you to be both of these things, because you are generous, like all true friends and brothers. I have been much deceived in all accounts that have been given to me concerning this expedition. Nevertheless, we have come safely to this point; and I am grateful to my friends and brothers for their help. I hope my friends and brothers will continue to help us. If they will do this we will be very much obliged to them. Likewise, we will pay them ten dollars a month and a bounty of two dollars, find them their provisions and give them liberty to choose their own officers."

Now this was generous, and I could see Paul was pleased. He knew Natanis would remain with me, which would leave Paul to be chosen captain by his Abenakis. All of them were doubly pleased when Arnold, after shaking hands with them again, summoned Captain Oswald and made a great to-do about how these were his brothers, and would hereafter draw rations with the rest of the army, and at once be given a bounty of two dollars in hard money.

Oswald gave me a comical look and asked whether I was to receive the two dollars as well. Arnold shook his head doubtfully and said he would talk to me and Natanis in private—persuade us, perhaps, to settle for three dollars for the two of us.

So we found ourselves alone with him, and he threw himself down behind his plank table, saying bitterly that he supposed now I was satisfied making him look and feel like a fool. His eyes roamed around the room, as if looking for a stout projection on which he could chin himself and laugh down at us.

I told him that all our misunderstandings had been due to Treeworgy—the man I knew to be Hook: that Hook had been responsible for my father's death and would have killed him with his own hands if he had not been bound by the letter of the Ten Commandments; that he would have been happy to be responsible for my death as well.

"What I want to know," I said, "is how you came to learn of Treeworgy? Who recommended that this army use bateaux to travel up the Kennebec? Who told you Natanis was a spy?"

"I can see," he said, popping out his eyes at me, "that you think there's a connection between these things; but there isn't. It's all quite simple. While I was at Ticonderoga with that boor Ethan Allen, who has just been sent to England in irons, which may enable him to learn a few lessons in politeness, I opened a correspondence with friends in Quebec and Montreal, having this expedition in mind and wishing to learn the sentiment in both towns.

"Treeworgy came up the lake in a canoe, carrying letters from two Tories in the Plymouth Company who had it in mind to run away to England. My men captured him; and after I had looked at the letters and found he had been a clergyman, I sounded him as to carrying messages for me. He agreed, provided I sent nothing contrary to the interests of his employers and remained silent concerning his former calling; for he said he was shamed to have left it."

"That man was shamed of nothing," I said. "He hated all the world. As soon as he hated a man he tried to send him to hell fire by the quickest road. Paul Higgins says he left the ministry because he hated God for not being quick enough at punishing the unrighteous."

"It may be," Arnold said. "Nay," he added hastily, seeing me begin to simmer, "it must be! At any rate, he seemed to me like a heaven-sent opportunity, and I believed him. What's more, he returned with answers to my letters."

"Who did you write to?"

"Old business acquaintances; fine men. Halsted, Gregory, Maynard, Mercier, Manir, your old friend Guerlac——"

"There!" I shouted in triumph. "I was sure of it! Guerlac!"

"No, no!" Arnold said. "Guerlac had nothing to do with it. I asked him nothing save the feelings of the French toward us; and this he told me, very simple and straightforward."

"Who told you about the bateaux?" I asked. "And about Natanis?"

"Why, now," he said, opening his eyes wide, "that's something I shouldn't tell; nor would I, if I hadn't treated you so badly. It was Captain William Gregory I asked about the Kennebec and the Chaudière, thinking he might know it or know of someone who knew it. When his reply came back, there was a secret message under the wafer: a message that this was best known to John Woodward, who had access to government papers; that letters would reach him at the inn Le Chat Qui Pêche, the Fishing Cat."

"And Eneas. How did you learn of him as a messenger?"

"He was with Treeworgy, paddling him, when Treeworgy returned with answers to my letters. What do you think? That he betrayed me? Or was he captured, as he claimed?"

"I don't know, but I'll try to find out. And who is Woodward? Do you know Woodward?"

"Only through letters," Arnold said. "I had letters about him from Gregory. Gregory vouched for him; and I know Gregory. A fine gentleman: as dependable as the tides!"

"But it was Woodward, a man you don't know," I persisted, "who told you Natanis was a spy?"

Arnold narrowed his eyes at me. "Yes: it was Woodward who said that nothing but a bateau could live in the quick water of the upper Kennebec and Chaudière; that Colonel McLean had received reports from Natanis: reports on all persons traversing Dead River in both directions. Reports written in French and signed."

"But you didn't know Woodward! How could you take his word about Natanis?"

"Because he sent me the proof!" Arnold said impatiently. "He sent me a copy of one of Natanis's reports: also one of his receipts for the pay he received from the British—a receipt for a month's pay."

"How much did he get a month?"

"Two shillings," said the colonel, laughing.

I told this to Natanis, who shrugged his shoulders. "I think I was overpaid," he said.

I spoke to him severely, reminding him that joking had already got him into trouble.

"Yes, Steven," he said, "you're right! Tell this colonel there must be something wrong with the story, because I can't write."

"He says it's a lie," I told Arnold. "He can't write in French, or English either."

The colonel gnawed at his nails, glowering at me with a dark, bulbous face. "By God!" he shouted, banging the table with the flat of his hand, "I've been had, and I'll admit it; but I've beaten him, whoever it was, at his own game, if it was his game to keep me from reaching Quebec. We're here, and we're as good as at Quebec. To the devil with all this chattering! Go puzzle it out for yourself. If you find Treeworgy, shoot him with my blessing. If I find John Woodward, I'll give him something he won't forget!"

I was starting out with Natanis, glooming over my failure to get at the bottom of this affair, when the colonel shouted after me.

"Here! Haven't you any sense? Haven't you any demands to make at all, seeing I've near ruined you, and raised the devil with your honor?"

"No. Treeworgy's going to pay for all that. Besides, you couldn't hurt my honor with my friends: not with Natanis and Phoebe——"

At this I bethought myself. "Yes, there *is* something! Phoebe—you remember Phoebe?"

Arnold shouted with laughter, slapping his thigh. "Why shouldn't I remember her! Clever little hussy!"

"No," I said, "she's no hussy: only a simple nuisance, but a good girl. Her husband died in the swamp by Maple Leaf Pond: he wasn't just right inside, I guess."

"I'm sorry to hear it," Arnold said, staring at me in a fixed, wide-eyed way that struck me as odd. "Very sorry. What'll she do now?"

"That was one of the things I had in mind. Will you take her in your headquarters to cook for you? Then she'll be out of the way of some of these devils with us."

"I will. That's doing no one a favor but myself."

"One other thing," I said. "Until we fight I'd like to be free to look for Treeworgy; and when we fight I'd like to go along behind you, with Natanis, or with Morgan's men."

"Anything! Anything!" he snapped, seeming to be suddenly exasperated. "Now get out of here and let me go to work!"

* * *

When we came out, Lieutenant Church and Lieutenant Steele and Major Bigelow were in front of the house. Bigelow lounged over to us. "My, my!" he said, and clicked with his tongue against the roof of his mouth. "I always wondered what a couple of spies looked like!" He turned to Steele.

"I don't see how you tell 'em when they're different colors, Archibald," he said, pretending to an exaggerated admiration in his voice and attitude. "One of 'em's brown, and one of 'em's white." He looked quickly back at me, seeming to scan my face closely. "Nearly white, that is."

He winked at Natanis and shook hands with him; then took me by the front of the shirt and shook me a little. "Well," he said, "it's a good thing you stopped playing spy, because now Steele can stop worrying. He was pretty sure you were one, he said, because you looked as if you had something on your mind. He isn't accustomed to people who look like that."

Steele came to me, shamed-like, and spit carefully to leeward.

"Glad you got back all right." He grinned sheepishly at Natanis and held out his hand.

"Lieutenant Steele," I told Natanis. "You remember him."

"He hopes," I translated to Steele for Natanis, "you enjoyed the two moose he sent you."

"He thought it was careless of him not to send cows instead of moose," Bigelow said. With that he burst into his wild, false laugh, and we were glad to laugh with him, all of us. Thus we were more at our ease together than if Arnold had called out all the drums and drummed us back into favor again.

There was a great to-do over Natanis; and since it was known that he spoke to the other Indians as Brother or Cousin, always, the word went about that Eneas and Sabatis and Hobomok and Natawammet and all the rest of them were either brothers or cousins of Natanis. This is a fair sample of how much the white man knows about the Abenakis.

*   *   *

We went on down the Chaudière to the village of St. Mary's—a village that sticks in my head because it was the scene of a mysterious occurrence, one that showed clearly how injustice often meets a stern and righteous reward.

There was an inn at St. Mary's, a whitewashed wooden inn with clay-chinked boards, and in it were Frenchmen selling food: turkeys, bad brandy, and Spanish wine. We went in to ask the prices, and found Burr already there, busy with the wine and jabbering with a French girl. Somehow he contrived to look courtly and pretty, in spite of his torn breeches. He winked at me knowingly, as if to say he would show this lady a thing or two, which I had no doubt he would. I think he couldn't keep from saying soft things to any woman so long as there was none other in sight that pleased him better.

When I found out the prices I was stonied by them, and left Burr to his gallantries, glad enough to go back to the beef and potatoes that Colonel Arnold had bought for us in bulk. Cap Huff, though, seemed to have something on his mind.

While we were eating, Major Bigelow and Captain Dearborn came up on horseback, the major riding close to Dearborn and supporting him. He was bent over the horse's neck with sickness, his face above his black beard looking like the parchment of a drumhead.

We went to help Dearborn, Cap among us, and the rat-faced Flood, who had gone with Asa Hutchins to kill Dearborn's dog. We had lowered the captain to the ground and were standing about, eager to do more, when I heard an enraged bellow from Cap, and saw him take Flood by the waist and throw him on the ground.

There was a turmoil. Flood was snatched to his feet. One of the men thrust his hand into Flood's breeches pocket and drew out a purse, which Bigelow took and gave to Dearborn. I heard Cap shout, "Whip him! Whip him!" People poured from the inn; and in the twinkling of an eye, while Flood shouted, "I never! I never!" he was spliced to a post, and two men were belaboring him with willow switches.

As for Cap, he had vanished—reluctant, I thought, to witness the punishment for which he was responsible.

At St. Mary's the army was formed into companies again and we struck away from the Chaudière and across the flat plains of Canada, with Arnold stopping to watch us every little while, and Major Bigelow and Captain Thayer and Captain Topham and Captain Morgan going up and down the straggling little line of men, all of them saying nothing but "Hurry, boys; hurry! Hurry on, boys; it's not far now! Hurry along! Hurry along!"

When we came up with Cap, he was sitting on an oval-shaped wooden keg. What was in it, he said, he didn't know; but he had found it and so brought it along. It was full of Spanish wine; so we managed to be cheerful as we plodded over the snow-covered ground and through the mud of the low spots, terrible going, the mud up to the middle of our legs.

Now I spoke of what happened at St. Mary's as mysterious, and in truth the incident was mysterious for all time to its victim Flood, but it was so no longer to me. I learned from Cap Huff how he had slipped the purse into Flood's pocket, so it might be found there, and under cover of the uproar that followed had filched the Spanish wine from the inn.

*   *   *

By the grace of God the weather was warm and sunny, so that the feet of the men were not torn to pieces. Provisions were plenty, and every ten miles there was a scattering of whitewashed houses with a papist chapel in their midst, so we could sleep under roofs at night. Around the houses were Frenchmen in blanket coats and red sashes and knitted caps, each with a queue down to his waist and in his mouth a smoldering pipe smelling like the fires we have in the spring in Arundel, when we burn the sweepings of the house and all the trash accumulated beneath the winter's snows.

I don't know why these Frenchmen have faces the color of my musket stock when it needs oil, a dusty grayish brown. But in all their houses there was no male who didn't smoke, even boys of three and four years old having short pipes at which they sucked; so I think the color is smoked into their faces, as into a ham.

It was the eighth of November when we shook ourselves free of a fresh fall of snow and came up a little rise on which stood Arnold and Bigelow and Steele and Church and a score more, looking off to the northward. Down beneath us was a wind-whipped river, so wide that two frigates lying in midstream looked no bigger than peapods. On the far side was a tremendous headland, higher at the upstream end, like a giant dog, all picked out in dazzling white because of the newly fallen snow.

There was a fringe of houses along the legs and belly of this giant dog, and a jumble of spires and gray stone buildings around its flanks. On its head were squat buildings with a blood-red flag flying above them.

We stood there silent. Others moved up the ridge, musket straps squeaking, rawhide moccasins rasping, and stood silent beside us as well. What the others thought I don't know; but I thought that in one of those jumbles of gray buildings was Mary Mallinson, beautiful and slender, with a dust of golden freckles on her white skin. I had a powerful fear I might somehow be prevented from going to her, now that I had waited all these years, and come through a terrible journey for the chance.

I might have had other and greater thoughts, but just then a boy from Thayer's company, a boy with no shoes, came up behind us, standing on one foot and then on the other, to keep the numbness from them.

He stared long across the river, silent with the rest of us. At last it was he that broke the silence.

"Gosh! Is that Quebec?"

BOOK IV

LADY OF THE SNOWS

XXVIII

Q UEBEC, scornful and aloof in her white mantle, put me in mind of a woman: caring nothing, to outward view, for these dirty, ragged, limping, hairy men who had accomplished the impossible and burst from the trackless wilderness to stare at her with hot and hungry eyes, yet watchful of their every move; eager to know their thoughts; fearful lest she succumb to them against her will; subject, even, to moments of weakness when, had we known, she might have softened at our touch.

I cannot tell how dangerous we were in those first few days that we lay strung along the high bank of Point Levis; but I know there was never a band of men who looked readier for rapine or murder. There were six hundred of us when the wanderers had straggled in; and none with anything to his name save the scurvy rags in which he stood, the shredded remnant of a blanket, a battered pack, and a musket foul with rust. Many had less; for even blankets had been torn from some by the rivers we had passed, or used long since for clothing.

There was a devilish wind each night, kicking up a chop that would swamp the staunchest canoe; so we could do nothing but lie where we were until the wind went down.

Here we heard how General Schuyler, commanding the army that aimed to come down the St. Lawrence, capture Montreal and join Colonel Arnold before Quebec, had been obliged to go away on other military matters, leaving the leadership of his regiments to General Richard Montgomery. Then there was incessant talk of Montgomery, how he had been a respected British officer, and had come over to us to fight against his own people because, some said, he had married an American, and because, according to others, he had not been treated justly by the British. We didn't care what the reason was, so long as he fought for us. In such a case, it seems to me, any reason becomes a good reason, just as any reason that leads a man to fight against us is considered a bad reason.

While we waited, the companies were mustered, and passed in review before Colonel Arnold; and I swear that any man who saw them without knowing what they had encountered would have laughed himself sick at such travesties on troops.

What with starvation, fluxes, coughs and rheumatics, they limped and wavered in their marching, more like cripples than soldiers. Half went barefoot in the snow, though the hides of our beeves had been turned into moccasins. Mostly they marched bareheaded to the cold Canadian wind, their hats long lost in the swamps of Megantic.

Their breeches were in shreds, held together by strips cut from the edges of blankets, or not held together at all. Stockings had vanished, and their legs were scarred beyond belief by the roots and brambles through which they had stumbled.

I have built many a scarecrow since that day, to keep the crows from our young corn in Arundel; and I have never done so without thinking how much more warmly and genteelly my scarecrows have been dressed than were the men who marched in review in sight of proud Quebec, white-cloaked and scornful in the distance.

It was on the thirteenth that the wind went down for the first time. I have little patience with those who fear the thirteenth day of any month as one that will bring disaster; but I would have been better pleased if we had crossed on some day other than the thirteenth; and so, too, would Colonel Arnold; for he had gnawed his fingers since our arrival at Levis on the eighth, fretting to get across and at the city's throat.

We had thirty-five canoes; four passengers to a canoe was all we could carry; for there were two British frigates in mid-stream, eager to blow us out of water, and so stationed that we must pass between them. Thus we had to go swiftly and silently; for with the discovery of one canoe, the entire flotilla, strung out on that mile-wide river, would be in danger.

At dark we brought the canoes out of hiding at Caldwell's mill, a stone building on the shore of the St. Lawrence where a little stream flows in. There the ragged army waited. The night was bitter cold, and dark as pine woods at midnight. We stood and shivered in this blackness when Arnold came among us and spoke to us. There was a rasping quality to his voice, always: irritating when he was in a rage; but one that moved his hearers to excitement when there were stirring things afoot. I think we shivered as much from the sound of his voice as from the cold.

"Now," he said, "don't spoil this by shouting or shooting. Be very quiet. Patrol boats pass between the frigates each hour. When one of us is discovered, we're all discovered. If we're *not* discovered, we can take Quebec this night. I hope by the grace of God we can do it; but if we can't, then we'll cut off its provisions and take it later. If ever any men earned the glory of taking this city, it's you! I believe no other men in the world could have endured what you have, and come as far as this, ready and willing to fight."

He went into the canoe with Lieutenant Church, Lieutenant Steele, Daniel Morgan, and a Mr. Halsted, who had come out from Quebec through friendship for Colonel Arnold and was now confident of leading us to a landing place at Wolfe's Cove, whence we could mount to the Plains of Abraham. Riflemen and musketmen packed themselves into the canoes, helter-skelter, until there were four in each besides the paddlers.

We slipped off after Arnold. I, paddling bow, could just see the glimmer of white at Steele's left shoulder, where his shirt had been torn so his skin showed through. There was no sound, only the sucking of the current at the canoe and the lapping of ripples against the sides; little to see save a fleck of light here and there on the far shore.

I so closely watched Steele's shoulder that my heart jumped into my throat when he sheered suddenly downstream, and there loomed on my left the blacker bulk of one of the British frigates, so near that a sailor, standing at her bulwarks, might have spat on us.

All in all, the crossing would have been peaceful, with nothing to distract me from thinking of Mary Mallinson and from framing the words I should say to her when we had at last entered Quebec—nothing except schools of villainous white porpoises, which Natanis said cruised perpetually in that tremendous stretch of waters.

These porpoises didn't roll languidly, as they roll on summer days near Arundel, but whizzed through the water in every direction in twos and fives and twenties, as if desperate to get somewhere.

There was a pale streak above each fish, like foam with moonlight glinting on it, a streak of cold, wavering, bluish-white fire. I have heard since that the antics of these white porpoises are admired by travelers, but when they darted between Steele's canoe and our own, I wished them all in hell.

Somehow the porpoises, and the cussedness of them, set me to thinking of Phoebe. I knew I must do something about her, lest she be left on the wrong side of the river and have to go to living in one of those whitewashed farms with a lot of long-tailed Frenchmen, so that she would turn all shriveled and leathery from their stinking pipes.

We came into smooth water where there were no more porpoises. I could feel, rather than see, a high bulk of land hanging over us. Canoe-bottoms grated on pebbles, and men splashed in shallows.

When we slid in beside Steele he whispered hoarsely: "Wolfe's Cove!" and there came to my mind that distant day when my father had drunk to red-headed James Wolfe for scaling the cliff from this very cove and taking Quebec.

I remember thinking to myself it ought to seem a mighty strange business, coming to this spot in the dead of night, following in the footsteps of James Wolfe; but it didn't seem strange at all: only a commonplace occurrence, like sculling down a guzzle at Swan Island to kill geese.

We could hear canoes coming in, upstream and downstream from us. Since we had three trips to make, we pushed off at once, and went back faster for being unloaded. Cap Huff was waiting patiently, watching over Phoebe and Jacataqua. I told him to have them ready for the third trip, and to say, in case of questioning, that both of them had been ordered to report to Arnold's headquarters at once.

Cap asked whether I had seen the frigates. When I said I had, he asked hoarsely whether it would be possible for a few of us to board one of them. I sniffed, thinking he must have stolen a keg of Spanish wine and drunk it all himself, and so become inflamed in the head. But it has occurred to me since that if he had known of a cash customer for a frigate, he might have found some way to acquire one that night.

It was after midnight when we set down our second load in Wolfe's Cove. There was a moaning of the wind in the tree branches above us: signs of breaking in the clouds that covered the moon—two portents I misliked, for I had no wish to be spilled into this bottomless river, nor any desire to be shot by a frigate's crew. Therefore we made haste on our third trip, knowing it would be our last.

Cap and his charges were waiting for us, and we took them aboard. Phoebe came close up behind me for warmth, and when she put her arms around my waist I could feel she was wearing her leather-bound shot on her wrist. When I asked her whether she had used it she said nothing, only put her head against the small of my back and shivered. I heard Jacataqua's yellow-faced dog climb in while she and Ivory and Noah were settling themselves, and then Burr's voice declaring he might as well go with us.

Having an overloaded canoe as it was, I told him to keep away lest I slap him with the paddle, calling to Natanis at the same time to push off. There were some things about Burr that were beginning to set ill on me, particularly when I was cold and hungry.

The wrack of clouds, whipped by a rising wind from the northwest, was thinner, so there began to be light from the hidden moon—a light that let us see other canoes faintly; and there was a wicked chop that slapped and slapped at our canoe, slapping water into our faces. I clung close to Steele, knowing he had a knack of coming through troublous times without taking hurt.

It's said we only remember pleasant things, but I've never forgotten that last crossing and there was nothing pleasant about it. Each of us had taken in more than was safe, knowing we couldn't get back that night. I could hear Natanis grunting with each stroke of his paddle, forcing the canoe against the bitter wind.

We slipped safely between the frigates; and it seemed to me the worst was past, when a school of white porpoises came suddenly on us, groaning and blowing spray as if contemptuous of our puny strivings, cutting through the water like mad things and lighting themselves on their way with streaks of pale blue fire.

While I cursed and struck at them with my paddle there came a half-strangled shout from Steele's canoe. I saw the two ends fly into the air. There was a sound of rattling and scrambling from it; and in an instant every man was in the water. The canoe, broken in the middle by a blow from one of those damnable, nonsensical fishes, wallowed half sunk and useless.

We were among the men at once. Jacataqua leaned over and took one of them by the neck—a tall Virginia rifleman, George Merchant by name, a reckless devil from Morgan's company.

The others caught the thwarts of canoes, or were held by men in them. We still followed Steele's torn shirt when we went on; for he had passed his arms over the stern of a canoe, and the paddler sat on them, so that when he was numbed by the icy water he couldn't lose his hold.

These men could not be taken into canoes in midstream and so we dragged them.

We were little more than halfway across; and our best speed, with the rising wind and the added weight, was poor enough. Phoebe sat far to the left, hanging over the water, so that Jacataqua could hold to her Virginian on the other side without swamping us; and hang to him she did, refusing to let Noah or Jethro come to her help. It may have been for the best. I could hear Jacataqua talking to this rifleman, and I could hear him answer, low and reckless. Once, hearing Phoebe sniff, I looked around, and it seemed to me Jacataqua's lips were closer to his than necessary; but it may be she made the blood run more rapidly in his veins than would have been the case if Noah or Jethro had held him, and that he was saved from a quinsy or from the sad fate of poor McClellan.

When we came ashore at last these poor men could not move their legs. Arnold, seeing what had happened, gave orders for the kindling of a fire in an empty house that stood near by, though he had forbidden fires to all others lest we be discovered. When this had been done and the castaways held before it, they soon thawed out.

We had crossed with no time to spare; for even as we made ready to mount the path to the Plains of Abraham there came, from the river, the sound of oars grinding between thole-pins. It drew nearer and nearer, and proved to be a patrol from a frigate, coming to see what had made our fire. One of our men shouted to the boat to come in, at which the rowing stopped. In the light of the pale moon we could dimly see the small craft drifting downstream. After a little it started to move out again, whereupon the rifles of the Virginians spat fire, and a crying and groaning arose from the boat, which continued to move outward, nevertheless.

We scrambled up a steep path, Colonel Arnold leading us, and came breathless to the top of the cliff to find ourselves on a snow-covered plain. Ahead of us, throngs of vague specters milled and muttered. They were forming into companies. I said to myself that we had done what we started to do, almost: we had reached Quebec, and now there was nothing left to do but take it. There was no excitement in the thought. After the cold and hunger and weariness we had endured, there was, it seemed to me, no excitement in anything.

A company of riflemen, headed by Captain Smith, came out of the gloom at our right, where there was a mass of houses or walls too distant to be distinguished, and I heard him report to Morgan that he had been the length of the walls, and that there was no suspicion of our presence. He added, too, that all the gates were tight shut, with no sentries in sight. Even while I listened I heard the cry of the watch in Quebec, shouting: "Five o'clock and all's well!"

Now I served in the army for some few years, at Quebec and later at Saratoga, where Arnold, with his wild courage and the help of

Daniel Morgan and this same Henry Dearborn whose black dog was taken away by Asa Hutchins to be eaten, gave Burgoyne the drubbing that took America from the British forever. In that time I heard strange tales, most of them false; for few persons know so little concerning what they are doing, or what is going on about them, as soldiers, unless it be sailors or hairdressers, both of whom brim with misinformation. Among these tales is one that went abroad among us within a day or so of the time when we set foot on the Plains of Abraham, when deserters and spies had come out to us from the city: the tale that St. John's Gate in the city walls had stood open all that first night, so that we might have walked in and made ourselves masters of Quebec.

It is God's truth that if we could have brought our scaling ladders across on our canoes—the scaling ladders our carpenters and blacksmiths had made in the five days we lay at Point Levis, waiting for the wind to die down—we would have scaled the walls that night; and as sure as we had scaled them the city would have fallen; for if ever men were desperate, our men were. So, too, were Colonel Arnold and Daniel Morgan; and I care not what any man may say of those two soldiers; or how he may point to what he may think they have been at this time or at another, or to what they may have done under one circumstance or the other circumstance. I knew them both, and I say this: neither among the Americans nor among the British during all our long war was there any leader after Washington who approached them in daring or recklessness, or exceeded them in bravery, ever.

And though I am sick of "ifs," and weary of listening to folk who tell what they would have done had they been twenty years younger or had events fallen out differently, I cannot help but set down what is the truth. Could we have finished our march a few days earlier we would have walked into the city and taken it, for it had neither defenders nor leaders worth the mentioning until the fifth of November, when a frigate and one hundred and fifty men came to Quebec from Newfoundland, followed on the twelfth by Colonel Allen McLean, who came down the St. Lawrence and into the city with another one hundred and sixty men, all of them recruits.

Yet these things are beside the mark. What I am getting at is this: Matthew Smith led his riflemen the length of the walls in the blackness of that bitter November morning, and he returned with the news that the gates were fast shut. I have no love for Matthew Smith, because of what he did at Conestoga and at Lancaster Gaol. None the less he was a fighter, reckless of the odds against him. So, too, were his riflemen, all of them willing to engage a regiment of men or devils, and all certain of success because of the deadly accuracy of their rifles. Therefore I say there was no gate open into Quebec that night; for if there had been Matthew Smith would have found it and gone in, for that was the sort of man Smith was.

✳   ✳   ✳

While I was hunting Goodrich's company in the dark, Burr came up to me, grumpy and sour.

"Here," he said, "I want you to do something about this!"

"About what?"

"Why, it's a shame and disgrace the way this red wench of yours has taken up with a common soldier—one of those damned Virginians, too! When I go to talk to her she treats me like the dirt under her feet and clings to that damned clod-hopping Virginian as if he were a gentleman!"

"I know nothing about it," I said. "She's no wench of mine, and I won't stick my nose into what doesn't concern me. I've seen too much of that in Arundel."

"Well," he said, "you take an interest in what she does, don't you?"

"Yes," I said, "I take an interest, but I won't try to regulate her. The law of the Abenakis says an Abenaki woman does as she pleases. If she wishes to marry a man, she goes to his bed and there's an end of it. If she wishes to divorce him, she leaves his bed and there's an end of *that*. That's one reason why our white poeple can never live in friendship with Indians. They can live with no one they can't regulate."

"Well, it's a shame and disgrace," Burr insisted. "If you wished, you could persuade her to go to headquarters with your friend Phoebe to help with the cooking."

"It seems to me no more shameful or disgraceful," I said, "than if she should travel to Quebec with you."

"Pah!" said Burr. "That's entirely different! What can this common soldier do for her?"

To this there were many answers in my mind, but it seemed wiser to withhold them. I growled a little, as Maine folk do when not wishful of answering, and set off again to look for Goodrich's company.

Phoebe had attached herself to Noah Cluff. "Look here," I told her, "go straight to the kitchen of whatever house Arnold takes as headquarters, and take Jacataqua with you."

"And have this little pickerel Burr darting around our feet day and night? I won't do it, Steven!"

"Now here!" I said. "I want none of this foolishness! You can do as you like about Jacataqua, of course; but I want you to waste no time getting to the kitchen."

"No," she said, "I'm not going to do it! Noah says he'll die if I leave him, so I'll stay with him. Then you won't worry about having me on your hands."

"Oh, for God's sake!" I said. "This is the most damnable thing I ever heard!"

"No," she said, "I don't choose you should have me on your hands."

"You *won't* be on my hands! Not as much as though you stayed with Noah. Noah indeed, the damned old fool!"

"Was you speaking about me?" asked Noah, yawning.

"Well, I won't be on your hands, and that's all there is to it," Phoebe said. "That's what you were afraid of when we left. Anyway, you've got another woman to think of now."

"Who?" I asked, thick-witted from the cold.

"Why," said Phoebe, speaking so mealy-mouthed as to sicken me, "why, somewhere I've had the thought there was someone in Quebec you had to save from a dreadful, dreadful fate!"

I looked at her sternly, but she returned my glance with such a steady long look of mockery that all I could do, it seemed, was turn from her disgustedly and go my ways.

*   *   *

A little before dawn Arnold and Morgan, followed by the riflemen and the rest of us, set off across the Plains of Abraham; and in the gray of the early morning we came up to a large manor house with workmen's cottages and barns and sheds, all forming a pile five times the size of our garrison house at Arundel, and all belonging, the officers said, to Major Henry Caldwell, commanding the British militia in Quebec.

When we surrounded the buildings and moved in on them, we found eight or ten servants loading food and furniture and pictures and rugs into teams, everything ready to hand. Yet we couldn't make free with these belongings, since Colonel Arnold ordered them to be taken into the house again. We dispersed in search of quarters, and I found myself with a part of Captain Goodrich's company in a small building beside the manor house, most of the rooms in the manor house having been seized by Morgan's riflemen.

I would have wasted no time in falling asleep had not Natanis come into the room and signaled to me to come out. He pointed to the roof of the manor house and on it I saw Cap Huff crouched with a stupendous armful of material. He threw it down to us, and we took it quickly to our quarters.

When Cap came in he wiped his sweaty face on a corner of the silk comforter in which his spoils were wrapped, and said he had been obliged to work like lightning to get ahead of Morgan's riflemen.

"Gosh!" he said angrily. "Those men don't think of *anything* but stealing! All I could do was clean out a closet and throw it into this comforter."

"What did you get?"

"I don't know. I didn't have time to look, but it was clothes, and we can trade clothes for *anything*."

We untied the comforter and found a number of garments belonging to the lady of the manor, among them some lace-trimmed inexpressibles, a haircloth bustle, a pair of stays, and two dresses of sprigged muslin. There were three pairs of breeches, but they were for a boy half the size of Phoebe, as were two roundabout jackets and three frilled shirts.

I expected Cap to burst into profanity that would set fire to the buildings; but the disappointment must have been too great. He rolled the things in the stays, made for a woman the size of a haystack, took them to where Phoebe was lying wrapped in her blanket beside Noah Cluff, and kicked the soles of her feet until she roused up and looked at him, her chopped-off hair sticking out from her head like that of a small boy. Still preserving an outraged silence, Cap hurled his bundle at her, so that it struck her on the chest. Then he swathed himself in the comforter and crawled in between Natanis and me.

*　　*　　*

It was late in the morning when I awoke. Cap was gone. The warmth of the room and the ceiling over my head—two unaccustomed luxuries—fuddled me completely. I though I was in Arundel and wiggled my nose for a whiff of Malary's coffee and bacon. Then it came to me that we were lying outside the walls of Quebec; that within those walls was Mary Mallinson, waiting to be taken from her captors and back to her own people.

We had wheat cakes and freshly killed pork from Phoebe, who told us proudly she could make good use of the garments Cap had given her. All she needed now, she added, with a sidelong glance at me, was some sort of fur garment, so she could clothe herself decently and play the spy in order to find out for me how my friends were progressing in the city.

Uneasy at her talk, I took Natanis and set off for the city walls, along the ridge at whose extremity lies Quebec.

If I had come as a farmer, looking for land to cultivate, I would have held this country in esteem; for the fields were smooth and rolling, well situated to attract summer rains and deep snows, which lend fertility to any soil. They fell away on our left into an enormous shallow valley; and at its far rim stood a long, long range of mountains, so there was a spaciousness to our surroundings that I had thought could only be found on the shore of the ocean.

Yet it was not as a farmer that I looked at it, but as one who had come to wrest it from its owners; so I could see little about it that was good. There was meager cover on those high plains; and I knew the wind and snows from the north would sweep down from the distant mountains and across that broad valley, piercing our poor rags as easily as newly sharpened scalping knives. Also if ever a place defied the devil himself to take it, it was this city of Quebec, built on a towering rock thrust out like a wedge to separate the St. Lawrence and the St. Charles rivers.

In the distance we could see the long, low line of the walls, with the spires and gables of the upper town rising above it; and between us and the walls three clusters of houses—to the left the suburb of St. Roque; in the center the suburb of St. John; and far over toward the right, the suburb of St. Louis. These suburbs were built around the city gates—St. Roque outside Palace Gate; St. John outside St. John's Gate; and St. Louis outside St. Louis's Gate.

On the extreme right the wall rose up to a high bastion on the peak of Cape Diamond; and because we had seen it from the far side of the river we knew it was perched on top of a perpendicular cliff towering three hundred feet above the St. Lawrence—though to us it seemed to rise from a rolling field. On the extreme left, too, where the wall ended at Palace Gate, we knew the land fell away to the St. Charles River. If, therefore, the wall was unscalable, there was only one method of attack: to go down to the shore of one of the two rivers, towering cliffs on one side and water on the other, and scramble all the way around the damned rock in the hope of finding a passageway from the lower town at the water's edge to the upper town, high up on the headland.

When we came closer to the wall we saw it was built of blocks of dirty gray stone. There were ports in it with the muzzles of cannon showing through; nor was there anything but wall to be seen, for its height cut off our sight of everything behind it.

We went close to the suburb of St. John, made up of neat small houses on rolling ground, with thickets of trees among them. While we debated whether we should go closer, there came a burst of shouts and a violent snarling from a thicket near the western edge of the suburb. We could see men struggling in the thicket. Almost at once a man ran toward the stragglers from trees far to their left, while another man started toward them from behind a hillock far to their right. These were our men, I could see. It came to me suddenly they were pickets, running toward another of our pickets who had been captured.

Ahead of us, among the houses of the suburb, there was incessant shouting and snarling. As we ran forward, we saw six men hurrying a seventh through the snow toward the wall. At their heels, snarling and slashing at them, was Jacataqua's yellow-faced dog, while closing in on them and being struck and thrown off again, was Jacataqua herself.

At this I knew that the captured man must be Jacataqua's new friend—George Merchant, the Virginia rifleman.

I stopped, primed my musket, and fired, but the distance was too great for accuracy. Heads showed along the top of the wall, and a faint noise of cheering came to us. Other riflemen came up, cursing, and wasted shots.

From the distant group a pistol was fired at the yellow-faced dog. He ran in a circle, biting at his tail. St. John's Gate swung open before the struggling men. All seven of them scurried through; and as they went, one of them struck Jacataqua and threw her into the snow beside the gate, which swung shut behind them.

Jacataqua picked herself up, went to the gate and beat against it with her fists, then turned to her dog. When he followed her, holding his rump gingerly, we saw the pistol ball had broken his tail near the base.

Natanis led me to the tracks of the seven men.

"Here is something to think about," he said, touching one footprint with his finger and then another. I failed to get his meaning.

He laughed. "You forget your lessons! Do you remember how Paul Higgins said to us that Treeworgy, like Hook, walked on the inside of his heels with his toes turned out, taking no grip on the ground?"

I looked again at the footprints. The marks of the heels were deep at the inner edge; those of the toes were shallow.

Jacataqua borrowed a knife from a rifleman and sliced off her dog's tail at the wound, so that he had less than an inch to wag.

She was quiet, showing no rage, only a little moodiness, such as a girl might show at dropping grease on a new ribbon; but from the way she hefted the knife in her right hand, I knew there was more than moodiness in her heart.

"Did you see anything familiar about those men?" I asked.

She said nothing for a time, but watched her dog staring reproachfully at the remnant of his tail, first from one side and then from the other.

At length she said: "No, but I won't forget the one with the brown beard and the white blanket coat—the one that shot Anatarso! His face——" She broke off suddenly and pointed her knife at me. "Why, yes! Treeworgy! That was Treeworgy!"

So Hook was in Quebec!

*   *   *

We could hear distant shouting, and the beat of a drum, and there was movement among those who stood behind the ramparts, watching us. Looking back along the road, we saw a column of troops coming down it.

Arnold led them, with Oswald, Ogden, Colonel Greene and Major Bigelow. I thought to fall in with Morgan's men, but Bigelow motioned me in beside him.

"What happened?" he asked. "We heard they were coming out."

"No," I said, "they caught Merchant, out of Morgan's company, in a hole and dragged him into the city before you could say Sam Adams."

"Well," he said, "the colonel thinks if they see what we look like they'll come out to drag all of us in. That's why he's parading us."

"I wish to God they would!" I said, thinking that if they did I might have a chance to get at Hook. "Maybe they will! They came out for Wolfe."

"The *French* came out for Wolfe," Bigelow corrected me. "Montcalm happened to go crazy on that particular day, and accidents like that don't happen twice in succession. Besides, these people are English. They won't go crazy. I can hear them in there now!"

He aped an Englishman's speech, chewing his words in the fore part of his mouth. "What! Go out among a lot of silly rebel tradesmen? Faugh, faugh! Pugh, pugh! Remember Montcalm!" He shook back imaginary lace from his wrist and took a pinch of imaginary snuff, affecting to sneeze horribly. I left him and fell in behind Morgan's men.

We were a sorry-looking crew, and fewer than I supposed, what with Captain Hanchet having been left at Point Levis with sixty men to guard our scaling ladders, and those who had been unable to get in the canoes, and the sick who had remained on the other side to regain their health.

When we deployed before the walls the folk on them set up a cheer and waved their hats. It may have been, as some thought, a friendly cheer; but to me it seemed ironical, as if they held our pretensions lightly. My suspicion was confirmed when, after our exchange of cheers, they let off a thirty-six pounder at us. I think they forgot to aim in their excitement, for the balls went every which way. Our men made contemptuous jeering noises by thrusting out their tongues and forcing air around them. Also they pursued the cannon balls through the snow, and brought them back to show to the garrison in derision. Some of the riflemen moved in closer to pick off a few lobster-backs, but the range was too long. From where we were we could see the icy patches on the walls we hoped to scale, and the deep stone trench below them like an open, icy grave—a most displeasing sight.

When it became apparent that the British were content to remain behind their ramparts, jeering at us and playing with their thirty-six pounder, Colonel Arnold sent Ogden forward to the gate under a flag of truce, with a demand that the city surrender. The garrison may have thought the white flag was a French flag; or they may merely have been British, great believers in their own nobility in war, but not so noble in actual practice, as we discovered on every occasion when we met them. At all events, they let off their thirty-six pounder at Ogden and his white flag when he was halfway to the gate, missing him, though not by a sufficient margin for comfort. He marched serenely back to us, but I suspect he had a shrinking feeling in his rear during the march, from the thought of receiving a thirty-six pound ball in that quarter.

So we went back again to Caldwell's manor house; and, knowing him to be the commander of the militia who had fired on our flag of truce, we slaughtered his cattle with clear consciences, which we would have done no matter who he was.

XXIX

WE LACKED many things in those first days before Quebec: breeches, shoes, razors, soap, shirts, blankets, hats, money, stockings, muskets, needles, thread, bayonets, pipes, tobacco. . . . No beggars, in short, could have had less than we.

Yet we might have endured our destitution without much trouble but for two things: we lacked men to set up a proper blockade of the roads going into Quebec, and powder to make a fight in case a force should come out from the city and take us front and rear. When our powder was measured there was enough to provide each man with four rounds; and four rounds is barely enough to smell up the barrel of a musket, let alone raise a dust on folk who are after your life.

Therefore the colonel, learning General Montgomery had captured Montreal and would soon march down river to join him, made up his mind to drop back out of danger and wait for Montgomery's arrival; then return to Quebec again with enough men to blockade the roads and cut off the city's provisions, and enough powder to blow holes in everybody.

When I heard the army was to fall back, I went hunting Cap Huff; for I hadn't seen him since he was disappointed in his personal looting of Major Caldwell's manor house.

Remembering his dislike of the French, and his determination to take home one of their queues as a souvenir, I was uneasy about him. It may be Cap was rude and uncouth, as some folk have ever believed and said, and seldom a beautification of the politer side of social life. Yet I found him restful because what he said never caused me to feel the need of thinking. The fact is that whatever he was, he was my friend. I need say no more to any man who has had a friend. One who has no friends could never understand my disquiet at this time, no matter how much I might say.

I asked here and there concerning him; but no man, it seemed, had seen or heard of him for days. I sent Natanis, Hobomok, and Jacataqua to find him if they could—Natanis along the road that skirts

the St. Lawrence, to the little town of Sillery; Hobomok along the
main road to Montreal, running out through the town of St. Foy's;
Jacataqua toward the settlements along the St. Charles River. While
they hunted I sat worrying and cursing Cap for an irresponsible fool;
for it had been decided that early on the following morning the army
would move back through St. Foy's to Pointe-aux-Trembles, some
twenty-four miles up the St. Lawrence; and God only knew what
would become of Cap if he were left alone.

Hobomok came back in the afternoon, declaring nobody in St.
Foy's had seen hide or hair of him; and toward dusk Jacataqua returned from the banks of the St. Charles with similar tidings. But
when Natanis came in, a little after nightfall, he had news. He had
gone out along the bluff of the St. Lawrence toward Sillery, passing
the tree-surrounded summer homes of wealthy Quebec folk, and had
found scuffed footprints wavering toward one of them. The footprints, big as bear-tracks, led to a side porch, where there was a
broken window. He entered the house and found himself in a kitchen,
in which were many empty brandy bottles, and a feather mattress
on the floor, and on the white wall the print of an enormous hand,
where its owner had leaned against the wall to raise the trap door
which, in all Canadian kitchens, conceals the staircase to the cellar.
This print, Natanis said, must have been made by the hand of Cap
Huff.

Cap had gone staggering off through the trees, bumping into them
and falling down, as Natanis could see from the tracks in the snow; so
Natanis trailed him. The tracks led to another summer house, where
there were more empty bottles, and on the kitchen floor a bed made
out of pillows.

"I think," Natanis said in conclusion, "that even still your friend
cannot go far without falling down in the snow. If we go at once to
Sillery, we may find him before he does himself a hurt."

We set off, the four of us, as soon as we could roll our packs. The
night was dark and the snow deep; and I was glad we were groping
for the roads of Canada rather than those of New England. They
have a custom in Canada, because of the violent snows, of marking
the roads on each side with upright pines, so that even though snow
falls each day, which it often does, there are always lines of pine
trees to guide the traveler on his way. It is the law, too, that after a
storm each Canadian must go out with a horse and one of the squat
sleighs they call carioles and drive along that portion of the road that
lies before his property. Thus the roads are always partly broken.

Natanis showed us the first house where signs of Cap's occupancy had been discovered. The second house, he said, was half a cross beyond—half the distance between two of the crosses that the papist French plant along their roads, as thick as fence posts in Maine, each cross surmounted with all manner of implements: shears, scaling ladders, hammers and tongs; frog-spears, bottles and roosters.

We came up to this second house to hear a tumult within, shouts and thumps and laughter, and then a bawling voice, familiarly hoarse, shouting the words of a song I came to know better, later:

> "Vive la Canadienne,
> Vole, mon cœur, vole;
> Vive la Canadienne
> Et ses jolis yeux doux!
> Et ses jolis yeux doux, doux, doux,
> Et ses jolis yeux doux!"

I opened the door and walked into a dark little hall and thence into a snug candle-lit kitchen with strips of colored paper pasted around the windows to keep out the bitter wind and the snow powder. There were Cap and an old, old Frenchman with a queue so long he could sit on the end of it, and a younger Frenchman and his brown-faced wife. There were three brown-faced girls, two about the age of Jacataqua and the other the size of a mosquito, and a brown-faced boy not more than five years old with a pipe between his teeth and a rope end braided into his queue to give it substance, all of them sitting before a pot-bellied iron stove red-hot around the neck.

The boy with the pipe was perched on one of Cap's knees, and the small girl on the other. When Cap saw my face at the door he leaped to his feet, spilling his young friends on the floor.

"Ho!" Cap bawled. "It's about time you got around! Hey, Zhulie! Hey, Lizette! Friend! Friend! Amee! Amee!"

He bellowed in a way to deafen everybody, as was his habit when he hoped to make himself understood by persons of alien speech. His French friends stared silently and timorously at the four of us: me with my rough clothes, and Natanis and Hobomok, and Jacataqua with her hand twisted in the scruff of Anatarso's neck. We must have had a look of wildness that would have quieted a gathering of New York gaolbirds, let alone a peaceable French family.

"What in God's name have you been doing?" I asked. "I've been in a state about you, you blundering ox!"

"What are you talking about!" he exclaimed. "Can't I take a little walk without being spied on?"

"A little walk!" I cried. "How many days do you need for a little walk? Didn't you get enough walking on the Chaudière?"

"What's the matter with you!" he growled benevolently, giving Jacataqua an affectionate slap in the ribs that made her cough.

"The matter is that the army moves back to Pointe-aux-Trembles at dawn to-morrow. I've been hunting you high and low so you wouldn't be left alone in this damned country, and spend the rest of your days in a British prison."

Cap rubbed his red face with his vast hands.

"To-morrow! They couldn't go to-morrow! They just got there!"

"You fool! How long do you think you've been away?"

"Two days," Cap said, scratching his head.

"Well, there's something wrong with your arithmetic, because all of us know you've been gone five days."

"Like hell I have! I slept in a kitchen night before last. Last night I slept here in this kitchen with Pierre Lemoine and his wife and his mother and his son and his three daughters and a dog, and I think there was a pig as well, though maybe it was a cow."

"It's not worth arguing about," I said, "but Natanis found two kitchens where you slept, both full of empty brandy bottles. God knows how many other places you occupied!"

Cap came close to me, smelling brutally of garlic and wearing a smirk that made his round red face look like the full moon coming up out of the ocean on a hot summer night. "That accounts for it! I was put to it to understand how all that stuff could have come out of one house." He came closer and breathed on me until I near choked. "Listen, Stevie: did you ever hear of Normandy cider?"

I shook my head, strangled by his nearness.

"Why wasn't we told about it, Steven?" he demanded. "Steven, that's a great drink! They got brandy in those cellars forty years old! Fifty, some of 'em! I want to tell you, Steven: you take a gallon of that Normandy cider and add a pint of old brandy to it, and you got a drink to put hair on a pumpkin!" He shook his head, as if recalling something that gave him pain. "Listen, Steven: I can talk French!" He rolled his eyes at the ceiling, put his head on one side, and ejaculated in a high, monotonous voice: "*On Normandee noo boovong doo see-druh.*"

"What did you mean," I asked, when I had pushed him away from me, "by saying you didn't understand how all that stuff could have come out of one house? All what stuff?"

Cap passed his hand reflectively over his moist red forehead. "Didn't I tell you about the picture? The picture of Philadelphia as Seen from Cooper's Ferry?"

I shook my head.

"Didn't I tell you about getting the cariole? Didn't I ask you whether you had any use for a fur coat or some silver knives and forks and spoons?"

"Nothing at all: you asked me nothing at all. We've just come here."

"Yes," he said thoughtfully, "I believe you're speaking the truth, since I ain't seen you for two days or five or something. Steven, I've got the most beautiful picture: Philadelphia as Seen from Cooper's Ferry."

"I could use knives and forks and spoons," I said. "Leastways, my mother could. And what was that about a fur coat?"

"Let me tell you about this picture," Cap insisted.

"What kind of fur was the coat? Was it a man's or a woman's?"

"I dunno," Cap said. "I can't hardly tell the difference between 'em. I think it was sable, though I disremember."

"Well," I said, "I want that coat."

"I got to tell you about this picture. This is the most beautiful picture in the world. Philadelphia as Seen from Cooper's Ferry. It's engraved. You can see ships on the river and people walking on shore, all as lifelike as if they was alive. I'd ruther have it than any picture I ever see! There's another one there, an oil painting, twice as big, of cows in a field; but I'd a thousand times ruther have my Philadelphia as Seen from Cooper's Ferry. You can see a cow any time, and there ain't anyone don't know what a cow looks like; but it ain't everyone that can get to Philadelphia, and looking at my picture is just like going there—better, too, in lots of ways. It don't take up near as much room as Philadelphia itself would."

He put his arm around me. My head throbbed from the fumes of his brandy-and-garlic breath. "Stevie, there ain't a man alive powerful enough to get that picture of Philadelphia as Seen from Cooper's Ferry away from me."

I got him silenced and pushed into a chair after a time. It was a quiet gathering at first, in spite of Cap's noisiness and his eagerness to have my opinion of Normandy cider strengthened with brandy. When all of us, even the brown-faced boy with the pipe, had sampled it a few times I saw that Natanis, who had been brought up in the

French-Abenaki town of St. Francis, could speak this whiny French tongue with ease, and that Jacataqua could make herself understood by the two brown-faced girls. After Cap had borrowed the stubby pipe from the little boy and sucked at it and then pretended to strangle, falling to the floor with a crash that shook the house and writhing there in seeming agony, there was more freedom among us.

The two brown-faced girls, Lizette and Zhulie, prepared the dinner for the next day, which they said they always did on the night before. Lizette climbed a ladder into the attic to cut a piece from the meat hanging there, and Zhulie climbed down a ladder into the cellar to get vegetables. When Cap tried to climb the ladder after Lizette, a rung broke so that he pitched down and wedged his beefy body into the hole. It seemed as though we might be obliged to cut the ladder from him, what with the bland, helpless way in which he lay where he was, refusing to move.

Nothing would do but I must master the song he had been singing; so we kept at it and kept at it, learning the verses from Lizette and Zhulie, who sat in our laps to teach us the better.

> "Nos amants sont en guerre,
> Vole, mon cœur, vole;
> Nos amants sont en guerre:
> Ils combattent pour nous!
> Ils combattent pour nous, doux, doux;
> Ils combattent pour nous!

> "On passe la carafe,
> Vole, mon cœur, vole;
> On passe la carafe;
> Nous buvons tous un coup.
> Nous buvons tous un coup, doux, doux;
> Nous buvons tous un coup!"

In the quiet of later days the verses would come back to me, a scrap here and a scrap there. They were about love and wine. Judging from the French songs we heard at the Taverne de Menut in St. Roque's outside of Palace Gate before we were through with Quebec, all French songs deal with these matters, nor do I know any better things for them to deal with.

My eye was taken by the dinner that Lizette and Zhulie prepared as well as they could for keeping out of the way of Cap, who would lean all over them whenever he moved, unless they dodged him, which it seemed to me they made no pointed effort to do.

They took a piece of meat, not as big as my fist, and put it in a kettle with a tight lid. With it they put a part of a cabbage and some garlic and a few potatoes and three or four turnips cut into pieces, after which they filled the kettle with water and set it on the stove. On the following day, at noon, they took it off and ate what was in it. They had put in, it seemed to me, less than enough to feed one man; but what they took out was a fine, meaty stew for six or seven persons. Meanwhile it had kept heat in the kitchen, which is a good thing in winter, since the kitchen is the place where the family sleeps, and guests as well, and any living thing that happens along.

Our host, Pierre Lemoine, said little; but what he said was to the point. When we spoke of the English, with Natanis interpreting between us, he used a word that Natanis did not know. He made an effort to get at the proper meaning of this word, but could not. He said it was not only a bad word, but a worse word than any of the bad ones he had heard used by Frenchmen.

What we did to the British, Lemoine said, he didn't care, provided we left no dead bodies in front of his farm during the day, to cause talk among the neighbors.

When I told this to Cap, to soften his hard feelings against the French, he nodded his head complacently, as if he had invented the French people. "That's right!" he said. "These frog-eaters ain't got no use at *all* for the British. I dunno how they'd be to fight, but they're powerful haters! They hate the English something *terrible!* They ain't bad people, either, once you get used to the awful stinks around their houses—garlic and manure and their pipes."

"Look here," I said, "I want to be sure to get that fur coat."

We finished our cider and brandy; and Cap, taking a lantern, led me through an adjoining grove of trees to one of the summer residences overlooking the St. Lawrence. It was a neat affair, a wooden house with gables; but the inside of it seemed to have been struck by a hurricane, everything overset and twisted out of place.

Cap apologized for its appearance. "I was in kind of a hurry, and I guess I wasn't standing up too well. Seems to me I never saw a house with so many things to fall over. I moved out a lot of stuff and packed it in the cariole."

"Whose cariole?"

"Well, that old Lemoine, he told me himself I drove up to his house in it, so I guess it must be mine."

He got the fur coat from a compartment beneath the stairs. It was, as he had said, a sable coat; one that would keep Phoebe as warm as though she nestled in a feather bed.

He showed me the cellar under the kitchen, and bragged of it as though he had not only built it but filled it. The bottles were all in racks, each bottle in a hole by itself, and I had a powerful desire to taste the different liquors, some of which I had never heard tell of.

Cap brought me a bottle with Beaune le Grève, 1761, printed on its label. He thought it must have been this, he said, on top of some brandy, that had rendered him unconscious for three days, while still leaving him able to walk about as though in full possession of his faculties. Knowing a half-bottle could do us no harm, we knocked off the neck and sampled it. I found it so pleasing that I took away four bottles, though warned by Cap that brandy was more helpful in this bitter weather, and safer.

We went back to Pierre Lemoine's farm, with the Great Dipper turning slowly above us and the tremendous cold flames of the Northern Lights marching across the sky. Lizette and Zhulie came out and helped us into the warm kitchen, where we sang "Vive la Canadienne" until long after the hour when honest people should be asleep.

XXX

I THOUGHT, when I looked at the weather-beaten farmhouses of Pointe-aux-Trembles, clustered drearily around a papist chapel on the desolate bank of the broad, ice-flecked St. Lawrence, that there would be no man of our little army, ever, who would speak good of the place, or hear its name without bursting into heartfelt curses. The snow was deep, and scarce a day passed without a fresh blanket of it being laid upon us; and full five hundred of our men had no rag to their backs save the tattered remnants of the garments in which they had marched out from Cambridge in the hot September sun.

Yet, miserable as they were, they had food to put in their bellies; and they lived in the warm, snug farmhouses of the long-queued French, neater and snugger than most of those on the frontiers of Virginia and Pennsylvania and Maine. Somehow, despite the scurviness of their appearance, they were followed about by the children and seldom spurned by the farmers' sprightly daughters. So in spite of eating themselves into stupors and heating themselves to the boiling point over pot-bellied kitchen stoves, and then going out into three feet of snow with their threadbare coverings, and suffering from coughs and quinsies and God knows what all, they contrived to endure their misery.

In after years I heard these very folk speak of Pointe-aux-Trembles with a wagging of their heads and a smacking of their lips, as though they had found it a place of heavenly pleasure; yet I remember how full of rancor they were at the time. Thus I have learned to disbelieve the tales men tell me of the delights of their younger days.

❄   ❄   ❄

I had thought to avoid trouble by persuading Cap Huff to give his mysterious horse and cariole to Pierre Lemoine; but Cap wouldn't hear to it.

"Steven," he said, "you ain't got the trading instinct! That horse and cariole was a gift right out of heaven; and we got to cart away a lot of stuff with us. We got to have that cariole."

"But you can't keep it! They'll take it away from you—a colonel or somebody."

"Not from me, they won't," Cap said. "Not while I got my health and my trading instinct."

We had some trouble with the packing of the cariole, because of the vast store of goods Cap had unearthed during his three days of unconsciousness. Bottles of brandy and Beaune and Spanish wine had to be protected between feather beds. On top of the beds we placed cushions, counterpanes, blankets, and other odds and ends, including a few garments for Phoebe, several dozen handsome case-knives and forks, and a set of dessert knives, which I knew would be gladly received by my mother if it should be my good fortune to return to Arundel. In among these things, where we could find room, we stowed firkins of butter and lard. On top of everything we balanced ourselves, Cap carrying the rolled-up picture of Philadelphia as Seen from Cooper's Ferry, he having made as much to-do over removing it from its frame as though it had been his major general's commission from Congress, engraved on gold.

There were some of Morgan's riflemen on guard at the edge of the town when we drove up to Pointe-aux-Trembles; and their faces steamed with excitement when they saw our cariole.

"Jeeminy!" said one of them, "where you been to get feather beds!"

He was huddled into himself with the cold. I remembered I hoped to go with these men in case there was fighting at Quebec, because they were wild enough to fight their way out of any difficulty.

"Where we've been," I told him, "there's enough truck to make you rich for the rest of the winter. You ought to be there instead of here."

The rifleman looked at me for a minute, then bawled down the road to another rifleman: "Hey, Buck! Tell Old Dan to come out here, 'n' hurry!"

He felt enviously of the blankets. "Any more of these left?"

"We can take you to hundreds," Cap said. "Blankets and brandy and silver and lard and beef and French girls just itching to sew up the holes in your shirt."

The hulking figure of Daniel Morgan bore down on us, his eyes a pale blue in the red of his face. "What's this?" he bellowed.

"They know where there's tons of this stuff," the rifleman said.

Morgan thrust his hand between the feather beds. I knew he felt the bottles, but he drew his hand out empty and rocked himself back and forth, missing no detail of our load.

"What's that?" he snapped, rapping his finger against the rolled picture.

"Philadelphia as Seen from Cooper's Ferry," Cap said. "Prettiest picture ever I saw."

Morgan grunted. "You never saw a picture of Winchester, Virginia, then! Where'd this stuff come from?"

"Down the road a piece," I said. "There's provision wagons passing all the time on that road. Seems as if there ought to be some men down there to stop 'em from carrying food into Quebec."

"One company enough?"

"Plenty! We could show you where these places are. I was kind of figuring there might be room for us in your company in case of an attack."

"Hell, yes!" Morgan said. He took a firkin of butter and two bottles of brandy from the cariole and started away.

"Take this, too," I said, fishing out a bottle of Beaune. "You'll be surprised if you never had any." He came back for it, tucked it under his arm with a growl that might have meant anything, and hurried down the road. I gave another bottle of brandy to the rifleman who had stopped us, and we trotted briskly toward Arnold's headquarters.

"I guess it's all right, Stevie," Cap said, caressing his picture of Philadelphia as Seen from Cooper's Ferry. "Your trading instinct ain't as bad as what I thought. I'd ruther fight under Morgan than under anyone except Arnold; but ain't they the thievingest lot you ever set eyes on?"

*   *   *

Cap took the cariole and our belongings to hunt for Goodrich's company while I went in to see the colonel, carrying two bottles of brandy and two bottles of Beaune hidden under my coat. Ogden was acting as adjutant, and he was a polite young man, handsome and at his ease.

"I want to see the colonel," I said.

Ogden looked at the lumps under my coat, and winked affably, a gay and frivolous officer, and a better fighter than more serious men I have known. "There's some gentlemen from Quebec with him just now, but as soon as they're out I'll put you in."

"How did they get here?"

"Carleton turned out everyone who won't bear arms against us."

"How did Carleton get to Quebec?"

"Down the river," he said angrily. "Damn him! Sailed down the day we marched here. Now we'll have hell's own time getting into the city. He's smart!"

When the Quebec gentlemen came out, solid-looking men in fur hats and coats, Ogden held the door open for me.

"Well!" Arnold said when I came in, "I was looking for you to carry word to Hanchet, at Point Levis, when we started back here. I thought you must have run into the city to pay a visit to your young woman!" He said it pleasantly enough, but his face was swarthy and nubbly. I suspicioned he was not overly pleased with me or anything else.

"I was hunting Cap Huff," I explained. "I wanted to make sure he got into no trouble with the French."

His eyes rested on the bulges around my waist, and he nodded doubtfully. "Well," he said, whipping out of his chair and spreading his coat-tails before the iron stove. "Any luck?"

I took the four bottles from under my coat and stood them on his desk.

"Whoo!" he said. "Beaune le Grève! 1761! Well, it might be worse! I'd rather have this than the word I just had about a friend of yours."

"What's that?"

"Colonel McLean and his detachment of Britishers had news of our coming while they lay in Sorel. That's why they hurried into Quebec three days before we reached Point Levis. These gentlemen out of Quebec say the news was brought to McLean by a dirty, ragged, sour-faced white man traveling in a canoe with an Indian. There's no doubt it was your friend Hook."

We looked at each other glumly.

"When's General Montgomery coming down?" I asked at length.

He shook his head, his face lumpy and bulbous. "Soon! Soon, I hope!" He glared at me. "Great grief! You'd think it was a thousand miles from Montreal, instead of a tenth of that!" I think both of us were recalling how his starving army had followed him from Lake Megantic to Point Levis in one week's time.

"Sir," I said, "you know how I feel about Mary Mallinson, she that you call Marie de Sabrevois. If Carleton's arrival puts Quebec out of our reach, I'd like to try getting in with Natanis: just the two of us."

"By God," Arnold said, picking up his chair and thumping it down on the floor so hard I thought the legs must shatter, "it *isn't* out of our reach! Not if Montgomery ever gets here, it isn't! I tell you I can take that city, Carleton or no Carleton or a dozen Carletons! All I ask is men that'll stick with me and go where I lead them, and not go whining around about danger. Danger, danger, danger! Damn it, to hear some of these namby-pambies talk, you'd think there wasn't any danger anywhere in the world except from bullets and cannon balls!" He flung himself into his chair and glared at me, moving his shoulders backward and forward inside his coat.

"Look here! It's senseless for you to think of going into the city. They'd catch you, sure as shooting. Then they'd put you in prison, and you'd be nowhere. You'd never get from the Lower Town to the Upper Town. It's like trying to climb the wall of a house without a ladder.

"Put that idea out of your head and wait till we capture it. I tell you I'm going into that city, unless all of you run away behind me! When we're in you can go where you please and do as you please. What do you say?"

I've heard a mass of lies about Colonel Arnold in these last years: how he was a horse jockey and a cheat and a braggart, and how all men hated him; but I'm setting down here the things I know from following him through two campaigns. Such tales are not so, none of them. He was a brave and determined man, nor was there any soldier serving under him who wouldn't, at his request, follow him anywhere at any time. Those who knew him had great love and respect for him, not only General Washington and General Schuyler, but all other men in his command except those who had aroused his displeasure and contempt—and God knows there were plenty to do that in those early days. Therefore I said what any other man would have said: that I'd wait. Then I went away to look for Phoebe, wishing she were well out of this numbing cold and back in our kitchen at Arundel, helping my mother hook a rug or chattering with my sisters as to what the women in Boston were wearing.

❀   ❀   ❀

All of these towns along the St. Lawrence are eight miles apart and as like as a basketful of potatoes, some having a few more eyes than others and some having more dirt than their fellows; but all smelling the same and nearly all of them called about the same, for that matter—Saint This and Saint That and Saint T'other. They are built with a single long street; and I had no trouble finding the quarters of Goodrich's company. The entire company was crowded around the cariole in which Cap still sat, not daring to move lest his picture be snatched from him.

When he saw me he let out a bellow of relief; and I suspected the men, thinking Cap aimed to keep everything for himself, were of a mind to take all from him, like the independent Sons of Liberty they were.

I said that we would proceed at once to a division, and appointed Noah Cluff bottle keeper for the company. We cleared a space in front of the farmhouse in which the men were billeted and then passed out the brandy and the Beaune, having twenty-two of the former and thirty of the latter; and while all the others were shouting over them and counting, I gave Phoebe the sable coat I had found in the summer house, a loose coat such as women of wealth wear in their carioles in winter. I thought, considering her fondness for a man's breeches and sea boots, that she wouldn't be overly excited by fripperies; but she squealed with joy at sight of it, and ran, still squealing, into the farmhouse.

After considerable bawling and bellowing it was decided the brandy should be mixed with Normandy cider according to the proportions advised by Cap Huff, and the Beaune drunk after the brandy had been consumed. We gave up the chair cushions and butter and lard for the men to divide as they saw fit, and carried the feather beds and the silver and the picture into the house for ourselves.

We found Phoebe in the kitchen, staring at herself in a cracked mirror. Her throat was creamy against the softness of the sable; and her cat's eyes, twisted around her forehead like a band of wampum, glowed against her hair. There was a redness under the brown of her cheeks, almost like the redness of the Beaune. I would scarce have known her, turning her head from side to side and striving to see all of herself in the fragment of mirror.

When she looked around and saw me gawking, she put her hand on her hip, stuck up her nose, and walked elegantly past the two of us, turning herself a little on each foot. In passing, she opened her eyes at Cap like a frightened calf, saying, *"Oh là! M'sieu!"*

Cap dropped everything and knelt on one knee, holding out his arms to her and shouting mournfully: *"On Normandee noo boovong doo see-druh!"*

"Here," I said, catching Phoebe by the arm, and noticing she was no longer the pitiful skeleton I had felt on the Chaudière, "here!

Stop this nonsense! Take these things to the attic and hide them where they can't be found."

There was dissatisfaction at first, that night, over Cap's drink of cider and brandy; but opinion changed as the night wore on. Among other things, the farmer's wife danced on a table for us, jubilant and frisky, and we taught the others to sing:

> *"Vive la Canadienne,*
> *Vole, mon cœur, vole;*
> *Vive la Canadienne,*
> *Et ses jolis yeux doux!*
> *Et ses jolis yeux doux, doux, doux,*
> *Et ses jolis yeux doux!"*

Now that I think back on it, Pointe-aux-Trembles was one of the pleasantest places I have ever known.

* * *

On the last day of November we heard that General Montgomery and his troops were near at hand, together with ammunition and the clothes that had never been so needed by any body of men, I do believe, since clothes were first worn. Toward noon on the next day, the first day of December, men went running up the road toward the point, their huge, rough, hay-stuffed moccasins flapping and padding in the snow as though they wore saddle bags on their feet. At the point we found three armed schooners, all loaded with troops, and on one of them the general.

We cheered when he came ashore; for there was no doubt he was a great leader, this tall, soldierly man, slender and of distinction, with the marks of smallpox heavy on his face. We could not cheer as heartily when we saw his aide, Aaron Burr, now a full-fledged captain, racing about on errands for his general like my dog Ranger when he suddenly comes on a spot where a fox has sat.

Nor was there a cheer in us for his troops, New Yorkers, little greater in numbers than ourselves and as worthless and unsoldierly-looking lot of knaves as could be found in any gutter. We were a sad-looking assemblage, God knows, after our struggle with starvation and the flux and the wilderness, nor were we any great shakes for discipline; yet we looked to be able to handle our muskets, and to endure whatever we might be set to doing, whereas these boys of Montgomery's looked like street rabble who knew how to do nothing save draw rations.

Having seen these poor wretches of his, we were not surprised, when we paraded before him that afternoon, to hear him speak highly of our soldierly appearance. Men near me opined, beneath their breaths, that he couldn't know much about soldiers, and that we might look more military if we had a few shirts among us; but just then the general announced in a ringing voice that to show what he thought of our exploit in marching to Quebec he would make each one of us a present of a suit of clothes and one dollar in hard money, and that we could draw these on the following day. Someone bawled, "Huzza for Richard Montgomery, our gallant general!" and such a cheering went up as must have made him think we considered him the greatest man in the world—which indeed we would have thought anyone who gave us garments to keep us warm and dry.

I have seen times when our army would have preferred to go naked rather than wear British uniforms; but this was not one of them. Those the general issued to us were British uniforms captured at Montreal, red coats and white woolen breeches and black woolen stockings and a white blanket coat to go over them, almost foppish; likewise a red cap lined with white that could be drawn down over the ears, if need be, to keep them from freezing. There was no coat big enough to fit Cap Huff. He growled and grumbled at this outrage, damning the British army for being an army of runts; but it was a circumstance for which we later had occasion to be grateful.

With the arrival of Montgomery there was tremendous activity, what with the distributing of ammunition and food, and the unloading of small cannon from the sloops—cannon so small, it seemed to me, that they might be good for the killing of geese in the guzzles of Swan Island, but no use at all for killing men inside the walls of Quebec.

With these new men we had enough to blockade the roads to the city, and so there were immediate preparations to march back again to the Plains of Abraham.

Having no wish to be once more in the bad graces of Colonel Arnold, I went with Cap Huff to the colonel's headquarters to let him know that we were going forward to Morgan's riflemen. We found a crowd of officers outside, Major Bigelow, Topham, Thayer, Church, Steele, Hubbard, Hanchet, and Goodrich, all of them neat in their white blanket coats and red caps.

Ogden came to the door, shouting for Captain Hanchet, and Hanchet hurried in, his lower jaw thrust forward disagreeably, and coughing a nasty, racking cough that seemed to start somewhere around his knees.

Bigelow watched him intently, and shook his head, as though there were something mislikable about Hanchet. "He was raving like a lunatic when he came up from Point Levis with his sixty men," he said. "Told everybody Arnold was giving him all the dirty jobs."

"What was the matter with Point Levis?"

"Oh," Bigelow said, "bad food and no good quarters for his men, and the likelihood of being surprised and captured by the British; and it was cold, and the river might have frozen any day."

"Yes," Captain Thayer said, as mildly as though admiring a peruke in his own hairdressing shop, "yes, and it's my understanding the wind was blowing, and might blow worse."

"Oh, much worse!" Bigelow said primly, "and it might snow; and Colonel Arnold, being angry at him, might have arranged for the sun not to shine on his side of the river!"

Thayer broke off in his laughing; for from headquarters there came a shouting in Colonel Arnold's voice. We could hear him as easily as though the windows had been open instead of sealed against the winter winds. "You're mad!" he shouted. "Mad! There isn't a man in this command that would say what you said! Danger! I'm ashamed to think one of my officers should speak of such a thing!"

Seemingly Captain Hanchet thrust in a reply here; for Arnold broke out again worse than before. "What if their enlistment *is* up on the first of January! This is December, I'll thank you to remember! They're subject to orders until midnight on December thirty-first! What do you think they are? New-born babes? By God, Hanchet, I'll put you under arrest for this!"

There was a banging of doors from inside headquarters. The front door flew open and Arnold stood before us, his face black and lowering. "Captain Topham!" he shouted. "Captain Thayer!"

Topham and Thayer moved forward, Topham, with his rosy cheeks, looking as though he were stepping up to receive a comfit for good behavior, and Thayer as meek and mild as an underpaid schoolmaster.

"Gentlemen," said Colonel Arnold, "our cannon must be taken from the sloops and carried to Sillery by bateaux; and the same bateaux must cross to Point Levis and return with our scaling ladders. I'm informed that this is a dangerous venture, because of the floating ice in the river. Would either of you be willing to undertake it?"

Topham looked at Thayer and said, "My men are handy with

bateaux!" Thayer looked at Arnold and said, "My men are ready to start at once."

Arnold smiled pleasantly. "In that case, gentlemen, I'll ask you to leave it to the fall of a coin."

The words were scarce out of his mouth when Thayer was flipping a shilling in the air.

"Heads!" Topham cried.

Thayer held out his hand, palm up, and Topham peered into it. Thayer laughed in his face, doubling up his fist and making as though to hit Topham a backhanded blow, and went in to get his orders from Arnold. Hanchet came out with a half-smile on his face, though I swear I'd never have smiled again if such a thing had happened to me; and Captain Goodrich and Captain Hubbard walked away with him down the road.

XXXI

THERE was a different reception waiting for us when we returned to Quebec. Carleton, to deprive us of shelter, had burned down Major Caldwell's manor house in which we previously lodged; and the houses in the suburb of St. John, nearest to the St. John Gate, had been destroyed as well. There was more snow, and a cold so bitter that eyelids froze together if held closed overlong. On top of everything Carleton had put cannoneers from the King's frigates on the walls, so when we struggled to our posts through the snow we were kept busy dodging shells and grape-shot.

Headquarters was at Holland House in the village of St. Foy's, three miles from St. John's Gate, but many of the men were lodged in the general hospital and nunnery, a mile outside the city on the St. Charles River; for the British, out of respect for the nuns, would not shell this building. Close as the hospital was to the walls, it was too far out for Morgan and his Virginians, who had no mind to waste time marching when there was fighting to be done; and shortly after I joined the riflemen, Morgan moved them into the very shadow of the walls, quartering them in the suburb of St. Roque.

The buildings of St. Roque comprised everything from small cottages, log cabins, shops and warehouses to stone dwellings and the most celebrated inn of all lower Quebec—the Taverne de Menut, which was a godsend to us in that awful cold. The whole suburb huddled against the base of the cliff on which the city stands; and in the space between the river and the cliff were the buildings, or what was left of them, that housed the greatest thief in all America: the palace of the chief trader of the French King. The Canadians called him the Intendant; and the stone barn where he stored the King's goods and sold them at murderous profits to the poor was called La Friponne, or The Cheat.

These were forts ready-made to our hand. Once we got into them, we could peer up at the high walls and see the sentries passing the gun ports; yet they couldn't shoot down at us without leaning far out over the parapet; and this, they soon discovered, wasn't healthy. Neither was it possible for them to depress their cannon sufficiently to hit us, so it gave us pleasure, each day, to slip into the ruins of the palace and La Friponne and practise our marksmanship on those who showed themselves on the wall.

We heard through spies that this diversion was considered un-gentlemanly by the British; but Morgan told us to go ahead and pop off all of them we could. They'd call it ungentlemanly, he said, even though we set off a rocket whenever we took aim; for no American could ever learn to talk or act or even think in a manner satisfactory to Britishers.

Yet those damned lobster-backs on the walls, finding they could bring no cannon to bear on us, pointed mortars so to drop thirteen-inch shells on the ledges above our stations. The shells, landing on the bank with a light charge of powder behind them, would roll down against the buildings near us and explode with a crash that led us for the first time in our lives to bless the French for building walls three feet thick.

*   *   *

We were strewn among the wrecked rooms of La Friponne one sunny morning toward the middle of December, pecking at British sentries, and enjoying our work because the sentries stood out against the sun whereas we lay in the shadow of the cliff, when one of the gunners rolled a pill against the side of our shelter at a moment when I was lying on my stomach with my head tilted far back, and my cheek and nose pressed tight against the stock of my musket.

The bomb let off with a thunderous roar and jar that almost broke my neck. At the moment of the explosion something was hurled against me so I thought the walls had fallen on me, and left me fit for nothing but a shallow grave in the snow.

I made a move to roll over, and found a body pinning me down. I threw it off and sat up. Phoebe had fallen across me, her eyes closed and a smutch of dirt on her face, so that she gave me such a fright as I have seldom had. I hauled her up with her back against the wall, and felt her all over to see whether she was hurt. She wasn't because in a moment she opened her eyes and said: "Why do you come to such a terrible place as this?"

"Look here," I said, angry at the turn she had given me, "what I do is none of your business! I won't have you coming out here! It's all right for a man, but you might be hurt, so stay where you belong!"

These Britishers, stupid as they are, have the luck of the devil; for one of them succeeded in rolling another pill against our walls. When it burst I thought Phoebe would burrow into my side.

"What have you done with your leather belt?" I asked, for I could feel it was no longer there.

"It near froze me, Steven, so I left it off."

"Yes," I said, at a loss to know why I was so put out at her, for it was pleasant to have her by me again, "yes, and not content with freezing and starving and God knows what all, you must come pushing your way into this place. What is it you want? What have you come here for?"

"I came to find you."

"Well," I said, "it wouldn't have hurt you to wait. It was in my mind to look for you to-night."

"To-night might have been too late."

"Too late for what?"

She plucked at the matted snow on the skirt of my blanket coat. "Did you know Montgomery sent a letter to Carleton asking for the surrender of the city? That Carleton won't receive any message, or let any man come near the gates, even under a white flag?"

"Yes," I said, "I heard so. There's no secrets in this army!"

"Steven, I think I can carry a message to Carleton. Will you give me the horse and cariole that you brought to Pointe-aux-Trembles?"

The thought fair graveled me. "How can you get in with such a message, when nobody else can?"

"Why," she said, "if I wear the fur coat you gave me, and a skirt, and drive up to the gate in a lather, early in the morning, with men running and shouting behind me, they'll never think of stopping me. If I say I have important information for Carleton, they'll let me in at once."

She was right: no doubt of that; yet I didn't want Phoebe mixed up in any such matter. Already there were too many people on the inside of Quebec, out of my reach, but weighing perpetually on my mind—Mary Mallinson, Guerlac, Ezekiel Hook.

I was gruff with her. "Let me hear no more of this! You might get into the city; but you'd be thrown into jail; maybe shot for a spy, even."

"Now, Steven," she said, in the same coaxing way she used when she went at me to buy the sloop, long ago, "you know the British won't shoot a woman. They won't even fire their cannon at the nunnery, though we're living in it. If they put me in gaol they'd soon let me out, for I'm no spy, and they know it; and they have too little food for themselves to feed another without need."

"Well," I said, "there's other ways of getting this letter to Carleton without having you carry it."

"What other ways?"

"Why, any God's quantity of ways. They could shoot the message over the walls with arrows in the night. They could send Mrs. Grier or Mrs. Warner with it, if you're so set on having a woman do it."

"Yes, and if they shot it over on arrows they might find it when the snow melts in the spring; or if they *did* find it, Carleton wouldn't take it, any more than he will now. As for Mrs. Grier and Mrs. Warner, they have husbands; and besides, Steven, they don't have a look that would incline the sentries toward letting them pass."

"Ho!" I said, annoyed at her assurance, "since when have people been taking you for a duchess or the governor's lady?"

"If you had eyes in your head and knew how to use them you'd know there are worse-looking women than I!"

"Belike."

She turned a little from me and did something to her hair and dress; then turned back again. "Look, Steven. *Haven't* you seen worse?" She laid hold of my arms, so that I had to look up at the triangle of creamy skin at her throat, and the pointed chin above it, and so to the rest of her: the oval cheeks, with the red blood close under them; the velvety brown of her eyes, and the thin black eyebrows that seemed traced with a quill; the peak of hair that came down low on her forehead, so her whole face was shaped like the hearts that Arundel boys carve on the old beech tree across the creek when waiting for their sweethearts.

"Haven't you?" she said, and shook me, and smiled a little on one side of her mouth. At this, for no reason I could understand, there came into my mind all of Arundel and the things I loved—blue sea and golden sunlight: brown reefs, and the white breakers tumbling toward the gray sand: the sweet, warm odors of the marsh; the fresh salt wind from over the water; the cricking of crickets on hot nights, and my mother's face, and Cynthy leaning against me to watch me eat a late supper; Ranger, with his ears cocked up and his lip curled in a grin, inviting me to take him for a hunt; the suck of the falling tide in the river, and the sweet perfume of young willow leaves in the spring.

"Haven't you?" Phoebe asked once more, while I sat and stared at her, with the rifles of the Virginians cracking on one side of us and then on the other, and the outrageous thudding of British cannon shaking the ruined wall against which we leaned.

I dropped my eyes and said, "Your nose is red." She only laughed.

"Here," I said, resolved to stop her nonsense once and for all, "such a thing as you propose is not what a woman should do: not a good woman."

"I didn't think of that," she said in a small voice. "What is a good woman, Steven?"

"You know as well as I do. A good woman doesn't go gallivanting off. She stays home and behaves herself."

"But, Steven, do you think I'm a bad woman?"

"Why, damn it," I said, not wishing to hurt her feelings, "not yet you aren't, but I don't want you to go hurroaring and hurrooing into Quebec. It wouldn't be decorum."

"You don't think ill of me for coming away with James?"

"No."

"Nor for continuing with Noah and Nathaniel and Jethro after James died?"

"No."

"Are you sure, Steven, you wouldn't think better of me if I stayed home always, instead of sailing the sloop, and lived in the kitchen, speaking ill of all my neighbors and growing to hate the faces I saw every day, like other good women in Arundel?"

"Now," I said, "all this argument is getting us nowhere! I don't propose to sit here and yawp all day. I don't think you should go, and there's an end of it. Why is it you want to do it, Phoebe?"

"Why? Why? Well, Steven, it seems to me things aren't right in the company. Goodrich and Hanchet are together all the time, talking in corners. Hubbard too. He's with them. Hanchet hates Arnold."

"That's no news!"

"I know, but he hates him worse than ever. Arnold ordered him to move into St. John with his company, and he wouldn't. Claimed it was too dangerous. Arnold said terrible things to him."

"He'd ought to shot him."

"No," Phoebe said; "he did better. He shamed him. He sent Topham and Thayer in his place, and they went. There was never anybody hated Arnold the way Hanchet does. He says he won't fight under him. Goodrich and Hubbard, they sit and listen to him, and drink brandy, and agree with everything he says."

"What else?"

"Steven, I think the men have caught it. Their enlistment is up the first of January. They want to go home. Some of them say they won't fight. Asa Hutchins says he won't. Noah and Nathaniel will, but there's a lot that won't."

She took a deep breath. "I want to be some use, instead of a burden on everyone's hands! If James could have come here and fought, then I'd have been some use. Maybe if I did something the men would be shamed into fighting. I can't sit and do nothing, Steven! I can't! I can't!"

She looked down at her hands. I saw they were clenched. The triangle of skin at her throat was as red as a maple leaf after a frost.

"Well," I said, feeling choked, "cover up your neck. I guess you can have the horse and cariole."

* * *

I drove out to St. Foy's with her that afternoon in the cariole, fair mazed by the figure she made. She had on a hat of sealskin, one that pulled close down onto her head. Cap Huff, she said, had got it from one of Morgan's men, paying a whole bottle of brandy for it. With it she wore the sable coat over a dress of gray wool begged from the nuns. On her feet were enormous winter boots, made of sealskin with the fur inside, such as Quebec ladies wear when they go in carioles.

I felt like a coachman, hunched down beside her in my dirty white blanket coat, my face bristly with beard; and I was shamed, stealing a look at her as she sat staring down at her mittened hands, to think I had spoken of her red nose, though God knows it was red, albeit not unpleasantly so.

She looked up at me as we went along, and caught me gawking at her; and though I had meant to speak to her of many things, I forgot them.

* * *

They had her to dinner at headquarters that night, while I ate pork and dumplings with the men in the kitchen. Once, when the door stood open, I heard the general speaking to her about her necklace of cat's eyes, and caught her reply, delivered straight and pleasant, Colonel Arnold and Burr and Ogden and Bigelow and the rest of them having fallen silent to hear her.

"Indeed," she said, "I didn't know it had so great a value; but I knew I wanted it; and what we New Englanders want is apt to have a high value. If we can avoid it, we never pay full value in money for what we want, though it may be we pay in other ways. You might say this necklace cost me a piece of rope; yet in the end it amounted to more than that. I had spliced a rope to make a running noose, back in my younger days, when I was captain of a vessel in the coasting trade——"

She waited for the shout of laughter to go down; then went on: "An Indian came aboard my sloop and hankered for the rope, so I traded it to him for a snake-skin case holding three needles made from mink bones. In Portsmouth I traded these to a lady who wished them for the running of ribbons through her fripperies; and in return I took a pistol with a brass knob on the end of the butt, big enough for knocking in the heads of molasses barrels. The pistol I traded for a parrot with a sailor from the Sugar Islands; and the parrot went to the captain of a Newburyport brig in return for two stone hatchets and a magnifying glass. The hatchets near wore holes in me before I came across the mate of a brig from Ceylon who was needful of them and the glass. He traded these cat's eyes for them; yet it may be the time and thought I put on the matter had a value, so that I didn't get the necklace for nothing."

They made much of her for this speech, though it seemed to me no more worthy of remark than many I had heard her make. In more ways than one they found her diverting, as I discovered from Captain Oswald coming into the kitchen to lean against the wall and take several deep breaths.

"Holy cats!" he said, when he saw me, "I never hoped to see that!"

"See what?"

"Why!" he said, "that young lady of yours was showing them the bauble on her wrist, that little leather-covered bauble, and Burr picked up her arm with both hands, pretty as you please, as if to help them see it." He wagged his head admiringly and moaned, as at a pleasant recollection.

"Where did it hit him?"

"She looked up in his face as innocent as a baby," Oswald continued. "Oh, dear! It was lovely! It just tapped his nose, by accident-like, and he's out in front, putting snow on it, to stop the bleeding."

*　　*　　*

We drove over to the Sillery Road, the one that leads into St. Louis Gate, before dawn the next morning, taking a few men with us. When it grew light we moved forward to where the straight road begins.

"Steven," she said, when I got out of the cariole, "couldn't you find an extra coat and wear a pair of them if you have to go back to lie in that awful place again."

"Don't you worry about me," I said, low in spirit to think I lacked the firmness to forbid her going. "All you have to do is finish your business and get back here where you belong."

"No message you want taken to anybody, is there?" she asked. For the life of me I couldn't think what she was getting at. While I gawked at her she whipped up the horse and went tearing around the bend onto the straight road, the rest of us pelting after and letting off our muskets.

Heads popped into sight on the bastions that flanked the gate, and we heard faint cheering. Still we ran on, shooting and whooping, while the cariole drew farther and farther away from us, and closer and closer to the gate. When we saw puffs of smoke along the top of the wall we came to a halt and had the pleasure of seeing the gate swing slowly open. Phoebe, plying her whip, dashed through and out of sight. We plodded slowly back, followed by the distant jeers of the city's brave defenders.

Each day, after that, I walked to headquarters to see whether word had come from Carleton in reply to the general's message, or whether Phoebe had returned; and it was such a time as comes now and again to every man—a time when everything happens except what ought to happen.

Our men had built a five-gun battery in the snow near the suburb of St. John; and the path to headquarters from our turkey-shooting post in the ruins of La Friponne led behind this battery. It was a poor thing, not only because of the small bore of the cannons, but also because the ground was hard as rock, so that the battery walls were made of snow on which water had been thrown. When, therefore, our battery began to play, the British opened on it with every cannon and mortar on the walls. There was a steady whanging and banging from the city, and shells and grape-shot racketing past at all hours, and a hellish and inconvenient bursting of bombs where they were not expected. The walk to headquarters was no pleasure at all, what with diving into the snow every few yards to escape something that could not be escaped, if so be it was bound for you.

I have heard wiseacres in New England say knowingly, when the air is sharp and biting, that it's too cold to snow; but I have seen snow aplenty fall outside the walls of Quebec when we dared not open our mouths for fear our tongues would freeze.

Along with the increase in cannon balls we had another foot of snow, and then we had a cold snap that made the preceding cold seem like a gentle, harmless spell of weather.

With these things came sicknesses among the men, mostly lung troubles that drove them out of their heads and set them to babbling of their homes and of maids they had known in other days. On top of everything came smallpox, bowling over five men here and three men there and half a dozen in another quarter. We took turns piling them into carioles and driving them out to Sillery and putting them into empty summer houses, to die or get well.

*   *   *

Thus there was much happening; but day after day went by with no sign of Phoebe, until four days before Christmas. On that day, along about noon, which was the hour when the cannonading grew slack and the turkey-shooting, as our men called their popping at British sentries, was lightest, there was a prolonged rolling of drums behind St. John's Gate—a rolling so noisy that it brought our men running to St. John from every part of the Plains of Abraham, thinking the British must be sallying on us.

From the sound, every drum in the city had been gathered in one spot. There were heads showing above the walls, all facing inward, watching what went on within.

After a deal of drumming the gates swung open and a motley throng of drummers poured out, to form a line on each side of the entranceway. When their drums were rattling and rolling with renewed violence, a small figure came marching out between those massive doors: a lonely figure, like a little boat running on a vast sea before a wall of towering thunderheads. It was Phoebe, walking stiffly erect, even proudly, and looking neither to right nor left.

We could hear the folk on the walls jeering at her; and through it all ran the beating of the drums, rolling and thudding in time to her steps.

It's no pretty sight to see any person drummed out of a city; and I cursed the British for lousy knaves as I ran down the road to meet this small and lonely figure.

News travels fast in an army, and it must be there was knowledge of who she was and what she'd done; for as she drew nearer, our men came out toward her from the houses of St. John, cheering and

waving their hats. Yet we never reached her; for a cariole slid past
with a scattering of snow wads from the horse's hoofs—a cariole with
Burr in it. It dashed out to her, whirled around, and picked her up in
less time than it takes to shell a pea pod. So back she came in it,
riding proud and straight; and the shouting and hat-waving grew
violent as they came up to the houses of St. John.

I thought she wouldn't see me; for Burr was so busy being polite
to her that he might have been a puppy snuffling at a wall after a
woodchuck. But as she passed me Phoebe leaned back and called,
"Come to the nunnery for supper!" With that she was gone.

❋   ❋   ❋

The general hospital for the city of Quebec, which was also a nunnery, was a long stone building overlooking the winding course of the
St. Charles. It was a mile from the city walls, and on the road running past the ruins of La Friponne and through the suburb of St.
Roque, where the Virginians lived. I was on my way to it before
dark, decently shaved and my head cropped by a proper barber for
the first time in three months, so that I felt as slick as a mackerel.

It had a dank and sour smell, that hospital and nunnery; and it
was in my mind, as I prowled along the corridor, peering into room
after room to find Goodrich's company, that there was smallpox in
the very air, and that I wouldn't like to have Phoebe broke out with
this horrible sickness, which leaves a person scarred forever if he
lays a finger to the sores that craze him with their itching.

I found her with Jacataqua and Noah Cluff and others from the
company in the big room that lets off from the kitchen. She had
gone back into her gray blanket coat with its gay red sash and her
blanket breeches stuffed into moccasins. She was in no amiable humor with those about her, though pleasant enough with me, bringing
me a dish of meat boiled with potatoes, and a stick of French bread,
log-shaped and hard; less fitted for eating purposes than for shooting
from a five-inch cannon.

She took me into a corner with Jacataqua, turning her back on the
rest of the company. I thought she had become haughty from dining
with generals and going about with beautiful aides.

"Well," she said, "I suppose you're glad to see me back."

"Yes."

"Ah," she said insolently, "if I'd known you were suffering as much
as all that, I'd have come out sooner."

"If you could have come out sooner and didn't, with me walking across the plains behind that battery of sparrow-guns of ours every day, so to get to headquarters to see whether you were back——"

"Hindsight's easier than foresight," Phoebe said. "It may be I'd have got out sooner if I'd hit 'em harder."

"Hit who?"

"The men who came to the cell."

"Cell!" I exclaimed.

"Of course! Did you think I had the royal apartments in the castle?"

Jacataqua burst into tears. "They sent my darling George to England in a warship to show to the King!"

"Now here!" I said. "I can't eat my supper in peace unless I have this story in order. I don't want a word out of you, Jacataqua, until Phoebe tells me the tale from the beginning."

"Steven," Phoebe said, "I could have killed that man Treeworgy!"

"Get back to the beginning quickly," I ordered.

"Well," she said, "they took me to Carleton, a quiet, pleasant gentleman. When he asked what I wanted, I took Montgomery's letter from my dress and handed it to him.

"'What's this?' he asked, and opened it, looking first for the signature. When he saw the name he dropped the letter on the floor and set his foot on it, saying, 'I hold no communication with traitors or rebels.' Then he called an orderly and sent for someone. While he waited he never so much as turned his eyes toward me. At length the door opened and Treeworgy came in.

"'Do you recognize this woman?' Carleton asked him.

"Treeworgy looked at me as he would at something bad, and said, 'Yes, she's a camp-follower: one of the hangers-on after the men in Arnold's army.'

"If I could have reached him, Steven, I'd have crushed his skull with my little club like breaking an egg; but there were guards beside me and a table between us. Oh, Steven, I could have torn out his throat with my fingers!"

"Yes, I know! That will come in good time! Get on with your tale."

"He sent Treeworgy away," she continued, "and called his orderly again, telling him to take me to the Seminary and confine me there. With that he stalked from the room without my having said a word in my own behalf." She shook her fist at me. "I was in such a rage at Treeworgy I couldn't think! Damn it, I couldn't think!"

"For God's sake!" I said angrily, "do you think I haven't waked up a score of nights sweating to get at him?"

"Well," she went on, "they took me to the Seminary: pushed me into a freezing cold room no bigger than a hogshead, with bars in the door and window. When I was able to think again I knew they had no business to put me in a cell. I screamed and wept to be taken back to Carleton. The guards laughed at me. Whenever one of them came near, I hit him with my little club and demanded an officer. I broke the hands of three of them. Two started into my cell to take away my club, but I broke the head of one. He had to be carried away. The other wouldn't come in.

"An officer came, and I told him they'd have to kill me to keep me quiet. I'd done no wrong and was determined to see Carleton again.

"He was polite, even though he laughed at me. He went away; and when he returned he led me to Carleton.

"As soon as I saw Carleton I went to talking, telling him I'd done nothing, only brought him a message from a man as honorable as he, who was fighting in a better cause—a message that any gentleman should receive as openly as it was sent; and who was he, I asked him, to sit in judgment on his fellow men when he refused, even, to hear what they had to say for themselves—and how would he like to be judged, on Judgment Day, by a Judge who would hold no communication with those he judged?

"He began to glower and blow out his mustaches, ready to tell me to be still, so I whacked his desk a fearful whack with my little club and said Treeworgy was a snake and a liar and a traitor—a disgrace to him and his army: that I was a plain sailor woman from Arundel, master of my own sloop, and married decently and in order to James Dunn of Arundel, who died of exposure in the marshes of Lake Megantic: that if he didn't let me out so I could go back to you —I mean so I could go back to my own people before Christmas—he would be what every New Englander says every English general is.

"He roared until orderlies popped their heads in at the door. When I was silent he said he'd turn me loose, and glad to be rid of me, but would drum me out of the city so nobody could hear the damnable wagging of my tongue—so I might remember the contempt in which every decent Englishman holds a deluded, traitorous rebel."

"Whew!" I said, "couldn't you think of something more to say to him?"

Phoebe laughed shortly. "I thought of plenty to say to him, but I was in a hurry to get away. I didn't feel comfortable in skirts, not in this weather!"

She turned from me, her hands on her hips, to stare at a score of Goodrich's men who, having finished their supper, had drawn close to hear Phoebe. I saw Noah Cluff and Nathaniel Lord and Jethro Fish, and the butcher from York, his face red and shiny, and one Butts from Wells, with an Adam's apple that jumped up and down in his throat almost like a frog; but I saw no sign of Asa Hutchins.

"Where's Asa?" I asked.

Phoebe stamped her foot. "He deserted, that's what Asa did! Walked up to the gate last night and joined the British! Asa Hutchins from Arundel! There's a nice tale to take home! Marched through the snow and the ice with the rest of us, and starved with us, and froze, and left the blood of his bare feet on the roads, and killed Dearborn's dog, and then went and joined the British, so he could get up high in the world and shoot at us from behind stone walls!"

The men stared at her, motionless and unwinking.

"Now, Phoebe," Noah Cluff said, "Asa's young. He don't——"

"Don't tell me anything about Asa Hutchins!" she cried. "He's a deserter! He ran away! What's more, I hear there's more of you want to run away! I hear there's a lot of you came up here to fight for your country, but kind of think you'd better go home without fighting. What's the matter: don't you have a country except when it's warm? Aren't you interested in Liberty when there's snow on the ground?"

"Lot you know about it!" growled the butcher from York.

Phoebe darted to him through the men as quickly as a mackerel gull dives into a breaker for a sand eel. "Don't I!" she cried, standing a scant six inches from him. "Don't I! I know the way to fight is to fight! What was it you came up here for? To see how far you could walk?"

The butcher from York turned away. She caught him by the sleeve and turned him back again. "Go ahead! Let's have the rest of it, now you've started shouting it's a lot I know about it! Did you come up here to fight or run?"

"There ain't no woman going to talk to me like that," the butcher said, his face redder and shinier than ever.

"Why, bless me!" said Phoebe, standing up to him like a bantam, "you don't mean to say you *can* fight if you don't like the way I talk, do you? Not *fight!* Not with your enlistment running out in a week! You've got to go home in a week! You couldn't run the risk of getting hurt before then, could you?"

Noah Cluff laid his hand on her shoulder. "Phoebe, they's some things you don't understand, I guess."

"Is that so! Is that so! What is it that's so clear to you mental giants, but beyond my comprehension?"

"Now, Phoebe," Noah said, patting her as one might soothe a restive horse, "you know the colonel's a hard driver, and if so be we got to serve under him——"

"Don't say it!" she cried, taking Noah by the front of the coat. "Do you suppose I don't know what you're going to say, and where you got it? All that stuff comes from Hanchet. Every last scrap of it comes from Hanchet! Hanchet, the man that's got a grievance! You remember the time the pumpkin pies were stolen at Fort Western, and how Hanchet came whining around after them? He made a personal grievance out of it! Yes, and he did the same thing when Arnold took all the bateaux and hurried to Sartigan to get food for the rest of us. He didn't worry about how much *we* needed food, or how near *we'd* come to dying if somebody didn't hurry to get it for us! Not Hanchet! We could die and be damned for all he cared! The only thing worried him was the way Arnold seized his bateaux. He was insulted! When he was put in command on Point Levis, it was a personal grievance! When Arnold asked him to take down the cannon it was a personal grievance! Did he think about helping us, or helping the colonies? He did not! He thought about his nasty little self with his sticky-out jaw! You've got a gall to tell me I don't understand it! How many Treeworgys and Hanchets are we going to have in this army to keep us from taking Quebec?" She stamped her foot. "I understand a cry-baby when I see one, and that's what Hanchet is! He's a cry-baby! He's got Goodrich and Hubbard to crying with him; and now you've begun to cry because you see your captains crying."

"'Tain't so," said Butts from Wells, and his Adam's apple moved convulsively. "What I say is, an enlistment's an enlistment. We enlisted till the fust of January, and what they're trying to do is get us into a fix where the fust of January won't mean nothing."

"Nothing at all!" said the red-faced butcher.

"Nothing at all, like your talk," Phoebe said. "I never heard the beat of it! According to your argument, you wouldn't eat your Thursday supper if you didn't get it till Friday morning. You know as well as I do that if you'd been asked to enlist to the first of February instead of the first of January you'd have done so. You'd have enlisted for a year! Now you're whining you can't fight because you got to go home the first of January!"

She whirled on Noah Cluff. "Are you going to fight or quit?"

"I don't rightly know, yet, Phoebe," Noah said slowly.

"What about you?" she asked Nathaniel Lord.

"Why," Nathaniel said, "I came up here to fight; so if others decide they can't, I'll go with Dearborn's company."

"How about the rest of you?"

From some of them came a grumbling murmur; from most of them, silence.

"Well," Phoebe said, "let me know when you make up your minds. As long as there's any doubt, I'm ashamed to be seen anywhere near you. I've got to look out for my reputation. Come on, Steven."

Phoebe and Jacataqua and the yellow-faced dog went back to St. Roque with me, and I got them a lodging with Mother Biard, an old brown-faced French woman who lived in a log house stuck against the cliff like a sea urchin against the side of a pool, not three minutes from the Taverne de Menut. She sold charms, which was how I came to know about her. I have no faith in such matters, but her charms were too cheap to be passed lightly by. For one shilling she would sell a charm certain to bring its owner safe to the one he loved, or so she said. I bought one from her, since she declared she would give back the money if the charm proved ineffective. I have it still, tucked in the corner of my green seaman's chest.

XXXII

IF THE liquors we drank at Menut's tavern had proved one tenth
as false as the tales we heard there, the defenders of Quebec might
have thrown away their muskets, for we would have been poisoned
and helpless in no time at all.

It was a pleasant place, this tavern, on a December night with the
northwest wind whining across the St. Charles and setting the snow
dust to whispering against the broad front door and the little dia-
mond-shaped panes of its windows. On the ground floor was a big
room, walled with rough plaster and timbered overhead with oak
beams as broad as Cap Huff. Two deep fireplaces yawned at each
other across the room; and at the back was a door into the kitchen,
flanked on one side by a staircase and on the other by a handsome
broad bar behind which stood Moshoo Menut himself when he was
able to stand, which was not often. The staircase led to a large upstairs room with two fireplaces and gaming tables, where, according
to the boasts of Moshoo Menut, all the bloods of Quebec and the
garrison did their gaming before we arrived. That was the only name
by which Cap would address Menut—Moshoo. It was American
French, he said, and he liked to speak American French; whereas
Frenchified French, like the word Menut, sounded so namby-pamby
he was ashamed to say it.

When we started coming to the tavern the walls were covered
with proclamations in French from the old days, and flyspecked ballads brought from French ports by sailors. Among them was a pompous printed sheet signed by McLean, the commandant of Quebec,
telling what fine things would be done for any man who would enlist
in the Royal Highland Emigrants to fight against the rebels. He
would be given two hundred acres of land in any province of North
America, with fifty acres extra for his wife, if he was married, and
fifty for each child, and a present of one guinea on enlisting.

All the proclamations and ballads we carried away with us, but
this sheet we left; for the men took pleasure in spitting neatly

around it on entering or leaving the room, so it was framed in a dark wreath that grew constantly darker.

God knows where the men got the information they passed out so freely at Menut's—how more than fifteen hundred French folk in the city were ready to join us if we should ever get in; how Montgomery was going to allow each one of us eight hundred dollars in loot if we should take the city; how five hundred scaling ladders had been constructed to replace the overshort ones built at Point Levis; what Hanchet had last said to Captain Goodrich about Colonel Arnold; and how the British were sending trollops from the city infected with smallpox so that more of us might catch it.

That's the way with most soldiers: they believe anything, no matter how wild, and can't rest until they unburden themselves of their misinformation. We were uneasy at the loose talk we heard, and doubly uneasy over the manner in which a man here and a man there deserted to the British each day. Since new scaling ladders had been made, we knew plans must be afoot to make an attack on the walls; and even Cap Huff, with all his recklessness, could see we might find ourselves in a mess if the British, thanks to our deserters, got wind of our attack.

"It ain't safe," Cap said angrily, "it ain't safe, the way they talk! By God, Stevie, if they ever make me a general, I won't have nobody in my army but deaf and dumb soldiers that can't read or write! I'll take ten thousand men like that and knock the daylights out of all the men that England can send over here—yes, and France and Russia too!"

I had gone to the tavern with Cap, the day after Phoebe returned, to get warm and to show him the drawing that Arnold's friend, Mr. Halsted, had made for me of the location of Guerlac's house. I was determined Cap should have this plan in his mind, so that if anything happened to me in the attack, he could go for Mary and bring her away.

I drummed it into his thick head while he gulped down his Normandy cider with brandy; how, after ascending the long flight of steps from the Lower Town to the Upper Town and coming into the Market Place that lies before the cathedral, we must turn sharp to the right and walk one hundred and thirty paces; turn to the left into a narrow street; walk eighty paces along it; turn to the right and walk thirty paces down a steep incline and thus come to Guerlac's house, a one-story house with an arched bombproof roof, on the right-hand side of the street.

"What's the name of the street?" Cap asked, calling for more cider.

"Never mind the name. All you've got to know is that you go thirty paces along it."

"Suppose we come at it from the other end?"

"You poor fool!" I said, "you *can't,* if you don't know the name. All you can do is climb into the Market Place and start counting. To the right, one hundred and thirty; to the left, eighty; to the right, thirty."

"You want to get the name of the street," Cap said.

Before we came to words over it the door of the inn opened and Captain Smith of the Pennsylvania riflemen stumbled in, kicking snow from his moccasins. What it was that set me against Smith I think was not one thing, but many, including the manner in which he was known to have slaughtered the Indians in Lancaster Gaol, and the way he wet down his black hair on his low forehead, and the way he gabbed, gabbed, gabbed with anyone that would listen to him, as well as for his suspicion of me on Seven Mile Stream. At all events, I had no love for him; so I watched him when he came in, and thought to myself he was in liquor from the way he lifted up his feet too high off the floor.

Instead of going upstairs, as was customary with the officers who came to Menut's, he walked over to a table where there were some of his own men, among them a young volunteer cadet officer named Henry, a good woodsman. Smith clapped Henry on the shoulder, laughed foolishly, and said thickly: "Now you boys got something to keep you busy! We're going to attack. Yes, sir, we had a council! We're going to attack! 'Bout time, too, if you ask me! If we hadn't, those lousy Easterners would have run away and left us flat on our backsides."

I could see young Henry redden at the freedom with which this information was thrust on him. A baby, I thought, would have known better than to talk in a public place of what had been decided in a council of war.

The men at the table stared down at their drinks, saying nothing. The rest of the drinkers in the room were silent as well. Smith unknotted the sash of his blanket coat, and swayed on his feet, as if wondering what to say next. Then he chuckled. "Going to attack: and when we *do* attack, they won't forget it in a hurry! You know what we're going to do? There's going to be a false attack at St. John's Gate; and while it's going on, Arnold and the rest of us'll go into the Lower Town through St. Roque, and Montgomery by way of Cape Diamond. Yes, sir! When we meet we're going to catch the

women and the priests and the children and put 'em in with the
troops and march up the steps into the Upper Town! Let 'em try to
stop us *then*, by God!"

Such a stillness had fallen on the room that we could hear, in the
fireplaces, the hissing of the sap boiling from the ends of the logs.
Young Henry's chair scraped on the sanded floor. He stood up, a
fresh-faced, curly-haired boy. It was plain to be seen he was sorely
distressed by his captain. "Sir," he said protestingly, "sir——"

Smith gave him a jovial slap that forced him back into his chair.
"Yesh! It'll be on you 'fore you know it! You know when we march?
It'sh——"

He hiccuped. His eyes wandered, as if noting the unwinking
stares fixed on him. He seemed to take pride in being the center of
interest.

Cap drained the cider from his mug of shiny black earthenware,
stood up quickly astride his chair, and threw the mug at Smith, hard
and straight; but hard and straight as he threw it, he was not quick
enough. While the mug was in the air we heard the words "To-
morrow night!" Then the mug shattered against the back of that
hard, round head, and Smith went down on the floor.

On the moment every man's tongue was wagging. Fingers were
pointed at Cap, who had sat down immediately and was bellowing
loudly for more cider. It seemed to me it might be well for us to make
a run for it through the kitchen; but before I could suggest it there
was a clattering on the stairs and down came Major Bigelow, followed by Captain Thayer and Captain Topham.

"Here, here!" Bigelow said. "What's going on here?" He pushed
through the men, who were crowding up toward Cap in a way I
misliked. "Who did this?" he asked, looking down at Smith.

A dozen hands pointed at Cap.

"Well, for God's sake!" Bigelow said, staring at us. "What happened?"

"Major," Cap said, "it was an accident."

There was a murmur of protest. "He up and threw it!" cried a
little weasel-faced man from one of Montgomery's regiments.

"Why, Major," Cap said, "that feller's mistaken! I wouldn't have
done *nothing* to interrupt the captain, I was that eager to hear what
he was talking about. That mug just slipped out of my hand!"

Bigelow looked from Smith to the table where we stood at attention. "Slipped!" he said doubtfully.

"What was it you wanted to hear?" Captain Thayer asked.

"He was telling everybody about the attack," Cap said. "Letting everybody know which way we'd got to go, and how we'd get from the Lower Town to the Upper Town. When he come to telling when it was going to be, I got afeared I'd be the only one in St. Roque that wouldn't hear about it—maybe the only one in Canada. I put my hand up to my ear to hear better, and the mug slipped out of my fingers and caught him right on the back of the head."

"Could you hear him?" Bigelow asked quickly.

"Yes, sir," Cap said. "It hit him half a second after he said 'To-morrow night.'"

Bigelow and Topham and Thayer looked at each other, a blank, horrified look. Bigelow scratched his jaw and watched two of Montgomery's undersized New Yorkers sidle out into the night. "It appears to me," he said, "that this was an accident."

"I've seen several just like it," Thayer agreed. "It comes from using those slippery black mugs. They're apt to fly out of your hand any minute."

"Dangerous, I call 'em," Topham said.

"I saw him!" the little weasel-faced man persisted. "He hauled back and slung it."

Bigelow looked around. His eyes finally rested on Henry, who had been sitting with his back to us when Smith fell.

"You saw this, didn't you?" Bigelow asked.

"Oh, yes, sir," Henry said.

"And it seemed to you to be an accident, didn't it?" Bigelow persisted.

"Yes," Henry said earnestly. "It slipped right out of his hand!"

"You see!" Thayer said. "It comes from using those slippery black mugs. What they need is wooden mugs with the bark on."

*   *   *

In the morning one of Montgomery's men who had been in the tavern deserted to the British; so the plans of which Smith had spoken were abandoned. Nevertheless, we knew an attack was close at hand. It was high time, Cap Huff said; for he had spent all his pay, and exhausted the coins sewed in the tail of his shirt to boot, so he needed to get into Quebec to replenish his store. There were other reasons besides this one of Cap's; and these we had on Christmas Day, a clear day so cold we kept an eye on each other, lest our faces freeze.

There was an order that morning for Colonel Arnold's troops to parade in front of the colonel's headquarters, and this we did toward sundown. Cap Huff and I fell in at the rear of Captain Goodrich's company for reasons of our own; and when we had paraded, General Montgomery, tall and thin and pockmarked, came out of the colonel's quarters and talked to us, a straight, sensible talk.

We could not, he told us, take Quebec by siege, because we could neither make trenches in the frozen ground nor live in them if they were made, nor could we breach the walls with our light cannon. Neither could we invest the town, because our army was not large enough to shut off food and fuel from it. Only one plan remained, and that was to take the city by storm. We could, he told us, select our own place of attack, thus keeping the garrison on the watch both day and night, exhausting them; and the chances of success and glory were good. Yet there was hazard to it; so it seemed right to him that we should have some say in the matter.

He had paraded us, he said, so that we might, company by company, give our opinion as to whether we should attempt to storm the city or whether we should desert our countrymen who were fighting for liberty at Boston and at New York—desert them as Colonel Enos had deserted us on Dead River.

He went to Captain Morgan's company, saying to them: "Shall we storm?" The shout of "Yes!" that came from those tall riflemen, who had set their hearts on looting the city, must have been heard back at Pointe-aux-Trembles, eight leagues away. Indeed, I think if there had been one among them to shout "No," Morgan would have dragged him from the ranks and hatcheted him.

There was never a "No" among the two companies of Pennsylvania riflemen; and as for the companies of Topham and Thayer and Dearborn, they would have followed their captains into any sort of mess, as they had shown repeatedly, and so shouted "Yes!" with as much eagerness as the riflemen, albeit more raggedly.

Then the general came to Goodrich's company, and before he got the words out of his mouth Cap and I began to bellow "Yes! Yes!" In a hoarse and penetrating whisper Cap added: "I'll kill the louse that says 'No'!"

How many said "Yes" I have no way of knowing. Not all of them, by any means; yet none said "No." As for the companies of Hanchet and Hubbard, some said "Yes" without much vigor, while some uncertainly said "No"; and then a shouting of "Yes!" and "No!" arose among them, and there was unseemly and unsoldierly fist-fighting, at which Hanchet and Hubbard raged at the men and struck them with their muskets, for all officers had taken to carrying muskets except Montgomery and Arnold.

Montgomery turned his back on all this rioting and said loudly he would give a Christmas present of two shillings to each man of us to drink success to the storming.

We did little drinking that night; for when we went to have our dinner with Phoebe and Jacataqua, and told Phoebe how Goodrich's company had not voted "No," she set off at once, the rest of us with her, to have Christmas dinner with Noah Cluff and Nathaniel and Jethro and the rest, so they might know she was no longer shamed of them.

*   *   *

I think we would have stormed the city on the day after Christmas except it was so cold we couldn't have charged or primed our muskets, once they were fired, because of numb fingers.

On the second day after Christmas there was a thick snowstorm, which had been hoped for, since the garrison couldn't see us if we approached in a heavy fall of snow. We weren't surprised when word came to all the barracks, taverns and drinking places for the men to assemble at midnight in the streets of St. Roque, each man with a sprig of spruce or hemlock in his cap, so we might be distinguished from the British, whose clothing and ours were similar.

When I had this word I went to see Phoebe, and we sat in Mother Biard's kitchen—Mother Biard and Phoebe and Jacataqua and Mother Biard's white-and-yellow cat with a smudged face that made her look as though she had been rubbing against the bottom of a fry-pan, and the dog Anatarso, who sat at my feet and stared with moon eyes at the cat on my knees as though in love with it.

"Well," I said, when Mother Biard had heated a poker red hot in the stove and thrust it into a mug of cider to mull it for me, "we'll be away from here before long, and there's matters to be discussed, whether or no." I took a long drink of cider and scratched the cat's chin and wished myself elsewhere; for I had no desire to raise unhappy thoughts in Phoebe's head.

We sat in silence for a long time. Finally Phoebe looked up at me with a one-sided smile. "Did you say something?"

"I'm fishing about in my mind," I said. "I don't choose to have you refuse what I ask."

"Why, Steven," Phoebe said, her voice flat and low, "I won't refuse it."

"How can you be sure, when you don't know what I'll ask?"

"I always know what you're going to ask; but even if I didn't, I'd agree."

"Well," I said, when I'd taken another drink of cider, "I want you to go home. You and Jacataqua must go home. Now that the snow is deep you can go easily on snowshoes. I want you to get away from here and go back to Arundel."

"When do you want us to go?" she asked meekly, which was a surprise. I had looked for her to be contentious.

"When? Why, as soon as something happens. If we don't come out at once from the city, go immediately. I've saved some money for you. Jacataqua can find an Abenaki somewhere and hire him to help you across the Height of Land and the Chain of Ponds.

"I don't want any argument about this," I said, when she made no reply. "I want someone to look after my mother——"

"I'm not arguing."

"Here's another thing," I said, "I've written this out on paper so you can take it with you. My mother must have the garrison house for her own, because of my sisters and my brother; but the money in the keg under the kitchen is enough to buy a ship: a small ship, but a good ship. It's my wish a ship be built, one half of it to belong to you and one half to my mother. I've said in the paper that you should oversee the building of it; and in cases where you and my mother hold different opinions, she should remember you've had more sailing and trading experience than she. Also you're to have a home in the garrison house as long as you desire it, and I've made provision for Jacataqua because she's been my friend—for Jacataqua and for anything that might happen because of Burr. It's all in the paper."

"I need nothing," Jacataqua said.

"You can't tell. You might."

Phoebe took the paper. "What are you doing this for?"

"Just to be on the safe side. There won't be any need of it; but it's a good thing to have, so to know where everything stands."

"No, I mean *why* are you doing it? Why are you giving me half the ship?"

"Why? Why? Why, because you know how to sail a ship! That's the reason. I'll feel safer, knowing you're going to be around my mother, making money for her and looking after things."

She nodded and was silent, creasing the paper in her fingers, first along one fold and then along the other. At length, not looking up, she coughed a dry cough. "If you find Mary, I'll tear this up."

"You let it alone! I wrote it, and if there's any tearing up to be done I'll do it myself. We'll cross that bridge when we come to it."

Mother Biard hobbled about, fixing her next day's dinner in the covered kettle, after the manner of all French people. She put me in mind of Malary; and Malary put me in mind of the curlew pasties she was accustomed to make, piling curlews around a cup in a bowl and building the crust over the cup. I thought of Ranger, and how he would go through waves with his eyes shut to pick up curlews when I shot them: I thought of Eunice and the long gray crescent of beach; the white sand on the floor of the gathering-room in Arundel, and the fire roaring in the fireplace. From the fire my mind went to the sawmill, and to the new wharf I wished to build below the mill-dam in the creek. I thought of the creek and the river and the pollocks and the eels and the gulls, and of the skiff and how it needed calking. We spoke of all these things, and I had an overpowering desire to leave this land of long-queued Frenchmen and the crashing of bombs, and snow and ice and winds that froze the face, and get back to my own piece of land and my own people.

We might have talked all night but for a rattling at the door. "That's Natanis," I said. It had been agreed that Natanis and Hobomok would go forward with Cap and me, and that Natanis should bring word when all was in readiness. "It's Natanis, and I must go." I picked up my musket and went to the door, and it was Natanis.

"The snow has stopped," he said in Abenaki. "There is a moon. Word has come from the great chief there will be no attack this night."

The shadow of the cliff lay like a blotch of ink against the silver of the snow-filled street. Those on the walls could have picked us off like tethered turkeys if we had come out from the shelter of the buildings. I heard Jacataqua translating his words to Phoebe; but when I went to say good-night to her she was wrapped in her blankets in a corner, and didn't answer me when I spoke; so I went softly out and joined Natanis, thinking to myself that I must talk less if, when I spoke, I sent a person to sleep as quickly as all that.

*   *   *

I think those in Quebec were in a frenzy during the days that followed, knowing or suspecting they would surely be attacked if the weather turned thick. They kept up a steady cannonading on St.

Roque during the hours of daylight, and I couldn't run out to our advance posts in La Friponne, which we still did in spite of the great cold, without a shrinking feeling in my back—a feeling a dog must have when he hastens sideways, his tail tucked tight between his legs, past a man intent on kicking him.

We drew closer and closer to the day when the enlistment of Hanchet's and Hubbard's and Goodrich's men expired. The twenty-eighth and twenty-ninth of December were clear and perishing cold —so cold our necks ached; and at night the moon glared in a pallid sky like an imitation sun of polished ice. On the thirtieth there were wisps of clouds, the merest shreds, all disarranged, as though what wind there was, in that high air, were moving in a dozen directions; and the scar on my forehead throbbed.

On the thirty-first the wisps of cloud lengthened into streamers from the northeast. The day grew grayer as it progressed, and the cannonading of the British waxed more violent; and our lowness of spirit, when darkness fell, drove us to Menut's and to the little taverns of St. Roque for cider and brandy and warmth.

Menut's was in a turmoil that night because of a game called "Doctor Liberty," invented by Cap Huff.

There were many of our men, at this time, especially in Hanchet's and Goodrich's and Hubbard's companies, who didn't wish to fight, nor would they if they could escape. They assumed illnesses they didn't have, either moaning they were coming down with smallpox, or placing tobacco under their arms so to become pale and sick. Some scratched their fingers with knife blades dipped in the sores of smallpox sufferers, so they might catch the disease.

To cure these malingerers, Cap Huff, with a few Virginians and three or four from Topham's and Thayer's companies and Nathaniel Lord from Goodrich's, organized the Liberty Apothecaries.

It was the duty of the Liberty Apothecaries to discover men who were feigning illness. Once discovered, halters were placed around their necks and they were dragged before Doctor Liberty, who held his consultations in the corner of Menut's large downstairs room.

It was a pleasing game to watch, for it resulted, usually, in refreshments for all well-disposed onlookers. When I came to Menut's on that last night of the year, low in mind from the penetrating cold, and low in pocket because I had given Phoebe most of my money, Cap was officiating as Doctor Liberty, flanked on each side by brother Apothecaries. Two Virginians had just dragged before him the round-faced butcher from York, whose name I disremember.

As Doctor Liberty, Cap donned an apron borrowed from Moshoo Menut, and wore on his head a red fisherman's toque.

He drank heartily from his mug of cider and brandy; then looked at the red-faced butcher in a lofty manner.

"What is the complaint the patient complains of?" he asked, huge-some and dignified.

"Doctor," said one of the Virginians, "he complains of having smallpox symptoms complicated with bilious *combusto internalis* and the pip."

"Has he got 'em? Has he got 'em all?"

"Doctor, in the opinion of the Worshipful Company of Liberty Apothecaries, he ain't got any!"

"Well, what *has* he got?" the Doctor demanded with professional callousness.

"Doctor, the investigation ain't been pushed to the limit, but it's known to the Liberty Apothecaries he's got two hard dollars, and three shillings over."

"Is it the opinion of the Company that this patient should be cured of what he's got?" the Doctor asked, taking a two-foot kitchen knife from the table and passing his thumb across the edge with a rasping sound.

"Yes!" bellowed the Liberty Apothecaries.

"Sir and patient," the Doctor said, "if you can pay to the Worshipful Company of Liberty Apothecaries the sum of two hard dollars, and three shillings over, the Apothecaries will pronounce you cured and free of what ails you, and you will be at liberty to fight for your home and your fellow men. If you cannot pay us——"

With this the Doctor picked up his mug of cider and brandy, which was by way of being a signal to the Liberty Apothecaries, and they at once bawled "Liberty or Death!"

"Liberty or Death!" Cap said, setting down his mug with a bang. "Will you pay and fight, or will you sicken and die?"

The Apothecaries brought in eleven men that night, and all were hearty in preferring liberty to death. We filled them with brandy and cider until they declared themselves willing to fight the British, or any man in the room for that matter; and out of the money we took from them we bought cider and brandy for all who would drink confusion to the old year and success to the new. Somehow, Cap was able to withhold enough to purchase three mutton pasties for the Apothecaries, of whom I was made a member.

When Moshoo Menut brought the pasties, Cap embraced him and

made us a speech about the French, for whom he professed great love. He said that of all the people in all the Americas who wore queues, the French were the most generous and friendly, and their queues without peers. The French, he said, would be perfect companions if only they would learn to get along without garlic, or if we would only learn to eat it. Sometimes, he said, it almost made him cry to think two nations should be kept apart by a mere vegetable, root, fungus, or berry, if garlic were indeed any of these; and he, for one, would be willing to devote the rest of his life to helping the French give up the use of garlic.

All this was pleasing to Moshoo Menut, and he sent cider in to us at his own expense. Cap drank his health, and said, with a knowing leer, "*On Normandee noo boovong doo* see-*druh;*" then suddenly fell silent, staring and rubbing his face with his great red hands, as if caught in a drift of spider webs.

When we looked where he was staring we saw a sergeant major from headquarters standing by our table—a sergeant major whose blanket coat, all down the breast and sleeves and on the shoulders, was matted with snow. He straightened his arms with a snap. Wads of snow flew out of the creases in his sleeves, plopping on the table before us and striking coldly against our faces.

"She's come!" Cap whispered hoarsely.

"You bet she has," the sergeant major said. "A northeaster: thicker than gurry and getting thicker every minute."

He looked around the room and our gaze followed his. Men were going out of the door, two and three at a time. Others were struggling into their blanket coats.

"Orders are to go to your barracks, put yourself in readiness, and get what sleep you can," he said. "They'll tell you the rest of it at barracks."

He turned away and went to the next table. We knotted the sashes of our coats and drew our caps over our ears. One of the Virginians stopped in front of McLean's proclamation offering land to recruits in any part of the American colonies. "They won't get no part of my land!" he said. He threw a cider mug at the proclamation. It smashed full against the paper. We went out into the snow.

When we reached Mother Biard's, the thought came to me that if I wished to speak to Phoebe once more I must do it now. The Virginians went on and left us before the house.

"What you want to talk to her about?" Cap asked.

I knew there was something, but for the life of me I couldn't remember what.

"To hell with it!" Cap said. "She'll know you're gone soon enough! Let her sleep."

That was the sensible thing to do, though I would have liked her opinion on the new ship and Ranger and the garrison house and the building of a bridge across the creek and a new dress for my mother. I went closer to the door and saw the snow had drifted high against it.

Cap pulled me by the sleeve. "Come on! It's too cold to stand here all night."

We went on. The snow muttered and hissed in my ear. I was wrapped in gloom, instead of filled with joy that at last the time had come to go in search of Mary Mallinson.

XXXIII

IT WAS four in the morning when we were awakened by the bellowing of Daniel Morgan. We were belted into our blanket coats and out into the storm before, almost, we had dug the sleep from our eyes. Scaling ladders and pikes were pushed into our hands as we went out—a ladder for every twenty men, and a pike for every four; and I made up my mind, when I felt the weight of the pike that was shoved at me, that I would give it to Cap as soon as I could and depend on my musket butt for killing Britishers.

I thanked God, when I got out into the snow, that Morgan's men had been billeted so close to the walls; for we had slept until the last minute, while the others had been marched in from the hospital, with the snow driving hard into their faces.

The street was full of men, drawn up in double ranks. We filed silently between them. Hendricks's riflemen, dimly seen, were hunkered down in the rear, their backs to the storm and their scaling ladders leaning against them, already coated with snow. Beyond them we passed Goodrich's company. Later I heard Hanchet and Goodrich and Hubbard had been shamed into going when they saw parts of their companies would have gone without them. The weak companies had been placed between strong ones. Ahead of Goodrich's company was Captain Ward's, then Captain Thayer's and Captain Topham's, after which Hubbard's and Hanchet's were led by Smith's Pennsylvania riflemen. Smith, still suffering from Cap Huff's mug-throwing, had been replaced by Lieutenant Steele.

Beyond Steele there were no men, only a snow-filled street; and we formed in a double line, heading the column. I wondered what had become of Paul Higgins and his Indians; and even as I thought it, Natanis and Hobomok came running up through the snow. I drew them in behind me. Paul, Natanis said, was following slowly with his men. Eneas, he told me, had gone into Quebec the day before, and Sabatis too. "I think," Natanis said, "that Eneas is against us, but that Sabatis goes with Eneas only because he is his friend."

In our rear we heard a confused gabbling. Captain Oswald with thirty advance pickets plodded through the snow between us, all with their heads down and free of scaling ladders. A little behind them came Colonel Arnold, talking to the men in that rasping voice of his that set anyone who heard it to breathing more quickly.

"Now, boys," he was saying, "we'll all have a shot at it! Nobody can stop us if you fight the way you can! Don't stop! Never give up! Stick to me, boys! The general depends on us, boys!"

So he went past us, broad-shouldered and laughing, and moving as lightly and easily through the drifts as he had moved across our yard at Arundel years before, doing his feats of skill. On his right was the hulking figure of Daniel Morgan, and on his left young Matthias Ogden; and the three of them continued on into the snow after Oswald and his advance pickets. We fell in and moved ahead.

We could hear nothing because of the doleful yowling and moaning of the northeast wind and the hiss of snowflakes pouring into our faces and against our garments.

I have been out on dark nights and on cold nights; but I have never been out on a worse night than this, with the snow cutting into our eyes, and the icy wind sucking the breath out of our lungs so that we hung our heads almost to our waists to shield our mouths. The snow dragged at my feet, so once again I moved to the rhythm of my mother's spinning wheel. We couldn't move faster than a crawl. The wall towered above us, a black bulk beyond the whirling flakes, and I knew we couldn't go on much farther without discovery. This was what troubled me; I expected each moment that the bombs and grape-shot of the British would rip into us, and the suspense was like a nest of mice in my vitals—as bad, almost, as the snow.

If I speak over-often of the snow, it is because we struggled in a smothering, strangling universe of snow—a whirling world of snow: snow that froze to our guns: snow that clogged our eyes: snow that slipped up our sleeves and down our collars and under our caps: that bit our lips and stung our throats and numbed our cheeks and chins: that made our eyebrows and eyelashes into ice-cakes and our hands into vast and painful iron knobs. However we turned or screened ourselves, the flakes hissed and spat against us as if in scoffing derision at our puny shivering efforts.

We passed the ruins of La Friponne and the palace, which lie near the beginning of the walls; then entered a narrow way between the St. Charles River and the cliff on which the walls were built.

This was the beginning of the Lower Town, and we had never come in so far as this, any of us.

We were pinched between the river and the cliff. Against the cliff were warehouses; and the high tides had thrown ice-cakes close against their fronts, so that we picked our way between and over blocks of ice, painfully and slowly, slipping and stumbling.

We were bearing to the right, rounding into the Lower Town. The drive of the snow was against the sides of our heads and not into our faces. Cap had just turned to me and said hoarsely: "They passed back word the Hôtel Dieu's up there, if that makes you any warmer," when far off we heard a harmless thud, as though a twig had slapped a pillow. More thuds followed in quick succession.

A bell clanged high up above us in the snow and the darkness; and other bells joined in. Dogs barked. We could hear shouts from the towering cliff at our right. There was a rattle of musketry behind us; and from the cliff came stabs of flame, ghostlike in the whirling snowflakes. The whole side of the cliff burst out with flashes. Above them were sheets of light and the crash of cannon, stupendous bellowing crashes that seemed to press snow into my ears and hold it there.

I heard Cap foolishly shouting: "They seen us! They seen us!"

I strove to find a mark at which to shoot. When I would have shot at a flash, my musket missed fire and I was jostled forward by those behind. There were no shots at all from our column, for our powder and everything else had been wetted by the driving snow.

Somehow those on the cliff threw fire balls over our heads: balls that sent up a red flame the height of a man, even when they fell in deep drifts. We moved between the walls and the fire balls, through a hideous tumult of bell-ringing and musket fire and the smashing of bombs and cannon. There were flirtings in the air, like the whir of the little birds that fly from underfoot when one hunts in a marsh in the late summer. These flirtings were the sound of passing bullets.

I saw one of the Virginians on his hands and knees beside the path. When Cap reached out and pulled him to his feet and released him, he fell full length in the snow. We went on by him; for the labor of getting through the drifts was great, and there was no use dragging a wounded man.

We came to three more sprawled beside the path. One of them, face up, said something in a wheezy, bubbly voice. When I stooped over him, he asked to be turned face down. I did as he asked, and hurried ahead, hoping to God I wouldn't meet the same end.

Since there was a wider space between the cliff and the river, I shouted to Cap and we moved out of the footsteps of those that preceded us and struggled along more quickly.

This did us no good; for the column stopped. Before we knew it we came up with a cluster of men standing there as if wondering whether to go on or go back.

I heard a man say, "Get me up! Get me up!" It was Arnold's rasping, excited voice.

"Jesus!" Cap said. "They got Arnold!"

I could see him, then, hanging to Ogden's neck: at his foot a black stain in the snow.

"Spread out, boys!" he said. "Spread out, so you won't be a mark! And for God's sake get forward!"

Morgan began to bellow: "God damn it! Who's in command!"

"Greene!" Arnold said. "It doesn't matter! Get forward! We're not fifty yards from the barrier! Get at it!"

"Let me have 'em!" Morgan shouted. "I've been through this before!"

"Go ahead!" Arnold snapped.

Morgan shook his fist at us. "Come on!" he roared. "We'll show 'em, by God!" He went plowing through the snow like an angry moose. The rest of us followed, as fast as we could for our muskets and pikes and scaling ladders. I saw Ogden catch at a Virginian to help him with Arnold, and heard Arnold shouting: "Don't give up! Go on, boys! Go on, boys!"

It made me a little sick to hear his voice fading behind us, urging on the others, urging them on; for this was the end of all his laboring and scheming, and the end had been plucked out of his hands, leaving him hurt and bleeding in the snow, and the rest of us without his resourcefulness and his wild courage.

The cliff and the river seemed to come together. We ran shouting around a shoulder of the cliff and into a narrow street, the Sault-au-Matelot—a narrow, narrow street, barred by a stockade of logs. The stockade would have been higher than our heads but for the snow which had drifted so deep against it that we could scramble across. Morgan was over it with a bellow, and close behind him those who were unburdened with ladders or pikes. The rest of us heaved over the pikes and ladders as best we could and went blundering after, into the teeth of the howling storm.

There was a higher barrier beyond the stockade, a barrier with two ports in it. One of the ports burst in my face, a hot white glare that seemed to rip the lids off my eyeballs. It must have been that the charge went over our heads; for we came safe to the foot of the wall, all of us. There were four scaling ladders against it in less time than it takes to peel an onion.

Cap blew out his breath at me with a great whoosh. "My God! I don't like it!"

There were men crouched on each ladder, as if waiting to be pushed up. Morgan reached out and caught one of them, pulling him backward into the snow. "Get up here!" he bawled in that bellowing teamster's voice of his, and was up it like a cat—up it and into a blaze of light from the muzzles of a dozen muskets. He fell backward off the ladder, and his Virginians set up an angry roar.

"Jesus!" Cap said, "they got Morgan, too!" He went to the nearest ladder and pulled a Virginian off it, going clumsily up. Before he reached the top Morgan had scrambled out of the snow and up his ladder, yelling like a madman. I threw my pike after Cap and went up too, jumping blindly into the pit beyond and scrambling forward so those behind me might not break my neck. I seemed to be on a gun platform, for I fell off it headfirst into the snow. Cap was there, snapping the hammer of his musket at running figures, and cursing wildly when it missed fire, which it steadily did.

Morgan hobbled in a circle near us, favoring his right leg and shouting for the men to hurry. We could see them scrambling over the wall behind us; hear them falling and cursing on the gun platform.

I scuffed in the snow for my pike without finding it. Musket fire began to smash against our faces from the windows of a log house into which the running figures had disappeared.

"Prime your guns!" Morgan shouted. "Get down here and prime your guns! Prick 'em out; they're wet!"

We went to priming and snapping at the windows of the house. Melted snow must have run down the barrels, for never a one would fire.

"To hell with that!" Morgan roared. "Run 'em out!"

He went lumbering at the house. When we scrambled through the windows with our pikes and bayonets, we found the guards tumbling frantically out of the rear door. A Virginian caught one of them on his pike and pitchforked him screaming through a window.

Morgan's shouts were deafening. "Ladder men!" he bawled. "Ladder men! Bring over three ladders and leave one! Get 'em over here! The rest of you get after those guards! Get 'em before they reach the next barrier!"

We stumbled out of the guardhouse and hurried after the others. The street was narrow—so narrow the buildings seemed toppling on us in the pallid, snow-swept dark, but there was no musketry or cannon fire to pester us. I doubt any Britisher could have kept up with me in my running, because of my eagerness to get under the second barricade before its defenders opened on us. It may be the others felt as I did; for we were on the guards and they disarmed in little more time than it had taken us to get in and out of the guardhouse.

We pushed them against a wall, fifty of them, and were taking their muskets for our own use when there came another spatter of musketry from farther along the street. Cap Huff found me in the press and dragged me after him.

"Come on!" he shouted. "I want to get at these lice with a dry musket! By God, Stevie, they're scareder than I am, and I'm damned scared!"

Natanis and Hobomok were clinging to him. We set off again down the narrow street, holding our new muskets under our coats to keep them dry. We saw a musket flash from a window on the right and heard Morgan shouting to get them. The Virginians started a sort of jeering howl and ran up under the windows, thrusting their new muskets through the panes and letting them off in the rooms, at which there arose a crying and complaining from the interior.

Cap Huff put his shoulder against the door and smashed it in, shouting, "Come out!" There stumbled into the street a motley throng of folk, business men playing at soldier, all muddled and heavy with drink. At their head was a portly gentleman with a splendid uniform showing under his blanket coat, but so drunk he could scarce stand up without catching at one of us. By good luck or ill, he caught hold of Cap, and Cap held him firmly.

He was indignant, this fine gentleman, and wished to talk about it in spite of the cold and the snow. "Very unsporting!" he said. "Not thing do 'tall, swear 'tain't, not Noorsheve—not Noorearsheave."

He hiccupped noisily.

"Take their arms!" Morgan shouted. "Push 'em in a corner and put 'em with the others. Take 'em back in the house, Huff, and stand guard until the others come up. Come on, boys."

We herded these raddled fighters back into their house while Morgan and his men ran on. Cap held their leader until the last.

"That's a lovely uniform you got on, Captain," I heard him say.

"Man after m'own heart!" the leader said, pawing Cap. "Not sporting thing do, come interfering gen'lemen Noorearseve, bu's all right. S'pose you're one those damned Americans, eh?"

"Listen!" Cap said, shaking him fiercely, "I want those clothes! Take 'em off!"

The fine gentleman pawed protestingly at Cap. "No! Not clothes! Shoard! You want shoard! Fortunes war!"

Cap snarled at him. "Sword and clothes too! Quick about it if you don't want this pin pushed through you!" He jabbed his bayonet against his captive's stomach.

"Not sporting!" the captive protested.

Cap snatched his fine laced hat from him and clapped it on. "This ain't sport! Leastways, I ain't seen none yet! Get out of those two coats!" He seized the Englishman's blanket coat and had him out of it like stripping the husks from an ear of corn. "Now the uniform coat! Off with it!"

He seized the uniform coat as well; then threw his own stained coats, sodden with snow, to the protesting captive. Seeing that some of Goodrich's men had caught up with us, Cap, important in his fine new garb, issued orders concerning the prisoners with as much assurance as Morgan himself. Then he took me by the arm and hurried onward.

How far we had come I couldn't tell. We must have been more than half a mile from Palace Gate; and from the manner in which we had curved to the right, it seemed we must be near the center of the Lower Town, and approaching the tip of the point on which Quebec stands sentinel at the juncture of the two rivers.

We passed more prisoners, hunched over miserably, their backs to the driving sheets of snow, and came suddenly on the second barrier with our men milling at its foot. They, too, had prisoners. Between the two barriers we must have captured more than one hundred and twenty men. There was a turmoil at the barrier, with Virginians and Maine men and Rhode Islanders mixed together seemingly without leaders. From their way of speaking and moving I knew their nerves were frayed and jumpy, like my own. It seemed to me we had floundered through the snow for hours; yet there were no signs that day would ever break.

Far back, in the direction from which we had come, there was still the confused noise of cannonading and musketry fire. Captain Thayer ran past me and kicked open the door of a house close to the barricade. I followed, asking for Morgan.

"Good grief!" he said, "he's gone ahead alone to see what's happening."

"Can't we go ahead too?"

He hissed despairingly. "We're stuck! We've got more prisoners than ourselves. If they get away, they can turn the guns on us from either barricade!"

"Where the hell are the others?" Cap growled, crowding behind me.

"Where's Montgomery?" Thayer countered. "Montgomery ought to be here! This is where we meet! Mountain Street's just beyond the barrier. We can't even set fire to the town till we know where he is. The wind might carry the flames down on him!"

"Gosh!" Cap said, looking at the dark buildings that leaned over us, "what a box to be caught in!"

"We'll have to take to the houses!" Thayer said, stamping through the doorway. "At least we can shoot from 'em with dry powder if we have to!"

Natanis came close to us where we stood looking after Thayer. "There is a door in the barrier. The street is empty beyond. The guards have run in a panic."

We followed him to the log face of the barrier. At the left end, where it joined a house, there was a narrow sally port, closed with a tight-fitting door of logs, a loopholed door. Hobomok stood by the door, his eye at a loophole. As we came up he opened the door and went through, and so did we. Beyond the barrier the street bent to the right, then divided, one of the divisions curving upward and the other running along the base of the cliff, as had the Sault-au-Matelot. The streets lay empty and snow-filled before us, shrouded in a pallid, wind-swept darkness.

"I'm going up into the other town," Cap said. "This curving street is Mountain Street. Somewheres beyond it are the steps that go up into the Market Place. What was it you said? A hundred and thirty paces to the right; turn to the left and go eighty paces; turn to the right and go thirty paces downhill; and the house is on the right. That's it, ain't it?"

"We can't leave them this way!" I protested.

Cap took me by the sash of my blanket coat and ran me into the shelter of the houses on the lower street, Natanis and Hobomok following in our footsteps. "You damn fool! We've fought our way into the city! What's going to happen if Montogomery doesn't come, and the garrison comes back and catches 'em in that street? Do you think they'll ever get out of that trap?"

"Let's get them through."

"Not by a damned sight! They can't move till Morgan comes back to tell 'em what to do. For that matter, they can't move anyway. They've got more prisoners than they can handle. They're finished as soon as any man fires a gun, because the prisoners will jump on their backs. You can't help anybody by staying behind that barrier; and you'll never get another chance to see Guerlac and Mary if the city ain't taken to-night."

"My God!" I said, "if Arnold was only here!"

"Well, he ain't!" Cap said. He started off up the street and we followed him. He turned back to us. "Listen! You're my detachment. If anybody speaks to us, keep your mouths shut while I talk English to 'em." He went ahead again, hulking and swaggering in his jaunty hat and his new coat, a fine figure of an officer. Far away to our right there were dull reports still; near at hand nothing but silence, as though the tall houses stared down at us with bated breaths.

A door creaked open at our shoulders and a woman scuttled out, an old woman with a bundle. She squeaked when she saw us; turned to scuttle back; then slipped and fell. I suspected how she felt; my heart had leaped within me, as at a partridge roaring from under foot, when the door opened. Cap pulled her to her feet, observing gravely, "On Normandee noo boovong doo see-druh!"

The woman burst into a flux of French, kissed Cap's hand, and went spraddling through the snow ahead of us. We overtook her. Cap picked her up, bundle and all, and swung her onto his shoulder. An old man and two women, one of the women dragging a child, popped out of an alley, stopped at the sight of us, then came on again, panting and struggling at our sides. I took the child under my arm, for it sank to its withers in the snow; and its mother, if mother it was, seemed to lack strength to drag it.

Ahead of us we saw five or six women and old men, each with a child or two, and some of the children crying, thin and futile in the whirling snow.

There was grayness in the air, the grayness of dawn. We came into a small square. On its far side was a steep-roofed papist chapel. We went past the chapel, and saw the folk ahead of us turn sharp to the right. In the snow were many footprints, all bearing to the right;

so we guessed there had been a panic in the Lower Town, and a great fleeing to the Upper Town.

There was a gate, flanked by small guardhouses, where these folk had turned. When we ourselves turned we saw a long, long flight of steps, walled with a stockade of logs in which there were small bastions for light artillery and muskets: a flight of steps so long and so steep that its top was shrouded in the storm. For all we knew, it led into the clouds or into heaven. It was spotted with climbers, slipping and falling as they climbed. With no word to each other we started up behind them.

I don't know to this hour whether the guards of the stairway, which was one of the two methods of getting from the Lower Town to the Upper Town, had gone to repulse an attack at some other place, or whether they had fled in a panic, as had the guards at the second barrier, or whether they were hidden in their guardhouses and failed to challenge us because we were dressed as the British were dressed and were helping fleeing citizens of the Lower Town. I think they had fled in panic, as they had done at nearly every barricade in the city at certain times during our attack. None of us cared why they weren't there: we cared only that they weren't, and thanked God for it.

By using our muskets as staves we came safely up the broad treads of the stairway, mounted a steep road that continued upward from it, and found ourselves in a wide square with a great building at each end, one of them a church with towering steeples. The wind howled dolefully across the square, piling up the snow in drifts. Those we had helped spewed out a tangle of French at us and lurched off into the snow. We turned sharp to our right in the dim gray light, plodding after Cap.

"One hundred and thirty!" Cap said.

We were at the entrance of a narrow street, wider than those in the Lower Town, but none too wide in case there were musketmen peering at us from the shuttered windows.

We turned into it. The houses were one story high and close together. Between and behind them we could see tall trees which creaked in the furious wind. I could hear Cap counting under his breath. When he reached eighty we were abreast of a narrow street pitching steeply downward to our right. The houses on it were large and surrounded by trees.

"That's the street!" I said to Cap. "Thirty! Hurry! It's getting light!"

We hurried on, stepping in Cap's footsteps to leave as little trail as might be. We could hear a cheering from the town below us, coming straight down wind; then, from the direction of the second barricade, scattered musket shots. A bell clanged and clanged, mournful in the high wind, the sound swelling and dying as though the bell suffered for those who had fought and died in the snow.

"Thirty!" Cap said.

On our right was a white house with a curved roof, such as Quebec folk build as protection against cannon shot—a house sheltered among tall trees. My heart was pounding. The musketry fire in the Lower Town had grown so heavy I could scarce think. "Into the trees," I ordered. Cap went into them with long strides, the rest of us after him.

"What if it ain't the house?" he asked.

"It's the house," I said. "I can feel it. How'll we do it, Cap?"

"Send Hobomok to pound on the front door while the rest of us go in the back."

"No," I said, "all the men in this town are being used to defend it. It's best to leave no marks at the front door in case they come home. If any man comes to this house we can't have him scared away."

"Not till we're ready to scare him," Cap agreed. "We'll rip off a blind and throw you through a window."

"All right! Work fast and make no noise. When we're in, close and bolt everything behind us. Get at it!"

"I hope to God we'll find something to drink!" Cap whispered hoarsely.

"I hope to God we'll find Mary!" I said.

We stole out from the trees in single file and made for the back of the house.

I remembered an old saying of my father's—"Try the simplest ways; they work oftenest." I hissed at Cap, ran up the steps outside the back door, and tried the handle gently. It turned in my hand. The door opened and I went in.

XXXIV

THERE was a fat woman in a decent gray habit standing over the stove, a spoon raised to her lips. Beside her, holding a tray, was a comely wench in a black dress. Sitting at a table near by was a serving girl, a small pretty thing, her gray skirts bunched in her lap and one hand thrust into the leg of her stocking so she might ply a needle on it with greater ease. Over everything was a smell of coffee, a rich, pungent, delicious odor that set my mouth watering.

Misliking the manner in which the white showed around the fat woman's eye when she turned her head from her spoon and saw me over her shoulder, I went quickly to her and took the hand that held the spoon, swinging her down upon the floor, where I could get my hand comfortably over her mouth or around her neck. The comely wench dropped the tray with a clatter, but before the gurgle in her throat became a shriek, Cap had her. I could tell from the way he looked at the serving girl, who had wrenched her arm in her agonized haste to get her hand out from her stocking and her skirts down where they belonged, that it pained him to be unable to deal with the two of them.

Natanis had the serving girl before she could cry out, though I doubt she could have uttered a sound.

"The first one that screams," I whispered, giving the fat cook's face a sharp squeeze, "gets a hatchet in the head." I told Natanis to repeat it in French, which he did. I set Hobomok to hunting for the door into the cellar, which is beneath the kitchen in these Quebec houses.

A bell in the corner began to jangle. Hobomok took the cook from me and hustled her through the trap in the floor, while I made fast the door through which we had entered. The bell jangled again while Cap and Natanis dragged the others after the cook. I listened at the inner door, and in a moment there came a faint voice, soft and pleasant, calling, "Justine! Justine!"

"Get a rope and fasten them down there," I said to Cap. "I'm going in."

*   *   *

I opened the door quietly and went into a long corridor. There were doors on each side, and at the end a larger door, which I took to be the front door. The corridor was warm and had the heavy feel of a house still asleep or half asleep—that, and a sweet odor of violets. I stood there listening, uncertain which door to open until the voice called again, impatient and peremptory, for Justine.

I moved down to the door. It opened. The girl who stood there, wild-eyed at the sight of me, was the same brown-legged Mary Mallinson who had last looked at me from the shadow of the pines across the creek from our garrison house. She had on a nightdress that clung to her, as I could see by the light of a candle she carried in her right hand. Her hair was thick and golden, and she was working at it with her left hand, as women will, to twine it into the semblance of order. Across her nose, from cheek to cheek, was a faint golden dust of freckles. I saw she was beautiful; yet I could see no great likeness between her and my Mary because her face was twisted from the fright I had given her.

I cleared my throat to speak. She threw the candle at me, darting back and pushing at the door, screaming as she did so, a shrill, terrified scream, that must, I thought, go out through the walls of the house and into every other house in Quebec as sharply as it pierced my own ears. I stopped the door from closing with my foot, forced it open, and caught her before she could scream again.

"Mary," I said, putting my hand over her mouth, "Mary, don't scream! I'm Steven Nason. You remember me, Mary!"

She wrenched herself away and screamed again—or started to; for before she could get on with it I clutched her tight against me and choked off her breath. The caked snow from my blanket coat was melting from the heat of the room. Her nightdress was as wet from it as though she had stood in a rainstorm.

"You keep your mouth shut," I said. "Keep it shut tight! I've come too far to get a bullet through me because a woman can't be quiet!"

My mind should have had room for no one but Mary, who had held my heart and my love from the first day I knew about such things. Yet my thoughts turned to Phoebe. What, I wondered, would Phoebe say if she could see me dripping water on Mary's nightdress? What would she do? Would she laugh? Would she jeer at me? Would she twist her cat's eyes between her fingers and sniff, and cough her hard, dry cough? Phoebe!

"Cap!" I shouted, still clinging to Mary and clutching her mouth none too gently with a hand that must have felt to her like a rough and wrinkled boot.

"Right here!" He seemed to have been standing behind me, listening.

"Get lights," I said. "Put Natanis at the front of the house and Hobomok at the rear, so we'll know if anyone comes. And get lights!"

Mary struggled and squirmed in my arms like a soft warm kitten, but her fingernails scratched me like the claws of a cat. I damned her and shook her until she lay quiet.

Cap hurried back, a candle in one hand and a bottle of brandy in the other. He went around the room lighting the candles that stood in sconces against the wall, enough candles to have lit ten rooms. The bed was the size of a sloop; and raised above it on four posts like masts was a red velvet tent, rich and useless. There were velvet curtains at the windows, and on the floor a quantity of skins, mostly white bearskins. There were chairs, all carved and cushioned; and on the bed were silken coverlets. The heady scent of violets had, in this room, become almost piercing. I still held Mary tight in my arms while I looked around; and the thought in my head fair graveled me, for it was that I must remember everything in order to tell Phoebe. Phoebe! for God's sake! I said to myself. I dragged Mary to the bed and threw her onto it, drawing the coverlets over her wet nightdress.

"Now listen to me," I said, with my hand still over her mouth, while Cap stood at the foot of the bed, sipping from his brandy bottle and eyeing Mary and dripping snow water from his coat on the silken coverlets. "If you scream when I take my hand away I'll gag you so your tongue will be pushed half down your throat." I freed her and stepped away, stripping off my sodden coat.

"Good idea!" Cap said. He removed his own, carrying the two of them from the room.

Shivering and cowering in the bed, Mary burst into a flux of French. She sobbed and snuffled and poured out French at me. Her blue eyes, peering out over the edge of the silken coverlet, never once moved from my face.

"Mary," I said, "I don't know a word you say. "I'm Steven Nason from Arundel. The other is Cap Huff, who threw Guerlac into the mud when we were children. We'll do you no harm if you're honest with us. You'll have to speak English."

Again she rattled at me in French, emphatic and indignant.

I could tell she was insisting that her name was De Sabrevois—insisting, too, that I should leave the house.

Cap came back with his brandy bottle and wandered around the room, picking up small silver articles from tables, examining them carefully, and peering into drawers.

"Cap," I said, "she doesn't remember any English."

Cap took a small leather case from the back of a drawer and opened it. "Don't be a damned fool! She stopped screaming, didn't she?"

Her glance traveled from Cap to me. Cap tossed the leather case into the drawer and turned sharply on her. "Hark, little lady! Do you think we dodged bullets and cannon balls and climbed into this lousy city to have you make a fool of us with your damned frog-eating French?"

She watched him without speaking.

Cap snapped his fingers impatiently. "Speak up!" Seemingly as an afterthought he laughed and added, "Sister!"

"What do you want?" she asked faintly.

I was stonied by the suddenness of the question, and racked my brains for a reply. Cap spoke up again. "I want something to eat. That's what I want and it's what you want, too, Stevie."

"Yes," I said, "I do. So does Mary. We broke in on her breakfast. She can get dressed while we're in the kitchen."

"She can get dressed while we're right here," Cap said, pulling out another drawer and rummaging among its contents. "She's too tricky to suit me."

I protested we couldn't shame her so.

"Shame her be damned! Let her dress under the bedclothes if she thinks we want to peep at her. I'd rather shame her than be caught like a rat because of her trickiness."

He picked delicate garments from a chair, peered at them curiously, sniffed loudly at them, expelled his breath in a noisy, ecstatic sigh, and pitched them onto the bed. "Get into those!"

"You great beast!" Mary said. "I'll touch nothing you've had in your hands."

"Oh, ho!" Cap said. "You've got finicky since you used to go bare-legged and wear blue cotton in Arundel. Put 'em on, or I'll put 'em on you myself." Again he paused, adding "Sister!" in a mincing tone.

"Cap," I said, "I don't like the way you talk! It's no way to talk to—to—it's no way to talk to Mary."

"No, it ain't, and that's a fact; not to Mary." He took a silver-backed brush from a dresser and attacked his hair with it. "That's a nice brush," he said, looking at it admiringly "H. G. deS. Those your initials, Sister?"

Mary was under the bedclothes and couldn't answer.

"Cap," I said, "I won't have it. You've got to stop."

Cap pulled me out in the hall, leaving the door open so he could keep an eye on Mary and her squirming beneath the coverlets. "Listen, Stevie," he whispered hoarsely. "We can't get out of this house till dark, if we get out at all. We might have to stay in here all day! God knows how we'll get out, in that case, or who may come while we're here. Guerlac might, for one, unless he's dead, and I'll bet he ain't. Now don't go getting soft about this Mary of yours until you know she won't stick a knife in your back if she gets a chance. She ain't our kind of folks any more, Stevie. She's a lady, and we're nasty, terrible people."

"No," I said. "She's frightened, poor thing."

"That won't hurt her none!" Cap growled, going back into the bedroom.

She was dressed by now in a gown of heavy blue stuff that clung to her. It had a collar that turned back from her white neck, and sleeves that came down over the backs of her hands. I had never seen a dress so fine or a face so beautiful as Mary's. There was a fragile, disdainful look to her: a look as though the labor of smiling would be more than she cared to undertake, and one that might crack her face into the bargain. There was a golden dust beneath her eyes, the dust that had caused the Frenchman Sharl to call her a Lily of France when he told me of her; and the braids of her hair seemed as golden and heavy as the loops of golden candy my sister Cynthy makes from molasses at Christmas time and pulls over an iron hook with butter on her hands. Yet I couldn't keep from thinking what would have become of this hair and this soft white skin in the swamps of Lake Megantic.

I stood looking at her. Truth to say, I stared and stared like an owl, and had no more to say than an owl. For, grown man as I was, I was like a boy who has a long daydream broken into suddenly. That was the case of it with me, in true fact; but the boyhood daydream had lasted within me over years. How many thousand times had I pictured my meeting with Mary when I should come to rescue her, what I should say to her and what she should say to me. And now the meeting had come to pass at last; but here was no Mary Mallinson at all before me. Here was a fine lady, Frenchified and delicate; and it was in her eyes that she thought of me just what she would have thought of an oversized, wet, and grotesque black bear out of the shaggy woods, if such a creature had come blundering into this exquisite bedchamber.

So I looked and looked at her and tried to speak, but instead I swallowed; and then, to find at last the makings of some sort of sound to make easier a kind of misery within my chest, I coughed several times as heartily as I could.

"Well——" I said, coughing again. "Well——" And saying no more I went to the front of the house and stood there.

After a little I turned into a room at the left of the corridor, and found Natanis peering out through a peephole in the closed shutter. There was an iron stove in this room, and fur rugs on the floor and paintings on the wall. Hanging from the ceiling, in glittering festoons, was a candleholder, made all of pieces of glass.

"The snow has let up," Natanis said, "but I think it will storm again. There has been no man on the street. This house is strong. There's an iron shutter on each window, and two doors, both iron."

I went to the door and unbolted it. It was as Natanis said. The first door opened inward; and three feet beyond it was the outer door, also of iron, opening outward. I showed Natanis that I was unbolting the outer door and leaving the inner door fastened.

"If any man comes, call me. Then open, and hide yourself behind the door as he enters. Between us we'll have no trouble. Keep watch. Soon there'll be food. I think we'll come well out of this."

I went into the kitchen. Hobomok sat against the back door, watchful; and in the middle of the room there was Mary sitting in a chair, looking straight at the wall. Cap, standing before her, was in no pleasant mood.

"Damn her!" he said. "She swears to God she don't know how to cook, and I'm beginning to believe her. It's a disgrace to the town of Arundel and the whole damned province of Maine, if you ask me! Can't cook! Gosh! I never expected to live to see the day a Maine woman couldn't cook!"

Mary never looked at him, nor at me, but she spoke in a husky voice. "Maine woman? I? You take me for a filthy Bostonnais?"

Cap's jaw dropped. He put a hand on each knee, squatting, open-mouthed, to stare at her the more strickenly. "Filthy who?"

"Mind your own business!" I told him. "There's plenty of women in Maine that can't cook, either, not any more than a chipmunk can, though they call it cooking. Why don't you cook your own breakfast?"

"Well, mebbe I better," Cap said, straightening up. "Us filthy Bostonnais have got to have our food."

"What can we have?" I asked.

"Why," said Cap, in some surprise, "there ain't nuthin' left in the world but pork, is there? Pork and wine wouldn't be bad for breakfast, Stevie: a little pork and a lot of wine." He turned to Mary, and the tone in which he addressed her was more polite than his words. "Where's the pork, Sister?"

"Where are my servants?" Mary asked.

"Everything's in the cellar," I told Cap. "You know it well enough. Bring up two dozen eggs and some of that Beaune if there is any."

Cap went down into the cellar with a candle, and there was a sound of squealing from below as he went. At this Mary turned her eyes on mine so that I was fair sickened by the uncomfortableness that her glance put upon me, but made shift to answer what seemed to be a scornful question in her look.

"The womenfolk are down there, but they'll come to no harm," I told her gruffly. Then, with what I knew to be a loutish awkwardness, and most lamely, while her eyes still remained upon me, I tried to say some of the things I had so many, many times dreamed I should say to her some day. But I failed, of course. I stammered, and was not able to conclude a sentence, so that my speech, like my presence of mind, was all fragments.

"I—I followed you with my father, but——" I said. "We tried to rescue—we tried—and after that every year I thought that I could—I always meant to come—I never forgot——"

She broke in on me with a cold little laugh. "There's one thing I know," she said, sliding her eyes toward me in a way that had stayed in my heart for many years, "and that is that this man wouldn't be where he is if the Bostonnais had captured the city." She meant Hobomok and his watching at the door with his musket between his knees.

"Mary," I stammered, "of course I always meant to come some day —on account of my promise——"

"Promise? You made a promise?"

"Why, I mean the promise after we'd had the lobsters in the dunes —when you—you kissed me and made me promise to marry you."

She had a wisp of a handkerchief in her hand. She dabbed at her lips with it. Her eyes sank until they rested on my feet. Then she lifted them and looked at my hands as though they weren't clean, though I think they were because of the deal of snow that had melted on them since I had started out of the barracks into the storm.

I swallowed again. "I think we can find some way of getting you out of the city, Cap and I, if so be you'll come. We can go back to Arundel. I've always expected to take you back to Arundel."

She raised her eyes to mine again. They were as blue as my mother's teacups that Captain Callendar brought her from England; as blue and as hard.

"Arundel! That stinking nest of log huts among the fish bones?"

"What!" I said, gaping at her. "Is that what you think of it?"

"You!" she cried suddenly and loudly, hurling the word out of her throat with such a fury of disgust in it that I almost staggered back from her. "You—you peasant! You innkeeper!"

"Well, for God's sake! What are you talking about!"

"Look around you!" she bade me fiercely. "Are you such a fool that you cannot see what this house is? There's no finer house in all Quebec! Do you know who comes to it? The governor comes to it! There's no man in Canada who is not honored to come to this house and eat at my table! Do you know how many men would give their souls to kiss this slipper?" Almost to my horror she thrust out at me her little foot in gilded leather, with a high red heel. "And do you know who they are, and do you know their quality? The highest here! Officers and gentlemen! And you talk to me of going back to your fisherman's cesspool! You boor, with your dirty, smelly clothes and your nasty rough face! You'd never be allowed in this house unless you came like a thief, you and your gaol-bird companions!"

"Good God!" I muttered. "Good God!"

There was a clatter behind me. Cap dropped the trapdoor with a bang and stowed an armful of meat and eggs and bottles on the table. "Gosh!" he said, walking over to Mary and staring hard at her face. "I heard what she just said, Stevie; and now I know who she reminds me of! It's her father, Stevie! He never said a sensible word in his life, and she's inherited it from him!"

He poked the fire and reached for a saucepan, when Natanis opened the door and spoke quickly in Abenaki.

"Take care of her, Cap," I said. "No noise!"

With that I went out after Natanis. He had said that Guerlac was coming to the house, alone.

*   *   *

I went close to the front door with Natanis and stood there. We could hear a fumbling at the outer latch, and catch the faint whine of hinges. There was a metallic banging at our very ears. My heart leaped as Natanis drew the bolt and opened the door. It folded back and hid the two of us in that dim corridor. Guerlac stepped jauntily past us, tugging at his sash and his blanket coat.

"Marie!" he called. "Marie!" As I closed the door behind him, he added in French some words I could not understand, following them with what he may have considered an imitation of our own nasal New England speech. "Couldn't do nawthin'l!" he shouted gaily. "Captured or killed every mother's son of 'em, the damned dirty rabble!"

He stopped and listened. "Marie!" he shouted again. He turned, his coat in his hand, seemingly with the intention of tossing it to the person who had opened to him, and saw Natanis standing there, not two feet distant.

He sprang away, clawing for his sword, and put himself squarely in my grasp. As I closed my hands around his arm Natanis took the other. He strained against us for a moment; then went slack.

"This is unexpected," he said, in the dry, delicate, displeasing tones I well remembered from my one meeting with him. "My eyes are dulled by the snow. To whom am I indebted for this greeting?"

"Old friends of yours," I said. "Old friends. You have a slit ear to help you remember my father, who gave it to you; and you may recall giving me the scar on my own forehead. There's another old friend of yours with us: one who hasn't seen you since he kicked you into the mud, where you belonged."

The door at the end of the corridor flew open on the candle-lit kitchen and Cap Huff peered out to see what we were about. I tightened my hold on Guerlac, thinking he might try to break from us at the sight that met our eyes—Mary bound hand and foot in a chair and gagged with a towel, done by the forethought of Cap Huff to keep her from trying to warn Guerlac of what awaited him; Hobomok leaning against the door with his musket between his knees, glowering at us; and Cap towering over both of them, a gaudy figure in his British officer's garb.

We took Guerlac to the kitchen, where Cap lashed his feet together; and we made him fast to a chair with his hands tied behind him. Then we took the gag from Mary's mouth, an easement that in a way seemed useless, since she sat silent.

"So!" Guerlac said, staring at us coolly. "Four deserters who ran from comrades in peril!"

This was no time to lose our tempers, I knew, and I could see Cap knew it too. I studied Guerlac. He had changed little since his visit to our inn at Arundel. His hair was gray over his ears, and there was a scar across his right cheek and ear where my father's arrow had clipped him. Beneath his chin there was a little fullness; but otherwise he was as slender and haughty as the picture of him that had clung in my mind.

Cap sliced pork into the saucepan. "Gosh! What with tending this wench, and waiting for this damned light-fingered murderer you just brought in, I'm starving!" He slammed the saucepan on the fire, where it sizzled bravely, sending out a cloud of fragrant smoke.

"Yet," said Guerlac, "it should be nourishment enough to know that when your comrades are rotting in gaol, you'll be hanged for spies. That will happen, I take it, as soon as my friends come here and find you."

"Get some cups, Stevie," Cap said. "We want to make a kind of holiday out of this. 'Tain't every day you catch a murderer in his own house, and it's New Year's Day and all! We wouldn't want to drink this man's wine out of a bottle, not even if we *are* filthy Bostonnais."

He fished the pork from the saucepan and broke a dozen eggs into the sizzling grease. We found bread in a box beneath the table and made a fair breakfast, with two dozen eggs and the pork, and cups a third full of the coffee the cook had left on the stove and two thirds full of wine, a fine satisfying wine called Mersault. God knows I needed something to hearten me, what with the hours we had kept and our fight in the Lower Town and the manner in which Mary had spoken to me, and now this news of Guerlac's that our men had been killed or captured. Whether to believe it or not, I didn't know; but I knew that if I showed him I wanted to know he would lie to me fit to tangle my brain like a wet anchor rope.

Cap tilted back in his chair when he had finished and looked with a cold eye at Guerlac. "I'm surprised, I vow I am, that you haven't got Mallinson's scalp hanging up as a decoration."

Guerlac sat silent, his eyelids drooping.

"I thought of you often," I told him, "after you took Mary and did your best to split my skull in doing it. Lately I've wondered why you, a captain in the regiment of Béarn—you, an English-hater—should now be fighting with the English against Americans. All other Frenchmen are with America, to be revenged on the English."

"Why," he said, "you're as ignorant as all Bostonnais! Some of us in Quebec recognize the justice of the British cause. Colonel Voyer and Captain Dambourges and Captain Maroux and Captain Alexandre Dumas fought with the English in the Sault-au-Matelot, this very day, against your rabble."

"That may be," I said, disregarding his attempts to enrage me and watching his face carefully, "but you gave Colonel Arnold to believe you sympathized with him."

He laughed lightly. "To be sure! I had sympathy for him until I learned he seriously intended to be such a fool as to attack Quebec. Then I withdrew my sympathy."

"And his letters," I said, "I suppose you gave to the government."

"Why," he said, "you're as good as a lawyer! I've had no letter from Colonel Arnold in three or four months."

I saw I could get nothing from him, nor was I sure he had anything for me to get.

We were silent, a strange, uncomfortable company; and the stillness lasted until there was a movement from Hobomok. He hissed a warning and got up from his chair, bringing his musket to his hip.

"No shooting!" I whispered.

Cap picked up the poker from beside the stove and wagged it lightly between Guerlac and Mary. "A little noise from anybody now," he whispered, "even from a lady, would be awful dislikable!"

There was a fumbling at the latch of the bolted door, and then a sharp rap.

"How many?" I asked Hobomok softly.

"Two! Eneas and Hook!"

*   *   *

I shot the bolt and tore open the door. It was Hook who had rapped, and Eneas stood behind him. I had already made up my mind what to do, and instantly I leaped out at Hook; but he was quicker than I: my reaching hands did not touch him. I stumbled and fell flat in the snow, the leap carrying me clear of the doorstep.

Now this was a mischance that proved a grave one; for we had to deal with men not only powerful in muscle, but nimble and quick-witted in fighting; and within a trice they were near to our undoing.

Eneas jumped upon me before I could move. He had his knee into my back so that the breath left me, and he jerked upward with his hands beneath my chin, to break my neck. His act was so quick and so violent that I seemed to be in a paralysis and had no power to throw him off, but only to stiffen the muscles of my throat as much as I could. I seemed to feel them breaking, and the spine that braced them cracking.

With eyes starting out of my head, I saw Hobomok a little before me, and it seemed to me he was running away, as if stricken with panic. Then I heard a dreadful groaning kind of grunt, which I knew to be in the voice of Cap Huff; and a great scarlet body seemed to hurtle through the air as if heaved by some mighty power, and it flopped down beside me and lay inert, a crimson splotch in the white snow. It was Cap Huff, apparently dead.

From behind me I heard the report of a musket and saw Hobomok stagger, so I knew he was shot.

Thus, in a trice, we seemed undone, so sudden, sometimes, are the overturnings that may befall men just when they are most cocksure. We four, Natanis, Hobomok, Cap and I, had no thought that misfortune could overwhelm us in any such manner. Opposed to us were only two men, attacked by surprise, and a man tied to a chair, and a girl; and in less than half a minute they had turned the tables against us and we were on the point of ruin. Nay, for myself, I was worse than that: I was at the point of death, and I knew it: my sight wavered, and such spouts of pain burst through all my upper parts and zigzagged in lightnings of anguish through my brain that never had I felt the like before, and was all too sure no one could thus suffer long and yet be alive.

It is wonderful that a man can be in so desperate a posture and still think; yet I did have thoughts, and wonderings, even then. It seemed to me there was something in what men call the ironical: to have dreamed of Mary Mallinson so long; to have come, after all my dreaming, to rescue her—to rescue her who would not be rescued, but despised me; and then, to top this off, to perish ignobly in such a pass, with my neck broke by an Indian spy. And what I wondered was how the devil it could be happening.

That helpless question is one that Cap Huff will, to his last hour, resent my putting to him. When Eneas leaped upon me Natanis ran to help me, Hobomok being engaged with Hook; and Cap made the blunder of going to the door to see how we fared. Rightfully I should not reproach him for this. It was his solicitude for me that caused the error; but he had two alert and quick-moving enemies behind him in the room, and they were not likely to miss their chance. Mary got a knife from the table and cut Guerlac's ropes. Hobomok had left his musket in the room, and Guerlac used the stock of it upon the back of Cap Huff's skull, then fired at Hobomok to save Hook.

The blow with the stock must have been delivered with a mighty swing, for it carried the whole weighty person of Cap as far as my leap from the door carried me, and laid him beside me, out of action. He was no worse than out of action—a fact for which credit must be given to his ancestors, who left him, as that very blow demonstrated, the thickest head-bone structure, undoubtedly, on the North American continent. But the fight was over; for he sat up and joined me in a great mutual puzzlement as to whether we were alive or no.

It was Natanis who saved us. His hatchet finished Eneas abruptly; my head, almost unseated, resumed its proper posture upon an aching neck; the intolerable weight upon my back was removed; and with eyes still wavering I saw Hobomok halt. He was not running away: it was Hook who was running away, with Hobomok after him —Hobomok with a bleeding left shoulder, as we saw from the red stain on his white blanket coat. He poised his tomahawk and threw, using the overhand swing with which the Abenakis hurl this weapon. The hatchet struck Hook in the middle of the back, near the waist; and he bent backward as if his body had been hinged, falling into the snow and lying there with no movement save a groping of his right hand, as if to catch hold of something and drag himself up.

I did not know until later that day how well and quickly Natanis thought and acted in these, our moments of overthrow. The blow fell upon Cap Huff at the very instant of the hatcheting of Eneas; and if Natanis had not sprung instantly back to the door, that door would have been closed: Guerlac and Mary would have run through to the front of the house and raised the town upon us.

But Natanis was too quick, and he was at the door before the latch could fall; Hobomok returned, running, and together they forced their way back into the house; so that even before I got Cap, groaning, to his feet, Guerlac was fast to his chair again, and Mary sat white and staring in hers.

Natanis and Hobomok ran out to Hook, took him by the arms, dragged him into the kitchen, and laid him on the floor. Cap and I staggered in. We shut the door and bolted it. Cap found a rag, soaked it in water, applied it to the back of his head, and stood looking at Guerlac with profound respect.

"Don't you ever do that again!" he said. "You might have hurt me! And besides, if this happened to be any other day, shooting off a gun like that right in town might have made a whole lot of folks come around to see what was going on. Of course, after all the bim-banging and everything last night and this morning, I expect no-

body's going to notice it; but don't you do it again! You know yourself we don't want the neighbors in here."

Natanis took the white coat from Hobomok and dressed the latter's wound, Hobomok sitting impassive, which was more than I
could have done; for the ball had lacerated the shoulder muscles,
and Natanis's methods of bandaging were heroic. Not a moan escaped from the Indian's lips; he was silent as the dying Hook upon
the floor near by.

While I hated Hook more than any man in the world—more, even,
than Guerlac—my hatred seemed to go from me when I saw his eyes
rolling from me to Cap and from Cap to Hobomok and Natanis with
the same fierceness I had seen in them when he went away from
our inn with a broken jaw, leaving my father dying upstairs.

It was the look, I thought, of a wounded fish-hawk; and it flashed
into my mind that there was more joy in having an enemy to pursue
than in catching and destroying him.

"Well," I said to Cap heavily, "there it is. That's what we suspected: a connection between Hook and Guerlac: between Eneas
and Hook and Guerlac."

*   *   *

We left Hobomok in the kitchen to watch the three of them, while
Cap and Natanis and I began a search of the house. Wherever there
was a locked door we broke it open. We examined every drawer,
tapped the floor of every room for hiding places; pried beneath the
stoves in search of loosened bricks. It was Cap who felt a weakness
at the top of a column which supported the mantel in the front room.
When he forced it from its position he found it concealed an opening
in which lay a long tin box.

"Here," said Cap, handing it to me, "see if this ain't what you want."
He went on with his search, thumping the walls and looking behind
pictures.

There were maps in the box, and deeds to property, and a roll of
gold coin. Last of all, at the bottom, was a bundle of letters. The
uppermost letter was addressed to John Woodward, Esqre., Le Chat
Qui Péche, Quebec. There it was before me: Guerlac had received
the messages written to Woodward. Woodward *was* Guerlac.

When I slipped the band from these letters and flipped them over,
I found one addressed to Captain William Gregory in Colonel Ar-
nold's handwriting. I knew I needed to look no further; for Colonel
Arnold had told me that he had asked questions concerning the Ken-

nebec of Captain William Gregory, and that under the seal of Captain Gregory's reply had been the information that John Woodward was the man who knew these things.

It seemed to me I should be filled with pleasure at discovering the letters in Guerlac's possession and having Guerlac where I could put my hand on him. Yet I had no such feelings: only a sense of loss and unhappiness. I picked up the roll of gold and hefted it, saying to myself it would buy many a fine article for Phoebe's cabin on the *Ranger.*

So thinking, I dropped it in my pocket. As it left my fingers there dawned on me a sudden understanding of my own utter blindness and stupidity, and of the manner in which Phoebe had grown around me and into me so that my world was no world at all if I couldn't have her a part of it.

Then I saw that Phoebe had always been first in my thoughts, no matter where I went or what I did; and I, like a surpassing fool, was where I might never see her again. I burst into a sweat at my folly, remembering how I had let her go into the hands of James Dunn, nor even known why I was in such a rage at both of them when they were married. Other foolishnesses popped out of the corners of my mind until I was revolted to think I could have been so witless.

There swept over me such a longing for her and for Arundel, and for the sight and the smell of the sea and the marshes, that I went in search of Cap to tell him my troubles.

He had returned to Mary's sweet-smelling bedroom; and when I found him he was playing with glittering shoe buckles, oval ones studded with brilliants.

"Were they the papers you wanted?" he asked, stuffing the buckles into his pocket.

"Cap," I said, "there's no greater fool in all New England than I!"

"Has somebody found us?" he asked, looking apprehensively over my shoulder.

"Cap, I've sent Phoebe home! And look at us—the fix we're in!"

"Yes, I hope she's a damned long way nearer home than we are! I take it you'd like to see her again?"

"Yes, I would."

He scratched his head. "So would I, if she's anywhere near home. This is a nice house: an awful nice house; and the hell of it is, we've got to stay here till after dark, and even then get buried somewhere, near and handy, if we ain't awful careful—and maybe anyhow, no matter how careful we are!"

What he said was the truth. "Well, what was your plan for getting out?" I asked.

He scratched his head again. "Stevie, it seems to me I've been altogether too busy learning how to get in. What was your own plan for getting out?"

"Me? I didn't have any."

"Well, we can't go by the Lower Town. If we try to go down those steps we'll have more holes in us than your ma's lace collar!"

"No, not by the Lower Town. God knows I've seen enough of those barricades. We'll decide what to do with Guerlac and then how we'll get out."

"You mean how we'll try to!" Cap said.

*   *   *

If there was any change in Guerlac's face when I returned to the kitchen and threw the tin box on the table, I couldn't detect it. It may be his eyes watched me more closely; but certainly his face was no paler, nor his bearing less haughty and unafraid.

I emptied the box on the table and ran through the letters. "Now," I said, "here's the proof of certain things. Hook, who was called Treeworgy in our army, was sent to Quebec by the Tories of Boston to help the British. He was an intelligent man, who knew the Abenakis and the forests; so they made him a paid spy. When he had fooled Colonel Arnold into entrusting him with letters, he brought all of them straight to Guerlac. Here are letters from Carleton to Guerlac about Hook, and from McLean to Guerlac, thanking him for his efforts, and assuring him his services won't be forgotten. So Guerlac, you see, was a spy also."

"How much did they pay him?" Cap asked.

"Well, now," I said, watching Guerlac closely, "I think they didn't pay him anything. I think his travels among us taught him he could never be happy living among the bigots and hypocrites of America —men so intolerant as to throw him in the mud instead of reverencing his sneers, and to spoil his beauty with a slit ear when he grew too free with women. I think he'd cast in his lot with any king to keep canting peasants like us from his houses and goods."

Guerlac smiled his lofty, contemptuous smile, and said nothing.

"Well," I said, "here's Arnold's letter to John Woodward, whose name was given to Colonel Arnold in Captain Gregory's letter. Here's Arnold's letter to Captain Gregory. Hook brought the letter to Guerlac instead of to Gregory, and Guerlac forged the reply. It's plain from these letters that Guerlac himself was John Woodward. In return for whatever it was that the English government gave them, money or security or honor, he and Hook undertook to do what they could to defeat Colonel Arnold's expedition."

"If they'd worked harder," said Cap, draining a bottle of Mersault, "they might have kept us from getting onto this side of the river."

"They did enough! It was John Woodward who recommended the use of bateaux. It was John Woodward who sent Arnold the forged proof that Natanis was a spy. Thus if all the bateaux were not destroyed, which they were almost certain to be, they made sure Natanis would either be killed or shunned, and the army robbed of the one guide who knew every trail and by-path between Dead River and Quebec. That meant the army would probably starve in the wilderness.

"It was John Woodward who instructed Hook to spread discontent and fear among the poorest soldiers of the expedition, so they would turn back, as you can see by this letter from Hook to Guerlac. It was Eneas, at Hook's orders, who betrayed Arnold by delivering his private letters into Guerlac's hands. Thus the Lieutenant Governor of Quebec was warned of our coming. It was Hook who ran to McLean in Sorel and blabbed to him of Arnold's approach, so he was able to hurry down the St. Lawrence with a few defenders on the very same day we came marching up to Point Levis."

"Can you prove all that?" Cap asked.

"It's all here."

We sat silent. Natanis spoke to me in Abenaki, asking whether Guerlac was the man who had done all the evil to us. When I said he was, he asked how I would kill him. At this Guerlac spoke up, smiling a cold, level smile, and I saw he had not forgotten the Abenaki tongue.

"I warn you," he said, "not to touch me. Your turn-coat general, Montgomery, was killed at the barrier under Cape Diamond last night, and the rest of his beggarly rabble ran like whipped dogs without even attempting to pick him up. All of Arnold's men were either captured or killed in the Sault-au-Matelot, all of them. You're alone in the city, and you're sure to be caught. Do you think you'll have a better chance to escape hanging if I come to any harm at your hands?"

We stared at him, sickened by what he told us. It seemed to be the truth.

"Well," I said at length, "I know we'll never leave the town alive if you get free; so we'd be showing only simple caution if we killed you."

Mary, it seemed to me, had not sensed the meaning of our words until just now. She had sat with a distant look on her face and her head poised a little to one side, as though absorbed in secret contemplation of her own perfection, and sure all those in the room were casting admiring looks at her pale beauty, which we were not, God knows.

At my last words, however, she looked quickly at me. The languidness went from her eyes. "What are you talking about? What's this talk of killing?"

"Haven't you understood? I think you have!"

"You're trying to blame Henri for something that happened. It's not true!"

"Yes, it's all true! Because of what he and Hook did, there are dead men rotting in the forest beside the path we traveled."

She laughed lightly. "Well, why shouldn't there be?"

"We're done with Hook," I told her then. "His back's broke. He'll never leave this room alive. But we aren't done with Guerlac."

"You'll not touch him." She laughed again. "You'll not touch him."

"Why hasn't he ever married you?"

"Pouf!" she said. "What a boor you are! I never cared whether he did or not, and he has a wife in France."

At that I turned away, for I could no longer look at her. So this was Mary Mallinson!

XXXV

I HAD found a map of Quebec among Guerlac's papers, and I laid it on the kitchen table, studying it.

We had seen no good maps of Quebec, only the rough ones deserters had made for us; and this of Guerlac's was good, the streets marked out neatly, the houses inked in by hand, and the ports in the ramparts indicated, together with the guardhouses and the steps to the parapets. I found the long stairway from the Lower Town, and traced our route to Guerlac's house. I found the sites of the old palace and of La Friponne, where we had lain on our bellies in the snow to pop at the sentries on the walls above.

No sooner had the tip of my finger touched them than I shouted for Cap. It had come to me how we could go safe from the city and take Guerlac with us as a present to Arnold—if Arnold was still alive!

❋   ❋   ❋

Darkness fell by mid-afternoon—a thick, snow-sprinkled darkness; for the wind hung in the northeast and seemed to be of two minds about inflicting another storm on this snow-covered world. We ate once more, and studied the map, rehearsing the parts we must play. We had put Mary and Guerlac in the bedroom, making sure they couldn't escape from their ropes.

Cap, bulging with brandy bottles and other knickknacks, saw that what had happened in this strange meeting with Mary had weighed heavily on me; and he strove to hearten me against a merciful inclination, of which I had muttered something to him.

"Stevie," he said, wiping his mouth with the back of his hand, "I've learned a heap about women these last few years. They're all alike about one thing, so far as I can see. It never bothers 'em when they lose a man. Somehow they all bear up, Stevie! It appears to me Mary ain't different from the rest of 'em. She'll have another man in a week, Stevie, if Guerlac doesn't come back to her; and she'll never know the difference! There ain't been a woman in Kittery or Portsmouth either, for that matter, to die because of the loss of a man; and the widows, whether seventeen or seventy, get other husbands and act smugger than ever!"

He poured me a drink of brandy. I took it and put a little more zest into our preparations.

It must have been five o'clock when Cap went into the cellar and readjusted the bindings of one of the serving maids—the one who had sat mending her stocking when we entered the house. He trussed her to a chair with a rope knotted in a hundred places, and fastened her to the wall so she must free herself to reach the others. On her hands he put no rope at all. Thus, in an hour or more, she might unknot her bonds and loose her fellow captives.

When it came to tying Guerlac so we could carry him with us, Natanis said here was one prisoner who would have no opportunity of escaping. He and Cap labored long and diligently over the Frenchman's bonds. Both his arms were lashed tight to a rope that passed around his waist, so they hung straight at his sides and appeared to be unbound. His legs were joined below the knee by a slender rope that permitted him to walk, though not to run; and to this rope was attached a longer rope to be held by one of us. His gag was left in his mouth and his jaws held together by a cloth running under his chin and knotted at the top of his head. When we pulled down his cap over his ears and pinned the collar of his blanket coat so it was turned up around his mouth, there was little to show, even in broad daylight, that he was tied in any way.

I heard Natanis say to Guerlac in Abenaki, while he was binding him, that if Guerlac made any sign or sound that led to our capture, he would shear off his face with his hatchet and leave him alive, to fill women and children with terror for the rest of his days.

When Cap and Natanis took Guerlac into the kitchen to make ready for the start, Mary, lying bound on the bed, pleaded with me to leave Guerlac behind. I could have, she said—and of course Guerlac had told her what to say—a thousand pounds for my own if I would do this; and Guerlac would make sure we got safely from the city. If I would join the British, Guerlac would have me made a major and I would be given five thousand acres when the war was done; and so on and so on, until my stomach turned over in me to know how small and mean I figured in her mind.

"You're wasting your breath," I said shortly.

She persisted in her pleading, staring at me piteously. "You'd be leaving nothing at all if you left this rabble you're with! Henri says nothing like it was ever seen before: it's a disgrace to fight against such folk or with them either! Their officers are nothing but hairdressers and blacksmiths and innkeepers and butchers and farmers, all thinking themselves gentlemen and as good as anyone."

I thought of Thayer and Steele and Morgan and Topham and Dearborn and the other officers, giving up their little portions of meat in the meadow at Seven Mile Stream so the soldiers under them might have more; as kind and gentle with their men as any titled Britisher or Frenchman could be. I carried her into the cellar and left her there with no further words.

Hook, lying in the corner of the kitchen, watched us belting up our coats and drawing the loads from our muskets so to reload for safety's sake. His eyes were half glazed with the nearness of death, but there still was hatred in them, so stubborn was that man.

When we were ready to go I told him that if he had a message to send to any person in New England before he died, I'd carry it.

"You deluded fool!" he said, showing his teeth at me between lips as gray as wood ashes. "You'll never get out of the city! St. Louis Gate and St. John's Gate are watched by a hundred men. The Lower Town's alive with sailors. No matter what road you take, you'll be full of bullets in half an hour." He panted a little and grinned horribly. "The forces of Belial have gone down before the armies of the Lord! The truth is mighty and shall prevail! Montgomery is dead, and your army of thieving blasphemers rotting in prison." His breath dragged in his throat. "You'll burn in hell this night, blasphemer!"

"Go ahead!" I said to Cap.

He shot back the bar on the kitchen door and went out into the snow. Natanis walked behind him; then Guerlac; then Hobomok; and last of all myself, where I could watch Hobomok, in case he weakened from his wound. It was dark, so dark that Cap, at the head of our little file, was only an indistinct bulk to me. The snow was falling steadily; and what with it being New Year's Day, and the city in no further danger of attack, and the citizens and garrison wearied by their long vigil and the night of terror through which they had just passed, I knew there would be none abroad save those who might be driven by necessity.

*   *   *

Our plan of escape was simple—too simple, it seemed to me, to fail. Later in the winter, indeed, a score of our men, at one time and another, broke from their cells and escaped in this self-same manner, sometimes by themselves and sometimes accompanied by their gaolers, who deserted.

Guerlac's house was near the great building of the Jesuits; and this, in turn, was only five or six blocks from the wall by Palace Gate. Beneath and beyond this section of the wall was the suburb of St. Roque and the ruins of La Friponne; and as a result of the hours I had spent on my belly in La Friponne, popping up at sentries on the walls above me, I remembered certain things of value.

I remembered that sentries walking on the parapet had been clearly visible through portholes to us below them; and that the portholes were large enough for a man to pass through. Also I remembered that the wall rose a full thirty feet above the bank, which was itself high; but that with each succeeding snowstorm the snow, driven always from the northeast or the northwest, had drifted higher and higher against the foot of the wall. Thus I knew that after the raging storm during which we made our attack this drift must have grown to an enormous size, so that one who leaped from the top of the wall would be no worse off than if he dropped into a pile of feather beds. Consequently our plan required only that we traverse the six blocks between Guerlac's house and the wall, mount to the parapet, and jump.

* * *

We came out from among the trees that sheltered Guerlac's house, looking like any squad of men engaged in changing guard or patrolling the streets, except that one of us—Guerlac—was without a musket. No man could have told that Natanis and Hobomok were Indians, for between their pulled-down caps and their turned-up collars there was no part of their faces visible.

We followed the steep street upward to our left, then turned sharp to our right. Immediately we encountered a lone officer trudging toward us through the snow. His chin was sunk in a cape, and he glanced up sideways at Cap as he came abreast of him, muttering some indistinguishable words cheerfully enough. To this Cap made an equally indistinguishable reply, chewing it in the forepart of his mouth and spitting it into the collar of his blanket coat; yet it seemed to content the Britisher, for he pulled his head back into his cape like a turtle and went trudging past.

When we reached the street of St. John's Gate we stopped in the lee of the house on the corner to see what might be seen. It was well we did so; for we had no sooner halted than a sentry paced across the end of the street we were on, not twenty feet from us.

We couldn't delay, for there was no telling when others might follow in our footsteps and come across us standing there. Cap went ahead, weaving and pitching in his walk, and we heard the sentry's challenge. By way of reply there was a violent hiccup from Cap, and a maudlin murmur of "Besh Newyearsh brandy." There came a silence, followed by a faint rattle and a sound of choking. We knew Cap was throttling him. Hobomok and I seized Guerlac under the arms and dragged him across the street of St. John's Gate, Natanis ranging ahead like a shadow on the snow.

Cap caught up with us at once, breathing a little quickly. We pushed rapidly into the narrow streets of the northwesternmost corner of the city. We had but three blocks to go before reaching the open space between the houses and that portion of the wall for which we were aiming, and on these steep dark streets we met no one.

We knew from the map that the last building to be encountered before we ventured into the open space was the barracks; and somehow we gained courage, when we reached its shelter, to find its windows lighted and to hear a discordant singing and bellowing from within.

"Hell," Cap whispered contemptuously, "there ain't a Britisher but what's drunk to-night. Disgusting! We'll go over that wall as easy as going upstairs to bed."

Natanis and Hobomok went across the field ahead of us, as we had planned. They were invisible against the drifts when they had gone six paces; so we took a firm grip on Guerlac's arms and followed. The wall loomed out of the snow when we had walked thirty paces—a low wall compared to its appearance from the far side. We saw the steps, and beside them a small guardhouse. Against the steps Natanis and Hobomok crouched, waiting. There was, Natanis whispered, a sentry on the wall: he would pass the head of the steps soon, and we could then go up safely.

My breast and throat were filled with the thumping of my heart, and I was near choking with the fear we might be found and stopped less than ten steps from safety. We cowered in the snow, waiting, and odd thoughts came into my head: the suspicion that a small taste of garlic might do no harm to my mother's cucumber relish; the thought of Cap's distress if he should be obliged to go home without his picture of Philadelphia as Seen from Cooper's Ferry; the recollection of how, ages ago, I had dreamed of entering Quebec with the Continental Army, marching stoutly between the tall stone houses, while laughing maids and cheering men welcomed us gladly from roadside and windows.

There was a sound of crunching from the parapet above us: slow footsteps in the snow. I hung my mouth as wide open as the bung-hole of a hogshead, so that my breathing might not reach the sen-try's ears. Little by little the sound of his feet grew fainter.

Natanis and Hobomok went crouching up the steps. Cap and I pulled Guerlac to his feet and followed. As we mounted, Cap slipped and fell with such a noise as might be made by the toppling of a tall clock on a stair landing. There was a sound of splintering glass and a powerful stench of brandy.

Off to our left I heard the sentry's challenge. By the time the sec-ond challenge came, we had Guerlac on the parapet. As we hustled him toward the port, Natanis fired past my ear. There was an an-swering shot from the sentry and a shout from the guardhouse. I saw Natanis dive through the port as Hobomok's rifle spat a streak of fire downward, and realized I was arousing the town with my bellowing to Cap and Hobomok to jump and get out of my way.

Cap scrambled through the port, grunting and growling, and Hobomok slid after him as the musket of the sentry at the guard-house flashed behind us.

Guerlac jerked upward; then sagged and hung limp in my arms. I could hear the shouting of other sentries along the wall. There was no time to pry into the manner in which the Frenchman had been injured; so I picked him up by the sash and stuffed him through the port and into space, scrambling blindly after him.

I could feel myself turning slowly in the air. I strove to hunch my-self together, so to offer a smaller mark to those on the parapet. My legs sprawled wildly as I turned and turned, listening always for musket shots above me. In the midst of a turn my shoulders struck an unyielding substance. There was a white flash in my brain, like that which had blotted out the world when Guerlac, years before, had driven his hatchet against my head.

*   *   *

God knows how much brandy Cap poured into me before I be-gan to cough it back at him. I rolled over onto my knees to let it drain out, and coughed until my lungs felt as though pounded on my own anvil.

"Thank God for that!" Cap said. "I thought I was wasting my last bottle on a corpse! You had a neck on you as limber as an old stocking." From the gurgle that followed, it seemed likely that Cap was doctoring himself for his fright.

I could feel that we were surrounded by walls, though I could see nothing for the dense blackness. "What happened?" I asked. From the soreness of my neck, I was none too sure but what it was broke. "What happened, and where's Natanis and Hobomok?"

The two of them spoke from near at hand.

"What happened," Cap said, "is that we're out of Quebec safe and sound, except that I'll be picking pieces of glass out of myself until I'm a hundred and fifty years old."

A fog began to move from my brain. "Where's Guerlac? I think a bullet hit him in the back."

"No," Cap said, "an Arundel Nason hit him!"

"That couldn't be!" I protested. "It was when the sentry fired that he jerked and almost fell."

"Well," Cap said, "we felt him all over to see what ailed him. We couldn't bother with anybody in that drift unless he was worth bothering with. You'd oughter seen that drift! It was big as Mount Agamenticus, and a damned sight solider!

"You came off the wall like a bull pine," he went on. "I couldn't see much through being fearful I might get one of your heels in the teeth, but it looked to me as though you landed on Guerlac with your neck and shoulders. Least ways, the muzzle of your rifle hit him in the back of the head. It was stuck there when we pulled you off him. You could have put your whole thumb in the hole."

"Wasn't there a bullet hole in him?"

"Nary a scratch!"

"And he was dead?"

"Deader than Job's turkey!"

I was pleased that Guerlac had died after this fashion, since he had played the fox in pretending to be hit; and God knows he had almost fooled me. I had nearly left him for dead on the parapet. Also I had feared all along that if I got him safely to Arnold he might be exchanged, or somehow escape alive; and it had also been in my mind that Cap or Natanis, impatient at being burdened with him and wishful of being revenged, might incontinently split open his head with a hatchet. I would have blamed them little for so doing; yet I misliked the idea and wouldn't have wanted it on my conscience.

The sentries on the walls, Cap said, had been unable to see us because of our white blanket coats. While they had shot blindly into the snow, Natanis and Hobomok and Cap had dug downward into the drift, dragging me behind them, and so slipped down into the shelter of the walls of La Friponne.

* * *

Cap raised a rumpus when we left La Friponne and set off into the black deserted streets of St. Roque, along which the whole of us had marched through the storm less than fifteen hours before.

There was glass all through him, he complained bitterly, like seeds in a watermelon. We stopped, therefore, at Menut's Tavern, which only yesterday had been so warm and cheery. When we cautiously opened the door we found the place a heap of wreckage, and Moshoo Menut, together with a few servants, laboring by candle-light to patch holes in the walls and scour dark stains from the floors. They scrambled under tables when we entered; but seeing we meant no harm, they crawled out, moaning and jabbering, while Cap stripped off his brandy-soaked and glass-filled garments.

Leaving my three friends to hear the tale, I hastened to the little house of Mother Biard, backed against the high bank like a baby rabbit backed against a bush. There was no light in it, nor in any of the other houses. The street was filled with litter—boards; pieces of thatch; heaps of chimney bricks; a smashed cariole. I pounded for admittance, and at length heard Mother Biard's voice behind the door. When she opened it a crack I pushed in and slammed it behind me.

Out of her few mangled words of English I learned that Phoebe and Jacataqua had remained with her until after daylight, watching the passing of the wounded Americans, who had been picked up by carioles and carried out to the hospital, some with feet and hands and faces frozen; some crying out and moaning; and some laughing and cursing, all very terrible. In the middle of the morning, a column of British had come out from Palace Gate and set off toward the hospital. A few Americans had opened on them with artillery and driven them back into the city, while the cannon balls tore through the houses of St. Roque, bursting rooms to bits and overthrowing chimneys.

Then there were no more wounded, for the British had captured all that were left and carried them into the Upper Town. On that Phoebe and Jacataqua rolled their blankets, bade Mother Biard farewell, and trudged off toward the north.

I gave her a piece of Guerlac's gold and hastened back for Cap and Natanis and Hobomok. From Menut they had learned more: how our men had remained between the two barricades in the Lower Town for four hours, waiting for reinforcements; and how they were then caught front and rear by constantly growing forces and so had surrendered.

"Does he know how many were captured?"

"He says all those not wounded or killed were captured, all of them, Virginians and all. He says there's God knows how many men dead under the snow—men that won't be found until the spring thaw." Cap cursed in a way to make me think Guerlac had been fortunate to die so easily.

"Where's Phoebe?" he asked, when he had cursed away a part of his rage.

"Gone."

Cap rubbed his round red face with his vast hands and tightened his coat around him. We left Moshoo Menut and his tavern and set off on the road to the General Hospital.

There was a light in every window of this sprawling building, and a powerful unpleasant odor of sickness inside, with nuns going back and forth carrying basins and bandages. There was a sentry in the hall, his face pitted beyond recognition, so we knew he had recently recovered from the smallpox. When we told him our business he went to the door of the main hospital room, and shortly thereafter the young surgeon of the army, Dr. Senter, came hurrying out, a blood-spattered sheet around his middle and blood halfway up his arms, looking ready to drop with weariness.

"What's this about Colonel Arnold?" he demanded irascibly. "Colonel Arnold's badly hurt. He's writing dispatches: can't be seen unless the matter's important."

"Well, God knows whether it is or not," I said. "We escaped from the city an hour ago. He might like to see us."

Senter gawped at us. "You came out of Quebec!"

We heard Arnold's rasping voice, that never failed to excite me, calling loudly for Senter. Senter scurried away and returned immediately.

"He wants you at once! Get out of those coats." He rubbed his forehead with the back of his wrist, seeming to be in a temper. "Damn him! He's a devil! I wanted him carried out beyond St. Foy's, where he'd be safe from capture in case of a sally; but all he did was have his sword brought to him and call for a loaded musket to be put at each man's bed. He'll fight 'em sick and lying down as quick as on his feet!" He herded us toward the door of the main room. "Christ!" he said. "What a piece of luck! Arnold and Montgomery, both of them, the first shot out of the box!"

*   *   *

There was a double row of beds stretching down this long, dim, whitewashed room. Nuns moved among them. At the head of each bed a musket leaned against the wall. Somewhere, near at hand, a man babbled rapid, meaningless words. Another coughed slowly and painfully, with a horrid wet sucking noise between each cough.

Arnold lay next to the door, cut off from the others by sheets hung on poles. He was propped up in bed, his field desk on a stool beside him. His coarse linen shirt, open at the throat, gave him a mild, pale look; but his eyes were hard and bright. They popped out at us until they seemed large as eggs.

He snapped his fingers impatiently when we saluted. "Out with it! Where've you been since the attack?"

"Sir," I said, "we were in the Upper Town." His eyes leaped from one to the other of us. I fumbled in my shirt, drew out Guerlac's papers, and handed them over. "We caught the three of them: Guerlac and Hook and Eneas."

He ran through the papers quickly. His face lengthened with his familiar reckless smile. "Good enough! Why didn't you bring Guerlac himself, along with the papers?"

"Sir," I said, "we tried. We tried hard; but we slipped going up the wall. The sentries opened on us. When we jumped, Guerlac was killed."

Arnold nodded. His face was expressionless. I wondered whether he doubted what I told him. Seemingly the same thought came into Cap's head, for he took a sword from behind his back and said, "This is his. I brought it along, thinking you could use it." He laid it on the bed. Arnold picked it up and loosened it in its sheath.

"What became of his sister?" he asked, peering at the blade.

"We found her," I said. "She was—she was different than I expected."

Cap bellowed angrily. "Different! I guess she *was* different! Do you know what she was?"

I took him by the elbow. He looked at me: then fell to humming, an absent-minded, unmelodious humming.

Arnold eyed me gravely. "I could have told you all that years ago, but you wouldn't have believed me."

"No."

"Well," Arnold said impatiently, "let's hear the rest! How in God's name did you get into the Upper Town?"

"Sir," I said, "there was no one at the second barrier when we reached it. We went through as Morgan had done."

"What do you mean? Did Morgan pass the second barrier? How do you know?"

"Captain Thayer told us. Thayer said Morgan went ahead to spy out the land, leaving the others to guard the prisoners from turning against us."

"Did you see Morgan beyond the second barrier?"

"No, sir. We saw no one, only women and children fleeing to the Upper Town."

Arnold gnawed his fingernails. His face darkened and grew lumpy. "If that's true, twenty men could have set fire to the whole Lower Town in an hour; and the Upper Town would have fallen to us in less than a month without the loss of a man!"

"Thayer told us they were afraid of sending the smoke and flame down on Montgomery."

Arnold nodded moodily. "Montgomery wasn't a child! He could have looked out for himself if he'd been in the Lower Town instead of dead in the snow."

"Sir," I said, "I wished to God a hundred times you could have been there."

Arnold nodded again. "We'd have kicked up a dust somehow."

"What would you have done?"

"God knows," he said wearily, "because I don't know how good your information is. There's one thing about it: prisoners or no prisoners, I'd never have stood four hours behind the second barrier and done nothing. If you're out to do something there's one sure way of not doing it, and that's by doing nothing. I'd rather be killed doing something than do nothing and come off safe."

He looked at me reflectively. "I can't tell what I'd have done. The time to decide such things is when the decision must be made; not before. With Morgan and his Virginians to follow me, and no one to stop us at the barrier, I'd have put the Lower Town in a blaze and got free somehow."

He shook his head and laughed. "Fortunes of war! We'll have them yet! Get on with your tale."

I told him the rest of it. When I had finished he lay silent, fingering a rip in the blanket. A wounded soldier in a near-by bed broke into a hiccuppy sobbing, like a child recovering from a spell of weeping, and called loudly for his mother.

"Sir," I said, "what happened to Montgomery?"

"Well," he said slowly, "it's too soon to be sure of these things. He attacked at Cape Diamond when we attacked through St. Roque. The carpenters sawed posts out of the first stockade, and Montgomery led the New York troops through—Montgomery and his aides: Captain Cheeseman and Captain McPherson and Captain Burr. There was a cannon loaded with grape beyond the stockade, and there was one shot fired before the British guards ran. One shot, and because the path was narrow and the attackers crowded together, it killed Montgomery, Cheeseman, McPherson, and a dozen soldiers."

He fell silent again, fingering the rip.

Cap cleared his throat, like a mill saw striking a pine knot. "Is that all?"

"Yes. That's all. They marched back to St. Foy's. It seemed too dangerous to go on."

"Who led them back?" Cap asked, growing redder and redder, as though on the edge of exploding.

"Lieutenant Colonel Donald Campbell of the New York Line," Arnold said.

"Lieutenant Colonel Donald Campbell," Cap repeated. "I guess Lieutenant Colonel Donald Campbell of the New York Line disremembered the rest of us might be caught in a box if he didn't get on. If you want to know what I think——"

"Fortunes of war!" Arnold said again. He pulled at the rip in the blanket.

"Be damned to that!" said Cap loudly. "We could have taken the city if he'd had the gizzard of a louse! I s'pose if you'd been in Lieutenant Colonel Donald Campbell's place you'd have run back to St. Foy's, screaming it was too dangerous! Like hell you would! If you want to know what I think——"

Arnold looked up at Cap's shining red face and laughed heartily. "The first thing you must learn in this business they call war is that when a thing's done, it's done. Forget it and lay your plans for the next step! If a soldier kept his mind on the things he lost through others' blunders, he'd go mad."

"All right," Cap said, sticking out his great barrel of a chest as if to drum on it, "but I know damned well you'd have gone ahead, if you'd been there! The troops would have gone too, even those pie-faced New York rats. What I think about this Lieutenant Colonel Donald Campbell is that he and Roger Enos ought to get into petti-coats and sell gingerbread cakes up an alley! It's all they're good for! Why, our Phoebe would have done better than this Lieutenant Colonel Donald Campbell of the New York Line!"

Arnold nodded as Cap's ferocious explosions faded to grumblings and sputterings. "I have no doubt she would. She's a smart young lady. Smart as they come! She'll make a good wife for some man." He looked hard at me. I felt myself go as red as a British coat.

"She'll make a good wife for me if I can ever find her."

"Ho ho!" Arnold cried, "you waked up at last, did you? She told me years ago you had a fondness for her, but didn't know what ailed you. She said you had this pale-faced wench of Guerlac's on the brain like a maggot."

I moved uncomfortably and said nothing.

"As to finding her," said Arnold, hitching himself into an easier position, "she came into this hospital at noon to-day to look for her townsfolk among the wounded, and to tell me you told her to go home. If I'm any judge you haven't lost her, any more than a child can lose its mother." He laughed, a familiar mocking, adventurous look in his eyes.

"I hope to God you're right!" I said. "For all she knows, I'm dead. Once before she married the most childish man in our town, though why she did it, if she's as smart as you say she is, I don't know. If she did it once, she might do it again before I catch up with her."

"So," Arnold said, moving his wounded leg under the bedclothes and wrinkling his face with the effort, "she never told you why she married him! You surprise me!"

From the derisive way he said it, I could tell I didn't surprise him at all. The whole thing was beyond me. I felt weary, and wishful of seeing Phoebe.

Arnold picked up Guerlac's sword and went to snapping it in and out of the sheath. "Here," he said, "why don't you do this? Why don't you go up the river a few miles above Pointe-aux-Trembles, where the ice is solid and a path cut through the blocks in the middle? That's where she has to go to cross. You can catch her there."

He scratched his chin and popped out his pale eyes at me, struck by an idea. "No! I'll do more than that for you! What do these Indians of yours consider the shortest route to Boston, and how long would it take to travel it?"

I already knew the answer. "They say," I told him, "that the passage of the army up the Kennebec and down the Chaudière has made a road that, with this snow, will be as smooth and level as our beach at Arundel. On snowshoes we could easily reach Boston in two weeks unless we met heavy storms, which isn't likely."

"Good!" Arnold said. "I'll send you express to Cambridge with dispatches for General Washington, all four of you. You can catch up with this Phoebe of yours and give her an escort to her home. She deserves one, after what she did for us."

"Sir," I said, "I'm mighty grateful."

"I know," he said, "and I'm grateful too." He opened his field desk, screwed together his saucer candlesticks, and kindled his candles from the one on the stool beside him. "Go out and wait in the hall. I'll send for you when I've finished. You'll want orders." He scratched names on a sheet of paper, but hesitated over one. "Huff! I never learned your first name. What is it?"

Cap looked at his feet uncomfortably, so I was moved to answer for him. "Saved From Captivity."

"Was he indeed!" Arnold said politely. "And what's his first name?"

"That's it. Saved From Captivity. It means nothing to any man unless written plain Cap."

Arnold snorted pleasantly. "Plain Cap it is." He waved us into the hall; and as we went, I saw Cap was in a black mood because of this airing of his name, and eager to vent his spleen on anyone that came to hand.

XXXVI

I MIGHT have clapped my arms around the first nun that passed, such was my delight over this providential stroke of fortune that would take me both to Phoebe and to Arundel, had we not encountered Burr in the hall—Captain Burr, to give him the new rank to which he had been elevated by Montgomery. He was asking to see his friend Matthias Ogden, and looking mighty important, after the manner of small men.

He pursed up his lips when he saw us, and nodded ominously, as though he took a gloomy pleasure in adversity.

"By God," he said, "I never thought to see you alive and free! We heard all of you who weren't killed or wounded were captured. Now you can tell me where I can find that slippery hussy Jacataqua."

Cap glowered at him, having come to mislike him even more than I, but I was in a state of mind to give any man a fair answer. "What you heard is about true," I said. "I think we'd either be wounded or captured if we hadn't got into the Upper Town by good luck and squared accounts with Treeworgy and the man who hired him."

"The Upper Town!" he exclaimed, and whistled. From the look in his sallowish pretty face, he doubted what I said.

Wishful of having no trouble with any man, and above all with an officer, now that we were on the edge of leaving this snow-ridden land, I was content to nod and grin at him, and wish heartily he would get along in to his friend and leave us be. Yet Cap couldn't remain quiet, but must hitch at his breeches and rub at his face with his hairy hands, a sure sign a storm was rising within him.

"I think more of us could have gone up," I said, hoping to forestall Cap, "except for Montgomery's misfortune at Cape Diamond."

Burr pressed his lips together. "It was awful! A terrible business! Montgomery and Cheeseman and McPherson dead at the first shot, and a score more groaning in the snow! I swear fifty grape-shot passed me within a whisker's width!" He slapped the fist of one hand into the palm of the other. "And Campbell, rot him, would not go forward!"

"It don't sound good!" Cap growled. "How far from you was Montgomery when he got it?"

"Not ten feet! He went down like a tree, and never moved nor made a sound."

Cap grunted. "A lousy Frenchman in the Upper Town told us all Montgomery's men ran like whipped dogs when he was killed: never even tried to pick him up and carry him away."

He stared at Burr and Burr stared at him, both of them motionless. "Why," said Burr at length, dropping his head and peering at us from under his eyebrows, so that he looked a little like a snake, "he was a liar! We could see nothing, any of us! You don't know how dark it was, with the howling wind and the snow!"

"Oh, don't we!" Cap exclaimed. "What do you think we were doing when all this happened? Reading a book? There was plenty of snow where we were—plenty; but we could see well enough to take Arnold back to the hospital and fight our way into the Lower Town, too! And they tell me those at Cape Diamond could see well enough to find their way back to the hole in the stockade! How big was that hole, anyway? Just about the size of Montgomery, wasn't it?"

"Are you meaning to accuse me of cowardice?" Burr asked softly.

"No," I said, laying hold of Cap's arm to twist some sense into him, "no, he's not! No man's a coward who came here with Arnold."

We heard Arnold calling us from the main room. "I'll tell you when I come out," said Cap to Burr in a whisper so hoarse and rasping that it seemed to flutter the white headgear on a pair of passing nuns. We went back to Arnold, and found him dropping wax on his letters.

"Saved From Captivity," he said, not looking up, "I want you to put a curb on your tongue. To say what you think is always a luxury and often a curse; for since you're only human, like the rest of us, your thoughts, a large part of the time, are doubtless wrong."

He pressed his thumb against a lump of hot wax and looked coldly at Cap. "You don't know what went on in the dark at Cape Diamond, any more than I know what you have in your pockets to bulge them out. It's not your place to talk of cowardice to your equals, let alone to your superiors. If you must fight, fight the British. Let your own people alone. Do you understand this, Saved From Captivity?"

"Well, my Gosh——" Cap began, puffing heavily. He gulped and

tried again. "I never liked——" Once more he started afresh. "Yes, sir!"

"Good," Arnold said. "I'll appreciate it if you'll apologize to Captain Burr when you go out. We've all of us had troubles enough this day without adding to them by hasty speech." In his impatience he spoke more roughly. "You big damned fool! Aaron Burr is just about the nerviest little gamecock in the army!"

He handed me the letters. "These to be handed to His Excellency in person. You can draw what rations you need. It may be we have a little hard money left."

"Why," I said, feeling uncomfortable, "we were so fortunate as to find some of that in—in Quebec, so we need none."

"Ah!" said Arnold noncommittally. "In that case be off soon, and make all possible speed. Give out no news except to General Washington. I'll be on my feet in three months' time. If they can spare me the men, I'll take this city as sure as there'll be green leaves in May." He shook hands, quick and impatient, as if glad to be rid of us, though I knew better.

"Here," he said, as I turned away. "I forgot something!" He opened a drawer in the back of his field desk and took out a seal ring set with a fat green stone. There was a coat of arms cut in the stone, and Arnold showed me the motto at the bottom of the seal—*Gloria mihi sursum.* "Glory above all things," he said, a reckless light in his pale eyes. "Give this to your Phoebe, and tell her it's a wedding present from a sincere admirer."

He wagged his hand and we went out, leaving behind us a brave and gallant gentleman who, if it had not been for the terrible thing that later happened, would be acknowledged by all soldiers to be second only to General Washington in daring and brilliance in military matters. He had all the qualities of a great soldier—observation, right judgment, quickness, leadership, determination, energy, and courage—and all of them, it seemed to me, in the highest degree.

This, too, I must add, because it's the truth, though a truth that displeases many: in none of my readings have I ever learned of anyone so persecuted and disappointed and unrewarded as this same brave and gallant gentleman. If the commissioning of officers had been in the hands of General Washington, where it should have been, instead of in the hands of the petty little argufiers of Congress, Benedict Arnold would never have suffered the cruel injustices that were heaped on him until, weakened by wounds, he was coaxed or driven to his awful crime.

*   *   *

There was no more swagger to Cap when he stepped into the hall to ask Burr's pardon than there is to a wet dish-towel; but there was no one in the hall save the sentry and two nuns with their heads together over a pile of bandages. When I would have asked Captain Burr's whereabouts from the sentry, Cap stopped me. "To hell with him!" he said in a rasping whisper. "If we get out of here fast enough we may never have to look at his liver-colored face again."

In a quarter-hour's time the four of us were stowed snugly in a cariole, jangling through the snow toward Pointe-aux-Trembles; and it was many a long day before our paths were crossed by Aaron Burr.

The leather-faced French made us welcome at the small hotel of Pointe-aux-Trembles, filling us full of roasted chicken and cider, even though it was midnight when we drew up before it. Snowshoes they said they'd get for us in the early morning, and blankets and provisions and all the things we needed for our march; and so we slept in peace. I, for one, felt as though I'd broken from a tomb that had been all but sealed over me.

I woke with a start a little before dawn, mindful of the silver knives and forks that had come from the summer house at Sillery; and something possessed me to go alone in search of them. I left Cap on his back snoring fiercely, and set off down the single street of Pointe-aux-Trembles for the farmhouse where Goodrich's troops had been quartered when we lay there waiting for Montgomery.

There was smoke rising from its chimney against the dull gray sky, and a gleam of light at the windows; so I pushed open the door and went into the kitchen. A long-queued Frenchman and his family stood near the stove, watching an Indian roll a blanket into a pack. He looked up at me. It was Sabatis. There were two other blankets by him, unrolled, and a coat of sable fur. The dog Anatarso sat on a corner of one of the blankets as if possessed of dower rights in it. I knew, when Sabatis nodded gravely at me, that we had already come up with Phoebe and Jacataqua, and that Sabatis must have deserted Eneas and come back like a faithful dog to his true friends.

Phoebe, I thought, would be in the attic uncovering my silver. I went up the ladder at the side of the room, opened the trapdoor at the top, and stepped up onto the floor.

At the far end of the attic I saw Jacataqua digging in the thatch. In the middle of the barren square space was Phoebe, on her knees before a double row of silver. I thought to call to her, but there was a fullness in my chest and throat, most embarrassing.

Although I made no sound, she suddenly looked over her shoulder into my face. She turned away, as though to find Jacataqua; then whirled to stare at me again. It seemed to me my appearance was strange to her, or not to her liking.

I looked down at my blanket coat, to make sure it was properly belted, and felt of my face, which had less beard than usual, because we had shaved before we fought. Finding these things in order, I rid myself of the tightness in my throat and chest by main force and said, though it was not at all what I wished to say, that I had come to see whether the silver was still here.

She scrambled to her feet, small and straight in her gray blanket coat and blue sash, her French snow leggins over her gray breeches, and her little fur cap pulled tight over her hair. She looked, in that shadowy, cold room, like a half-grown boy. She came up to me and put her hand against my chest, then nodded, twining her fingers in the string of cat's eyes at her throat.

"It's all here," she said, "and Cap's picture. I was going to take it home. Do you want me to take it home? Shall I—shall I take Cap's picture home?" She drew a deep breath, and pools of tears came into her eyes and hung on her lashes. When they spilled down her cheeks, the life came back into me and I got my arms around her at last.

I wondered how I could ever have thought her back was hard and flat. She was softer against me than Mary Mallinson with all her smell of French perfume and her night rail that could be seen through when wet.

"Now here," I said, feeling an unpleasant hotness in my own eyes, "I won't have any of this crying nonsense!" I picked her up in my arms, finding her no more in them than a young lamb, and carried her to a bale of straw, so I could sit down with her and get her fur cap off her head and my fingers into her hair.

After a time she tightened her arm around my throat so I couldn't breathe. "You've got to answer me!" she said, when I took steps to break her hold. "I've asked you four times about Cap." I saw then that Jacataqua had come around in front of us and was watching us with interest.

"He's well," I said, motioning to Jacataqua to get back to her thatch. "I left him snoring fit to knock the chimney off the inn, and Natanis and Hobomok with him."

She held me off again with an arm as rigid as a steel band. "For
God's sake!" I said, in a rage, "will you stop pushing me away from
you when I've wasted God knows how many years; or don't you want
to be kissed?"

"I don't mind being kissed," she said. "You can see how I feel about
it from this." She showed me what she meant, and I saw she had
spoken the truth. "What I must know," she went on at length, "is
how long a leave have you got from the army?"

"Why," I said, "I'm traveling express to Cambridge for Colonel
Arnold, and Cap and Natanis and Hobomok with me, and we have
orders to act as your escort. I have a wedding present for you from
Colonel Arnold. We can be married by the priest here at this place
unless you think you'll be everlastingly damned if a papist is mixed
up in it. We ought to be at it, what's more, for we must buy snowshoes, and I'd like to be across the river by noon."

"Well," she said, "I don't mind the papist, but I don't see how I
can be married without proper clothes."

"Proper clothes! Since when did you begin thinking of them?"

"Why," she said, eyeing me reproachfully, "you told me once that
breeches were no fit garb for a woman. Since I love you dearly, I
must please you by wading through the snow in long skirts."

"Phoebe," I asked, "shall we be married now?"

"I'll die if we aren't!" she whispered, and then fell silent.

"Steven," she said, after a little, "when the guns pounded and the
wind screamed at the windows and the men began to come back,
staggering and falling down and dragging each other, and leaving
blots of red in the snow—I watched for you—and watched for you.
I saw Colonel Arnold carried past, and Matthias Ogden with the
shoulder of his coat a smear of blood. The butcher from York came
by with poor Nathaniel Lord across his shoulders like a sheep, a
bullet through his lungs. When I ran to Nathaniel to see what word
I could take to his people, he choked and died.

"There were none of the others, Steven! Noah and Jethro and
Ivory and the rest of them didn't come back—nobody! Morgan and
Steele and Topham and Thayer and Goodrich and Dearborn and
Bigelow and Greene and Meigs and all the rest—they none of them
came back: none of them! I was afraid you—afraid you wouldn't
come either!"

She clung to me. After a time I told her that most of them had
been captured and would come safe home at last. Then there was a

bellowing and hallooing below us, and I knew Cap had come hunting for his picture of Philadelphia as Seen from Cooper's Ferry.

"Steven," said Phoebe, while the ladder was rattling at the trapdoor, "you found Mary——"

"Yes, we found her."

Phoebe said no more, but lay against me, stroking my shoulder. It seemed to me I had never known, before this moment, what it was to be at peace.

There was a roar from the trapdoor, and we looked up to see Cap's face, mouth and eyes wide open, shining at us over the door's edge like a pumpkin in the light of a harvest moon.

"So it's you?" I asked him. "What do you want?"

Cap stared. "What do I want? My God, what do you *think* I want? Where's my picture!"

Phoebe pointed, and his whole face brightened as his eye fell upon the rolled engraving of Philadelphia as Seen from Cooper's Ferry. He pounced on it with a delighted bellow.

When he had unrolled it and studied it for a time, he sat himself down on his heels and looked at us with the air of one who has made a great resolve. "I'm no fool," he said. "I can see the two of you are thinking of entering the holy bonds of matrimony."

"I don't know what makes you think such a thing," I said, "but it happens you're right."

Cap stood looking at us, then at the picture he held in his hands, and then back at us. He swallowed painfully. "I'll do it!" he said, his voice trembling a little. "I've got to make you a wedding present, of course, and it ought to be a good one. I'll give you my picture of Philadelphia as Seen from Cooper's Ferry!"

The distress in his face was all too plain, and evidence of what a sacrifice his generosity was forcing him to make; and I told him immediately we couldn't accept. "It's too fine and valuable a picture," I said, "for the simple house we plan to live in."

"Damn it!" he roared, "why don't you give Phoebe a say in it! She's the one that's going to have the say, anyhow."

"Nay," said Phoebe hastily, "we can't take the picture, Cap. We'll be living on a ship much of the time. If we took it with us on a ship it would soon become stained and moldy."

"Well," Cap sighed, and it was pleasant to see how he wiped his forehead in relief, "if you won't, you won't; but if I ever find a copy of it you've got to take it. Here: I've got some other things with me. Maybe there's one or two of 'em you could use."

He emptied the pockets of his breeches and his coat, pouring out silver shoe buckles, gold spoons, pieces of lace, a gold watch with a jeweled fob, two miniatures on ivory, a small gold box, a silver-backed hairbrush, four gold scent bottles, a heap of gold coin, a bag of soft yellow leather, a set of razors with silver handles, pieces of scented soap, and several small objects, such as rings and buckles and seals.

"Now here," Cap said, dragging something from the depths of his breeches pocket, "here's something Phoebe might use." He opened his clumsy fingers to disclose a band of jewels that seemed, in that dim attic, to be filled with blue and red fires.

"Those are diamonds," he said, "and this contraption is for a woman to wear, like in one of those miniatures."

Phoebe sat erect on my knee, took it from him, and snapped it around her forehead, so that it bound her tousled hair. She sat there with her hands in her lap, a half-smile on her lips, as though she held some secret from us that we would never learn. Jacataqua came from her delving in the thatch and leaned against Cap's shoulder, and the two of them stared at her in silence. As for me, I wondered how, if I had lacked the wit to see she was beautiful, I could have had the brain to eat and sleep and go about my business.

She shook her head at length, and took the thing off, turning it in her hand so that fiery glints flashed from it. "I can't wear this. It must be worth a fortune. Take it back."

Cap waved his hand airily. "Keep it. If you can't wear it, sell it or trade it." Phoebe dropped the band of jewels at his feet, and he picked it up and polished it on the front of his blanket coat. "Well ——" he said. "Well ——" He wriggled his hand into the yellow leather pouch and took out a string of round white beads, soft and velvety looking.

"Here's something you *can* wear."

"Mary's!" she said.

"What do you care?"

Phoebe looked quickly at me, and I saw what I had never noticed before: that there were flecks of gold in her eyes. She turned back to Cap and shook her head gently. "No," she said.

Cap hefted the string, as if pondering what to do with it. Jacataqua slipped under his arm and hung there, wedged against him, as she had wedged herself against me many months before and so aroused Phoebe's ire. Cap closed his thick fingers over the pearls and tightened his arm around Jacataqua until she squeaked a little, though not distressfully.

"Well, now," he said, frowning at her severely, "I might have knowed this would happen. If I'd got me some pearls long ago, maybe you wouldn't gone running off after other folks like Burr or George Merchant."

"Maybe I wouldn't," Jacataqua said, rolling her eyes at him enticingly.

"Yes, and maybe you would!" He dangled the pearls from his forefinger and whirled them in the air, at which she made a snatch at them, a snatch that was unsuccessful because of his grip on her.

"Now, now! None of that! That won't get 'em for you. You got to be a nice quiet girl, and look out for Phoebe going home, and not run after anyone we come across, and then maybe you can have 'em." He closed his hand over the pearls again. "Yes," he added suspiciously, "and how did that damned red Sabatis get out here with you?"

Phoebe struggled to her feet, pulled her sealskin cap over her hair, tightened the knitted sash of her blanket coat, and buttoned the coat around her neck. "He came out of the city when the attack began, and went with Paul Higgins and his Abenakis. He guided them across the bay of the St. Charles so that they got away. His place, he said, was with his brothers from the Kennebec. He's a good Indian. He'll help us get home. We're lucky to have him, and it's time we started."

"Where's Paul and his men?" I asked, feeling that she was right, and that Sabatis had done what he was bidden to do by Eneas, all with no thought of doing wrong.

"Gone to Indian Lorette," she said, "to make snowshoes and dry some meat for their trip home. They wouldn't stay with Arnold any longer, because they say this isn't their kind of fighting. Will you look for the priest, Steven, or shall I hunt him myself?"

Cap stowed his loot in his pockets. We packed up the silver and the picture of Philadelphia as Seen from Cooper's Ferry and scrambled down the ladder to find the leather-faced French waiting for us below.

They went readily enough to hunt the priest when they learned there was to be a marriage, with cider and brandy. By the time we had stopped at the tavern for the brandy and located the priest in the pleasant house beside the papist chapel, we had fifty Frenchies tagging along behind us, laughing and screaming in their silly twittery lingo and singing countless verses of "Vive la Canadienne."

They brought us all the snowshoes in the town as soon as they discovered we had the money with which to pay for them. I believe Cap was right when he said there are no people more obliging or politer than the French, once they know you have money to spend and are willing to spend it.

It may be there are some priests to the papist French not blue-jowled and not powerfully scented with garlic; but all I saw looked so and smelled the same. It was so with the one who married us, Claude-Marie Delacroix.

When he stood up before us in his long black dress like a night rail and jabbered French, we would have been at a loss except for Jacataqua. At times she would poke Phoebe and Phoebe would say "Yes"; and at times she would poke Cap, who stood close behind me, and Cap would almost push his forefinger through my back, whereat I would say "Yes."

The affair went smoothly, except at a point where Jacataqua whispered anxiously to Cap, and Cap fumbled in the pocket that held the largest part of his loot, while I wondered at his fumblings. He worried out a ring, which he handed to the priest; and all of us stood staring at it. It held a red stone as large as Ranger's eye, a stone as brilliant and fiery as though cut from a red sunset. Around it were small glittering diamonds; and it must have graveled the priest, lying in Cap's chapped paw, as unexpected as a thousand-pound note. Before the priest could reach out for it I got back my wits. Telling Cap to put away his bauble, I took Arnold's ring from the pocket of my buckskin shirt, and we were wed with it.

When, later, I asked Phoebe whether she felt married with the words that joined us being spoke in such a lingo, she said she would have felt married if an Abenaki *m'téoulin* had united us in the sign language.

*   *   *

The day was still young when we set off up the river for the crossing place, where a passage had been cut through the tumbled mass of ice cakes that are jammed up into mountain ranges in the middle of the river by the force and strength of the current. Nor am I ashamed to say I had liefer face a dozen Guerlacs or Hooks, or find my way out of Quebec ten times over, than cross the frozen St. Lawrence. When we came to the passage through the ice cakes there were thunderous bangings and crashings on both sides of us and beneath our feet, louder than any artillery, and a trembling of the ice, and a fearful coldness that bit through our garments as though they had been made of cotton. I was in a freezing sweat for fear the ice would open under Phoebe and swallow her up.

My fears came to naught, as do most fears; and we set off down the St. Lawrence, traveling rapidly in single file, Natanis in the lead, and then Jacataqua and the dog Anatarso and Cap and Sabatis and Phoebe and myself, and in the rear Hobomok. That night we reached the town of St. Mary's on the Chaudière, and lodged at the inn where Cap had found the keg of Spanish wine. Here they made us welcome and set out a wedding feast of chicken pasties and bear meat and apple pies and Spanish wine and a villainous brandy.

It was here, in the middle of our feast, that it came into my head to ask Phoebe why she had married James Dunn. She looked at me with a queer, misty smile and said nothing at all, so that I didn't learn; nor did I ask her again, ever, because I didn't care.

In spite of the weight of pork and flour we carried, we moved quickly; for our hearts were light and there were no heavy storms to hinder us, only snow flurries, and those mostly at night while we lay snugly on spruce branches in our snow-walled shelters. There was no day on which we failed to travel forty miles; for the lakes and ponds and swamps we had crossed with such labor during our march to Quebec had become broad white thoroughfares; and the jagged stumps that tripped us on the new-made trails over the Height of Land and the Great Carrying Place were hidden deep beneath a level covering.

On the third day after we left St. Mary's we crossed the ice of Lake Megantic, ascended the serpentine curves of Seven Mile Stream to the beautiful meadow, and scaled the Height of Land as easily as walking from Saco to Arundel.

Here we found ourselves at last upon a descending trail; and although the dawns were slow in coming, and darkness fell early, we covered fifty miles a day, a prodigious journey.

As we went over the snow, and at night, lying upon spruce boughs, I thought a thousand times—as I have thought ten thousand times since then—of all our labor and our anguish as we struggled along this same way upon the march to Quebec. I thought of the groaning and sweating men of that little army, half dead with exhaustion and the pain of torn and ailing bodies: starving and freezing, yet ready with heroic laughter, and never stopped by what still seems to me the very incarnate demon of ill-fortune.

I thought of lost muskets, of broken bateaux, of torn fragments of tents, down below us, frozen into the ice; and more, I thought of terrible stark forms, staring upward, eyeless, from deep beneath our feet. And it seemed strange and like a dream that we should pass now so easily and lightly over the way that had been agony. And in the murmur of the forest it seemed to me always that I could hear, as I can hear in the woods of Arundel to this day when I go into them, the voices of the bateaumen, the cries of stragglers, the shouts of officers—all the voices of Arnold's army.

*　　*　　*

Three days after we passed the Height of Land we came to deserted Norridgewock and lodged there; and on the following day we came to Fort Western, whence we had started four months earlier. Here we learned how the British captain, Mowat, who must have been, as Cap Huff firmly swore, the lousiest knave that ever wore a British uniform, had warped his two ships of war up to the Falmouth docks on the eighteenth day of October, bombarded the defenseless town, and burned more than four hundred buildings, leaving the entire population of the town without shelter for the winter. For that reason there were none of the settlers left along the Kennebec. The burning of Falmouth had destroyed their source of supplies, so they had gone down to the coast, all of them, to live on clams and whatever else they could take from the salt water.

It was two days later, toward dusk of a gray January day, that we reached the marshy banks of the Arundel River. The tide was on the make, and the steel-gray water brought up to us the fresh, heartening smell of the sea. There was a familiar odor of wood smoke blended with it; and as we followed the river toward its mouth I found myself short of breath, as I ever do when I near my home after an absence.

Cap lifted up his voice and began to bawl about old Benning Wentworth, and Phoebe came back beside me and pushed her hand into the sash of my coat. In no time at all we stood on the little sandy beach across from our garrison house. We could see a light in a window, and hear the far-off barking of a dog; and the plume of smoke that rose from the chimney wavered and flattened itself above the roof as though it had no notion what to do.

It seemed to me I could smell baked beans and new bread mixed

with the salt tang of the sea; and I stood on the shore, wavering
like the plume of smoke, gawking across the dark water and clutching Phoebe to me. I might have stood there until midnight except
for Cap, who blew at the ferry horn as though to blow its insides out.

A new ferry boy came to us, rattling his oars and staring white-
eyed at Natanis and Hobomok.

When he had set us across we went around by the kitchen door
and Phoebe opened it. My mother, with Ranger at her feet, sat at
her spinning wheel, and my muscles tightened at the clicking it
made when the door flew open. My sister Cynthia stood by the
brick oven holding a bean pot cover in her hand and peering at the
beans; while Malary, moaning querulously, prodded at the crusts of
brown loaves with a long-handled fork.

At the opening of the door my mother looked up; her eyes widened and widened, as if never in her life could she come to believe
that she saw what she saw before her; and then, as her face slowly
changed from that blank disbelief and became radiant, I could see
it no longer, nor anything else with distinctness, for the room and
all it contained grew wavery before me with the wetness in my eyes.
I was home again—in Arundel.

AUTHORITIES

On the Abenaki Indians of New England, on their relations with the early settlers of Maine, and on Indian warfare, magic-making, hunting, folk-lore, and customs: Baxter, Rev. J., *Journal of Several Visits to the Indians on the Kennebec River;* Bourne, E. F., *History of Wells & Kennebunk;* Bradbury, C., *History of Kennebunkport;* Colman, E. L., *New England Captives Carried to Canada;* Drake, S. G., *Book of the Indians* and *Tragedies of the Wilderness;* Hanson, J. W., *History of Norridgewock & Canaan* and *History of Gardiner, Pittston & W. Gardiner;* Leland, C. G., *Algonquin Legends of New England;* Lincoln, Gov. E., *Language of the Abenakis;* Nash, C., *Indians of the Kennebec;* Nicolar, J., *Life & Traditions of the Red Man;* Parkman, F., *Half Century of Conflict* and *Montcalm & Wolfe;* Pope, S., *Hunting with the Bow & Arrow;* Pote, W., *Journal During His Captivity in the French & Indian War;* Reed, P. M., *History of the Lower Kennebec;* Remich, D., *History of Kennebunk;* Vetromile, Father E., *The Abenakis & Their History;* Whitney, S. H., *The Kennebec Valley;* Williamson, W. D., *History of Maine;* Willis, W., *History of Portland,* Vol. 2.

On events preceding the Revolution, on Arnold's expedition through the Maine wilderness, on individuals who participated in the expedition, and on the attack on Quebec: Adams, J. T., *Revolutionary New England;* Allen, W., *Arnold's Expedition;* Arnold, Benedict, *Journal* and *Letters,* Maine Historical Society Collections, Series 1, Vol. 1; Arnold, I. N., *Life of Benedict Arnold;* Codman, J., *Arnold's Expedition to Quebec;* Dearborn, Henry, *Journal of the Quebec Expedition;* Fobes, Simeon, *Journal of a Member of Arnold's Expedition;* French, Allen, *Siege of Boston;* Graham, J., *Life of Daniel Morgan;* Haskell, C., *Diary of Arnold's Expedition;* Hayden, Rev. H. H. (in Magazine of American History, Vol. 13), *Gen. Roger Enos: A Lost Chapter of Arnold's Expedition to Quebec;* Henry, J. J., *Campaign Against Quebec;* Hill, G. C., *Life of Benedict Arnold;* Hughes, Rupert, *George Washington;* Lossing, B. J., *Field Book of the Revolution;* Minnegerode & Waddell, *Aaron Burr;* Meigs, Return J., *Journal of Arnold's Expedition;* Melvin, J., *Journal of Expedition to Quebec;* Parton, J., *Life & Times of Aaron Burr;* Senter, Dr. Isaac, *Journal on a Secret Expedition to Quebec;* Smith, Justin H., *Arnold's March from Cambridge to Quebec;* Thayer, S., *Journal Describing the Perils and Sufferings of the Army under Colonel Benedict Arnold.*

On life in and about Quebec during the Revolutionary period: Anburey, Lt. Thomas, *Travels through the Interior Parts of America, 1776–1781;* Henry, J. J., *Campaign Against Quebec.* The conformation of Quebec in 1775 and the exact route of Arnold's attack on the Lower Town was reconstructed from a French engineer (manuscript) map supplied by the Library of Congress, and from measurements and surveys made with Lt.-Col. G. E. Marquis of the Dominion Government.

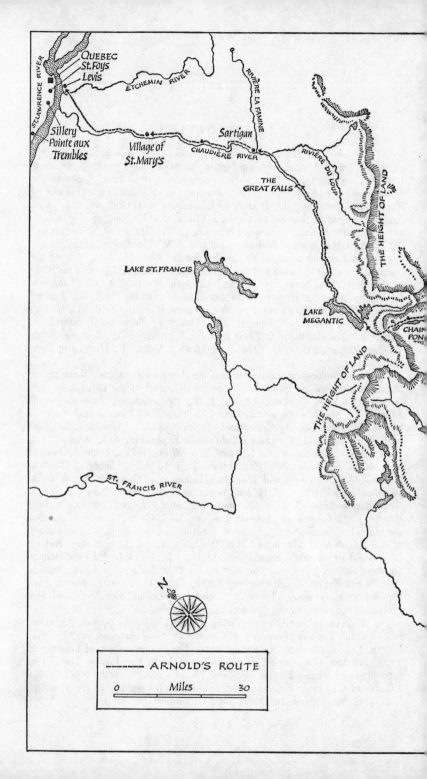

QUEBEC
St.Foys
Levis

ST.LAWRENCE RIVER

ETCHEMIN RIVER

RIVIÈRE LA FAMINE

Sillery
Pointe aux
Trembles

Village of
St. Mary's

Sartigan

CHAUDIÈRE RIVER

RIVIÈRE DU LOUP

THE GREAT FALLS

THE HEIGHT OF LAND

LAKE ST. FRANCIS

LAKE
MEGANTIC

CHAIN
PON

THE HEIGHT OF LAND

ST. FRANCIS RIVER

N

------ ARNOLD'S ROUTE

0   Miles   30

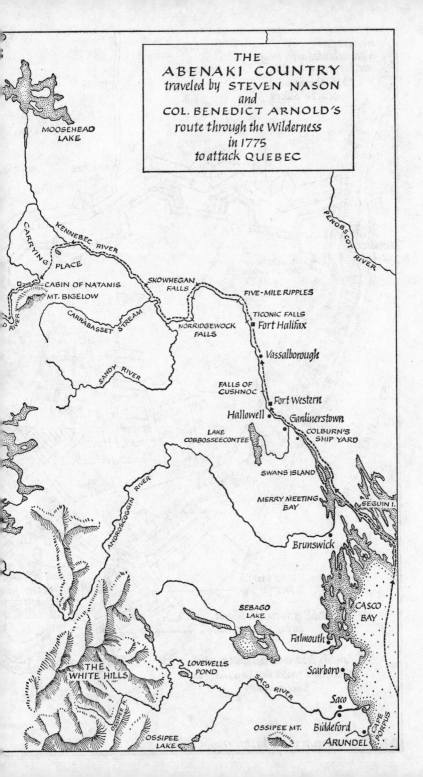

THE
ABENAKI COUNTRY
traveled by STEVEN NASON
and
COL. BENEDICT ARNOLD'S
route through the Wilderness
in 1775
to attack QUEBEC

MOOSEHEAD
LAKE

PENOBSCOT
RIVER

CARRYING
KENNEBEC RIVER
PLACE

CABIN OF NATANIS
MT. BIGELOW

SKOWHEGAN
FALLS

FIVE-MILE RIPPLES

TICONIC FALLS
Fort Halifax

CARRABASSET STREAM

NORRIDGEWOCK
FALLS

SANDY RIVER

Vassalborough

FALLS OF
CUSHNOC

Fort Western
Hallowell
Gardinerstown
COLBURN'S
SHIP YARD

LAKE
COBBOSSEECONTEE

SWANS ISLAND

ANDROSCOGGIN RIVER

MERRY MEETING
BAY

SEGUIN I.

Brunswick

CASCO
BAY

SEBAGO
LAKE

THE
WHITE HILLS

LOVEWELLS
POND

Falmouth

Scarboro

SACO RIVER

Saco

OSSIPEE MT.
Biddeford

CAPE PORPUS

OSSIPEE
LAKE

ARUNDEL

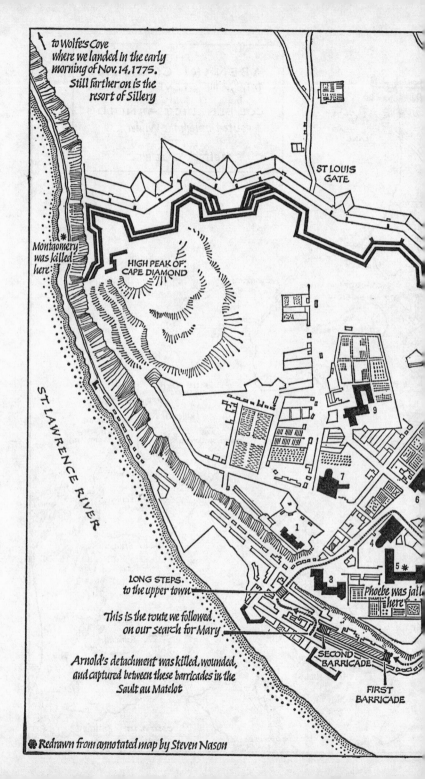

to Wolfe's Cove where we landed in the early morning of Nov. 14, 1775. Still farther on is the resort of Sillery

ST LOUIS GATE

Montgomery was killed here

HIGH PEAK OF CAPE DIAMOND

ST. LAWRENCE RIVER

9

7

6

1

4

5

LONG STEPS to the upper town

3

Phoebe was jailed here

This is the route we followed on our search for Mary

SECOND BARRICADE

Arnold's detachment was killed, wounded, and captured between these barricades in the Sault au Matelot

FIRST BARRICADE

Redrawn from annotated map by Steven Nason

to the Hospital

Morgan's men lodged here
and from here
our attack started

MENUTT'S
TAVERN

o St. Foys and
Pointe aux
Trembles

ST. JOHNS
GATE
where Phoebe
was drummed
from the city

SUBURB OF
ST. ROQUE

LA TRIPONNE

This is where we jumped from the walls into the deep snow
Jan. 1, 1776

THE INTENDANT'S
PALACE
from which we sniped at the
sentries on the walls

Here was the Palace Gate

GUERLAC'S
HOUSE

This is the route
of our attack

Arnold
was wounded here

ST. CHARLES RIVER

PLAN de la Ville de
QUEBEC
—1775

1 Le Château
2 Le Palais
3 Le Palais Episcopal
4 La Cathédrale
5 Le Seminaire
6 Les Jesuites
7 Les Recoletes
8 L'Hôtel Dieu
9 Les Ursulines

Henri Guerlac de Sabrevois

taken January 1, 1776, by
Steven Nason of Arundel